THE DIVINE COMEDY
OF DANTE ALIGHIERI

THE DIVINE COMEDY

OF

DANTE ALIGHIERI

Edited and Translated by
ROBERT M. DURLING

Introduction and Notes by
RONALD L. MARTINEZ
AND ROBERT M. DURLING

Illustrations by
ROBERT TURNER

Volume 1
INFERNO

OXFORD UNIVERSITY PRESS
NEW YORK OXFORD

Oxford University Press

Oxford   New York
Athens   Auckland   Bangkok   Bombay
Calcutta   Cape Town   Dar es Salaam   Delhi
Florence   Hong Kong   Istanbul   Karachi
Kuala Lumpur   Madras   Madrid   Melbourne
Mexico City   Nairobi   Paris   Singapore
Taipei   Tokyo   Toronto

and associated companies in
Berlin   Ibadan

First published in 1996 by Oxford University Press, Inc.,
198 Madison Avenue, New York, New York 10016

First issued as an Oxford University Press paperback, 1997

Oxford is a registered trademark of Oxford University Press

Library of Congress Cataloging-in-Publication Data
Dante Alighieri, 1265–1321.
[Divina commedia. English & Italian]
The divine comedy of Dante Alighieri / edited and translated
by Robert M. Durling ; introduction and notes, Ronald L. Martinez
and Robert M. Durling ; illustrations by Robert Turner.
p.   cm.   Includes bibliographical references
and index.   Contents: v. 1. Inferno.
ISBN 0-19-508740-2
ISBN 0-19-508744-5 (Pbk.)
I. Durling, Robert M.   II. Title.
PQ4315.D87   1996
851'.1—dc20   95-12740

1 3 5 7 9 10 8 6 4 2

Printed in the United States of America
on acid-free paper

PREFACE

A Note on the Text and Translation

In this first volume of our projected edition and translation of the *Divine Comedy*, the text of the *Inferno* is edited on the basis of the critical edition by Giorgio Petrocchi, sponsored by the Società Dantesca Italiana, *La Commedia secondo l'antica vulgata* (Copyright © 1994, Casa Editriee Le Lettre). We have departed from Petrocchi's readings in a number of cases, however, which are discussed under the rubric "Textual Variants" (page 585), and we have somewhat lightened Petrocchi's excessively heavy punctuation and have treated quotations according to American norms.

The translation is prose, as literal as possible, following as closely as practicable the syntax of the original; there is no padding, such as one finds in most verse translations. The closely literal style is a conscious effort to convey in part the nature of Dante's very peculiar Italian, notoriously craggy and difficult even for Italians. Dante is never bland: his vocabulary and syntax push at the limits of the language in virtually every line; there must be some tension, some strain, in any translation that respects the original. While we hope the translation reads well aloud, there is no effort to mirror Dante's sound effects—meaning and syntax are much more important for our purposes. Latin words and phrases are left untranslated and are explained in the notes; they add an important dimension.

The translation begins a new paragraph at each new terzina; the numbers in the margins are those of the first Italian line of each terzina. This format continually reminds the reader that the original is in verse. It helps approximate the narrative and syntactic rhythm of the original. It calls attention to Dante's frequent, emphatic enjambments between terzinas (the translation keeps the syntax distributed among the terzinas as closely as possible). It is designed to direct the reader's attention over to the original, and we believe it facilitates reference to particular lines and words: the reader of the translation can always identify the corresponding Italian, even finding the middle line of a terzina without difficulty.

A Note on the Notes

The notes make no pretension to scholarly completeness, but they are fuller than those found in many current translations; they are designed for the first-time reader of the poem. We have tried to strike a balance among the interests that compete for inclusion: information essential for comprehension, often about historical events and intellectual history; clarification of obscure or difficult passages; and illumination of the complexity of the language, the allusiveness, the intellectual content, and the formal structures of this masterpiece of late Gothic art. We have tried to give some idea of the tradition of commentary on the poem, now roughly 650 years old, and of current developments in Dante studies, many taking place on this side of the Atlantic. We have borrowed freely from earlier commentators and critics. Rather than take the readers' hands at every step and tell them exactly what to feel or think, we hope to present some of the materials with which they can build their own views of the poem.

Although fairly extensive, the notes are subject to limitations of space. In countless cases, it simply is not possible to cite differing views or shades of opinion. Usually, when a matter has been the subject of dispute, we call attention to the fact and list in the Bibliography suggestions for further study; but for the most part, we state our own position, with some of its reasons, and pass over in silence the views that we do not accept, many of them recent and set forth with great learning and cogency by their authors, whose indulgence we entreat. Any other approach would have swelled the notes beyond reason; furthermore, we really do not think it would be appropriate, in a commentary meant for readers approaching the poem for the first time, to include the details of scholarly disputes.

But of course your two annotators are human, and some of the details we have excluded from the notes themselves can be found in the "Additional Notes" at the end of the volume. Here each of us has taken the bit in his teeth on a few subjects dear to his scholarly heart. The titles of these short essays are self-explanatory, we believe; each carries an indication of the part of the poem it concerns or the place in the poem where the issues it discusses have emerged.

Acknowledgments

We have received generous help and encouragement from many friends and colleagues, and it is a pleasure to thank them. Robert McMahon and David Quint read portions of the manuscript at various stages of its evolution and made helpful suggestions. Ken Durling read the entire translation and the introduction; his criticisms were extremely helpful. Sarah Durling was a great help with the introduction. Richard Kay, Edward Peters, and R. A. Shoaf read selected cantos, both translation and commentary, and Charles T. Davis listened to the entire translation on tape;

we have adopted many of their suggestions. Ruggero Stefanini's counsel on textual matters was invaluable. Paul Alpers, Nicholas J. Perella, and Regina Psaki read the entire manuscript; they have saved us from a number of errors, and we have adopted a large percentage of their suggestions. Like those already mentioned, Margaret Brose, Rachel Jacoff, Victoria Kirkham, and Francesco Mazzoni have given us generous encouragement that has been important to us. Nancy Vine Durling has read the manuscript in all its versions; she has caught many mistakes, and her suggestions have been most useful. Mildred Durling, though her eyesight was failing, proofread the entire text of translation and notes and helped us avoid a significant number of errors. We thank Jean-François and Sabine Vasseur of Sceaux (France) and Doug Clow of Minneapolis for the cordial hospitality that made possible prolonged meetings of the collaborators. An NEH fellowship for university teachers granted to Ronald L. Martinez for a Dante-related project (1993–1994) contributed significantly to this venture as well. Our greatest debt is to Albert Russell Ascoli, who repeatedly gave both the translation and notes extremely detailed and searching scrutiny. In both, he saved us from errors, recalled us to balance and fairness, and made so many useful suggestions that there is hardly a page that does not reflect his influence. He and our other friends are not to blame, of course, for the errors and shortcomings that may remain. Finally, the patience, forbearance, and active help of our wives, Nancy Vine Durling and Mary Therese Royal de Martinez, have been essential.

In a very real sense, this book owes its existence to the extraordinary skill and care of Linda Robbins, Irene Pavitt, and Donna Ng of Oxford University Press; it is a pleasure to thank them.

The text of Giorgio Petrocchi's edition of the *Inferno* is reprinted (with the qualifications noted above) with the kind permission of the Società Dantesca Italiana and of the present publisher, Casa Editrice Le Lettere, Florence.

Translations of biblical passages are from the Douay version, except as noted; unless otherwise identified, all other translations in the notes are our own.

Berkeley   R. M. D.
Minneapolis   R. L. M.
October 1995

CONTENTS

Contents

ADDITIONAL NOTES

MAPS

FIGURES

Italy, ca. 1300.

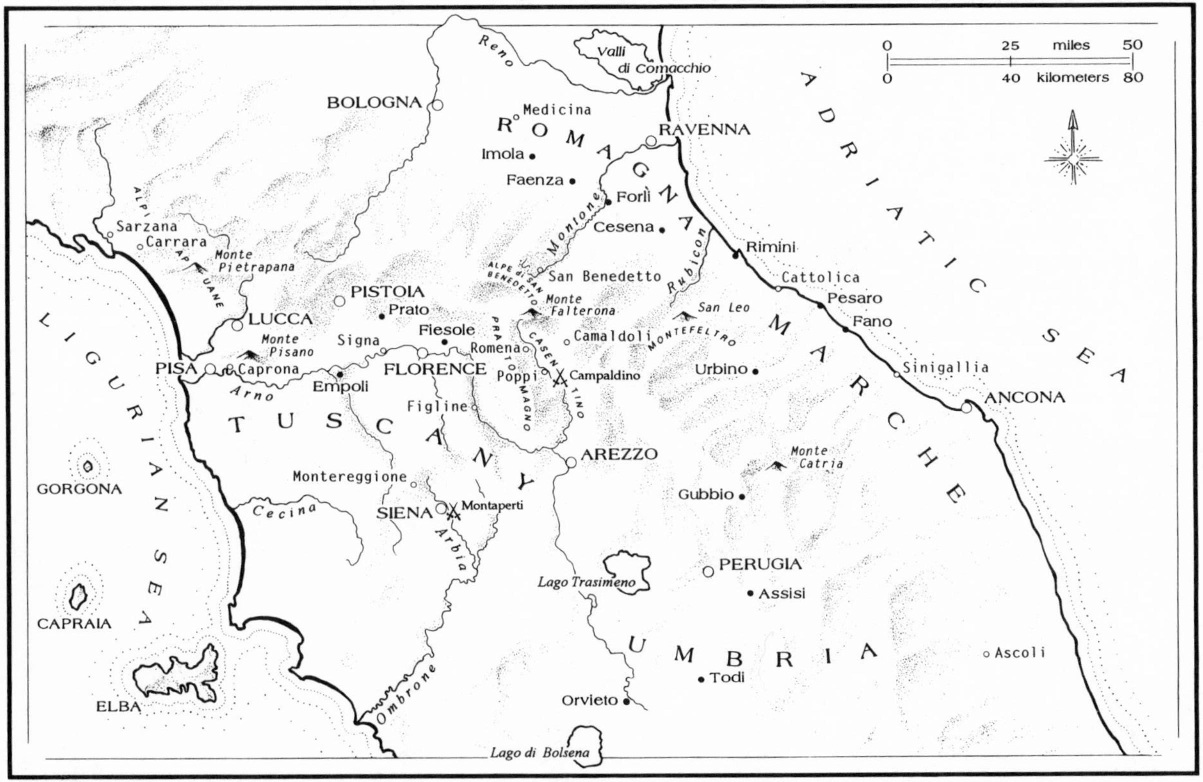

ADRIATIC SEA

LIGURIAN SEA

MARCHE

ROMAGNA

TUSCANY

UMBRIA

RAVENNA
BOLOGNA
Medicina
Imola
Faenza
Forlì
Cesena
Rimini
Cattolica
Pesaro
Fano
Sinigallia
ANCONA
Ascoli
San Leo
Urbino
Monte Catria
Gubbio
PERUGIA
Assisi
Todi
AREZZO
Orvieto
Lago Trasimeno
Lago di Bolsena
San Benedetto
Monte Falterona
Camaldoli
MONTEFELTRO
Campaldino
Poppi
CASENTINO
PRATOMAGNO
Romena
Figline
SIENA
Montaperti
Arbia
Ombrone
Montereggione
Cecina
FLORENCE
Fiesole
PISTOIA
Prato
Signa
Empoli
LUCCA
Monte Pisano
Caprona
PISA
Arno
Carrara
Monte Pietrapana
Sarzana
ALPI
APUANE
GORGONA
CAPRAIA
ELBA
Reno
valli di Comacchio
Montone
Rubicone
ALPE DI SAN BENEDETTO

miles
0   25   50
0   40   80
kilometers

Romagna and Tuscany, ca. 1300.

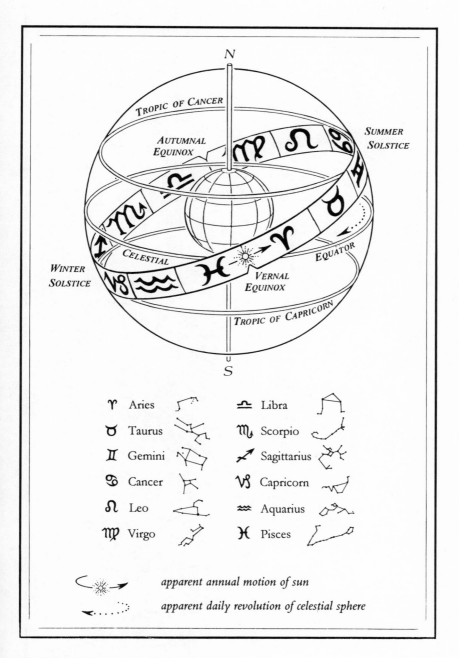

The Celestial Sphere and the Zodiac.

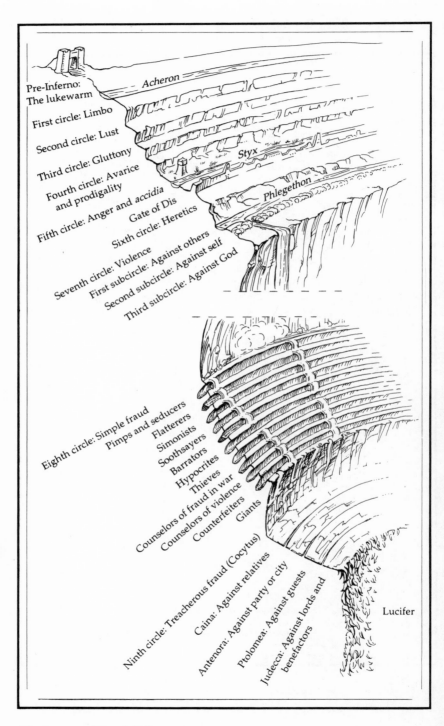

The Structure of Dante's Hell.

ABBREVIATIONS

Acts	The Acts of the Apostles
Aen.	Vergil, *Aeneid*
Apoc.	The Apocalypse of Saint John
Commentarii	Macrobius, *Commentarii in Somnium Scipionis*
Consolation	Boethius, *Philosophiae Consolatio*
Cor.	Saint Paul's Epistles to the Corinthians
Dan.	Daniel
Deut.	Deuteronomy
Eccles.	Ecclesiastes
Ecclus.	Ecclesiasticus
E.D.	*Enciclopedia dantesca*
Eph.	Saint Paul's Epistle to the Ephesians
Ex.	Exodus
Ezek.	Ezekiel
Gal.	Saint Paul's Epistle to the Galatians
Gen.	Genesis
Inf.	*Inferno*
Is.	Isaiah
Jer.	Jeremiah
John	The Gospel According to Saint John
Luke	The Gospel According to Saint Luke
Mark	The Gospel According to Saint Mark
Matt.	The Gospel According to Saint Matthew
Met.	Ovid, *Metamorphoses*
Par.	*Paradiso*
Peter	Saint Peter's Epistles
P. L.	*Patrologia Latina*
Prov.	The Book of Proverbs
Purg.	*Purgatorio*
Romans	Saint Paul's Epistle to the Romans
Servius	*Servii grammatici qui feruntur in Vergilii carmina commentarii*
Summa theol.	Thomas Aquinas, *Summa theologiae*

Theb.	Statius, *Thebaid*
Thess.	Saint Paul's Epistle to the Thessalonians
Wisdom	The Wisdom of Solomon

Authors' names not followed by dates (e.g., Singleton) refer to commentaries that are listed in the Bibliography under "Commentaries on the *Divine Comedy*"; authors' names followed by dates (e.g., Singleton 1966) refer to items listed in the Bibliography under "Modern Works." Primary sources are for the most part cited by author and abbreviated title; references are to editions listed under "Works by Dante" and "Primary Texts."

THE DIVINE COMEDY
OF DANTE ALIGHIERI

INTRODUCTION

The seventh centennial of Dante's death will take place in September 2021, at this writing little more than a quarter century in the future. After seven centuries his masterpiece, the *Divine Comedy*, continues to engage and fascinate readers all over the world, both those approaching it for the first time and those who know it intimately, from students and amateurs to professional scholars, in spite of the fact that the culture from which it springs is so distant and so different from our own. As even those who have not read the poem know, it recounts the journey of its protagonist (the poet himself) through the three realms of the medieval Catholic Otherworld: Hell, Purgatory, and Paradise. On this basic narrative thread of a complete tour of the cosmos and the moral universe that it embodies, with its great central theme of the education of the protagonist, is strung a series of remarkably vivid encounters with the inhabitants of the three realms. Under the guidance first of the soul of the poet Vergil,* then of his beloved Beatrice, who, he tells us in the *Vita nuova,* had died at the age of twenty-four, the protagonist meets the souls of those who have determined the nature of European history.

Dante's ultimate subject might be described as the ways the great cosmic and historical drama of God's creation of the world, man's fall, and humanity's redemption from sin is visible in history and in his own personal experience; his experience is always conceived as firmly located in place (Florence and the Italy of his day) and time (the late thirteenth century). For Dante, as for most medieval thinkers, the fate of the individual is inextricably bound up with that of society as a whole, but the great principles are always seen in terms of the actions and words of concretely represented individuals, as often as not contemporaries of the poet, usually those prominent in political life. More than any other major European poem, the *Comedy* is a detailed commentary on the political, economic, and social developments of its author's times.

Many of the historical events and individuals so important in Dante's experience are all but forgotten today, except among medieval historians (and, of course, students of the *Comedy*). But Dante's age was in fact a major turning point in European history, fraught with developments and problems whose results are still with us today, albeit in very different

*Modern scholarship has established that *Vergilius* is the correct spelling of Vergil's name; Dante follows the traditional medieval spelling in writing *Virgilio.* We shall maintain the distinction, using *Vergil* to refer to the historical Vergil, and *Virgil* to refer to the character in Dante's poem.

form: they include early capitalism, already revealing its tendency to engulf cities and local interests in the network of an international economy, closely associated with the development of international finance, in which Dante's city, Florence, was the acknowledged leader; the menacing rise of the nation-state, still in the form of feudal monarchy but increasingly centralized, ruthless, and violent, with the accompanying collapse of medieval internationalism; and the increasing involvement of the Christian Church in the economic and political struggles of the day, with the resultant corruption and compromise of its spiritual mission.

One of the reasons for the *Comedy*'s enduring vitality is that Dante saw so deeply into the nature of these problems. He also acknowledged very clearly that it was increasingly difficult to discern a providential plan, though he continued to believe there must be one. The terms of his analysis and of his imagined remedies are medieval, of course, which means theological, moralistic, and metaphysical, as opposed to structural, economic, or sociological in any modern sense. His grasp of the historic urgency of contemporary events, however, has largely been vindicated, and we can still learn from his powerful analysis—structural and sociological in its own way—of the nature of greed-motivated fraud, which Dante identified as a major social problem. And, like the question of the direction history is taking, the great moral and spiritual issues remain, though few today would wish to inhabit the cosmos Dante supposed was the theater of human action or the society he wished to see established.

We devote the bulk of this introduction to providing, in condensed and abbreviated form, some of the historical and biographical background essential to understanding the poem; much of this material is also discussed in the notes to the individual cantos. A brief concluding section discusses the form of the *Comedy*.

Dante's Times, Life, and Works

Dante Alighieri was born in Florence in 1265, probably in late May, to Bella and Alighiero degli Alighieri. His mother, perhaps of the prominent Abati family, died while Dante was still a boy. His father was a modest moneylender and speculator in land, descended from an old but much declined noble family; he died when Dante was about eighteen. At the time of Dante's birth, Florence, though already an important center of trade and banking, was scarcely more than a town of about 45,000, of whom only several thousand—males who were over thirty, owned property, and were related to powerful families—were eligible to vote and hold public office. By 1301, the date of the great disaster of Dante's life, his going into exile, Florence was one of the largest and most important cities in Europe, equal in size and importance to Paris, with a population of over 100,000 and financial and commercial interests that extended as far as England and Constantinople and even beyond. Like other independent city-states, Florence had always been deeply implicated in Italian and European politics, especially the great struggle between the emperors and the popes, and its phenomenal expansion during Dante's lifetime made its involvement ever deeper. The increasing commercialization of Florentine life and the corruption of the papacy seemed to Dante the two principal causes both of his own misfortunes and of the troubling developments he saw throughout Europe.

Dante followed Florentine tradition in dating the expansion of the city from the beginning of the twelfth century—thus during the lifetime of his ancestor Caccaguida degli Elisei, who appears in the poem in *Paradiso* 15–18—an era the poet idealized as one of peace, simplicity, and civic virtue. Favorably located on the trade routes between the Mediterranean basin and northern Europe, Florence developed important wool-finishing and silk industries early and began to assert its power in the surrounding countryside and against the smaller towns of central Tuscany: Fiesole, a chief rival, was conquered and destroyed in 1125. The population of Florence expanded steadily; the city walls Cacciaguida had known, built around 1072, were replaced after 1172 with a new circle of walls, enclosing three times the earlier area. During Dante's youth the expansion became even more rapid: in 1284 new walls were begun, designed to enclose eight times the area of 1172 (they were not finished until 1333). Ambitious projects for churches, bridges, and public buildings were undertaken: Santa Maria Novella, the Dominican church, was begun in 1279; Santa Croce, the Franciscan church, was expanded in 1295; Santa Maria del Fiore, the new cathedral, or Duomo, was begun in 1294; the Baptistery of San Giovanni was entirely renovated in the 1290s, with resplendent internal mosaics that may or may not have been finished when Dante went into exile. Two hundred years of exploding wealth, population, and civil strife help explain Dante's condemnation of acquisitiveness and political factionalism as well as his changing views on republican versus imperial forms of government.

For several centuries the jockeying for commercial and dynastic advantage among Europe's growing national powers had been overshadowed by the bitter struggle for hegemony between the increasingly ambitious popes and the Holy Roman Emperors. The emperors were the feudal heads of an "empire" more legal and traditional than real, embracing much of central western Europe, including Italy; it was often claimed to be continuous with the Roman empire founded by Augustus, by virtue of its supposed restoration when the pope crowned Charlemagne emperor in the year 800. The long rivalry had reached a decisive stage during the two decades preceding Dante's birth, when Frederick II of Hohenstaufen, grandson of the great emperor Frederick Barbarossa and heir through his mother to the Norman kingdoms of Naples and Sicily, was made emperor (1212). Among Frederick's holdings were feudal dependencies in northern Italy, including a number of prosperous cities, as well as in southern Italy and Sicily; his lands thus completely encircled the traditional possessions of the popes, the so-called patrimony of Saint Peter, comprising parts of modern Latium, Umbria, Romagna, and the Marches (see the maps on pages xiii–xvi). Frederick II was known as *Stupor mundi* [Wonder of the World] because of his formidable abilities and the brilliance of his court, which welcomed Moslem as well as Christian scientists and artists and first developed courtly poetry in Italian (including the sonnet). He was in many respects an enlightened ruler, but throughout his reign he was forced to struggle against his papal antagonists, Gregory IX, Innocent IV, and Clement IV, who considered his power and influence a danger to the Church. Excommunicated and declared deposed by the council of bishops held at Lyons in 1245, beleaguered but still in power, Frederick died suddenly in 1250. This was an opportunity Clement IV could not ignore; he promised Charles of Anjou, the brother of Louis IX of France, all of southern Italy and Sicily as a papal fief if he could conquer it.

All over Europe the conflict between the popes and the emperors had split local communities: supporters of the popes were known as Guelfs (after the powerful Welf family, dukes of Bavaria—the *w* → *gw* shift is common in the Romance languages), and those of the emperors were known as Ghibellines (after the castle of Waibling, traditionally owned by the emperors). Florence was no exception, and historians have shown that its division into Guelf and Ghibelline parties was the expression of long-standing rivalries between clans of similar economic and social profiles rather than the reflection of differences of class or ideology, though these soon emerged. Originally rural landowners, the clans took up residence in the city as its importance increased, building fortress-like palaces equipped with high towers—useful for both defense and reconnaissance—from which they continued their vendettas. The city's tradition of representative government grew out of the necessity of controlling the clans' rivalries and inclinations toward private war. Some clans adhered to the traditional loyalty to the empire, of which Tuscany was still a fief, while others saw an opportunity to expand their own interests in alliance with the popes.

According to the Florentine chroniclers, Guelfs and Ghibellines coexisted peacefully in the city until Buondelmonte de' Buondelmonti, a prominent Guelf, broke his engagement to a daughter of the Ghibelline

Donati family and married another; to avenge this slight the Donati and their relatives the Lamberti murdered Buondelmonte on Easter, 1215, near the Ponte Vecchio. Thenceforth violence became increasingly prevalent. While this single event scarcely explains the social tensions within the city, it does suggest how networks of rival clans could polarize it. Over time these networks became ever more entangled, so that by Dante's day, when the Guelfs themselves split into "White" and "Black" factions, it is almost impossible to say why one family saw its interests lying more with one side than with another. By then, however, new lines of antagonism had emerged, pitting the members of the trade guilds against the more powerful families, the "Magnates."

One of Frederick II's last maneuvers had been to furnish a troop of cavalry that helped the Florentine Ghibellines drive out the Guelfs in February 1248. The Guelfs returned victorious in January 1250, after Frederick's death, driving the Ghibellines out in their turn. Guelf domination coincided with a major change in the constitution of the city, known as the *Primo popolo* [literally, first (government of the) people], reflecting a new assertiveness in the increasingly powerful trade guilds. The new government prohibited private towers higher than 150 feet (all exceeding that height were ordered reduced) and established a new official, the *Capitano del popolo* [captain of the people], charged with maintaining the peace, alongside the traditional *podestà* [mayor]. Meanwhile, with the help of Frederick II's natural son Manfred, king of Naples and Sicily, the Ghibellines all over Italy were mobilizing against Charles of Anjou. The Tuscan (especially Florentine and Sienese) Ghibellines, along with German troops furnished by King Manfred, massacred the Florentine Guelfs at Montaperti, near Siena, in 1260, a battle still remembered with great bitterness forty years later, according to Dante (see *Inferno* 10, with notes). Ghibelline rule was short-lived, however, for in 1266, Charles of Anjou and his largely French army defeated and killed Manfred at Benevento (see map), and in 1268, in a battle at Tagliacozzo (see map), captured Frederick's eighteen-year-old grandson Conradino, later beheaded in Naples. Charles was thus established as the ruler of Sicily and southern Italy, under the overlordship of the pope, and his hegemony extended much further; he was made *podestà* of Florence, where he ruled through *vicarii* [vicars]. The Angevin "protectorate" thus replaced Hohenstaufen "tyranny," until the death of Charles of Anjou in 1285 and especially the election of Pope Boniface VIII in 1294; once again the balance of power had shifted.

Many Italian cities remained Ghibelline after Charles's victory; some of the more prominent were Verona, Siena, and Pisa. Guelf Florence was continually at war with its Tuscan Ghibelline rivals. According to a letter written by Dante (now lost), Dante was in the first line of cavalry at the battle of Campaldino in June 1289, when the Guelfs defeated the Ghibellines of Arezzo; in *Inferno 22* he tells us that he saw the surrender of Caprona, a Pisan stronghold, which took place later in the same year. Periods of uneasy peace alternated with armed conflict; Florence was to achieve definite victory over its hated rival Pisa only in the sixteenth century.

There were efforts to reconcile Ghibellines and Guelfs within Florence, the most important of which took place in 1280; after its failure, the city embarked on a new process of democratizing its constitution (the *Secondo popolo*), which shifted all power of choosing city officials to the trade guilds, while eventually expanding the number of enfranchised guilds from seven to twenty-one. A decade after the creation in 1282 of a board of six *Priori* [priors] as the executive branch of the government, the process of democratization came to a head with the promulgation of the *Ordinamenti di giustizia* [Ordinances of Justice] in 1293, whose main provision was to exclude from public offices all members of noble families sufficiently powerful to be classed as Magnates; soon thereafter, however, several of the more rigid restrictions were relaxed (1295), and it became possible for nobles who were guild members to hold public office. This made it possible for Dante to enter politics, and he became eligible to do so by joining the guild (*Arte*) of doctors and apothecaries.

The election of Benedetto Caetani, member of a powerful Roman clan, to the papacy as Boniface VIII brought to the throne of Saint Peter a particularly able, ambitious, and ruthless man, eager to consolidate and extend the power of the Church everywhere in Europe. He claimed that with the imperial throne vacant, jurisdiction over Tuscany reverted to the papacy, and he was determined to break the Florentine habit of independence. Dante advanced through a series of minor offices and at last, in 1300, was elected to serve a (normal) two-month term as one of the six priors (June 15–August 15), but his rise to political influence took place in circumstances that were increasingly dangerous, particularly since the antagonism between the White Guelfs (Dante's party) and the Black Guelfs became increasingly hostile, culminating in bloody riots on May 1 and June 23 (perhaps intentionally fostered by the pope). The six priors, Dante among them, exiled the leaders of the two factions, including the turbulent Guido Cavalcanti, Dante's friend (see the notes to Canto 10); the Blacks, however, refused to abide by the sentence, and the next group of priors recalled the Whites as well.

These troubles were the subject of many anxious public meetings, at which it seems clear that Dante took a leading role. Those who, like Dante, were desirous of moderation and reconciliation decided to appeal to the pope to mediate between the two parties, unaware that he secretly favored the Blacks, and to this end the city sent two embassies to Rome, one in November 1300 and one in October 1301. Dante was a member of at least one of these delegations, though it is not entirely certain which one; according to early biographers, he was in Siena, on his way home from the second of them in November 1301, when he learned of the events that would mean he would never again see his beloved native city.

For Boniface had secretly connived both with the Blacks and with a young brother of Philip IV (the Fair) of France, the adventurer Charles of Valois (Lackland), who was leading an army south to attempt the reconquest of Sicily, which had rebelled against the Angevins in 1282. On November 1, 1301, as the official peacemaker appointed by the pope, Charles gained entry to Florence with his army. Once inside, according to his agreement with the pope (documentation of which still exists), he cooperated with the Blacks in their violent coup d'état, during which the leading White Guelfs were killed or driven from the city and had their property confiscated or destroyed.

Dante was accused and tried in absentia (January 1302) on trumped-up charges of forgery, embezzlement, and opposition to the pope; when he did not respond he was, in subsequent proclamations, stripped of his property and condemned, if captured, to be burnt at the stake. Confiscation of property, exile, and loss of citizenship were even more severe to a Tuscan of 1300 than the equivalent would be today; there was no provision for "naturalization" into some other community; also, as Dante complained, the unthinking supposed that official condemnation must be justified.

By the time of his exile Dante was known as a poet and intellectual of some distinction. Precisely where he began the education that ultimately made him one of the best-informed individuals of his age is not fully known. He probably had private tutoring as a boy, which taught him the rudiments of Latin and a few of the elementary Latin classics, like Phaedrus's *Fables* and the *Distichs* of Cato. He may have attended the cathedral school, and there is a strong possibility that he was able to attend lectures accessible to laymen at the *studia* of Santa Maria Novella and Santa Croce, where he might have heard teachers like the Dominican Remigio de' Girolami, who had strong views on the importance of civic institutions, and Peter John Olivi, a radical Franciscan critic of ecclesiastical wealth. It is virtually certain that Dante went to Bologna in the late 1280s (one of his poems was copied there in 1287); there he would have come into contact with the dominant intellectual trend of Aristotelian natural science, though in what capacity we do not know. That he had any direct schooling from Brunetto Latini, the prehumanist described by the chronicler Villani as the "refiner of the Florentines," is uncertain, but Brunetto—a man of letters, the political theorist of the *Secondo popolo,* and a trusted political counselor to the Florentine commune from 1266 until his death in 1293—provided him with an important early example of civic engagement inspired by classical models.

The high culture of the Middle Ages had always been dominated by Latin, the language of the Bible, of the Church, of government, diplomacy, theology, philosophy, science. Only recently, first in Provence with the upsurge, beginning in the early twelfth century, of a brilliant courtly civilization whose most characteristic product was the poetry of the troubadors, had poetry and prose in a European vernacular begun to attract international notice. The movement caught on at the French-speaking court of the Angevin kings of England and in northern France, especially in the aristocratic circles of prosperous cities, often the courts of minor rulers. Concomitantly with the development of the Gothic cathedrals came the spread of courtly romance, including Arthurian romance, courtly love poetry, and courtly ideals of behavior and style, especially through the influence of the poet Chrétien de Troyes (active in Champagne ca. 1170–1180). With the rise of the universities, poetry in the vernacular became increasingly learned. Paris became an important literary as well as intellectual center, and philosophical poetry in the vernacular was born with the continuation and completion (ca. 1274) of the *Romance of the Rose* by the bourgeois intellectual Jean de Meun. Literary prose came into existence in French as vast cycles of Arthurian romance were compiled in the early thirteenth century: the so-called Vulgate Cycle, centering on Lancelot and Guinevere, and the Tristan Cycle. The fashions spread to Austria, Spain, England, Italy, and elsewhere.

In Italy the themes and forms of troubador verse were introduced, as we have mentioned, at the court of Frederick II, which traveled both in the north and in the south and kept in contact with new trends everywhere. Frederick's courtiers and officials adapted the Provençal *canso* to create the Italian *canzone,* and they invented the sonnet. Soon after midcentury the movement was spreading to Tuscany, with the satirical, moralizing canzoni of Guittone d'Arezzo, and to the Italian university cities, especially Bologna, where Guido Guinizelli, probably a prominent judge, created a new suavity and philosophical intensity in love poetry; Dante was to call Guinizelli "the father of me and of all my betters who ever used sweet, graceful rhymes of love" (*Purg.* 26.97–99). Legal circles in Bologna took keen interest in the new poetry, and the fashion arose of filling out the spaces at the bottom of parchment legal documents (as an attestation of the integrity of the pages) with quotations from it, a fashion that enables us to document the early circulation of Dante's lyrics and of the *Inferno*.

In Florence, in ferment with its new expansion and prosperity, the fashion caught on with characteristic elegance and intensity. When Dante was in his teens there were a score of accomplished writers of sonnets and canzoni: lawyers, physicians, and aristocrats. Dante began writing poetry—mainly sonnets and canzoni—under the influence especially of Guinizelli, from whom he adopted the theme of the so-called *donna angelicata*, the lady so pure and beautiful as to seem an angel, named Beatrice [she who makes blessed] in Dante's poems. His entrance on the Florentine literary scene was characteristically self-conscious, if it followed a typical mode of the day. He sent a sonnet (later made the first poem in the *Vita nuova*) to "many of those who were famous poets in those days," as he says in the *Vita nuova*, including the most elegant and gifted of them, Guido Cavalcanti, whom we have already met as a turbulent Guelf. The sonnet asked for interpretation of a portentous love-dream; three replies survive, including one from Cavalcanti, which Dante says was "quasi lo principio de l'amistà tra lui e me" [almost the beginning of the friendship between him and me]. In retrospect Dante's entrance on the literary scene can seem portentous. His works, and those of his followers Petrarch and Boccaccio, established the Tuscan vernacular as a literary medium worthy of comparison with Latin and Greek. This prestige in turn led to the great revolution of literary style of the Renaissance as Italian influence spread throughout Europe in the fifteenth and sixteenth centuries.

The *Vita nuova*, Dante's first important work, completed by 1295, is a selection among his early poems about Beatrice, accompanied by a prose narrative that explains the occasion of each, arranged so that they form an idealized account of how Beatrice's miraculous influence shaped his life, both as lover and as poet. At the center of the book is her death, recorded as occurring on June 8, 1290; the second half relates a period of grief and disorientation until a vision of her in Heaven calls the writer's devotion back to her memory. The elaborate dating of her death suggests that Beatrice was a historical figure, but although she has been plausibly identified with Beatrice Portinari, daughter of Folco Portinari and wife to Simone de' Bardi, a wealthy banker (to whom she bore several children), the book bears no trace of these domestic circumstances; there is likewise no trace of the fact that Dante himself had been married in the mid-1280s to Gemma Donati, to whom he had been betrothed in 1277 while still an adolescent.

Though in some respects appreciably juvenile, the *Vita nuova* already demonstrates Dante's genius for arranging complex, cumulative verbal structures; it reflects deep, if not wide, reading, especially of Boethius's

Consolatio Philosophiae [Consolation of Philosophy] and of several of Cicero's dialogues, as well as of Provençal, French, and Italian poetry. It also introduces Dante's complex, in many ways mysterious relationship with his friend and poetic rival Guido Cavalcanti, whose sympathy with heretical philosophical doctrines—such as the mortality of the individual human soul—Dante deplored.

Dante continued to write poems, and not long after completing the *Vita nuova*, probably in 1296, he wrote a group of four canzoni, usually called the *rime petrose* [stony rhymes], poems of challenging power and formal difficulty addressed to a lady called "stone" (*petra*), in which the poet's frustrated sexuality and feelings of violent resentment toward the conventional "lady" of amatory verse are given scope to a degree unusual for the Middle Ages. Trends incipient in the *Vita nuova*—representation of the poet as a microcosm, the idea of the human being as the horizon of the material and spiritual (a Platonic problematic considered an existential predicament until the mid-seventeenth century), the function of poetry as the salve or sublimation of the poet's failures, whether erotic or political—are brought to a remarkable focus in the *petrose* and serve, we have argued, as a principal proving ground for the work that still lay in the future.

In the years following his exile, Dante's movements are difficult to trace exactly: he lingered in Tuscany and participated, along with other exiled Whites, in abortive attempts to reenter the city (1302–1303). He received hospitality from Bartolommeo della Scala, lord of Verona, in 1303 and 1304 (he would later dedicate the *Paradiso* to Bartolommeo's son Can Grande). Early in 1304 Dante broke decisively with the Whites, and, astonishingly for the times, dissociated himself from all political parties and became "a party by [himself]," as he has his ancestor Cacciaguida say in *Par.* 17.69. The years 1305 to 1307 saw Dante in northeastern Italy, in the region then known as the March of Treviso; he was in Padova in 1306, where he may have met Giotto at work on the Scrovegni chapel, and in Lunigiana in 1307 on an errand for the Malaspina family; in 1308 he seems to have been in Forlì and may have stopped in Lucca. Boccaccio and the chronicler Villani claim he journeyed to Paris in 1308 to 1309 but offer no corroborating evidence. Around 1310 to 1311, Dante is in the Casentino, near the headwaters of the Arno, probably at the castle of Poppi (see map) with Guido da Battifolle; in 1312, he may have met the emperor Henry VII in his camp near Pisa.

During the years 1310 to 1313, Dante followed closely the efforts of Henry VII of Luxembourg, the Holy Roman Emperor (elected 1308), to reimpose imperial authority in northern and central Italy, a campaign upon which Dante based great hopes for the reform of Italian and European political life. In 1313, after the failure of the long-awaited (and too-long-delayed) siege of Florence, a center of resistance to him, Henry fell sick and died. By then Dante had written several impassioned letters hailing him as the appointed savior of Italy and had also written to the Florentines condemning in the harshest terms their resistance to Henry's claims. After the collapse of imperial hopes, Dante's later years were spent as the guest of Can Grande della Scala at Verona (perhaps 1314–1316) and then, from perhaps about 1317, of Guido minore da Polenta (the nephew of Francesca da Rimini) in Ravenna, then a peaceful and palpably archaic city, dotted with ancient Christian temples decorated with shimmering mosaics. In Ravenna Dante enjoyed considerable status, gathering around him a coterie of disciples (though he did no formal teaching); he was joined there by his sons Jacopo and Pietro, who had fallen under a reiteration of their father's condemnation (1315) upon reaching majority; his daughter Antonia was a nun there, with the name Beatrice. Of Dante's wife, Gemma, there is no word. In 1321, after fulfilling a diplomatic mission in defense of his hosts before the Venetian council of state, Dante caught a fever (probably malaria) while traversing the swampy Comacchio region of the Po estuary; he died in Ravenna on September 13 or 14 of the same year.

Thus most of Dante's works, including the *Comedy,* were written in exile, a fact to which most of them allude. Probably the most important work, next to the *Comedy,* is the *Convivio* [Banquet], planned as a feast of wisdom offered to its readers, written in Italian because its intended audience was those who followed the active life with no leisure for study and who thus knew no Latin. It is a prose commentary, deploying a formidable mixture of Aristotelian and Neoplatonic lore for the explanation of three previously composed canzoni. Although the commentary is coordinated with the poems, Dante finds room to hold forth on the relation of the vernacular and Latin, on the hierarchy of the liberal arts in relation to theology and the structure of the cosmos, and on the correlation of the Aristotelian virtues to the ages of man. In its present form—only four of fifteen projected books (on fourteen canzoni) were completed—the work is organized around the writer's devotion to the personified lady Philosophy, a form of the biblical *Sapientia* [Wisdom], who is presented as the successor to Beatrice.

Probably between the composition of the third and fourth books of the *Convivio,* Dante began a Latin treatise, *De vulgari eloquentia* [On eloquence in the vernacular], also left unfinished. After a preamble on the necessity of language itself, a critique of the various dialects in use in

Italy in the thirteenth century leads to the suggestion that the proper language of vernacular poetry—referred to as the "illustrious vernacular"—exists in no single court of Italy (for Italy lacks a unifying court), but rather virtually, in the use of all who write well. The illustrious vernacular once established, Dante uses examples culled from Provençal, French, Sicilian, and north-central Italian poets to derive the preferred forms and diction of the canzone.

Certainly after 1309, very possibly as late as 1317, Dante wrote a treatise on world government, the *Monarchia*, which argues for the necessity of a single all-powerful emperor as ruler of the world on a priori, historical-theological, and polemical grounds: a single emperor is necessary because the single human race, with the single goal of full actualization of its intellectual powers, requires peace, which only a single emperor can guarantee; the present emperor is the successor of Caesar and of Augustus, under whose authority Christ chose to be born, thus Rome's power was providentially established by God; the papal arguments denying the equal competences, in their separate spheres, of pope and emperor are therefore demonstrably false.

Dante wrote other, less important works during his exile: several more canzoni and short poems; a number of letters, some of them with important political content; one letter, of debated attribution, expounding the prologue (really the first eighteen lines) of the *Paradiso* for Can Grande della Scala of Verona; a scholastic disputation on the distribution of earth and water on the surface of the earth; and two Latin eclogues in response to poems by Giovanni del Virgilio, an early Bolognese humanist, encouraging Dante to write in Latin and to accept being crowned in Bologna with the laurel.

Not the least of the consequences of Dante's exile is that his work was done in the unpropitious circumstances of a wandering existence, with no fixed residence or library, no real status except that conferred on him ad hoc by his various hosts. Dante's memory, like that of Aquinas, must have been prodigious, allowing him to quote scores of texts known by heart. Among other effects of his exile were his sense, often attested in the poem, of the diverse linguistic traditions and dialects of Italy, and his resulting awareness of the need for a common literary language and a universal monarchical government that might stem the factionalism of the Italian cities.

The most important labor of Dante's exile was, of course, the vast *Comedy*—not vast in length (it is 14,233 lines long), but in scope and power. Current thinking suggests that the *Inferno* was published around 1314 (including revisions; a first version was probably ready by 1310) with the *Purgatorio* following shortly thereafter, and that the *Paradiso* was brought to completion by 1320 in Ravenna. Dante's poem could have taken the form that it did, and acquired the finish that it possesses, at few other moments in history: that is, at any time other than just before the breaking up of the attempt, begun by scholastics like Albertus Magnus and Thomas Aquinas, to harmonize the philosophy of Aristotle with the teaching of the Catholic Church.

For Dante came to maturity when the most sweeping and exciting intellectual revolution of the Middle Ages had just crested. The years 1190 to 1250 had witnessed the introduction of the majority of the corpus of Aristotle's writings, including works on physics, biology, ethics, psychology (in the older sense, the study of the embodied rational soul), politics, and metaphysics. These far surpassed in scope and power anything else available and made possible much broader and more intelligent and sympathetic observation of natural phenomena and human institutions. The renewed natural and human sciences were proposed, moreover, through Aristotle's own methods of inquiry and argument (logic, dialectic, and rhetoric), of great power and persuasiveness; little wonder that scholars of the day seem to have felt they might come to know virtually everything. This movement was inextricably bound up with the rise of the cities and their new universities, and roughly contemporaneous with the rise of literature in the vernaculars.

Although the first Latin versions of Aristotle (from translators in Toledo, Spain, and in southern Italy) began to circulate toward the end of the twelfth century, it was not until 1255 that Aristotle's *Nichomachean Ethics* was actually a required text at the University of Paris, the center of the Aristotelian revival. From the very beginning, however, there had been reaction from traditional theological circles, who saw in the works of Aristotle (and in their dissemination, especially by masters from the Dominican order) both a challenge to their domination over the diffusion of knowledge—not to mention the control of university chairs—and, as the best young minds began to subject questions of faith to the razors of dialectic, a dangerous invasion of the sanctum of Christian truth by rationalistic ideas and styles of thought. A number of episcopal injunctions early in the century culminated in 1277 with the condemnation by Etienne Tempier, bishop of Paris, of over two hundred propositions: even a number of positions taught by Thomas Aquinas (d. 1274) were declared erroneous. Such discouragement did not, however, much diminish the spread of Aristotle's influence, and many of his views and methods became part of the common heritage of learned inquiry. Dante was the heir and product of this intellectual ferment, and the unique combination of conceptual clarity and vivid, realistic presentation of the natural and human world we see in the *Comedy* is one expression of a thirteenth-century worldview shaped by the scholastic interpretation of Aristotle and the shift of interest to natural phenomena that accompanied it.

The *Comedy* was also deeply shaped by another influence, that of the Franciscan movement, history's most revolutionary protest against the wealth of the Church. Saint Francis of Assisi (1181?–1226, canonized 1228) was the son of a rich merchant; he publicly renounced his patrimony before the bishop in order to espouse a life of utter poverty and severely ascetic penitence, all in a spirit of spontaneous joyfulness and loving identification with the suffering Christ. Disciples flocked to the *poverello di Dio* [God's poor little one] as he became known; in a few years the Order of Lesser Brothers (*Ordo fratrum minorum*), verbally authorized by the pope in 1210, later confirmed with a charter, grew into one of the largest and most powerful organizations in Europe. In spite of Francis's efforts to maintain the purity of his original conception, the order became immensely rich (and inevitably corrupt) and was split by bitter disputes on the issue of property (the saint's will prohibiting the owning of property by the order or its members was declared invalid by the pope in 1230). A large group within the order, however, did continue the polemic in favor of apostolic poverty.

Saint Francis himself had written the first great Italian lyric, the "Cantico di frate Sole" [Canticle of Brother Sun], in rapturous praise of the beauty of creation, and the Franciscan movement, with its essentially democratizing impulse, gave powerful impetus to Italian as a medium of devotional poetry. Along with their rivals the Dominicans, the Franciscan masters dominated instruction in theology at the universities; they were leaders in forming the new scientific orientations of the fourteenth century, and by the time of Dante's death the principles on which Albertus and Aquinas had built their remarkable syntheses were under withering attack from a new generation of nominalist scholastics, chief among them the Franciscans Duns Scotus (1265?–1308) and William of Occam (d. 1350): like the first general of the Franciscan order, Saint Bonaventura (1221–1274), they remained faithful to an Augustinianism that emphasized God's omnipotent will rather than rational continuities. The influence of the Franciscan movement and its characteristic sensibility is visible everywhere in thirteenth- and fourteenth-century art (Giotto is the leading example), architecture, and literature.

As C. H. Grandgent observed long ago, a number of medieval literary genres are digested and combined in Dante's poem: the dream-vision (exemplified by the Old French *Romance of the Rose*), which included first-person narration and a global perspective achieved in a dream; accounts of journeys to the Otherworld (such as the *Visio Pauli*, Saint Patrick's

Purgatory, the *Navigatio Sancti Brendani*), which contributed the ideas of distinct areas of punishment and of bringing news of punishment to spark repentance; philosophical allegory, sometimes of the *prosimetrum* (mixed verse and prose) variety, such as Boethius's *Consolatio Philosophiae* (the *Vita nuova* and, in a sense, the *Convivio* are *prosimetra*); the medieval encyclopedia (e.g., Isidore, Brunetto Latini, Vincent of Beauvais, Bartholomew of England), which brings together information on all subjects; and finally, the supreme work of the medieval theologian, the comprehensive presentation of theological knowledge in a *summa*.

Dante frames a number of problems in the poem as scholastic *quaestiones*; but the parallel with scholastic method goes deeper. We might here recall Erwin Panofsky's thesis that the same principles governed the scholastic *summae* and the great Gothic cathedrals: the cathedrals, like the highly rationalized sequence of topics of a *summa*, exhibit clarity for clarity's sake, manifesting the exhaustive articulation of their parts; but, like the balancing of authorities and reason in the scholastic response to a question, they also embody a principle of concord, or reconciliation of contradictory views, in that the history of solutions to specific problems (like the insertion of a rose window into a markedly vertical facade) begins by sharpening and concludes by reconciling opposing tendencies. Both clarity of articulation and concord can be found at work in the *Comedy*, for example in Virgil's account of love in *Purgatorio* 17–18, or in *Paradiso* 4, where Dante reconciles Platonic and Christian views on the influence of the planets. And an even more fundamental parallel links the form of the *Summae* of Alexander of Hales and Aquinas, and no doubt others, and of the *Comedy*: the order of subjects discussed in these *Summae* is explicitly conceived as a procession from God, through the creatures and man, then back to God via the mediation of human will and the Incarnation. A similar procession and return is discernible in Dante's poem, which begins with the descent of Beatrice to help Dante, lost in the wood of error, and then returns through Hell, Purgatory, and the heavenly bodies to the universal source in God.

Dante's most important literary models, however, were Vergil's epic poem, the *Aeneid*, and the Vulgate, or Latin Bible. The *Aeneid* is the epic of Rome, the city that would one day be the seat of the papacy and the source of the imperial authority to which Dante looked for the restoration of justice in the world; its author is imagined to be Dante's guide through the first two parts of the poem, which is partly to say that Dante's account of Hell and Purgatory is ruled to a considerable extent by precedents in the *Aeneid*. In the tradition of its late antique commentators, Dante viewed Vergil's poem as a work that embraced the whole cosmos and all of history; but the *Comedy* exceeds even that measure, for it depicts this life and the next; it traverses Hell, Purgatory, and Heaven. As Auerbach showed, it exhibits all levels of style and draws from all genres, a diversity of register impossible for classical epic.

Such breadth and variety can be matched within a single book only by the Bible, which is itself a miscellaneous compilation of verse and prose, myth, chronicle, prophecy, allegory, and sententious wisdom, high style and low (although always sublime in some sense, being the transcription of God's word). Medieval study of the Bible also affects how we interpret Dante's poem, for Dante's views of the multiple meanings possible for a text derive directly from techniques of biblical interpretation typical of his age (although by Dante's day even works written by pagans— Ovid's *Metamorphoses,* for example—were interpreted in a similar way). Although the manner and extent of Dante's application of such schemes to his own poem is hotly disputed, that the richness of the poem's meaning is in some sense analogous to that of the Bible (as then interpreted) has been an influential view among modern students of the poem.

The *Comedy* is much too complex a poem for us to attempt to give a full account of it in this brief introduction. Instead, we conclude this section with discussion of one important image that can stand, metaphorically, for the whole *Comedy*: the "ladder of creation," sometimes called the "great chain of being" or "Homer's golden chain." Dante's poem is the fullest representation ever made of this ancient concept, so influential in Western thought. Its most significant implication is that the hierarchy of logical classes (species and genera) coincides with the hierarchy of being and value; thus every created thing has a unique and inevitable place in the order of the cosmos.

That the various, hierarchically arranged levels of creation are viewed as a "ladder" or (preferably) "stairway" becomes explicit in the *Paradiso,* with Jacob's ladder—Dante specifies that it is "golden"—which reaches from the sphere of Saturn to the Empyrean, beyond space and time, in Cantos 21–22. Thus all creation descends from God stepwise in a "great chain of being," described by the Neoplatonist Macrobius as "an uninterrupted connection of interlocking links from the supreme deity as far as the last dregs of things"; Macrobius identifies this chain with the "golden chain of Homer" (actually, a rope) mentioned in the *Iliad.* Although thus explicit only in *Paradiso* (why this is so we will see in a moment), the image of the pilgrim's journey as proceeding gradually along a stairway recurs throughout the poem: frequently in the *Purgatorio* to describe the penitential climb through the seven realms of purgation (3.50–56; 11.40–44; 17.60–62; 27.122–24) and sparingly in *Inferno,* notably in the description of both Geryon and Lucifer as "ladders" necessary to the traversing of Hell (17.82–86; 34.82–86; note the same line numbers) and in Virgil's description of Hell in Canto 11 (cf. "descending step by step," lines 17–18). Repeatedly Dante rhymes words for stairway or ladder (*scala, scale*) with the words for wings (*ale, ali*) and for climbing (*sale, salire*) or descending (*cala, calare*). These recurring rhymes correlate, and reiterate, the essential aspects of the pilgrim's journey as first a descent, then an ascent along the stairway of being; they are links in the chain and correlate the narrative of the poem with the concatenation of its rhymes.

For Dante, the image of the great chain of being had been filtered through late antique Neoplatonism; in addition to Macrobius, the idea is important to Augustine, Boethius, and especially Dionysius the Areopagite, the extraordinarily influential sixth-century writer who successfully imposed on the whole Middle Ages his claim to be the Dionysius converted by Saint Paul in Acts 17 (Saint Denis, the patron saint of France). In the twelfth and thirteenth centuries the image reappears among the Platonizing writers associated with the school of Chartres, while monastic writers pair it with the biblical image of Jacob's ladder (Gen. 28.12). Contemporary with Dante, Jacob's ladder as the "ladder of being" is readily found in the widely read *Journey of the Mind to God* by the Franciscan Saint Bonaventura, where the visible creation is treated as a ladder to be ascended through contemplation to the vision of God:

> Since, then, we must mount Jacob's ladder before descending it, let us place the first rung of the ascension in the depths, putting the whole sensible world before us as a mirror, by which ladder we shall cross over to God, the Supreme Creator, that we may be true Hebrews crossing from Egypt to the land promised to our fathers; let us also be Christians crossing with Christ from this world over to the Father. (John 13.1)

The parallel Bonaventura draws here between the Exodus from Egypt and the Atonement is fundamental to the *Comedy*, as the epistle to Can Grande says. Bonaventura fuses it with the idea of the ladder, and this fusion is also part of Dante's conception. When the pilgrim, in the heaven of Mars, is told by his ancestor Cacciaguida that during his approaching exile he will experience "what a hard path it is to descend and mount by another's stairs" (*Par.* 17.58–60), his basic images for the poet's journey to God—the way or road, and the stairway—are fused in the description of the pain of exile. (In portions of the passage we do not quote, the images of arrow and bread gain similar double meanings; see the notes to *Paradiso* 17.) Such a nexus of words, images, and rhymes is another link in the chain. In this profoundly Boethian passage, misfortune is recast as blessing, and one of Dante's most heartfelt insights into how his life and his poem have become unified crystallizes around the figure of the stairway of being.

A number of other important dimensions of the poem are linked to the idea of the great chain: the poem's numerological form, by which it may be said to be "bound" by number (cf. Wisdom 11.21, and see "A Note on the Form of the Poem"); the oft-remarked scheme of parallel cantos (by which the popes in *Inferno* 19 are answered by one in *Purgatorio* 19); even the many references, pointed out by Curtius, to the "image of the book," may suggest the ancient notion, well known in the Middle Ages, of a book as a "chain," or *catena* of passages designed for memorization.

All of these aspects of the poem articulate or imply a catenary structure. Since the golden chain depends from God, this scheme also implies, consistent with Dante's intellectual formation, that the *Paradiso*, though reached last in the narrative (and the last of the three *cantiche* to be composed), is the origin and cause of the whole poem. The poem ends where it logically, causally, began, in its final/first cause: the blessedness that is humanity's destiny and the reason for its having been created. This "return to origins" is evident everywhere in the *Paradiso*: the pilgrim meets his remote physical origins (first his ancestor Cacciaguida, then the "first father," Adam) and is told why he should write down his vision, so that we witness the logical genesis of the poem. These moments of origin are the narrative and autobiographical equivalents of cosmic structure, which provides that the heavenly spheres (and the angelic intelligences that drive them) are the cooperating agents (secondary causes) in bringing about what happens on earth, far below. The inescapable corollary is that if we wish to fully understand Dante's poem on its own terms, we must follow it through to its end, which is its real beginning: everything both derives from it and hangs from it.

A Note on the Form of the Poem

The *Inferno*, like the rest of the *Divine Comedy*, is written in the normal eleven-syllable line of Italian poetry. The prestige of this line was established by the poets of the Sicilian school (mid-thirteenth century), who invented the sonnet and introduced the high courtly lyric into Italy, and by those of the so-called *dolce stil novo*, Bolognese and Tuscan poets of the generation before Dante's and later. Dante's own treatise on poetry in the vernacular, the *De vulgari eloquentia* (unfinished, ca. 1306), set forth theoretical grounds for the superiority of the hendecasyllable to other line lengths, but it was the *Divine Comedy* itself that definitively established the preeminence of the hendecasyllable and, to some extent, that of its formal rhyme pattern, terza rima, for narrative poetry.

The hendecasyllable corresponds to the normal ten-syllable verse of English poetry as practiced by Chaucer and Milton. This was not a metrical scheme in the sense of requiring a fixed pattern of metrical feet, as it became in the nineteenth century. Rather the nature of the line was determined by the number of syllables (normally ten in English but eleven in Italian, since most Italian words are accented on the next-to-last syllable, the penult), with certain syllables, which might be called the anchors of the line, being accented. In both English and Italian the tenth syllable must be accented as well as either the fourth or the sixth. There must be a caesura, or break in the line, normally near its middle. Beyond this, there is a virtually unlimited flexibility: any number of syllables in any additional positions may be accented. Two famous lines of Milton's illustrate the principle (accented syllables are underlined; the caesura is marked with |):

> Of <u>Man's</u> <u>First</u> Diso<u>bed</u>ience, | and the <u>Fruit</u> . . .

Note that the fourth and eighth syllables are not accented, but the second, third, sixth, and tenth are; this is not iambic pentameter. In

> <u>Hurl'd</u> <u>head</u>long <u>flam</u>ing | from th' E<u>the</u>real <u>Sky</u> . . .

the first, second, fourth, eighth, and tenth syllables are accented, but not the sixth.

Compare Dante's verse (5. 142)

> E <u>cad</u>-di, | co-me <u>cor</u>-po <u>mor</u>-to <u>ca</u>-de.

One additional principle needs to be added to complete the picture: ordinarily, contiguous vowels are elided. Thus (in line 2 of the *Inferno*) "u-na sel-va os-cu-ra" counts as six syllables, not seven, because the *a* ending *selva* is combined in pronunciation with the *o* beginning *oscura*. (For the rules of Italian pronunciation, the reader should consult an elementary grammar text.) Here are the opening four lines:

> Nel <u>mez</u>-zo del cam-<u>min</u> | di <u>nos</u>-tra <u>vi</u>-ta,
> mi ri-tro-<u>vai</u> | per u-na <u>sel</u>-va os-<u>cu</u>-ra,
> ché la di-<u>rit</u>-ta <u>via</u> | e-ra smar-<u>ri</u>-ta.
> <u>Ahi</u> <u>quant</u>-o a <u>dir</u> qual <u>er</u>-|a è <u>co</u>-sa <u>du</u>-ra . . .

In line 4, there are three contiguous vowel pairs that must be elided: *ahi, o a, a è*. The frequency of them in this and the following line is unusual and contributes strongly to the breathless, anxious effect they create (as does, of course, the highly unusual position of the caesura in both). Of course it often happens that two contiguous vowels both have to be pronounced. This can be seen, in fact, in the third line of the poem. The strong caesura after *via* requires the two vowels of that word to be elided. As one can readily see, the repertoire of expressive possibilities in Italian verse is very great indeed, and although there were fine poets before him, Dante was the first poet to explore them with anything like thoroughness.

One last item of terminology. An Italian hendecasyllable normally has a full eleven syllables, having one unaccented syllable after the accented tenth one. This type of line and line-ending is called *piano* [smooth]. But, like an English line, though more rarely, it can end after the tenth syllable, as in 4.60:

> e con Ra-<u>che</u>-le, per cui <u>tan</u>-to <u>fè</u>,

in which case it is called *tronco* [truncated], or it can have two unaccented syllables after the tenth, as in 24.66:

> a pa-<u>ro</u>-le for-<u>mar</u> <u>dis</u>-con-ve-<u>ne</u>-vo-le,

in which case it is called *sdrucciolo* [sliding]. The *verso piano* is by far the most numerous of the three types.

The rhyme scheme of the *Comedy*, invented by Dante, is called *terza rima* (literally, third [i.e., triple] rhyme). Here is the opening of the poem:

Nel mezzo del cammin di nostra vita	A (–ita)
mi ritrovai per una selva oscura,	B (–ura)
ché la diritta via era smarrita.	A (–ita)
Ahi, quanto a dir qual era è cosa dura,	B (–ura)
esta selva selvaggia e aspra e forte	C (–orte)
che nel pensier rinova la paura!	B (–ura)
Tant' è amara che poco è più morte;	C (–orte)
ma per trattar del ben ch' i' vi trovai,	D (–ai)
dirò de l'altre cose ch'i' v'ho scorte.	C (orte)
Io non so ben ridir com' i' v'intrai,	D (–ai)
tant' era pien di sonno a quel punto	E (–unto)
che la verace via abbandonai.	D (–ai)

After the first group of three lines (called a *terzina*), each terzina begins and ends with the middle rhyme of the previous one, introducing a new one into its own second position. It is easy to see from the punctuation that the syntactic units generally follow the division into terzinas. At the same time, the rhyme scheme forms a kind of interlocking chain that links each terzina with the previous and subsequent ones. Each rhyme appears three times, except for the ones that open and close cantos, which appear only twice. Here is the end of the first canto:

E io a lui: "Poeta, io ti richeggio	X (–eggio)
per quello Dio che tu non conoscesti,	Y (–esti)
acciò ch'io fugga questo male e peggio,	X (–eggio)

che tu mi meni là dov' or dicesti,	Y (-esti)
sì ch'io veggia la porta di san Pietro	Z (-etro)
e color cui tu fai cotanto mesti."	Y (-esti)
Allor si mosse, e io li tenni dietro.	Z (-etro)

Thus the end of a canto is a kind of mirror image of its beginning.

Terza rima is an extremely supple and flexible medium. In the *Divine Comedy* there is no set number of lines in a canto; the cantos range in length from 115 to 160 lines. It is clear that Dante associated the triplicities of the form (groups of three lines, interlocking chains of three rhymes) with the idea of the Creator as triune and with the idea of the chain of being. In the wake of Saint Augustine's *De trinitate*, he saw the marks of the Creator's triple unity everywhere in creation—in the structure of time (past, present, and future), in the triple structure of man's nature (rational, appetitive, and vegetative), and in the three "first things" (form and matter, separate and conjoined)—and he regarded his verse medium, terza rima, as one of the ways his creation of the poem imitated God's creation of the universe: others are, of course, that the poem has three parts and that it consists of a "perfect" number of cantos, 100—or, after the prologue of the first canto, three parts of thirty-three cantos each. (John Freccero's 1983 essay "The Significance of *Terza Rima*" discusses further implications of the form; see the Bibliography.)

Suggested Readings

Barbi, Michele. 1954. *Life of Dante*. Edited and translated by Paul G. Ruggiers. Berkeley: University of California Press.

Carroll, John S. [1904] 1971. *Exiles of Eternity: An Exposition of Dante's Inferno*. Port Washington, N.Y.: Kennikat Press.

Freccero, John, ed. 1965. *Dante: A Collection of Critical Essays*. Twentieth Century Views. Englewood Cliffs, N.J.: Prentice-Hall.

Gilson, Etienne. 1936. *The Spirit of Mediaeval Philosophy (Gifford Lectures, 1931–1932)*. Translated by A. H. C. Downes. New York: Scribner.

Holmes, George. 1980. *Dante*. Past Masters. Oxford: Oxford University Press.

———. 1986. *Florence, Rome, and the Origins of the Renaissance*. Oxford: Clarendon Press.

Hughes, Robert. 1968. *Heaven and Hell in Western Art*. New York: Stein and Day.

Jacoff, Rachel, ed. 1993. *The Cambridge Companion to Dante*. Cambridge: Cambridge University Press.

Keen, Maurice. 1968. *A History of Medieval Europe*. London: Routledge & Kegan Paul.

Lectura Dantis Virginiana. Dante's Inferno: Introductory Readings. 1990. Charlottesville: University of Virginia Press.

Singleton, Charles S. 1949. *An Essay on the "Vita nuova."* Cambridge, Mass.: Harvard University Press.

————. 1954. *Dante's Commedia: Elements of Structure*. Cambridge, Mass.: Harvard University Press.

Southern, R. W. 1970. *Western Society and the Church in the Middle Ages*. Vol. 2 of *The Pelican History of the Church*. London: Penguin Books.

INFERNO

CANTO 1

1   Nel mezzo del cammin di nostra vita
mi ritrovai per una selva oscura,
ché la diritta via era smarrita.

4   Ahi quanto a dir qual era è cosa dura
esta selva selvaggia e aspra e forte
che nel pensier rinova la paura!

7   Tant' è amara che poco è più morte;
ma per trattar del ben ch'i' vi trovai,
dirò de l'altre cose ch'i' v'ho scorte.

10   Io non so ben ridir com' i' v'intrai,
tant' era pien di sonno a quel punto
che la verace via abbandonai.

13   Ma poi ch'i' fui al piè d'un colle giunto,
là dove terminava quella valle
che m'avea di paura il cor compunto,

16   guardai in alto, e vidi le sue spalle
vestite già de' raggi del pianeta
che mena dritto altrui per ogne calle.

19   Allor fu la paura un poco queta
che nel lago del cor m'era durata
la notte ch'i' passai con tanta pieta.

22   E come quei che con lena affannata,
uscito fuor del pelago a la riva,
si volge a l'acqua perigliosa e guata:

25   così l'animo mio, ch'ancor fuggiva,
si volse a retro a rimirar lo passo
che non lasciò già mai persona viva.

28   Poi ch'èi posato un poco il corpo lasso,
ripresi via per la piaggia diserta
sì che 'l piè fermo sempre era 'l più basso.

CANTO 1

The dark wood—the three beasts—Virgil—the prophecy of the greyhound—the plan of the journey

1   In the middle of the journey of our life, I came to myself in a dark wood, for the straight way was lost.

4   Ah, how hard a thing it is to say what that wood was, so savage and harsh and strong that the thought of it renews my fear!

7   It is so bitter that death is little more so! But to treat of the good that I found there, I will tell of the other things I saw.

10   I cannot really say how I entered there, so full of sleep was I at the point when I abandoned the true way.

13   But when I had reached the foot of a hill, where the valley ended that had pierced my heart with fear,

16   I looked on high and saw its shoulders clothed already with the rays of the planet that leads us straight on every path.

19   Then was the fear a little quieted that in the lake of my heart had lasted through the night I passed with so much anguish.

22   And like one with laboring breath, come forth out of the deep onto the shore, who turns back to the perilous water and stares:

25   so my spirit, still fleeing, turned back to gaze again at the pass that has never yet left anyone alive.

28   After I had a little rested my weary body, I took my way again along that deserted slope, so that my halted foot was always the lower.

31   Ed ecco, quasi al cominciar de l'erta,
        una lonza leggera e presta molto,
        che di pel macolato era coverta;

34   e non mi si partia dinanzi al volto,
        anzi 'mpediva tanto il mio cammino
        ch'i' fui per ritornar più volte vòlto.

37   Temp' era del principio del mattino,
        e 'l sol montava 'n sù con quelle stelle
        ch' eran con lui quando l'amor divino

40   mosse di prima quelle cose belle;
        sì ch' a bene sperar m'era cagione
        di quella fiera a la gaetta pelle

43   l'ora del tempo e la dolce stagione.
        Ma non sì che paura non mi desse
        la vista che m'apparve d'un leone.

46   Questi parea che contra me venisse
        con la test' alta e con rabbiosa fame,
        sì che parea che l'aere ne tremesse.

49   Ed una lupa, che di tutte brame
        sembiava carca ne la sua magrezza,
        e molte genti fé già viver grame,

52   questa mi porse tanto di gravezza
        con la paura ch' uscia di sua vista,
        ch' io perdei la speranza de l'altezza.

55   E qual è quei che volontieri acquista,
        e giugne 'l tempo che perder lo face,
        che 'n tutti suoi pensier piange e s'attrista:

58   tal mi fece la bestia sanza pace,
        che, venendomi 'ncontro, a poco a poco
        mi ripigneva là dove 'l sol tace.

61   Mentre ch'i' rovinava in basso loco,
        dinanzi a li occhi mi si fu offerto
        chi per lungo silenzio parea fioco.

64   Quando vidi costui nel gran diserto,
        "*Miserere* di me," gridai a lui,
        "qual che tu sii, od ombra od omo certo!"

67   Rispuosemi: "Non omo, omo già fui,
        e li parenti miei furon lombardi,
        mantoani per patrïa ambedui.

31   And behold, almost at the beginning of the steep, a leopard, light and very swift, covered with spotted fur;

34   and it did not depart from before my face but rather so impeded my way that I was at several turns turned to go back.

37   The time was the beginning of the morning, and the sun was mounting up with those stars that were with it when God's love

40   first set those lovely things in motion; so that I took reason to have good hope of that beast with its gaily painted hide

43   from the hour of the morning and the sweet season; but not so that I did not fear the sight of a lion that appeared to me.

46   He appeared to be coming against me with his head high and with raging hunger, so that the air appeared to tremble at him.

49   And a she-wolf, that seemed laden with all cravings in her leanness and has caused many peoples to live in wretchedness,

52   she put on me so much heaviness with the fear that came from the sight of her, that I lost hope of reaching the heights.

55   And like one who gladly acquires, and the time arrives that makes him lose, who in all of his thoughts weeps and becomes sad:

58   so she made me, that restless beast, who, coming against me, little by little was driving me back to where the sun is silent.

61   While I was falling down into a low place, before my eyes one had offered himself to me who through long silence seemed hoarse.

64   When I saw him in the great wilderness, "*Miserere* —on me," I cried to him, "whatever you may be, whether shade or true man!"

67   He replied: "Not a man, I was formerly a man, and my parents were Lombards, Mantuans both by birth.

70　　　Nacqui *sub Iulio*, ancor che fosse tardi,
　　　e vissi a Roma sotto 'l buono Augusto
　　　nel tempo de li dèi falsi e bugiardi.

73　　　Poeta fui, e cantai di quel giusto
　　　figliuol d'Anchise che venne di Troia
　　　poi che 'l superbo Ilïón fu combusto.

76　　　Ma tu perché ritorni a tanta noia?
　　　Perché non sali il dilettoso monte
　　　ch' è principio e cagion di tutta gioia?"

79　　　"Or se' tu quel Virgilio e quella fonte
　　　che spandi di parlar sì largo fiume?"
　　　rispuos' io lui con vergognosa fronte.

82　　　"O de li altri poeti onore e lume,
　　　vagliami 'l lungo studio e 'l grande amore
　　　che m'ha fatto cercar lo tuo volume.

85　　　Tu se' lo mio maestro e 'l mio autore,
　　　tu se' solo colui da cu' io tolsi
　　　lo bello stilo che m'ha fatto onore.

88　　　Vedi la bestia per cu' io mi volsi:
　　　aiutami da lei, famoso saggio,
　　　ch' ella mi fa tremar le vene e i polsi."

91　　　"A te convien tenere altro vïaggio,"
　　　rispuose, poi che lagrimar mi vide,
　　　"se vuo' campar d'esto loco selvaggio;

94　　　ché questa bestia, per la qual tu gride,
　　　non lascia altrui passar per la sua via,
　　　ma tanto lo 'mpedisce che l'uccide;

97　　　e ha natura sì malvagia e ria,
　　　che mai non empie la bramosa voglia,
　　　e dopo 'l pasto ha più fame che pria.

100　　　Molti son li animali a cui s'ammoglia,
　　　e più saranno ancora, infin che 'l veltro
　　　verrà, che la farà morir con doglia.

103　　　Questi non ciberà terra né peltro,
　　　ma sapïenza, amore e virtute,
　　　e sua nazion sarà tra feltro e feltro.

106　　　Di quella umile Italia fia salute
　　　per cui morì la vergine Cammilla,
　　　Eurialo e Turno e Niso di ferute.

70   I was born *sub Iulio*, though it was late, and I
lived in Rome under the good Augustus in the time
of the false and lying gods.

73   I was a poet, and I sang of that just son of
Anchises who came from Troy, when proud Ilion
was destroyed by fire.

76   But you, why do you return to so much suffering?
why do you not climb the delightful mountain that is
origin and cause of all joy?"

79   "Now are you that Virgil, that fountain which
spreads forth so broad a river of speech?" I replied
with shamefast brow.

82   "O honor and light of the other poets, let my long
study and great love avail me, that has caused me to
search through your volume.

85   You are my master and my author, you alone are
he from whom I have taken the pleasing style that
has won me honor.

88   See the beast for which I have turned back: help
me against her, famous sage, for she makes my veins
and pulses tremble."

91   "You must hold to another path," he replied, after
he saw me weep, "if you wish to escape from this
savage place;

94   for this beast at which you cry out lets no one
pass by her way, but so much impedes him that she
kills him;

97   and she has a nature so evil and cruel that her
greedy desire is never satisfied, and after feeding she
is hungrier than before.

100   Many are the animals with whom she mates, and
there will be more still, until the greyhound shall
come, who will make her die in pain.

103   He will feed on neither earth nor pelf, but on
wisdom, love, and power, and his birth will be
between felt and felt.

106   He will be the savior of that humble Italy for
which the virgin Camilla died of her wounds, and
Euryalus, Turnus, and Nisus.

109   Questi la caccerà per ogne villa,
fin che l'avrà rimessa ne lo 'nferno,
là onde 'nvidia prima dipartilla.

112   Ond' io per lo tuo me' penso e discerno
che tu mi segui, e io sarò tua guida,
e trarrotti di qui per loco etterno,

115   ove udirai le disperate strida,
vedrai li antichi spiriti dolenti,
ch'a la seconda morte ciascun grida;

118   e vederai color che son contenti
nel foco, perché speran di venire,
quando che sia, a le beati genti.

121   A le quai poi se tu vorrai salire,
anima fia a ciò più di me degna:
con lei ti lascerò nel mio partire;

124   ché quello Imperador che là sù regna,
perch' i' fu' ribellante a la sua legge,
non vuol che 'n sua città per me si vegna.

127   In tutte parti impera e quivi regge;
quivi è la sua città e l'alto seggio:
oh felice colui cu' ivi elegge!"

130   E io a lui: "Poeta, io ti richeggio
per quello Dio che tu non conoscesti,
acciò ch'io fugga questo male e peggio,

133   che tu mi meni là dov' or dicesti,
sì ch'io veggia la porta di san Pietro
e color cui tu fai cotanto mesti."

136   Allor si mosse, e io li tenni dietro.

109 He will drive her from every town until he has put her back in Hell, whence envy first sent her forth.

112 Thus for your good I think and judge that you shall follow me, and I shall be your guide, and I will lead you from here through an eternal place,

115 where you will hear the desperate shrieks, you will see the ancient suffering spirits, who all cry out at the second death;

118 and you will see those who are content in the fire, because they hope to come, whenever it may be, to the blessed people.

121 To whom then if you shall wish to rise, there will be a soul more worthy of that than I; with her I shall leave you when I depart;

124 for that Emperor who reigns on high, because I was a rebel to his law, wills not that I come into his city.

127 In every place he commands, and there he rules; there is his city and high throne: O happy the one he chooses to be there!"

130 And I to him: "Poet, I beg you by that God whom you did not know, so that I may flee this evil and worse,

133 that you lead me where you have just now said, so that I may see the gate of Saint Peter and those whom you call so woebegone."

136 Then he moved, and I followed after him.

NOTES

1. In the middle of the journey of our life: Later passages (e.g., 21.112–14) place the action of the poem in April 1300; if, as is probable, Dante was born in May 1265, he would be thirty-five in 1300, midway in the normative biblical lifespan, "threescore years and ten" (Psalm 90.10), mentioned by Dante in *Convivio* 4.23 (cf. Is. 38.10: "In the midst of my days I shall go to the gates of Hell"). The line suggests, with the plural possessive "our," that the pilgrim is a representative human being, an Everyman. Dante omits or postpones the traditional "topics of exordium," such as announcement of subject, dedication, and invocation of the muse; the abruptness of this beginning is highly unconventional in medieval as well as classical narrative.

2. I came to myself: The traditional translation of *mi ritrovai* is "I found myself." In our view, the prefix *ri-*, rather than denoting repetition here, serves to intensify the inward nature of the event: Dante is describing a moral awakening. We believe there is also, both here and in line 11, a (very understated) reference to the literary genre of dream-vision, in which the dream regularly begins with an awakening (early illustrations often show a "sleeping" poet-as-author at the beginning); this question is more fully discussed in the note on *Par.* 32.139 (see the note to 2.8).

2. a dark wood: The "wood" of error and sin (cf. *Convivio* 4.24.12); there may be a reference to the "ancient forest, deep dwelling of beasts" near the mouth of Hades in *Aen.* 6.179. There is probably a reference to the Platonic idea of matter (*silva* in the Latin translation of the *Timaeus*) and also to the forest of Arthurian romance. Dante is perhaps drawing on the beginning of his teacher Brunetto Latini's allegorical poem the *Tesoretto*, in which the narrator loses his way in a wondrous forest, where the goddess Nature appears to instruct him.

3. the straight way: The course of the just man, leading to God (see Psalm 23.3, Prov. 2.13–14, 2 Peter 2.15). If *ché* is taken as *che*, the so-called modal conjunction (the orthography of Dante's time did not distinguish them), the line could mean "where the straight way was lost."

4–7. Ah, how hard . . . death is little more [bitter]: Note the characteristic stress on an identity between the writing of the poem and the experience it relates: though in terms of the fiction the narrator has seen God, he is still subject to all the terrors of the journey as he narrates them.

8. to treat of the good that I found there: *Trattar* [to treat systematically] is a semi-technical term, like *good*; this is an oblique announcement of the subject of the poem, for the "good" he found there would seem to be the undertaking of the journey (cf. 2.126).

11. so full of sleep: The sleep of sin and moral oblivion (as in Romans 13.11–14), again, we believe, with implicit reference to dream-vision (see the note to line 2).

13. a hill: Like the sea and the dark wood, the hill, later called a mountain, is part of a traditional symbolic landscape we intuitively understand as representing the position of human beings between the depths and the heights (Dante may well have in mind the famous instance in the Old French *Queste del saint Graal*, pp. 91–92). For the "Lord's holy mountain," see Psalms 24.3, 43.3, 121.1 and Is. 2.2–5.

17–18. the planet that leads us straight: The expression emphasizes the role of the sun as revealer of knowledge and wisdom. In *Convivio* 3.12, Dante discusses the sun as the chief visible analogue of God. The sun is a "planet" (wanderer) like the six others, moving against the background of the fixed stars.

20. lake of my heart: Medieval physiology thought of the heart not as a pump, but as a reservoir of blood and pneuma ("spirit"): fear would rush them back to the "lake," leaving the limbs pale and weak. Compare *Vita nuova* 2.4 and the canzone "Così nel mio parlar voglio esser aspro," lines 45–47 (translated in Durling and Martinez 1990, pp. 286–90).

21. anguish: Dante's word is *pieta*, a form of *pietà*, which includes the meanings "pity," "pitiable suffering," even "piety."

22. like one with laboring breath: The first formal simile: the pilgrim has metaphorically escaped shipwreck ("slope" at line 29 can also mean "shore"), as Aeneas does literally at the beginning of the *Aeneid*. Hollander (1969) explores an elaborate system of parallels with the opening of the *Aeneid* in the first cantos of the *Inferno*.

27. the pass that has never yet left anyone alive: Probably damnation itself (see Prov. 12.28).

28. my weary body: The presence of the pilgrim's body, of which this is the first mention, will be insisted on throughout *Inferno* and *Purgatorio*.

30. my halted foot was always the lower: Freccero (1959) has given the best explanation of this famous crux. In the act of walking, one foot must be fixed to support the body while the other moves; according to Aristotle and others, we naturally begin to walk by lifting the right foot, so that the left can be referred to as the naturally fixed or halted foot. Thus the pilgrim's left foot is dragging behind his right one, is always "the lower."

The soul was said to walk (i.e., to move toward its objects) on the two "feet" of its two chief faculties, intellect and will (desire); the left foot of the soul (will, for the heart is on the left side) drags behind the right foot (intellect) because of the laming wound in man's nature inflicted by Adam's Fall: intellect is able to see the goal clearly, but will moves toward it only haltingly.

32. a leopard: Commentators do not agree on the significance of this and the other beasts—lion and she-wolf—that drive back the pilgrim, which Dante's Italian ties together with alliteration (*lonza, leone, lupa*). Various possibilities have been suggested; the most likely correlates them with the triple division of Hell into sins of disordered appetite (she-wolf), violence (lion), and fraud (leopard); other identifications, such as the leopard with lust and the she-wolf with fraud, though traditional, seem arbitrary. The poem does seem to call out for labels here, but it is important to see that at this point it is withholding definitive clues: the pilgrim may be as mystified as the reader, and only later experience will explain the beasts.

37–43. The time was . . . the sweet season: This second astronomical reference identifies the beginning of the action as related to the spring equinox (March 21 by convention, March 14 in fact, in Dante's time); medieval tradition held that at the moment of creation the sun was at the first point of Aries. Other evidence in the poem suggests the date of April 8, 1300.

44–48. but not so . . . tremble at him: Note the repeated emphasis on Dante's fear. The dreamlike character of the scene raises the question to what extent the beasts are projections of internal dangers.

49–54. And a she-wolf . . . of reaching the heights: Why the pilgrim should be most afraid of the she-wolf is not explained (cf. line 97, with note).

55. gladly acquires: The economic simile (first of many) targets a society, the Florence of Dante's youth and young adulthood, only recently become wealthy and acquisitive.

60. the sun is silent: That is, where knowledge is darkened and hope is gone. The sun is traditionally associated with speech (e.g., Psalm 18.2–3).

62–63. before my eyes . . . seemed hoarse: Virgil is now introduced, to become Dante's guide. The elaborately contorted phrasing, which the translation renders literally, is striking in two respects. First, the pluperfect "had been offered" suggests that in some sense Virgil has been there for some time; second, the passive suggests that Dante must see Virgil before Virgil can speak to him. These features are particularly appropriate if the figure of Virgil is taken to refer to the codex of the historical Vergil's works (for our spellings, see below), where his voice does exist for the eye; they are most probably to be connected with an allegorical meaning: a reading of Vergil's works, especially of the *Aeneid*, would seem to have played a prominent role in the spiritual crisis of 1300 (cf. Leo 1951). Thus the conventional allegoresis of Dante's Virgil as representing "human reason," while at times undeniably valid, is much too narrow. The figure of Virgil in the poem should be taken to refer to the soul of the historical Vergil, expressed in his voice—his poetry—but in possession of added knowledge because he is dead, though still subject to some of his old limitations. Virgil's hoarseness has been variously explained (the Italian allows "dim" or "weak" as well as "hoarse"): his Latin is no longer understood; his works have been disregarded (whether by Dante or others); or he is a shade like those of the Vergilian underworld.

Modern scholarship has established that *Vergilius* is the correct spelling of Vergil's name; Dante follows the traditional medieval spelling in writing *Virgilio*. We shall maintain the distinction, using *Vergil* to refer to the historical Vergil, and *Virgil* to refer to the character in Dante's poem.

65. *Miserere* [have mercy]: The Latin here derives most immediately from the Psalms (especially Psalm 51 [Vulgate 50], liturgically the most important penitential psalm).

67. Not a man: Because dead, a disembodied soul. In Dante's Christian Aristotelian view, a human being is the union of body and soul (see the note to 6.109–111).

70. born sub Iulio: Publius Vergilius Maro was born in 70 B.C. at Andes, near Mantua, then in Cisalpine Gaul; he died at Brundusium in 19 B.C., leaving the *Aeneid*, on which he had spent eleven years, incomplete. At the order of Augustus, Vergil's literary executors disregarded the poet's wish that it be burned. Vergil's other principal works are his pastoral *Eclogues* or *Bucolics*, which strongly influenced Dante, and his versified treatise on agriculture and husbandry, the *Georgics*, which has left fewer apparent traces in Dante's work. Vergil was born "under Julius," when Julius Caesar, born about 100 B.C., had barely qualified for the Senate; he was only twenty-six when Caesar was assassinated in 44 B.C. Although Caesar was not in power at Vergil's birth, Dante wishes to associate the poet of the Roman empire with the figure that he considered its founder (see the note to 2.20–24).

72. false and lying gods: Christian opinion, based on Psalm 96.5 [Vulgate 95], and established since Augustine, was that the gods of the pagan world (Jove, Juno, Mars, etc.) were demons that had led humanity astray through the oracles, which were silenced at Christ's birth (see *City of God* 2.2, 2.10); certain individuals, such as Plato and Aristotle, and often Vergil, were thought to have been essentially monotheists though they used polytheistic terminology. Dante frequently uses the names *Jove* and *Apollo* to refer to the Christian God (e.g., 31.92, *Par.* 1.13).

73–74. just son: Justice, the noblest of the moral virtues, is attributed to Aeneas, son of the goddess Venus and Trojan Anchises, founder of Rome after the destruction of Troy ("proud Ilion") by the Greeks (see *Aen.* 1.544–45). Vergil sang of Aeneas in his *Aeneid*, vessel of one of the Middle Ages' most significant myths: the descent of Europeans from Aeneas and other Trojans.

78. origin and cause of all joy: The mountain is designated as the origin of happiness following Aristotle's analysis of causation, in which the final cause (the *telos*, the goal or end) is also the first cause (the *archē* origin).

79–80. are you that Virgil . . . river of speech: That Vergil's poetry was like a great river was a traditional topic in ancient and medieval literary criticism. In the Middle Ages, the *Aeneid, Georgics,* and *Eclogues* were thought to define the levels of poetic style: "tragic" or "high," "middle" or "rustic," and "low" or "bucolic," respectively.

79. are you that Virgil: Compare *Aen.* 1.617: "Tune ille Aeneas quem . . ." [Are you that Aeneas whom . . .], in Dido's first speech to Aeneas.

85. You are my master and my author: The translation will uniformly translate *maestro* as "master," though the word also means "teacher"; the modern "author" no longer conveys the meaning the term *autore* had for the Middle Ages. An *auctor* is one whose formative influence on others has been so great and so widespread that he has acquired *authority* in the strongest possible (positive) sense: he is "worthy of faith and obedience" (*Convivio* 4.6).

87. the pleasing style that has won me honor: There are traces of Vergil's stylistic influence on Dante as early as the *Vita nuova* (ca. 1294) and the *rime petrose* (1296). Dante was already well known as a poet in 1300.

91. You must hold to another path: The pilgrim cannot proceed directly up the mountain; he must first descend. See Romans 6.3–4:

> Know ye not, that all we, who are baptized in Christ Jesus are baptized in his death? For we are buried together with him by baptism into death: that as Christ is risen from the dead by the glory of the Father, so we also may walk in newness of life.

The penitential descent into Hell imitates Christ's death on the Cross and is parallel to baptism, the sacramental death to sin, followed by "newness of life." The pattern by which the believer's experience is a figural imitation of Christ is fundamental to the poem.

97. she has a nature . . . : Virgil's account of the she-wolf, obscure as it is, makes clear that, as the pilgrim sensed in line 51, she is a terrible external power and a major force in history.

100. the animals with whom she mates: The language is that of the Old Testament prophets, for whom unfaithfulness to Jehovah is "fornication" (cf. Is. 1.21, Jer. 3.1, and Apoc. 18.3).

101–5. the greyhound . . . felt: Innumerable explanations have been offered of this prophecy. There are two main families of interpretation: (1) the greyhound refers to the Second Coming of Christ or to an ecclesiastical figure prefiguring it; (2) the greyhound refers to a secular ruler, who would also prefigure the Second Coming. Prime candidates for the latter figure are Can Grande della Scala, the Ghibelline leader of the Veronese noble house that offered Dante hospitality during his exile (his title, derived from *khan*, also means "dog," hence greyhound), and Emperor Henry VII, whose descent into Italy in 1311 to 1313 seemed to Dante to promise, before his untimely death, the reform of religious and political institutions for which he yearned. "Between felt and felt" has been taken to mean a geographical location (between the towns of Feltre and Montefeltro), an astrological sign (the Gemini, Dante's own natal sign, were sometimes shown with felt caps), the two mendicant orders (Franciscans and Dominicans), and a technique of election (counters dropped into felt-lined boxes), perhaps with reference to an emperor. Along with the prophecy in the last canto of the *Purgatorio* (to which it is closely related), this passage remains one of the most obscure in the poem. The best discussion is Davis 1976.

106. that humble Italy: Dante adapts *Aen.* 3.522–23, where the term *humilis* [low-lying] refers to the physical appearance of the Italian shore as seen by Aeneas's crew. Note the contrast with line 75, "proud Ilion," itself an echo of *Aen.* 3.2–3 (*superbum/Ilium*).

107–8. virgin Camilla . . . Nisus: Dante lists some of the fallen in the Trojan-Italian war described in the last six books of Vergil's epic, including Turnus, the chief antagonist of Aeneas as rival for the hand of Lavinia. But Trojans (Nisus and Euryalus) and native Italians (the Rutulian Turnus, the Volscian Camilla) are carefully interwoven in Dante's list, their former antagonisms elided. The lines suggest patriotism as the motive of these deaths.

111. whence envy first sent her forth: See Wisdom 2.24: "by the envy of the devil, death came into the world." The devil's envy of man's favored status is the traditional reason for his enmity.

117. the second death: The death of the soul in eternal damnation, following the first, physical death; for the expression, see Apoc. 20.15, 21.8.

118–19. content in the fire: Souls undergoing the fire of purgation. A metonymy for all of Purgatory, which includes a diversity of punishments; the identification of Purgatory with fire is traditional, resting on 1 Cor. 3.13–15 ("the fire shall try every man's work . . . but he himself shall be saved, yet so as by fire").

120–26. the blessed people . . . into his city: The blessed are thought of as inhabiting, along with the angels, the "Empyrean," a sphere of fire beyond the confines of the cosmos; this is "his city," to which the pilgrim ascends in the *Paradiso*.

122. a soul more worthy: Unmistakably, Beatrice, the poet's lady celebrated in the *Vita nuova* (see 2.53).

124–25. that Emperor . . . a rebel to his law: For the question of how Virgil was a "rebel" against God's law, see 4.33–39, with notes.

134. the gate of Saint Peter: The gate to Purgatory (see *Purg.* 9.73–145).

CANTO 2

1   Lo giorno se n'andava, e l'aere bruno
toglieva li animai che sono in terra
da le fatiche loro; e io sol uno

4   m'apparecchiava a sostener la guerra
sì del cammino e sì de la pietate,
che ritrarrà la mente che non erra.

7   O muse, o alto ingegno, or m'aiutate;
o mente che scrivesti ciò ch'io vidi,
qui si parrà la tua nobilitate.

10   Io cominciai: "Poeta che mi guidi,
guarda la mia virtù s'ell' è possente,
prima ch'a l'alto passo tu mi fidi.

13   Tu dici che di Silvïo il parente,
corruttibile ancora, ad immortale
secolo andò, e fu sensibilmente.

16   Però, se l'avversario d'ogne male
cortese i fu, pensando l'alto effetto
ch'uscir dovea di lui, e 'l chi e 'l quale,

19   non pare indegno ad omo d'intelletto;
ch' e' fu de l'alma Roma e di suo impero
ne l'empireo ciel per padre eletto:

22   la quale e 'l quale, a voler dir lo vero,
fu stabilita per lo loco santo
u' siede il successor del maggior Piero.

25   Per quest' andata onde li dai tu vanto,
intese cose che furon cagione
di sua vittoria e del papale ammanto.

28   Andovvi poi lo Vas d'elezïone,
per recarne conforto a quella fede
ch'è principio a la via di salvazione.

CANTO 2

1
The day was departing, and the darkened air was releasing all living creatures on the earth from their toils; and I alone

4
prepared myself to undergo the war both of the journey and of pity, which memory, unerring, will depict.

7
O muses, O high wit, now help me; O memory that wrote down what I saw, here will your nobility appear.

10
I began: "Poet who are my guide, consider my strength, if it is powerful enough, before you entrust me to the deep pass.

13
You say that the father of Silvius, still in corruptible flesh, went to the immortal realm and was there with his senses.

16
Therefore, if the adversary of all evil was liberal to him, considering the high effect that was to come forth from him, and who and what he was,

19
it does not seem unworthy to a man of intellect; for he in the Empyrean heaven had been chosen to be father of mother Rome and her empire:

22
and Rome and her empire, to tell the truth, were established to be the holy place where the successor of great Peter is enthroned.

25
Through this journey that you claim for him, he understood things that were the cause of his victory and of the papal mantle.

28
Later the chosen Vessel went there, to bring back strengthening for that faith which is the beginning of the way of salvation.

31   Ma io, perché venirvi? o chi 'l concede?
Io non Enëa, io non Paulo sono;
me degno a ciò né io né altri 'l crede.

34   Per che, se del venire io m'abbandono,
temo che la venuta non sia folle.
Se' savio; intendi me' ch'i' non ragiono."

37   E qual è quei che disvuol ciò che volle
e per novi pensier cangia proposta,
sì che dal cominciar tutto si tolle:

40   tal mi fec' ïo 'n quella oscura costa,
perché, pensando, consumai la 'mpresa
che fu nel cominciar cotanto tosta.

43   "S'i' ho ben la parola tua intesa,"
rispuose del magnanimo quell' ombra,
"l'anima tua è da viltade offesa,

46   la qual molte fïate l'omo ingombra
sì che d'onrata impresa lo rivolve,
come falso veder bestia quand' ombra.

49   Da questa tema acciò che tu ti solve,
dirotti perch' io venni e quel ch' io 'ntesi
nel primo punto di te mi dolve.

52   Io era tra color che son sospesi,
e donna mi chiamò beata e bella,
tal che di comandare io la richiesi.

55   Lucevan li occhi suoi più che la stella;
e cominciommi a dir soave e piana,
con angelica voce, in sua favella:

58   'O anima cortese mantoana,
di cui la fama ancor nel mondo dura,
e durerà quanto 'l mondo lontana,

61   l'amico mio, e non de la ventura,
ne la diserta piaggia è impedito
sì nel cammin, che volt' è per paura;

64   e temo che non sia già sì smarrito
ch'io mi sia tardi al soccorso levata,
per quel ch'i' ho di lui nel cielo udito.

67   Or movi, e con la tua parola ornata
e con ciò c'ha mestieri al suo campare,
l'aiuta sì ch'i' ne sia consolata.

31   But I, why come there? or who grants it? I am not Aeneas, I am not Paul; neither I nor others believe me worthy of that.

34   Therefore, if I abandon myself to the journey, I fear lest my coming may be folly. You are wise, you understand better than I speak."

37   And like one who unwills what he just now willed and with new thoughts changes his intent, so that he draws back entirely from beginning:

40   so did I become on that dark slope, for, thinking, I gave up the undertaking that I had been so quick to begin.

43   "If I have well understood your word," replied the shade of that great-souled one, "your soul is wounded by cowardice,

46   which many times so encumbers a man that he turns back from honorable endeavor, as a false sight turns a beast when it shies.

49   That you may free yourself from this fear, I will tell you why I came and what I heard in the first moment when I grieved for you.

52   I was among those who are suspended, and a lady called me, so blessed and beautiful that I begged her to command me.

55   Her eyes were shining brighter than the morning star; and she began to speak gently and softly, with angelic voice, in her language:

58   'O courteous Mantuan soul, whose fame still lasts in the world and will last as far as the world will go,

61   my friend, not the friend of fortune, on the deserted shore is so blocked in his journey that he has turned back for fear;

64   and I am afraid that he may be already so lost that I have risen too late to help him, according to what I have heard of him in Heaven.

67   Now go, and with your ornamented speech and whatever else is needed for his escape help him so that I may be consoled.

70   I' son Beatrice che ti faccio andare;
vegno del loco ove tornar disio;
amor mi mosse, che mi fa parlare.

73   Quando sarò dinanzi al segnor mio,
di te mi loderò sovente a lui.'
Tacette allora, e poi comincia' io:

76   'O donna di virtù, sola per cui
l'umana spezie eccede ogne contento
di quel ciel c'ha minor li cerchi sui,

79   tanto m'aggrada il tuo comandamento
che l'ubidir, se già fosse, m'è tardi;
più non t'è uo' ch'aprirmi il tuo talento.

82   Ma dimmi la cagion che non ti guardi
de lo scender qua giuso in questo centro
de l'ampio loco ove tornar tu ardi.'

85   'Da che tu vuo' saver cotanto a dentro,
dirotti brievemente,' mi rispuose,
'perch' i' non temo di venir qua entro.

88   Temer si dee di sole quelle cose
c'hanno potenza di fare altrui male;
de l'altre no, ché non son paurose.

91   I' son fatta da Dio, sua mercé, tale
che la vostra miseria non mi tange,
né fiamma d'esto 'ncendio non m'assale.

94   Donna è gentil nel ciel che si compiange
di questo 'mpedimento ov' io ti mando,
sì che duro giudicio là sù frange.

97   Questa chiese Lucia in suo dimando
e disse:—Or ha bisogno il tuo fedele
di te, e io a te lo raccomando.—

100   Lucia, nimica di ciascun crudele,
si mosse, e venne al loco dov' i' era,
che mi sedea con l'antica Rachele.

103   Disse:—Beatrice, loda di Dio vera,
ché non soccorri quei che t'amò tanto
ch'uscì per te de la volgare schiera?

106   Non odi tu la pieta del suo pianto,
non vedi tu la morte che 'l combatte
su la fiumana ove 'l mar non ha vanto?—

70   I am Beatrice who cause you to go; I come from the place where I long to return; love has moved me and makes me speak.

73   When I shall be before my lord, I will praise you frequently to him.' Then she was silent, and I began:

76   'O lady of power, through whom alone the human race rises above all the contents of that heaven whose circles are smallest,

79   so pleasing to me is your command that obeying, had it already taken place, is slow; no more is needed than to unfold your desire.

82   But tell me the reason why you do not shrink from coming down here, into this center, from the spacious place where you desire to return.'

85   'Since you wish to know so deeply, I will tell you in brief,' she replied, 'why I do not fear to come inside here.

88   One must fear only those things that have the power to harm; not other things, for they are not fearful.

91   I am made by God, in his mercy, such that your misery does not touch me, the flame of this burning does not assail me.

94   There is a noble lady in Heaven, who grieves for this impediment to which I send you, so that she vanquishes harsh judgment there on high.

97   She called Lucia in her request and said:—Now your faithful one has need of you, and I put him in your hands.—

100   Lucia, enemy of all cruelty, moved and came to the place where I was sitting with the ancient Rachel.

103   She said:—Beatrice, true praise of God, why do you not help him who loved you so, who because of you came forth from the common herd?

106   Do you not hear the anguish of his weeping, do you not see the death that attacks him there, by the torrent where the sea has no boast?—

109   Al mondo non fur mai persone ratte
a far lor pro o a fuggir lor danno,
com' io, dopo cotai parole fatte,

112   venni qua giù del mio beato scanno,
fidandomi del tuo parlare onesto,
ch'onora te e quei ch'udito l'hanno.'

115   Poscia che m'ebbe ragionato questo,
li occhi lucenti lagrimando volse,
per che mi fece del venir più presto.

118   E venni a te così com' ella volse:
d'inanzi a quella fiera ti levai
che del bel monte il corto andar ti tolse.

121   Dunque che è? perché, perché restai,
perché tanta viltà nel core allette,
perché ardire e franchezza non hai,

124   poscia che tai tre donne benedette
curan di te ne la corte del cielo,
e 'l mio parlar tanto ben ti promette?"

127   Quali fioretti dal notturno gelo
chinati e chiusi, poi che 'l sol li 'mbianca,
si drizzan tutti aperti in loro stelo:

130   tal mi fec' io di mia virtude stanca,
e tanto buono ardire al cor mi corse,
ch'i' cominciai come persona franca:

133   "Oh pietosa colei che mi soccorse!
e te cortese ch'ubidisti tosto
a le vere parole che ti porse!

136   Tu m'hai con disiderio il cor disposto
sì al venir con le parole tue,
ch'i' son tornato nel primo proposto.

139   Or va, ch'un sol volere è d'ambedue:
tu duca, tu segnore e tu maestro."
Così li disse; e poi che mosso fue,

142   intrai per lo cammino alto e silvestro.

109   In the world there have never been persons so swift to seek their advantage or to flee their loss, as I, after hearing such words spoken,

112   came down here from my blessed throne, trusting in your virtuous speech, which honors you and those who have heeded it.'

115   After she had spoken all this to me, she turned her shining eyes, shedding tears, which made me quicker to come here.

118   And I have come to you as she willed: from before that beast I have taken you, that deprived you of the short path up the mountain.

121   Therefore what is it? why, why do you stand still? why do you nurse such cowardice in your heart? why do you not have boldness and freedom,

124   seeing that three such blessed ladies have a care for you in the court of Heaven, and my speech promises you so much good?"

127   As little flowers, bowed and closed in the chill of night, when the sun whitens them straighten up all open on their stems:

130   so did I become with my tired strength, and so much good boldness ran to my heart, that I began like a person freed:

133   "Oh full of pity she who has helped me! and you courteous, who have quickly obeyed the true words she offered you!

136   Your words have so filled my heart with desire to come with you, that I have returned to my first purpose.

139   Now go, for one same will is in both: you are leader, you lord, and you master." So I said to him; and when he had set forth

142   I entered upon the deep, savage journey.

NOTES

1–3. The day was departing . . . and I alone: Like Canto 1, Canto 2 begins with an indication of time and of the pilgrim's isolation; whereas he slept in Canto 1, here he alone is awake. The contrast between the protagonist and the peace permeating nature draws on several passages in the *Aeneid*, such as 8.26–27:

> Nox erat et terras animalia fessa per omnis
> alituum pecudumque genus sopor altus habebat,
> cum pater . . .
>
> [It was night and through all lands deep sleep held the tired
> living creatures, the winged ones and the flocks,
> while the father . . .]

and 9.224–25:

> Cetera per terras omnis animalia somno
> laxabant curas et corda oblita laborum
>
> [Other creatures through all lands in sleep
> loosened their cares and their hearts, forgetting their labors]

and compare 4.522–32.

7–9. O muses . . . appear: The appearance of an invocation to the muses here retrospectively turns the entire first canto into a kind of *propositio* [announcement of subject]; compare the sequence of Vergil's *Aeneid*, Book 1: lines 1–7, proposition ("Arms and the man I sing . . ."), and lines 8–11, invocation ("Muse, remind [*memora*] me of the causes . . ."). The opening invocations of *Purgatorio* and *Paradiso* constitute an ascending series with this one.

7–8. O muses, O high wit: The identification of the muses (the "daughters of memory") with the powers of the poet's own mind or with the lore of the craft was common in the Middle Ages. We use "wit" to translate Dante's term

---

ingegno, regularly used by Dante to refer to the innate qualities of mind as opposed to those acquired by practice or knowledge; the term is further discussed in the notes to *Par.* 22.1–9.

8. O memory that wrote down: Dante's word is *mente* [mind], closely related in derivation to *memoria* (cf. *memora* [*Aen.* 1.8] and compare the English verb *to mind*, as in "Mind your p's and q's"). Implicit here is the idea of memory as a book, basic to the entire *Vita nuova* (see especially Chapter 1).

Chaucer adapted this and the following lines in the Prologue to Book 2 of the *House of Fame*, lines 523–28:

> O Thought that wrot al that I mette,
> And in the tresorye hyt shette
> Of my brayn, now shal men se
> Yf any vertu in the be,
> To tellen al my drem aryght.
> Now kythe thyn engin and myght.

> [O Thought that wrote down all I dreamed,
> And shut it in the treasury
> Of my brain, now shall men see
> If there be any virtue in thee
> To tell all my dream aright.
> Now make known thy skill and might.]

The lines strongly suggest that Chaucer thought of the *Comedy* as a dream-vision (see the notes to 1.2 and 1.11).

13. the father of Silvius: Silvius was the posthumous son (*Aen.* 6.760–66) of Aeneas, whose journey to the underworld is related in *Aeneid* 6, one of Dante's chief models, especially for the *Inferno*. Here, as elsewhere, Dante writes as if he considered the events of the *Aeneid* to be historical fact.

14–15. still . . . with his senses: That Aeneas journeyed to Hades in the flesh, rather than in dream or in the spirit, is repeatedly emphasized in Vergil's account. See, for example, *Aen.* 6.290–94, 413–14; at the end of the book, however, he leaves Hades by the gate of false dreams (lines 893–99).

17. the high effect: This is specified in lines 20–24. Line 19 may also be taken to mean "he [Aeneas] does not seem unworthy."

20–24. for he . . . great Peter: Dante's view that the Romans were a second chosen people, and that the establishment of the Roman empire was part of God's providential preparation for the coming of Christ and the establishment of the Church, underlies the entire *Divine Comedy* and is set forth in his *Convivio* (4.4–5) and *Monarchia* (Book 2).

24. the successor of great Peter: The pope; Christ's gift to Saint Peter of the keys of the kingdom (Matt. 16.13–20) was interpreted by the Roman Church as signifying Peter's appointment as the first pope.

26–27. the cause . . . papal mantle: That is, Aeneas's journey to the under-world was the cause of his victory in Latium and thus, according to Vergil, of the Roman empire; for Dante, the cause of the eventual establishment of the papacy as well.

28. the chosen Vessel: *Vas electionis*, the phrase used by God to refer to Saul/Paul in Acts 9.15. Saint Paul relates his vision of the "third heaven" in 2 Cor. 12.1–7. There is an account of Saint Paul's visit to Hell in the fifth- or sixth-century Latin "Apocalypse of Paul" (*Visio Pauli*; see Elliott).

32. I am not Aeneas, I am not Paul: After the periphrases of lines 13 and 28, the use of the names themselves is climactic. In addition to developing the theme of the pilgrim's fear (see below), the raising of this question serves to emphasize the iconoclastic, in fact epoch-making importance of a journey to the other world being claimed by a layman and politically active private individual.

43–45. If I have . . . cowardice: A continuation of the theme of the pilgrim's fear, a chief obstacle in Canto 1 (see 1.19, 44, 52, 90). The terzina opposes magnanimity (largeness of spirit) with baseness or smallness of spirit, in this case the pilgrim's unwillingness to believe he is destined for great things and his reluctance to trust Virgil; the concepts are discussed in *Convivio* 1.11, on the basis of Aristotle's *Nichomachean Ethics* (4.3).

52–117. I was among those . . . quicker to come here: Virgil answers the pilgrim's fears with an account of how he was sent to the pilgrim, which reveals the hierarchical chain of mediation of God's grace (Virgin Mary–Saint Lucy–Beatrice–Virgil) that his presence implies. His authority is guaranteed by his connection with the highest (God) via the hierarchical chain (note that his knowledge of the upper levels is itself mediated by Beatrice's account). On the importance of the "great chain of being" in the *Comedy,* see Introduction, pp. 18–20.

52. those who are suspended: The souls in Limbo (see Canto 4).

53–57. a lady . . . in her language: The style of Virgil's description of Beatrice derives from the lyric poetry of the *dolce stil novo* (itself deriving from the long medieval tradition of narrative and lyric exaltation of ladies) and especially the *Vita nuova,* which narrates Dante's youthful love for her before and after her death and establishes her status as a miracle. Florentine tradition, related by Boccaccio, identified her with a Beatrice Portinari, a young married woman who died on the appropriate day; the name *Beatrice* means "she who makes blessed."

61. not the friend of fortune: That is, he loved her without regard to personal advantage.

67. your ornamented speech: Virgil's rhetorical power, praised also in lines 113–14 and exemplified in this entire account (see the note to line 126).

71. the place . . . return: The Empyrean (see the note to lines 120–26).

76–78. O lady . . . smallest: This is the first reference in the poem to the allegorical dimension of Beatrice; in addition to being the soul of the Florentine lady Dante loved, she represents, variously, the principles of mediation, accommodation, revelation, and divine grace.

78. that heaven whose circles are smallest: That of the moon. Change was thought to be confined to the sublunar realm, since all the heavenly bodies, beginning with the moon, were perfect and changeless.

82–114. But tell me . . . those who have heeded it: Virgil's question and Beatrice's answer reproduce the structure governing the canto as a whole: the pilgrim's question expressing his fears (lines 10–36) and Virgil's answer, followed by its result (lines 43–142). Like Virgil, Beatrice answers a question about fear of Hell (in this case, her own lack of it) with the narrative of how she was sent.

91. your misery does not touch me: Beatrice's use of the verb *tangere* [to touch] echoes the risen Jesus' words to Mary Magdalen (John 20.17): "Noli me tangere" [Do not touch me].

94. noble lady: The Virgin Mary.

97. Lucia: Saint Lucy of Syracuse, the patroness of vision (probably because her name seems derived from the Latin word for "light"). There has been much discussion of the question of Dante's devotion to her, about which nothing more is known except her appearance helping Dante in *Purg.* 9.35–63 and *Par.* 32.136–38.

102. Rachel: The story of Jacob's love for Rachel, for whom he served seven years, and then another seven years when her older sister Leah was substituted for her, is told in Genesis 29–30. The two sisters were traditionally interpreted as symbolic of the contemplative life (Rachel) and the active life (Leah) (see *Purg.* 27.94–108).

105. came forth . . . herd: That is, Dante's love for Beatrice itself distinguished him, and it also motivated him to seek acclaim as a poet.

108. the torrent . . . no boast: A deliberately obscure line, variously interpreted; in our view, the reference is the same as in 1.26–27, "the pass that has never yet left anyone alive," in other words the abyss or flood of sin/Hell (Boccaccio). On the assumption that the torrent is a separate river, however, parallels have been suggested with Acheron and Jordan, which do not flow into the sea (Freccero 1966b).

126. my speech: Looking back on Virgil's speech, one notes its formal rhetorical structure: proem with *propositio* (lines 43–51), narration (lines 52–120), emotive peroration (lines 121–26). Despite the pilgrim's disclaimer, the sanctions for his journey do strictly parallel the precedents of Aeneas and Saint Paul, though with important differences. Of his two guides, Virgil is a representative of the Roman empire, Beatrice of the Church. But the pilgrim's claim on each is that of an individual, a layman, not someone authorized by institutional status: his claims are his devotion to Virgil's poetry and his being himself a poet (cf. 1.79–87), which of course already place him in an exalted literary tradition, though a secular one (the epoch-making decision to write in the vernacular is also at stake here), and his human love for the earthly Beatrice (cf. 2.61, 103). Virgil's role in the pilgrim's journey will be to prepare him for the coming of Beatrice (implied in 1.121–23), a process analogous to the historical function of Rome as Dante saw it, that of bringing the world under the rule of law in preparation for the coming of Christ. Though it seems to concern only the pilgrim's salvation, the passage in fact lays the foundation for the view of the poem as a providentially inspired intervention in current history, set forth especially in

Paradiso 17 and 27. Jacoff and Stephany (1989) discuss many of the interpretive issues in this canto.

127–132. As little flowers . . . a person freed: The canto began with the approach of night and the pilgrim's fears; here, in simile, it is dawn again (cf. 1.37–42).

CANTO 3

1   PER ME SI VA NE LA CITTA' DOLENTE,
PER ME SI VA NE L'ETTERNO DOLORE,
PER ME SI VA TRA LA PERDUTA GENTE.

4   GIUSTIZIA MOSSE IL MIO ALTO FATTORE;
FECEMI LA DIVINA PODESTATE,
LA SOMMA SAPÏENZA E'L PRIMO AMORE.

7   DINANZI A ME NON FUOR COSE CREATE
SE NON ETTERNE, E IO ETTERNO DURO.
LASCIATE OGNE SPERANZA, VOI CH'INTRATE.

10   Queste parole di colore oscuro
vid' ïo scritte al sommo d'una porta,
per ch'io: "Maestro, il senso lor m'è duro."

13   Ed elli a me, come persona accorta:
"Qui si convien lasciare ogne sospetto,
ogne viltà convien che qui sia morta.

16   Noi siam venuti al loco ov' i' t'ho detto
che tu vedrai le genti dolorose
c'hanno perduto il ben de l'intelletto."

19   E poi che la sua mano a la mia puose
con lieto volto, ond' io mi confortai,
mi mise dentro a le segrete cose.

22   Quivi sospiri, pianti e alti guai
risonavan per l'aere sanza stelle,
per ch'io al cominciar ne lagrimai.

25   Diverse lingue, orribili favelle,
parole di dolore, accenti d'ira,
voci alte e fioche, e suon di man con elle

28   facevano un tumulto, il qual s'aggira
sempre in quell'aura sanza tempo tinta,
come la rena quando turbo spira.

CANTO 3

*Hell Gate—the trimmers—the Acheron—Charon and the damned
souls—the pilgrim's faint*

1   THROUGH ME THE WAY INTO THE GRIEVING CITY,

    THROUGH ME THE WAY INTO ETERNAL SORROW,

    THROUGH ME THE WAY AMONG THE LOST PEOPLE.

4   JUSTICE MOVED MY HIGH MAKER;

    DIVINE POWER MADE ME,

    HIGHEST WISDOM, AND PRIMAL LOVE.

7   BEFORE ME WERE NO THINGS CREATED

    EXCEPT ETERNAL ONES, AND I ENDURE ETERNAL.

    ABANDON EVERY HOPE, YOU WHO ENTER.

10   These words I saw written with dark color above
a gate, and I said: "Master, their sense is hard for
me."

13   And he to me, like one alert: "Here one must
abandon every suspicion, every cowardice must die
here.

16   We have come to the place where I told you you
will see the grieving peoples who have lost the
good of the intellect."

19   And, putting his hand on mine with a cheerful
glance from which I drew strength, he introduced me
into the secret things.

22   There sighs, weeping, loud wailing resounded
through the starless air, for which at the outset I shed
tears.

25   Strange languages, horrible tongues, words of
pain, accents of anger, voices loud and hoarse, and
sounds of blows with them,

28   made a tumult that turns forever in that air
darkened without time, like the sand when a
whirlwind blows.

31   E io ch'avea d'orror la testa cinta,
   dissi: "Maestro, che è quel ch' i' odo?
   e che gent' è che par nel duol sì vinta?"

34   Ed elli a me: "Questo misero modo
   tegnon l'anime triste di coloro
   che visser sanza 'nfamia e sanza lodo.

37   Mischiate sono a quel cattivo coro
   de li angeli che non furon ribelli
   né fur fedeli a Dio, ma per sé fuoro.

40   Caccianli i ciel per non esser men belli,
   né lo profondo inferno li riceve,
   ch'alcuna gloria i rei avrebber d'elli."

43   E io: "Maestro, che è tanto greve
   a lor che lamentar li fa sì forte?"
   Rispuose: "Dicerolti molto breve.

46   Questi non hanno speranza di morte,
   e la lor cieca vita è tanto bassa
   che 'nvidïosi son d'ogne altra sorte.

49   Fama di loro il mondo esser non lassa;
   misericordia e giustizia li sdegna:
   non ragioniam di lor, ma guarda e passa."

52   E io, che riguardai, vidi una 'nsegna
   che girando correva tanto ratta
   che d'ogne posa mi parea indegna;

55   e dietro le venìa sì lunga tratta
   di gente, ch'i' non averei creduto
   che morte tanta n'avesse disfatta.

58   Poscia ch'io v'ebbi alcuno riconosciuto,
   vidi e conobbi l'ombra di colui
   che fece per viltade il gran rifiuto.

61   Incontanente intesi e certo fui
   che questa era la setta d'i cattivi,
   a Dio spiacenti e a' nemici sui.

64   Questi sciaurati, che mai non fur vivi,
   erano ignudi e stimolati molto
   da mosconi e da vespe ch'eran ivi.

67   Elle rigavan lor di sangue il volto,
   che, mischiato di lagrime, a' lor piedi
   da fastidiosi vermi era ricolto.

31   And I, my head girt with horror, said: "Master, what is this I hear? and what people is this who seem so overcome by grief?"

34   And he to me: "This wretched measure is kept by the miserable souls who lived without infamy and without praise.

37   They are mixed with that cowardly chorus of angels who were not rebels yet were not faithful to God, but were for themselves.

40   The heavens reject them so as not to be less beautiful, nor does deep Hell receive them, for the wicked would have some glory from them."

43   And I: "Master, what is so grievous that it makes them lament so loudly?" He replied: "I will tell you very briefly.

46   They have no hope of death, and their blind life is so base that they are envious of every other fate.

49   The world permits no fame of them to exist; mercy and justice alike disdain them: let us not speak of them, but look and pass on."

52   When I looked again, I saw a flag running in circles so rapidly that it seemed to scorn all pause;

55   and after it there came so long a train of people, that I would not have believed death had undone so many.

58   After I had recognized several, I saw and knew the shade of him who in his cowardice made the great refusal.

61   Immediately I understood and was certain that this was the sect of cowards, displeasing both to God and to his enemies.

64   These wretches, who never were alive, were naked and much tormented by large flies and wasps that were there.

67   These streaked their faces with blood which, mixed with tears, at their feet was gathered up by disgusting worms.

70   E poi ch'a riguardar oltre mi diedi,
vidi genti a la riva d'un gran fiume,
per ch'io dissi: "Maestro, or mi concedi

73   ch'i' sappia quali sono, e qual costume
le fa di trapassar parer sì pronte,
com' i' discerno per lo fioco lume."

76   Ed elli a me: "Le cose ti fier conte
quando noi fermerem li nostri passi
su la trista riviera d'Acheronte."

79   Allor con li occhi vergognosi e bassi,
temendo no 'l mio dir li fosse grave,
infino al fiume del parlar mi trassi.

82   Ed ecco verso noi venir per nave
un vecchio, bianco per antico pelo,
gridando: "Guai a voi, anime prave!

85   Non isperate mai veder lo cielo:
i' vegno per menarvi a l'altra riva
ne le tenebre etterne, in caldo e 'n gelo.

88   E tu che se' costì, anima viva,
pàrtiti da cotesti che son morti."
Ma poi che vide ch'io non mi partiva,

91   disse: "Per altra via, per altri porti
verrai a piaggia, non qui, per passare:
più lieve legno convien che ti porti."

94   E 'l duca lui: "Caron, non ti crucciare:
vuolsi così colà dove si puote
ciò che si vuole, e più non dimandare."

97   Quinci fuor quete le lanose gote
al nocchier de la livida palude,
che 'ntorno a li occhi avea di fiamme rote.

100   Ma quell' anime, ch'eran lasse e nude,
cangiar colore e dibattero i denti,
ratto che 'nteser le parole crude.

103   Bestemmiavano Dio e lor parenti,
l'umana spezie e 'l loco e 'l tempo e 'l seme
di lor semenza e di lor nascimenti.

106   Poi si ritrasser tutte quante insieme,
forte piangendo, a la riva malvagia
ch'attende ciascun uom che Dio non teme.

70 And when I gazed beyond them, I saw people on the bank of a great river; so I said, "Master, now grant

73 that I may know who those are, and what disposition makes them seem so ready to cross over, as I can discern in spite of the weak light."

76 And he to me: "These things will be made known to you when we stay our steps on the gloomy shore of Acheron."

79 Then with eyes shamefast and cast down, afraid that my speaking might displease him, I refrained from speech until we reached the river.

82 And behold coming toward us in a boat an old man, white with the hairs of age, crying: "Woe to you, wicked souls!

85 Never hope to see the sky: I come to lead you to the other shore, to the eternal shadows, to heat and freezing.

88 And you who are over there, living soul, separate yourself from these here, who are dead." But when he saw that I did not leave,

91 he said: "By another way, through other ports will you come to shore, not by crossing here: a lighter vessel must carry you."

94 And my leader to him: "Charon, do not torture yourself with anger: this is willed where what is willed can be done, so ask no more."

97 Then were quiet the woolly jowls of the pilot of the livid swamp; around his eyes he had wheels of flame.

100 But those weary, naked souls changed color and gnashed their teeth, as soon as they heard his harsh words.

103 They cursed God and their parents, the human race and the place and the time and the seed of their sowing and of their birth.

106 Then all of them together, weeping loudly, drew near the evil shore that awaits each one who does not fear God.

109 Caròn dimonio, con occhi di bragia,
loro accennando tutte le raccoglie;
batte col remo qualunque s'adagia.

112 Come d'autunno si levan le foglie
l'una appresso de l'altra, fin che 'l ramo
vede a la terra tutte le sue spoglie:

115 similemente il mal seme d'Adamo
gittansi di quel lito ad una ad una
per cenni, come augel per suo richiamo.

118 Così sen vanno su per l'onda bruna,
e avanti che sien di là discese,
anche di qua nuova schiera s'auna.

121 "Figliuol mio," disse 'l maestro cortese,
"quelli che muoion ne l'ira di Dio
tutti convegnon qui d'ogne paese;

124 e pronti sono a trapassar lo rio,
ché la divina giustizia li sprona
sì che la tema si volve in disio.

127 Quinci non passa mai anima buona;
e però, se Caron di te si lagna,
ben puoi sapere omai che 'l suo dir suona."

130 Finito questo, la buia campagna
tremò sì forte che de lo spavento
la mente di sudore ancor mi bagna.

133 La terra lagrimosa diede vento
che balenò una luce vermiglia
la qual mi vinse ciascun sentimento,

136 e caddi come l'uom cui sonno piglia.

109   Charon the demon, with eyes like glowing coals, making signs to them, gathers them all in; he beats with his oar whoever lingers.

112   As in autumn the leaves remove themselves one after the other, until the branch sees all its raiment on the ground:

115   so the evil seed of Adam throw themselves from that shore one by one, when beckoned to, each like a falcon to its lure.

118   Thus they go off across the dark waves, and before they have disembarked over there, over here again a new flock gathers.

121   "My son," said my courteous master, "those who die in God's anger all come together here from every land;

124   and they are ready to cross over the river, for God's justice so spurs them that fear turns to desire.

127   No good soul ever passes this way; and so, if Charon complains of you, you can well understand what his words mean."

130   As he finished, the dark landscape trembled so violently that in terror my memory bathes me again with sweat.

133   The tearful earth gave forth a wind that flashed

136   with a crimson light which overcame all feeling in me, and I fell like one whom sleep is taking.

NOTES

1–9. **THROUGH ME . . . YOU WHO ENTER:** Like Vergil, Dante gives Hell both an outer and an inner gate (see 8.68 and 9.104, with notes). The early commentators identify the "speaking gate" as a personification; Morpurgo (1926; cited in Simonelli 1993) studied the genre of "gate-inscriptions" in medieval Latin; he found they typically include a statement of intent, often anaphorically with *per me* [through me] (cf. lines 1–3); the name of the builder (cf. lines 4–6); and the date of building (cf. line 7). Compare John 10.9, where Christ says, "I am the door [*osteum*]. Through me, if any man enter in, he shall be saved."

1. **GRIEVING CITY:** The grieving city derives from the biblical personification of Jerusalem mourning its destruction in 586 B.C. See Lamentations 1.1–2:

> How doth the city sit solitary. . . . Weeping she hath wept in the night, and her tears are on her cheeks: there is none to comfort her.

The destruction of Jerusalem was regarded by the exegetes as a figure of the Last Judgment and thus as applicable to Hell (this figure is discussed further in the note on 30.58–61). Dante quotes the first verse both in the *Vita nuova* (Chapter 29, on the death of Beatrice) and in a political epistle. That both Heaven and Hell are referred to as cities (cf. 1.126, 128) derives from Augustine's theory of the Earthly and Heavenly Cities in the *City of God*.

5–6. **DIVINE POWER . . . PRIMAL LOVE:** Power is the attribute of the Father, wisdom of the Son, and love of the Spirit: all creation is the work of the Trinity. The central theme of the *Inferno*, of course, is the carrying out of God's justice on sin.

7–8. **NO THINGS . . . EXCEPT ETERNAL ONES:** In *Par.* 29.22–36, Dante notes that the three eternal creatures are the angels (pure form or act), prime matter (pure potentiality), and the heavens (potentiality partially realized in act).

7. **CREATED:** That Hell was prepared for the rebel angels is biblical (Matt. 25.41: "the everlasting fire . . . was prepared for the devil and his angels"); the rebellion of the angels and their casting out from Heaven is mentioned in Apoc. 12.9:

And that great dragon was cast out, that old serpent, who is called the devil and Satan, who seduceth the whole world: and he was cast unto the earth, and his angels were thrown down with him.

See also 2 Peter 2.4.

10. dark color: The expression can refer both to the appearance of the writing and to the obscure and harsh meaning ("rhetorical" color).

11. above a gate: The gate stands open, like that of Vergil's Hades (*Aen.* 6.127: "noctes atque dies patet atri ianua Ditis" [all night and all day the gate of black Dis stands open]), but for Dante it was not always so (see 4.52–63 and note).

12. sense is hard: See John 6.61: "durus est hoc sermo" [this saying is hard], said by the disciples hearing Christ offer his flesh as food. See also 9.61–63, *Purg.* 8.19–22, with notes.

13–15. Here one must abandon . . . must die here: Note the antithesis with line 9. The sense echoes the Sybil in *Aen.* 6.261: "Nunc animis opus, Aenea, nunc pectore firmo" [Now there is need, Aeneas, of bravery, of a strong heart]; the relation between the pilgrim and his guide Virgil is patterned in many respects on that between Aeneas and the Sybil. In this canto Dante alludes to or quotes Aeneas's entrance into Hades (*Aen.* 6.261–414) more than a dozen times.

18. good of the intellect: The intellectual vision of God. The Aristotelian source of the phrase *(Nichomachean Ethics* 6.2.1139a) is quoted by Dante at *Convivio* 2.13.6: "as the Philosopher says . . . , the truth is the good of the intellect."

21. the secret things: Knowledge of the other world. Compare *Aen.* 6.264–67:

Di, quibus imperium est animarum, umbraeque silentes
et Chaos et Phlegethon, loca nocte tacentia late,
sit mihi fas audita loqui, sit numine vestro
pandere res alta terra et caligine mersas.

[Gods, whose power controls the shades [of the dead], and you, silent shadows,
and Chaos and Phlegethon, broad places silent in the night,
let it not be impious for me to speak things heard, let it be with your power
that I set forth things drowned in the deep earth and darkness.]

22–27. loud wailing . . . sounds of blows: Compare Matt. 13.42: "There shall be weeping and gnashing of teeth," also echoed in line 101, where the meaning of "chattering" includes "gnashing." See also *Aen.* 6.557–59 (of the gate to Tartarus):

> Hinc exaudiri gemitus et saeva sonare
> verbera, tum stridor ferri tractaeque catenae
>
> [From there wailing and fierce blows were heard,
> then the grating of irons and chains dragging]

23. starless air: Compare *Aen.* 6.534: "tristis sine sole domos" [gloomy sunless dwellings]; the last word of each cantica of the poem is *stars.*

24. I shed tears: The first of the pilgrim's varying emotional responses to Hell.

25. Strange languages, horrible tongues: The first hint of Hell's kinship with Babel, the place of confused speech.

29. darkened without time: Air darkened forever, beyond time.

31. my head girt with horror: In other words, the pilgrim's scalp is bristling (Latin *horreo,* to bristle) all around his head. The line echoes *Aen.* 2.559: "At me tum primum saevus circumstetit horror" [Then a dreadful horror first encircled me]; Aeneas is describing the decapitation of Priam, king of Troy.

36. without infamy and without praise: Dante's journey will bring infamy to those in Hell and renewed or better reputations to the blessed; but the neutrals are barred from any preservation of their reputations or "names." This verse is usually taken as a reference to Apoc. 3:15–16, spoken by Christ the Judge in reproof of Laodicea: "because thou art lukewarm, and neither cold nor hot, I will begin to vomit thee out of my mouth" (see the note to line 64).

37–39. They are mixed . . . for themselves: The legend of the neutral angels, mentioned in numerous medieval texts, including the *Voyage of Saint Brendan,* goes back at least as far as Clement of Alexandria (Gmelin). This mixing of human and angelic is not observed anywhere else in the poem.

39. but were for themselves: The rebel angels first averted themselves from God and then actively turned to evil with Satan, but the neutrals, once averted from God, did not act further (Freccero [1960] prefers the translation "stood by themselves"); theirs is a "double negation," and lines 36–52 offer a number of examples where the double exclusion of the neutrals assumes a characteristic syntactic form (Freccero 1983).

52–53. flag running in circles: The first instance of Dante's *contrapasso* [counter-suffering]—the fitting of the punishment to the sin (see 28.142). The flag acts as the lure, the wasps and flies as prods or stimuli, punishing the neutrals' purpose-lessness and lack of affiliation.

56–57. death had undone so many: The infinite number of the dead is a classical topos, discussed in the note to lines 112–17, but Dante's point is more barbed. Eliot translated this line in *The Waste Land*.

59–60. him who in his cowardice . . . great refusal: This unnamed soul has been identified as Pontius Pilate, Esau, and a host of others. But Pietro dal Morrone, the pious monastic reformer (he founded the order of Celestines) elevated to the papacy in 1294 as Celestine V and canonized shortly after his death, is the choice of the earliest commentators (the expression "saw and knew" suggests that Dante had seen him, and Pietro was in Florence in 1280, though the phrase is also used of Hector and Aeneas in Canto 4). Celestine is a plausible candidate because his abdication cleared the way for the accession of Benedetto Caetani as Boniface VIII, Dante's corrupt enemy (see 19.52–57, 27.85–105). Celestine's act would thus have been a "neutral" failure to oppose a patent evil, resulting from *viltà* [cowardice] (see Virgil's words to the pilgrim in 2.45), but all identifications are inconclusive.

62–64. sect of cowards . . . wretches: The word for "coward" here, *cattivo* (used also in line 37), still retained for Dante the meaning of "captive" (cf. 30.16).

64. never were alive: See Apoc. 3.1 (of the Church at Sardis): "I know thy works, that thou hast the name of being alive: and thou art dead."

65–69. large flies and wasps . . . worms: In Dante's day, flies, wasps, and worms were thought to be born of putrefaction.

70–78. I saw people . . . Acheron: Dante clusters a number of references to Vergil's poem in this part of the canto (a dozen in lines 70–105 alone), where the subject is the boundary river of Hades, the Acheron (Dante has rearranged the traditional rivers of the underworld, which are not clearly distinguished in Vergil's treatment). Compare *Aen.* 6.318–20:

Dic, ait, o virgo, quid vult concursus ad amnem?
quidve petunt animae? Vel quo discrimine ripas
hae linquunt, illae remis vada livida verrunt?

[He says: Say, virgin, what means this crowding at the river?
what do the souls seek? Or by what decision
do these remain on the shore, while those others beat the dark waters with oars?]

77–81. when we stay our steps . . . until we reached the river: See *Aen.* 6.295: "Hinc via Tartarei quae fert Acherontis ad undas" [From here the way ied down to the waters of infernal Acheron], and 6.384: "Ergo iter inceptum peragunt fluvioque propinquant" [They took up their journey again and approached the river].

82–111. And behold . . . whoever moves slowly: In these lines, Dante adapts Vergil's portrait of Charon, the traditional ferryman of the Styx, *Aen.* 6.298–305:

Portitor has horrendus aquas et flumina servat
terribili squalore Charon, cui plurima mento
canities inculta iacet, stant lumina flamma,
sordidus et umeris nodo dependet amictus.
Ipse ratem conto subigit velisque ministrat
et ferruginea subvectat corpora cumba,
iam senior, sed cruda deo viridisque senectus.

[A fearsome ferryman guards these waters, this river:
Charon. His filth is frightening, thick gray straggly
whiskers cover his chin; his eyes are flames.
A dirty cloak hangs from his shoulders by a knot.
With a pole he steers and tends the sail
of the iron-hued skiff that conveys the bodies across.
He is old now, but a god's eld is green and raw.]

Note, in Dante's text, 82 "old man" (cf. *senior*), 83 "white with hairs of age" and 97 "woolly cheeks" (cf. *canities mento inculta*), 99 "wheels of flame," "eyes like glowing coals" (cf. *stant lumina flammae*). For this last, compare Apoc. 1.14: "his eyes were as a flame of fire."

Dante makes Charon a devil (line 109), as he does other figures from the Vergilian/classical underworld, in keeping with biblical/Augustinian tradition (see the note to 1.72).

88–89. living soul, separate yourself from these here: Compare *Aen.* 6.391–94:

> Fare age quid venias iam istinc, et comprime gressum.
> Umbrarum hic locus est, somni noctisque soporae:
> corpora viva nefas Stygia vectare carina.

> [Say at once from there, why do you come, and halt your steps.
> This is the place of shades, dreams, and the sleep of night:
> it is sacrilege to carry living bodies in the Stygian hull.]

91–93. By another way . . . must carry you: Aeneas crosses in Charon's boat, but how the pilgrim crosses Acheron is left unspecified. Charon's words imply that the pilgrim is destined for salvation. The "lighter vessel" appears in *Purg.* 2.40–42.

95–96. this is willed . . . ask no more: The first of several passages where Virgil quells protest by invoking the theological commonplace of God's omnipotence (see 5.22–24, which are identical to these lines, and 7.10–12). These lines have the distinction of being the first attested quotation from the *Inferno*, found on the inside front cover of a register of criminal acts written in Bologna by the notary Gano degli Useppi of San Gimignano in 1317 (this is important evidence of the circulation of the *Inferno* during Dante's lifetime [Livi 1918]) (see the note to 5.23).

103–5. They cursed God . . . and of their birth: See Jer. 20.14: "Cursed be the day wherein I was born: let not the day in which my mother bore me, be blessed." See also Job 3.1 and Hosea [Vulgate Osee] 9.11.

111. beats with his oar: This vivid detail, not in Vergil, is vividly rendered by Michelangelo in the Sistine Chapel's *Last Judgment.*

112–17. As in autumn . . . to its lure: See *Aen.* 6.309–12:

> Quam multa in silvis autumni frigore primo
> lapsa cadunt folia, aut ad terram gurgite ab alto
> quam multae glomerantur aves, ubi frigidus annus
> trans pontum fugat et terris immittit apricis.

[As numerous as in the forest at the first chill of autumn,
the leaves fall, let loose, or on the land from the deep waves
the many birds gather, when the cold season
drives them overseas to warmer climes.]

This famous simile, in Vergil an imitation of Homer, was taken up by Milton for the multitudes of rebel angels and by Shelley for dead leaves driven by the West Wind. Where Vergil's simile gives two views of large numbers—the multitude of souls as dead leaves, as birds—for Dante the shift from one metaphor to the next (closely linked by the leaf and the bird being single) follows the transformation in the souls, as their reluctance is changed into a desire to cross.

115. the evil seed of Adam: Those of Adam's descendants who are damned (even those who did not sin voluntarily are damned by the sin inherited from Adam unless redeemed by faith in Christ). The image draws on the medieval commonplace of the tree of Adam's progeny.

117. each like a falcon to its lure: Dante's term is the generic *uccello* [bird], but the reference is clear and is the first of a large number of images drawn from falconry. Falconers used the lure, often consisting of shiny pieces of metal that could be whirled by an attached cord, to recall their birds after the hunt.

118. dark waves: Compare *Aen.* 5.2, "fluctusque atros."

123. together here from every land: Dante gives itineraries for the soul after death at 13.27 and *Purg.* 2.101–5; the idea of a gathering of birds, introduced in the simile of lines 112–17, is still at work here, as in line 119.

125–26. God's justice ... turns to desire: See the note to lines 112–17. Compare *Aen.* 6.313–14:

> stabant orantes primi transmittere cursum
> tendebantque manus ripae ulterioris amore.

> [the first stood praying to be taken across,
> they stretched out their hands in desire for the farther shore.]

130–133. the dark landscape ... a wind: Medieval geology, based on Seneca's *Natural Questions* and Aristotle's *Meteorology*, understood earthquakes as the result of violent winds pent up in the earth (cf. *Purg.* 21.56–57); like winds in the atmosphere, subterranean winds could produce lightning and thunder. The cause of this subterranean wind would not seem to be natural.

131–32. my memory . . . with sweat: Another instance of the narrating poet's being caught again in the experience narrated, discussed in the note to 1.4–7.

136. one whom sleep is taking: For other "sleeps" and "swoons" of the pilgrim, see 1.2, 1.6, 5.142, and *Purgatorio* 9, 19, 27, and 31.

CANTO 4

1   Ruppemi l'alto sonno ne la testa
un greve truono, sì ch'io mi riscossi
come persona ch'è per forza desta;

4   e l'occhio riposato intorno mossi,
dritto levato, e fiso riguardai
per conoscer lo loco dov' io fossi.

7   Vero è che 'n su la proda mi trovai
de la valle d'abisso dolorosa
che 'ntrono accoglie d'infiniti guai.

10   Oscura e profonda era e nebulosa
tanto che, per ficcar lo viso a fondo,
io non vi discernea alcuna cosa.

13   "Or discendiam qua giù nel cieco mondo,"
cominciò il poeta tutto smorto.
"Io sarò primo, e tu sarai secondo."

16   E io, che del color mi fui accorto,
dissi: "Come verrò, se tu paventi
che suoli al mio dubbiare esser conforto?"

19   Ed elli a me: "L'angoscia de le genti
che son qua giù, nel viso mi dipigne
quella pietà che tu per tema senti.

22   Andiam, ché la via lunga ne sospigne."
Così si mise e così mi fé intrare
nel primo cerchio che l'abisso cigne.

25   Quivi, secondo che per ascoltare,
non avea pianto mai che di sospiri
che l'aura etterna facevan tremare;

28   ciò avvenia di duol sanza martìri
ch'avean le turbe, ch'eran molte e grandi,
d'infanti e di femmine e di viri.

CANTO 4

First circle: Limbo—the unbaptized—Virgil's account of the Harrowing of Hell—the ancient poets—the Noble Castle—the illustrious pagans

1 Breaking the deep sleep within my head, a heavy thunder-clap made me shake myself like one forcibly awakened;

4 and I turned my rested eye about, standing erect, and gazed fixedly, to know the place where I might be.

7 In truth, I found myself on the brink of the sorrowful valley of the abyss, which gathers in the thundering of infinite woes.

10 Dark and deep it was, and so clouded that though I probed with my sight to the bottom I discerned nothing there.

13 "Now let us descend down here into the blind world," began the poet, all pale. "I will be first, and you will be second."

16 And I, who had perceived his color, said: "How can I come, if you are afraid, who when I have fears have ever brought me strength?"

19 And he to me: "The suffering of the peoples who are here below, paints on my face that pity which you perceive as fear.

22 Let us go, for the long way urges us." So he put himself, and so he made me enter, into the first circle girding the abyss.

25 Here, as far as could be heard, there was no weeping except of sighs which caused the eternal air to tremble;

28 these resulted from grief without torture, felt by the crowds, which were many and large, of infants and of women and of men.

31   Lo buon maestro a me: "Tu non dimandi
che spiriti son questi che tu vedi?
Or vo' che sappi, innanzi che più andi,

34   ch'ei non peccaro; e s'elli hanno mercedi
non basta, perché non ebber battesmo,
ch'è porta de la fede che tu credi;

37   e s'e' furon dinanzi al cristianesmo,
non adorar debitamente a Dio:
e di questi cotai son io medesmo.

40   Per tai difetti, non per altro rio,
semo perduti, e sol di tanto offesi
che sanza speme vivemo in disio."

43   Gran duol mi prese al cor quando lo 'ntesi,
però che gente di molto valore
conobbi che 'n quel limbo eran sospesi.

46   "Dimmi, maestro mio, dimmi, segnore,"
comincia' io per volere esser certo
di quella fede che vince ogne errore:

49   "uscicci mai alcuno, o per suo merto,
o per altrui, che poi fosse beato?"
E quei, che 'ntese il mio parlar coverto,

52   rispuose: "Io era nuovo in questo stato,
quando ci vidi venire un possente
con segno di vittoria coronato.

55   Trasseci l'ombra del primo parente,
d'Abèl suo figlio e quella di Noè,
di Moïsè legista e ubidente,

58   Abraàm patrïarca e Davìd re,
Israèl con lo padre e co' suoi nati
e con Rachele, per cui tanto fè,

61   e altri molti, e feceli beati.
E vo' che sappi che, dinanzi ad essi,
spiriti umani non eran salvati."

64   Non lasciavam l'andar perch' ei dicessi,
ma passavam la selva tuttavia,
la selva, dico, di spiriti spessi.

67   Non era lunga ancor la nostra via
di qua dal sonno, quand' io vidi un foco
ch'emisperio di tenebre vincia.

31 My good master to me: "You do not ask what spirits are these you see? Now I wish you to know, before you walk further,

34 that they did not sin; and if they have merits, it is not enough, because they did not receive baptism, which is the gateway to the faith that you believe.

37 And if they lived before Christianity, they did not adore God as was needful: and of this kind am I myself.

40 Because of such defects, not for any other wickedness, we are lost, and only so far harmed that without hope we live in desire."

43 Great sorrow seized my heart when I understood him, because I knew that people of great worth were suspended in that limbo.

46 "Tell me, my master, tell me, lord," I began, wishing to be assured of that faith which overcomes all error:

49 "has anyone ever gone forth from here, either through his own merit or through another, so as to become blessed?" And he, who understood my veiled speech,

52 replied: "I was still new in this condition, when I saw a powerful one come, crowned with a sign of victory.

55 He led forth from here the shade of our first parent, of Abel his son, and that of Noah, of Moses, lawgiver and obedient,

58 Abraham the patriarch and David the king, Israel with his father, and his children, and Rachel, for whom he did so much,

61 and many others, and he made them blessed. And I would have you know that before them no human spirits were saved."

64 We did not cease walking because he spoke, but kept on passing through the wood, the wood, I say, of crowding spirits.

67 Our way had not led far from where I had slept, when I saw a fire that overcame a hemisphere of shadows.

70   Di lungi n'eravamo ancora un poco,
        ma non sì ch'io non discernessi in parte
        ch'orrevol gente possedea quel loco.

73   "O tu ch'onori scïenzïa e arte,
        questi chi son c'hanno cotanta onranza,
        che del modo de li altri li diparte?"

76   E quelli a me: "L'onrata nominanza
        che di lor suona sù ne la tua vita,
        grazïa acquista in ciel che sì li avanza."

79   Intanto voce fu per me udita:
        "Onorate l'altissimo poeta:
        l'ombra sua torna, ch'era dipartita."

82   Poi che la voce fu restata e queta,
        vidi quattro grand'ombre a noi venire:
        sembianz' avevan né trista né lieta.

85   Lo buon maestro cominciò a dire:
        "Mira colui con quella spada in mano,
        che vien dinanzi ai tre sì come sire:

88   quelli è Omero, poeta sovrano;
        l'altro è Orazio satiro che vene;
        Ovidio è 'l terzo, e l'ultimo Lucano.

91   Però che ciascun meco si convene
        nel nome che sonò la voce sola,
        fannomi onore, e di ciò fanno bene."

94   Così vid' i' adunar la bella scola
        di quel segnor de l'altissimo canto
        che sovra li altri com' aquila vola.

97   Da ch'ebber ragionato insieme alquanto,
        volsersi a me con salutevol cenno,
        e 'l mio maestro sorrise di tanto;

100   e più d'onore ancora assai mi fenno,
        ch'e' sì mi fecer de la loro schiera,
        sì ch'io fui sesto tra cotanto senno.

103   Così andammo infino a la lumera,
        parlando cose che 'l tacere è bello,
        sì com' era 'l parlar colà dov' era.

106   Venimmo al piè d'un nobile castello,
        sette volte cerchiato d'alte mura,
        difeso intorno d'un bel fiumicello.

70   We were still some distance from it, but not so far
as to keep me from discerning in part that people worthy
to be honored possessed the place.

73   "O you who honor knowledge and art, who are
these who receive so much privilege as to be
separated from the manner of the others?"

76   And he to me: "The honor with which their names
resound up in your life, wins grace in Heaven that
thus advances them."

79   Meantime a voice was heard by me: "Honor the
highest poet: his shade returns, that had departed."

82   When the voice had ceased and was silent, I saw
four great shades coming toward us: their expression
was neither sad nor happy.

85   My good master began to speak: "Behold the one
with that sword in his hand, coming in front of the
other three as if their lord:

88   that is Homer, the supreme poet; the next is
Horace the satirist; Ovid is the third, and the last,
Lucan.

91   Because they all share with me that name which
the single voice pronounced, they do me honor, and
in this they do well."

94   So saw I come together the lovely school of that
lord of highest song, who soars above the others like
an eagle.

97   When they had spoken together for a time they
turned to me with sign of greeting, and my master
smiled at that;

100   and they did me an even greater honor, for they
made me one of their band, so that I was sixth
among so much wisdom.

103   Thus we went as far as the light, speaking things
of which it is good to be silent now, as it was good
to speak them there where I was.

106   We came to the foot of a noble castle, seven times
encircled by high walls, defended all around by a
lovely little stream.

109   Questo passammo come terra dura;
   per sette porte intrai con questi savi;
   giugnemmo in prato di fresca verdura.

112   Genti v'eran con occhi tardi e gravi,
   di grande autorità ne' loro sembianti:
   parlavan rado, con voci soavi.

115   Traemmoci così da l'un de' canti
   in loco aperto, luminoso e alto,
   sì che veder si potien tutti quanti.

118   Colà diritto, sovra 'l verde smalto,
   mi fuor mostrati li spiriti magni,
   che del vedere in me stesso m'essalto.

121   I' vidi Eletra con molti compagni,
   tra ' quai conobbi Ettòr ed Enea,
   Cesare armato con li occhi grifagni.

124   Vidi Cammilla e la Pantasilea;
   da l'altra parte vidi 'l re Latino,
   che con Lavina sua figlia sedea.

127   Vidi quel Bruto che cacciò Tarquino,
   Lucrezia, Iulia, Marzïa e Corniglia;
   e solo, in parte, vidi 'l Saladino.

130   Poi ch'innalzai un poco più le ciglia,
   vidi 'l maestro di color che sanno
   seder tra filosofica famiglia.

133   Tutti lo miran, tutti onor li fanno:
   quivi vid' ïo Socrate e Platone,
   che 'nnanzi a li altri più presso li stanno,

136   Democrito che 'l mondo a caso pone,
   Dïogenès, Anassagora e Tale,
   Empedoclès, Eraclito e Zenone;

139   e vidi il buono accoglitor del quale,
   Dïascoride dico; e vidi Orfeo,
   Tulïo e Lino e Seneca morale,

142   Euclide geomètra e Tolomeo,
   Ipocràte, Avicenna e Galïeno,
   Averoìs che 'l gran comento feo.

145   Io non posso ritrar di tutti a pieno,
   però che sì mi caccia il lungo tema
   che molte volte al fatto il dir vien meno.

109 This we passed over like solid ground; through seven gates I entered with these sages; we came into a meadow of fresh green.

112 Here were people with slow, grave eyes and great authority in their countenances: they spoke seldom, and with soft voices.

115 Therefore we drew to one side, to a place open, bright, and high, whence all of them could be seen.

118 There opposite, on the bright green grass, all the great spirits were shown to me, so that I am still exalted within myself at the sight.

121 I saw Electra with many companions, among whom I recognized Hector and Aeneas, Caesar in armor with hawklike eyes.

124 I saw Camilla and Penthesilea; on the other side I saw King Latinus, who was sitting with Lavinia his daughter.

127 I saw the Brutus who drove Tarquin out, Lucretia, Julia, Marcia, and Cornelia; and alone, to the side, Saladdin.

130 When I lifted my brow a little higher, I saw the master of those who know, sitting among a philosophical company.

133 All gaze at him, all do him honor: there I saw Socrates and Plato, standing closer to him, in front of the others,

136 Democritus, who assigns the world to chance, Diogenes, Anaxagoras, and Thales, Empedocles, Heraclitus, and Zeno;

139 and I saw the good gatherer of qualities, Dioscorides I mean; and I saw Orpheus, Tullius and Linus, and Seneca the moralist,

142 Euclid the geometer and Ptolemy, Hippocrates, Avicenna and Galen, Averroës who made the great commentary.

145 I cannot describe them all in full, because my long theme so drives me that often the word falls short of the fact.

148   La sesta compagnia in due si scema:
per altra via mi mena il savio duca
fuor de la queta, ne l'aura che trema.

151   E vegno in parte ove non è che luca.

148   The company of six is reduced to two: along another way my wise leader conducts me out of the quiet, into the trembling air.

151   And I came to a place where no light shines.

NOTES

1. the deep sleep: Echoing 3.136, and recalling also 1.2 and 1.11.

2. a heavy thunder-clap: Perhaps the sound of the lightning flash of 3.134. Except for line 67, no further reference is made to either passage.

8. valley of the abyss: The expression "pit of the abyss" (the "abyss" is literally the "bottomless") is biblical (Apoc. 9.1–2).

11. I probed with my sight: According to Plato, vision results from the joining of light emitted by the eye with external light. Aristotle conclusively refuted this view, but Dante's terminology regularly reflects it.

14–21. all pale . . . you perceive as fear: Virgil's pity seems restricted to the souls in Limbo. Though it is not fear that causes his pallor here, it does cause it later (see 9.1–3).

24. the first circle: The existence of a Limbo (the term means "edge" or "fringe") for unbaptized children and for the faithful waiting for Christ was asserted by the fathers of the Church; Aquinas placed it underground, below Purgatory (also underground) but above Hell itself (*Summa theol.* Suppl., q. 94). Dante's placing unbaptized adults and virtuous pagans there is original with him and contrary to Church doctrine. The best discussion is Padoan 1970.

29–30. the crowds . . . and of men: There is an echo here of Vergil's description of the dead crowding the shores of Styx (*Aen.* 6.306–8), which Dante also drew on in 3.70–78:

> matres atque viri defunctaque corpora vita
> magnanimum heroum, pueri innuptaeque puellae,
> impositique rogis iuvenes ante ora parentum

> [mothers and men and the bodies reft of life
> of great-souled heroes, boys and unwedded girls,
> youths placed on the pyre before the eyes of their parents]

34–42. they did not sin . . . live in desire: For Dante, beatitude cannot be earned but is the result of a free gift by God predicated on faith in Christ (strictly speaking, faith itself is a gift of grace), though faith alone, without works, is insufficient (Dante will give numerous instances of late repentants who are saved, however). "Merits" refers to deserving acquired by works; Virgil may seem to imply that those who lived before Christ were saved if they "adored" God (or "prayed" to him) rightly; in *Paradiso* 19, in a passage about the salvation of a Trojan from the time of the Trojan War, the pilgrim is told that no one has ever been saved without believing in Christ. Dante's theory of salvation, thoroughly orthodox in medieval terms (unlike his Limbo), is set forth in *Paradiso* 7.

35–36. baptism, which is the gateway: This is a traditional metaphor; as Dante writes in *Par.* 25.10–11, by baptism he "entered into the faith." See also *Inferno* 19, especially lines 16–21.

39. and of this kind am I myself: Virgil identifies himself as one who, living before Christianity, "did not adore God as was needful"; since he has explicitly stated that the souls in Limbo "did not sin" (line 34), his account here really does not explain his statement (1.123) that he was "a rebel" against God's law. This question hovers over Dante's entire portrayal of Virgil (see, with notes, Cantos 8 and 9 and *Purgatorio* 21, 22, and 30).

42. without hope we live in desire: They desire the beatific vision of God but cannot hope to reach it; compare with Augustine, *Confessions* 1.1: "you have made us for yourself, and our heart is unquiet until it rest in you."

47–50. assured of that faith . . . to become blessed: Lines 47–48 can be taken to mean that the pilgrim desires a high degree of certainty or that he desires clarification of his Christian belief. Chiavacci Leonardi suggests that his question reflects Dante's awareness that Christ's descent into Hell (between his death and resurrection) had been made an article of faith only in 1215 (reasserted in 1274); he is obviously asserting it as correct.

52–63. I was still new . . . no human spirits were saved: Virgil's account refers to the so-called Harrowing of Hell, narrated in the apocryphal *Gospel of Nicodemus* (third century A.D.), itself based on scattered biblical passages (e.g., Eph. 4.9) and no doubt founded on earlier beliefs: Christ was supposed to have descended into the underworld, violently breaking down its outer gate (cf. 3.1–12) against the opposition of the devils, and to have led to Heaven in triumph the souls of all those who had believed the prophecies of his future coming. This theme became one of the most widely represented in the Middle Ages, in poems, mosaics, sculptures, paintings, and plays. The Byzantine *anastasis*, the earliest type of pictorial representation of the triumphant Christ, showed him trampling the shattered gates of Hell (and, underneath them, Satan) while taking by the hand Adam at the head of a line of Old Testament figures; good examples are the apse mosaic at Torcello and the internal mosaic at San Marco in Venice (reproduced in Singleton, plate 2).

52. I was still new: Vergil died in 19 B.C.; by Dante's reckoning he would have been dead for about fifty-two years when Christ died.

53. a powerful one: Virgil does not seem to have recognized Christ as anything more than a man; Augustine (*Enarrationes in Psalmos*, 48.1.5) expressed the view that at the Last Judgment the damned would not be able to see Christ's divinity (see the note to 34.115).

54. crowned . . . victory: Virgil probably saw a classical laurel wreath rather than the cruciform nimbus, a sign of divinity, which crowns the triumphant Christ in the *anastasis* and later images (see previous note); the line may echo Hebrews 2.9: "But we see Jesus . . . crowned with glory and honor."

59–60. Israel . . . did so much: Jacob (named Israel after his struggle with the angel, Gen. 32.28), his father Isaac, his twelve sons (the progenitors of the twelve tribes of Israel), and his wife Rachel (see the note to 2.100).

69. a fire . . . shadows: The hemisphere of light is a symbol both of the enlightenment achieved by classical civilization and of the knowledge (the memory) of the classical world possessed by Dante and his contemporaries (the "honorable mention," or fame, of line 76). Although Dante realized that his time possessed only fragmentary knowledge of antiquity, he could not have foreseen that the generation of Petrarch (1304–1374) and Boccaccio (1308–1375) would double the number of ancient texts accessible to readers and consequently further revolutionize European conceptions of history.

88. Homer: Dante had no direct knowledge of Homer or any other Greek poets; his ideas were derived from Aristotle, Cicero, Vergil, and other Latin authors. He apparently knew nothing of Aeschylus, Sophocles, Pindar, or Sappho, to mention only a few (Euripides and several others are mentioned in *Purg.* 22.106–7).

89. Horace the satirist: Quintus Horatius Flaccus (65–8 B.C.) was, with Vergil, the leading poet of the Augustan age. Dante refers to the *Ars poetica,* which circulated separately, in *De vulgari eloquentia* 2.4.4 but never mentions the other *Epistles* or the *Odes*.

90. Ovid . . . Lucan: Publius Ovidius Naso (43 B.C.–ca. A.D. 17) and Marcus Annaeus Lucanus (A.D. 39–65). Dante knew all or most of Ovid's works, of which he most frequently cites the *Metamorphoses;* Lucan is the author of the *Pharsalia,* an epic on the civil war between Caesar and Pompey. The only major Latin epic poet omitted here is Statius, whom we meet in Purgatory; Dante does not seem to have known Propertius.

98–105. they turned to me . . . there where I was: A transparent autobiographical allegory, referring to Dante's learning the craft of poetry by studying the ancients and his conviction that he is worthy of their company (no false modesty here).

102. so that I was sixth: The phrase seems to echo Ovid's naming of himself as fourth in the line of elegiac poets in *Tristia* 4.10.54: "fourth of these in the succession of time was I myself." There is, no doubt, a numerological significance in the pilgrim's being sixth; in the *Purgatorio,* with the addition of Statius, he becomes seventh (for the significance in the poem of the number seven, see the notes to *Purgatorio* 17).

106. a noble castle: Like the hemisphere of light, this is another symbol of classical civilization, usually identified as the castle of wisdom, the seven walls symbolizing the seven classical virtues (four moral, the so-called cardinal virtues: prudence, temperance, fortitude, and justice; three intellectual: understanding, knowledge, and, again, prudence), the seven gates symbolizing the seven liberal arts (the Trivium [triple path], arts of language: grammar, rhetoric, and dialectic; and the Quadrivium [fourfold path], sciences of the cosmos: music, arithmetic, geometry, and astronomy), also inherited from antiquity (see Curtius 1953). The stream is often glossed as representing eloquence; several early commentators take it to refer to worldly temptations which must be shunned for the sake of learning. As the early commentators point out, the green meadow derives from Vergil's Elysian Fields (*Aen.* 6.637–892).

115–17. Therefore we drew . . . could be seen: The elevation from which the group contemplate the great souls of antiquity seems to echo the hill from which Aeneas and Anchises see the future heroes of Rome (*Aen.* 6.754–55).

118–20. There opposite . . . at the sight: At the autobiographical level of the allegory, the entire episode of the hemisphere of light must of course refer to Dante's reading of classical writers and his acquisition of classical lore. Along with lines 97–102, this is a clear expression of the excitement he felt.

121. Electra: Not the daughter of Agamemnon but of Atlas; she was the mother of Dardanus, a founder of Troy (*Aen.* 8.134–35; Dante refers to her again in *Monarchia* 2.3.2). She is appropriately grouped with the Trojans Hector and Aeneas and with Julius Caesar (descended, according to Vergil, from Aeneas).

124–26. Camilla . . . Lavinia his daughter: Figures from the *Aeneid* (cf. 1.107–8): Camilla and Penthesilea are virgin warriors: Camilla, an invention of Vergil's, is an ally of the Latins (*Aen.* 7.803–17, 11.648–835), and Penthesilea, the queen of the Amazons, was an ally of Troy according to a Greek tradition mentioned by Vergil (*Aen.* 1.490–93). King Latinus, the king of the Latins, betrothed his daughter to Aeneas before hostilities broke out; from the union of Trojans and Latians sprang the Romans.

127–29. Brutus . . . Cornelia: Figures from Roman history, known to Dante from Livy, Lucan, and others. Tarquin, according to Roman tradition, was the last of the kings; his son's rape of Lucretia resulted in their expulsion and the founding of the republic, which Dante notes in *Convivio* 4.5.12 as lasting from Brutus, its first consul, to Julius Caesar. Cornelia was Julius Caesar's wife and the mother of Julia, who was married to Pompey the Great. Marcia was the wife of Cato the Younger, whom we meet in *Purgatorio* 1.

129. Saladdin: Saladdin (Salah ad-Din, 1137–1193) was the sultan of Egypt who drove the Crusaders entirely out of the Holy Land, except for the fortress of Acre, which fell in Dante's day. Many stories and legends gathered about this impressive figure; Dante mentions him in *Convivio* 4.11.14 as an example of liberality.

130. When I lifted my brow a little higher: The heroes of the contemplative life—philosophers, poets, and scientists—are placed higher than those of the active life.

131. the master of those who know: Aristotle (384–322 B.C.), widely known simply as "the philosopher," all of whose surviving works had by Dante's time been translated into Latin. One of the most impressive achievements of the Middle Ages was the assimilation and mastery during the twelfth and thirteenth centuries of all the works of Aristotle.

134. Socrates and Plato: Dante knew Plato only indirectly, mainly through Augustine's adaptation of Neoplatonic lore, except for the incomplete translation of the *Timaeus* by the fourth- or fifth-century Christian bishop Calcidius, who also wrote a commentary on it. Although Dante makes Plato subordinate to Aristotle, the "Aristotle" he knew was more Platonic than not, since, in common with his time, Dante ascribed to him several works by late followers of Plato and read him in a Neoplatonic key.

136–38. Democritus . . . Zeno: Diogenes and Zeno Dante had read of in manuals; the others are pre-Socratics discussed by Aristotle in his *Physics* in order to refute their views.

139. Dioscorides: The traditional author of the most widely used collection of works on *materia medica*; the qualities referred to are those of plants.

140–42. Orpheus . . . Seneca: Orpheus and Linus are legendary poets mentioned in Vergil's *Eclogues* and *Georgics*; Tullius is Marcus Tullius Cicero (106–46 B.C.); Seneca the moralist is Lucius Annaeus Seneca the younger (4 B.C.–A.D. 65), also the author of tragedies. Some works by both Cicero and Seneca were known to Dante. The inclusion of poets among philosophers reflects the

Ciceronian tradition of identifying poetry with wisdom, as well as the fact that many of the pre-Socratics wrote in verse.

142–44. Euclid . . . Averroës: Scientists and philosophers, all translated into Latin. Euclid's (third century B.C.) *Elements* and *Optics* were widely studied in Dante's time. Ptolemy's (second century A.D.) *Almagest* was the leading astronomical textbook, as his *Tetrabiblos* was the dominant influence in astrology. Hippocrates (fifth century B.C.) was the most famous physician of ancient Greece, to whom works by many authors were ascribed. Galen (second century A.D.) was the founder of experimental medicine; his influence dominated European medicine from the late Middle Ages into the seventeenth century.

Dante treats the Muslim philosophers almost as extensions of Greco-Roman civilization. Avicenna (Ibn-Sina, d. 1036) was the leading Muslim Neoplatonic philosopher and the author of an influential handbook of medicine that Dante probably knew. The Spanish Arab Averroës (Ibn-Rushd, d. 1198), who suffered persecution from the Islamic fundamentalists of his day, was the greatest of the medieval commentators on Aristotle, widely known simply as "the Commentator" (the "great commentary" refers to his commentary on Aristotle's *De anima*); the extent to which Dante accepted his influential doctrine of the unity of the intellect (combatted by Aquinas) has been hotly debated.

CANTO 5

1   Così discesi del cerchio primaio
giù nel secondo, che men loco cinghia
e tanto più dolor che punge a guaio.

4   Stavvi Minòs orribilmente, e ringhia;
essamina le colpe ne l'intrata;
giudica e manda secondo ch'avvinghia.

7   Dico che quando l'anima mal nata
li vien dinanzi, tutta si confessa;
e quel conoscitor de le peccata

10   vede qual loco d'inferno è da essa;
cignesi con la coda tante volte
quantunque gradi vuol che giù sia messa.

13   Sempre dinanzi a lui ne stanno molte;
vanno a vicenda ciascuna al giudizio,
dicono e odono e poi son giù volte.

16   "O tu che vieni al doloroso ospizio,"
disse Minòs a me quando mi vide,
lasciando l'atto di cotanto offizio,

19   "guarda com' entri e di cui tu ti fide:
non t'inganni l'ampiezza de l'intrare!"
E 'l duca mio a lui: "Perché pur gride?

22   Non impedir lo suo fatale andare:
vuolsi così colà dove si puote
ciò che si vuole, e più non dimandare."

25   Or incomincian le dolenti note
a farmisi sentire; or son venuto
là dove molto pianto mi percuote.

28   Io venni in loco d'ogne luce muto,
che mugghia come fa mar per tempesta,
se da contrari venti è combattuto.

CANTO 5

Minos—second circle: the lustful—Francesca da Rimini and
Paolo Malatesta

1 Thus I descended from the first circle down to the
second, which encloses a smaller space, but so much
more suffering that it goads the souls to shriek.

4 There stands Minos bristling and snarling: he
examines the soul's guilt at the entrance; he judges
and passes sentence by how he wraps.

7 I say that when the ill-born soul comes before
him, it confesses all; and that connoisseur of sin

10 sees which is its place in Hell; he girds himself
with his tail as many times as the levels he wills the
soul to be sent down.

13 Always many stand before him; each goes in turn
to judgment, they speak and hear and are cast into
the deep.

16 "O you who come to the dolorous hospice," said
Minos when he saw me, leaving off the exercise of
his great office,

19 "beware how you enter and to whom you entrust
yourself: be not deceived by the spacious entrance!"
And my leader to him: "Why still cry out?

22 Do not impede his going, which is decreed: this is
willed where what is willed can be done, so ask no
more."

25 Now the grief-stricken notes begin to make
themselves heard; now I have come where much
weeping assails me.

28 I came into a place where all light is silent, that
groans like the sea in a storm, when it is lashed by
conflicting winds.

31 La bufera infernal, che mai non resta,
mena li spirti con la sua rapina;
voltando e percotendo li molesta.

34 Quando giungon davanti a la ruina,
quivi le strida, il compianto, il lamento;
bestemmian quivi la virtù divina.

37 Intesi ch'a così fatto tormento
enno dannati i peccator carnali,
che la ragion sommettono al talento.

40 E come li stornei ne portan l'ali
nel freddo tempo, a schiera larga e piena,
così quel fiato li spiriti mali

43 di qua, di là, di giù, di sù li mena;
nulla speranza li conforta mai,
non che di posa, ma di minor pena.

4⁴ E come i gru van cantando lor lai,
faccendo in aere di sé lunga riga,
così vid' io venir, traendo guai,

49 ombre portate da la detta briga;
per ch'i' dissi: "Maestro, chi son quelle
genti che l'aura nera sì gastiga?"

52 "La prima di color di cui novelle
tu vuo' saper," mi disse quelli allotta,
"fu imperadrice di molte favelle.

55 A vizio di lussuria fu sì rotta
che libito fé licito in sua legge,
per tòrre il biasmo in che era condotta.

58 Ell' è Semiramìs, di cui si legge
che succedette a Nino e fu sua sposa:
tenne la terra che 'l Soldan corregge.

61 L'altra è colei che s'ancise amorosa,
e ruppe fede al cener di Sicheo;
poi è Cleopatràs lussurïosa.

64 Elena vedi, per cui tanto reo
tempo si volse, e vedi 'l grande Achille,
che con Amore al fine combatteo.

67 Vedi Parìs, Tristano"; e più di mille
ombre mostrommi e nominommi a dito,
ch'Amor di nostra vita dipartille.

31 The infernal whirlwind, which never rests, drives the spirits before its violence; turning and striking, it tortures them.

34 When they come before the landslide, there the shrieks, the wailing, the lamenting; there they curse God's power.

37 I understood that to this torment were damned the carnal sinners, who subject their reason to their lust.

40 And as their wings carry off the starlings in the cold season, in large full flocks, so does that breath carry the evil spirits

43 here, there, down, up; no hope ever comforts them, not of lessened suffering, much less of rest.

46 And as the cranes go singing their lays, making a long line of themselves in the air, so I saw coming toward us, uttering cries,

49 shades borne by the aforesaid violence; so I said: "Master, who are those people whom the black wind so chastises?"

52 "The first of those about whom you wish to learn," he said to me then, "was empress over many languages.

55 So broken was she to the vice of lust that in her laws she made licit whatever pleased, to lift from herself the blame she had incurred.

58 She is Semiramis, of whom we read that she succeeded Ninus and was his wife: she ruled the lands the Sultan governs now.

61 The next is she who killed herself for love and broke faith with the ashes of Sichaeus; next is lustful Cleopatra.

64 Behold Helen, who brought such evil times, and see the great Achilles, who battled against Love at the end.

67 Behold Paris, Tristan"; and more than a thousand shades he showed me, and named them, pointing, whom Love parted from our life.

70   Poscia ch'io ebbi 'l mio dottore udito
nomar le donne antiche e ' cavalieri,
pietà mi giunse, e fui quasi smarrito.

73   I' cominciai: "Poeta, volontieri
parlerei a quei due che 'nsieme vanno
e paion sì al vento esser leggeri."

76   Ed elli a me: "Vedrai quando saranno
più presso a noi; e tu allor li priega
per quello amor che i mena, ed ei verranno."

79   Sì tosto come il vento a noi li piega,
mossi la voce: "O anime affannate,
venite a noi parlar, s'altri nol niega!"

82   Quali colombe dal disio chiamate
con l'ali alzate e ferme al dolce nido
vegnon per l'aere, dal voler portate,

85   cotali uscir de la schiera ov' è Dido,
a noi venendo per l'aere maligno,
sì forte fu l'affettüoso grido.

88   "O animal grazïoso e benigno
che visitando vai per l'aere perso
noi che tignemmo il mondo di sanguigno,

91   se fosse amico il re de l'universo,
noi pregheremmo lui de la tua pace,
poi c'hai pietà del nostro mal perverso.

94   Di quel che udire e che parlar vi piace,
noi udiremo e parleremo a voi,
mentre che 'l vento, come fa, ci tace.

97   Siede la terra dove nata fui
su la marina dove 'l Po discende
per aver pace co' seguaci sui.

100   Amor, ch'al cor gentil ratto s'apprende,
prese costui de la bella persona
che mi fu tolta, e 'l modo ancor m'offende.

103   Amor, ch'a nullo amato amar perdona,
mi prese del costui piacer sì forte
che, come vedi, ancor non m'abbandona.

106   Amor condusse noi ad una morte.
Caina attende chi a vita ci spense."
Queste parole da lor ci fuor porte.

70   After I had heard my teacher name the ancient ladies and knights, pity came upon me, and I was almost lost.

73   I began: "Poet, gladly would I speak with those two who go together and seem to be so light upon the wind."

76   And he to me: "You will see when they are closer to us; and then beg them by the love that drives them, and they will come."

79   As soon as the wind bends them toward us, I sent forth my voice: "O wearied souls, come speak with us, if another does not forbid it!"

82   As doves, called by their desire, with wings raised and steady come to their sweet nest through the air, borne by their will,

85   so did they emerge from the flock where Dido is, coming to us through the cruel air, so compelling was my deepfelt cry.

88   "O gracious and benign living creature who through the black air go visiting us who stained the world blood-red,

91   if the king of the universe were friendly we would pray to him for your peace, since you have pity on our twisted pain.

94   Of whatever it pleases you to hear and to speak we will listen and speak to you, while the wind is quiet for us, as it is now.

97   The city where I was born sits beside the shore where the Po descends to have peace with its followers.

100   Love, which is swiftly kindled in the noble heart, seized this one for the lovely person that was taken from me; and the manner still injures me.

103   Love, which pardons no one loved from loving in return, seized me for his beauty so strongly that, as you see, it still does not abandon me.

106   Love led us on to one death. Caina awaits him who extinguished our life." These words were borne from them to us.

109   Quand' io intesi quell' anime offense,
china' il viso, e tanto il tenni basso
fin che 'l poeta mi disse: "Che pense?"

112   Quando rispuosi, cominciai: "Oh lasso,
quanti dolci pensier, quanto disio
menò costoro al doloroso passo!"

115   Poi mi rivolsi a loro e parla' io,
e cominciai: "Francesca, i tuoi martìri
a lagrimar mi fanno tristo e pio.

118   Ma dimmi: al tempo d'i dolci sospiri,
a che e come concedette Amore
che conosceste i dubbiosi disiri?"

121   E quella a me: "Nessun maggior dolore
che ricordarsi del tempo felice
ne la miseria; e ciò sa 'l tuo dottore.

124   Ma s'a conoscer la prima radice
del nostro amor tu hai cotanto affetto,
dirò come colui che piange e dice.

127   Noi leggiavamo un giorno per diletto
di Lancialotto come amor lo strinse;
soli eravamo e sanza alcun sospetto.

130   Per più fiate li occhi ci sospinse
quella lettura, e scolorocci il viso;
ma solo un punto fu quel che ci vinse.

133   Quando leggemmo il disïato riso
esser basciato da cotanto amante,
questi, che mai da me non fia diviso,

136   la bocca mi basciò tutto tremante.
Galeotto fu 'l libro e chi lo scrisse:
quel giorno più non vi leggemmo avante."

139   Mentre che l'uno spirto questo disse,
l'altro piangëa sì che di pietade
io venni men così com' io morisse,

142   e caddi come corpo morto cade.

109   When I understood those injured souls, I bent my face downward, and I held it down so long that the poet said: "What are you pondering?"

112   When I replied, I began: "Alas, how many sweet thoughts, how much yearning led them to the grievous pass!"

115   Then I turned back to them and spoke, and I began: "Francesca, your sufferings make me sad and piteous to tears.

118   But tell me: in the time of your sweet sighs, by what and how did Love grant you to know your dangerous desires?"

121   And she to me: "There is no greater pain than to remember the happy time in wretchedness; and this your teacher knows.

124   But if you have so much desire to know the first root of our love, I will do as one who weeps and speaks.

127   We were reading one day, for pleasure, of Lancelot, how Love beset him; we were alone and without any suspicion.

130   Many times that reading drove our eyes together and turned our faces pale; but one point alone was the one that overpowered us.

133   When we read that the yearned-for smile was kissed by so great a lover, he, who will never be separated from me,

136   kissed my mouth all trembling. Galeotto was the book and he who wrote it: that day we read there no further."

139   While one spirit said this, the other was weeping so that for pity I fainted as if I were dying,

142   and I fell as a dead body falls.

NOTES

1–3. Thus . . . shriek: Limbo is thus identified as the uppermost circle of Hell, although in important respects it is different from all the others. The narrower compass of this second circle is the first indication that Hell is funnel-shaped and that effects of compression and crowding will become increasingly prominent.

4. There stands Minos: According to Greco-Roman tradition, Minos, son of Zeus and Europa and king of Crete, and his brother Rhadamanthus became judges in the underworld (cf. *Aen.* 6.566–69). Further references to Cretan legend are found in *Inferno* 12 (the Minotaur, Theseus, and Ariadne) and 14 (the Old Man of Crete), *Purgatorio* 26 (Pasiphaë), and *Paradiso* 13 (Ariadne) (see the note to 12.12).

6–12. by how he wraps . . . wills the soul to be sent down: In other words, the number of times Minos's tail is wrapped about his body indicates the number of circles the soul must descend to find its permanent place. This representation of the overall structure of Hell associates its successively lower levels with the body. (Michelangelo includes a striking Dantean Minos in his Sistine Chapel *Last Judgment.*)

16. hospice: The use of the term for a monastic guesthouse is bitterly sarcastic.

20. spacious entrance: See Matt. 7.13: "wide is the gate and broad is the way that leadeth unto destruction."

23. this is willed where . . . can be done: The second of Virgil's reproofs of infernal custodians, identical with the first (3.95–96).

25. Now the grief-stricken notes: This first region of Hell proper (but second circle) is marked by the onset of the discordant "music" of Hell, the accumulated dissonances of its grieving souls.

28. all light is silent: That is, where all knowledge ceases (cf. 1.60).

31–33. The infernal whirlwind . . . tortures them: Like many of the punishments in Dante's Hell, the whirlwind is a taking literally of a common metaphor, in this case a figure for the power of passion; note the implication of conflicting impulses in line 30. For the theory of *contrapasso*, see the note to 28.142.

34. before the landslide: For this detail, see 12.32 (another canto involving conspicuous references to myths about Crete).

39. who subject their reason to their lust: Note the political metaphors: the sovereign function of reason is usurped by desire. *Talento* [talent], Dante's word for "desire" here, originally referred to the unit of weight of silver used in antiquity; see the parable of the talents in Matt. 25.14–30. One's desire is thus one's "weight," one's dominant inclination (see Augustine, *Confessions* 13.9.10). The metaphor is maintained throughout the canto. Lust (Latin *luxuria*) was traditionally regarded as the least serious of the seven deadly vices.

40–44. And as their wings . . . down, up: The first of three bird similes (starlings, cranes, and doves) that track the pilgrim's shifts of attention; starlings and doves were associated in the medieval bestiaries with lust (Ryan 1976).

43. here, there, down, up: These directions correspond to the four classical "perturbations" of the spirit (love, hate, fear, and joy) (see the note to 10.58 and cf. Cicero, *Tusculan Disputations* 5.6).

46. as the cranes . . . their lays: Bestiaries familiar to Dante (e.g., the one included in his teacher Brunetto Latini's *Trésor*) compare the formations of migrating cranes to knights in battle lines (Ryan 1976). The emergence of the line of noble lovers (and there is a reference to the medieval vogue of stories of adulterous love in Breton *lais*) suggests that the starlings may represent more plebeian lovers.

54. empress over many languages: Semiramis, widow of King Ninus, legendary founder of Babylon and its empire, hence "over many languages." "She made licit whatever pleased" (in the Italian, only a single letter distinguishes *libito* from *licito*, the "pleasing" from the "lawful"), that is, she legalized incest, allegedly because she herself was guilty of it with her son. For these details and for his general knowledge of Semiramis, Dante follows hostile Christian accounts (Augustine's *City of God*, Orosius's *Seven Books against the Pagans*, and Brunetto's *Trésor*).

60. the lands the Sultan governs now: In Dante's day, Syria, though not Baghdad, was ruled by the Mameluke Sultans of Egypt.

61–62. she who killed herself for love: An echo of *Aen.* 4.552: Dido committed suicide when abandoned by Aeneas (see also 6.450–51); she had previously vowed to be faithful to the memory of her husband Sichaeus. Dante could have known from Macrobius that according to ancient tradition Aeneas and Dido lived several hundred years apart and that Dido was legendary for her chastity. Dido's story had both charmed and alarmed Christian moralists since at least the time of Augustine (cf. *Confessions* 1.13).

63. lustful Cleopatra: Queen of Egypt, famous for her liaison with Julius Caesar and her marriage with Mark Antony, which led to war between him and

Octavian (later Augustus). As was the custom of the Ptolemies, Cleopatra morganatically married her brother; the theme of incest was introduced with Semiramis.

64. Behold Helen: Helen of Troy, wife of Menelaus, king of Sparta, blamed by Homer and Vergil for the Trojan War (cf. *Aen.* 2.567–88; the *Roman de Troie* 28426–33, etc.).

65–66. great Achilles: Dante conserves the classical epithet (cf. Statius, *Achilleid* 1.1, "magnanimum" [great-souled]), but the Achilles who fell in love with Polyxena, daughter of Priam, and was thus led to ambush and death was in the foreground in the Middle Ages, thanks to both Latin (Dictys Cretensis, Dares Phrygius) and vernacular (*Roman de Troie*) versions of the story.

67. Paris, Tristan: Paris, the son of the Trojan king Priam and Helen's abductor, and a single figure from medieval romance—the final position is telling—round out the list of love's victims (seven in number, only the last three are men). Tristan's love affair with Iseult, the wife of his uncle, King Mark, ending with the death of the lovers, was the most famous love story of the Middle Ages. All seven examples involve the subversion of political or military responsibility by adulterous passion.

69. whom Love parted from our life: See *Aen.* 6.442: "quos durus amor crudeli tabe peredit" [those whom harsh love destroyed with cruel death]; the Sybil is identifying a division of the underworld by its denizens.

71. ancient ladies and knights: Such anachronistic description of classical and ancient figures is frequent in Dante's time.

72. pity came upon me . . . almost lost: The pilgrim's strong reaction of sympathy begins a process that reaches its climax at the end of the canto. His word for "lost" here, *smarrito*, was used in 1.3 of the straight way.

82–84. As doves . . . by their will: For the comparison, see *Aen.* 5.213–17 and 6.190–92, when the doves of Venus guide Aeneas to the golden bough, the key to entering Hades. This is the last of the bird similes, which move toward smaller groups and "nobler" birds and from classical to modern examples (Shoaf [1975] surveys doves in the *Comedy*).

82–84. called by their desire . . . borne by their will: Such phrases, continue the principle of the whole canto: the wind that drives the soul is the force of desire.

88–108. O gracious and benign . . . from them to us: Francesca (she is identified in line 116) begins with a courteous salutation meant to capture the listener's attention and good will (the *captatio benevolentiae* of classical rhetoric), and the gracious tone is maintained throughout her carefully organized speeches.

90. stained the world blood-red: Francesca is alluding to Ovid's tale of Pyramus and Thisbe, residents of Semiramis's Babylon (see *Met.* 4.55–166): Pyramus's blood stains the mulberry first red, then, when it dries, black.

93. our twisted pain: The Latin/Italian *pervertere* means literally "to turn in an evil direction."

97–99. The city . . . with its followers: Francesca was born in Ravenna, where, during the Middle Ages, one of the branches of the Po entered the Adriatic. She uses the language of pursuit to describe the relation between the Po and its tributaries. Her yearning for peace was evident also in lines 91–92.

100–107. Love . . . extinguished our life: Each of these three terzinas begins with the word *Love* (anaphora): first of Paolo's love for Francesca (Love "seized" him), then of her love for him (also a "seizing"—note the contrast between Francesca's claim that anyone beloved must love in return and Virgil's parallel but quite different statement in *Purg.* 22.10–12), and last of its result, death (Love "led" them). In each case it is the personified god of love that is made the agent, rather than the human actors. Note the etymological figure in the central terzina, *Amor . . . amato . . . amar.*

Hardt (1973) observed that of the nineteen instances of the word *amor, amore* in the *Inferno*, this canto has the central nine (i.e., five precede Canto 5, five follow it), of which these are the central three.

100. Love, which is swiftly kindled: Francesca echoes the canzone "Al cor gentil rempaira sempre amore" [To the noble heart love always repairs], by the Bolognese poet Guido Guinizelli (d. 1276?), whom Dante admired and called "the sage" (when quoting the same canzone in *Vita nuova* 20) and "my father" (*Purg.* 26.97); he is one of the founders of the "sweet new style" (*dolce stil novo*) proclaimed by Bonagiunta of Lucca in *Purg.* 24.57. For Francesca's words, see especially "Al cor gentil," line 11, "Foco d'amor in gentil cor s'aprende/come vertute in petra preziosa" [The fire of love is kindled in the noble heart /as is the power in a precious stone]. Francesca's speech is a tissue of allusions to the fashionable poetry of love, including Dante's own early poems.

106. Love led us on to one death: In the Italian the first word, *amor*, is included in the last two: *una morte.*

107. Caina awaits him: "Caina" is the division of Cocytus—the lowest circle of Hell—assigned to those who murder relatives, named for Cain (*Caino*).

111. What are you pondering: The translation emphasizes the etymological force of Italian *pensare* [to think], from Latin *pensum* [a weight of flax to be spun], continuing the series of metaphors of weight. Compare the movements of the pilgrim's head in these lines with those ascribed to the lovers later.

113. sweet thoughts: The expression is almost a technical term in the medieval theory of love deriving from Andreas Capellanus and refers to the obsessive presence of the beloved's image in the imagination.

116. Francesca: Only here is the identity of this soul revealed; the pilgrim has either recognized her or inferred her identity from her words. It is Francesca da Rimini (her companion, Paolo Malatesta, remains silent), a member of the Polenta family of Ravenna (her nephew, Guido Novello da Polenta, would be Dante's host in Ravenna from 1317 to 1320), who was married around 1275 to Gianciotto Malatesta, ruler of Rimini (the cruelty of his successors is denounced in 27.6–48 and 28.76–90). According to Dante's early commentators (the story left no trace in the chronicles), around 1285 Francesca's husband discovered her with his younger brother Paolo and murdered both of them. Boccaccio, who interviewed her family, asserts that Francesca had fallen in love with Paolo, his brother's proxy at the betrothal, supposing it was he she was to marry.

119. how did Love: The pilgrim follows Francesca's rhetoric of attributing agency to "Love" rather than to the human actors.

121. no greater pain: If Francesca is taken at her word, Dante's visit would involve considerable intensification of her suffering. Despite the apparent nod to Virgil here ("and this your teacher knows"), the commentators cite Boethius, *Consolation* 2.4.3–6. The idea is a commonplace, however (cf. Augustine, *Confessions* 10.14), like its converse, the pleasure of recalling past misery once free of it (e.g., *Aen.* 1.203: "perhaps at some time we will be glad remembering these things") (see the notes to 6.96 and 10.34).

124. But if you have so much desire: Compare the beginning of Aeneas's tale of the fall of Troy (*Aen.* 2.10). Again, Francesca draws on lofty literary models.

127. We were reading: Paolo and Francesca were reading some version of the *Book of Lancelot of the Lake,* part of a vast early-thirteenth-century prose compilation, the so-called Vulgate Cycle, and specifically the scene where Lancelot, coaxed by his friend and go-between Galehault, confesses his love to Guinevere and the lovers exchange their first kiss (the scene was often illustrated).

130. Many times: Like *volta* [turning, from *volgere*], *fiata* [occasion]—from Old French *fiee* (or directly from VL *vicata*, according to DeVoto & Oli, crossed with *fiato*, breath)—was for Dante a normal word for "occasion." Whatever the derivation, Dante often seems to associate *fiata* with *fiato*; here the association contributes strongly to the tension; cf. 10.48.

130–31. that reading . . . turned our faces pale: The reading is now made the active agent; note the emphasis on the motions of the head. And see Ovid's *Art of Love* 1.573–74.

132. one point alone . . . overpowered us: See the use of the term *punto* in 1.11, 7.32; again, the rhetoric places the agency in something other than the human beings.

133. the yearned-for smile was kissed: The use of the passive again avoids naming the agent. In the surviving Old French Lancelot romances, it is invariably Guinevere who kisses Lancelot, not vice versa; so also in the iconographic tradition. For another reference to this scene, see *Par.* 16.14–15 (the "first recorded fault of Guinevere").

137. Galeotto was the book: *Galeotto* is the Italian form of *Galehault*, the name of the knight who, as Lancelot's friend, arranged the meeting with Guinevere (see the note to line 127). Because of the prominence in it of this character, the second third of the *Book of Lancelot of the Lake* was commonly called the *Galehault*. As Francesca's remark shows, the name had by Dante's time already become current in Italian as a common noun for "go-between"; compare the English word *pander*, originally the name of the character in Chaucer's *Troilus and Criseyde*.

138. that day we read there no further: If they had finished reading the Vulgate Cycle, they would have read how Lancelot's and Guinevere's adultery (with Arthur's incest) eventually destroys the entire Arthurian world (the blows by which Arthur and his son Mordred kill each other are recalled in 32.61–62), though the lovers themselves repent and die saintly deaths.

141–42. for pity I fainted . . . falls: Given the emphasis on the motions of the head throughout the canto, it seems likely that the pilgrim falls head first (cf. 6.92–93). The pilgrim's pity, which will frequently figure in the rest of Hell, is presented as highly questionable. His symbolic death imitates Francesca's (death-bringing) surrender to passion, just as she and Paolo had imitated the book; like her surrender, it is a response to a text. At the end of Canto 3, the pilgrim had fallen "like one whom sleep is taking."

CANTO 6

1 Al tornar de la mente, che si chiuse
   dinanzi a la pietà d'i due cognati,
   che di trestizia tutto mi confuse,

4 novi tormenti e novi tormentati
   mi veggio intorno come ch'io mi mova
   ch'io mi volga, e come che io guati.

7 Io sono al terzo cerchio, de la piova
   etterna, maladetta, fredda e greve;
   regola e qualità mai non l'è nova.

10 Grandine grossa, acqua tinta e neve
   per l'aere tenebroso si riversa;
   pute la terra che questo riceve.

13 Cerbero, fiera crudele e diversa,
   con tre gole caninamente latra
   sovra la gente che quivi è sommersa.

16 Li occhi ha vermigli, la barba unta e atra
   e 'l ventre largo, e unghiate le mani;
   graffia li spirti ed iscoia ed isquatra.

19 Urlar li fa la pioggia come cani;
   de l'un de' lati fanno a l'altro schermo;
   volgonsi spesso i miseri profani.

22 Quando ci scorse Cerbero, il gran vermo,
   le bocche aperse e mostrocci le sanne;
   non avea membro che tenesse fermo.

25 E 'l duca mio distese le sue spanne,
   prese la terra, e con piene le pugna
   la gittò dentro a le bramose canne.

28 Qual è quel cane ch'abbaiando agogna
   e si racqueta poi che 'l pasto morde,
   ché solo a divorarlo intende e pugna,

CANTO 6

Third circle: the gluttons—Cerberus—the Florentine Ciacco—civil strife in Florence: causes, prophecy—famous Florentines in Hell—intensity of sufferings after the Last Judgment

1   When consciousness returned, after closing itself up before the pity of the two in-laws, which utterly confounded me with sadness,

4   new torments and new tormented ones I see around me wherever I walk, and wherever I turn, and wherever I look.

7   I am in the third circle, with the eternal, cursed, cold, and heavy rain; its rule and quality never change.

10   Great hailstones, filthy water, and snow pour down through the dark air; the earth stinks that receives them.

13   Cerberus, cruel, monstrous beast, with three throats barks doglike over the people submerged there.

16   His eyes are red, his beard greasy and black, his belly large, and his hands have talons; he claws the spirits, flays and quarters them.

19   The rain makes them howl like dogs; they make a shield for one of their sides with the other; castout wretches, they turn over frequently.

22   When Cerberus, the great worm, caught sight of us, he opened his mouths and showed his fangs; not one of his members held still.

25   And my leader opened his hands, took up earth, and with both fists full threw it into those ravenous pipes.

28   Like a dog that baying hungers and is silent once he bites his food, for he looks and struggles only to devour it,

31 cotai si fecer quelle facce lorde
de lo demonio Cerbero, che 'ntrona
l'anime sì ch'esser vorrebber sorde.

34 Noi passavam su per l'ombre che adona
la greve pioggia, e ponavam le piante
sovra lor vanità che par persona.

37 Elle giacean per terra tutte quante,
fuor d'una ch'a seder si levò, ratto
ch'ella ci vide passarsi davante.

40 "O tu che se' per questo 'nferno tratto,"
mi disse, "riconoscimi, se sai:
tu fosti, prima ch'io disfatto, fatto."

43 E io a lui: "L'angoscia che tu hai
forse ti tira fuor de la mia mente,
sì che non par ch'i' ti vedessi mai.

46 Ma dimmi chi tu se' che 'n sì dolente
loco se' messo e hai sì fatta pena
che, s'altra è maggio, nulla è sì spiacente."

49 Ed elli a me: "La tua città, ch'è piena
d'invidia sì che già trabocca il sacco,
seco mi tenne in la vita serena.

52 Voi cittadini mi chiamaste Ciacco;
per la dannosa colpa de la gola,
come tu vedi, a la pioggia mi fiacco.

55 E io anima trista non son sola,
ché tutte queste a simil pena stanno
per simil colpa." E più non fé parola.

58 Io li rispuosi: "Ciacco, il tuo affanno
mi pesa sì ch'a lagrimar mi 'nvita;
ma dimmi, se tu sai, a che verranno

61 li cittadin de la città partita;
s'alcun v'è giusto; e dimmi la cagione
per che l'ha tanta discordia assalita."

64 E quelli a me: "Dopo lunga tencione
verranno al sangue, e la parte selvaggia
caccerà l'altra con molta offensione.

67 Poi appresso convien che questa caggia
infra tre soli, e che l'altra sormonti
con la forza di tal che testè piaggia.

31   so became those filthy snouts of the demon
Cerberus, who thunders over the souls so that they
wish they were deaf.

34   We were passing through the shades that the
heavy rain weighs down, and we were placing our
soles on their emptiness that seems a human body.

37   They were lying on the ground, all of them, save
one, who raised himself to sit as soon as he saw us
passing before him.

40   "O you who are led through this Hell," he said to
me, "recognize me if you can: you were made before
I was unmade."

43   And I to him: "The anguish that you have perhaps
drives you from my memory, so that it does not
seem I have ever seen you.

46   But tell me who you are, who are put here in so
painful a place, and have such a punishment that if any
is greater, none is so disgusting."

49   And he to me: "Your city, which is so full of envy
that the sack already overflows, kept me with her
during my sunny life.

52   You citizens called me Ciacco; because of the
damnable sin of the gullet, as you see, I am broken
by the rain.

55   And I, wretched soul, am not alone, for all these
endure similar punishment for similar guilt." And he
spoke no further word.

58   I replied: "Ciacco, your trouble weighs on me so
that it calls me to weep; but tell me, if you know, to
what will come

61   the citizens of the divided city; if any there is just;
and tell me the reason so much discord has assailed
it."

64   And he to me: "After much quarreling they will come
to blood, and the party from the woods will drive
out the other with much harm.

67   Then later this party must fall within three suns
and the other rise, with the power of one who now
hugs the shore.

70   Alte terrà lungo tempo le fronti,
tenendo l'altra sotto gravi pesi,
come che di ciò pianga o che n'aonti.

73   Giusti son due, e non vi sono intesi;
superbia, invidia e avarizia sono
le tre faville c'hanno i cuori accesi."

76   Qui puose fine al lagrimabil suono.
E io a lui: "Ancor vo' che mi 'nsegni
e che di più parlar mi facci dono.

79   Farinata e 'l Tegghiaio, che fuor sì degni,
Iacopo Rusticucci, Arrigo e 'l Mosca,
e li altri ch'a ben far puoser li 'ngegni,

82   dimmi ove sono e fa ch'io li conosca;
ché gran disio mi stringe di savere
se 'l ciel li addolcia o lo 'nferno li attosca."

85   E quelli: "Ei son tra l'anime più nere;
diverse colpe giù li grava al fondo:
se tanto scendi, là i potrai vedere.

88   Ma quando tu sarai nel dolce mondo,
priegoti ch'a la mente altrui mi rechi:
più non ti dico e più non ti rispondo."

91   Li diritti occhi torse allora in biechi;
guardommi un poco e poi chinò la testa:
cadde con essa a par de li altri ciechi.

94   E 'l duca disse a me: "Più non si desta
di qua dal suon de l'angelica tromba,
quando verrà la nimica podesta:

97   ciascun rivederà la trista tomba,
ripiglierà sua carne e sua figura,
udirà quel ch'in etterno rimbomba."

100   Sì trapassammo per sozza mistura
de l'ombre e de la pioggia, a passi lenti,
toccando un poco la vita futura;

103   per ch'io dissi: "Maestro, esti tormenti
crescerann' ei dopo la gran sentenza,
o fier minori, o saran sì cocenti?"

106   Ed elli a me: "Ritorna a tua scïenza,
che vuol, quanto la cosa è più perfetta,
più senta il bene, e così la doglienza.

70   Long will they hold high their brows, keeping the others down under heavy weights, no matter how they weep or are shamed.

73   Two are just, and no one heeds them; pride, envy, and greed are the three sparks that have set hearts ablaze."

76   Here he put an end to the tearful sound. And I to him: "Again I wish you to instruct me and make me the gift of further speech.

79   Farinata and Tegghiaio, who were so worthy, Iacopo Rusticucci, Arrigo and Mosca, and the others who turned their wits to doing well,

82   tell me where they are and cause me to know them; for great desire urges me to understand if Heaven sweetens or Hell poisons them."

85   And he: "They are among the blacker souls; various sins weigh them toward the bottom: if you descend so far, you can see them there.

88   But when you are back in the sweet world, I beg you, bring me to people's minds: no more do I say to you and no more do I answer you."

91   His direct eyes then he twisted into oblique ones; he stared at me a little and then bent his head; with it he fell level with the other blind ones.

94   And my leader said to me: "Never again will he arise this side of the angelic trumpet, when he will see the enemy governor:

97   each will see again his sad tomb, will take again his flesh and his shape, will hear what resounds eternally."

100   Thus we passed through a filthy mixture of shades and rain, with slow steps, touching somewhat on the future life;

103   so I said: "Master, these torments, will they grow after the great Judgment, or will they be less, or equally hot?"

106   And he to me: "Return to your philosophy, which teaches that the more perfect a thing is, the more it feels what is good, and the same for pain.

109   Tutto che questa gente maladetta
in vera perfezion già mai non vada,
di là più che di qua essere aspetta."

112   Noi aggirammo a tondo quella strada,
parlando più assai ch'i' non ridico;
venimmo al punto dove si digrada.

115   Quivi trovammo Pluto, il gran nemico.

109   Even though these cursed people will never enter into true perfection, on that side they can expect to have more being than on this."

112   We followed that path in a curve, speaking much more than I recount; we came to the point where it descends.

115   There we found Plutus, the great enemy.

NOTES

2. the pity of the two in-laws: Paolo and Francesca were brother- and sister-in-law, a degree of relation that in the eyes of the Church would have made their relationship incestuous as well as adulterous.

7–12. I am in the third circle . . . the earth stinks: The rain, hail, and snow and resulting mud are versions of the food and drink to which the gluttons were addicted: in the last analysis merely versions of the elements earth and water. Dog imagery dominates (lines 14, 19, and 28), but the gluttons wallow like pigs (as in line 52; cf. 8.49) in material implicitly compared to excrement (line 12). Chiavacci Leonardi notes a parallel in Wisdom 16.16, where the wicked are said to be punished by "strange waters, and hail, and rain." Gluttony is the second of the seven deadly vices or sins; on their traditional ranking, see *Purg.* 17.115–39, with notes; for their relation to the arrangement of Hell, see the note to 11.70–73.

9. its rule and quality never change: The rule is the quantity and direction, the quality is the nature, of what is coming down.

13–32. Cerberus . . . thunders: The three-headed dog, in Greek mythology the guardian of the entrance to Hades. Dante is drawing on Vergil's description, *Aen.* 6.417–22:

> Cerberus haec ingens latratu regna trifauci
> personat adverso recubans immanis in antro.
> Cui vates horrere videns iam colla colubris
> melle soporatam et medicatis frugibus offam
> obicit. Ille fame rabida tria guttura pandens
> corripit obiectam, atque immania terga resolvit
> fusus humi totoque ingens extenditur antro.

> [These regions gigantic Cerberus with his three-throated barking
> makes resound, lying huge across the path in his den.
> When the priestess saw the snakes already beginning to rise around his neck,
> she threw him a cake drugged with honey and soporific grain.
> He in his raging hunger opened his three gullets,
> and seized it as it was thrown, and relaxed his enormous bulk,
> lying on the ground; enormous, he fills the whole cave.]

The traditional classical interpretation of Cerberus saw him as the earth, devourer of corpses (Servius). Dante makes him into a personification of gluttony and a demon (line 32—a minor devil, like Charon), debasing him and scaling h'm down, aptly turning the three throats to the account of gluttony and adding other quasi-human details (the greasy beard, large belly, hands) appropriate to it.

Cerberus's thundering over the souls (line 32) and his mauling of them (line 18) have a quasi-political dimension (see the note to lines 91–93).

14, 16, 18. latra [barks] . . . atra [black] . . . isquatra [quarters]: The same three rhymes appear in the last of the *rime petrose*, "Così nel mio parlar voglio esser aspro" (lines 54, 55, and 56), discussed in Durling and Martinez 1990.

20–21. they make a shield. . . turn over frequently: An important parallel exists between this description and the characterization of Florence as a sick woman in *Purg.* 6.148–51.

21. castout wretches: Dante's term is *profani* [profane], etymologically referring to those barred from the *fanum,* or sanctuary. As Gmelin observes, the sinners here are like drunkards lying in the gutter.

22. the great worm: That Cerberus is a worm is appropriate to the gastronomic theme, but there is also an association with Satan himself, called the "evil worm that gnaws the world" in 34.108 (see also 6.115, "the great enemy").

36. their emptiness that seems a human body: "Human body" translates Dante's *persona* [person]; compare Francesca's use of the term in 5.101. In addition to the vivid visual effect here, the line is a comment on gluttony itself, like line 101.

40–42. O you . . . I was unmade: Note the etymological figure in *fatto/disfatto* [made/unmade]. The line can be taken to mean that Ciacco recognizes the pilgrim; his phrase "if you can" would then refer to his disfigurement. Of course, as Dante's readers knew, and as becomes clear in Canto 16, a Florentine of the upper class was recognizable by his clothes, and the pilgrim's age is obvious.

49–51. Your city . . . kept me: Note the implicitly digestive image of the sack. Ciacco is the first Florentine the pilgrim encounters; these lines introduce the important theme of Florentine political affairs and Dante's involvement in them.

50. envy: Compare 1.111, where the devil's envy is made responsible for the she-wolf's presence in the world.

52. You citizens called me Ciacco: Note the repeated emphasis on the theme of the city; *cittadino,* used here and in line 61, means "city dweller." Ciacco is otherwise unknown; the name may be a corruption of French *Jacques* or even of *Cecco,* the nickname for Francesco; it also means "hog."

53. the damnable sin of the gullet: Italian *gola* [throat]; from *gula,* the standard medieval Latin term for gluttony.

58–59. your trouble . . . calls me to weep: Note the parallel with the pilgrim's words to Francesca (5.116–17), whom the pilgrim also may have recognized (see the note to lines 36–42).

60–63. but tell me . . . has assailed it: The pilgrim asks three questions, which are answered in order in lines 64–72, 73, and 74–75, respectively.

61. the divided city: The term refers directly to the division of Florence into parties and the dominant role played by violent partisanship, but it also resonates with the Augustinian concept of the two cities (the Earthly and the Heavenly), which coexist in this life (*City of God,* Book 11).

64–72. After much quarreling . . . they weep or are shamed: Ciacco foretells the events of 1300 to 1302. The rival Guelf factions, the Whites ("the party from the woods," to which Dante belonged, so called because its nucleus, the Cerchi family, was originally from a rural area outside Florence) and the Blacks ("the other," led by Corso Donati), rioted violently on May 1, 1300. In June (while Dante was one of the six priors of the city, the chief executive committee), during the temporary dominance of the White party, the troublemakers from both parties were exiled, including Dante's close friend and fellow poet Guido Cavalcanti, a turbulent member of the White faction; in June 1301, all the Black leaders were exiled.

"One who now hugs the shore" refers to Pope Boniface VIII, who for a long time seemed impartial, though he secretly favored the Black faction. In 1301 both sides appealed to him to make peace; he sent Charles of Valois, a brother of the French king, as peacemaker; Charles, after gaining entrance to the city with an armed force, supported the Blacks in their violence against the Whites, many of whom were killed, others fleeing into exile (early November 1301). The Black victory, begun in the spring of 1302, was complete by the fall, thus "within three suns [years]" from the spring of 1300; they dominated Florence during the rest of Dante's lifetime. For the effect of these events on Dante's life, see 10.79–81 and notes.

65. to blood: That is, to shedding blood. Note the repetition of *verranno* [they will come] from line 60.

73. Two are just: Who Ciacco/Dante means is never specified (15.61–66 supports the view that Ciacco refers to Dante as one of the two). The existence in corrupt cities of a small number of "just men" is a biblical motif, as in Gen. 18.23–33 and Ezek. 14.13–14.

74. pride, envy, and greed: Note the similar line, again with *invidia* [envy] at the center, at 15.68. There would seem to be an important relation with the three beasts of Canto 1.

79–80. Farinata . . . Mosca: All are prominent Florentines of earlier generations. For Farinata degli Uberti, see Canto 10; for Iacopo Rusticucci and Tegghiaio Aldobrandi, see Canto 16; for Mosca, see Canto 28.103–11; Arrigo, presumably Arrigo di Cascia, is not mentioned again.

84. if Heaven sweetens or Hell poisons: Note the food metaphors.

91–93. His direct eyes . . . the other blind ones: Ciacco has been looking directly at Dante; now he turns his head away, still looking at Dante, but obliquely, that is, sidelong; then he bows his head, and the rest of his body follows his head downward (cf. the movements of Dante's head in Canto 5). The sidelong gaze is traditionally characteristic of envy (*invidere* [to envy] was traditionally derived from the privative prefix *in-* and the verb "to see"; note the blindness mentioned in line 93); compare Ovid's portrait of Envy in *Met.* 2.770–82, especially line 776: "nusquam recta acies" [her eyebeam is never straight]. While speaking with the pilgrim and gazing at him directly, Ciacco was momentarily restored to community; his weird withdrawal may be in part a comment on the disregard of civic responsibility implicit in gluttony.

96. the enemy governor: The *podesta* (usually *podestà*, from Latin *potestas, potestatis*) was the chief executive in the medieval Italian city-states, often brought from the outside, usually for six months or a year. Virgil is referring to the Last Judgment and Christ's coming as Judge (once again, as in 4.53–54, without any reference to his divinity) on the basis of Matthew 24–25, the so-called Little Apocalypse.

99. will hear . . . eternally: The damned will hear the definitive sentence condemning them to Hell for eternity (Matt. 25.41).

106–9. Return to your philosophy . . . pain: "Your philosophy" is equivalent to philosophy as such (cf. the same usage in *Hamlet* 1.5.167), meaning, of course, the current Aristotelianism. The axiom Virgil cites appears in Aristotle's *Nichomachean Ethics* 10.4.

109–11. Even though these cursed people . . . than on this: For Plato and the Neoplatonic tradition, human nature was complete in the soul; the union with the body was a fall. For Aristotle the soul was the form of the body; he inclined toward mortalism (the doctrine that the soul dies with the body). Since the Bible taught that God created Adam's and Eve's bodies directly, Christians could not accept the Platonic view, for the body must be good in its kind. The medieval adaptation of Aristotle's doctrine was that the nature of human beings is the *union* of the immortal soul with the body (cf. 13.37–39 and notes). Thus only when body and soul are reunited can human beings be complete, or "perfect" in their natures. The accepted view, therefore, was that the sufferings of the damned will be more intense after the Resurrection. The effect on the damned of the ending of time is discussed in 10.58.

115. Plutus: We interpret the Italian *Pluto* (which appears in the *Comedy* only here and in 7.2) as referring to the traditional god of riches, Plutus, rather than the god of the underworld, Pluto (also called Dis and Hades), whom Dante identifies with Satan and regularly refers to as Dis or Lucifer. However, Dante was aware of a special association between the two (of which he had read in Cicero and Isidore of Seville), based on gold and silver coming from underground and on the importance of greed as a source of ills. That Plutus is called "the great enemy" (cf. "the great worm," line 22 and note) strengthens the connection.

CANTO 7

1   *"Pape Satàn, pape Satàn aleppe!"*
cominciò Pluto con la voce chioccia;
e quel savio gentil, che tutto seppe,

4   disse per confortarmi: "Non ti noccia
la tua paura; ché poder ch'elli abbia
non ci torrà lo scender questa roccia."

7   Poi si rivolse a quella 'nfiata labbia
e disse: "Taci, maladetto lupo!
consuma dentro te con la tua rabbia.

10   Non è sanza cagion l'andare al cupo:
vuolsi ne l'alto, là dove Michele
fé la vendetta del superbo strupo."

13   Quali dal vento le gonfiate vele
caggiono avvolte, poi che l'alber fiacca:
tal cadde a terra la fiera crudele.

16   Così scendemmo ne la quarta lacca,
pigliando più de la dolente ripa
che 'l mal de l'universo tutto insacca.

19   Ahi giustizia di Dio! tante chi stipa
nove travaglie e pene quant' io viddi?
e perché nostra colpa sì ne scipa?

22   Come fa l'onda là sovra Cariddi,
che si frange con quella in cui s'intoppa:
così convien che qui la gente riddi.

25   Qui vid' i' gente più ch'altrove troppa,
e d'una parte e d'altra, con grand' urli,
voltando pesi per forza di poppa.

28   Percotëansi 'ncontro; e poscia pur lì
si rivolgea ciascun, voltando a retro,
gridando: "Perché tieni?" e "Perché burli?"

CANTO 7

*Fourth circle: the avaricious and the prodigal—Plutus—Virgil on
Fortune—fifth circle: the angry and sullen—Styx—the tower*

1   "*Pape Satàn, pape Satàn aleppe!*" began Plutus
with his clucking voice; and that noble sage, who
knew all things,

4   said, to strengthen me, "Let not your fear harm
you; for whatever power he may have shall not
prevent us from going down this cliff."

7   Then he turned back to that swollen face and
said: "Silence, cursed wolf! consume yourself with
your rage within.

10   Not without cause is our descent to the depths: it
is willed on high, where Michael avenged the proud
onslaught."

13   As when sails swollen by the wind fall tangled,
when the mast gives way: so did that cruel beast fall
to earth.

16   So we descended into the fourth pit, taking in
more of the sorrowing bank that bags all the evil of
the universe.

19   Ah, justice of God! who stuffs in so many strange
travails and punishments as I saw? and why does
our own guilt so destroy us?

22   As the waves do there above Charybdis, breaking
over each other as they collide: so the people here
must dance their round.

25   Here I saw people more numerous than before, on
one side and the other, with great cries rolling
weights by the force of their chests.

28   They would collide, and then right there each one,
reversing directions, would look back, crying: "Why
do you hold?" and "Why do you toss?"

31   Così tornavan per lo cerchio tetro
da ogne mano a l'opposito punto,
gridandosi anche loro ontoso metro;

34   poi si volgea ciascun, quand' era giunto
per lo suo mezzo cerchio a l'altra giostra.
E io, ch'avea lo cor quasi compunto,

37   dissi: "Maestro mio, or mi dimostra
che gente è questa, e se tutti fuor cherci
questi chercuti a la sinistra nostra."

40   Ed elli a me: "Tutti quanti fuor guerci
sì de la mente in la vita primaia
che con misura nullo spendio ferci.

43   Assai la voce lor chiaro l'abbaia,
quando vegnono a' due punti del cerchio
dove colpa contraria li dispaia.

46   Questi fuor cherci, che non han coperchio
piloso al capo, e papi e cardinali,
in cui usa avarizia il suo soperchio."

49   E io: "Maestro, tra questi cotali
dovre' io ben riconoscere alcuni
che furo immondi di cotesti mali."

52   Ed elli a me: "Vano pensiero aduni:
la sconoscente vita che i fé sozzi
ad ogne conoscenza or li fa bruni.

55   In etterno verranno a li due cozzi;
questi resurgeranno del sepulcro
col pugno chiuso, e questi coi crin mozzi.

58   Mal dare e mal tener lo mondo pulcro
ha tolto loro, e posti a questa zuffa:
qual ella sia, parole non ci appulcro.

61   Or puoi, figliuol, veder la corta buffa
d'i ben che son commessi a la Fortuna,
per che l'umana gente si rabuffa;

64   ché tutto l'oro ch'è sotto la luna
e che già fu, di quest' anime stanche
non poterebbe farne posare una."

67   "Maestro mio," diss' io, "or mi dì anche:
questa Fortuna di che tu mi tocche,
che è, che i ben del mondo ha sì tra branche?"

31   Thus they would return around the dark circle on
either hand to the point opposite, again shouting at
each other their shameful meter;

34   then each would turn back, once he had arrived
through his half-circle to the other jousting. And
I, my heart almost pierced through,

37   said: "Master, now explain to me what people this
is, and if these tonsured ones to our left were all
clerics."

40   And he to me: "Every one of them was so cross-
eyed of mind in the first life, that no measure
governed their spending.

43   Very clearly do their voices bay it out, when they
come to the two points of the circle where their
opposing faults disjoin them.

46   These were clerics, who have no hairy covering to
their heads, and popes and cardinals, in whom
avarice does its worst."

49   And I: "Master, among this last kind, I should
certainly be able to recognize some who were soiled
with those ills."

52   And he to me: "You are gathering empty thought:
the undiscerning life that befouled them makes them
dark now to all recognition.

55   For eternity they will come to the two buttings:
these will rise from the tomb with closed fists, these
with hair cut short.

58   Bad giving and bad keeping has deprived them of
the lovely world and set them to this scuffling:
whatever it is, I prettify no words for it.

61   Now you can see, my son, the brief mockery of
the goods that are committed to Fortune, for which
the human race so squabbles;

64   for all the gold that is under the moon and that
ever was, could not give rest to even one of these
weary souls."

67   "My master," said I, "now tell me also: this
Fortune that you touch on here, what is it, that has
the goods of the world so in its clutches?"

70   E quelli a me: "Oh creature sciocche,
quanta ignoranza è quella che v'offende!
Or vo' che tu mia sentenza ne 'mbocche.

73   Colui lo cui saver tutto trascende
fece li cieli, e diè lor chi conduce
sì ch'ogne parte ad ogne parte splende,

76   distribuendo igualmente la luce.
Similemente a li splendor mondani
ordinò general ministra e duce

79   che permutasse a tempo li ben vani
di gente in gente e d'uno in altro sangue,
oltre la difension d'i senni umani;

82   per ch'una gente impera e l'altra langue,
seguendo lo giudicio di costei,
che è occulto come in erba l'angue.

85   Vostro saver non ha contasto a lei;
questa provede, giudica, e persegue
suo regno come il loro li altri dèi.

88   Le sue permutazion non hanno triegue;
necessità la fa esser veloce,
sì spesso vien chi vicenda consegue.

91   Quest' è colei ch'è tanto posta in croce
pur da color che le dovrien dar lode,
dandole biasmo a torto e mala voce;

94   ma ella s'è beata e ciò non ode;
con l'altre prime creature lieta
volve sua spera e beata si gode.

97   Or discendiamo omai a maggior pieta:
già ogne stella cade che saliva
quand' io mi mossi, e 'l troppo star si vieta."

100   Noi ricidemmo il cerchio a l'altra riva
sovr' una fonte che bolle e riversa
per un fossato che da lei deriva.

103   L'acqua era buia assai più che persa;
e noi, in compagnia de l'onde bige,
intrammo giù per una via diversa.

106   In la palude va c'ha nome Stige
questo tristo ruscel, quand'è disceso
al piè de le maligne piagge grige.

70 And he to me: "O foolish creatures, how great is
the ignorance that injures you! Now I would have
you drink in my judgment.

73 He whose wisdom transcends all things fashioned
the heavens, and he gave them governors who see that
every part shines to every other part,

76 distributing the light equally. Similarly, for
worldly splendors he ordained a general minister and
leader

79 who would transfer from time to time the empty
goods from one people to another, from one family
to another, beyond any human wisdom's power to
prevent;

82 therefore one people rules and another languishes,
according to her judgment, that is hidden, like the
snake in grass.

85 Your knowledge cannot resist her; she foresees,
judges, and carries out her rule as the other gods do
theirs.

88 Her permutations know no truce; necessity makes
her swift, so thick come those who must have their
turns.

91 This is she who is so crucified even by those who
should give her praise, wrongly blaming and
speaking ill of her;

94 but she is blessed in herself and does not listen:
with the other first creatures, she gladly turns her
sphere and rejoices in her blessedness.

97 But now let us go down to even greater pity:
already every star is falling that was rising when I
set out, and too long a stay is forbidden."

100 We cut across the circle to the other shore, beside
a spring that boils and spills into a ditch leading away
from it.

103 The water was much darker than purple; and we,
beside the murky wave, entered a strange, descending path.

106 Into the swamp called Styx goes this sad stream,
when it has come down to the foot of the evil grey
slopes.

109   E io, che di mirare stava inteso,
vidi genti fangose in quel pantano,
ignude tutte, con sembiante offeso.

112   Queste si percotean, non pur con mano
ma con la testa e col petto e coi piedi,
troncandosi co' denti a brano a brano.

115   Lo buon maestro disse: "Figlio, or vedi
l'anime di color cui vinse l'ira;
e anche vo' che tu per certo credi

118   che sotto l'acqua è gente che sospira,
e fanno pullular quest' acqua al summo,
come l'occhio ti dice, u' che s'aggira.

121   Fitti nel limo dicon: 'Tristi fummo
ne l'aere dolce che dal sol s'allegra,
portando dentro accidïoso fummo:

124   or ci attristiam ne la belletta negra.'
Quest' inno si gorgoglian ne la strozza,
ché dir nol posson con parola integra."

127   Così girammo de la lorda pozza
grand' arco, tra la ripa secca e 'l mézzo,
con li occhi vòlti a chi del fango ingozza.

130   Venimmo al piè d'una torre al da sezzo.

109　And I, gazing intently, saw people muddied in that slough, all naked, with indignant expressions.

112　They kept striking each other, and not only with hands, but with head and breast and feet, tearing each other apart with their teeth, piece by piece.

115　My kind master said: "Son, now behold the souls of those whom anger vanquished; and I would have you believe, too, as a certainty,

118　that under the water are people who are sighing, making the water bubble at the surface, as your eye will tell you wherever it turns.

121　Fixed in the mire, they say: 'We were gloomy in the sweet air that the sun makes glad, bearing within us the fumes of sullenness:

124　now we languish in the black slime.' This hymn they gurgle in their throats, for they cannot fully form the words."

127　So we wound about a large arc of the filthy swamp, between the dry bank and the wetness, our eyes turned on those who swallow mud.

130　We came to the foot of a tower at the last.

NOTES

1. *Pape Satàn . . . aleppe*: This line has been much discussed. It is clearly intended to convey an impression of incomprehensibility and is connected with the idea of Hell as Babel. However, the early commentators agree in taking *pape* as an interjection expressing surprise (Latin, *papae*) and *aleppe* as the first letter of the Hebrew alphabet; they disagree on whether *aleppe* is to be taken as equivalent to "alas," or as meaning "first" (thus "God"). There may also be a mordant allusion, in the cry of *pape*, to the avarice of the popes (Latin, *papa, papae*), explicitly attacked later in this canto and elsewhere. The name Satan occurs nowhere else in the *Comedy*.

2. Plutus: The name is discussed in the note to 6.115.

8. cursed wolf: The line establishes a special connection between avarice (or, more broadly, cupidity) and the she-wolf of Canto 1 (see especially lines 94–102). See also *Purg.* 20.10, where the she-wolf is explicitly identified as a symbol of avarice.

11. willed on high: Virgil's formula defeats Plutus, as it silenced Charon and Minos. Here the claim of a providential reason for the pilgrim's passage is the first hint of a main theme of the canto, the relation of Fortune and Providence, which becomes explicit in lines 73–96.

12. Michael . . . proud onslaught: The archangel Michael was traditionally the commander of the angelic host that expelled the rebel angels (cf. 3.7 and note).

13–15. As when sails . . . to earth: Plutus is being compared to a dismasted vessel in danger of shipwreck. For the Middle Ages, shipwreck was an instance of the *Fortuna maris*, the fortune of the sea. Although associated with avarice, Plutus's puffed-up appearance ("swollen face," line 6) and rabid behavior also suggest pride and wrath. For Dante's scheme of sins in Cantos 5–8, see the note to lines 73–96.

18. bags: "Bagging" is of course suitable to the greedy. Compare the words of the simoniac Pope Nicholas III at 19.72: "I pocketed . . . myself down here." Clerics, proverbial for their avarice, are conspicuous in many medieval visual representations of Hell, such as Giotto's *Last Judgment* in the Scrovegni Chapel in Padova (ca. 1306), which it is conceivable Dante helped plan: he was in the vicinity at what may have been the appropriate time.

22–25. As the waves . . . dance their round: Like Ulysses, Aeneas must sail near the whirlpool Charybdis and the monster Scylla: part-human, part-wolf, and part–dolphin. Ancient and medieval authorities located them in the Strait of Messina between Italy and Sicily (*Aen.* 3.420–23):

> Dextrum Scylla latus, laevum implacata Charybdis
> obsidet, atque imo barathri ter gurgite vastos
> sorbet in abruptum fluctus rursusque sub auras
> erigit alternos, et sidera verberat unda.
>
> [On the right side Scylla, on the left implacable Charybdis
> threatens and three times into the deep whirl of the abyss
> it suddenly sucks a great flood and again into the air
> spews it forth, and the wave lashes the stars.]

Dante's simile compares the collision of the avaricious (on the left) with the prodigal (on the right) to that of the currents in the strait. The two phases of Charybdis's cycle ("sucks into . . . spews forth," emphasized also in Ovid's descriptions in *Met.* 7.63 and 13.730) are reflected again in the contrasting reproaches of line 30, discussed in the note to line 32.

The concept of virtue as a middle path between extremes was early identified in Homer's paired dangers; the identification of Charybdis with avarice/prodigality became proverbial. Dante's conception depends on the fourth book of Aristotle's *Ethics*, where liberality, a virtue, is explained as the mean between tightfistedness and prodigality. Although Canto 7 implies the Aristotelian view of virtue as a mean (discussed by Dante in *Convivio* 4.17.5–7), this does not seem true of Cantos 5, 6, and 8, on lechery, gluttony, and wrath.

24. dance their round: Dante's word for "round" is *ridda*, a round dance in which the dancers go in a circle but also weave in and out.

25. people more numerous: That the avaricious are multitudinous is proverbial; see *Aen.* 6.610–11:

> aut qui divitiis soli incubuere repertis
> nec partem posuere suis, quae maxima turba est.
>
> [or those who, having found wealth, crouched over it
> nor shared any with relatives, which is the largest crowd.]

27. rolling weights: See *Aen.* 6.616: "saxum ingens volvunt alii" [others roll a huge rock], an allusion to the myth of Sisyphus, condemned for his robberies to roll a rock up a hill, only to have it endlessly roll back down.

33. shameful meter: The use of *metro* [meter], referring to verse—measured speech—sarcastically alludes to the lack of measure (i.e., moderation) inherent in avarice and prodigality.

36. my heart almost pierced through: Note the close parallel with 1.15.

39. tonsured ones to our left: All the avaricious the pilgrim sees are members of the clergy. The term *clericus* originally meant "chosen by lot," and Dante seems to be ironically referring to the dominance of Fortune as well as to the fact that the *cherici* [clerics] are *chercuti* [tonsured]; compare "no hairy covering" in line 45: the shaving of a portion of the head signified the renunciation of worldly desires.

40–42. so cross-eyed . . . their spending: These terms, like "undiscerning" in line 52, imply that the avaricious and prodigal failed to discern the "mean," the "right measure" between extremes (see the note to lines 22–25). One notes the recurrence of the *in-vidia* [non-seeing] theme (see the note to 6.91–93).

47. popes: In Italian, *papi* (see line 1, with note).

57. these with hair cut short: By the same logic as clerical tonsure, the shearing of the prodigals suggests mortification of the indulgence implied by abundant hair. The closed but empty fist and the shorn forelock suggest abortive economic transactions: the greedy can no longer seize, the lavish no longer proffer. Compare Dante, "Doglia mi reca ne lo core ardire," lines 83–84, an attack on avarice: "you have gathered and hoarded with both hands that which so quickly slips from your grasp" (tr. Foster and Boyde).

58. Bad giving and bad keeping: See Aristotle, *Nichomachean Ethics* 4.1.1121a: "prodigality and meanness are excesses and deficiencies, and in two things: in giving and in taking."

64. for all the gold . . . the moon: The universe beneath the sphere of the moon (the sublunar) is the domain of mutable riches and honors (see the note to 2.78). The goddess Fortuna (discussed in the note to lines 73–96) and the ever-changing moon were commonly associated, and this passage and *Par.* 16.82–83 associate Fortune's wheel (see line 96) with the lunar sphere (Figure 1). The passage reflects Boethius, *Consolation* 2.2.1–14.

64–66. all the gold . . . weary souls: On God as the natural object of human desire, see 4.42, with note.

69. its clutches: The pejorative term for Fortune's grip sets off Virgil's exposition of Fortune as the instrument of Providence. Reference to Fortune's "claws" (*branche*) may be an echo of Fortune-as-Scylla.

72. drink in my judgment: Virgil offers the milk of elementary knowledge, like that given when Philosophy instructs Boethius about Fortune (*Consolation* 1.2.2).

Figure 1. Fortune and her wheel. (Based on a drawing in Hildegard of Bingen's *Liber Scivias*)

73–96. He whose wisdom . . . rejoices in her blessedness: Virgil's account of Fortune rests on the analogy between earthly wealth and power ("splendors" in that they make people illustrious) and the bright heavenly bodies, whose influence governs all natural change. As the heavenly spheres are governed by the angels, so "worldly splendors" are governed by Fortune. The analogy implies a seriously intended parallel between the structure of society and that of the universe, supported by the many references in the canto to the cycles and circles that characterize the movement of the heavens as Dante understood them. Despite human condemnation of Fortune, her work is providential: there is no discontinuity between apparent chance and divine order (see Aquinas on Providence: *Summa theol.* 1a, q. 22, a. 2–3; *Summa contra gentiles* 3.94). Virgil's condensed account draws on Boethius's in *Consolation* 4.6, where Philosophy explains the divine causality of seemingly random events. Appearing just before the passage to the second subdivision of Hell (see Cantos 8–9), the cosmic order revealed in Virgil's speech also reflects the order of the poem thus far. Fortune's power is implicit in the circles of the lustful and the gluttonous; the Trojan War, remembered in 5.64–65, was for the Middle Ages perhaps the most frequently cited instance of Fortune's domination in history (cf. 30.13–15); while the alternating rule of parties in Florence (cf. 6.67–69: one party rising, the other falling) exemplifies the shifting of power among groups. But the sequence of Cantos 5, 6, and 7 is also one of growing scope: the domestic tragedy of Francesca in Canto 5 is followed in Canto 6 by civic disturbances in Florence, and in Canto 7 by the universal pattern by which Fortune distributes good and ill to the world.

74. governors: These are the angels, identified in medieval thought with the intelligences Aristotle saw as governing the celestial spheres. Aquinas (*Summa contra gentiles* 3.80) notes that the principalities, an angelic order, are especially charged with transferring political domination among peoples (Gmelin).

84. like the snake in grass: See Vergil's *Eclogues* 3.93, where a "snake lurks in the grass," threatening pastoral tranquillity.

87. the other gods: For Dante's references to the angels (or "intelligences") as "gods," see *Purg.* 32.8 and *Par.* 28.121; he explains the usage in *Convivio* 2.4.4–6.

90. so thick come those . . . their turns: Compare 5.13–14 (the souls before Minos).

91. she who is so crucified: The complaint against Fortune is a medieval commonplace; see Boethius, *Consolation* 2.1.26, 2.2.29–31, 2.m.1.5–6, and Dante's *Convivio* 4.11.6–9, where Fortune's gifts are said to take no account of merit.

96. turns her sphere: Usually referred to as a wheel, the "sphere" is important for the analogy with the heavenly intelligences. The chief source for the image of Fortune's wheel (the rotating heavens are often called a wheel) is Boethius; see *Consolation* 2.1.60–62: "Can you really try to stop the momentum of her flying wheel?" and 2.2.29–31: "For this is my strength, this game I continually play: I turn my wheel in swift cycles, I enjoy shifting the lowest to the highest, the highest to the lowest." Manuscripts of the *Consolation* had a rich tradition of illustrations of such images (Courcelle 1967).

98. every star is falling that was rising: The reference to the whirling of the outermost visible cosmic wheel closes Virgil's account of Fortune as a celestial minister on a cosmic note that contrasts strongly with the violent half-circles of the avaricious and prodigal. See also the conclusion to Canto 11.

105. the swamp called Styx: Servius, on *Aen.* 6.323, notes that the name of the Styx means "sorrow" (*tristitia*). Macrobius interprets it as "whatever immerses human souls in the gulf of hatreds"; these allegories are discussed in Additional Note 2.

116. those whom anger vanquished: The phrase recalls the self-defeating wrath of Plutus, the monster of avarice, at the beginning of the canto.

123. the fumes of sullenness: Whether Dante wished to subdivide the angry into two groups, those "whom anger vanquished" and the passively angry (or sullen), or whether the second group represent another category of deadly sin, the slothful (referred to in Italian as *accidiosi*, here translated "sullen"), has caused much disagreement. We incline to the view of Russo (1967), in which the unifying category of the fifth circle is *tristitia* [sorrow, grief], which is a passion that includes as its "effects" pride, envy, wrath, and *accidia* or sloth. See the discussion of incontinence in the notes to 11.70–75.

125–26. This hymn they gurgle in their throats: A final reference to singing, "music," and distorted language.

130. at the last: The canto ends with a word of finality; we are approaching one of the principal divisions of Hell (see 11.70–90).

CANTO 8

1   Io dico, seguitando, ch'assai prima
che noi fossimo al piè de l'alta torre,
li occhi nostri n'andar suso a la cima

4   per due fiammette che i vedemmo porre,
e un'altra da lungi render cenno
tanto ch'a pena il potea l'occhio tòrre.

7   E io mi volsi al mar di tutto 'l senno;
dissi: "Questo che dice? e che risponde
quell'altro foco? e chi son quei che 'l fenno?"

10   Ed elli a me: "Su per le sucide onde
già scorgere puoi quello che s'aspetta,
se 'l fummo del pantan nol ti nasconde."

13   Corda non pinse mai da sé saetta
che sì corresse via per l'aere snella,
com' io vidi una nave piccioletta

16   venir per l'acqua verso noi in quella,
sotto 'l governo d'un sol galeoto,
che gridava: "Or se' giunta, anima fella!"

19   "Flegïàs, Flegïàs, tu gridi a vòto,"
disse lo mio segnore, "a questa volta:
più non ci avrai che sol passando il loto."

22   Qual è colui che grande inganno ascolta
che li sia fatto e poi se ne rammarca,
fecesi Flegïàs ne l'ira accolta.

25   Lo duca mio discese ne la barca
e poi mi fece intrare appresso lui;
e sol quand' io fui dentro parve carca.

28   Tosto che 'l duca e io nel legno fui,
segando se ne va l'antica prora
de l'acqua più che non suol con altrui.

CANTO 8

Signals—Phlegyas and his boat—crossing Styx—Filippo Argenti—the
walls of Dis—the gate of Dis—the devils—parley—Virgil excluded

1   I say, continuing, that well before we reached the
foot of the high tower, our eyes went up to its
summit

4   because of two small flames we saw placed there,
and another replying from so far away that the
eye could hardly seize it.

7   And I turned toward the sea of all wisdom; I said:
"What does this one say? and what does that other
fire answer? and who are those doing this?"

10   And he to me: "Over the slimy waves you can
already make out what they are waiting for, if the
fumes of the swamp do not hide it."

13   A bowstring never propelled an arrow to fly
through the air so swiftly as a little boat I saw

16   come toward us in that instant over the water,
governed by a single oarsman, who was shouting:
"Now you are caught, wicked soul!"

19   "Phlegyas, Phlegyas, you are shouting uselessly,"
said my lord, "this time; you will have us no longer
than passing over the bog."

22   As one who hears of a great deception done to
him and then mutters of it, so became Phlegyas in
his contained anger.

25   My leader stepped down into the boat and then
had me enter after him; and only when I was aboard
did it seem laden.

28   As soon as my leader and I were in the bark, the
ancient prow set forth, cutting more of the water
than it does with others.

31   Mentre noi corravam la morta gora,
dinanzi mi si fece un pien di fango,
e disse: "Chi se' tu che vieni anzi ora?"

34   E io a lui: "S'i' vegno, non rimango;
ma tu chi se', che sì se' fatto brutto?"
Rispuose: "Vedi che son un che piango."

37   E io a lui: "Con piangere e con lutto,
spirito maladetto, ti rimani;
ch'i' ti conosco, ancor sie lordo tutto."

40   Allor distese al legno ambo le mani;
per che 'l maestro accorto lo sospinse,
dicendo: "Via costà con li altri cani!"

43   Lo collo poi con le braccia mi cinse;
basciommi 'l volto e disse: "Alma sdegnosa,
benedetta colei che 'n te s'incinse!

46   Quei fu al mondo persona orgogliosa;
bontà non è che sua memoria fregi:
così s'è l'ombra sua qui furïosa.

49   Quanti si tegnon or là sù gran regi
che qui staranno come porci in brago,
di sé lasciando orribili dispregi!"

52   E io: "Maestro, molto sarei vago
di vederlo attuffare in questa broda
prima che noi uscissimo del lago."

55   Ed elli a me: "Avante che la proda
ti si lasci veder, tu sarai sazio:
di tal disïo convien che tu goda."

58   Dopo ciò poco vid' io quello strazio
far di costui a le fangose genti,
che Dio ancor ne lodo e ne ringrazio.

61   Tutti gridavano: "A Filippo Argenti!"
e 'l fiorentino spirito bizzarro
in sé medesmo si volvea co' denti.

64   Quivi il lasciammo, che più non ne narro;
ma ne l'orecchie mi percosse un duolo,
perch'io avante l'occhio intento sbarro.

67   Lo buon maestro disse: "Omai, figliuolo,
s'appressa la città c'ha nome Dite,
coi gravi cittadin, col grande stuolo."

31 While we were coursing the dead channel, before
me rose up one covered with mud, who said: "Who
are you, who come before your hour?"

34 And I to him: "If I come, I do not remain; but who
are you, who have become so foul?" He replied:
"You see that I am one who weeps."

37 And I to him: "With weeping and mourning,
cursed spirit, now remain; for I recognize you,
though you are filthy all over."

40 Then he stretched out toward the boat both his
hands; but my master, alert, pushed him off, saying:
"Away, over there with the other dogs!"

43 My neck then with his arm he embraced; he
kissed my face and said: "Disdainful soul, blessed be
she who was pregnant with you!

46 In the world he was a person filled with pride;
there is no act of goodness to adorn his memory:
therefore his shade is so furious here.

49 How many consider themselves great kings up
above, who here will be like pigs in the mire, leaving
behind horrible dispraise of themselves!"

52 And I: "Master, much would I desire to see him
ducked in this broth before we leave the lake."

55 And he to me: "Before the shore lets itself be seen,
you will be satisfied: it is fitting that such a desire
be fulfilled."

58 A little later I saw him torn apart by those muddy
people in such a way that I still praise God and
thank him for it.

61 All were crying: "At Filippo Argenti!" and the wild
Florentine spirit turned on himself with his teeth.

64 There we left him, I tell no more of him; for my
ears were now struck by a shrieking that made me
open wide my eyes, intent on what lay ahead.

67 My good master said: "Now, my son, we approach
the city whose name is Dis, with the weighty citizens,
the great host."

70   E io: "Maestro, già le sue meschite
là entro certe ne la valle cerno,
vermiglie come se di foco uscite

73   fossero." Ed ei mi disse: "Il foco etterno
ch'entro l'affoca le dimostra rosse,
come tu vedi in questo basso inferno."

76   Noi pur giugnemmo dentro a l'alte fosse
che vallan quella terra sconsolata;
le mura mi parean che ferro fosse.

79   Non sanza prima far grande aggirata,
venimmo in parte dove il nocchier forte
"Usciteci," gridò: "qui è l'intrata."

82   Io vidi più di mille in su le porte
da ciel piovuti, che stizzosamente
dicean: "Chi è costui che sanza morte

85   va per lo regno de la morta gente?"
E 'l savio mio maestro fece segno
di voler parlar loro segretamente.

88   Allor chiusero un poco il gran disdegno
e disser: "Vien tu solo, e quei sen vada
che sì ardito intrò per questo regno.

91   Sol si ritorni per la folle strada:
pruovi, se sa; ché tu qui rimarrai,
che li ha' iscorta sì buia contrada."

94   Pensa, lettor, se io mi sconfortai
nel suon de le parole maladette,
ché non credetti ritornarci mai.

97   "O caro duca mio, che più di sette
volte m'hai sicurtà renduta e tratto
d'alto periglio che 'ncontra mi stette,

100   non mi lasciar," diss' io, "così disfatto;
e se 'l passar più oltre ci è negato,
ritroviam l'orme nostre insieme ratto."

103   E quel segnor che lì m'avea menato
mi disse: "Non temer, ché 'l nostro passo
non ci può tòrre alcun: da tal n'è dato.

106   Ma qui m'attendi, e lo spirito lasso
conforta e ciba di speranza buona,
ch'i' non ti lascerò nel mondo basso."

70 And I: "Master, already I discern its mosques there clearly within the moat, as red as if they had just come out of the fire."

73 And he said to me: "The eternal fire that burns within it makes them glow red, as you see in this lower Hell."

76 Now we arrived within the deep moats that fortify that unconsolable city; the walls seemed to me to be of iron.

79 Not without first making a large circle did we reach a place where the pilot loudly cried: "Get out. Here is the entrance."

82 At the gate I saw more than a thousand that had rained down from Heaven, who were saying angrily: "Who is he there, that without death

85 goes through the kingdom of the dead?" And my wise master made a sign that he wished to speak with them secretly.

88 Then they restrained somewhat their great disdain and said: "You come alone, and send him away, who so boldly entered this kingdom.

91 Let him return alone along his foolhardy path; let him try if he can; for you will remain here, who have escorted him across so dark a territory."

94 Think, reader, if I became weak at the sound of those cursed words, for I did not believe I would ever return here.

97 "O my dear leader, who more than seven times have kept me safe and saved me from deep peril that stood against me,

100 do not leave me," I said, "so undone; and if passing further is denied us, let us retrace our footsteps quickly together."

103 And that lord who had led me there, said: "Do not fear, for our passage no one can prevent, it is granted by such a one.

106 But here await me, and strengthen your weary spirit, feeding it with good hope, for I will not leave you in the underworld."

109   Così sen va, e quivi m'abbandona
lo dolce padre, e io rimagno in forse,
ché sì e no nel capo mi tenciona.

112   Udir non potti quello ch'a lor porse;
ma ei non stette là con essi guari,
che ciascun dentro a pruova si ricorse.

115   Chiuser la porta que' nostri avversari
nel petto al mio segnor, che fuor rimase
e rivolsesi a me con passi rari.

118   Li occhi a la terra e le ciglia avea rase
d'ogne baldanza, e dicea ne' sospiri:
"Chi m'ha negate le dolenti case?"

121   E a me disse: "Tu, perch' io m'adiri,
non sbigottir, ch'io vincerò la prova,
qual ch'a la difension dentro s'aggiri.

124   Questa lor tracotanza non è nova,
ché già l'usaro a men segreta porta,
la qual sanza serrame ancor si trova:

127   sovr' essa vedestù la scritta morta.
E già di qua da lei discende l'erta,
passando per li cerchi sanza scorta,

130   tal che per lui ne fia la terra aperta."

109 Thus my sweet father goes off and abandons me
there, and I remain in doubt, for "yes" and "no"
quarrel in my head.

112 I could not hear what he proffered them; but he
hardly stood with them there, before they vied to run
back inside.

115 They closed the gate, those adversaries of ours, in
my lord's face, who remained outside and turned
back to me with slow steps.

118 His eyes were on the ground, his brow shorn of
all boldness, and he was saying, as he sighed: "Who
has denied me the sorrowing houses?"

121 And to me he said: "You, though I am angered, do
not be dismayed, for I will overcome this test,
however they scurry about inside to prevent it.

124 This overweening of theirs is not new; they used it
once before at a less secret gate, which still cannot be
barred:

127 above it you saw the dead writing. And already,
on this side of it, there comes down the slope,
passing through the circles without a guide,

130 such a one that by him the city will be opened to
us."

NOTES

1. I say, continuing, that well before: The unusual "continuing" and the return to a narrative moment logically earlier than the end of the previous canto (7.130) have occasioned comment. Padoan (1993) argues that they are evidence that the first seven cantos of the *Inferno* had already been published (ca. 1315; see 3.95–96 with note) and therefore could no longer be revised.

According to Boccaccio's *Esposizioni* and his biographies of Dante, Dante had written the first seven cantos of the poem before his exile but had left the manuscript behind in Florence, receiving it again only a number of years later. There is no other evidence for this idea, however, and it is extremely unlikely, on the evidence of Dante's other works, that the *Comedy* was begun before 1306. An interruption at some later date may of course have taken place.

4–6. two small flames . . . hardly seize it: As will become clear later in the canto, the devils consider themselves still in a state of war, driven back into their city walls, with outposts like this tower in the surrounding countryside (like that surrounding an Italian city-state).

17. a single oarsman: Dante's term is *galeoto* (from *galea*, galley), literally a slave rowing in a galley, not the same word as *Galeotto* in 5.137 (see note). There is no further reference to the boat's means of locomotion.

18. Now you are caught, wicked soul: Phlegyas is presumably addressing the pilgrim, whom he mistakes for a soul condemned to the Styx.

19. Phlegyas: A figure in Greek mythology, a king of Thessaly who avenged his daughter's rape by Apollo by burning the god's temple at Delphi; Vergil makes him an exemplary figure (*Aen.* 6.618–20):

> Phlegyasque miserrimus omnis
> admonet et magna testatur voce per umbras:
> discite iustitiam moniti et non temnere divos.

> [And most wretched Phlegyas
> warns all and testifies with a great voice through the shadows:
> Learn justice being warned, and not to contemn the gods.]

Dante associated Phlegyas's name with the Greek root *phleg-*, which he knew from Servius and elsewhere to refer to fire (as in the the the name of the river Phlegethon, in Greek the present participle of a verb "to burn").

27. only when I was aboard . . . laden: Only the pilgrim has a body to weight the boat. The incident derives from Aeneas's crossing the Styx in Charon's boat (*Aen.* 6.412–16):

> Simul accipit alveo
> ingentem Aenean. Gemuit sub pondere cumba
> sutilis et multam accepit rimosa paludem.
> Tandem trans fluvium incolumis vatemque virumque
> informi limo glaucaque exponit in ulva.
>
> [At once he accepts into his boat
> the gigantic Aeneas. The bark groans with the weight,
> being sewn together, and admits through its rifts much of the swamp.
> Finally beyond the river he deposits unharmed both the prophetess and
> the hero
> on the gray shore with its shapeless mud.]

29–30. cutting more . . . with others: It is lower in the water because of the pilgrim's weight. Compare *Aen.* 5.2, of sailing: "fluctusque atros Aquilone secabat" [he cut the dark flood before the north wind].

32–51. before me rose up one . . . horrible dispraise of themselves: The episode of Filippo Argenti (he is named in line 61) is the subject of a famous panting by the French painter Eugène Delacroix (1798–1863), *Dante and Virgil Crossing the Styx*, now in the Louvre.

36. You see that I am one who weeps: The line echoes a sonnet by Guido Cavalcanti, "Vedete ch'i' son un che vo piangendo" [You see that I am one who go weeping]; like Filippo Argenti, Cavalcanti was notoriously quarrelsome.

43–45. My neck then . . . pregnant with you: Virgil's enthusiasm for the pilgrim's violent anger against Filippo Argenti seems to assert the difference between a justified anger against sin and the anger and sullenness punished here. Still, a major theme of the journey through Hell is that the pilgrim usually shares in the sin he is contemplating, at least in the sense of having the potentiality for it within himself (the most striking instance so far is in Canto 5).

A further peculiarity of these lines is that they seem to be the only reference in the entire poem to Dante's mother and clearly, if somewhat diffusely, echo the "Ave Maria": "Blessed art thou among women and blessed is the fruit of thy womb . . ." (cf. Luke 1.28).

61. Filippo Argenti: This was a Florentine, according to Boccaccio a member of the Adimari family (Black partisans denounced by Dante in *Par.* 16.115–20), who was so arrogant that he had his horse shod with silver, hence his surname; in *Decameron* 9.8 Boccaccio relates an incident involving his temper. Nothing more is known about the man, though several early commentators relate that his brother gained possession of some of Dante's property when it was confiscated.

63. turned on himself with his teeth: Like the souls in 7.114.

65. shrieking: Dante hears the shrieking from within the City of Dis; in *Aen.* 6.557–61, Aeneas and the Sybil hear cries, blows, and rattling chains from inside the walls of Dis (see the note to line 68).

68. the city whose name is Dis: Dante's division of Hell into two main parts (upper and lower Hell; cf. line 74) derives from Vergil's. Within the "walls of Dis" (*moenia Ditis* [*Aen.* 6.541, 548–49]), which Aeneas and the Sybil do not enter, lies the pit of Tartarus, where the worst criminals and rebels against the gods are punished, described to Aeneas by the Sybil (*Aen.* 6.562–627). For the name *Dis*, see the note to 6.115.

69. the weighty citizens, the great host: The devils, angels fallen from Heaven (Apoc. 12.7–9), still continuing the war.

70. mosques: Dante is repeating the common medieval Christian slander that Islam was a form of devil worship and that the characteristic architecture of the mosque and minaret was inspired by the devils.

77. that unconsolable city: See 3.1, "THE GRIEVING CITY," with note.

78. the walls seemed . . . of iron: So Vergil says of the gate of the walls of Dis: *Aen.* 6.554 (*ferrea turris*, iron tower) and *Aen.* 6.630–31 (spoken by the Sybil):

> Cyclopum educta caminis
> moenia conspicio atque adverso fornice portas. . . .
>
> [I discern the walls brought forth from the Cyclops's furnaces
> and the gates with their projecting vaults. . . .]

82–117. I saw more than a thousand . . . with slow steps: This initial phase of the exciting episode of Virgil's being blocked at the city of Dis (the entire episode takes up most of Cantos 8 and 9), in addition to emphasizing the obstinacy characteristic of the devils and of the sins of malice punished within the city (see 11.22–66), is also a comment on the fact that in the *Aeneid* Aeneas and the Sybil may not enter there. The Sybil's explanation for this is that no virtuous person may cross its threshold. Virgil is blocked here because, in Dante's view, this is where Vergil was blocked in life, as the sixth book of the *Aeneid* shows (see the note to 9.38–42); the question of the relevance of this episode to Virgil's damnation is discussed in the notes to *Purgatorio* 22.

What the Sybil tells Aeneas in *Aen.* 6.553–54, that "not even the power of the heaven dwellers can beat down in war" the gates of Dis, is untrue for the Christian Dante. In the context of the entire *Inferno*, Dante is establishing an important difference between Vergil's imperfect knowledge of the underworld and his own Christian reliance on God, which enables the believer, with God's help, to confront the lowest depths of evil, including Satan himself; see Romans 8.38–39:

> For I am confident that neither death, nor life, nor angels, nor principalities, nor powers, nor things present, nor things to come, nor might, nor height, nor depth, nor any other creature, shall be able to separate us from the love of God, which is in Christ Jesus our Lord.

Compare Matt. 16.18:

> Thou art Peter; and upon this rock I will build my church, and the gates of Hell shall not prevail against it.

87. he wished to speak with them secretly: Discussed in the note on lines 118–23.

90. so boldly . . . his foolhardy path: The devils' phrases echo the dialogue about the pilgrim's fears in Canto 2 (cf. 2.35 *folle*, and 2.123 *ardire*), as they perhaps know.

94–96. Think, reader . . . ever return here: The first apostrophe of the reader in the poem, signaling the importance of the episode. Gmelin pointed out that there are seven such apostrophes in each cantica. The others in the *Inferno* are 9.61–63, 16.127–30, 20.19–22, 22.118, 25.46–48, and 34.22–24. The present episode is the only one in the *Inferno* to have *two* such heightenings of tone (here and at 9.61–63) (see the notes to 9.61–63 and 34.22–24).

96. I did not believe: The phrase is obviously not to be taken in the strong sense of despair, the utter loss of faith and hope, which would in itself constitute damnation, but in a state of doubt. The possibility of despair may, however, be the ultimate threat of the Medusa (9.52–63).

97. more than seven times: This is a biblical turn of phrase, but the statement is accurate, as the reader can verify.

115. adversaries: "Adversary" is the literal meaning of the Greek *diabolos* [devil], literally, one who throws (something) against one or opposes one; the shutting of the gate is a literal enactment of the root idea of the term.

116. in my lord's face: The Italian *nel petto al mio segnor* means literally "in (or against) my lord's breast," helping suggest the significance of the walls of Dis in the overall body analogy discussed in Additional Note 2.

118–22. His eyes were on the ground . . . I will overcome this test: Virgil's discouragement and his repeated references to himself ("Who has denied me," line 120; "I will overcome this test," line 122) suggest that he has been overconfident, has supposed that his own strength would be sufficient to overcome the rebellious devils here, as it had been with Charon, Plutus, and others.

124–26. This overweening . . . still cannot be barred: A reference to the resistance of the devils to the Harrowing of Hell by Christ (see the notes to 4.52–63), of which this episode in its entirety is a figural reenactment (see Musa 1974).

127. the dead writing: The writing proclaiming death (i.e., damnation) in 3.1–9. At the beginning of the *Purgatorio*, the *Inferno* will be referred to as "la morta poesì" [dead poetry]. Note the connection between "Abandon every hope, you who enter" and the present episode.

128–30. already, on this side of it . . . the city will be opened to us: Virgil's thought has moved from his own defeat here to the Harrowing of Hell—that is, from his human helplessness to a chief instance of God's omnipotence—and he suddenly has what can only be called a visionary moment: he *knows,* perhaps *sees,* that the one who will open the city (the next canto will show this to be an angel) is already some distance within the outer gate. Virgil's knowledge is discussed further in the notes to 9.7–9, 38–42, 61–63, and 10.100–108.

CANTO 9

1   Quel color che viltà di fuor mi pinse,
veggendo il duca mio tornare in volta,
più tosto dentro il suo novo ristrinse.

4   Attento si fermò com' uom ch'ascolta;
ché l'occhio nol potea menare a lunga
per l'aere nero e per la nebbia folta.

7   "Pur a noi converrà vincer la punga,"
cominciò el, "se non . . . Tal ne s'offerse.
Oh quanto tarda a me ch'altri qui giunga!"

10   I' vidi ben sì com' ei ricoperse
lo cominciar con l'altro che poi venne,
che fur parole a le prime diverse;

13   ma nondimen paura il suo dir dienne,
perch' io traeva la parola tronca
forse a peggior sentenzia che non tenne.

16   "In questo fondo de la trista conca
discende mai alcun del primo grado,
che sol per pena ha la speranza cionca?"

19   Questa question fec' io; e quei: "Di rado
incontra," mi rispuose, "che di noi
faccia il cammino alcun per qual io vado.

22   Ver è ch'altra fïata qua giù fui,
congiurato da quella Eritón cruda
che richiamava l'ombre a' corpi sui.

25   Di poco era di me la carne nuda,
ch'ella mi fece intrar dentr' a quel muro
per trarne un spirto del cerchio di Giuda.

28   Quell' è 'l più basso loco e 'l più oscuro,
e 'l più lontan dal ciel che tutto gira:
ben so 'l cammin; però ti fa sicuro.

CANTO 9

Virgil's dismay—the Furies—Medusa—the heavenly messenger—the
gate opened—sixth circle: the heretics

1   The color that cowardice brought out on my face,
seeing my leader turn back, caused him more quickly
to master his own new pallor.

4   He stood still, attentive, like one who listens; for
his glance could not go far through the black air and
the thick fog.

7   "Still, we must win the fight," he began, "if not . . .
Such a one was offered to us. Oh how long it
seems to me until someone arrives!"

10   I saw well how he covered up his beginning with
what came next, words different from the first;

13   but nonetheless his speech made me afraid, for I
drew from his truncated words a meaning worse
than perhaps they held.

16   "Into this depth of the sad pit does anyone from
the first level ever come, of those whose only
punishment is to have hope cut off?"

19   Such was my question; and: "Rarely does it
happen," he replied, "that any of us makes the
journey I am taking.

22   It is true that I have been down here once before,
conjured by that harsh Erichtho who called souls
back to their bodies.

25   My flesh had been naked of me only a little while,
when she made me enter those walls, to bring up a
spirit from the circle of Judas.

28   That is the lowest place and the darkest and the
farthest from the sky that turns all things: well
do I know the way; therefore be free of care.

31 Questa palude che 'l gran puzzo spira
cigne dintorno la città dolente,
u' non potemo intrare omai sanz' ira."

34 E altro disse, ma non l'ho a mente;
però che l'occhio m'avea tutto tratto
ver' l'alta torre a la cima rovente,

37 dove in un punto furon dritte ratto
tre furïe infernal di sangue tinte,
che membra feminine avieno e atto,

40 e con idre verdissime eran cinte;
serpentelli e ceraste avien per crine,
onde le fiere tempie erano avvinte.

43 E quei, che ben conobbe le meschine
de la regina de l'etterno pianto,
"Guarda," mi disse, "le feroci Erine.

46 Quest' è Megera dal sinistro canto;
quella che piange dal destro è Aletto;
Tesifón è nel mezzo"; e tacque a tanto.

49 Con l'unghie si fendea ciascuna il petto;
battiensi a palme e gridavan sì alto
ch'i' mi strinsi al poeta per sospetto.

52 "Vegna Medusa: sì 'l farem di smalto,"
dicevan tutte riguardando in giuso;
"mal non vengiammo in Tesëo l'assalto."

55 "Volgiti 'n dietro e tien lo viso chiuso;
ché se 'l Gorgón si mostra e tu 'l vedessi,
nulla sarebbe di tornar mai suso."

58 Così disse 'l maestro; ed elli stessi
mi volse, e non si tenne a le mie mani,
che con le sue ancor non mi chiudessi.

61 O voi ch'avete li 'ntelletti sani,
mirate la dottrina che s'asconde
sotto 'l velame de li versi strani.

64 E già venìa su per le torbide onde
un fracasso d'un suon pien di spavento,
per cui tremavano amendue le sponde,

67 non altrimenti fatto che d'un vento
impetüoso per li avversi ardori,
che fier la selva e sanz' alcun rattento

31   This swamp that breathes forth the great stench,
girds the grieving city all about, where now we
cannot enter without wrath."

34   And he said more, but I do not remember it; for
my eyes had made me all intent on the high tower
with its glowing summit,

37   where suddenly, in an instant, stood up three
Furies of Hell, stained with blood, who had the limbs
and gestures of women

40   and were girt with bright green water snakes;
little asps and horned serpents they had for hair,
which wound about their fierce temples.

43   And he, who well knew the maid-servants of the
queen of eternal weeping, "Look," he told me, "at the
ferocious Erinyes.

46   This is Megaera on the left; she who weeps on the
right there is Allecto; Tisiphone is in the middle," and
he fell silent.

49   With her nails each was tearing at her breast; they
beat themselves with their palms and shrieked so
loudly that for fear I drew closer to the poet.

52   "Let Medusa come: so we will turn him to
concrete," they were all saying, looking down; "we
did ill in not avenging on Theseus his attack."

55   "Turn around and keep your eyes closed; for if the
Gorgon appears and you should see her, there would
never be any going back up."

58   So spoke my master; and he himself turned me,
and he did not stop with my hands, but closed me up
with his own as well.

61   O you who have sound intellects, gaze on the
teaching that is hidden beneath the veil of the strange
verses.

64   And already, over across the turbid waves, came
the crashing of a fearful sound, at which both the
banks were shaking,

67   not otherwise than of a wind made impetuous by
conflicting heats, that strikes the wood and without
any resistance

70 li rami schianta, abbatte e porta fori;
dinanzi polveroso va superbo,
e fa fuggir le fiere e li pastori.

73 Li occhi mi sciolse e disse: "Or drizza il nerbo
del viso su per quella schiuma antica
per indi ove quel fummo è più acerbo."

76 Come le rane innanzi a la nimica
biscia per l'acqua si dileguan tutte
fin ch'a la terra ciascuna s'abbica:

79 vid' io più di mille anime distrutte
fuggir così dinanzi ad un ch'al passo
passava Stige con le piante asciutte.

82 Dal volto rimovea quell' aere grasso,
menando la sinistra innanzi spesso,
e sol di quell' angoscia parea lasso.

85 Ben m'accorsi ch'elli era da ciel messo,
e volsimi al maestro; e quei fé segno
ch'i' stessi queto ed inchinassi ad esso.

88 Ahi quanto mi parea pien di disdegno!
Venne a la porta e con una verghetta
l'aperse, che non v'ebbe alcun ritegno.

91 "O cacciati del ciel, gente dispetta,"
cominciò elli in su l'orribil soglia,
"ond' esta oltracotanza in voi s'alletta?

94 Perché recalcitrate a quella voglia
a cui non puote il fin mai esser mozzo,
e che più volte v'ha cresciuta doglia?

97 Che giova ne le fata dar di cozzo?
Cerbero vostro, se ben vi ricorda,
ne porta ancor pelato il mento e 'l gozzo."

100 Poi si rivolse per la strada lorda,
e non fé motto a noi, ma fé sembiante
d'omo cui altra cura stringa e morda

103 che quella di colui che li è davante;
e noi movemmo i piedi inver' la terra,
sicuri appresso le parole sante.

106 Dentro li 'ntrammo sanz' alcuna guerra;
e io, ch'avea di riguardar disio
la condizion che tal fortezza serra,

70   shatters the branches, beats them down, and
carries them away; full of dust it goes proudly on
and makes the beasts and shepherds flee.

73   He loosed my eyes and said: "Now direct your
beam of sight out over that ancient foam, there where
the smoke is darkest."

76   Like frogs before the enemy snake, who scatter
themselves through the water until each huddles on
the bottom:

79   so saw I more than a thousand shattered souls
fleeing before one who was walking across Styx with
dry feet.

82   From his face he was moving that greasy air,
waving his left hand before him frequently, and only
of that discomfort did he seem weary.

85   Well did I perceive that he was sent from Heaven,
and I turned to my master, who made a sign that I
should stand still and bow to him.

88   Ah, how full of disdain he seemed to me! He
came to the gate and with a little wand he opened it,
for nothing held it.

91   "O driven forth from Heaven, despised people," he
began on the horrid threshold, "how is this
overweening nursed in you?

94   Why do you kick back against that Will whose
ends can never be cut short and which has many
times increased your suffering?

97   What is the good of butting against fate? Your
Cerberus, if you remember, still has his chin and
gullet stripped because of it."

100   Then he turned back along the filthy way and said
not a word to us; he had the look of a man whom
other cares urge and gnaw

103   than his who stands before him; and we directed
our feet toward the city, unafraid after the holy
words.

106   We entered in without any battle; and I, in my
desire to examine the conditions enclosed by such a
fortress,

109   com' io fui dentro, l'occhio intorno invio:
e veggio ad ogne man grande campagna,
piena di duolo e di tormento rio.

112   Sì come ad Arli, ove Rodano stagna,
sì com' a Pola, presso del Carnaro
ch'Italia chiude e suoi termini bagna,

115   fanno i sepulcri tutt' il loco varo,
così facevan quivi d'ogne parte,
salvo che 'l modo v'era più amaro:

118   ché tra li avelli fiamme erano sparte,
per le quali eran sì del tutto accesi
che ferro più non chiede verun' arte.

121   Tutti li lor coperchi eran sospesi,
e fuor n'uscivan sì duri lamenti
che ben parean di miseri e d'offesi.

124   E io: "Maestro, quai son quelle genti
che, seppellite dentro da quell' arche,
si fan sentir coi sospiri dolenti?"

127   E quelli a me: "Qui son li eresïarche
con lor seguaci, d'ogne setta, e molto
più che non credi son le tombe carche.

130   Simile qui con simile è sepolto,
e i monimenti son più e men caldi."
E poi ch'a la man destra si fu vòlto,

133   passammo tra i martìri e li alti spaldi.

109   as soon as I was inside, send my eye around; and I see on every hand a broad plain, full of grief and harsh torments.

112   As at Arles, where the Rhone makes its delta, as at Pola, near the Carnaro that encloses Italy and bathes its boundaries,

115   tombs variegate the place, so they did here on every side, except that the manner was more bitter:

118   for among the tombs flames were scattered, by which they were so entirely fired that no art asks for iron that is hotter.

121   All their covers were lifted, and from them came forth laments so grievous that they surely seemed those of wretches suffering within.

124   And I: "Master, who are the people buried within these arks, who make themselves heard with anguished sighs?"

127   And he to me: "Here are the chiefs of heresies with their followers, of every sect, and much more than you believe are the tombs laden.

130   Like with like is buried here, and the monuments are more and less hot." And when he had turned to the right,

133   we passed between the torments and the high battlements.

NOTES

1–3. The color ... new pallor: That is, Virgil, seeing that the pilgrim has turned pale with fear, more energetically represses his own pallor, causing his blood (!) to flow more freely into his face. *Viltà* [cowardice] was used of the pilgrim's fear in 2.45.

5–6. his glance ... the thick fog: Again the theme of the difficulty of sight, in terms of the Platonic theory of vision discussed in the note to 4.11.

7–9. Still, we must win ... until someone arrives: Virgil's listening attitude and these words show that he has lost the clear knowledge of the location of the "one" to whom he referred in the last words of Canto 8. His "still" (Italian, *pur*) has the force in this context of "even if the messenger is not in fact coming." If perhaps only rhetorically, he entertains the possibility that they will not "win the fight" (i.e., gain entrance to the city), momentarily envisaging the negative consequences ("if not . . ."). As the pilgrim notices in lines 10–12, the next sentences (from "Such a one" to "until someone arrives") are meant to cover up his spontaneous expression of uncertainty.

8. Such a one was offered: The Italian pronoun in *s'offerse* has no gender, but the reference is presumably to Beatrice's implicit offer of heavenly assistance related in Canto 2. Note the parallel with the use of the verb *offrirsi* in 1.62.

15. a meaning worse than perhaps they held: That is, Virgil was perhaps not expressing fear; perhaps he was exploring the logical implications of the assurance he was given: if they are not to enter the gate, some other path through Hell will have to be found.

16–18. Into this depth ... hope cut off: The pilgrim's anxiety and curiosity prompt the natural question (see the note to 8.82–117). Compare "hope cut off" with "truncated words" (line 14) and "cut short" (line 95).

22–30. It is true ... be free of care: The story of Virgil's soul having been sent by the sorceress Erichtho to the lowest part of Hell is apparently of Dante's invention, based on an episode in Lucan's *Pharsalia* in which Erichtho (Lucan's invention, called by him *effera* [savage]) conjures up a dead soldier to learn the outcome of the imminent battle of Pharsalus, in which Julius Caesar defeated Pompey the Great (48 B.C.). This is one of the few places in the *Comedy* where Dante even faintly associates his Virgil with the medieval traditions of the historical Vergil's having been a sorcerer. This earlier descent of the pilgrim's guide was perhaps suggested by the Sybil's (*Aen.* 6.562–65).

27. the circle of Judas: Judecca, the place of the worst traitors (Canto 34). As we know from 5.107, some circles of Hell are named for their most famous occupants.

29. the sky that turns all things: The Crystalline Heaven, or Primum Mobile; possibly, the Empyrean (the Italian can also mean "that surrounds all things").

38–42. three Furies . . . about their fierce temples: Vergil's Sybil describes Tisiphone and her sisters (the three Furies, or Erinyes, punishers of crimes of blood) as the gatekeepers of the city of Dis (*Aen.* 6.570–75):

> . . . continuo sontis ultrix accincta flagello
> Tisiphonē quatit insultans, torvosque sinistra
> intentans anguis vocat agmina saeva sororum
> tum demum horrisono stridentes cardine sacrae
> panduntur portae. Cernis custodia qualis
> vestibulo sedeat, facies quae limina servet?
>
> [. . . always, taker of vengeance for crime, brandishing her whip,
> Tisiphonē towering shakes her frightful snakes
> and, holding them out, calls forth the fierce battle line of her sisters.
> Then finally the cursed gates, resounding fearfully on their hinges,
> are opened. Do you see what kind of guardian
> she makes sitting at the entrance, what kind of face guards the threshold?]

Dante clearly saw this passage as one of the keys to Vergil's conception of why Aeneas cannot descend to Tartarus (see the note to 8.82–117). Allecto, in the *Aeneid* a personification of war fever, is described as having hydras (poisonous water snakes) for hair (*Aen.* 7.447).

49–50. With her nails . . . with their palms: Traditional classical gestures of rage and grief.

52. Let Medusa come: Dante's principal source on the Medusa was the account, in *Met.* 4.606–5.249, of how Neptune raped one of the three Gorgons, sisters, in the temple of Minerva, who turned her into the monster with snakes for hair, turning all who saw her to stone. Perseus, using Mercury's winged sandals and Minerva's shield, was able to kill her by looking at her reflection in the shield. The Furies' snakes (lines 40–42) anticipate the Medusa's. The episode as a whole is discussed in the note to lines 61–63. The Furies' use of the term for "concrete" is humorous.

54. we did ill . . . his attack: That is, we should have killed Theseus. According to the myth, Theseus was imprisoned in Hades after Pirithous was killed by Cerberus; Hercules rescued him (for the traditional Christian interpretation of this story, see the note to line 98). In *Aen.* 6.392–97, Charon challenges Aeneas:

Nec vero Alciden me sum laetatus euntem
accepisse lacu, nec Thesea Pirithoumque,
dis quamquam geniti atque invicti viribus essent.
Tartareum ille manu custodem in vincla petivit
ipsius a solio regis traxitque trementem;
hi dominam Ditis thalamo deducere adorti.

[Nor did I rejoice, when Alcides [Hercules] went down,
to accept him on the lake, nor Theseus and Pirithous,
though they were begotten by gods and unvanquished in their strength.
The first sought out the watchdog with chains
and from the very threshold of the king dragged him up trembling;
the others were attempting to carry off Dis's queen from his bed.]

55–60. Turn around . . . with his own as well: That is, Virgil turns the pilgrim to face away from the walls, has the pilgrim cover his eyes with his hands, and places his own hands over the pilgrim's. Since he is now facing away from the Medusa, it is not clear what function (other than a purely symbolic one) the multiple coverings (veilings) have (see the note to lines 61–63).

61–63. O you . . . the strange verses: This is the second of the apostrophes of the reader in the *Inferno* (see the note to 8.94). "The strange verses" most probably refers to the entire episode, not merely to lines 52–62. There has been considerable discussion of the nature of the danger represented by the Medusa. The medieval commentators on Ovid interpret his Medusa as representing fear so intense as to paralyze (they also preserve the interpretation that saw her as a prostitute so beautiful she destroyed men). Dante's commentators vary in their interpretations. Boccaccio pointed out that the walls of Dis enclose the obstinate, hardened sinners who resist God's efforts to convert them, and he saw the Medusa as obstinate sensuality blind to spiritual matters, thus relating the episode to the recurrent theme of the difficulty of sight. Others see her as heresy (Lana), terror, or despair (most fourteenth-century commentators).

A noteworthy modern interpretation is Freccero's (1972), which calls attention to parallels with Dante's *rime petrose*, especially with "Io son venuto al punto de la rota" [I have come to the point on the wheel], and sees the danger as that of a kind of erotic fixation on the literal surface of texts, as opposed to a spiritual or allegorical view that sees beneath the veil (this is actually a version of Boccaccio's interpretation). In support of such a reading is the common metaphor of entering into or penetrating a text when understanding its "inner" meanings, often compared to entering a building; for instance, Augustine points out that those who approach the Bible in pride, especially the Old Testament, cannot understand it, for they will not stoop (humble themselves) to enter its door (*Confessions* 3.5.9; cf. 6.4ff.). The entire episode focuses sharply on the nature of Dante's poem as a text. Further discussion of the Medusa will be found in the notes to 32.130–31, 33.55–57, and in Additional Note 15 (cf. *Purgatorio* 22).

64–72. And already . . . beasts and shepherds flee: There are Vergilian precedents for this magnificent simile, for instance, *Aen.* 2.416–19 (describing the destruction of Troy):

adversi rupto ceu quondam turbine venti
confligunt, Zephyrusque Notusque et laetus Eois
Eurus equis; stridunt silvae saevitque tridenti
spumeus atque imo Nereus ciet aequora fundo.

[as opposing winds breaking forth from a whirlwind
collide, west wind, south wind, and, with the horses
of the dawn, the east wind; the woods shriek and with his trident
Nereus rages and foaming urges the deeps to the very bottom.]

The early commentators point out the scientific accuracy of correlating the violence of a wind with the difference in temperatures of the contiguous air masses.

The thundering sound represents the approach of the messenger from Heaven (line 85), though it strangely subsides when he becomes visible. It draws on the account of the Harrowing of Hell in the *Gospel of Nicodemus* (see the note to 4.52–63), where the wind heralds the approach of Christ, reinforcing the parallel of the present episode with it.

73–74. Now direct your beam of sight: See the note to 4.11–12, and compare lines 5–6.

76–78. Like frogs . . . huddles on the bottom: See Ovid's account of the transformation of the churlish Lycians (*Met.* 6.370–81), especially lines 370–73:

iuvat esse sub undis
et modo tota cava submergere membra palude,
nunc proferre caput, summo modo gurgite nare,
saepe super ripam stagni consistere, saepe
in gelidos resilire lacus. . . .

[they enjoy being under the waves,
and now to submerge all their members in the deep pond,
now to put forth their heads, now their nostrils above the flood,
often they sit still on the bank of the pool, often
jump back into the freezing water. . . .]

See the note to 7.117–26, derived from the same passage.

81–85. one who was walking . . . he was sent from Heaven: The phrase "sent from Heaven" is equivalent to "an angel from Heaven" (the Greek **angelos**, Greek, *angelos*, like the Hebrew word it translates, is derived from the verb "to send"). Note the parallel here with Virgil's reference to Christ in 4.53 (with note); the brightness of the angel is dimmed both by the atmosphere of Hell and by the pilgrim's unreadiness to see it (on the gradual increase of the brightness of angels in the *Purgatorio*, see *Purg.* 24.142–44, with notes). The angel's walking on the water recalls Christ's doing so on the Sea of Galilee (Matt. 14.24–32), as well as the figure of Mercury in Statius (*Theb.* 2.1–3), slowed by the thick air of Styx.

89. with a little wand: Because of the implications of the episode for Dante's theory of interpretation (see the note to lines 61–63), Freccero (1972) suggests that the wand is meant to recall Mercury's caduceus, Mercury being the patron of hermeneutics and the pagan messenger of the gods.

94. Why do you kick back: This line echoes the words of Christ to Saul/Paul at his conversion, "It is hard for you to kick [*calcitrare*] against the goad" (Acts 9.5, cited also in Acts 26.14); the metaphor is of a horse or ox.

94–95. that Will whose ends can never be cut short: Compare Virgil's rebukes of Charon (3.94–96) and Minos (5.22–24).

97. fate: The messenger speaks classically: Latin *fatum* (plural, *fata*) means literally "what has been said"—that is, decreed.

98. Your Cerberus . . . because of it: A reference to Hercules' chaining of Cerberus (see the note to lines 52–54). Because of his preeminence among the heroes as a benefactor of humanity, his descent to Hades to rescue Theseus, and his apotheosis at death, Hercules was regarded in the Middle Ages as a chief mythic parallel to Christ; thus in terms of Dante's syncretism, always seeking to establish continuities between the classical and Christian worlds, this pagan reference seems much less outlandish than it does to moderns; for a survey of the Christological references to Hercules in the *Inferno*, see Miller 1984.

112–15. As at Arles . . . tombs variegate the place: The references are to Roman cemeteries. According to a widespread legend, the tombs at Arles miraculously enclosed the Christian dead after a great battle of Charlemagne's against the Muslims.

121. All their covers were lifted: The Italian is *sospesi* [suspended] (see the note to 10.8–9).

125. arks: Cassell (1984) points out the implicit reference to Noah's ark and the iconography of baptism (see the note to 10.33).

127–28. Here are the chiefs of heresies: Heresy, the obstinate rejection of all or part of orthodox Christian faith and the adherence to a separate group (thus a tearing of the unity of the Church, often compared to Christ's "tunica inconsutilis" [seamless garment], John 19.23), was seen as distinct from schism, which need not involve theological error, and from error itself, which need not be willful or obstinate. It was regarded as both heinous and a major threat to the Church and was vigorously investigated (the term "Inquisition" means "investigation") and prosecuted, especially from the early thirteenth century on; the Dominican order was founded expressly to combat it, and the Franciscans also became prominent in the Inquisition. Heresy is not included in Virgil's discussion of the arrangement of Hell in Canto 11, and its placement here, associated with the unusual turn to the right in line 132, has occasioned discussion. We discuss it in Additional Note 2.

132. when he had turned to the right: As the commentators have noticed, on only two occasions in Hell are Virgil and the pilgrim said to turn to the right (here and at 17.31), but this instance is really unique, for in 17.31 there is of course only one direction in which the two can descend. In association with the walls of Dis, the turn may have been in part suggested by *Aen.* 6.540–43 (Grandgent):

> Hic locus est partis ubi se via scindit in ambas:
> dextera quae Ditis magni sub moenia tendit,
> hac iter Elysium nobis; at laeva malorum
> exercet poenas et ad impia Tartara mittit.

> [Here is the place where the path splits in two directions:
> the right one, which leads under the walls of great Dis,
> will be our path to Elysium; but the left one punishes
> the wicked and leads to the crimes of Tartarus.]

This is a version of the so-called Pythagorean choice: the left path leads downward; the right one, upward. Aeneas and the Sybil turn right *outside* the walls of Dis: they may not enter, since in Vergil's classical terms evil is simply to be shunned. This turn of the pilgrim and Virgil *inside* the walls helps emphasize the difference: the pilgrim must see evil in its entirety (see the notes to 30–51 and 8.82–117). See also 10.22–28, with note.

CANTO 10

1   Ora sen va per un secreto calle
     tra 'l muro de la terra e li martìri
     lo mio maestro, e io dopo le spalle.

4   "O virtù somma, che per li empi giri
     mi volvi," cominciai, "com' a te piace,
     parlami, e sodisfammi a' miei disiri.

7   La gente che per li sepolcri giace
     potrebbesi veder? già son levati
     tutt' i coperchi, e nessun guardia face."

10   E quelli a me: "Tutti saran serrati
     quando di Iosafàt qui torneranno
     coi corpi che là sù hanno lasciati.

13   Suo cimitero da questa parte hanno
     con Epicuro tutti suoi seguaci,
     che l'anima col corpo morta fanno.

16   Però a la dimanda che mi faci
     quinc' entro satisfatto sarà tosto,
     e al disio ancor che tu mi taci."

19   E io: "Buon duca, non tegno riposto
     a te mio cuor se non per dicer poco,
     e tu m'hai non pur mo a ciò disposto."

22   "O Tosco che per la città del foco
     vivo ten vai così parlando onesto,
     piacciati di restare in questo loco.

25   La tua loquela ti fa manifesto
     di quella nobil patrïa natio
     a la qual forse fui troppo molesto."

28   Subitamente questo suono uscìo
     d'una de l'arche; però m'accostai,
     temendo, un poco più al duca mio.

CANTO 10

*The Epicureans—Farinata degli Uberti—Guelfs and Ghibellines—
prophecy of Dante's exile—Cavalcante de' Cavalcanti—Florentine
hatred of Farinata—foreknowledge of the damned*

1 Now my master walks along a secret path,
between the wall of the city and the torments, and I
at his back.

4 "O highest power, who wheel me through the
wicked circles as you please," I began, "speak to me
and satisfy my desires.

7 The people who are lying in the sepulchers, could
they be seen? for all the covers are lifted, and no one
is standing guard."

10 And he to me: "All will be closed when from
Jehoshaphat they return with the bodies they left up
there.

13 Epicurus and his followers have their cemetery in
this part, who make the soul die with the body.

16 Therefore your request will soon be satisfied here
within, and also the desire you leave unspoken."

19 And I: "Kind leader, I hide my heart from you
only in order to speak briefly, and you have so
inclined me, not only just now."

22 "O Tuscan who through the city of fire, alive, walk
along speaking so modestly, let it please you to stop
in this place.

25 Your speech makes you manifest as a native of
that noble fatherland to which perhaps I was too
harmful."

28 Suddenly this sound came forth from one of the
arks; therefore I shrank, afraid, somewhat closer to
my leader.

31   Ed el mi disse: "Volgiti! Che fai?
Vedi là Farinata che s'è dritto:
da la cintola in sù tutto 'l vedrai."

34   Io avea già il mio viso nel suo fitto;
ed el s'ergea col petto e con la fronte
com' avesse l'inferno a gran dispitto.

37   E l'animose man del duca e pronte
mi pinser tra le sepulture a lui,
dicendo: "Le parole tue sien conte."

40   Com' io al piè de la sua tomba fui,
guardommi un poco, e poi, quasi sdegnoso,
mi dimandò: "Chi fuor li maggior tui?"

43   Io, ch'era d'ubidir disideroso,
non gliel celai, ma tutto gliel' apersi;
ond' ei levò le ciglia un poco in suso;

46   poi disse: "Fieramente furo avversi
a me e a miei primi e a mia parte,
sì che per due fïate li dispersi."

49   "S'ei fur cacciati, ei tornar d'ogne parte,"
rispuos' io lui, "l'una e l'altra fïata;
ma i vostri non appreser ben quell'arte."

52   Allor surse a la vista scoperchiata
un'ombra, lungo questa, infino al mento:
credo che s'era in ginocchie levata.

55   Dintorno mi guardò, come talento
avesse di veder s'altri era meco;
e poi che 'l sospecciar fu tutto spento,

58   piangendo disse: "Se per questo cieco
carcere vai per altezza d'ingegno,
mio figlio ov' è? e perché non è teco?"

61   E io a lui: "Da me stesso non vegno:
colui ch'attende là per qui mi mena
forse cui Guido vostro ebbe a disdegno."

64   Le sue parole e 'l modo de la pena
m'avean di costui già letto il nome;
però fu la risposta così piena.

67   Di sùbito drizzato gridò: "Come
dicesti? 'elli ebbe'? non viv' elli ancora?
non fiere li occhi suoi il dolce lume?"

31 And he said: "Turn! What are you doing? See there Farinata who has stood erect: from the waist up you will see all of him."

34 I had already fixed my eyes in his; and he was rising up with his breast and forehead as if he had Hell in great disdain.

37 And the spirited, quick hands of my leader pushed me among the sepulchers toward him, saying, "Let your words be counted."

40 When I stood at the foot of his tomb, he gazed at me a little, and then, as if scornful, asked me: "Who were your forebears?"

43 I, desiring to obey, did not hide it, but opened it all to him; and he raised his brows a little upwards;

46 then he said: "Fiercely were they opposed to me and to my ancestors and to my party, so that twice I scattered them."

49 "If they were driven out, they returned from every side," I replied, "the first time and the second; but your people did not learn that art well."

52 Then a shade rose up, discovered to sight as far as the chin, alongside the first one; I think it had risen to its knees.

55 It looked around me, as anxious to see whether another were with me; and after its peering was entirely spent,

58 weeping it said: "If through this blind prison you are going because of height of intellect, where is my son, and why is he not with you?"

61 And I to him: "I do not come on my own: he who is waiting over there leads me through here, perhaps to one your Guido had in disdain."

64 His words and the manner of his punishment had already read to me his name; therefore was my reply so full.

67 Of a sudden risen to his feet, he cried: "How did you say? 'he had'? Is he no longer alive? Does the sweet light no longer strike his eyes?"

70 Quando s'accorse d'alcuna dimora
ch'io facëa dinanzi a la risposta,
supin ricadde e più non parve fora.

73 Ma quell'altro magnanimo, a cui posta
restato m'era, non mutò aspetto,
né mosse collo, né piegò sua costa;

76 e sé continüando al primo detto,
"S'elli han quell'arte," disse, "male appresa,
ciò mi tormenta più che questo letto.

79 Ma non cinquanta volte fia raccesa
la faccia de la donna che qui regge,
che tu saprai quanto quell'arte pesa.

82 E se tu mai nel dolce mondo regge,
dimmi: perché quel popolo è sì empio
incontr' a' miei in ciascuna sua legge?"

85 Ond' io a lui: "Lo strazio e 'l grande scempio
che fece l'Arbia colorata in rosso,
tal orazion fa far nel nostro tempio."

88 Poi ch'ebbe sospirando il capo mosso,
"A ciò non fu' io sol," disse, "né certo
sanza cagion con li altri sarei mosso.

91 Ma fu' io solo, là dove sofferto
fu per ciascun di tòrre via Fiorenza,
colui che la difesi a viso aperto."

94 "Deh, se riposi mai vostra semenza,"
prega' io lui, "solvetemi quel nodo
che qui ha 'nviluppata mia sentenza.

97 El par che voi veggiate, se ben odo,
dinanzi quel che 'l tempo seco adduce,
e nel presente tenete altro modo."

100 "Noi veggiam, come quei c'ha mala luce,
le cose," disse, "che ne son lontano:
cotanto ancor ne splende il sommo duce.

103 Quando s'appressano o son, tutto è vano
nostro intelletto, e s'altri non ci apporta
nulla sapem di vostro stato umano.

106 Però comprender puoi che tutta morta
fia nostra conoscenza da quel punto
che del futuro fia chiusa la porta."

70   When he perceived a certain delay I made before replying, he fell back supine and appeared no more outside.

73   But that other great-souled one, at whose request I had stopped, did not change his expression, nor move his neck, nor bend his side;

76   but, resuming his earlier speech: "If they have learned that art badly," he said, "that torments me more than this bed.

79   But not fifty times will be rekindled the face of the lady who reigns here, before you will know how much that art weighs.

82   And as you hope ever to return to the sweet world, tell me: why is that people so cruel against mine in all its laws?"

85   Therefore I to him: "The slaughter and the great loss that stained the Arbia red, causes such orations to be made in our temple."

88   After he had moved his head, sighing, "In that I was not alone," he said, "nor certainly without cause would I have moved with the others.

91   But I alone, there where all others would have suffered Florence to be razed, was the one who defended her openly."

94   "Ah, so may your seed at some time rest," I begged him, "untie the knot that has entangled my judgment here.

97   It seems that you see beforehand, if I hear well, what time will bring, but in the present have a different mode."

100   "We see, as does one in bad light, the things," he said, "that are distant from us: so much the highest Leader still shines for us.

103   When they approach or are present, our intellect is utterly empty; and if another does not bring news, we know nothing of your human state.

106   Thus you can comprehend that our knowledge will be entirely dead from that point when the door of the future will be closed."

109   Allor, come di mia colpa compunto,
dissi: "Or direte dunque a quel caduto
che 'l suo nato è co' vivi ancor congiunto;

112   e s'i' fui, dianzi, a la risposta muto,
fate i saper che 'l fei perché pensava
già ne l'error che m'avete soluto."

115   E già 'l maestro mio mi richiamava;
per ch'i' pregai lo spirto più avaccio
che mi dicesse chi con lu' istava.

118   Dissemi: "Qui con più di mille giaccio:
qua dentro è 'l secondo Federico
e 'l Cardinale; e de li altri mi taccio."

121   Indi s'ascose; e io inver' l'antico
poeta volsi i passi, ripensando
a quel parlar che mi parea nemico.

124   Elli si mosse; e poi, così andando
mi disse: "Perché se' tu sì smarrito?"
E io li sodisfeci al suo dimando.

127   "La mente tua conservi quel ch'udito
hai contra te," mi comandò quel saggio;
"e ora attendi qui," e drizzò 'l dito:

130   "quando sarai dinanzi al dolce raggio
di quella il cui bell' occhio tutto vede,
da lei saprai di tua vita il vïaggio."

133   Appresso mosse a man sinistra il piede;
lasciammo il muro e gimmo inver' lo mezzo
per un sentier ch'a una valle fiede

136   che 'nfin là sù facea spiacer suo lezzo.

109   Then, as if repentant of my fault, I said: "Now will
you tell that fallen one his son is still joined with the
living;

112   and if, earlier, I was silent before replying, make
him know that I did it because I was already
thinking in the error that you have untied for me."

115   And already my master was calling me back;
therefore more hurriedly I begged the spirit to tell me
who was there with him.

118   He told me: "Here with more than a thousand I
lie: here within is the second Frederick and the
Cardinal; and of the others I do not speak."

121   Then he hid himself; and I turned my steps
toward the ancient poet, thinking back on that speech
which seemed hostile to me.

124   He moved on; and then, walking, he said: "Why
are you so dismayed?" And I answered his question
fully.

127   "Let your memory preserve what you have heard
against you," that sage commanded me; "and now
pay attention here," and he raised his finger:

130   "when you are before her sweet ray whose lovely
eye sees all, from her you will know the journey of
your life."

133   Then he moved his foot toward the left: we turned from
the wall and walked toward the center, along a path that
cuts straight to a valley

136   whose stench was displeasing even up there.

NOTES

1. secret path, between the wall . . . and the torments: Since Virgil and the pilgrim have turned to the right, the wall is now to their right, the field of sarcophagi to their left.

5. wheel me . . . as you please: A reference to the unusual turn (see the note to 9.132).

8–9. all the covers are lifted . . . standing guard: The open tombs and the mention of guards introduce two prominent iconographic features of the Resurrection of Christ (*levati* [lifted] can also mean "removed"; in 9.121 the covers are said to be "suspended"; the question of their position is probably resolved by 11.6–7, which imply that they are leaning against the tombs). Dante is drawing a parallel between the pilgrim's visit to the tomb and the visit of the Marys to Christ's tomb on Easter morning (Matt. 28.1–8; Luke 24.1–10).

11. Jehoshaphat: The locale of the Last Judgment, according to the prophet Joel (3.2 and 12).

14–15. Epicurus . . . make the soul die with the body: Although in *Convivio* 4.6 Dante included Epicurus among the noteworthy Greek philosophers, drawing on Cicero's *De finibus,* here his attitude seems to be determined by Augustine's hostile discussions, to which Epicurus's denial of immortality is central. That those who deny immortality "make [*fanno*] the soul die" has a double sense: (1) they *assert* that it dies, and (2) their adherence to that belief (against all reason and authority, in Dante's view; see *Convivio* 2.9) *causes* the death of their souls (i.e., their damnation).

The categories that govern their presentation here are based largely on Saint Paul's denunciation of those who denied the Resurrection of Christ and partook unworthily of the Eucharist (1 Cor. 11 and 15.12–32), as interpreted by Augustine, *Sermo de scripturis* 150: "Now if Christ be preached, that he arose again from the dead, how do some among you say, that there is no resurrection of the dead? But if there be no resurrection of the dead, then Christ is not risen again. And if Christ be not risen again, then is our preaching vain, and your faith also is vain. . . . If (according to man) I fought with beasts at Ephesus, what doth it profit me, if the dead rise not again? *Let us eat and drink, for tomorrow we shall die* [1 Cor. 15.12–14, 32]." Augustine identifies the italicized sentence as the characteristic Epicurean attitude. In having the souls of the heretics buried in sarcophagi, Dante is drawing on Psalm 49 [Vulgate 48].11, "their sepulchres shall be their houses forever."

18. the desire you leave unspoken: Presumably the desire to see Florentines, perhaps specifically Farinata (cf. 6.79).

19–21. I hide my heart . . . not only just now: As in 3.75–81, for example.

22–29. O Tuscan . . . one of the arks: Since the pilgrim cannot see him, Farinata must be behind him and to his left (as the damned are to Christ's left; references to the Last Judgment are particularly frequent in this canto; see 9.132). His address identifies the pilgrim first as a Tuscan (Farinata's larger allegiance), then as a Florentine.

25. Your speech makes you manifest: A close translation of Matt. 26.73, "loquela tua manifestum te facit," spoken to Peter, whose Galilean accent revealed him as one of the followers of Jesus; in the verse that follows, Peter denies Christ for the third time. For denial of the Resurrection as denial of Christ, see 1 Cor. 11 and 15.

32. See there Farinata: Manente degli Uberti (ca. 1205–1264), called Farinata, was, from 1239 until his death, the leader of the Florentine Ghibellines (representing principally the old military aristocracy); in 1248 they had driven the Guelfs out of the city, only to be driven out themselves three years later. Farinata then led a coalition of Tuscan Ghibellines against Florence, slaughtering them in a bloody battle in 1260, on the plain of Montaperti, near Siena, crossed by the river Arbia. A subsequent council of Ghibellines in Empoli proposed to raze Florence, but Farinata's single-handed opposition dissuaded them.

After Charles of Anjou defeated and killed King Manfred at Benevento in 1266, a major disaster for the Ghibelline cause throughout Italy, an uprising in Florence drove out the Ghibellines. Farinata's descendants were explicitly excluded from the attempted reconciliation of 1280, as they were from later amnesties. In 1283 the Franciscan inquisitor for Florence, fra Salamone da Lucca, posthumously condemned Farinata and his wife as adherents to the heresy of the Paterines (a branch of the Cathars); their bodies were exhumed and burned, their ashes scattered on unhallowed ground.

33. from the waist up: In numerous respects the figure of Farinata alludes ironically to a famous iconographic motif, the so-called *Imago pietatis*, showing the dead Christ from the waist up, with bowed head, and hands crossed in front of him; it has been shown to be a representation of the Real Presence of the Body of Christ in the consecrated host (cf. the note to lines 14–15); thirteenth-century efforts to combat heresy stressed the doctrine of transubstantiation as the limit case of the testimony of faith against that of the senses. Farinata also recalls the iconography of baptism, and the use of the term *ark* may remind the alert reader that Noah's ark was widely interpreted as a figure of baptism as well as of the Church. For further discussion of this and other points in the notes on this canto, see Mazzotta 1979, Cassell 1984, and Durling 1981b.

34. fixed my eyes in his: The face-to-face confrontation of Farinata and the pilgrim is another allusion to the Last Judgment (note also lines 8–12, 35–36, 106–8), when all will see Christ the Judge face to face (1 Cor. 12.12); the pilgrim obviously corresponds to Christ the Judge, in spite of Farinata's pretensions.

35–36. and he was rising up . . . in great disdain: Dante's description of Farinata's imposing figure, emphasizing breast and forehead,

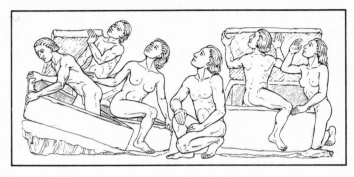

Figure 2. The Resurrection of the dead. (Based on the central tympanum, west front, Amiens Cathedral)

seats of the courage and foresight of a great leader (on his "magnanimity," see the note to line 73), as well as pride and rebellion, forces us to entertain, if only momentarily, the possibility of such a soul's actually being superior to the sufferings of Hell. But the ironies with which Farinata is encompassed are manifold. Not the least is that in the iconography of the Resurrection the dead are often represented as hearing the angelic trumpet and sitting up or standing up in their tombs (Figure 2); Farinata's and Cavalcante's standing up in their tomb abortively imitates this.

42. Who were your forebears: Farinata is still attached to the obsessive political and class concerns of his life. Note that he uses the familiar *tu* to the pilgrim.

46–48. Fiercely were they opposed to me . . . twice I scattered them: Dante has Farinata grant Dante's forebears a social status sufficiently close to his own for them to be identifiable as direct opponents, but there is no mention of them in the surviving lists of exiles. The scatterings referred to are those of 1248 and 1260. "Twice" translates Dante's *per due fiate* [literally, by/in two breaths] (cf. Francesca's use of the same term in 5.130, with note).

49–51. If they were driven out . . . did not learn that art well: That is, the pilgrim's forebears returned from exile twice, but not Farinata's people. The pilgrim, too, is caught up in the old party animosity. Note his use of the term *art* for returning from exile, a version of the traditional use of the term for politics (cf. line 77). It is striking that the pilgrim answers both Farinata and Cavalcante with the possessive derived from the respectful *voi* (cf. *direte*, line 110), according to Florentine social usage. To only one other individual in Hell, Brunetto Latini in Canto 15, does he use the respectful forms.

52–72. Then a shade rose up . . . appeared no more outside: The pilgrim must infer the identity of this shade (lines 64–66); Dante had evidently never met him. It is Cavalcante de' Cavalcanti (d. ca. 1280; Dante's friendship with his son Guido began ca. 1283), a leading Guelf, and, by Dante's assertion here (line 64), well known as a denier of the Resurrection. His son Guido (ca. 1255–1300) is Dante's "first friend" *(Vita nuova* 25), and the leading Florentine poet during Dante's youth. As part of a peacemaking effort in 1266, Guido had been betrothed to Farinata's daughter Beatrice (calling attention to the close family connections between members of opposing parties is part of Dante's commentary on Florentine civil dissension). After the riots of May 1300 (see the note to 6.64–72), Dante, as one of the priors of the city, voted for Guido's relegation to Sarzanà, where he became ill; in August the next group of priors voted to allow him and others to return to Florence; he died that month. (The fact that the pilgrim refers to Guido as still alive is an important indication that the fictional date of the journey is April 1300.)

55–57. It looked . . . entirely spent: As we soon learn, Cavalcante expects to see his son. Although the pilgrim had to infer his identity, Cavalcante knows who the pilgrim is and that he is Guido's friend, perhaps by the foreknowledge discussed in lines 97–108.

58. through this blind prison: The underworld. Cavalcante's phrase echoes Anchises' description of life in the body, which infects the soul with its perturbations *(Aen.* 6.730–34):

> Igneus est ollis vigor et caelestis origo
> seminibus, quantum non noxia corpora tardant
> terrenique hebetant artus moribundaque membra.
> Hinc metuunt cupiuntque, dolent gaudentque, neque auras
> dispiciunt clausae tenebris et carcere caeco.

> [A fiery vigor is theirs and a heavenly origin
> of those seeds, to the extent that their noxious bodies do not slow
> or their earthly limbs and death-bound members weaken.
> Thence they fear and desire, grieve and rejoice, nor do they see
> the heavens, shut up in shadows and a blind prison.]

Ironically, Vergil's lines fit Cavalcante, both during his life and now. Vergil's assertion that the body is the source of evil was vigorously criticized by the Church fathers, who devoted much attention to his portrayal of the underworld; it was central to the Gnostic tradition, including the Cathars.

59. because of height of intellect: As later passages make clear (especially *Par.* 17.124–42), the pilgrim's poetic genius is indeed a reason for his journey. But Cavalcante does not envisage the pilgrim's being led by grace, supposing rather that his journey expresses philosophical proficiency or loftiness of mind; his question implicitly attributes competitiveness to the two friends.

61. I do not come on my own: The first part of the pilgrim's reply singles out the first part of the question: he is relying on higher powers, and he points to Virgil as his guide. In his sermon on Acts 17.16–18 (referred to above), Augustine identified the Epicureans and Stoics (who question Saint Paul in Athens) as the philosophical sects of human self-sufficiency. Dante clearly has it in mind: Cavalcante corresponds to the Epicureans, whom Augustine accuses of following fleshly impulse, Farinata to the Stoics (because of his reliance on self-command and superiority to suffering, as well as his concern with political action).

63. perhaps to one your Guido had in disdain: One of the most famous cruxes in the poem, about which gallons of ink have been spilt. The Italian is intentionally obscure; the main obscurities result from (1) the pronoun *cui* (translated "to one to whom"), which can mean "whom" or "to whom," and whose referent is debatable; (2) the verb *ebbe* [had], a past tense of the verb *avere* [to have], which can mean "just now had," "definitively had," "once had," or "no longer has." (All these possibilities, and others, have actually been advocated.) Freccero (1988) has suggested that Dante is echoing Augustine's "they disdain [*dedignantur*] to learn from [Christ]" (*Confessions* 7.21.27), said of the pride of the Neoplatonists. Most critics have accepted the interpretation proposed by Pagliaro ([1953] 1967): "he who is waiting over there is leading me to one to whom your Guido disdained to come." Most also have taken the view that Dante is here asserting that Guido shared his father's sin. While Dante is expressing misgivings about Guido, in our view he seems with this elaborately obscure line to avoid saying anything definite about Guido's ultimate fate (see the note to lines 67–69).

67–69. How did you say? 'he had' . . . strike his eyes: Cavalcante takes Dante's obscure *ebbe* in the last of the senses listed in the note to line 63 under (2): he thinks Guido *no longer disdains*, but in a negative sense, because he is no longer alive (since Guido is still alive, as this mistake shows, "no longer disdains" may have a positive sense). The father's questioning of the pilgrim in these lines is strikingly parallel to God's questioning of Cain about Abel in Gen. 4.9–11: "Ubi est frater tuus?" [Where is your brother], "Quid fecisti?" [What have you done]. The existence of an unresolved node of guilt and anxiety connected with Guido is palpable (see the notes to *Purg.* 11.97–99 and *Par.* 13.133–42).

70–72. When he perceived . . . fell back supine: Cavalcante's despair at the idea of his son's death is part of the punishment of one who saw nothing after death. He falls supine as if struck by a blow on the forehead. His concern for his son and his son's fame, like Farinata's concern for his descendants and his own reputation, are for Dante instances of human beings' universal concern for what will happen after their deaths. Cavalcante is thus acting out impulses that should have taught him that the soul is immortal, and his misinterpretations of the pilgrim's presence and of his *ebbe* are part of a system of negative misinterpretation of experience.

73. that other great-souled one: Dante's term for "great-souled" is *magnanimo*, a key term contrasting Farinata with Cavalcante's pusillanimity. Scott (1977) demonstrated the double-edged nature of this idea, with its background in Aristotle's *Nichomachean Ethics;* for the Middle Ages it can mean "overweening." It thus has quite a different significance according to whether Farinata's worldly values or the pilgrim's Christian ones are asserted.

79–81. not fifty times . . . how much that art weighs: This is the second prophecy by a Florentine, this time foretelling Dante's exile as a result of the troubles predicted by the first (6.64–72). "The lady who reigns here" is Hecate (in classical mythology the wife of Dis, also called Proserpina), commonly identified with the moon. Fifty months would take us to the summer of 1304, just before the Whites were defeated in their effort to reenter Florence by force of arms (July). Dante had apparently repudiated them some months before. Farinata's prophecy is couched in the terms of the pilgrim's earlier speech (line 51).

83. why is that people so cruel against mine in all its laws: Legislation against Farinata's descendants continued to be passed in Florence (see the note to lines 32–33).

85–87. The slaughter . . . to be made in our temple: The slaughter of Guelfs at Montaperti. "Our temple" has been identified with a number of Florentine churches, where meetings of qualified voters were held. Orations (*orazioni*) thus has two meanings: "speeches" and "prayers."

88–93. After he had moved his head . . . who defended her openly: Farinata shakes or perhaps bows his head—his only movement in the entire scene, perhaps acknowledging the depth of his suffering; it particularly focuses the parallel with the *Imago pietatis*. Dante seems to be expressing a considerable complexity of attitude toward the historical Farinata—both dramatizing the pride, rigidity, self-absorption, and intellectual/moral confusion involved in turning against his homeland (and in his heresy), and suggesting that the Florentine vengefulness, decades after the man's death, was excessive. The dialogue that began with party animosity has moved toward some degree of mutual sympathy.

97–108. It seems that you see . . . will be closed: What Farinata describes, where events "distant" in the future are clear but those in the present or near future are not seen, is a kind of inversion of the pattern of memory: events distant in the past are obscure, those in the present or near past are clear. The "bad light" refers to twilight (perhaps moonlight: cf. *Aen.* 6.270: "quale per incertam lunam, sub luce maligna" [because of an uncertain moon, under bad light]), when distant things are outlined against the horizon. The "highest Leader" is God, or more precisely the Logos, second person of the Trinity and principle of intellect, here compared to the sun (on the analogy, see the note on 1.17–18), and referred to with the first of Cicero's famous epithets for the sun, *dux* (*Somnium Scipionis* 4.2). Farinata's explanation may shed some light on the failure of Virgil's foreknowledge at the beginning of Canto 9.

107. that point when the door of the future will be closed: The end of time. Dante, like Aquinas, believed that after the Last Judgment the turning heavens would be immobilized. The moment of the ending of time is the furthest reference to the future made in the *Inferno*; it is striking that it should be made by Farinata.

110–14. Now will you tell . . . you have untied for me: Note the contrast between Cavalcante's frantic jumping to negative conclusions and the pilgrim's careful inquiry into the cause of the misunderstanding; compare Eph. 4.14: "Be no more children tossed to and fro and carried about with every wind of doctrine."

119. the second Frederick and the Cardinal: Frederick II of Hohenstaufen (d. 1250), Holy Roman Emperor, called *Stupor mundi* [Wonder of the World], who, although he passed severe laws against heresy, in the later part of his reign was bitterly opposed by the popes and accused by the Guelfs of being an Epicurean and a mortalist; their animus against him was caused in part by the fact that he maintained friendly diplomatic relations with Muslim rulers (he regained Jerusalem and other parts of the Holy Land by peaceful negotiation), welcomed Muslim scientists and scholars to his court, and founded a city for his Muslim subjects where they were permitted to practice their faith openly. He was the author of a noted treatise on falconry. "The Cardinal" is the pro-Ghibelline Ottaviano degli Ubaldini (d. 1273), whom early commentators report as having said, "If I have a soul, I have lost it a hundred times for the Ghibellines."

129. he raised his finger: The timeless gesture of admonition, for Dante a very emphatic one.

131. before her sweet ray: When face to face, not with Farinata (line 34), but with Beatrice, whose eyes (emphasized in Virgil's narrative, 2.55 and 116), seeing all, contrast with the blindness of the Epicureans and will be a central focus of attention when she appears in *Purgatorio* 29–33 and throughout the *Paradiso*. But the pilgrim will in fact learn the details of his exile from his ancestor Cacciaguida (*Par.* 17.37–93).

CANTO 11

1　　　In su l'estremità d'un'alta ripa
che facevan gran pietre rotte in cerchio,
venimmo sopra più crudele stipa;

4　　　e quivi, per l'orribile soperchio
del puzzo che 'l profondo abisso gitta,
ci raccostammo, in dietro, ad un coperchio

7　　　d'un grand' avello, ov' io vidi una scritta
che dicea: "Anastasio papa guardo,
lo qual trasse Fotin de la via dritta."

10　　　"Lo nostro scender conviene esser tardo,
sì che s'ausi un poco in prima il senso
al tristo fiato; e poi no i fia riguardo."

13　　　Così 'l maestro; e io: "Alcun compenso,"
dissi lui, "trova che 'l tempo non passi
perduto." Ed elli: "Vedi ch'a ciò penso."

16　　　"Figliuol mio, dentro da cotesti sassi,"
cominciò poi a dir, "son tre cerchietti
di grado in grado, come que' che lassi.

19　　　Tutti son pien di spirti maladetti;
ma perché poi ti basti pur la vista,
intendi come e perché son costretti.

22　　　D'ogne malizia, ch'odio in cielo acquista,
ingiuria è 'l fine, ed ogne fin cotale
o con forza o con frode altrui contrista.

25　　　Ma perché frode è de l'uom proprio male,
più spiace a Dio; e però stan di sotto
li frodolenti, e più dolor li assale.

28　　　D'i vïolenti il primo cerchio è tutto;
ma perché si fa forza a tre persone,
in tre gironi è distinto e costrutto.

CANTO 11

Delay—the divisions of lower Hell: violence, fraud, treachery—
distinction between malice and incontinence—art/industry as Nature's
child, God's grandchild

1
At the edge of a high cliff, made by great rocks
broken in a circle, we came above a crueler crowding;

4
and there, because of the horrible excess of stench
cast up by the abyss, we moved back beside the lid

7
of a great tomb, where I saw writing which said:
"I hold Pope Anastasius, whom Photinus drew from
the straight way."

10
"Our descent will have to be delayed, so that our
sense can become a little accustomed to the evil
smell; and then we can disregard it."

13
So my master; and I to him: "Find something to
compensate, so that the time may not be lost." And
he: "You see I am considering it."

16
"My son, within these rocks," he then began to
say, "are three smaller circles descending step by
step, like those you are leaving.

19
All are full of cursed spirits; but so that later the
mere sight of them may suffice, hear how they are
constricted and why.

22
Of every malice gaining the hatred of Heaven,
injustice is the goal, and every such goal injures
someone either with force or with fraud.

25
But because fraud is an evil proper to man, it is
more displeasing to God; and therefore the
fraudulent have a lower place and greater pain
assails them.

28
Of the violent the first circle is full; but because
violence can be directed against three persons, the
circle is divided and constructed in three subcircles.

31 A Dio, a sé, al prossimo si pòne
far forza, dico in loro e in lor cose,
come udirai con aperta ragione.

34 Morte per forza e ferute dogliose
nel prossimo si danno, e nel suo avere
ruine, incendi e tollette dannose;

37 onde omicide e ciascun che mal fiere,
guastatori e predon, tutti tormenta
lo giron primo per diverse schiere.

40 Puote omo avere in sé man vïolenta
e ne' suoi beni; e però nel secondo
giron convien che sanza pro si penta

43 qualunque priva sé del vostro mondo,
biscazza e fonde la sua facultade,
e piange là dov' esser de' giocondo.

46 Puossi far forza ne la deïtade
col cor negando e bestemmiando quella,
e spregiando natura e sua bontade;

49 e però lo minor giron suggella
del segno suo e Soddoma e Caorsa
e chi, spregiando Dio col cor, favella.

52 La frode, ond' ogne coscïenza è morsa,
può l'omo usare in colui che 'n lui fida
e in quel che fidanza non imborsa.

55 Questo modo di retro par ch'incida
pur lo vinco d'amor che fa natura;
onde nel cerchio secondo s'annida

58 ipocresia, lusinghe e chi affattura,
falsità, ladroneccio e simonia,
ruffian, baratti e simile lordura.

61 Per l'altro modo quell'amor s'oblia
che fa natura e quel ch'è poi aggiunto,
di che la fede spezïal si cria;

64 onde nel cerchio minore, ov' è 'l punto
de l'universo in su che Dite siede,
qualunque trade in etterno è consunto."

67 E io: "Maestro, assai chiara procede
la tua ragione, e assai ben distingue
questo baràtro e 'l popol ch'e' possiede.

31   To God, to oneself, and to one's neighbor one can do violence, that is, to them and to their possessions, as you will hear with clear reason.

34   Death by violence and painful wounds can be inflicted on one's neighbor, and on his possessions ruin, fires, and wrongful extortion;

37   thus homicides and whoever wrongfully strikes, spoilers, and bandits, all are tormented in the first subcircle in different groups.

40   One can turn a violent hand against oneself or one's own possessions; therefore in the second subcircle each must uselessly repent

43   whoever deprives himself of your world, or utterly squanders and undermines his wealth, and weeps where he should be happy.

46   One can use force against the Deity by denying it and cursing it in one's heart or by scorning Nature and its goodness;

49   and therefore the smallest subcircle stamps with its seal Sodom and Cahors and whoever speaks with scorn of God in his heart.

52   Fraud, which bites at every mind, a man can use against one who trusts in him or against one who has in his purse no cause for trust.

55   This latter mode seems to cut solely into the bond of love that Nature makes; thus in the second circle find their nest

58   hypocrisy, flattery, casters of spells, impersonators, thievery and simony, panders, embezzlers, and similar filth.

61   The former mode forgets the love that Nature makes and also that which is added to it, from which special trust is created;

64   thus in the smallest circle, at the point of the universe where Dis is enthroned, whoever is a traitor is eternally consumed."

67   And I: "Master, your reasoning proceeds most clearly and divides very well this pit and the people it possesses.

70 Ma dimmi: quei de la palude pingue,
che mena il vento, e che batte la pioggia,
e che s'incontran con sì aspre lingue,

73 perché non dentro da la città roggia
sono ei puniti, se Dio li ha in ira?
e se non li ha, perché sono a tal foggia?"

76 Ed elli a me: "Perché tanto delira,"
disse, "lo 'ngegno tuo da quel che sòle?
o ver la mente dove altrove mira?

79 Non ti rimembra di quelle parole
con le quai la tua Etica pertratta
le tre disposizion che 'l ciel non vole,

82 incontenenza, malizia e la matta
bestialitade? e come incontenenza
men Dio offende e men biasimo accatta?

85 Se tu riguardi ben questa sentenza
e rechiti a la mente chi son quelli
che sù di fuor sostegnon penitenza,

88 tu vedrai ben perché da questi felli
sien dipartiti, e perché men crucciata
la divina vendetta li martelli."

91 "O sol che sani ogne vista turbata,
tu mi contenti sì quando tu solvi,
che, non men che saver, dubbiar m'aggrata.

94 Ancora in dietro un poco ti rivolvi,"
diss' io, "là dove di' ch'usura offende
la divina bontade, e 'l groppo solvi."

97 "Filosofia," mi disse, "a chi la 'ntende,
nota, non pure in una sola parte,
come natura lo suo corso prende

100 dal divino 'ntelletto e da sua arte;
e se tu ben la tua Fisica note,
tu troverai, non dopo molte carte,

103 che l'arte vostra quella, quanto pote,
segue, come 'l maestro fa 'l discente;
sì che vostr' arte a Dio quasi è nepote.

106 Da queste due, se tu ti rechi a mente
lo Genesì dal principio, convene
prender sua vita e avanzar la gente;

70   But tell me: those of the greasy swamp, those driven by the wind and beaten by the rain, and those who collide with such harsh words,

73   why are they not punished inside the ruddy city, if they are under God's wrath? and if not, why are they treated so?"

76   And he to me: "Why does your wit," he said, "so wander from its usual course? or where does your mind gaze mistaken?

79   Do you not remember the words with which your *Ethics* treats so fully the three dispositions that Heaven refuses,

82   incontinence, malice, and mad bestiality? and how incontinence offends God less and acquires less blame?

85   If you consider this judgment well and bring to mind who those are that undergo their penitence higher up and outside,

88   you will see clearly why they are separated from these wicked ones and why God's justice hammers them less wrathfully."

91   "O sun that heals every clouded sight, you content me so when you resolve questions, that doubting is no less pleasurable than knowing.

94   Turn back a little yet again," I said, "to where you say that usury offends God's goodness, and untie that knot."

97   "Philosophy," he said, "to one who understands it, notes, and not merely in one place, how Nature takes its course

100   from the divine intellect and art; and if you take good note of your *Physics*, you will see, after not many pages,

103   that your art follows Nature as much as it can, as a disciple follows the master; so that your art is almost God's grandchild.

106   From these two, if you bring to mind the beginning of Genesis, we must draw our life and advance our people;

109   e perché l'usuriere altra via tene,
per sé natura e per la sua seguace
dispregia, poi ch' in altro pon la spene.
112   Ma seguimi oramai, che 'l gir mi piace;
ché i Pesci guizzan su per l'orizzonta,
e 'l Carro tutto sovra 'l Coro giace,
115   e 'l balzo via là oltra si dismonta."

109 and because the usurer holds another way, he scorns Nature in herself and in her follower, since he puts his hope in something else.

112 But follow me now, for I desire to go; the Fishes are wriggling up over the horizon, and the Wain lies entirely above the northwest wind,

115 and it is far to the place where we must climb down this bank."

NOTES

4. excess of stench: This is the "stench of sinners" (*foetor peccatorum*) and "stench of evil" (*foetor mali*) of the *Visio Pauli*, which also requires caution on approach (Silverstein 1937; the idea is also scriptural [e.g., Prov. 10.7]). See also Virgil's *Aen.* 6.201: "fauces grave olentis Averni" [the jaws of evil-smelling Avernus]; also 6.239–42.

7. writing: The first inscription since that on Hellgate in Canto 3, and the last in Hell. Canto 11, like Canto 3, is one of transition.

8–9. Pope Anastasius . . . the straight way: Identification of these figures is uncertain (perhaps intentionally so), particularly since the syntax is ambiguous: either *Anastasio* or *Fotin* could be either the subject or the object of the verb. In both cases the heresies are early ones and concern the divinity of Christ. Dante's names here form a series of ironic puns: Anastasius, "the resurrected," in a tomb; Photinus, "the little light" of error.

16–111. My son, within these rocks . . . his hope in something else: Dante now puts in Virgil's mouth an explanation of the structure of Hell as a whole and the classification of sins on which it is based: first (lines 16–66), he discusses three of the four circles of lower Hell, enclosed within the walls of the city of Dis, those of violence, simple fraud, and treacherous fraud, after first establishing that they are all for sins of malice; then, in answer to the pilgrim's first question (lines 67–75), he accounts for the circles they passed through before reaching the walls (lines 76–90); finally, in answer to the pilgrim's second question (lines 91–96), he clarifies a particular point, the classification of usury (lines 97–111). Virgil's account is incomplete (it omits the neutrals, Limbo, and heresy [the first circle inside the walls]; however, of these only the last is subject to Minos) and perhaps in some respects inconsistent (see the notes to lines 76–90). Kirkham (1992) suggests that the medieval interpretation of the number eleven as signifying transgression (it "goes beyond" the perfect number, ten) helps explain the placing of this explanation (Virgil's lesson, she notes, concludes at 11.111; cf. 1.111).

22–24. Of every malice . . . injures someone: Virgil first asserts the distinguishing characteristic of lower Hell: malice, the express purpose ("the goal") of which is to act contrary to the law (*iniuria*, from *ius*, law) and consequently (since the purpose of the law is to ensure that all are treated justly) to inflict harm. Virgil does not distinguish here between God's law and natural law or human law; many of his distinctions are drawn from Roman law, broadly understood (cf. *Digest* 47.10).

24. either with force or with fraud: This is to be understood as an exhaustive classification; it, too, is derived from Roman law (*Institutes* 4.4.2).

25–27. But because fraud ... greater pain assails them: Fraud is more displeasing to God than violence because it involves corruption of what is more distinctive of man, his intellect (cf. *Convivio* 3.2.14–19; that violence is shared with the beasts is implied here). It should be noted that in Dante's view the devil also practices fraud and that Virgil's words "proper to man," if taken to mean "exclusive to man," are mistaken (Cantos 21–23 suggest that Virgil in fact does not understand the nature of the devils).

28–51. Of the violent ... scorn of God in his heart: The circle of the violent is divided into three subcircles corresponding to the person injured: God, oneself, or one's neighbor. The conception derives from Matt. 22.37–40 (cf. Mark 12.29–39):

> Jesus said to him: Thou shalt love the Lord thy God with thy whole heart, and with thy whole soul, and with thy whole mind. This is the greatest and the first commandment. And the second is like to this: Thou shalt love thy neighbor as thyself. On these two commandments dependeth the whole law and the prophets.

The theologians interpreted this order as quite logical: it is natural to love God first, as one's origin and the source of all value, and it is more natural to love oneself than to love others (cf. Aquinas, *Summa theol.* 2a 2ae, q. 118). Thus the sequence of increasing gravity of violence against others or their possessions (least serious, because in a sense more natural, lines 34–39), oneself and one's possessions (lines 40–45), and God and his possessions (lines 46–51). That acts of violence against possessions are ranked according to the possessor is ultimately derived from Roman law (see the entries under *iniuria* in *Digest* 4.10.21).

It should be remembered that in the Neoplatonic tradition accepted by medieval Christianity love is also the bond that unites the entire cosmos with its golden chain. An important text for Dante is Book 2, metrum 8 of Boethius's *Consolation*, especially lines 13–30 (on love, cf. Chaucer's *Knight's Tale*, 2987–93):

> Hanc rerum seriem ligat
> terras ac pelagus regens
> et caelo imperitans amor.
> Hic si frena remiserit,
> quidquid nunc amat invicem
> bellum continuo gerens,
> et quam nunc socia fide
> pulchris motibus incitant,
> certent solvere machinam.

[Love binds this series of things,
ruling the lands and the sea,
commanding from the heavens.
If love released the reins,
all things that now love mutually,
suddenly waging war,
this fabric of things which
now with mutual trust
they drive in lovely motions,
they would strive to dissolve.]

The chain of love, with the closely associated "great chain of being," is implicit even in Hell, in the notion of its concentric circles (cf. those of the planets) and in that of descent by degrees.

40–45. One can turn . . . where he should be happy: The squanderers punished here are clearly to be distinguished from the spendthrifts of Canto 7 as being expressly self-destructive rather than simply uncontrolled (see lines 72, 82–84). Line 45 would seem to refer to the squanderers rather than the suicides.

46–51. One can use force . . . in his heart: "Sodom" refers to sodomy; "Cahors," from a city in southern France noted for its moneylenders, refers to usury. The idea that blasphemy, sodomy, and usury offend God more than murder derives partly from the ordering of persons noted in lines 31–33, but it rests also on a notable shift in the meaning of the term *violence* as applied to these sins, and in the relation between possessor and things possessed. Perhaps in no other aspect of the *Inferno* is the distance so pronounced between Dante's medieval conceptions, on the one hand, and, on the other, modern or even Greek (Aristotelian) ones. The Christian condemnation of homosexuality as against nature stems largely from Saint Paul (Rom. 1.26–27), but of course goes back to the Old Testament (see the note to 14.8–39). For associating sodomy and usury with violence against God, see Aquinas, *Summa theol.* 2a 2ae, q. 154, a. 12: "in sins against nature, in which the very order of nature is violated, an injury is done to God himself, who sets nature in order."

Identification of the sin of Sodom has generated much discussion. A number of critics have argued that Dante is condemning other sins under this name; the most prominent are Pézard (1950), for whom the sin is preferring a foreign language to one's mother tongue, and Kay (1978b), who offers a great wealth of material on the complexity of the idea of Sodom for the Middle Ages, arguing that here the sin is opposition to the Holy Roman Empire. The traditional, and the majority view, which we share, is that "Sodom" here refers to homosexuality. See Additional Notes 4 and 5.

49–50. stamps with its seal: For the metaphor, probably one of coining, see the note to lines 55–56.

51. scorn of God in his heart: Ps. 13.1, 52.1: "The fool says in his heart: there is no God."

52–66. Fraud . . . eternally consumed: Fraud against God would be impossible, given his omniscience; only fraud against others is explicitly classified, and it is again divided according to the persons injured: those who have a special reason to trust their deceiver (treacherous fraud), and those who do not (simple fraud). For the metaphor of coin for trust, see next note.

55–56. This latter mode . . . that Nature makes: That is, simple fraud does not violate a bond of special trust between individuals, but only the natural bond of love between human beings. It is on this bond that the possibility of civil society rests, and therefore even simple fraud weakens society itself, as implied by Dante's term *incida* ("cuts into," not "severs"). Compare Aquinas, *Summa theol.* 2a 2ae, q. 109, a. 3: "One must say that because man is a social animal, by nature each man owes to the other that without which human society cannot be preserved. For men cannot associate with each other unless they believe they are telling each other the truth." In this light the coin metaphor of line 54 itself raises the issue of the social significance of fraud. The perversity of the city of Dis *as a city* is subjected to particularly detailed analysis in the Malebolge (see next note).

57–60. in the second circle . . . and similar filth: The Malebolge [Evil pouches], described in Cantos 18–30, is the second of the three lower circles mentioned in line 17, subdivided into ten concentric ditches or "pouches." Virgil is far from exhaustive and names occupants of only eight of the ten "pouches."

57. find their nest: Nesting animals include both vermin and reptiles; Dante refers to Florence as a "nest of so much malice" in 15.78.

61–66. The former mode . . . eternally consumed: "The former mode" refers to lines 53–54 and is correlated with "this latter mode" of line 55. Thus "the smallest," the third circle, Cocytus (accented on the second syllable), punishes those who, forgetting both the natural bond among men and also the particular bonds of love that join them to individuals, deceive persons who have reason to trust them. The additive principle (traitors break both bonds, the general and the special) also holds, in the lowest reaches of Hell, for the relation of violence and fraud: Dante's traitors are all, directly or indirectly, murderers.

64–65. the point of the universe: In Dante's cosmos, this is the deepest point, where the weight of the entire universe impinges.

70–75. those of the greasy swamp . . . treated so: The pilgrim lists, but not in order, the sinners of Cantos 5–8. These, Virgil will explain, are the sins of incontinence; Dante associates them with material elements (swamp, wind, rain, and stone, or earth). This was traditional: the different personality types were explained by the predominance of one or another humor in the body, and the humors (phlegm, blood, bile, and black bile) were associated with the four elements and the four qualities (wet, dry, hot, and cold). (See also Vergil, *Aen.* 6.730–43, on the infection of the body and the cycle of reincarnation.) If we accept Russo's (1967) explanation of the sins punished in the Styx (see the note to 7.123), it is easy to see why a number of the early commentators considered that all seven deadly vices (seen as passions to which the sinners gave way) are punished in the circles of incontinence.

76–90. Why does your wit . . . less wrathfully: Virgil explains that those outside the city sinned by incontinence rather than "malice" or "mad bestiality." For the concept see Aquinas, *In Ethica Nichomachea* 7.8 (1151a12–13): "whereas the incontinent still judges rightly about what he should do or avoid, and only his passions are astray, in the intemperate man reason itself is perverted: he approves of his corrupt desires." Virgil introduces here the Aristotelian concept of *disposition*, the habit or inner inclination toward bad (or good) actions, acquired through repetition. The earlier discussion (lines 22–24) classified sins according to the *intention* ("the goal," line 23) of acting unjustly, the *mode* or *means,* and the direct *result.* Now the emphasis shifts to include the habitual state of the sinner, whether expressed in his sin or the result of his sin.

76. wander: Boccaccio explains that Dante's verb for "wander" here, *delirare,* means literally "to depart from the furrow that is being plowed."

80. your *Ethics*: Aristotle's *Nichomachean Ethics*, which the pilgrim has evidently studied.

81–83. the three dispositions . . . mad bestiality: "Bestiality" is a new term in Virgil's discussion, and there has been disagreement about its reference. Most critics take it to refer to the circle of violence, especially to those violent against others; support for this view is offered by the frequency of references in Canto 12 to the bestiality of anger. But this seems inconsistent with lines 22–24: would the tendency to violence be distinct from malice? Others (led by Mazzoni 1953, 1986) point out that Virgil's words draw on a passage in the *Nichomachean Ethics*, where Aristotle (who of course says nothing about God's displeasure with sin) distinguishes three "moral states to be avoided . . . vice [somewhat inaccurately translated in the Middle Ages as *malitia*], incontinence, brutishness." By "brutishness," as a later chapter (1148b15–1150a8) makes somewhat clearer, Aristotle means the extremes of cruelty "beyond the limits of vice [that is, the customary vices of civilized Greeks]" (1149a1); most of his examples of "brutishness" involve cannibalism. Since cannibalism is an explicit feature of Cocytus, this view argues that in these lines "incontinence" refers to the sins punished outside the city, "malice" to all sins punished within the city (violence and both types of fraud), and "mad bestiality" only to the sin of Cocytus (treacherous fraud). Both views involve overlapping categories.

87. penitence: Not of course in any profitable sense; the term here means "undergoing of punishment" (Latin *poenitentia,* from *poena,* punishment).

91–96. O sun . . . untie that knot: The pilgrim's second question asks why usury is condemned. He does not question the condemnation of sodomy or ask to have it explained (a fact that supports the majority view); for the analogy between usury and sodomy, see the note to lines 110–11.

96. untie that knot: Treating a problem as a knot is traditional. There may also be a hint here of usurious debt as a bond, the opposite of the "bond of nature" that usury offends.

97–111. Philosophy . . . in something else: Virgil explains that usurers evade God's decree (Gen. 3.17–19): "In the sweat of thy face shalt thou eat bread" (Luke 6.35 was another important text often cited against charging interest on loans). Nature (in the Middle Ages the term usually refers to the influence of the heavenly bodies) is God's art (cf. *Monarchia* 1.3.2) because it carries out his creative plan and fashions the sublunar. Nature is thus analogous to a human craftsman (the analogy is spelled out in *Par.* 2.112–32) and the model for all human making (Aristotle, *Physics* 2.2: "art follows nature insofar as it can"). "Your art" is thus metaphorically the child of Nature, the child of God. "Philosophy" here, as in 6.106, refers to the current Aristotelianism, for which the concept of a beneficent—and "reasonable"—Nature was crucial. For further discussion of these concepts, see *Monarchia* 2.2.3.

106. From these two: That is, from Nature and industry (art).

110–11. he scorns Nature . . . in her follower: The usurer scorns both Nature and art. The third circle of violence, then, holds those who scorn God directly (the blasphemers), those who scorn Nature directly and thus God indirectly (the homosexuals), and those who scorn Nature indirectly and God doubly indirectly (the usurers). Like the usurers, the sodomites evade a divine commandment, to "be fruitful and multiply" (Gen. 1.22), not dissimilar, in Dante's view, from the injunction to productive work. In the traditional Greek terminology for interest paid to moneylenders, it was called *tókos* [offspring]; Aristotle considered it unnatural that coin should *breed* or *beget* money *(Politics* 1.10.1258b); cf. Aquinas's commentary: "thus a kind of birth occurs when money grows from money. For this reason this acquisition of money is especially contrary to Nature."

112–114. the Fishes . . . the northwest wind: It is April, and the sun is in Aries: if the Fish, which form the preceding constellation, are just rising, and the Wain, or Big Dipper, is in the direction of the northwest wind (Corus), then it is a few hours before sunrise, about 4:00 A.M. As in the case of Canto 7, Virgil's concluding his discourse with an indication of time according to the positions of the stars suggests his "inner eye" is fixed on the circlings of the heavens, the model of rationality and order.

CANTO 12

1   Era lo loco ov' a scender la riva
venimmo alpestro e, per quel che v'er' anco,
tal ch'ogne vista ne sarebbe schiva.

4   Qual è quella ruina che nel fianco
di qua da Trento l'Adice percosse,
o per tremoto o per sostegno manco,

7   che da cima del monte, onde si mosse,
al piano è sì la roccia discoscesa
ch'alcuna via darebbe a chi sù fosse:

10   cotal di quel burrato era la scesa;
e 'n su la punta de la rotta lacca
l'infamïa di Creti era distesa

13   che fu concetta ne la falsa vacca;
e quando vide noi, sé stesso morse,
sì come quei cui l'ira dentro fiacca.

16   Lo savio mio duca inver' lui gridò: "Forse
tu credi che qui sia 'l duca d'Atene,
che sù nel mondo la morte ti porse?

19   Pàrtiti, bestia, ché questi non vene
ammaestrato da la tua sorella,
ma vassi per veder le vostre pene."

22   Qual è quel toro che si slaccia in quella
c'ha ricevuto già 'l colpo mortale,
che gir non sa, ma qua e là saltella:

25   vid' io lo Minotauro far cotale;
e quello accorto gridò: "Corri al varco;
mentre ch'e' 'nfuria, è buon che tu ti cale."

28   Così prendemmo via giù per lo scarco
di quelle pietre, che spesso moviensi
sotto i miei piedi per lo novo carco.

CANTO 12

Seventh circle: the violent—descent of the landslide—the earthquake at Christ's death—first subcircle: the violent against others—the centaurs—the river of blood

1   The place where we came to descend the bank was mountainous, and, because of what else was there, such that every sight would shun it.

4   Like that landslide which struck the flank of the Adige this side of Trento, because of an earthquake or the failing of support,

7   where from the summit of the mountain, whence they fell, down to the plain, the rocks lie so strewn that they would provide a path for one who was above:

10   such was the descent into that valley; and at the very point where the slope had broken, the infamy of Crete was stretched out,

13   the one conceived in the false cow; and when he saw us, he bit himself like one broken within by anger.

16   My wise one shouted toward him: "Perhaps you believe the duke of Athens is here, who put you to death up in the world?

19   Away, beast, for this man does not come taught by your sister, but goes to see your punishments."

22   Like a bull that wrenches free at the moment it has received the mortal blow, that is unable to walk but jumps here and there,

25   so I saw the Minotaur do; and that alert one cried: "Run to the crossing; it is good to go down while he is in his fit."

28   So we took our way down along that scree, and the stones kept moving under my feet, because of their new burden.

31 Io gia pensando; e quei disse: "Tu pensi
forse a questa ruina, ch'è guardata
da quell'ira bestial ch'i' ora spensi.

34 Or vo' che sappi che l'altra fïata
ch'i' discesi qua giù nel basso inferno,
questa roccia non era ancor cascata.

37 Ma certo poco pria, se ben discerno,
che venisse colui che la gran preda
levò a Dite del cerchio superno,

40 da tutte parti l'alta valle feda
tremò sì ch'i' pensai che l'universo
sentisse amor, per lo qual è chi creda

43 più volte il mondo in caòsso converso;
e in quel punto questa vecchia roccia,
qui e altrove, tal fece riverso.

46 Ma ficca li occhi a valle, ché s'approccia
la riviera del sangue in la qual bolle
qual che per vïolenza in altrui noccia."

49 Oh cieca cupidigia e ira folle,
che sì ci sproni ne la vita corta,
e ne l'etterna poi sì mal c'immolle!

52 Io vidi un'ampia fossa in arco torta,
come quella che tutto 'l piano abbraccia,
secondo ch'avea detto la mia scorta;

55 e tra 'l piè de la ripa ed essa, in traccia
corrien centauri, armati di saette,
come solien nel mondo andare a caccia.

58 Veggendoci calar, ciascun ristette,
e de la schiera tre si dipartiro
con archi e asticciuole prima elette;

61 e l'un gridò da lungi: "A qual martiro
venite voi che scendete la costa?
Ditel costinci; se non, l'arco tiro."

64 Lo mio maestro disse: "La risposta
farem noi a Chirón costà di presso:
mal fu la voglia tua sempre sì tosta."

67 Poi mi tentò, e disse: "Quelli è Nesso,
che morì per la bella Deianira
e fé di sé la vendetta elli stesso.

31   I walked thoughtful; and he said: "You are thinking perhaps of this landslide, guarded by that bestial anger I just now put out.

34   Now I would have you know that the other time I came down here into lower Hell, this cliff had not yet fallen.

37   But certainly, if I remember well, a little before he came who took from Dis the great spoils of the highest circle,

40   on every side this deep, foul valley trembled so that I thought the universe must be feeling love, by which, some believe,

43   the world has often been turned back into chaos: and at that point this ancient cliff, here and elsewhere, was broken down.

46   But probe the valley with your sight, for we are approaching the river of blood, in which are boiling those who harm others with violence."

49   Oh blind cupidity and mad rage, that so spur us in this short life, and then in the eternal one cook us so evilly!

52   I saw an ample, curving ditch that embraces the entire plain, according to what my guide had said;

55   and between the foot of the cliff and it, centaurs were running in file, armed with arrows, as they used to go hunting in the world.

58   Seeing us come down, each stopped, and from the file three came forth with bows and with arrows they had selected first;

61   and one cried from afar: "To what punishment do you come, you who are climbing down the bank? Speak from there; otherwise I draw my bow."

64   My master said: "The reply will we make to Chiron, close over there; to your harm has your will always been so hasty."

67   Then he nudged me and said: "That is Nessus, who died because of fair Deianira and himself avenged himself.

70   E quel di mezzo, ch'al petto si mira,
è il gran Chirón, il qual nodrì Achille;
quell'altro è Folo, che fu sì pien d'ira.

73   Dintorno al fosso vanno a mille a mille,
saettando qual anima si svelle
del sangue più che sua colpa sortille."

76   Noi ci appressammo a quelle fiere isnelle;
Chirón prese uno strale, e con la cocca
fece la barba in dietro a le mascelle.

79   Quando s'ebbe scoperta la gran bocca,
disse a' compagni: "Siete voi accorti
che quel di retro move ciò ch'el tocca?

82   Così non soglion far li piè d'i morti."
E 'l mio buon duca, che già li er' al petto,
dove le due nature son consorti,

85   rispuose: "Ben è vivo, e sì soletto
mostrar li mi convien la valle buia;
necessità 'l ci 'nduce, e non diletto.

88   Tal si partì da cantare *alleluia*
che mi commise quest'officio novo;
non è ladron, né io anima fuia.

91   Ma per quella virtù per cu' io movo
li passi miei per sì selvaggia strada,
danne un de' tuoi a cui noi siamo a provo

94   e che ne mostri là dove si guada;
e che porti costui in su la groppa,
ché non è spirto che per l'aere vada."

97   Chirón si volse in su la destra poppa,
e disse a Nesso: "Torna, e sì li guida,
e fa cansar s'altra schiera v'intoppa."

100   Or ci movemmo con la scorta fida
lungo la proda del bollor vermiglio,
dove i bolliti facieno alte strida.

103   Io vidi gente sotto infino al ciglio;
e 'l gran centauro disse: "E' son tiranni
che dier nel sangue e ne l'aver di piglio.

106   Quivi si piangon li spietati danni;
quivi è Alessandro, e Dïonisio fero,
che fé Cicilia aver dolorosi anni.

70   The one in the middle, who is gazing at his breast, is the great Chiron, who brought up Achilles; that other is Pholus, who was so full of anger.

73   Around the ditch they go by thousands, shooting with arrows whatever soul emerges from the blood more than his guilt allots."

76   We drew near those swift beasts: Chiron took an arrow, and with the notch he moved his beard back from his jaw.

79   When he had uncovered his great mouth, he said to his companions: "Have you noticed that the one behind moves what he touches?

82   The feet of the dead usually do not so." And my good leader, who already stood at his breast, where the two natures are wedded,

85   replied: "He is indeed alive; and thus alone I must show him the dark valley; necessity induces us, and not pleasure.

88   One left off singing *hallelujah* who entrusted me with this strange task: he is not a robber nor I a thievish soul.

91   But by that Power through which I move my steps along so wild a road, give us one of yours to guide us

94   and show us where the ford is, and carry this one on his rump, for he is not a spirit that can walk upon the air."

97   Chiron turned on his right breast, and said to Nessus: "Go back and guide them, and, if you meet another company, make them give way."

100   Now we go with our trusty escort along the bank of the red boiling, where the boiled ones were uttering high shrieks.

103   I saw people immersed as far as the brow; and the great centaur said: "They are tyrants who put their hands to blood and to others' goods.

106   There they weep for their pitiless crimes: there is Alexander and fierce Dionysius, who gave Sicily such grievous years.

109 E quella fronte c'ha 'l pel così nero
è Azzolino; e quell'altro ch'è biondo
è Opizzo da Esti, il qual per vero
112 fu spento dal figliastro sù nel mondo."
Allor mi volsi al poeta, e quei disse:
"Questi ti sia or primo, e io secondo."
115 Poco più oltre il centauro s'affisse
sovr' una gente che 'nfino a la gola
parea che di quel bulicame uscisse.
118 Mostrocci un'ombra da l'un canto sola,
dicendo: "Colui fesse in grembo a Dio
lo cor che 'n su Tamisi ancor si cola."
121 Poi vidi gente che di fuor del rio
tenean la testa e ancor tutto 'l casso;
e di costoro assai riconobb' io.
124 Così a più a più si facea basso
quel sangue, sì che cocea pur li piedi;
e quindi fu del fosso il nostro passo.
127 "Sì come tu da questa parte vedi
lo bulicame che sempre si scema,"
disse 'l centauro, "voglio che tu credi
130 che da quest'altra a più a più giù prema
lo fondo suo, infin ch'el si raggiunge
ove la tirannia convien che gema.
133 La divina giustizia di qua punge
quell'Attila che fu flagello in terra,
e Pirro e Sesto; e in etterno munge
136 le lagrime che col bollor diserra
a Rinier da Corneto, a Rinier Pazzo,
che fecero a le strade tanta guerra."
139 Poi si rivolse e ripassossi 'l guazzo.

109　　　And that forehead with such black hair is
Azzolino; and that other blond one is Obizzo da Este,
who truly

112　　　was murdered by his bastard up in the world."
Then I turned to my poet, and he said: "Let him now
be first for you, and I second."

115　　　A little further along, the centaur stopped above
people who seemed to emerge from the boiling
stream as far as the throat.

118　　　He pointed to a soul by itself to one side, saying:
"That one cleft, in the bosom of God, the heart that
still drips blood along the Thames."

121　　　Then I saw people who held their heads out of the
river and then all their trunks; and of them I
recognized many.

124　　　Thus the blood became shallower and shallower,
until it was cooking only feet; and there was our
passing of the ditch.

127　　　"Just as on this side you see the boiling stream
diminish," said the centaur, "I would have you
believe

130　　　that on this other side it lowers its bed deeper and
deeper, until it reaches the depth where tyranny
must moan.

133　　　Over there God's justice pierces that Attila who
was a scourge on earth, and Pyrrhus and Sextus, and
for eternity milks

136　　　the tears unlocked by the boiling from Rinier da
Corneto and Rinier Pazzo, who waged such war on
the roads."

139　　　Then he turned and passed back over the ford.

NOTES

2. what else was there: This phrase is explained in lines 11–14.

4–9. Like that landslide . . . who was above: The landslide makes it possible for one to climb down to the foot of the mountain (see the note to 31–45). As the commentators have shown, this passage follows closely one in Albertus Magnus's *Meteorologica* (3.6) describing the famous Slavini di Marco, south of Rovereto, between Trento and Verona, which can in fact be descended on foot.

12. the infamy of Crete: The Minotaur—half-bull, half-man—is stretched out across the path. Pasiphaë, wife of King Minos of Crete (cf. 5.4, with note), fell in love with a white bull, with which she copulated disguised in a wooden cow built by Daedalus, the great inventor and artist. She gave birth to the Minotaur, for whom Minos had Daedalus build the labyrinth (in which he also imprisoned Daedalus). Defeated in war by the Cretans, the Athenians gave a yearly tribute of youths and maidens, supposedly devoured by the monster, until Theseus (9.54, with note), helped by Ariadne, penetrated the labyrinth and slew the Minotaur.

Dante knew this widely commented-upon myth mainly from Ovid (*Art of Love* 2.1–32; *Met.* 8.152–82) and Vergil (*Aen.* 6.14–33). Vergil relates that after his escape with the wax-and-feather wings, during which he lost his son Icarus (cf. *Inf.* 17.109–11), Daedalus built the temple to Apollo at Cumae, where the Sybil was priestess, and represented these events on its gate. Vergil thus establishes a parallel, which did not escape Dante, between the Cretan labyrinth, and Aeneas's path through the underworld and wanderings between Troy and Italy (Doob 1990). Like the centaurs, whom we meet later, the Minotaur represents the problematic union of rational and animal in human beings. For other myths about Crete, see 14.94–120, with notes.

15. like one broken within by anger: Note the parallels of phrasing with the passage on Plutus (7.9 and 14) and the self-biting anger of Filippo Argenti (8.62–63).

17. duke of Athens: In the wake of the Old French *Roman de Thèbes* (which retells the events of Statius's *Thebaid*), Theseus is frequently identified as the duke, rather than the king, of Athens (in the thirteenth and fourteenth centuries Athens was in fact a dukedom).

20. your sister: Ariadne, daughter of Minos and Pasiphaë (see the note to line 12).

22–25. Like a bull . . . the Minotaur do: Compare the famous simile in *Aen.* 2.222–24:

> qualis mugitus, fugit cum saucius aram
> taurus et incertam excussit cervice securim.

> [such bellowing, as when the wounded bull flees the altar
> and shakes from his neck the uncertain axe.]

Compare also Seneca, *Oedipus* 342–43:

> taurus duos
> perpessus ictus huc et huc dubius ruit

> [a bull, enduring two
> blows, rushes half-conscious here and there]

The vivid touch of the bull hopping on four legs perhaps implies that Dante imagines the Minotaur as having the body of a bull and the head of a man (perhaps also a human breast, like the centaurs) rather than a human body and bull's head, as in most of the representations in ancient art (not available to Dante). Ovid's "semibovemque virum semivirumque bovem" [both a man half-bull and a bull half-man] (*Art of Love* 2.24) is ambiguous.

29–30. the stones kept moving . . . new burden: Again note the emphasis on the novelty of the presence of the pilgrim's body (as in 8.27 and 30). There is the suggestion that Virgil's next comments are prompted by its presence.

31–45. You are thinking perhaps . . . broken down: Virgil now explains that the landslide happened just before the Harrowing of Hell (lines 37–39; cf. 4.52–73); Virgil is apparently unable to make the connection with the death of Christ (Matt. 27.45–51):

> Now from the sixth hour there was darkness over the whole earth, until the ninth hour. . . . And Jesus again crying with a loud voice, yielded up the ghost. And behold the veil of the temple was rent in two from the top even to the bottom, and the earth quaked, and the rocks were rent.

The explanation applies, of course, to all the landslides in Hell, and now it becomes clear that the damned shriek and curse God as they pass the one in 5.34 because it reminds them of the redemption from which they are excluded, Singleton (1965) pointed out (see also 11.1, 23.133–38). The great landslide, like its explanation, is appropriate to the circle of violence: for Dante the Crucifixion was the worst act of violence ever committed, and the union of rational and animal nature in man is implicitly related to the union of the divine and human natures in Christ. On the landslides providing the pilgrim's path, see Additional Note 16.

41–43. I thought the universe . . . into chaos: Another moment of remarkable insight on the part of Virgil. The traditional explanation of the darkening of the sun and the earthquake at Christ's death (Matt. 27.45, 51) was that both Heaven and Hell testified that he was the Creator who had died (Jerome, cited in Aquinas, *Catena aurea*; in *Super Matthaeum*, Albertus Magnus writes, "at [Christ's] cry so many signs appeared because the entire universe exclaimed that it could not endure that death"; in his commentary on Sacrobosco, Michael Scot recorded the tradition that the universe felt compassion). That Virgil's true insight into the cause of the earthquake is lost when he refers it to Empedocles' doctrine and thus discredits it, is probably another clue to his fate (see 8.128–30, 9.1–15, with notes). Empedocles (mentioned in 4.138), according to Aristotle (e.g., *Physics* 1.4–5), held that the universe alternates between a phase when strife predominates, driving things apart, and one when love draws things together, back toward the original chaos.

47. the river of blood: Clearly to be connected, in the body analogy (see Additional Note 2), with the great blood vessels surrounding the heart (the explicit comparison of the bloodstream with a river is frequent in Aristotle and other writers known to Dante); the association of irascible temperament with the element of fire in the blood is ancient. As Virgil will later explain (14.134–35), this is the river Phlegethon (*Aen.* 6.550–51; cf. 8.19 with note). The river of fire or blood is also a standard element of the popular traditions of the other world (Morgan 1990). Dante seems to have got the idea of correlating degree of immersion with seriousness of sin from the *Visio Pauli* or one of its descendants, perhaps through Vincent of Beauvais, where it is the punishment of tyrants (Silverstein 1937).

49–51. Oh blind cupidity . . . cook us so evilly: Greed and anger are thus identified as the chief motives leading to violence; both are implicitly compared with fire in the metaphor of spurs and cooking. The spurs also introduce the horse metaphor: comparing the interaction of the rational with the irascible-appetitive and that of a human being with a horse goes back to antiquity; in Plato (*Phaedrus* 246–48) the rational soul is a charioteer with two horses; in medieval versions (e.g., *Queste del saint Graal*, pp. 91–92) it is a mounted knight. Dante uses the metaphor frequently (e.g., *Convivio* 4.17.4; *Monarchia* 3.15.9); it underlies his entire treatment in the *Purgatorio* (see *Purg.* 16.85–96, with notes).

56. centaurs: Dante knew of the centaurs—half-man, half-horse—mainly from his poets and the mythographers. Unlike the other guardians of Hell, his centaurs seem not to be conceived as demons; they are apparently exempt from the punishment of the violent, though they were traditionally portrayed as being so. In addition to the myths mentioned below, the centaurs were famous for having attempted to carry off the bride and other women from the wedding of Theseus's friend Pirithous; the resulting fight—interpreted as rationality versus bestiality (see previous note)—was a favorite subject of Greek art and a main focus of Ovid's *Metamorphoses*, Book 12.

The centaurs inevitably suggest the figure of the mounted warrior (the early commentators compare them to the mounted mercenaries frequent in Italy); the ancients speculated that the myth originally derived from the surprise of those who first saw mounted invaders from Thessaly (where the centaurs were said to originate).

67–69. That is Nessus . . . avenged himself: According to the myth, after agreeing to carry Hercules' wife Deianira across the river Euenus, Nessus attempted to carry her off; Hercules killed him with an arrow dipped in the blood of the fire-breathing Lernaean Hydra. Dying, Nessus told Deianira that his shirt, dipped in his blood, would be an infallible love charm. Years later, hoping to regain his love, Deianira sent Hercules the shirt, which consumed his flesh. Hercules built and lit his own funeral pyre; his human part was purged away, and he became a god (cf. 9.98 and note).

71. Chiron: The wisest of the centaurs, especially learned in medicine, music, and astronomy, said to have been the teacher of both Hercules and Achilles (Statius, *Achilleid*, Book 1), and to have become the constellation Sagittarius at his death.

72. Pholus: Referred to by Vergil (*Georgics* 2.256), Ovid (*Met.* 12.306), and Lucan (*Pharsalia* 6.391) as particularly violent.

83–84. his breast, where the two natures are wedded: Where man leaves off and horse begins. In human beings the locus of the union of rational and animal being, according to Aristotle, is the breast, for he believed that the soul, with all its powers, dwells in the heart (see the note to 13.37–39); mind and passion meet and struggle there. Chiron's gaze would seem to refer to the wisdom about his double nature that enables him to rule.

85–96. He is indeed alive . . . upon the air: Virgil's appeal to Chiron is quite different from the harsh peremptory replies to Charon, Minos, and Plutus. The assumption seems to be that Chiron and the centaurs are not at war with God, "that Power" in line 91 (apparently indicated also in the fact that in line 119 Nessus mentions God).

88. One left off singing *hallelujah*: The reference is of course to Beatrice in Canto 2. Dante would have known that the Hebrew *hallelujah* [praise God] included one of the names of God.

97–99. Chiron . . . give way: The choice of Nessus as a guide is perhaps meant to emphasize the contrast between the centaurs, who are now guided by the rational Chiron in spite of their violence in life, and the souls being punished here. He is now a "trusty escort" for them, though he was not for Deianira.

104. tyrants: Dante glosses the term *tyrant* in the *Monarchia* (3.4.10) as referring to "those who attempt to twist the laws not to the common good but their own."

107. Alexander and fierce Dionysius: Probably Alexander the Great (third century B.C.) and Dionysius the tyrant of Syracuse (d. 397 B.C.), both of whom Dante's sources (Valerius Maximus, Paulus Orosius, and Brunetto Latini) identify as especially bloodthirsty.

110. Azzolino: Or Ezzelino III da Romano, lord of Treviso (d. 1259), head of the northern Ghibellines, called a son of the devil because of his cruelty (see *Par.* 9.25–63, with notes).

111–12. Obizzo da Este . . . up in the world: Obizzo II da Este, lord of Ferrara (d. 1293), a notoriously cruel ruler, was rumored to have been murdered by his son and successor Azzo VIII, whose illegitimacy Dante here apparently asserts (though *figliastro* may also mean "degenerate son").

119–20. That one cleft . . . drips blood along the Thames: The reference is to Guy of Montfort's murder of Henry of Cornwall, a cousin of Edward I of England, in Viterbo in 1271. The murder took place in church, during the assembly of cardinals to choose a pope. *Si cola,* translated here "drips blood," is uncertain; it may mean "is venerated." The first, stronger meaning would be a commentary on the fact that the murder, committed in the presence of the kings of France and of Naples, was never avenged or punished.

119. in the bosom of God: Nessus is one of the few speakers in Hell who refer to God without periphrasis (see the notes to lines 85–96).

134. Attila who was a scourge: Attila the Hun (d. A.D. 453), popularly called the "scourge of God," whom Dante erroneously credits with the destruction of Florence (13.148–49).

135. Pyrrhus . . . Sextus: "Pyrrhus" is probably the king of Epirus (third century B.C.), a compulsive fighter who gave his name to any victory so bloody for the victor as to constitute a defeat; or it may be Achilles' son, who kills King Priam in *Aen.* 2.526–58. "Sextus" is probably Sextus Pompeius, son of Pompey the Great (see the note to 9.22–27), a pirate, denounced by Lucan (6.419–22).

137. Rinier da Corneto . . . Rinier Pazzo: Notorious highwaymen of the thirteenth century, active respectively in southern and northern Tuscany. The name *Pazzo* means "crazy."

CANTO 13

1   Non era ancor di là Nesso arrivato,
quando noi ci mettemmo per un bosco
che da neun sentiero era segnato.

4   Non fronda verde, ma di color fosco,
non rami schietti, ma nodosi e 'nvolti,
non pomi v'eran, ma stecchi con tòsco.

7   Non han sì aspri sterpi né sì folti
quelle fiere selvagge che 'n odio hanno
tra Cécina e Corneto i luoghi cólti.

10   Quivi le brutte Arpie lor nidi fanno,
che cacciar de le Strofade i Troiani
con tristo annunzio di futuro danno.

13   Ali hanno late, e colli e visi umani,
piè con artigli, e pennuto 'l gran ventre;
fanno lamenti in su li alberi strani.

16   E 'l buon maestro "Prima che più entre,
sappi che se' nel secondo girone,"
mi cominciò a dire, "e sarai mentre

19   che tu verrai ne l'orribil sabbione.
Però riguarda ben; sì vederai
cose che torrien fede al mio sermone."

22   Io sentia d'ogne parte trarre guai
e non vedea persona che 'l facesse,
per ch'io tutto smarrito m'arrestai.

25   Cred' ïo ch'ei credette ch'io credesse
che tante voci uscisser, tra quei bronchi,
da gente che per noi si nascondesse.

28   Però disse 'l maestro: "Se tu tronchi
qualche fraschetta d'una d'este piante,
li pensier c'hai si faran tutti monchi."

CANTO 13

Seventh circle, second subcircle: the violent against themselves—the poisoned wood—Pier della Vigna—the chase of prodigals—the anonymous Florentine

1   Not yet had Nessus reached the other side, when we entered a wood that no path marked.

4   Not green leaves, but dark in color, not smooth branches, but knotted and twisted, no fruit was there, but thorns with poison.

7   Not such harsh thickets nor so dense do those wild beasts hold, that hate the cultivated places between Cécina and Corneto.

10   There the ugly Harpies make their nests, who drove the Trojans from the Strophades with dire prophecy of their future woe.

13   Their wings are broad, their necks and faces human, their feet have claws, and their great bellies are feathered; they utter laments on the strange trees.

16   And my good master: "Before you enter, know that you are in the second subcircle," he began to say, "and will be until

19   you come to the horrible sands. Therefore look carefully; and you will see things that would make you disbelieve my speech."

22   I heard cries of woe on every side but saw no person uttering them, so that all dismayed I stood still.

25   My belief is that he believed that I must believe that so many voices, among those thickets, came forth from people hidden from us.

28   Therefore my master said: "If you break off some little twig from one of these plants, the thoughts you have will all be cut off."

31   Allor porsi la mano un poco avante
e colsi un ramicel da un gran pruno;
e 'l tronco suo gridò: "Perché mi schiante?"

34   Da che fatto fu poi di sangue bruno,
ricominciò a dir: "Perché mi scerpi?
non hai tu spirto di pietade alcuno?

37   Uomini fummo, e or siam fatti sterpi:
ben dovrebb' esser la tua man più pia
se state fossimo anime di serpi."

40   Come d'un stizzo verde ch'arso sia
da l'un de' capi, che da l'altro geme
e cigola per vento che va via:

43   sì de la scheggia rotta usciva insieme
parole e sangue, ond'io lasciai la cima
cadere, e stetti come l'uom che teme.

46   "S'elli avesse potuto creder prima,"
rispuose 'l savio mio, "anima lesa,
ciò c'ha veduto pur con la mia rima,

49   non averebbe in te la man distesa;
ma la cosa incredibile mi fece
indurlo ad ovra ch'a me stesso pesa.

52   Ma dilli chi tu fosti, sì che 'n vece
d'alcun' ammenda tua fama rinfreschi
nel mondo sù, dove tornar li lece."

55   E 'l tronco: "Sì col dolce dir m'adeschi
ch'i' non posso tacere; e voi non gravi
perch' ïo un poco a ragionar m'inveschi.

58   Io son colui che tenni ambo le chiavi
del cor di Federigo e che le volsi,
serrando e diserrando, sì soavi

61   che dal secreto suo quasi ogn'uom tolsi;
fede portai al glorïoso offizio,
tanto ch'i' ne perde' li sonni e ' polsi.

64   La meretrice che mai da l'ospizio
di Cesare non torse li occhi putti,
morte comune e de le corti vizio,

67   infiammò contra me li animi tutti;
e li 'nfiammati infiammar sì Augusto
che ' lieti onor tornaro in tristi lutti.

31   Then I stretched out my hand a little before me and plucked a small branch from a great thornbush; and its stem cried out: "Why do you split me?"

34   When it had become dark with blood, it began again: "Why do you pluck me? Have you no spirit of pity at all?

37   We were men, and now we have become plants: truly your hand should be more merciful had we been the souls of serpents."

40   As when a green log is burnt at one end, from the other it drips and sputters as air escapes:

43   so from the broken stump came forth words and blood together, and I let the tip fall and stood like one afraid.

46   "If he could have believed first," replied my sage, "O wounded soul, what he has seen only in my rhymes,

49   he would not have stretched out his hand against you; but the incredible thing made me induce him to do what pains me as well.

52   But tell him who you were, so that as a kind of amends he may refresh your fame in the world above, where he is permitted to return."

55   And the branch: "You so tempt me with sweet speech that I cannot be silent, and let it not vex you that I am lured to speak a little.

58   I am he who held both the keys to the heart of Frederick and turned them, locking and unlocking, so gently

61   that I excluded almost everyone else from his intimacy; I kept faith with my glorious office, so much that because of it I lost sleep and vigor.

64   The whore who never turns her sluttish eyes away from Caesar's dwelling, the common death and vice of courts,

67   inflamed against me all spirits; and those inflamed inflamed Augustus so that my bright honors turned to sad mourning.

70   L'animo mio, per disdegnoso gusto,
        credendo col morir fuggir disdegno,
        ingiusto fece me contra me giusto.

73   Per le nove radici d'esto legno
        vi giuro che già mai non ruppi fede
        al mio segnor, che fu d'onor sì degno.

76   E se di voi alcun nel mondo riede,
        conforti la memoria mia, che giace
        ancor del colpo che 'nvidia le diede."

79   Un poco attese, e poi: "Da ch'el si tace,"
        disse 'l poeta a me, "non perder l'ora;
        ma parla, e chiedi a lui, se più ti piace."

82   Ond' ïo a lui: "Domandal tu ancora
        di quel che credi ch'a me satisfaccia;
        ch'i' non potrei, tanta pietà m'accora."

85   Perciò ricominciò: "Se l'om ti faccia
        liberamente ciò che 'l tuo dir priega,
        spirito incarcerato, ancor ti piaccia

88   di dirne come l'anima si lega
        in questi nocchi; e dinne, se tu puoi,
        s'alcuna mai di tai membra si spiega."

91   Allor soffiò il tronco forte, e poi
        si convertì quel vento in cotal voce:
        "Brievemente sarà risposto a voi.

94   Quando si parte l'anima feroce
        dal corpo ond' ella stessa s'è disvelta,
        Minòs la manda a la settima foce.

97   Cade in la selva, e non l'è parte scelta,
        ma là dove fortuna la balestra,
        quivi germoglia come gran di spelta.

100   Surge in vermena e in pianta silvestra;
        l'Arpie, pascendo poi de le sue foglie,
        fanno dolore e al dolor fenestra.

103   Come l'altre verrem per nostre spoglie,
        ma non però ch'alcuna sen rivesta,
        ché non è giusto aver ciò ch'om si toglie.

106   Qui le strascineremo, e per la mesta
        selva saranno i nostri corpi appesi,
        ciascuno al prun de l'ombra sua molesta."

70 My spirit, at the taste of disdain, believing by death to flee disdain, made me unjust against my just self.

73 By the strange new roots of this wood, I swear to you that I never broke faith with my lord, who was so worthy of honor.

76 And if either of you goes back to the world, strengthen my memory, languishing still beneath the blow that envy dealt it."

79 My poet waited a little, and then, "Now that he is silent," he said, "do not lose the moment, but speak, ask him what you will."

82 And I to him: "You ask him again about what you think will satisfy me; for I could not, so much pity weighs on my heart."

85 Therefore he began again: "So may one do liberally for you what your speech has begged, imprisoned spirit, let it please you still

88 to tell us how the soul is bound in these knots; and tell us, if you can, if anyone ever unties himself from such limbs."

91 The broken branch hissed loudly, and then that wind was converted into these words: "Briefly will you be answered.

94 When the fierce soul departs from the body from which it has uprooted itself, Minos sends it to the seventh mouth.

97 It falls into the wood, and no place is assigned to it, but where chance hurls it, there it sprouts like a grain of spelt.

100 It grows into a shoot, then a woody plant; the Harpies, feeding on its leaves, give it pain and a window for the pain.

103 Like the others, we will come for our remains, but not so that any may put them on again, for it is not just to have what one has taken from oneself.

106 Here we will drag them, and through the sad wood our corpses will hang, each on the thornbush of the soul that harmed it."

109   Noi eravamo ancora al tronco attesi,
       credendo ch'altro ne volesse dire,
       quando noi fummo d'un romor sorpresi:

112   similemente a colui che venire
       sente 'l porco e la caccia a sua posta,
       ch'ode le bestie, e le frasche stormire.

115   Ed ecco due da la sinistra costa,
       nudi e graffiati, fuggendo sì forte
       che de la selva rompieno ogne rosta.

118   Quel dinanzi: "Or accorri, accorri, morte!"
       E l'altro, cui pareva tardar troppo,
       gridava: "Lano, sì non furo accorte

121   le gambe tue a le giostre dal Toppo!"
       E poi che forse li fallia la lena,
       di sé e d'un cespuglio fece un groppo.

124   Di rietro a loro era la selva piena
       di nere cagne, bramose e correnti
       come veltri ch'uscisser di catena.

127   In quel che s'appiattò miser li denti,
       e quel dilaceraro a brano a brano;
       poi sen portar quelle membra dolenti.

130   Presemi allor la mia scorta per mano,
       e menommi al cespuglio che piangea
       per le rotture sanguinenti in vano.

133   "O Iacopo," dicea, "da Santo Andrea,
       che t'è giovato di me fare schermo?
       che colpa ho io de la tua vita rea?"

136   Quando 'l maestro fu sovr' esso fermo,
       disse: "Chi fosti, che per tante punte
       soffi con sangue doloroso sermo?"

139   Ed elli a noi: "O anime che giunte
       siete a veder lo strazio disonesto
       c'ha le mie fronde sì da me disgiunte,

142   raccoglietele al piè del tristo cesto.
       I' fui de la città che nel Batista
       mutò 'l primo padrone, ond' ei per questo

145   sempre con l'arte sua la farà trista.
       E se non fosse che 'n sul passo d'Arno
       rimane ancor di lui alcuna vista,

109   We were still attentive to the broken branch,
believing it had more to say, when we were
surprised by a noise:

112   like one who hears the boar and the hunt
approaching his post, who hears the beasts, and the
branches breaking.

115   And behold two on our left, naked and scratched,
fleeing so fast that they were breaking every
opposing branch in the forest.

118   The one in front: "Now hurry, hurry, death!" And
the other, who seemed to himself too slow, "Lano,
not so nimble were

121   your legs at the jousts at Toppo!" And perhaps
because his breath was failing, he made one clump of
himself and a bush.

124   Behind them the wood was full of black bitches,
ravenous and running like greyhounds loosed from
the chain.

127   They set their teeth to the one that had squatted,
tearing him to pieces, bit by bit; then they carried off
those suffering members.

130   My guide then took me by the hand and led me
to the bush that wept through its bleeding wounds in
vain.

133   "O Iacopo," it was saying, "di Santo Andrea, what
did it profit you to make a shield of me? how am I to
blame for your wicked life?"

136   When my master stopped above it, he said: "Who
were you, who through so many splintered branches
puff out with blood your sad speech?"

139   And he to us: "O souls who have arrived to see
the shameful rending that has so divided my leaves
from me,

142   gather them together at the foot of my sad shrub.
I was from the city that for the Baptist changed its
first patron, who for this

145   with his art will always grieve it. And were it not
that at the crossing of Arno there still remains some
trace of him,

148   que' cittadin che poi la rifondarno
       sovra 'l cener che d'Attila rimase,
       avrebber fatto lavorare indarno.
151   Io fei gibetto a me de le mie case."

148   those citizens who refounded it upon the ashes
left by Attila, would have labored in vain.
151   I made a gibbet for myself of my houses."

NOTES

1–9. Not yet ... Corneto: Dante begins each of the first three tercets of the canto with a negative, as well as each line of the middle tercet; compare the use of anaphora in the inscription of 3.1–9 and in Francesca's speech in 5.100–108.

1. the other side: Of the river of blood, traversed in 12.126.

3–6. a wood ... thorns with poison: The only vegetation in Hell, this trackless wood recalls that of Canto 1. The unnatural forest is a commonplace of ancient accounts of the approaches to Hades; compare Seneca, *Hercules* 689, 698–702 (Gmelin); Lucan, *Pharsalia* 3.400–414; and Statius, *Theb.* 4.419–42 (cf. 7.24–63).

9. Cécina and Corneto: The Cécina, a stream in Tuscany, and the hamlet of Corneto Tarquinia, in Latium, were on the boundaries of the Maremma, a swampy area, rich with wild animals, in west-central Italy.

10–12. Harpies ... future woe: The Strophades are small islands in the Ionian sea. In the *Aeneid*, the Harpies befoul the meal of the Trojan exiles and predict that they will one day have to eat their plates; the prophecy is fulfilled harmlessly (*Aen.* 3.210–57 and 7.111–34). The Harpies are described at *Aen.* 3.216–18, 225–28:

> Virginei volucrum voltus, foedissima ventris
> proluvies uncaeque manus et pallida semper
> ora fame. . . .
> At subitae horrifico lapsu de montibus adsunt
> Harpyiae et magnis quatiunt clangoribus alas
> diripiuntque dapes contactuque omnia foedant
> immundo, tum vox taetrum dira inter odorem.
>
> [The birds' faces are girlish, disgusting is the
> flow of their bellies, their hands are claws and
> always pale are their faces with hunger. . . .
> Suddenly in terrifying descent from the mountains
> the Harpies arrive and noisily shake their great wings;
> they tear at the food, and with their filthy touch all is
> polluted, then the dire voice is heard over the foul smell.]

15. laments on the strange trees: As the commentators have pointed out, the adjective *strani* [strange] can modify either *lamenti* [laments] or *alberi* [trees]. Benvenuto pointed out that both alternatives make sense; the ambiguity is probably intended.

17. you are in the second subcircle: That of the suicides. Dante draws both on classical views about suicide and on Christian ones stemming from Saint Ambrose and Saint Augustine. Plato's Socrates argues that suicide is like a soldier's leaving his post in battle without an order from his commander (*Phaedo* 62); the Judeo-Christian condemnation of suicide follows from the commandment "Thou shalt not kill" (Ex. 20.13), a view developed by Augustine in a rigorous critique of the Stoic and Epicurean theory of suicide as permissible or even noble (*City of God* 1.17). See also the notes to lines 72, 73–75.

21. things that would make you disbelieve my speech: They would not be believable if I were to relate them. This line begins a series of references to the theme of trust and belief in the canto.

25–27. My belief . . . hidden from us: The mannered triple construction, which coordinates the narrating poet's awareness of Virgil's awareness of the pilgrim, distributed over several tenses and distinct moods of the verb (present, simple past, and imperfect subjunctive), has excited much comment. De Sanctis and his followers saw it as alluding to the highly mannered style of Pier delle Vigne's Latin epistles; later views (Spitzer 1942) see these and the other contortions of the language of the canto as expressive of the problematic of suicide (see the notes to lines 70–72). We see this passage as one of several devices expressing the tension between the living (thus, integrated) Dante and the suicides, who violently destroy the unity of soul and body. The lines render the pilgrim's hesitation and puzzlement as well as pointing to the special, sometimes telepathic relation he shares with Virgil (for another example, see 23.21–22, with notes).

26. voices, among those thickets: The scene suggests a parallel with Adam and Eve's hiding among the trees of the Garden after the Fall (Gen. 3.8), which, according to Saint Paul, caused a "war" to break out "within the members" of the human person (Romans 7.23) (see the note to line 72).

31–44. Then I stretched . . . like one afraid: According to *Aen.* 3.13–65, Aeneas, in Thrace in his first landfall after leaving Troy and wishing to sacrifice to the gods, plucks wood in a thick grove; the roots bleed, and from underground, Polydorus, youngest son of Priam, tells of his murder (*Aen.* 3.39–48):

(Eloquar an sileam?) gemitus lacrimabilis imo
auditur tumulo et vox reddita fertur ad auris:
Quid miserum, Aenea, laceras? iam parce sepulto,
parce pias scelerare manus . . .
nam Polydorus ego. Hic confixum ferrea texit
telorum seges et iaculis increvit acutis.
Tum vero ancipiti mentem formidine pressus
obstipui steteruntque comae et vox faucibus haesit.

[Shall I speak or keep silent? from the depths
of the mound a tearful moan is heard and a voice comes to my ears:
"Why do you tear the miserable, Aeneas? spare one who is buried,
keep your pious hands from pollution . . .
for I am Polydorus. Murdered here, an iron crop
of spears and sharp javelins has grown up to cover me."
Then truly, my mind oppressed by wavering fear,
I froze, my hair stood on end and my voice caught in my throat.]

32. plucked a small branch: In the Polydorus episode, Aeneas pulls up plants by the roots. The pilgrim's plucking of a branch may have been suggested by *Aen.* 6.133–47, where the Sybil tells Aeneas that he must obtain the golden bough if he is to enter Hades and return. In *Aen.* 3.22–40, the "plucking" of the bleeding branch, sure sign that Thrace is not his destined home, is a negative anticipation of the plucking of the golden bough.

33. its stem cried out . . . split me: The "stem" (*tronco*) is the part of the branch still on the tree. The soul speaks appropriately, since he is now a plant (cf. "pluck," line 35): this tension between human and vegetable persists through the canto and involves rhetorical figures creating difficulty (antithesis, etymological figures, alliteration, catachresis, and others).

37–39. We were men . . . souls of serpents: Paratore (1968) observes that in this tercet Piero refers to the three levels of animate being: humans ("men"), animals ("serpents"), and plants ("sticks"). For other such triplets, see lines 64–75. Canto 13 maintains the parallel of the circle of violence with the human breast (see Additional Note 2). It draws on traditional metaphors (the heart was a forest in its multitude of desires, as in Augustine's *Confessions* 2.1.1; desires are like birds; etc.) and on Aristotle's doctrine that the heart was the dwelling of the soul, from which it exerted all its powers, rational, animal (sensation, appetite, and motion), and vegetative (nutrition, growth, and reproduction). (Aristotle thought that the function of the brain, like that of the lungs, was to temper the vital heat in the heart, the "hearth" of the body.)

Combining the principle of the unity of the soul with that of the essence of humanity being the *union* of body and soul (6.110–12 and *Purg.* 4.1–12, 25.37–75, with notes), one can see the *contrapasso* here: since the suicides destroy the most basic unity of the human being, that of body and soul, they suffer a reduction and dispersal of the soul's complex powers, all now fulfilled, if at all, in distorted and painful ways. Note the frequency of the terminology of binding and knotting, the traditional language for the union of body and soul (e.g., John Donne, "The Extasie," line 64: "The subtle knot that makes us man"; cf. Shakespeare, *Antony and Cleopatra* 5.2.303–4).

40–44. As when a green log . . . words and blood: For the suicides to speak—to express themselves—they must suffer wounds, like those which caused the death of their bodies.

45. like one afraid: See *Aen.* 3.29–30 and 47–48, describing Aeneas's terror at the bleeding, speaking plants.

46–51. If he could have believed . . . pains me as well: Virgil must subject Piero to violence similar to what the Harpies inflict, so that the pilgrim may be instructed. In his first *Sermon on the Song of Songs*, Bernard of Clairvaux draws an extended analogy between the "opening" (interpretation) of a text of scripture and the breaking of the Eucharistic bread; this traditional analogy would seem to underlie this passage, in which the breaking of Piero is necessary to the disclosure of the nature of suicide.

55. You so tempt me: Literally, "you lure me with bait." " I am lured" (line 57) translates *m'inveschi* (literally, "I am enlimed," a metaphor derived from the use of birdlime, a sticky substance used in hunting small birds). This ceremoniously rhetorical opening suggests Piero's elaborate chancery style. Beyond that, they are richly ironic, given the Harpies and Piero's being "bound" in his thornbush. In addition, it is probably relevant that falconry was a favorite occupation of Piero's lord, the emperor Frederick II (see 10.119 and note).

58–61. I am he . . . from his intimacy: The speaker, never named but immediately identifiable, is Pietro or Piero delle Vigne (or della Vigna), born into a modest family in Capua in southern Italy (Kingdom of Naples and Sicily) around 1190. After law studies at Bologna, Piero became in 1231 a notary in the imperial chancery, the most important nonecclesiastical bureaucracy of the period. He rose rapidly to great influence and by 1234 was a principal author of the *Constitutions of Melfi* or *Liber augustalis*, Frederick's epoch-making code of laws. Piero was famous as a jurist and judge and in 1246 was appointed protonotary (in charge of government publications) and logothete (official spokesman). He was well known as a Latin prose stylist, especially in his widely circulated letters, and wrote vernacular poetry; he is cited as an exemplar of rhetorical skill in Brunetto Latini's treatise on rhetoric (see Canto 15). In 1248 Frederick was excommunicated a second time by the pope; in the same year, Piero was implicated, probably falsely, in a conspiracy against him. Arrested in 1249, he was blinded and killed himself, apparently by dashing his head against a wall. Frederick later held up Piero as an example of corruption in office, a traitor, and a "Simon" (Simon Magus; cf. Canto 19); it is beyond dispute that Piero had reaped enormous financial gain while in office.

At the height of his influence, just as his namesake Peter the Apostle held "the keys of the kingdom" (Matt. 16.19), Piero held the "keys" of influence with Frederick, whose propaganda proclaimed him God's vicar on earth. A letter from a friend of Piero's describes him as the keyholder of the emperor: "he closes and none opens; he opens and none can close," borrowing, like Dante here, the formula from Is. 22.22, which is in turn the basis for Matt. 16.19 and again for Apoc. 3.7. The smoothness of Piero's operations as key turner stands in stark contrast to the violence of his death. And there is further irony: in Italian, *soave* [gently] is a pun on the name of Frederick's hereditary lands, Swabia (Italian, *Soave*).

62. I kept faith with my glorious office: Coming so emphatically after the mention of the emperor's name (Italian, *Federigo*), Piero's assertion of faith (Italian, *fede*) inescapably suggests a play on the first two syllables of the name, perhaps also on the last two syllables (as equivalent to *ricco*, rich).

63. I lost sleep and vigor: A similar phrase to 1.90, describing the pilgrim's terror before the wolf.

64–66. The whore . . . vice of courts: Envy, the typical vice of courts, here personified; note the triple periphrasis for Envy, capped by the explicit naming only in line 78 (on envy, cf. 1.111, 6.74, and 15.68).

67–68. inflamed against me . . . inflamed Augustus: The contiguity of the three forms of the verb *infiammare* [to inflame] suggests the spreading of the fire by contagion. A number of commentators cite Piero's *Eulogy* for Frederick II, which ends with the word *inflammet* ("let it enflame," said of how examples of fidelity incite others). This is also a key example of the triple constructions we have been following, closely related to the triple periphrasis of Envy; to the three honorific terms for Frederick, named only in verse 58 (Caesar, 65; Augustus, 68; and Lord, 75); to the sequence on *degno* [worthy] and its compound *disdegno* [scorn] in 70, 71, and 75; and to the sequence on "unjust" and "just" (*ingiusto* and *giusto*) in 72, and "I swear" (*giuro*) in 74.

68–69. bright honors turned to sad mourning: The fire imagery is maintained in the changes from honors (*lieti* [Latin, *laeti*] associates the honors with the traditional white color of festive garments) to the ashes represented by the black of mourning. Piero's fate follows the structure of a typical medieval tragedy, the sudden overturning of good fortune and descent into misfortune.

70–72. My spirit . . . against my just self: That is, Piero killed himself to avoid scorn and humiliation, or perhaps to avoid the contempt of his lord, Frederick, but in committing suicide he committed a crime against his own innocence. In his attack on the Stoic idealizing of suicide, to him equivalent to murder, Augustine maintains that the suicide of an otherwise innocent person is a more serious crime than that of a guilty one (*City of God* 1.17; cf. the note to line 87).

70. at the taste of disdain: There has been no satisfactory explanation of the phrase *per disdegnoso gusto* [through disdainful taste], though there is some agreement that it cannot refer to taste in the sense of temperament. We follow Guido da Pisa and Buti, who understood it to refer to Piero's undergoing scorn; others take it to refer to Piero's scorn for his enemies.

72. made me unjust against my just self: In the Italian, this line is centered on the paradox of suicide in the phrase *me contra me* [me against me], which condenses and almost spatializes the self-division of suicide; the order of terms, like Piero's act, gives first place to the injustice that destroys his innocence: that is, *ingiusto* [unjust] precedes *giusto* [just].

73–75. By the strange new roots . . . worthy of honor: Italian *nove* can mean "new," "strange," or even "nine."

These lines, which come at the middle of the canto and are the culmination of Piero's speech, are the focus of sharp disagreement. Most commentators take them as Dante's exoneration of Piero. This view is borne out by contemporary sources, most of which agree that the evidence against Piero was fabricated.

Still, Piero's suicide is itself an act of multiple disobedience: its victim is immediately the body, which the soul should care for; Piero's suicide also contravenes the emperor's prerogative of determining capital punishment, written by Piero into the *Constitutions of Melfi* (Title 14) of 1234, and this disobedience is compounded by violation of God's law. Aquinas's discussion of suicide draws both on Deut. 32.39 and on the idea, found in both Aristotle and Cicero's *Somnium Scipionis*, that in suicide the soul disobeys also by failing to care for the "servant" in its charge, the body. In a certain sense, then, Piero, the new Peter, "betrays" both Frederick and Christ. The question of "keeping faith" in the canto thus includes keeping faith with the self by husbanding and caring for both body and soul, as well as with Nature and God: principal subjects, as we have seen, of the circle of violence.

74. I never broke faith: See also line 62 and the words of Ovid's Dryope (*Met.* 9. 371–73):

> Si qua fides miseris, hoc me per numina iuro
> non meruisse nefas: patior sine crimine poenam!
> Viximus innocuae. . . .

> [If the miserable can be believed, I swear by the gods
> that I have not deserved this curse; I suffer punishment without a crime!
> I lived innocent. . . .]

84. so much pity weighs on my heart: As a lay intellectual cast out and condemned to death by his own city, Dante had strong reasons to identify with Piero (Olschki 1940).

87. imprisoned spirit: Virgil's phrase recalls Cavalcante's "blind prison" (10.58–59); the Epicureans who "make the soul die with the body" (10.13; the phrase applies also to the suicides) include the emperor Frederick. Rabuse (1958) showed that Dante's language for the imprisonment of the souls in the trees echoes the Neoplatonic argument that suicide, rather than freeing the soul from the body, binds it more tightly to materiality (Macrobius, *Commentarii* 1.13–14), and in Dante's version to a lower form of materiality than that of the human body (see the note to lines 97–100).

97–100. It falls into the wood . . . then a woody plant: The language distantly recalls Christ's parable of the sower (Matt. 13.1–23), where the seed is the word of God and the various places it falls (stony places, hard path, thorns, and good soil) reflect the way the word is received by those who hear it; the parable is combined here with the metaphor of the vine leaves (John 15.1–7), where Christ is the vine and his disciples its branches. Piero's name, "of the vine," and his status as a thornbush invoke the parallel with Christ as vine and tree of life (see also the parable of the vine in Is. 5.1–7, especially verse 6: "I will make it desolate . . . briers and thorns shall come up"). Killing himself, Piero has cast himself out of the vine (recalled by his own name) and cast the "seed" of his soul into the unfruitful wood of Hell. His suicide makes him one of those who could not conserve the word in their hearts when tribulation arose (Matt. 13.20–21); and see Boethius, *Consolation* 1.6: "The nature and strength of these troubles is such that they can dislodge a man, but they cannot tear him out and completely uproot him." Boethius's *Consolation* is directly relevant to Piero's suicide, for it is the Middle Ages' most influential discussion of the injustice of rulers: Boethius was accused, he claimed falsely, of conspiracy against the Gothic king Theodoric; his theme is the philosophical and spiritual victory over misfortune, injustice, and death. The first book of the *Convivio*, written early in Dante's exile, shows that Dante identified very strongly with Boethius's fate.

103–5. Like the others . . . taken from oneself: Dante departs from orthodoxy here, which calls for the return of all souls to their bodies on the Day of Judgment.

107. our corpses will hang: Cassell (1984) showed that the iconography of the corpse in the tree derives from that of the suicide of Judas (see the note to 34.63).

109–29. We were still attentive . . . suffering members: These lines show the punishment of the spendthrifts, after which we revert to the suicides. The link between suicide and prodigal waste is suggested in Aristotle's *Nichomachean Ethics* 4.1: "The destruction of the good through which man lives is a certain kind of destruction of himself" (cited in *Summa theol.* 2a 2ae, q. 119, a. 3).

112–14. like one . . . branches breaking: Gmelin notes that Dante abbreviates a simile of Statius (*Theb.* 4.494–99), describing Eteocles of Thebes as he waits for ghosts, conjured by Tiresias and Manto, who will predict the future of Thebes; the augury takes place near the Field of Mars, where the city's first inhabitants were sown as dragon seed. For Florence and Thebes, see the note to lines 143–44.

118–19. The one in front . . . And the other: Identified as, respectively, Arcolano da Squarcia di Riccolfo Maconi, a Sienese said by Boccaccio to be a member of the "spendthrifts' club" of Siena (see 29.130), killed in 1288 near Pieve al Toppo; and Iacopo da Santo Andrea, named in line 133, a member of the court of Frederick II, murdered by order of Azzolino da Romano (for Azzolino, see 12.110 and note). Lana records that Iacopo ordered the burning of his own property in order to satisfy a whimsical desire to see a fire.

118. Now hurry, hurry, death: Perhaps an appeal for extinction (and thus release from suffering) as some argue; but Lano's plea seems especially to reevoke the scene of his death in battle, which, according to the early commentators, he voluntarily sought as a solution to the ruin caused by his squandering.

123. he made one clump . . . a bush: Thus this squanderer's pose echoes the suicides, who have literally been joined to their bushes.

128. tearing him to pieces: See Ovid, *Met.* 3.250: "dilacerant falsi dominum sub imagine cervi" [they tear their master apart under the false image of a stag]. In the allegorical reading by Fulgentius, the story of Actaeon (grandson of the founder of Thebes) became an example of the destructive effects of excessive spending. In the Ovidian tale, Actaeon is torn apart by his own hounds after being transformed into a stag by Diana, goddess of hunting, outraged at being seen naked. For Fulgentius, this means that Actaeon renounced hunting when he saw its true nature (hence his mutation into a deer) but could not renounce his beloved dogs, who ate him out of house and home. For other tales of squandering, see Canto 29.

143–44. the city that . . . its first patron: The first patron of Florence was Mars, but when it was converted to Christianity the city took as its patron Saint John the Baptist; in Dante's day the Baptistery of Saint John was said to have formerly been a temple of Mars.

143–50. I was from the city . . . in vain: This unnamed suicide says that Florence, destroyed by Attila (besieged in fact by Totila in A.D. 410) and refounded in 801, traditionally by Charlemagne, would not have survived had not a fragmentary equestrian statue, thought to be of Mars, remained on the north side of the Arno, near what is now the Ponte Vecchio. The suicide's discourse seems pagan in attributing such influence to the offended god. However, it was believed that Florence had been refounded with Mars and Mercury in the ascendant; therefore the city was understood to be astrologically inclined both to warfare (Mars) and to commerce (Mercury).

The passage thus can be taken as a reflection on Florence as it changed from a small commune to a great commercial city, gradually exchanging feudal and military values for commercial ones (the image of Saint John the Baptist was stamped on the gold florin, the foundation of Florentine financial power; for the florin, see the notes to 30.89–90). Rabuse (1958) argues that there is in the *Inferno* a general pattern whereby the successive circles of Hell correspond to the order—and influence—of the planets; the circle of violence as a whole would reflect the astrological influence of Mars on the souls damned there and is the principal focus of his book.

151. I made a gibbet for myself of my houses: That is, the anonymous suicide hanged himself in his house. Since the first commentators, there has been no consensus as to his identity; his anonymity facilitates his being taken as a symbol of the "divided city" itself destroyed by its warring factions, its "houses." Lucan wrote that the people of Rome "in sua victrici conversum viscera dextra" [turned its victorious right hand against its own vitals] (*Pharsalia* 1.3); civil war is thus the suicide of the body politic, as suicide is civil war within the self. For the relation of the themes of civil war, suicide, and dismemberment in this canto, see MacKinnon [1988] 1989.

CANTO 14

1   Poi che la carità del natio loco
mi strinse, raunai le fronde sparte
e rende'le a colui, ch'era già fioco.

4   Indi venimmo al fine ove si parte
lo secondo giron dal terzo, e dove
si vede di giustizia orribil arte.

7   A ben manifestar le cose nove,
dico che arrivammo ad una landa
che dal suo letto ogne pianta rimove;

10   la dolorosa selva l'è ghirlanda
intorno, come 'l fosso tristo ad essa:
quivi fermammo i passi a randa a randa.

13   Lo spazzo era una rena arida e spessa,
non d'altra foggia fatta che colei
che fu da' piè di Caton già soppressa.

16   O vendetta di Dio, quanto tu dei
esser temuta da ciascun che legge
ciò che fu manifesto a li occhi mei!

19   D'anime nude vidi molte gregge
che piangean tutte assai miseramente,
e parea posta lor diversa legge.

22   Supin giacea in terra alcuna gente,
alcuna si sedea tutta raccolta,
e altra andava continüamente.

25   Quella che giva 'ntorno era più molta,
e quella men che giacëa al tormento,
ma più al duolo avea la lingua sciolta.

28   Sovra tutto 'l sabbion, d'un cader lento,
piovean di foco dilatate falde,
come di neve in alpe sanza vento.

CANTO 14

Seventh circle, third subcircle: the violent against God, Nature, or industry—the burning plain—Capaneus—the rivers of Hell—the Old Man of Crete

1   Compelled by love of my birthplace, I gathered together the scattered leaves and returned them to him, who was already silent.

4   Thence we came to the boundary where the second subcircle is divided from the third, and where one sees a horrible art of justice.

7   To make the new things clearly manifest, I say that we arrived at a plain that removes every plant from its bed;

10   the grieving wood is a garland around it, as the sad ditch is to the wood: we halted our steps at the very edge.

13   The floor was coarse, dry sand, not made differently from that once trodden by the feet of Cato.

16   O vengeance of God, how much must you be feared by everyone who reads what was made manifest to my eyes!

19   Of naked souls I saw many flocks, all weeping wretchedly, and different laws seemed to govern them.

22   Some were lying supine on the earth, some were sitting all huddled, and some were walking ceaselessly.

25   The flock that was walking was largest by far, and fewest were those lying to be tortured, but their tongues were looser to cry out.

28   Over all the sand there rained, with a slow falling, broad flakes of fire, like snow in the mountains without wind.

31 Quali Alessandro in quelle parti calde
d'Indïa vide sopra 'l süo stuolo
fiamme cadere infino a terra salde,

34 per ch'ei provide a scalpitar lo suolo
con le sue schiere, acciò che lo vapore
mei si stingueva mentre ch'era solo:

37 tale scendeva l'etternale ardore,
onde la rena s'accendea, com' esca
sotto focile, a doppiar lo dolore.

40 Sanza riposo mai era la tresca
de le misere mani, or quindi or quinci
escotendo da sé l'arsura fresca.

43 I' cominciai: "Maestro, tu che vinci
tutte le cose, fuor che ' demon duri
ch'a l'intrar de la porta incontra uscinci,

46 chi è quel grande che non par che curi
lo 'ncendio e giace dispettoso e torto,
sì che la pioggia non par che 'l maturi?"

49 E quel medesmo, che si fu accorto
ch'io domandava il mio duca di lui,
gridò: "Qual io fui vivo, tal son morto.

52 Se Giove stanchi 'l suo fabbro da cui
crucciato prese la folgore aguta
onde l'ultimo dì percosso fui—

55 o s'elli stanchi li altri a muta a muta
in Mongibello a la focina negra,
chiamando "Buon Vulcano, aiuta, aiuta!"

58 sì com' el fece a la pugna di Flegra—
e me saetti con tutta sua forza,
non ne potrebbe aver vendetta allegra."

61 Allora il duca mio parlò di forza
tanto, ch'i' non l'avea sì forte udito:
"O Capaneo, in ciò che non s'ammorza

64 la tua superbia, se' tu più punito;
nullo martirio, fuor che la tua rabbia,
sarebbe al tuo furor dolor compito."

67 Poi si rivolse a me con miglior labbia,
dicendo: "Quei fu l'un d'i sette regi
ch'assiser Tebe; ed ebbe, e par ch'elli abbia,

31   Like the flames that Alexander saw, in those hot parts of India, falling down on his host, whole all the way to the ground,

34   so that he provided for the earth to be trampled by his squadrons, since the burning was better extinguished while separated:

37   so the eternal burning was coming down, and the sand caught fire, like tinder beneath the flint, to double the suffering.

40   Without any rest ever was the dancing of their wretched hands, brushing away the fresh burning, now from there, now from here.

43   I began: "Master, you who overcome all things, save the hard demons who came out against us at the gate,

46   who is that great one who seems not to mind the fire, and lies there scornful and frowning, so that the rain does not seem to ripen him?"

49   And he himself, when he perceived that I was questioning my leader about him, cried out: "As I was alive, so am I dead.

52   Though Jove tire out his smith, from whom he wrathful took the sharp thunderbolt that struck me on the last day—

55   and though he weary the others, turn after turn, at the black forge in Mongibello, calling, 'Good Vulcan, help, help!'

58   as he did at the battle of Phlegra—and strike me with all his force, he could not have happy vengeance thereby."

61   Then my leader spoke more forcefully than I had ever heard him: "O Capaneus, since your pride

64   is not extinguished, you are punished more; no punishment, other than your rage, would be suffering of a measure with your fury."

67   Then he turned back to me with a better look, saying: "This was one of the seven kings who besieged Thebes; and he had, and seems still to have,

70   Dio in disdegno, e poco par che 'l pregi;
ma, com' io dissi lui, li suoi dispetti
sono al suo petto assai debiti fregi.

73   Or mi vien dietro, e guarda che non metti
ancor li piedi ne la rena arsiccia,
ma sempre al bosco tien li piedi stretti."

76   Tacendo divenimmo là 've spiccia
fuor de la selva un picciol fiumicello,
lo cui rossore ancor mi raccapriccia.

79   Quale del Bulicame esce ruscello
che parton poi tra lor le peccatrici,
tal per la rena giù sen giva quello.

82   Lo fondo suo e ambo le pendici
fatt' era 'n pietra, e ' margini dallato,
per ch'io m'accorsi che 'l passo era lici.

85   "Tra tutto l'altro ch'i' t'ho dimostrato
poscia che noi intrammo per la porta
lo cui sogliare a nessuno è negato,

88   cosa non fu da li tuoi occhi scorta
notabile com' è 'l presente rio,
che sovra sé tutte fiammelle ammorta."

91   Queste parole fuor del duca mio;
per ch'io 'l pregai che mi largisse 'l pasto
di cui largito m'avëa il disio.

94   "In mezzo mar siede un paese guasto,"
diss' elli allora, "che s'appella Creta,
sotto 'l cui rege fu già 'l mondo casto.

97   Una montagna v'è che già fu lieta
d'acqua e di fronde, che si chiamò Ida;
or è diserta come cosa vieta.

100   Rëa la scelse già per cuna fida
del suo figliuolo, e per celarlo meglio
quando piangea, vi facea far le grida.

103   Dentro dal monte sta dritto un gran veglio,
che tien volte le spalle inver' Dammiata
e Roma guarda come süo speglio.

106   La sua testa è di fin oro formata,
e puro argento son le braccia e 'l petto,
poi è di rame infino a la forcata;

70 God in disdain, and respects him little; but, as I
said, his spite is the ornament his breast deserves.

73 Now follow me, and beware that you not place
your foot on the burning sand as yet, but keep your
feet still close within the wood."

76 Silent we came to where a little stream spurts out
of the wood; its red color still makes me shudder.

79 As from Bulicame a river comes forth that the
sinning women then divide among themselves, so
this one flowed down across the sand.

82 Its bed and both its banks were made of stone,
and the margins on the sides, so that I perceived our
path lay there.

85 "Among all the other things I have shown you
since we entered the gate whose threshold is denied
to none,

88 nothing has been perceived by your eyes as
notable as the present river, which extinguishes all the
flames above it."

91 These were my leader's words, and I begged him
to grant me the food, since he had granted me the
hunger for it.

94 "In the midst of the sea lies a ruined land," he said
then, "called Crete, under whose king the world once
was chaste.

97 A mountain is there that once was happy with
water and foliage, called Ida; now it is desolate, like
an outworn thing.

100 Rhea chose it once to be the trusted cradle of her
son, and, the better to hide him when he cried,
ordered the shouting there.

103 Within the mountain stands erect a great old man,
with his back toward Damietta, looking toward Rome
as to his mirror.

106 His head is formed of fine gold, and pure silver
are his arms and breast; then he is of brass as far as
the fork;

109   da indi in giuso è tutto ferro eletto,
salvo che 'l destro piede è terra cotta;
e sta 'n su quel, più che 'n su l'altro, eretto.

112   Ciascuna parte, fuor che l'oro, è rotta
d'una fessura che lagrime goccia,
le quali, accolte, fóran quella grotta.

115   Lor corso in questa valle si diroccia;
fanno Acheronte, Stige e Flegetonta;
poi sen van giù per questa stretta doccia

118   infin, là ove più non si dismonta,
fanno Cocito; e qual sia quello stagno
tu lo vedrai; però qui non si conta."

121   E io a lui: "Se 'l presente rigagno
si diriva così dal nostro mondo,
perché ci appar pur a questo vivagno?"

124   Ed elli a me: "Tu sai che 'l loco è tondo;
e tutto che tu sie venuto molto,
pur a sinistra, giù calando al fondo,

127   non se' ancor per tutto 'l cerchio vòlto;
per che, se cosa n'apparisce nova,
non de' addur maraviglia al tuo volto."

130   E io ancor: "Maestro, ove si trova
Flegetonta e Letè? ché de l'un taci,
e l'altro di' che si fa d'esta piova."

133   "In tutte tue question certo mi piaci,"
rispuose, "ma 'l bollor de l'acqua rossa
dovea ben solver l'una che tu faci.

136   Letè vedrai, ma fuor di questa fossa,
là dove vanno l'anime a lavarsi
quando la colpa pentuta è rimossa."

139   Poi disse: "Omai è tempo da scostarsi
dal bosco; fa che di retro a me vegne:
li margini fan via, che non son arsi,

142   e sopra loro ogne vapor si spegne."

109   from there downward he is all refined iron, except
that his right foot is baked clay; and on that one,
more than on the other, he stands erect.

112   Each part of him, except his golden head, is
broken by a crack that drips tears, which, gathering,
bore through that cave.

115   Their course plunges into this valley; they become
Acheron, Styx, and Phlegethon; then they go on
down through this narrow duct,

118   until, where there is no further descent, they
become Cocytus; and what that pool is like you will
see, so that I do not describe it here."

121   And I to him: "If the present stream flows down
in this way from our world, why does it appear only
at this border?"

124   And he to me: "You know that the place is
circular; and although you have come a long way,
descending and turning always to the left, toward the
bottom,

127   you have not yet turned through the whole circle;
so that if we see some new thing, it should not bring
amazement to your face."

130   And I again: "Master, where are Phlegethon and
Lethe? for you are silent about the one, and the other
you say flows from this rain of tears."

133   "In all your questions, certainly, you please me,"
he replied, "but the boiling of the red water ought to
answer one of them.

136   Lethe you will see, but outside this ditch, there
where the souls go to be washed once their repented
guilt has been removed."

139   Then he said: "Now it is time for us to leave the
wood; see that you come behind me: the margins
provide a path, for they are not burned,

142   and above them every flame is extinguished."

NOTES

1–3. Compelled . . . already silent: Note the contrast between the pilgrim's "love," which attempts to gather and reunite, and the suicides' violent division of themselves.

3. him, who was already silent: The unnamed Florentine suicide of 13.130–51, who has fallen silent. Chiavacci Leonardi observes that this verse establishes that *fioco* could mean "mute" in 1.63 (see the note to 1.62–63).

6. a horrible art of justice: "Horrible" (*orribil*) means what causes one's hair to bristle (cf. 3.31, with note): the ingenuity of God's justice should terrify one.

8–39. a plain . . . to double the suffering: The punishment of the violent against God, nature, or industry (11.46–51) is derived from the biblical account of the destruction of the "cities of the plain," Sodom and Gomorrha, because of the violent homosexuality of the citizens (Genesis 19), especially verses 24–28:

> And the Lord rained upon Sodom and Gomorrha brimstone and fire from the Lord out of heaven. And he destroyed these cities, and all the country about, all the inhabitants of the cities, and all things that spring from the earth. And his [Lot's] wife looking behind her, was turned into a statue of salt. And Abraham got up early in the morning, and in the place where he had stood before with the Lord, he looked toward Sodom and Gomorrha, and the whole land of that country: and he saw the ashes rise up from the earth as the smoke of a furnace.

The destruction of the cities of the plain was said to be a figure of the Last Judgment as early as the New Testament (2 Peter 2.6–9). The burning plain of Cantos 14–17, like that of Sodom (cf. Gen. 13.10), and like the wood of the suicides, is an anti-Eden (on the desolation of Crete, see the note to lines 94–120).

In the body analogy, the burning plain represents a perversion of fundamental powers of the human soul, located, according to Aristotelian doctrine, in the heart (see the note to 13.37–39). The emphasis on sterility derives especially from the biblical condemnation of homosexuality as directly counter to God's injunction to Adam and Eve and to Noah to people the world (Gen. 1.28, 8.17, and 9.1). The thread of logic that links the three sins of this subcircle (blasphemy, sodomy, and usury)—to modern minds rather disparate (but see the note to 11.46–51)—is their relation to God's creative power, of which human reproduction and human industry are both analogues and instances. (For the view that "Sodom" is some other sin, see the note to 11.46–51.)

9. removes every plant from its bed: In contrast with the wood of the suicides, the implicit downward sequence (from human to animal to plant) is carried a step further; compare Gen. 19.25: "destroyed . . . all things that spring from the earth."

12. at the very edge: The Italian doublet (*a randa a randa*, literally "at the edge at the edge"), a characteristic mode of emphasis (cf. 17.134: *al piè al piè*, "at the very foot," also 17.101, 17.115), is the first of several instances in the canto.

13. coarse, dry sand . . . feet of Cato: The reference is to the crossing of the northern Sahara in Libya by Cato the Younger and his army during the war of the Roman Senate, supporting Pompey the Great, against Julius Caesar. Dante's many references to this episode (see also Cantos 24–25) derive especially from Lucan's *Pharsalia* (Book 9), as does his conception of Cato, the hero of Lucan's poem, who appears in *Purgatorio* 1. According to Ovid (*Met.* 2.236–37), the Sahara was the result of Phaëthon's loss of control of the chariot of the sun, which scorched the earth as it came too close.

16. how much must you be feared: This is one of Dante's few direct references to the traditional purpose of accounts of the next life: to affect men's conduct by instilling fear of punishment or desire of reward there (see, e.g., Macrobius, *Commentarii* 1.1.4–5).

22–24. Some were lying . . . walking: The three "laws" (line 21) obviously correspond to the three sins (blasphemy, usury, and sodomy, respectively) punished in this subcircle.

30. like snow in the mountains without wind: The line conspicuously echoes a famous *plazer* (a short poem—in Italian often, as in this case, a sonnet—listing delightful things) by Guido Cavalcanti, "Biltà di donna e di saccente core," line 6: "e bianca neve scender senza vento" [and white snow falling without wind]; the addition of "in the mountains" strikingly intensifies it, just as depicting fire as snow intensifies the biblical "rained . . . brimstone and fire."

31–36. Like the flames that Alexander saw . . . while separated: This wonder is derived, as the modern commentators note, from a passage in Albertus Magnus's *De meteoris* 1.4.8, which conflates two separate episodes in the Pseudo-Callisthenes' *Letter* (purportedly from Alexander to his tutor, Aristotle): "Alexander writes in his letter on the marvels of India a marvelous description, saying that ignited clouds fell from the air in the manner of snow and that he ordered his men to trample them" (*E.D.*).

35–36. the burning . . . while separated: That is, if each flame ("burning," *vapore*) was extinguished before it combined with others.

40. the dancing of their wretched hands: The Italian word we translate with "dancing" here is *tresca*, used for a vigorous peasant dance involving rapid movements of both hands and feet; the word apparently derives from an Old Gothic word meaning "to pound," and, with its derivatives, was often used as a derogatory sexual metaphor (DeVoto and Oli 1971).

46–72. that great one: Capaneus, one of the Seven against Thebes (line 68), known to Dante in Statius's version, the *Thebaid* (he appears in 3.598–670, 4.165–86, 5.563–87, 6.731–825, and 9.540–69; he is prominent in Book 10, his death narrated in 10.827–939, one of the most vigorous parts of the poem). He is portrayed as a gigantic, enormously proud warrior, a contemner of the gods, praying only to his own right hand (9.548–50, 10.482–86), comparable to the centaurs and Cyclops (3.604–5). The first to surmount the walls of Thebes, he disdains its earthly littleness, challenges Bacchus and Hercules (its patrons) to defend it, and then, disdaining lesser gods, challenges Jupiter himself; Jupiter strikes him with a thunderbolt (10.899–939)—another instance of fire from Heaven. For Dante's many other references to the Theban material, see the notes to 26.52–54, 30.1–27, and 33.88–90.

46–48. who seems not to mind . . . to ripen him: Note the parallel with Farinata, who seems to have Hell "in great disdain" (10.36; cf. 14.70). The sarcasm of line 48 derives from the antithesis implicit in the rain of fire (with allusion to Gen. 19.24–25) and the sterility that it causes (see "Textual Variants," p. 585).

47. scornful and frowning: The line echoes Statius's description of Capaneus's dead body as "torvus adhuc visu" [still frowning in appearance].

51. As I was alive . . . dead: A reference to the Stoic ideal of consistency and imperturbability, again involving allusion to Farinata.

52–60. Though Jove . . . happy vengeance thereby: Capaneus is claiming that Jupiter is terrified of him. Statius, following the tradition that had Jupiter's thunderbolts fashioned by Vulcan and his Cyclops helpers at his forge under Mount Aetna, has Jupiter demand the thunderbolts and refer to the Battle of Phlegra (where the giants, attacking the gods, were struck down by Jove's thunderbolts—see Vergil, *Georgics* 1.278–83, Ovid, *Met.* 10.149–51; in the *Inferno*, the giants appear in Canto 31) as he laughs at Capaneus's folly (*Theb.* 10.911).

Mongibello, the popular name for Mount Aetna, is a compound of Latin *mons* and Arabic *jabal,* both meaning "mountain."

55. turn after turn: In the Italian, *a muta a muta* [literally, in turn in turn] and *aiuto, aiuto* [help, help] (line 55) are further instances of the idiomatic emphasis by repetition (as in line 12)

61–66. Then my leader . . . with your fury: Virgil's spirited rebuke of Capaneus may remind us of Capaneus's difference from the hero of the *Aeneid,* the "dutiful" Aeneas (*pius Aeneas*).

63–64. your pride is not extinguished: Note the fire metaphor.

69–70. he had . . . God in disdain: The language again recalls Farinata (10.36); presumably Farinata is less a scorner of God than Capaneus, or he would be punished here; the correlations are perhaps meant to require the reader to consider the nuances of difference.

68, 70, 72. regi . . . pregi . . . fregi: The same rhymes (in two cases the same words) are used of the furious Filippo Argenti in 8.47, 49, and 51, as the commentators observe.

72. the ornament his breast deserves: Again the emphasis on the breast (see the note to lines 8–39).

76–78. Silent we came . . . shudder: The color makes the pilgrim shudder because it is that of blood, perhaps including the blood that issues from the wounded shrubs imprisoning the suicides; as we soon learn, it is a continuation of the river of blood of Canto 12.

79–80. As from Bulicame . . . divide among themselves: Bulicame (used by Dante as a common noun in 12.117 for the river of blood; the word means, literally, "boiled [or boiling] thing," often used for hot springs) is a sulfurous spring, colored red, near Viterbo. "The sinning women" was explained by the early commentators as a reference to prostitutes having special conduits for the waters of the Bulicame, perhaps as a curative (prostitutes were barred from the public baths). Some modern critics argue for the reading *pettatrici* [carders]—that is, industrial preparers of wool, who did use such streams; this reading is not supported by the manuscripts but could be related to other industrial images in the canto (those of the smithy in lines 55–56, pottery in line 110, and metallurgy [perhaps] in lines 106–9).

89–90. the present river . . . all the flames: Since the river extinguishes the flames and thus provides a safe path for the pilgrim, it is closely related to the path provided by the earthquake discussed in 12.31–45, and thus to Christ's death. In terms of the body analogy, "vapors" were said to rise upward from the bloodstream.

94–120. In the midst . . . describe it here: Dante's elaborate, syncretic myth of the Old Man of Crete has not been fully explained. It represents in some sense both the history and the present state of mankind. See Additional Note 3.

118–19. where there is no further descent . . . Cocytus: That is, Cocytus is located at the very bottom of Hell, "where Dis is enthroned" (11.65).

134. the boiling of the red water: In other words, the river of blood of Canto 12 is the classical Phlegethon (see the note to 8.19).

136. Lethe you will see: In the Earthly Paradise, the true Eden, at the summit of the mountain of Purgatory.

CANTO 15

1   Ora cen porta l'un de' duri margini,
e 'l fummo del ruscel di sopra aduggia,
sì che dal foco salva l'acqua e li argini.

4   Qual i Fiamminghi tra Guizzante e Bruggia,
temendo 'l fiotto che 'nver' lor s'avventa,
fanno lo schermo perché 'l mar si fuggia;

7   e quali Padoan lungo la Brenta,
per difender lor ville e lor castelli,
anzi che Carentana il caldo senta:

10   a tale imagine eran fatti quelli,
tutto che né sì alti né sì grossi,
qual che si fosse, lo maestro félli.

13   Già eravam da la selva rimossi
tanto ch'i' non avrei visto dov' era,
perch' io in dietro rivolto mi fossi,

16   quando incontrammo d'anime una schiera
che venian lungo l'argine, e ciascuna
ci riguardava come suol da sera

19   guardare uno altro sotto nuova luna;
e sì ver' noi aguzzavan le ciglia
come 'l vecchio sartor fa ne la cruna.

22   Così adocchiato da cotal famiglia,
fui conosciuto da un, che mi prese
per lo lembo e gridò: "Qual maraviglia!"

25   E io, quando 'l suo braccio a me distese,
ficcaï li occhi per lo cotto aspetto,
sì che 'l viso abbrusciato non difese

28   la conoscenza süa al mio 'ntelletto;
e chinando la mano a la sua faccia,
rispuosi: "Siete voi qui, ser Brunetto?"

CANTO 15

The literary sodomites—Brunetto Latini—prophecy of Dante's future

1
Now one of the hard margins carries us along, and the vapor from the river gives a shelter that protects the water and the banks from the fire.

4
As the Flemings, between Wissant and Bruges, fearing the tide that rises against them, make dykes to escape the sea;

7
and as the Paduans do along the Brenta, to protect their farms and castles, before Carinthia feels the thaw:

10
after that image were these made, though not so high nor so thick, whoever he may have been, the master-builder made them.

13
We had already come so far from the wood that I would not have seen where it was, though I had turned back,

16
when we encountered a band of souls coming along the barrier, and each was gazing at us as in the evening

19
people gaze at one another under the new moon; and they sharpened their brows toward us as the old tailor does at the eye of his needle.

22
Looked over in this way by such a company, I was recognized by one, who seized me by the hem and cried: "What a marvel!"

25
And I, when he stretched out his arm toward me, penetrated with my eye his baked appearance, so that his scorched face did not prevent

28
my intellect from recognizing him; and, reaching my hand down toward his face, I replied: "Are you here, ser Brunetto?"

31   E quelli: "O figliuol mio, non ti dispiaccia
se Brunetto Latino un poco teco
ritorna 'n dietro e lascia andar la traccia."

34   I' dissi lui: "Quanto posso, ven preco;
e se volete che con voi m'asseggia,
faròl, se piace a costui, che vo seco."

37   "O figliuol," disse, "qual di questa greggia
s'arresta punto, giace poi cent' anni
sanz' arrostarsi quando 'l foco il feggia.

40   Però va oltre: i' ti verrò a' panni,
e poi rigiugnerò la mia masnada,
che va piangendo i suoi etterni danni."

43   Io non osava scender de la strada
per andar par di lui, ma 'l capo chino
tenea com' uom che reverente vada.

46   El cominciò: "Qual fortuna o destino
anzi l'ultimo dì qua giù ti mena?
e chi è questi che mostra 'l cammino?"

49   "Là sù di sopra, in la vita serena,"
rispuos' io lui, "mi smarri' in una valle,
avanti che l'età mia fosse piena.

52   Pur ier mattina le volsi le spalle:
questi m'apparve, tornand' io in quella,
e reducemi a ca per questo calle."

55   Ed elli a me: "Se tu segui tua stella,
non puoi fallire a glorïoso porto,
se ben m'accorsi ne la vita bella;

58   e s'io non fossi sì per tempo morto,
veggendo il cielo a te così benigno
dato t'avrei a l'opera conforto.

61   Ma quello ingrato popolo maligno
che discese di Fiesole *ab* antico,
e tiene ancor del monte e del macigno,

64   ti si farà, per tuo ben far, nimico;
ed è ragion, ché tra li lazzi sorbi
si disconvien fruttare al dolce fico.

67   Vecchia fama nel mondo li chiama orbi;
gent' è avara, invidiosa e superba:
dai lor costumi fa che tu ti forbi.

31   And he: "O my son, let it not displease you if Brunetto Latino turns back with you a little and lets his troop run on."

34   I said to him: "As much as I can, I beg you; and if you wish me to sit down with you, I will do so, if he over there permits it, for I am going with him."

37   "O son," he said, "whoever of this flock stands still for an instant, must then lie for a hundred years without brushing off the fire that strikes him.

40   Therefore walk on; I will come along at your skirts, and then I will rejoin my crew, who go bewailing their eternal losses."

43   I did not dare descend from the path to walk level with him, but I kept my head bowed, as one might walk reverently.

46   He began: "What fortune or destiny leads you down here before your last day? and who is this showing you the way?"

49   "Up there above, under the clear sky," I replied, "I lost myself in a valley, before my age was full.

52   Only yesterday morning did I turn my back on it: he appeared to me as I was returning there again, and is leading me back home by this road."

55   And he to me: "If you follow your star, you cannot fail to reach a glorious port, if I perceived well during sweet life;

58   and if I had not died so early, seeing the heavens so kindly toward you I would have given you strength for the work.

61   But that ungrateful, malicious people who came down from Fiesole of old, and still smack of the mountain and the granite,

64   will become your enemies because of your just actions; and that is reasonable, for among the sour crab apples it is not fitting that the sweet fig bear its fruit.

67   Ancient fame in the world calls them blind; they are a people avaricious, envious, and proud: see that you keep yourself clean of their customs.

70   La tua fortuna tanto onor ti serba
        che l'una parte e l'altra avranno fame
        di te; ma lungi fia dal becco l'erba.

73   Faccian le bestie fiesolane strame
        di lor medesme, e non tocchin la pianta,
        s'alcuna surge ancora in lor letame,

76   in cui riviva la sementa santa
        di que' Roman che vi rimaser quando
        fu fatto il nido di malizia tanta."

79   "Se fosse tutto pieno il mio dimando,"
        rispuos' io lui, "voi non sareste ancora
        de l'umana natura posto in bando;

82   ché 'n la mente m'è fitta, e or m'accora,
        la cara e buona imagine paterna
        di voi quando nel mondo ad ora ad ora

85   m'insegnavate come l'uom s'etterna;
        e quant' io l'abbia in grado mentr'io vivo
        convien che ne la mia lingua si scerna.

88   Ciò che narrate di mio corso scrivo,
        e serbolo a chiosar con altro testo
        a donna che saprà, s'a lei arrivo.

91   Tanto vogli' io che vi sia manifesto,
        pur che mia cosciënza non mi garra,
        ch'a la Fortuna, come vuol, son presto.

94   Non è nuova a li orecchi miei tal arra:
        però giri Fortuna la sua rota
        come le piace, e 'l villan la sua marra."

97   Lo mio maestro allora in su la gota
        destra si volse in dietro e riguardommi;
        poi disse: "Bene ascolta chi la nota."

100   Né per tanto di men parlando vommi
        con ser Brunetto, e dimando chi sono
        li suoi compagni più noti e più sommi.

103   Ed elli a me: "Saper d'alcuno è buono;
        de li altri fia laudabile tacerci,
        ché 'l tempo saria corto a tanto suono.

106   In somma sappi che tutti fur cherci
        e litterati grandi e di gran fama,
        d'un peccato medesmo al mondo lerci.

70   Your fortune holds so much honor in store for you, that both sides will hunger for you; but let the grass be far from the goat.

73   Let the Fiesolan beasts make straw of each other, but let them not touch the plant, if any still sprout in their manure,

76   in which may live again the holy seed of the Romans who remained there when that nest of so much malice was built."

79   "If my request were all fulfilled," I replied to him, "you would not yet be banished from human nature;

82   for in my memory is fixed, and now it weighs on my heart, the dear, kind paternal image of you when, in the world, from time to time

85   you used to teach me how man makes himself eternal; and how grateful I am for that, as long as I live must be discerned in my language.

88   What you narrate about my path I am writing down and keeping to be glossed, with other texts, by a lady who will know, if I reach her.

91   This much I would make manifest to you, that as long as my conscience does not reproach me I am ready for Fortune, whatever she will.

94   This pledge is not new to my ears: therefore let Fortune turn her wheel as she pleases, and the peasant his hoe."

97   My master then turned around over his right cheek and gazed at me; then he said: "He listens well who takes note."

100   Nonetheless I go speaking with ser Brunetto, and I ask him of his more famous and accomplished companions.

103   And he to me: "To know of some is fitting; about the others silence is praiseworthy, for the time would be too short for so much noise.

106   In brief, know that they were all clerks and great men of letters, of great fame, all fouled with the same sin in the world.

109   Priscian sen va con quella turba grama,
        e Francesco d'Accorso anche; e vedervi,
        s'avessi avuto di tal tigna brama,

112   colui potei che dal servo de' servi
        fu trasmutato d'Arno in Bacchiglione,
        dove lasciò li mal protesi nervi.

115   Di più direi, ma 'l venire e 'l sermone
        più lungo esser non può, però ch'i' veggio
        là surger nuovo fummo del sabbione.

118   Gente vien con la quale esser non deggio.
        Sieti raccomandato il mio Tesoro,
        nel qual io vivo ancora, e più non cheggio."

121   Poi si rivolse, e parve di coloro
        che corrono a Verona il drappo verde
        per la campagna; e parve di costoro

124   quelli che vince, non colui che perde.

109   Priscian goes along with that wretched crowd, and
Francesco d'Accorso, too; and, if you had desired
such scurf, you could see there

112   him who by the Servant of servants was
transmuted from Arno to Bacchiglione, where he
left his ill-protended muscles.

115   I would say more, but my walking and my speech
can last no longer, for I see new smoke rising from the
sand over there.

118   People are coming with whom I must not be. Let
my *Treasure* be commended to you, in which I live
still, and I ask no more."

121   Then he turned back, and he seemed one of those
who at Verona race for the green cloth across the
fields; and of those he seemed

124   the one who wins, not the one who loses.

NOTES

2. vapor from the river: Discussed in the note to 14.89–90.

4–12. As the Flemings . . . the master-builder made them: Dante's simile compares the "margins" of the river of blood with the dykes that protect the Flemings from the tides and the Paduans from the annual flooding of the river Brenta. The river of blood is contained within these stone "banks" (14.82), which, with their wide margins on which the pilgrim and Virgil walk, are thought of as elevated, probably to somewhat less than the height of a man (see lines 23, 29, 35, and 40); in 17.6 the margins are said to be of marble.

4. Flemings, between Wissant and Bruges: Parodi (1920) pointed out that the Italian forms of these names (*Fiamminghi, Guizzante,* and *Bruggia*) sound like the words for "flaming" (*fiammeggia*), "wriggling" (*guizzante*), and "burning" (*brucia*). Puns and equivocal language are frequent in this canto of sodomy.

5. the tide: Dante may be echoing accounts of the tides in Ovid, Lucan, and Brunetto Latini, represented as the strife of the sea against the land.

9. Carinthia: This is a region in Austria; in Dante's time, the term was used to include the Carnic Alps, where Dante thought the Brenta originated.

15. though I had turned back: The line means, of course, that he did not turn back. The mention of looking back, in a context involving the destruction of Sodom, recalls Lot's wife, who, although warned by the angel, did look back and was turned into a "statue of salt" (Gen. 19.26).

16–21. we encountered a band . . . eye of his needle: From Virgil's exposition in 11.49–51 and from 14.22–24, we deduce that these souls are sodomites. The scene, which moved T. S. Eliot to his imitation in "Little Gidding," is of groups of people, out at night in the dark of the moon, near the walls of the city.

18–19. as in the evening . . . under the new moon: The commentators note the echo of *Aen.* 6.270–72:

> quale per incertam lunam sub luce maligna
> est iter in silvis, ubi caelum condidit umbra
> Iuppiter, et rebus nox abstulit atra colorem.

[like a path in the woods, because of an uncertain moon, under bad light
when Jupiter has hidden the sky with darkness,
and black night has taken away color from things.]

22. company: Dante's term here (*famiglia,* family) was used to refer to the servants and dependents of even a large household or enterprise, including a city (here it strongly suggests the night watch), or to a group linked by shared activity or ideals (e.g., of the philosophers in Limbo, 4.132); compare *masnada* (41), used of the body-servants of a lord.

23. seized me by the hem: Augustine's *Confessions* 8.11.26 suggests a context and meaning for this gesture: "My lovers of old, trifles of trifles and vanities, held me back. They plucked at my fleshly garment, and they whispered softly: 'Do you cast us off?' and 'From that moment we shall be no more with you forever and ever!'" (tr. Ryan) (see the note to line 124).

25–29. stretched out his arm . . . penetrated with my eye . . . reaching my hand down: Brunetto's scrutiny of the pilgrim and the pilgrim's of Brunetto are followed, in each case, by a physical gesture indicating both intimacy and affection.

27. his scorched face: Brunetto (whose name means "dark") is burned over his whole body; in some Italian cities (though not Florence), burning was a frequent civil penalty for sodomy.

30. Are you here, ser Brunetto: The pilgrim is apparently surprised to see Brunetto among the sodomites; in fact there is no mention in the chroniclers of his having been one. The title *ser* identifies Brunetto as a notary, and as was appropriate in addressing a distinguished elder, Dante addresses him with the respectful *voi* (see the note to 10.49–51).
Brunetto Latini was born in Florence about 1220, and died there about 1294. In 1260, when returning from an embassy to Alfonso X of Castile, he learned of the defeat of the Guelfs at Montaperti (1260) and changed his destination to Montpellier and then Paris, where he lived privately, supported by a merchant friend. After the victory of the Guelfs in 1266 Brunetto returned to Florence and was prominent in public life; in 1289 he was appointed public orator. Brunetto was an important figure in what might be called the proto-humanistic movement, urging the practice of civic virtue and the study of classical rhetoric; his most significant works were the *Trésor* (a short encyclopedia in French with emphasis on rhetoric and government), the *Tesoretto* (a didactic poem in Italian; see the note to 1.2), and translations into Italian of part of Cicero's *De inventione* and several of his orations. For the question whether Brunetto's sin was something other than homosexuality, see the note to 11.46–51.

31. O my son: The expression recurs in line 37. Since Brunetto was about forty-five years older than Dante, the expression is natural; the theme of Brunetto as a father figure is fundamental to the episode.

32. Brunetto Latino: Dante's having Brunetto refer to himself in the third person seems to echo a mannerism of Brunetto's (especially in the *Tesoretto*), revealing a devotion to personal fame.

33. turns back with you a little: For an allegorical reading of Brunetto's turn back with Dante, see the note to line 124.

36. if he over there permits it: Perhaps to emphasize the difference between Brunetto and his present guide, Dante avoids naming Virgil in the narrative of this canto.

38. must then lie for a hundred years: In other words, suffer for a hundred years the fate of the blasphemers (see 11.49–51).

40. I will come along at your skirts: Imposed by the difference in height between the top of the wall and the floor of the plain, Brunetto's position is of course symbolic of a radical reversal of roles (see the note to line 124). *Panni* is literally "cloths"; the reference is to the full, ankle-length skirts of Dante's garment. This line is the climactic one in a series of references to cloth and clothing. See also lines 21, 23–24, 111, 123–24.

46–48. fortune or destiny . . . showing you the way: See *Aen.* 6.531–34, where Deiphobus inquires of Aeneas:

> Sed te qui vivum casus, age fare vicissim,
> attulerint. Pelagine venis erroribus actus
> an monitu divum? An quae te fortuna fatigat,
> ut tristis sine sole domos, loca turbida, adires?

> [But what events—tell me—have brought you here alive?
> Driven wandering over the deep do you come,
> or at the bidding of the gods? What misfortune harasses you,
> that you visit these sad homes and sunless, this place of confusion?]

48. who is this: See the note to line 36.

50. I lost myself in a valley: Here the pilgrim for the first time describes his experience at the beginning of the poem in language similar to the terms of the poem itself (1.1–7); the parallel with the *Tesoretto* (see 1.2) is perhaps an acknowledgment of Brunetto's influence.

52. did I turn my back on it: See the note to line 33.

54. is leading me back home: Heaven is the fatherland, or home (see the note to line 56).

55. If you follow your star: Whether or not Brunetto refers here to Dante's natal sign, Gemini, to which he attributes his talent (*Par.* 22.112–14), is disputed (see the note to line 59).

56. a glorious port: Dante uses the metaphor of the port in *Convivio* 4.12–18 as part of his discussion of human life as the soul's journey back to God (to "glory"). Although many commentators take Brunetto's words to refer exclusively to earthly fame, there is no clear justification for so limiting their meaning. The complementary relation between astrological influence and grace is a major theme of the entire poem (see, e.g., 26.23–24).

58–60. if I had not died . . . strength for the work: Some would limit the meaning of "work" here to Dante's political career, which began in 1295, one year after Brunetto's death, but it seems artificial not to think of Dante's literary work, which began early and continued throughout his life.

59. seeing the heavens so kindly toward you: The reference is to benign astrological influences.

61–62. people who came down from Fiesole of old: *Ab antico* here means "in ancient times." The allusion is to the story, half-fact, half-legend, that Fiesole was led by Catiline's sympathizers to revolt against Rome (*Trésor* 1.37.1–2), and that after Fiesole had been razed by Julius Caesar, and Florence was built on the Arno not far away, the surviving Fiesolans, including descendants of Catiline's followers, were mixed in with the Roman colonists.

63. smack of the mountain and the granite: That is, they are rustic and resistant to civilized ways. This was a common Florentine view of the Fiesolans (see Davis 1967).

64. will become your enemies . . . just actions: Brunetto is referring to Dante's exile, predicted by Farinata (10.79–81). Dante puts in Brunetto's mouth the phrase *ben far,* which the pilgrim had used (6.81) when asking about other Florentines.

65–66. among the sour crab apples . . . bear its fruit: Brunetto is using biblical language; see especially Matt. 7.16–19:

> By their fruits ye shall know them. Do men gather grapes of thorns, or figs of thistles? Even so every good tree bringeth forth good fruit, and the evil tree bringeth forth evil fruit. A good tree cannot bring forth evil fruit, neither can an evil tree bring forth good fruit.

71. both sides: The Blacks, who exiled Dante, and the Whites, with whom Dante was still associated in the first years of his exile (1302–early 1304); he denounces the Whites in *Par.* 17.61–69.

72. the goat: The Italian here permits also "beak" or "snout."

76–77. holy seed of the Romans: A reference to the Romans who lived in Florence after the incorporation of the Fiesolans. The seed (descendants) of the Romans is holy because of the providential status of the Roman empire (2.13–33).

78. nest of so much malice: For analogous phrases, see 11.57 and *Purg.* 11.99. Throughout the *Inferno*, Florence will be compared with the Earthly City, whose archetype is Hell (as well as with Sodom and Thebes) (see the notes to 3.1 and 6.61).

79–81. If my request . . . from human nature: Since the pilgrim says "not yet," the sentence must refer to Brunetto's death: the pilgrim wishes Brunetto had not died so early (see line 58). But it must refer also to Brunetto's damnation (see 23.126, "the eternal exile," for damnation). (The tension here is closely related to that concerning Guido Cavalcanti in 10.52–72: if Guido is alive, he may still repent.)

82. in my memory is fixed: See Vergil's words (*Aen.* 4.3–4) on Dido's love for Aeneas: "haerent infixi pectore vultus/ verbaque" [his face and words are fixed deep in her breast].

83. kind paternal image: Here the pilgrim himself asserts the relation claimed by Brunetto in lines 31 and 37. (Dante's own father died when he was eighteen; Guido, of course, is metaphorically a brother.) Brunetto is the person, in addition to Virgil and Beatrice, to whom Dante attributes the most influence on his adult values and activities.

84. from time to time: The Italian is *ad ora ad ora* [literally, to time to time], another idiomatically repetitive expression (see the notes to 14.12 and 55).

85. how man makes . . . eternal: This is no doubt a reference to earthly glory, as in line 56. In the strictest sense, however, both lines also include reference to salvation. The quest for glory, particularly literary fame, is not regarded by Dante as inconsistent with salvation (see 1.79–87, 2.104–5, and 24.43–57).

The pathos of Brunetto's situation is that of one who understood (and in his works asserted) Christian values but, because he did not "chastise his body" (see lines 121–24, with note), forfeited eternity. Limiting lines 56 and 85 exclusively to the quest for secular fame is an impoverishment of the episode. After all, line 85 is spoken by the pilgrim.

86–87. how grateful I am . . . in my language: Given the number of echoes of Brunetto's works in the *Comedy* and other works, the pilgrim's words are no more than the truth. However, this canto is the only evidence that has survived attributing sodomy to Brunetto.

88–90. What you narrate . . . if I reach her: The lines echo 10.127–32, where Virgil tells the pilgrim, "Let your memory preserve what you have heard against you," since he will hear from Beatrice "the journey of your life." In *scrivo* [I am writing down] and *chiosar* [to gloss], the metaphor of the book of memory reappears. Segre (1986) notes that this is one of a number of expressions in the canto that recall the teacher–pupil relation; but this text will be glossed by a higher teacher.

90. lady who will know: Beatrice (see the note to 10.131).

93. ready for Fortune, whatever she will: *Aen.* 5.710: "Quidquid erit, superanda omnis fortuna ferendo est" [Whatever it will be, every fortune must be surmounted by being borne].

94. pledge: Dante's term is *arra*, which means, literally, a "down payment," a "deposit," or "earnest money." Note the introduction of commercial terminology.

95–96. let Fortune turn her wheel . . . the peasant his hoe: That is, let the world continue on its usual uneven course, since I am constant. The expression was apparently proverbial.

99. He listens well who takes note: This would seem to be a reference to 10.127–32: the pilgrim is learning Virgil's lesson well. (To note is to write down.)

106–7. clerks and great men of letters: The early commentators point out that sodomy was notoriously widespread among the clergy and the learned; this was a frequent reproach in the Middle Ages and was the basis of Alain of Lille's (early-thirteenth-century) poetic tract against it, the *De planctu Naturae*.

109. Priscian . . . wretched crowd: No independent tradition records that Priscian (Byzantium and Rome, 491–518), author of the most famous Latin grammar of the Middle Ages, was a homosexual.

110. Francesco d'Accorso: The son of one of the wealthiest jurists in history, d'Accorso (1225–1293) spent much of his career in England as the private counselor to King Edward I.

111. such scurf: Dante's term *tigna* (from Latin *tinea*, moth) was used to refer to mange and other diseases that cause loss of hair; in addition to expressing disdain for the next person mentioned, it calls attention to the fact that all the inhabitants of this circle have lost all their hair (see 16.35). See also the notes to lines 27 and 119.

112. him who . . . ill-protended muscles: Andrea de' Mozzi, of a powerful Florentine banking family, was appointed bishop of Florence in 1287. Accused of various abuses, he was transferred by the pope (the popes traditionally style themselves *Servi servorum Dei* [Servants of the servants of God]), in this case Boniface VIII, to the bishopric of Vicenza in 1294 (the Bacchiglione flows through both Vicenza and Padua); he died in 1295. *Protesi* [protended] is a Latinism from Latin *protendere* [to stretch forward].

117. I see new smoke rising: An allusion to Gen. 19.28: "he saw the ashes rise up from the earth as the smoke of a furnace."

118. People . . . I must not be: The different groups of sodomites are apparently strictly separate; the group now approaching, if it is the same as the one in the next canto, is made up of aristocrats.

119. Let my *Treasure* . . . I ask no more: Brunetto's *Treasure* is his *Trésor* (see the note to line 30). That Brunetto "asks no more" has suggested to numerous commentators a parallel with Matt. 6.19–21:

> Lay not up to yourselves treasures on earth: where the rust and moth consume, and where thieves break through and steal. But lay up to yourselves treasures in heaven. . . . For where thy treasure is, there is thy heart also.

(In the Vulgate, "moth" is *tinea*: see the note on "scurf" in line 111.)

121. Then he turned back . . . across the fields: Verona was the site of a footrace (*palio*), with a bolt of green cloth as the prize. The race took place on a wide plain outside the walls of the city; note that Brunetto is being observed from the top of a wall as he runs across the plain.

124. the one who . . . not the one who loses: Kay (1978b) was apparently the first to note the allusion here to 1 Cor. 9.24–27 (quoted by Dante in *Convivio* 4.22):

> Know you not that they that run in the race, all run indeed, but one receiveth the prize? So run that you may obtain. And every one that striveth for the mastery, refraineth himself from all things: and they indeed that they may receive a corruptible crown; but we an incorruptible one. I therefore so run, not as at an uncertainty: I so fight, not as one beating the air: But I chastise my body, and bring it into subjection: lest perhaps, when I have preached to others, I myself should become a castaway.

The full allusion is further evidence that Brunetto's sin is homosexuality and one of the many indications that the canto can be regarded as a commentary on the interaction of Dante and Brunetto in life. First are the reversals of direction (strongly negative or positive): line 15 (the allusion to Lot's wife; the pilgrim did *not* turn back), line 33 (Brunetto "turns back with you"); lines 52–53 (the pilgrim left the dark wood but was returning to it when Virgil intervened); and line 121 (Brunetto rejoins his companions). Second is the reversal of roles: Brunetto the teacher now walks along at the pilgrim's skirts like a child (line 40) and is partly instructed in how the pilgrim will reach immortality. Third is the allusion to sexual solicitation: the plucking of the pilgrim's garment (line 23).

If we interpret the episode as a veiled account of the relation between Dante and Brunetto, its implication would seem to be: Dante and Brunetto met going in opposite directions both on the arc of life and in relation to salvation; Brunetto was sexually attracted to Dante, and Dante perhaps to him (line 23 and Additional Note 5); Dante rejected Brunetto's advances, however, and for a time Brunetto turned back from his sinful life and followed Dante's example, was being led toward salvation (this would involve an important parallel with the call to Ugolino; see Additional Note 15); in the end he turned back to his sin. Such a reading, though speculative, has an extensive basis in the text and is consistent with Dante's treatment of such material elsewhere.

CANTO 16

1   Già era in loco onde s'udia 'l rimbombo
de l'acqua che cadea ne l'altro giro,
simile a quel che l'arnie fanno rombo,

4   quando tre ombre insieme si partiro,
correndo, d'una torma che passava
sotto la pioggia de l'aspro martiro.

7   Venian ver' noi, e ciascuna gridava:
"Sòstati tu ch'a l'abito ne sembri
essere alcun di nostra terra prava."

10   Ahimè, che piaghe vidi ne' lor membri,
ricenti e vecchie, da le fiamme incese!
Ancor men duol pur ch'i' me ne rimembri.

13   A le lor grida il mio dottor s'attese;
volse 'l viso ver' me, e: "Or aspetta,"
disse, "a costor si vuole esser cortese.

16   E se non fosse il foco che saetta
la natura del loco, i' dicerei
che meglio stesse a te che a lor la fretta."

19   Ricominciar, come noi restammo, ei
l'antico verso; e quando a noi fuor giunti,
fenno una rota di sé tutti e trei.

22   Qual sogliono i campion far nudi e unti,
avvisando lor presa e lor vantaggio
prima che sien tra lor battuti e punti:

25   così rotando, ciascuno il visaggio
drizzava a me, sì che 'n contraro il collo
faceva ai piè continüo vïaggio.

28   E: "Se miseria d'esto loco sollo
rende in dispetto noi e nostri prieghi,"
cominciò l'uno, "e 'l tinto aspetto e brollo,

CANTO 16

The noise of the great cataract—the three Florentine noblemen—
denunciation of Florence—the cataract—the pilgrim's belt—the
summoning of Geryon

1   Already I was in a place where one heard the
thundering of the water falling into the next circle,
like the rumbling that beehives make,

4   when three shades came running together out of a
herd passing by beneath the rain of the harsh
punishment.

7   They were coming toward us, and each was
shouting: "Stop, you who by your clothes seem to be
someone from our depraved city."

10   Alas, what wounds I saw in their members, recent
and old, burned into them by the flames! It still pains
me when I remember.

13   At their shouts my teacher paused; he turned his
face toward me and: "Now wait," he said, "to these
we should be courteous.

16   And if it were not for the fire that the nature of
the place pours down, I would say that haste would
more become you than them."

19   When we stood still, they began again their
former verse; and on reaching us they made a wheel
of themselves, all three.

22   As is the custom of wrestlers, naked and oiled,
spying out their holds and their advantage before
they come to blows and wounds:

25   so they wheeled, and each kept his face toward
me, so that their necks made a constant motion
contrary to their feet.

28   And: "If the wretchedness of this vile place brings
us and our prayers to scorn," one began, "and our
darkened, scorched appearance,

31   la fama nostra il tuo animo pieghi
a dirne chi tu se', che i vivi piedi
così sicuro per lo 'nferno freghi.

34   Questi, l'orme di cui pestar mi vedi,
tutto che nudo e dipelato vada,
fu di grado maggior che tu non credi:

37   nepote fu de la buona Gualdrada;
Guido Guerra ebbe nome, e in sua vita
fece col senno assai e con la spada.

40   L'altro, ch'appresso me la rena trita,
è Tegghiaio Aldobrandi, la cui voce
nel mondo sù dovria esser gradita.

43   E io, che posto son con loro in croce,
Iacopo Rusticucci fui, e certo
la fiera moglie più ch'altro mi nuoce."

46   S'i' fossi stato dal foco coperto,
gittato mi sarei tra lor di sotto,
e credo che 'l dottor l'avria sofferto;

49   ma perch' io mi sarei brusciato e cotto,
vinse paura la mia buona voglia
che di loro abbracciar mi facea ghiotto.

52   Poi cominiciai: "Non dispetto, ma doglia
la vostra condizion dentro mi fisse,
tanta che tardi tutta si dispoglia,

55   tosto che questo mio segnor mi disse
parole per le quali i' mi pensai
che qual voi siete, tal gente venisse.

58   Di vostra terra sono, e sempre mai
l'ovra di voi e li onorati nomi
con affezion ritrassi e ascoltai.

61   Lascio lo fele e vo per dolci pomi
promessi a me per lo verace duca;
ma 'nfino al centro pria convien ch'i' tomi."

64   "Se lungamente l'anima conduca
le membra tue," rispuose quelli ancora,
"e se la fama tua dopo te luca,

67   cortesia e valor dì se dimora
ne la nostra città sì come suole,
o se del tutto se n'è gita fora:

31   let our fame incline your spirit to tell us who you are, who so confidently step with your living feet through Hell.

34   This man, in whose steps you see me tread, though he now goes naked and hairless, was of higher degree than you believe:

37   he was the grandson of the good Gualdrada; Guido Guerra was his name, and in his life he accomplished much with wisdom and the sword.

40   The other, who wears the sand behind me, is Tegghiaio Aldobrandi, whose words should have been more pleasing in the world above.

43   And I, placed on the cross with them, was Iacopo Rusticucci, and certainly my fierce wife harms me more than anything else."

46   If I had been protected from the fire, I would have thrown myself down there among them, and I believe my teacher would have suffered it;

49   but because I would have burned and cooked myself, fear vanquished the good will that made me greedy to embrace them.

52   Then I began: "Not scorn, but grief was fixed in me by your condition, so great that it will long endure,

55   as soon as my lord here said words that made me think people such as yourselves were coming.

58   I am from your city, and always your works and your honored names I have repeated and heard with affection.

61   I am leaving the bitter and seek the sweet fruit promised me by my truthful leader; but first I must plunge as far as the center."

64   "So may your soul long guide your body," he replied then, "and so may your fame shine after you,

67   tell if courtesy and valor dwell in our city as they used to do, or if they have utterly forsaken it:

70   ché Guiglielmo Borsiere, il qual si duole
con noi per poco e va là coi compagni,
assai ne cruccia con le sue parole."

73   "La gente nuova e i sùbiti guadagni
orgoglio e dismisura han generata,
Fiorenza, in te, sì che tu già ten piagni."

76   Così gridai con la faccia levata;
e i tre, che ciò inteser per risposta,
guardar l'un l'altro com' al ver si guata.

79   "Se l'altre volte sì poco ti costa,"
rispuoser tutti, "il satisfare altrui,
felice te se sì parli a tua posta!

82   Però, se campi d'esti luoghi bui
e torni a riveder le belle stelle,
quando ti gioverà dicere 'I' fui,'

85   fa che di noi a la gente favelle."
Indi rupper la rota, e a fuggirsi
ali sembiar le gambe loro isnelle.

88   Un amen non saria possuto dirsi
tosto così com' e' fuoro spariti;
per ch'al maestro parve di partirsi.

91   Io lo seguiva, e poco eravam iti,
che 'l suon de l'acqua n'era sì vicino,
che per parlar saremmo a pena uditi.

94   Come quel fiume c'ha proprio cammino
prima dal Monte Viso 'nver' levante
da la sinistra costa d'Apennino,

97   che si chiama Acquacheta suso, avante
che si divalli giù nel basso letto,
e a Forlì di quel nome è vacante,

100   rimbomba là sovra San Benedetto
de l'Alpe, per cadere ad una scesa
ove dovria per mille esser recetto:

103   così, giù d'una ripa discoscesa,
trovammo risonar quell'acqua tinta
sì che 'n poc' ora avria l'orecchia offesa.

106   Io avea una corda intorno cinta,
e con essa pensai alcuna volta
prender la lonza a la pelle dipinta.

70   for Guiglielmo Borsiere, who has been grieving with us but a short time and goes there with our companions, causes us much pain with his words about it."

73   "The new people and the rapid gains have generated pride and excess, Florence, in you, so that you already weep for it."

76   So I cried with face uplifted; and the three, who took that as my reply, looked at each other as one looks at the truth.

79   "If at other times it costs you so little," they all replied, "to satisfy others, happy are you, if you speak so readily!

82   Therefore, if you escape these dark places and go back to see the beautiful stars, when it will be pleasant to say, 'I was,'

85   see that you speak of us to people." Then they broke the wheel, and their quick legs seemed wings to their flight.

88   An amen could not be said more quickly than they disappeared; so my master judged we should move on.

91   I was following him, and we had not walked far, when the sound of the water was so close to us that we could hardly have heard each other speak.

94   Like that river which is first to take its own course toward the east, after Monte Viso, on the left side of the Apennines,

97   which is called Acquacheta above, before it falls down into the low bed and loses that name at Forlì,

100   as it thunders there above San Benedetto de l'Alpe, when falling in one cascade where it usually descends by a thousand:

103   so down from a steep cliff we found that dark water resounding, such that in a short while it would have harmed our ears.

106   I had a cord girding me, and with it I had thought at times to capture the leopard with the spotted hide.

109 Poscia ch'io l'ebbi tutta da me sciolta,
sì come 'l duca m'avea comandato,
porsila a lui aggroppata e ravvolta.

112 Ond' ei si volse inver' lo destro lato,
e alquanto di lunge da la sponda
la gittò giuso in quell' alto burrato.

115 "E' pur convien che novità risponda,"
dicea fra me medesmo, "al novo cenno
che 'l maestro con l'occhio sì seconda."

118 Ahi quanto cauti li uomini esser dienno
presso a color che non veggion pur l'ovra,
ma per entro i pensier miran col senno!

121 El disse a me: "Tosto verrà di sovra
ciò ch'io attendo e che il tuo pensier sogna;
tosto convien ch'al tuo viso si scovra."

124 Sempre a quel ver c'ha faccia di menzogna
de' l'uom chiuder le labbra fin ch'el puote,
però che sanza colpa fa vergogna;

127 ma qui tacer nol posso, e per le note
di questa comedìa, lettor, ti giuro,
s'elle non sien di lunga grazia vòte,

130 ch'i' vidi per quell' aere grosso e scuro
venir notando una figura in suso,
maravigliosa ad ogne cor sicuro:

133 sì come torna colui che va giuso
talora a solver l'àncora ch'aggrappa
o scoglio o altro che nel mare è chiuso,

136 che 'n sù si stende e da piè si rattrappa.

109   After I had untied it from around me, as my leader had commanded me, I held it out to him knotted and wound.

112   And he turned toward his right side and somewhat far from the bank threw it down into that deep pit.

115   "Some new thing must answer," I was saying to myself, "the strange sign that my master is following with his eyes."

118   Ah, how cautious men should be in the presence of those who not only see our actions but with their wisdom see our inner thoughts!

121   He said to me: "Soon what I expect, what your thoughts are dreaming, will come up; soon it will be revealed to your sight."

124   Always to that truth which has the face of falsehood one should close one's lips as long as one can, for without any guilt it brings shame;

127   but here I cannot conceal it, and by the notes of this comedy, reader, I swear to you, so may they not fail to find long favor,

130   that I saw, through that thick dark air, a figure come swimming upward, fearful to the most confident heart,

133   as one returns who at times goes down to release an anchor caught on a rock or other thing hidden in the sea,

136   and reaches upward as he draws in his feet.

NOTES

1–3. Already . . . the rumbling that beehives make: The noise of the great cataract between the circle of violence and the Malebolge is mentioned also in 16.91–105 and 17.118–20, dominating these two transitional cantos. After the arrival at the bottom, it is not mentioned again. The comparison of the sound to that of beehives indicates that it is softened by distance; Dante may have expected his readers to remember the high status granted to beehives as exemplars of industrious commonwealths (*Aen.* 1.430–36; cf. *Georgics* 4.149–250). The food–poison antithesis (related to the bee–spider antithesis) will be prominent in the Malebolge, to which the cataract descends.

4–5. three shades . . . out of a herd: On the different groups identified here and in Canto 15, see Additional Note 5.

8. by your clothes: Just as Farinata recognized the pilgrim as Florentine by his speech, so these three do so by his characteristic Florentine garb (cf. 15.23–24 and 40).

9. our depraved city: Such expressions describing Florence are beginning to be taken for granted.

12. It still pains me . . . remember: Another instance of the poet's reliving the terrors and sorrows of the journey.

14–18. Now wait . . . you than them: Virgil emphasizes the need for courtesy, a central element in the encounter. It is quite striking that Virgil ranks the living—and elect—pilgrim below the three Florentine sodomites, at least in the protocol of courtesy; see Additional Note 5.

19–21. they began again . . . all three: Their "former verse" is probably a reference to the weeping mentioned in 14.20, which was interrupted by their shouting; for the cries of the damned as song or poetry, compare 5.46 "lays," 7.34 "meter," 7.125 "hymn" (and see line 128). The wheel the shades now form is a kind of dance (cf. 14.40–42, with note).

21–27. they made a wheel of themselves . . . contrary to their feet:
In other words, as the three wheel in their circle and their feet take them away
from Dante, their heads turn back in order to keep him in view (each describes
two circles: one with his steps, the other with his head). As the early com-
mentators point out, the comparison with wrestlers (the Italian *campioni* means
"champions") includes implicit reference to the athletes of ancient Greece
and Rome (as in *Aen.* 5.421–31 or *Theb.* 6.847–51); according to Lana, in
Tuscany trial by combat in minor cases could involve naked wrestling instead
of armed combat. In addition to the implicit homosexual reference, there is
probably also a comment here on the disparity of their high courtesy and
concern for the public good (the path of their heads) coexisting with their
homosexual conduct (the path of their feet); Brunetto Latini exhibits the same
paradox.

32–33. step with your living feet: Dante's Italian is *i vivi piedi freghi* [literally,
rub your living feet]; the pain of setting foot on the burning sands is implied.

34–45. This man . . . more than anything else: All three of these famous
Florentines of the last century are mentioned as "worthy" and as having "turned
their wits to doing well" in the pilgrim's questioning of Ciacco in 6.79–81.

38. Guido Guerra: Grandson of Gualdrada di Bellincion Berti de' Ravignani
(a distant kinswoman of Dante's, wife of Count Guido the Elder, regarded by
her contemporaries as a paragon of domestic virtue), Guido Guerra (1220–1272),
as one of the Conti Guidi, was a member of one of the most powerful noble
families of Tuscany. He was one of the chief leaders of the Tuscan Guelfs
(cf. "with wisdom") and distinguished himself (cf. "with the sword") at the Battle
of Benevento (1266).

41. Tegghiaio Aldobrandi: Another high-ranking nobleman of Guelf per-
suasion (dead by 1266), who attempted to dissuade the Florentines from march-
ing against the Sienese in what became the Battle of Montaperti.

43. placed on the cross: That is, paying the penalty for sin; this is one of
many indications in the *Inferno* that the punishments of the damned are distorted
reflections of the Crucifixion.

44. Iacopo Rusticucci: Apparently a member of the lesser nobility, flourished
around 1235 to 1254, still alive in 1266. Early commentators say that the hostil-
ity between him and his wife caused them to live apart and turned him against
women in general.

46–51. If I had been protected . . . greedy to embrace them: On Dante's "greediness," see Additional Note 5.

59. your works and your honored names: As Guelfs and as public benefactors. Note the contrast between the hostile initial interchange with Farinata, a Ghibelline, in Canto 10, and the concern for fame of all these shades.

67–68. tell if courtesy and valor dwell in our city: These are central aristocratic virtues for Dante. Compare the similar concerns voiced in *Purg.* 8.121–32 and 14.91–126. For Dante's idyllic view of earlier Florence, see *Paradiso* 15–16.

70. Guiglielmo Borsiere: The exact identity of this individual, who must have died shortly before the date of the journey, is uncertain; his being mentioned in this context and the fact that Rusticucci associates him with himself and the others as concerned for the aristocratic virtues suggests that he, too, is a nobleman. His surname means "purse-holder." Boccaccio makes him an exemplar of courtesy and liberality in *Decameron* 1.8.

73–75. The new people . . . weep for it: This ascription of the causes of the current troubles in Florence is consistent with others in the poem, most notably that offered by the pilgrim's ancestor, Cacciaguida, in *Paradiso* 15–16. To some extent it is already implied in Ciacco's image of Florence as a bag (6.49–50).

76. So I cried with face uplifted: The pilgrim lifts his face in the direction of Florence, on the surface of the earth, and addresses the city directly. This is a striking instance of his gradual assumption of the role of a prophet, like a biblical one, directly addressing his contemporaries, especially his fellow Florentines, though several other cities are apostrophized, as well as Italy as a whole and numerous individuals. This gradually assumed prophetic role is represented as leading directly to the writing of the poem. See also 19.88–123, 25.10–15, 26.1–12, and 33.79–90, *Purg.* 6.76–151, and *Par.* 17.106–42.

82–84. if you escape . . . to say, 'I was,': The last phrase echoes the famous line in *Aen.* 1.203 quoted in the note to 5.121. "Go back to see the beautiful stars" is a striking anticipation of the last line of the *Inferno*.

92–105. the sound of the water . . . would have harmed our ears: The increased loudness of the cataract is a measure of the distance Virgil and the pilgrim have walked since the opening of the canto. The steep cliff that bounds the inner edge of the circle of violence is, with the Styx (Canto 8), the second major division of Hell; its crossing is emphasized by covering two entire cantos (Cantos 16 and 17).

94–102. Like that river ... descends by a thousand: Monte Viso (or Monviso) is at the northwestern limit of the Apennines. Following the Apennines east from there (and necessarily facing south), the first river flowing down the left (i.e., the east) side of the range that had its own path (i.e., was not a tributary of the river Po) was in Dante's time the Montone. Dante thought of the Acquacheta (the name means "quiet water") as the upper Montone; it is now considered a tributary of the Montone. When in spate, the Acquacheta falls in a single cataract at San Benedetto delle Alpi (see the map of Romagna and Tuscany, p. xiv). There is a variant at line 102, discussed in "Textual Variants."

105. it would have harmed our ears: Dante is thinking here (as at line 2) of the din of the famous cataracts of the Nile, which according to Cicero make the inhabitants of the region deaf (*Somnium Scipionis* 5.3). Macrobius (*Commentarii* 2.4.14) compares their sound (negatively) to the music of the spheres.

106–14. I had a cord girding me ... threw it down: This cord represents one of the most famous cruxes in the poem, for which a vast number of symbolic interpretations have been proposed (they include, among others, self-reliance, law, temperance, chastity, "the bond of love that Nature makes," justice, pity, lust, and pride). One whole family of interpretation rests on the identification of the leopard of Canto 1 with lust; this, though defended by such scholars as Nardi (1966), seems to us excluded by the clear connection this passage establishes between the leopard and fraud (compare the leopard's spotted hide with that of Geryon in Canto 17). In the pilgrim's encounter with the leopard (1.31–39), there is no mention of the belt nor of the intention of capturing the beast, though the pilgrim takes "good hope" of it; and the pilgrim's giving up his belt here seems to have no consequences other than attracting Geryon; there is no further reference to it, except perhaps for the pilgrim's girding himself with a rush (apparently signifying humility) in *Purgatorio* 1 (this connection would supply support for the view that the throwing of the cord is a symbolic giving up of self-reliance: but that does not make it specific to entering the Malebolge).

The most satisfactory explanation seems to us to be that of the early commentators, who understood the pilgrim's cord to represent fraud, in other words the pilgrim's own inclination to fraud (or history of it); it attracts Geryon, who hopes to entrap him. The knotted cord would seem to reflect the iconography of personified Dialectic, who holds one signifying her ability to bind men's minds

(Masciandaro 1979); thus the cord would be part of the important theme of the relation to fraud of Dante's poetry itself (see Ferrucci 1971 and the notes on Geryon in Canto 17).

112. And he turned . . . and . . . threw it: That is, Virgil wheels on his right side in preparation for the throw (he is evidently right-handed).

118–20. Ah, how cautious . . . our inner thoughts: Preparation for the theme of fraud.

124–26. Always to that truth . . . it brings shame: In other words, when speaking a truth that seems a falsehood (as opposed to the lie that seems true, the theme of the circles of fraud), one may be blamed for lying without having done so (whereas the fraudulent, if successful, are credited with speaking the truth). That a truth may have the face or appearance of a lie implies, of course, that a truth may also have the face of truth, be obviously true, and be immediately believed; this seems to be the case in lines 76–78: and note the emphasis on *the pilgrim's* face in line 76 (the metaphorics of face and belly are discussed in Additional Note 13).

127–29. by the notes of this comedy . . . long favor: This is the third of the seven apostrophes of the reader in the *Inferno* (see the note to 8.94–96). Within the fiction, the oath contributes effectively to the mysterious and threatening emergence of the figure of Geryon, but it is important for other reasons as well. It contains the first appearance in the poem of what amounts to its title (the addition of the epithet "divine" became customary in the sixteenth century) (see the note to 21.2).

The "notes" by which the poet swears are, of course, the words of the poem (cf. the note to lines 19–20); it was customary to swear by what one held most dear (plausibly the case for Dante). That the poet swears to what is obviously a fiction has excited comment that has not always been attentive to the nature of the "truth" Dante claims for the figure of Geryon; the relation of the "face of falsehood" here to the true-seeming face of Geryon is discussed also in the notes to 17.10–27; here we may observe that in this oath, and by naming his poem here, close to the center of the *Inferno,* the poet is both asserting the importance of his analysis of fraud and problematizing the fictional-allegorical mode of the poem. See Additional Note 13.

130–36. I saw . . . draws in his feet: The vivid description of Geryon's flight describes it in terms of swimming, as the Florentines' running was compared to flight (line 87).

132. fearful: The Italian is *maravigliosa* [causing wonder or alarm]; compare with Brunetto's exclamation, 15.24.

133–36. as one returns ... draws in his feet: A vivid evocation of the motions of a swimmer. It should be remembered that Geryon is swimming/flying up from very deep in Hell, figurally the abyss, or the depths of the sea. Geryon is discussed in the notes to Canto 17.

CANTO 17

1   "Ecco la fiera con la coda aguzza,
che passa i monti e rompe i muri e l'armi!
Ecco colei che tutto 'l mondo appuzza!"

4   Sì cominciò lo mio duca a parlarmi;
e accennolle che venisse a proda
vicino al fin d'i passeggiati marmi.

7   E quella sozza imagine di froda
sen venne, e arrivò la testa e 'l busto,
ma 'n su la riva non trasse la coda.

10   La faccia sua era faccia d'uom giusto,
tanto benigna avea di fuor la pelle,
e d'un serpente tutto l'altro fusto;

13   due branche avea pilose insin l'ascelle;
lo dosso e 'l petto e ambedue le coste
dipinti avea di nodi e di rotelle:

16   con più color, sommesse e sovraposte,
non fer mai drappi Tartari né Turchi,
né fuor tai tele per Aragne imposte.

19   Come talvolta stanno a riva i burchi,
che parte sono in acqua e parte in terra,
e come là tra li Tedeschi lurchi

22   lo bivero s'assetta a far sua guerra:
così la fiera pessima si stava
su l'orlo ch'è di pietra e 'l sabbion serra.

25   Nel vano tutta sua coda guizzava,
torcendo in sù la venenosa forca
ch'a guisa di scorpion la punta armava.

28   Lo duca disse: "Or convien che si torca
la nostra via un poco insino a quella
bestia malvagia che colà si corca."

CANTO 17

Geryon, the "filthy image of fraud"—the usurers—descent on Geryon's back

1   "Behold the beast with the pointed tail, that passes through mountains and pierces walls and armor! Behold the one that makes the whole world stink!"

4   So my leader began speaking to me; and he gestured to it to come ashore near the end of our marble pathway.

7   And that filthy image of fraud came over and beached its head and chest, but did not draw up its tail as far as the bank.

10   Its face was that of a just man, so kindly seemed its outer skin, and the rest of its torso was that of a serpent;

13   it had two paws, hairy to the armpits; it had back and breast and both sides painted with knots and little wheels:

16   with more colors, in weave and embroidery, did never Tartars nor Turks make cloths, nor did Arachne string the loom for such tapestries.

19   As skiffs lie on the shore at times, partly in water and partly on land, and as there among the drunken Germans

22   the beaver positions itself to wage its war: so the wicked beast rested on the rim of stone that encloses the sand.

25   In the emptiness all its tail was wriggling, twisting upward the poisoned fork that armed its tip like a scorpion's.

28   My leader said: "Now our path must bend a little toward the evil beast that lies over there."

31   Però scendemmo a la destra mammella
e diece passi femmo in su lo stremo,
per ben cessar la rena e la fiammella.

34   E quando noi a lei venuti semo,
poco più oltre veggio in su la rena
gente seder propinqua al loco scemo.

37   Quivi 'l maestro: "Acciò che tutta piena
esperïenza d'esto giron porti,"
mi disse, "va, e vedi la lor mena.

40   Li tuoi ragionamenti sian là corti;
mentre che torni, parlerò con questa,
che ne conceda i suoi omeri forti."

43   Così ancor su per la strema testa
di quel settimo cerchio tutto solo
andai, dove sedea la gente mesta.

46   Per li occhi fora scoppiava lor duolo;
di qua, di là soccorrien con le mani
quando a' vapori, e quando al caldo suolo:

49   non altrimenti fan di state i cani
or col ceffo or col piè, quando son morsi
o da pulci o da mosche o da tafani.

52   Poi che nel viso a certi li occhi porsi,
ne' quali 'l doloroso foco casca,
non ne conobbi alcun; ma io m'accorsi

55   che dal collo a ciascun pendea una tasca
ch'avea certo colore e certo segno,
e quindi par che 'l loro occhio si pasca.

58   E com' io riguardando tra lor vegno,
in una borsa gialla vidi azzurro
che d'un leone avea faccia e contegno.

61   Poi, procedendo di mio sguardo il curro,
vidine un'altra come sangue rossa,
mostrando un'oca bianca più che burro.

64   E un che d'una scrofa azzurra e grossa
segnato avea lo suo sacchetto bianco,
mi disse: "Che fai tu in questa fossa?

67   Or te ne va; e perché se' vivo anco,
sappi che 'l mio vicin Vitalïano
sederà qui dal mio sinistro fianco.

31   Therefore we descended toward the right breast
and made ten paces to the edge, to be well beyond
the sand and the flames.

34   And when we had reached it, a little further, on
the sand, I see people sitting near the empty place.

37   There my master said to me: "That you may carry
away full experience of this subcircle, go, and see
their behavior.

40   Let your speech there be brief; until you return, I
will speak with this beast, that it may grant us its
strong shoulders."

43   So once more along the outer edge of that seventh
circle I walked all alone, where the mournful people
were sitting.

46   Through their eyes burst forth their pain; here,
there, they sought remedy with their hands at times
against the fire, at times against the hot ground;

49   not otherwise do the dogs behave in the summer,
now with muzzle, now with foot, when they are
bitten by fleas or gnats or horseflies.

52   When I turned my eyes to their faces, on which
the painful fire falls down, I recognized none; but I
perceived

55   that from the neck of each hung a bag of a special
color, with a special emblem, and their eyes seem to
feed there.

58   And as I come gazing among them, on a yellow
purse I saw blue that had the shape and bearing of a
lion.

61   Then, proceeding further with my scrutiny, I saw
another, red as blood, displaying a goose whiter than
butter.

64   And one who had his little white sack signed with
a fat blue sow, said to me: "What are you doing in
this ditch?

67   Now go away; and since you are alive, too, know
that my neighbor Vitaliano will sit here at my left
flank.

70   Con questi Fiorentin son padoano:
spesse fïate mi 'ntronan li orecchi
gridando: 'Vegna 'l cavalier sovrano,

73   che recherà la tasca con tre becchi!'"
Qui distorse la bocca e di fuor trasse
la lingua, come bue che 'l naso lecchi.

76   E io, temendo no 'l più star crucciasse
lui che di poco star m'avea 'mmonito,
torna'mi in dietro da l'anime lasse.

79   Trova' il duca mio ch'era salito
già su la groppa del fiero animale,
e disse a me: "Or sie forte e ardito:

82   omai si scende per sì fatte scale.
Monta dinanzi, ch'i' voglio esser mezzo,
sì che la coda non possa far male."

85   Qual è colui che sì presso ha 'l riprezzo
de la quartana c'ha già l'unghie smorte
e triema tutto pur guardando 'l rezzo:

88   tal divenn' io a le parole porte;
ma vergogna mi fé le sue minacce,
che innanzi a buon segnor fa servo forte.

91   I' m'assettai in su quelle spallacce;
"Sì," volli dir, ma la voce non venne
com' io credetti: "Fa che tu m'abbracce."

94   Ma esso, ch'altra volta mi sovvenne
ad altro forse, tosto ch'i' montai
con le braccia m'avvinse e mi sostenne;

97   e disse: "Gerïon, moviti omai;
le rote larghe, e lo scender sia poco:
pensa la nova soma che tu hai."

100   Come la navicella esce di loco
in dietro in dietro, sì quindi si tolse;
e poi ch'al tutto si sentì a gioco,

103   là 'v' era 'l petto, la coda rivolse,
e quella tesa, come anguilla, mosse,
e con le branche l'aere a sé raccolse.

106   Maggior paura non credo che fosse
quando Fetonte abbandonò li freni,
per che 'l ciel, come pare ancor, si cosse,

70 With these Florentines I am a Paduan: often they
thunder in my ears shouting, 'Let the reigning knight
come down,

73 who will bring the bag with the three goats.'" Here
he twisted his mouth and stuck out his tongue, like an
ox licking its snout.

76 And I, fearing lest a longer stay might displease
him who had warned me to be brief, turned back,
away from those weary souls.

79 I found my leader had climbed already onto the
fierce animal's rump, and he told me: "Now be strong
and bold:

82 henceforth we descend by stairs like these. Mount
in front, for I wish to be between, so that its tail
can do no harm."

85 Like one whose fit of the quartan fever is so close
that his nails are already pale and he trembles all
over merely looking at the shade:

88 so I became at the words I heard; but shame made
its threats, that makes a servant bold in the presence
of a good lord.

91 I positioned myself on those monstrous shoulders;
"Yes," I wanted to say, but my voice did not come as I
expected: "Be sure to hold me."

94 But he, who had supported me at other times, in
other dangers, as soon as I mounted clasped and
braced me with his arms;

97 and he said: "Geryon, now move; make your
wheelings large, your descent slow: consider the new
weight you carry."

100 As a little boat moves from its place backward,
backward, so he moved thence; and when he felt
himself entirely free,

103 he turned his tail where his breast had been, and,
extending it, he moved it like an eel's, and gathered
the air to himself with his paws.

106 I believe there was no greater fear when Phaëthon
abandoned the reins, so that the sky was scorched, as
still appears,

109   né quando Icaro misero le reni
      sentì spennar per la scaldata cera,
      gridando il padre a lui, "Mala via tieni!"

112   che fu la mia, quando vidi ch'i' era
      ne l'aere d'ogne parte, e vidi spenta
      ogne veduta fuor che de la fera.

115   Ella sen va notando lenta lenta;
      rota e discende, ma non me n'accorgo
      se non che al viso e di sotto mi venta.

118   Io sentia già da la man destra il gorgo
      far sotto noi un orribile scroscio,
      per che con li occhi 'n giù la testa sporgo.

121   Allor fu' io più timido a lo stoscio,
      però ch'i' vidi fuochi e senti' pianti;
      ond' io tremando tutto mi raccoscio.

124   E vidi poi, ché nol vedea davanti,
      lo scendere e 'l girar per li gran mali
      che s'appressavan da diversi canti.

127   Come 'l falcon ch'è stato assai su l'ali,
      che sanza veder logoro o uccello
      fa dire al falconiere: "Omè, tu cali!"

130   discende lasso onde si move isnello,
      per cento rote, e da lunge si pone
      dal suo maestro, disdegnoso e fello:

133   così ne puose al fondo Gerïone,
      al piè al piè de la stagliata rocca,
      e, discarcate le nostre persone,

136   si dileguò come da corda cocca.

109   nor when the wretched Icarus felt his loins unfeathering because of the heated wax, as his father shouted to him, "You're on a bad course!"

112   than was mine, when I saw that I was in the air on every side, and every sight put out save that of the beast.

115   It goes along swimming slowly, slowly; it wheels and descends, but I perceive its motion only by the wind on my face from below.

118   I could already hear at my right hand the torrent making a horrible roar beneath us, and so I lean out my head, looking down.

121   Then I became more afraid of falling, for I saw fires and heard weeping; so that all trembling I huddled back.

124   And then I saw what I had not seen before, our descending and turning against the great evils that came closer on every side.

127   As when a falcon has been long on the wing and, without seeing lure or prey, makes the falconer say, "Oh me, you are coming down!"

130   descending weary to the place it swiftly left, with a hundred circlings, and lands far from its master, full of disdain and spite:

133   so Geryon placed us on the bottom, at the very foot of the vertical rock, and, our persons unloaded,

136   disappeared like the notch from the bowstring.

NOTES

1–3. Behold the beast . . . the whole world stink: This unusual canto opening serves partly to heighten interest in the still undescribed creature that came swimming up at the end of the last canto. It also calls attention to the fact that, like Cantos 8 and 9, this canto forms a major transition between divisions of Hell, for we now move from the circle of violence to the two circles of fraud (simple fraud and treacherous fraud [see 11.52–66]; for the new elaborateness of canto openings in the Malebolge, see the note on 18.1–18).

Line 7 makes it explicit that Geryon is a personification of fraud. Fraud makes all physical barriers and defenses (mountains, walls, and armor) useless. It makes "the whole world stink" primarily with the venom of its scorpion-like tail (lines 25–27); this is a submerged reference to fraud as poison (truth is the food of the soul-mind, deception its poison; see Additional Note 13).

5. come ashore: Continues the nautical terminology of 16.131–36. See also the notes to lines 8–9, 19–24, and 100–101.

6. our marble pathway: That is, the margin of the river of blood, on which the pilgrim and Virgil are standing, first mentioned as their pathway in 14.84 (see the note to 15.4–11).

8. beached its head and chest: See the note to lines 19–24; another nautical image.

10–27. Its face . . . like a scorpion's: The description of Geryon draws on a wide variety of sources, such as the description in Apoc. 9.7–10 of the plague of locusts: "And their faces were as the faces of men. . . . And they had tails like to scorpions, and there were stings in their tails." (Geryon's being called a beast in line 1 may also recall the beast of Apoc. 11.7.) Dante also draws on the fabulous Manticore described by Pliny and by Brunetto Latini in *Trésor* 1.192, which combines parts of man, lion, and scorpion; and contemporary, especially Franciscan, discussions of the Antichrist (Friedman 1972). Geryon is a triple hybrid (the first in the poem; previous hybrids have been double), whose successive parts—man, beast (bear?), and serpent—descend on the scale of nature (the scorpion was classed as a worm) (see the note to line 97).

In Geryon, the pilgrim sees the process of fraud spatially, as it were from outside time (in itself an apocalyptic perspective). The succession of Geryon's parts is a spatial representation of the chronological sequence of a fraudulent "deal": the honest appearance engages initial trust, the bright colors and little wheels complicate and confuse, and the end of the process brings the sting, whether of loss or of death; at some point the claws begin acquiring.

10. Its face was that of a just man: In *Convivio* 4.12.3, Dante mentions "the traitor, who, in the face he puts forward, shows as a friend, but under it conceals his enmity" (cf. 16.124–26, 127–29, with notes). It was apparently a common belief in Dante's time that the scorpion's face resembled a human face.

12. its torso was that of a serpent: Like Cerberus, "the great worm" (6.22), and Minos (5.7–12), Geryon is part snake. The serpent was of course the first deceiver (Genesis 3); compare also the dragon of the Apocalypse (Apoc. 12.2–3 and 12.9).

14–18. it had back and breast . . . for such tapestries: Geryon's brightly "colored" (*dipinti*) torso recalls the "gaily painted hide" (1.42) of the leopard (cf. 16.108, "painted skin," *pelle dipinta*) and provides the basis of the most probable identification of the leopard, that it represents fraud.

The association of fraud (and the telling of tales) with spinning and weaving is ancient and virtually universal (compare such English expressions as "pull the wool over someone's eyes"). In Ovid's *Metamorphoses* (6.1–145) Arachne challenges Minerva to a weaving contest. While Minerva makes a tapestry showing the benefactions of the gods, Arachne's (which Ovid says is just as skillful as Minerva's) shows the disguises, deceptions, and crimes of the gods. The envious and enraged goddess strikes Arachne and destroys her work; Arachne attempts to hang herself but is changed by Minerva into a spider. In the medieval allegorical interpretations of Ovid, Arachne is identified as the devil.

Dante's "weave and embroidery" (line 16) and "painted" (line 15) refer to tapestries, for both Minerva and Arachne weave colored backgrounds and then embroider figures with gold thread (*Met.* 6.23: "pingebat acu" [she painted with the needle] and 6.68–69):

> illic et lentum filis immittitur aurum,
> et vetus in tela deducitur argumentum.
>
> [the pliant gold is inserted among the threads,
> and the old story is drawn into the weave.]

For Arachne and painting, see Barkan 1988.

19–24. As skiffs . . . the sand: As in lines 7–9, Dante here emphasizes that the beast is only halfway on the shore; half of his body remains in the void. We are now close to the midpoint of the *Inferno*; if we count Geryon, more than half of the *Inferno* is devoted to the sins of fraud. In terms of the body analogy (see Additional Note 13), this midpoint is the division between chest and abdomen.

22. the beaver positions itself to wage its war: That the beaver used its tail to attract fish which it then caught was a widespread belief.

27. like a scorpion's: Compare Ovid, *Met.* 2.195–97:

Est locus, in geminos ubi bracchia concavat arcus
Scorpius et cauda flexisque utrimque lacertis
porrigit in spatium signorum membra duorum.

[There is a place, where Scorpius curves in double arcs
his arms, and, with tail and legs curving on both sides,
extends his members over two signs of heaven.]

For the tale of Phaëthon, from which this passage is drawn, see the note to lines 106–11.

31. toward the right breast: For similar expressions, see 12.97, 15.98. Since the river of blood lies to their left, there is no other direction of descent from the high margin: everything they have seen from it (all the souls of this circle so far, and Geryon) has been to their right (see the note to 9.132).

35. a little further: That is, still to the right.

40–41. I will speak with this beast: Dante opens a parenthesis here, marked by the pilgrim's turns to and from the right: the pilgrim returns to the beast at line 79; within the parenthesis is the account of the usurers. Compare the "border" zones at the beginning of the poem (Limbo, the neutrals) and between incontinence and violence (the wrathful and slothful, the heretics) with the border of the circle of violence here, in a sense already within the orbit of "the image of fraud."

45. the mournful people were sitting: The third of the groups listed in 14.22–24. The sitting posture suits the idleness of usurers, whose "work" is done by their money (cf. line 78).

49. dogs behave in the summer: The commentators note the disparaging comparison of the usurers to animals here and in line 75, and in the animals on their associated bags (lines 60, 63, 64, 73).

51. gnats or horseflies: The Italian literally means "flies and horseflies."

54. I recognized none: Several of these figures have been identified, but Dante's point lies partly in the fact that conviction for usury often brought not only civil and religious penalties but also public infamy, which extended to children and relatives.

55. a bag of a special color: Contemporary accounts prove that bags were carried by moneylenders and placed on their changing tables (Salvemini 1901–1902); visual representations of Hell (e.g., the *Last Judgment* in the Scrovegni Chapel in Padua) typically show usurers holding bags.

57. their eyes seem to feed there: Compare Eccles. 4.8: "neither are his eyes satisfied with riches." The obsession of the usurers with both coats of arms and moneybags focuses Dante's condemnation of a class, many of whose members were recently knighted, that owed its wealth and influence to the practice of usury (see the note to lines 64–65). Dante's verb here, *pascere*, is normally used of the grazing of animals.

59. on a yellow purse . . . a lion: The device of the Gianfigliazzi family of Florence, prominent Guelfs after 1215 and followers of the Black Guelfs after 1300. The figure here is perhaps Catello di Rosso Gianfigliazzi, who practiced usury in France and became a knight on returning to Florence; he was dead by 1298.

62–63. red as blood . . . whiter than butter: The Ghibelline Obriachi were a Florentine family of the high aristocracy residing in the part of the Oltrarno that includes the modern Via dei Bardi. Closely allied with the Uberti, Farinata's family, they were well known as bankers and money changers.

64–65. sack signed with a fat blue sow: A blue sow big with young, rampant, was the device of the wealthy Scrovegni (from *scrofa*, sow) family of Padua (see line 70). Reginaldo Scrovegni, who died in 1290, made an immense fortune; his son Arrico obtained a knighthood. Arrico financed the Scrovegni Chapel at Padua, frescoed by Giotto in the first decade of the fourteenth century; it is conceivable that Dante, who seems to have been in Padua at an appropriate time, helped with the planning.

68. my neighbor . . . at my left flank: This expected usurer (the only one given a name), is usually identified with Vitaliano del Dente, who married a daughter of Reginaldo Scrovegni and served as *podestà* of several cities; there is little evidence, beyond this passage, for his having been a usurer. Scrovegni's phraseology may evoke the placing of the wicked thief, and of the reprobate at the Last Judgment, at Christ's left.

72–73. Let the reigning knight . . . three goats: Three goats in a gold field was the device of the Buiamonte family. Giovanni di Buiamonte de' Becchi was Gonfaloniere della Giustizia (commissioner and chief of police) of Florence in 1293, when only newly a knight.

74–75. Here he twisted . . . licking its snout: The usurer's grotesque gesture (he is the one with the sow on his bag) expresses both reduction to bestiality and a weird sluggishness perhaps associated with their sin.

81. Now be strong and bold: See 2.14–15, with note.

82. henceforth we descend by stairs like these: The figure of the "chain" or "ladder of being" is all but explicit (see the notes on 2.52–117 and 11.18, and Introduction, pp. 18–20). Geryon is a ladder not only in providing transport, but by representing in his body the descent from the human to the lowest of the beasts, as Minos's tail mapped the coils of Hell. See also 34.82, 119 and notes.

86–87. quartan fever . . . at the shade: Tertian and quartan fevers are forms of malaria whose attacks recur every forty-eight and seventy-two hours, respectively. The pilgrim's symptoms echo those of the frightened Phaëthon (*Met.* 2.200): "mentis inops gelida formidine" [his mind failed, frozen with fear]; see also *Met.* 2.180: "palluit, et subito genua intremuere timore" [he turned pale, and suddenly his knees shook with fear]. For Phaëthon, see also the note to lines 106–14.

96. clasped and braced me: As in lines 83–84, this may be taken allegorically, indicating the wayfarer protected by his guide, reason, from the threat of fraud. For Virgil carrying the pilgrim bodily, see 19.43–44, 124 and 23.49–51, 24.22–24.

97. Geryon: Only now is the "image of fraud" given a name, that of one of the classical monsters defeated by Hercules (like Cerberus in Canto 6; other defeated opponents of Hercules are Cacus, in Canto 25, and Antaeus, in Canto 31). According to Vergil, Geryon is triple-bodied (*Aen.* 6.289: "forma tricorporis umbrae" [the form of the triple-bodied shade]). By making him a triple hybrid, Dante metamorphoses Geryon into a fantastic creature like the classical Chimera (lion, goat, and serpent), mentioned along with Geryon at *Aen.* 6.288.

98–99. your wheelings large, your descent slow: Geryon is to avoid the extremes of too narrow an arc or of too precipitous a descent. For the relation of these instructions to those given to Phaëthon and Icarus, see the note to lines 106–11 and Additional Note 6, which also discusses the relation of Geryon's motion to that of the sun. See also 34.96 and note.

99. consider the new weight you carry: A reference to the pilgrim's physical body (see 8.27, with note). Benvenuto de' Rambaldi began the tradition of attributing a metaliterary implication to the pilgrim's flight on Geryon, associating the "new weight" with the new subject matter of the circles of fraud. Current criticism tends to see the flight on Geryon as metaphorical for the entire poem (Ferrucci 1971; Barolini 1992).

100–101. As a little boat . . . he moved thence: The figure of Geryon as a boat (see lines 5, 19) is continued. Ovid, in *Met.* 2.163–66, compares the chariot of Phaëthon (see next note) to a boat with insufficient ballast (Brownlee 1984), and at *Met.* 8.228 compares Icarus's wings to oars. For this comparison (used to illustrate metaphor in medieval handbooks of rhetoric), see the note to 26.125; the parallel between Ulysses' and the pilgrim's journeys begins to be established here.

106–11. I believe . . . bad course: To describe the pilgrim's fear of riding on the back of Geryon, Dante draws on a pair of Ovidian myths that were traditional examples of overreaching: in the first (*Met.* 1.747–2.332), Phaëthon requests, as proof of his divine origin, that his father Helios (the sun) allow him to drive the chariot of the sun for one day. Losing control of the horses, Phaëthon allows the chariot to veer from its track and burns both the heavens, leaving the Milky Way as a scorch mark (cf. lines 107–8; Dante mentions the Milky Way in *Convivio* 2.14), and the earth, making the Sahara Desert (*Met.* 2.237–38; see 24.85–90, with note), until felled by a lightning bolt from Jove.

The second myth (*Met.* 8.183–259) is that of Icarus, the son of Daedalus the craftsman. Escaping with him from the labyrinth of King Minos (see 12.12, 25 and notes) on wings fashioned by his father, Icarus disregards his father's advice to steer a middle course between sky and sea (hence the cry of Dante's line 111, which does not appear in Ovid) and flies too close to the sun, whose heat melts the wax holding his wings together; he falls into the sea and drowns. Mention of Icarus completes a series of references to Cretan myth in the middle area of Hell (see the note to 12.12 and Additional Notes 3 and 6).

106, 110. when Phaëthon abandoned . . . , when the wretched Icarus felt: As the commentators point out, Dante chooses the critical moments: when Phaëthon, terrified by the Scorpion (with a stinging tail, like Geryon), "abandons the reins" (*Met.* 2.200: *lora remisit*), and when Icarus, climbing too high, feels the wax melting (8.226: "mollit odoratas, pennarum vincula, ceras" [it softened the sweet-smelling wax, the bonds of his wings]).

120–26. I lean out . . . came closer on every side: The vividness and accuracy of Dante's imagining of night flight, particularly of the perception of descent by the sight of the lights on the ground, is striking.

127–32. As when a falcon . . . spite: The second of many images in the poem drawn from falconry (in the *Inferno*, see 3.117, 22.128–41, and 33.22). The falcon of this simile, returning without prey and unbidden by its master, is both like and unlike Geryon, who is bearing the load of the pilgrim, but not doing so willingly. The simile and the tercet that follows, juxtaposing Geryon's turnings at Virgil's bidding (see lines 97–99) with the direct flight of an arrow (line 136), expresses the reluctance of Geryon's obedience to Virgil, the strongest argument for the view of some commentators that Geryon—and his master—have been defrauded of expected prey.

132. its master: The point of view of the simile is that of the falconer (line 129); it is implied that the falconer is Satan, Geryon's lord (cf. 3.117).

136. like the notch from the bowstring: The comparison of directed motion to the flight of an arrow is frequent in Dante's work and in thirteenth-century writing on physics generally; see Aquinas, *Summa theol.* 1a, q. 1, a. 2: "thus an arrow directs itself to its determined end because it is set in motion by the bowman, who directs his action to an end" (cf. 8.13–14, on Phlegyas).

CANTO 18

1
Luogo è in inferno detto Malebolge,
tutto di pietra di color ferrigno,
come la cerchia che dintorno il volge.

4
Nel dritto mezzo del campo maligno
vaneggia un pozzo assai largo e profondo,
di cui *suo loco* dicerò l'ordigno.

7
Quel cinghio che rimane adunque è tondo
tra 'l pozzo e 'l piè de l'alta ripa dura,
e ha distinto in dieci valli il fondo.

10
Quale, dove per guardia de le mura
più e più fossi cingon i castelli,
la parte dove son rende figura:

13
tale imagine quivi facean quelli;
e come a tai fortezze da' lor sogli
a la ripa di fuor son ponticelli:

16
così da imo de la roccia scogli
movien che ricidien li argini e' fossi
infino al pozzo che i tronca e raccogli.

19
In questo luogo, de la schiena scossi
di Gerïon, trovammoci; e 'l poeta
tenne a sinistra, e io dietro mi mossi.

22
A la man destra vidi nova pieta,
novo tormento e novi frustatori,
di che la prima bolgia era repleta.

25
Nel fondo erano ignudi i peccatori;
dal mezzo in qua ci venien verso 'l volto,
di là con noi, ma con passi maggiori:

28
come i Roman per l'essercito molto,
l'anno del giubileo, su per lo ponte
hanno a passar la gente modo colto,

CANTO 18

Eighth circle: simple fraud—the plan of Malebolge—first bolgia:
panders and seducers—second bolgia: *flatterers*

1　　There is in Hell a place called Malebolge, made of
stone the color of iron, like the circle that encloses it.

4　　In the exact center of the evil field there gapes a
broad, deep pit, whose fashion I will tell *suo loco*.

7　　The belt that remains, then, is round, between the
pit and the foot of the high hard bank, and its
bottom is divided into ten valleys.

10　　As, where to guard the walls many moats gird
castles, their placing traces a pattern:

13　　such an image these valleys made there; and as
from the thresholds of such fortresses bridges lead to
the outside bank:

16　　so, from the base of the cliff, ridges moved that
cut across the banks and the ditches, as far as the pit
that truncates and gathers them in.

19　　In this place, shaken from Geryon's back, we
found ourselves; and my poet moved toward the left,
and I followed him.

22　　On my right hand I saw new cause for pity, new
torments and new wielders of the whip, of which the first
pocket was full.

25　　At the bottom were the sinners, naked; on this side
of the midpoint they came with their faces toward
us, on the other side in our direction, but with longer
steps:

28　　as the Romans, the year of the Jubilee, because of
the great throng, found a way to move people across
the bridge,

31   che da l'un lato tutti hanno la fronte
        verso 'l castello e vanno a Santo Pietro,
        da l'altra sponda vanno verso 'l monte.

34   Di qua, di là, su per lo sasso tetro
        vidi demon cornuti con gran ferze
        che li battien crudelmente di retro.

37   Ahi come facean lor levar le berze
        a le prime percosse! già nessuno
        le seconde aspettava né le terze.

40   Mentr' io andava, li occhi miei in uno
        furo scontrati, e io sì tosto dissi:
        "Già di veder costui non son digiuno."

43   Per ch' ïo a figurarlo i piedi affissi;
        e 'l dolce duca meco si ristette
        e assentio ch'alquanto in dietro gissi.

46   E quel frustato celar si credette
        bassando 'l viso; ma poco li valse,
        ch'io dissi: "O tu che l'occhio a terra gette,

49   se le fazion che porti non son false,
        Venedico se' tu Caccianemico.
        Ma che ti mena a sì pungenti salse?"

52   Ed elli a me: "Mal volontier lo dico,
        ma sforzami la tua chiara favella,
        che mi fa sovvenir del mondo antico.

55   I' fui colui che la Ghisolabella
        condussi a far la voglia del marchese,
        come che suoni la sconcia novella.

58   E non pur io qui piango bolognese;
        anzi n'è questo loco tanto pieno
        che tante lingue non son ora apprese

61   a dicer *sipa* tra Sàvena e Reno;
        e se di ciò vuoi fede o testimonio,
        rècati a mente il nostro avaro seno."

64   Così parlando il percosse un demonio
        de la sua scurïada, e disse: "Via,
        ruffian! qui non son femmine da conio."

67   I' mi raggiunsi con la scorta mia;
        poscia con pochi passi divenimmo
        là 'v' uno scoglio de la ripa uscia.

31   for on one side they are all turned toward the Castle and are going toward Saint Peter, and on the other they are going toward the mountain.

34   Here and there, along the dark rock, I saw horned demons with great whips, who were beating them from behind.

37   Ah, how the first blow made each lift his heels! none waited for the second or the third.

40   As I was walking, my eye fell on one; immediately I said: "I am certainly not fasting for sight of him."

43   And so I stopped my pace to make out his features; and my sweet leader stopped with me and consented that I walk a little backward.

46   And that whipped one thought to hide by lowering his face; but it little availed him, for I said: "O you who cast your eyes to the earth,

49   if your features are not false, you are Venedico Caccianemico. But what leads you to such pungent sauces?"

52   And he to me: "Unwilling I say it, but your clear speech compels me, reminding me of the former world.

55   It was I who induced Ghisolabella to do the marchese's will, however they tell the shameful tale.

58   And not only I weep here from Bologna, for this place is so full of us that not so many tongues have learned

61   to say *sipa* now between the Sàvena and the Reno; and if you want proof or testimony of that, bring to mind our greedy breast."

64   As he was speaking a demon struck him with his scourge, and said: "Away, pimp! here there are no females to coin."

67   I caught up with my guide; then after a few steps we came to where a ridge went out from the bank.

70   Assai leggeramente quel salimmo;
e vòlti a destra su per la sua scheggia
da quelle cerchie etterne ci partimmo.

73   Quando noi fummo là dov' el vaneggia
di sotto per dar passo a li sferzati,
lo duca disse: "Attienti, e fa che feggia

76   lo viso in te di quest' altri mal nati
ai quali ancor non vedesti la faccia,
però che son con noi insieme andati."

79   Del vecchio ponte guardavam la traccia
che venìa verso noi da l'altra banda,
e che la ferza similmente scaccia.

82   E 'l buon maestro, sanza mia dimanda,
mi disse: "Guarda quel grande che vene,
e per dolor non par lagrime spanda:

85   quanto aspetto reale ancor ritene!
Quelli è Iasón, che per cuore e per senno
li Colchi del monton privati féne.

88   Ello passò per l'isola di Lenno
poi che l'ardite femmine spietate
tutti li maschi loro a morte dienno.

91   Ivi con segni e con parole ornate
Isifile ingannò, la giovinetta
che prima avea tutte l'altre ingannate.

94   Lasciolla quivi gravida, soletta:
tal colpa a tal martiro lui condanna,
e anche di Medea si fa vendetta.

97   Con lui sen va chi di tal parte inganna;
e questo basti de la prima valle
sapere e di color che 'n sé assanna."

100   Già eravam là 've lo stretto calle
con l'argine secondo s'incrocicchia
e fa di quello ad un altr' arco spalle.

103   Quindi sentimmo gente che si nicchia
ne l'altra bolgia e che col muso scuffa,
e sé medesma con le palme picchia.

106   Le ripe eran grommate d'una muffa,
per l'alito di giù che vi s'appasta,
che con li occhi e col naso facea zuffa.

70   Easily we climbed it, and, turning to the right
along its spine, we left those eternal circlings.

73   When we were above where it gapes to give
passage to the whipped ones, my leader said: "Wait,
and let the sight

76   of these other ill-born ones strike you, many of
whose faces you have not seen, since they have
walked together with us."

79   From the old bridge we looked down on the file
that was coming toward us on the other side,
likewise driven by the lash.

82   And my good master, without my asking, said:
"Look at that tall one coming, who does not seem to
be shedding any tears for the pain:

85   how regal is his bearing still! That is Jason, who
by courage and wit robbed the Colchians of the ram.

88   He visited the island of Lemnos after the bold,
pitiless women had put all their males to death.

91   There with tokens and elaborate words he
deceived Hypsipyle, the young girl who, before that,
had deceived all the other women.

94   He left her there pregnant and alone: such guilt
condemns him to this punishment, and also for
Medea vengeance is taken.

97   Those walk with him who deceive in that
direction; and let this be enough to know about the
first ditch and those it grinds in its teeth."

100   Already we had come to where the narrow
passage intersects the second bank and makes of it
the support for another arch.

103   From there we heard people whimpering in the
next pocket, and puffing with their snouts, and
striking themselves with their palms.

106   The banks were encrusted with a mold from the
breath from below that condenses there, which
assailed both eyes and nose.

109   Lo fondo è cupo sì che non ci basta
loco a veder sanza montare al dosso
de l'arco, ove lo scoglio più sovrasta.

112   Quivi venimmo; e quindi giù nel fosso
vidi gente attuffata in uno sterco
che da li umani privadi parea mosso.

115   E mentre ch'io là giù con l'occhio cerco,
vidi un col capo sì di merda lordo
che non parea s'era laico o cherco.

118   Quei mi sgridò: "Perché se' tu sì gordo
di riguardar più me che li altri brutti?"
E io a lui: "Perché, se ben ricordo,

121   già t'ho veduto coi capelli asciutti,
e se' Alessio Interminei da Lucca:
però t'adocchio più che li altri tutti."

124   Ed elli allor, battendosi la zucca:
"Qua giù m'hanno sommerso le lusinghe
ond' io non ebbi mai la lingua stucca."

127   Appresso ciò lo duca: "Fa che pinghe,"
mi disse, "il viso un poco più avante,
sì che la faccia ben con l'occhio attinghe

130   di quella sozza e scapigliata fante
che là si graffia con l'unghie merdose,
e or s'accoscia e ora è in piedi stante:

133   Taïde è, la puttana che rispuose
al drudo suo quando disse, 'Ho io grazie
grandi apo te?': 'Anzi maravigliose!'

136   E quinci sian le nostre viste sazie."

109 　The bottom is so deep that no vantage point is
sufficient without climbing on the back of the arch,
where the ridge is highest.

112 　There we came; and from there I saw, down in the
ditch, people immersed in dung that seemed to have
come from human privies.

115 　And while I am searching with my eyes down
there, I saw one with his head so filthy with shit that
whether he was lay or clerk did not show.

118 　He scolded me: "Why are you so hungry to look
more at me than the other filthy ones?" And I to him:
"Because, if I recall well,

121 　I have seen you before with dry hair, and you are
Alessio Interminei of Lucca; therefore I eye you more
than all the others."

124 　And he again, beating his noggin: "I am
submerged down here by the flatteries with which
my tongue was never cloyed."

127 　After that, my leader told me: "See that you push
your eye a little further on, so that it attains the face

130 　of that filthy baggage with disordered hair who
is scratching herself with her shitty nails, now
squatting, now standing on her feet:

133 　that is Thaïs, the whore who, when he said, 'Do I
find great favor with you?' replied to her lover:
'Marvelous favor indeed!'

136 　And therewith let our eyes be sated."

NOTES

1–18. There is in Hell a place . . . gathers them in: This abrupt abandoning of the point of view of the pilgrim for that of the omniscient author provides a kind of proem to the Malebolge as a whole (Cantos 18–30); we now begin the second half of the *Inferno*. In Malebolge, Cantos 18–22, 24, 26, 28, and 30 (i.e., nine cantos out of thirteen) have proems emphasizing the craftsmanship of the poet; they contribute strongly to the formal unity of these thirteen cantos. (Cantos 23, 25, 27, and 29—in all but the last case the second of two or more cantos devoted to a single *bolgia*—continue the narrative without interruption.) This new self-conscious emphasis, which begins at 16.128–29 in connection with the introduction of Geryon, represents a marked change from the cantos preceding Malebolge; it is one of the ways Dante makes the entire poetic texture more elaborate and more intense, as well as keeping before the reader the problematic relation of poetry (fiction, allegory) to fraud.

1. There is in Hell a place . . . Malebolge: *Malebolge* means literally "evil pouches" or "sacks." The Italian word *bolgia* was borrowed from Old French *bulge* (from medieval Latin *bulga*, apparently Celtic in origin), a bulge or what bulges, thus a sack or purse (also in Middle English: see Skelton's "Bouge of Court"). The implicit comment on the greed that is said to motivate most of the fraudulent is clear enough (see 19.71–72, where the point is made explicit). The metaphor of the sack, especially appropriate to the "belly" of Hell, was used also in 6.49–50 and 7.18. See Additional Note 13.

For the expression *luogo è* [there is a place], compare Latin *est locus*, as in the story of Phaëthon quoted in the note to 17.27.

2. the color of iron: Dark gray.

5. broad, deep pit: The pit is Cocytus, where traitors are punished.

6. *suo loco*: Latin for "in its own place," that is, in Cantos 32–34.

7–9. The belt that remains . . . ten valleys: The ten valleys containing the ten varieties of "simple" fraud (see 11.52–60) are obviously imagined as concentric circles around the central pit.

10–18. where to guard . . . and gathers them in: The castle simile, deliberately contorted in syntax, rests on a noteworthy reversal at line 16, for the surrounding cliff is correlated with the *central* keep of a castle, and the central pit with the world *surrounding* the castle. The point is partly that this depth of Hell *is* a kind of perverted and inverted fortress, that of Satan, who is at war both with God and with the damned. That the pit "truncates" and "gathers in" the ridges emphasizes the ambiguous futility of the structure.

The imagined diagram of the valleys surrounding the central pit strongly suggests, also, the structure of the web of a spider, the traditional fraudulent hunter; Satan's position below this metaphorical web corresponds to that of the larger species of spider as discussed in Pliny and the bestiaries (the smaller species sit directly on the web).

22–24. On my right hand . . . was full: The sinners are on the pilgrim's right because he and Virgil have turned to the left and are walking along beside the pit. Note the parallel with 6.4–5.

25. At the bottom were the sinners, naked: Gmelin points out the parallel with the frequent medieval experience of looking down into pits where bears and other wild animals were kept.

28–33. as the Romans . . . toward the mountain: This is the first mention in the poem that 1300 (the year of the pilgrim's journey to the other world) was proclaimed by Boniface VIII in February to be a Jubilee year (an innovation at the time), according to which special plenary indulgences were granted for daily visiting of the basilicas of San Pietro in Vaticano and San Paolo fuori le Mura (some three miles distant from each other). According to the chronicler Villani, 200,000 pilgrims visited Rome during the Jubilee. Dante is the only writer to mention this invention of barrier-enforced two-way traffic, and his emphasis on ocular testimony is evidence of his having seen it himself.

The bridge is the Ponte degli Angeli [Bridge of the Angels], originally built in A.D. 132, still standing, though integrated with more modern structures and adorned with statues designed by Bernini (seventeenth century); it crosses the Tiber in front of "the castle," the Castel Sant'Angelo (the emperor Hadrian's tomb, turned into a fortress by the popes), and in Dante's time provided the quickest route from the center of Rome to the Vatican. The "mountain" is the Monte Giordano, a small hill opposite the Castel Sant'Angelo. This is the first of many references in Malebolge and Cocytus to Italian cities, usually denouncing them (Bologna is denounced in this canto in lines 58–63); there is a special irony in the parallel between Hell and the Rome of the Jubilee.

35. horned demons with great whips: The first appearance in the poem of the familiar medieval type of devil (see Figure 4), to which the closest approximation so far has been the figure of Minos (Canto 5). Public whipping through the streets was a frequent medieval punishment (see the note to line 72).

42. I am certainly not fasting for sight of him: In other words, I have seen him before. The food metaphor (the first of many in the Malebolge; see Additional Note 13) is picked up in line 51, as well as in the next *bolgia*.

43. to make out his features: Dante's term *figurarlo* [literally, to figure him; cf. French *figure*, face] connects this act of recognition with the "pattern" (*figura*) of the Malebolge (line 12).

50. Venedico Caccianemico: A prominent Bolognese Guelf nobleman, who in fact seems to have lived until 1302; he served as *podestà* of several cities (see the note to 6.96). His first name is derived from Latin *benedico* [I bless]; his family name means "drive away the enemy."

51. such pungent sauces: Use of the metaphor of highly seasoned sauce for punishment seems to derive from popular usage (Sapegno); compare line 42, with note. The early commentators also point out the existence of a common grave for executed criminals outside Bologna, called the *Salsa*. The use of the plural is odd, referring, it would seem, to the repeated whip blows.

52–54. Unwilling . . . the former world: We begin to find souls unwilling to be recognized and mentioned in the world of the living, in marked contrast to Ciacco (6.88–89), Pier delle Vigne (13.76–78), and others higher in Hell.

53. your clear speech: This seems an odd characterization of the pilgrim's scornful metaphors; it is sometimes taken to refer to the familiarity he reveals with Bolognese customs and ways of speech (Dante, who in all probability had spent a year or more in Bologna, praises the harmoniousness of the Bolognese dialect in *De vulgari eloquentia* 1.15.5–7; cf. lines 58–61).

55–57. It was I . . . the shameful tale: The incident referred to here has left no record in the chroniclers. The early commentators, though disagreeing as to the identity of the marchese (Azzo VIII of Este or Obizzo of Este), agree that Ghisolabella was Venedico's sister.

57. tale: The Italian *novella* [news] becomes the name of an entire literary genre in the wake of Boccaccio's *Decameron* (which, incidentally, singles out Bolognese flattery for satire, 7.7).

58–63. And not only I . . . our greedy breast: See the note to lines 28–33.

61. to say *sipa* now between the Sàvena and the Reno: *Sipa* is Bolognese dialect for "yes." The Sàvena and the Reno are rivers in and near Bologna.

66. here there are no females to coin: The pimps are identified as ones who turn women into coins; see the note to 11.110–11, on the generative terminology applied to usury. The first sin of fraud is metaphorically connected with the last sin of violence, usury.

70–79. we climbed . . . we looked down: This canto exemplifies what will be a frequent alternation between viewing the Malebolge from the bank parallel to the ditch and from the bridge crossing over it. In only two cases (in Cantos 19 and 23) do the poets actually descend into the *bolge*.

72. those eternal circlings: The Italian is *cerchie* (not *cerchi* [circles]): the feminine implies a concrete instance; the use of the term *cerchia* for public whipping is attested in medieval Tuscany.

73. gapes: Dante had already used the word *vaneggia* in line 5.

83–96. Jason: Dante knew the story of Jason from Ovid's *Met.* 7.1–424, *Heroides* 6, and Statius's *Theb.* 5.29–485.

85. how regal is his bearing still: The descriptive touches on Jason's noble appearance (line 83) and bearing may have been suggested by *Met.* 7.43–45, on the appeal for Medea of Jason's beauty and nobility. Jason was the son of Aeson, exiled king of Iolchis.

87. robbed the Colchians of the ram: Having sailed to Colchis, at the eastern end of the Black Sea, in the ship *Argo*, Jason won the Golden Fleece (the fleece of the ram that had carried Phryxus and Helle to Colchis; the ram was made the constellation Aries) with the help of Medea, daughter of the king, whom he carried off. Dante refers to this exploit repeatedly in the *Paradiso* (see *Par.* 2.16–18, 25.7, 33.94–96, with notes).

88–94. He visited . . . pregnant and alone: Made revolting to their husbands by Venus because of their failure to sacrifice to her, the women of Lemnos resolve to kill all their men. Only Hypsipyle, young daughter of the king, secretly spares her father's life and enables him to flee. When the Argonauts, on the way to Colchis, are forced by bad weather to stay for two years on Lemnos, the women take them as husbands. According to both Ovid and Statius, Hypsipyle and Jason were ritually married. According to *Heroides* 6.61–62, Hypsipyle is pregnant when Jason leaves; according to Statius, she gives birth before he does so. Hypsipyle is referred to in *Purg.* 22.112 and 26.95.

91. elaborate words: Literally, "ornate." Note the parallel emphasis on rhetorical ornamentation (and closely parallel phrasing) in Beatrice's words to Virgil in 2.67–69 (Mazzotta 1979).

96. also for Medea vengeance is taken: After begetting two children by Medea, Jason abandoned her to marry Glauce, daughter of the king of Corinth; on the wedding day Medea murdered the bride and both her own children in Jason's presence.

97. deceive: The third use of the verb *ingannare* (cf. lines 92 and 93).

103–36. From there . . . be sated: While the punishment of whipping for the pimps and seducers has no obvious metaphorical relevance to their sin (though perhaps it alludes to their urgings of their victims), that of the flatterers is clearly appropriate. It is the worthlessness of the flatteries themselves that is represented by the excrement, in a substitution of lower for upper products of the body; such inversions will be frequent in the Malebolge. Dante outdoes himself in the expression of scorn and the vivid evocation of sensory disgust.

106. encrusted with a mold: See also the notes on lines 117 and 126. Emphasis on viscous or oily substances that coat the sinners' bodies will be frequent in the Malebolge. See Additional Note 13.

117. whether he was lay or clerk: That is, whether a portion of his head had been shaved in the clerical tonsure; the clear implication is that both clerics and laymen are present.

118. hungry: Another food metaphor.

122. Alessio Interminei: There seems to be a play on the idea of endlessness in the shade's surname; the name Alessio derives from a Greek verb meaning "to protect."

126. with which my tongue was never cloyed: The Italian adjective *stucco/a* is itself a metaphor for stickiness derived from the noun *stucco* [plaster].

133–35. that is Thaïs . . . Marvelous favor indeed: Thaïs is a character in Terence's play *Eunuchus*; Dante is quoting one scene, which in all probability he read of in Cicero's *De amicitia*, where her reported reply is cited as an example of the exaggeration typical of flatterers, or in John of Salisbury's *Policraticus* (twelfth century), where flattery is identified as a species of fraud (Pézard 1948, Gmelin). It is noteworthy that the only prostitute we find in Dante's Hell is damned for flattery, not prostitution, whereas the panders—those who induce women to have sex for money and profit from it—are legion. For the women in Hell, see the note to 30.37–41.

136. sated: As if by food.

CANTO 19

1

O Simon mago, o miseri seguaci,
che le cose di Dio, che di bontate
deon essere spose, e voi rapaci

4

per oro e per argento avolterate,
or convien che per voi suoni la tromba,
però che ne la terza bolgia state.

7

Già eravamo, a la seguente tomba,
montati de lo scoglio in quella parte
ch'a punto sovra mezzo 'l fosso piomba.

10

O somma sapïenza, quanta è l'arte
che mostri in cielo, in terra e nel mal mondo,
e quanto giusto tua virtù comparte!

13

Io vidi per le coste e per lo fondo
piena la pietra livida di fóri,
d'un largo tutti e ciascun era tondo.

16

Non mi parean men ampi né maggiori
che que' che son nel mio bel San Giovanni,
fatti per loco d'i battezzatori;

19

l'un de li quali, ancor non è molt' anni,
rupp' io per un che dentro v'annegava:
e questo sia suggel ch'ogn' omo sganni.

22

Fuor de la bocca a ciascun soperchiava
d'un peccator li piedi e de le gambe
infino al grosso, e l'altro dentro stava.

25

Le piante erano a tutti accese intrambe,
per che sì forte guizzavan le giunte
che spezzate averien ritorte e strambe.

28

Qual suole il fiammeggiar de le cose unte
muoversi pur su per la strema buccia:
tal era lì dai calcagni a le punte.

CANTO 19

1   O Simon Magus, O wretched followers, you who the things of God, that should be brides of goodness, rapaciously

4   adulterate for gold and for silver, now the trumpet must sound for you, because you are in the third pocket.

7   We had already climbed to that part of the ridge that is exactly above the center of the next tomb.

10   O highest Wisdom, how great is the art you show in the heavens, on earth, and in the evil world, and how justly your Power distributes!

13   I saw, along the sides and the bottom, the livid rock perforated with holes, all of the same size, and each was round.

16   They seemed no less ample, nor greater, than those in my lovely San Giovanni, made as places for the baptizers;

19   one of which, not many years ago, I broke because of one drowning inside it: and let this be a seal to undeceive all men.

22   From the mouth of each protruded the feet and legs of a sinner, as far as the thighs, and the rest was inside.

25   All of them had both soles aflame; therefore they wriggled their joints so violently that they would have broken twisted withes or braided ropes.

28   As the flaming of oily things moves over just the outer rind: so did it there from heel to toes.

31 "Chi è colui, maestro, che si cruccia
guizzando più che li altri suoi consorti,"
diss' io, "e cui più roggia fiamma succia?"

34 Ed elli a me: "Se tu vuo' ch'i' ti porti
là giù per quella ripa che più giace,
da lui saprai di sé e de' suoi torti."

37 E io: "Tanto m'è bel, quanto a te piace:
tu se' segnore, e sai ch'i' non mi parto
dal tuo volere, e sai quel che si tace."

40 Allor venimmo in su l'argine quarto;
volgemmo e discendemmo a mano stanca
là giù nel fondo foracchiato e arto.

43 Lo buon maestro ancor de la sua anca
non mi dipuose, sì mi giunse al rotto
di quel che sì piangeva con la zanca.

46 "O qual che se' che 'l di sù tien di sotto,
anima trista come pal commessa,"
comincia' io a dir, "se puoi, fa motto."

49 Io stava come 'l frate che confessa
lo perfido assessin, che, poi ch'è fitto,
richiama lui per che la morte cessa.

52 Ed el gridò: "Se' tu già costì ritto,
se' tu già costì ritto, Bonifazio?
Di parecchi anni mi mentì lo scritto.

55 Se' tu sì tosto di quell' aver sazio
per lo qual non temesti tòrre a 'nganno
la bella donna, e poi di farne strazio?"

58 Tal mi fec' io quai son color che stanno,
per non intender ciò ch'è lor risposto,
quasi scornati, e risponder non sanno.

61 Allor Virgilio disse: "Dilli tosto:
'Non son colui, non son colui che credi!'"
E io rispuosi come a me fu imposto.

64 Per che lo spirto tutti storse i piedi;
poi, sospirando e con voce di pianto,
mi disse: "Dunque che a me richiedi?

67 Se di saper ch'i' sia ti cal cotanto
che tu abbi però la ripa corsa,
sappi ch'i' fui vestito del gran manto;

31   "Who is that one, master, who shows the torture
by wriggling more than his other companions," I
said, "and whom a ruddier flame sucks at?"

34   And he to me: "If you wish me to carry you there,
down the bank that is less steep, from him you will
learn of him and his wrongs."

37   And I: "So much is pleasant to me as pleases you:
you are my lord, you know that I do not depart from
your will, and you know what I leave unsaid."

40   Then we came to the fourth bank; we turned and
descended to the left, down there into the narrow,
perforated ditch.

43   My good master did not put me down from his
hip until we reached the place of him who was
weeping so with his shanks.

46   "O whatever you are, you who hold your up side
down, sorrowing soul, planted like a pole," I began
speaking, "if you can, say a word."

49   I was standing like the friar that confesses the
treacherous assassin who, once he is fixed in the
earth, calls him back so as to put off his death.

52   And he cried out: "Are you already standing
there, are you already standing there, Boniface? The
writing lied to me by several years.

55   Are you so soon sated by the wealth for which
you did not fear to marry the lovely lady
fraudulently, and then to tear her apart?"

58   I became like those who, not understanding what
is said to them, stand as if mocked, at a loss for a
reply.

61   Then Virgil said: "Tell him quickly, 'I am not he, I
am not he you suppose,'" and I replied as was
commanded me.

64   Therefore the spirit twisted its feet; next, sighing,
its voice full of tears, it said to me: "Then what do
you want from me?

67   If it matters so much to know who I am, that just
for this you have run down the bank, know that I
was clothed in the great mantle;

70 e veramente fui figliuol de l'orsa,
cupido sì per avanzar li orsatti
che sù l'avere e qui me misi in borsa.

73 Di sotto al capo mio son li altri tratti
che precedetter me simoneggiando
per le fessure de la pietra piatti.

76 Là giù cascherò io altresì quando
verrà colui ch'i' credea che tu fossi,
allor ch'i' feci 'l sùbito dimando.

79 Ma più è 'l tempo già che i piè mi cossi
e ch'i' son stato così sottosopra,
ch'el non starà piantato coi piè rossi;

82 ché dopo lui verrà di più laida opra,
di ver' ponente, un pastor sanza legge,
tal che convien che lui e me ricuopra.

85 Nuovo Iasón sarà, di cui si legge
ne' Maccabei; e come a quel fu molle
suo re, così fia lui chi Francia regge."

88 Io non so s'i' mi fui qui troppo folle,
ch'i' pur rispuosi lui a questo metro:
"Deh, or mi dì: quanto tesoro volle

91 nostro Segnore in prima da san Pietro
ch'ei ponesse le chiavi in sua balìa?
Certo non chiese se non: 'Viemmi retro.'

94 Né Pier né li altri tolsero a Matia
oro od argento, quando fu sortito
al loco che perdé l'anima ria.

97 Però ti sta, ché tu se' ben punito;
e guarda ben la mal tolta moneta
ch'esser ti fece contra Carlo ardito.

100 E se non fosse ch'ancor lo mi vieta
la reverenza de le somme chiavi
che tu tenesti ne la vita lieta,

103 io userei parole ancor più gravi;
ché la vostra avarizia il mondo attrista,
calcando i buoni e sollevando i pravi.

106 Di voi pastor s'accorse il Vangelista
quando colei che siede sopra l'acque
puttaneggiar coi regi a lui fu vista,

70 and truly I was a son of the she-bear, so greedy to advance her cubs, that I pocketed wealth up there, and myself down here.

73 Beneath my head are driven the others who preceded me in simony, squeezed into the cracks of the rock.

76 I, too, will fall down there, when he comes who I believed you to be, when I asked my sudden question.

79 But it has been a longer time that my feet have burned and that I have been upsidedown like this, than he will be planted with red feet:

82 for after him will come, from towards the west, a lawless shepherd of even uglier deeds, such that he will cover both him and me.

85 He will be a new Jason, like the one we read of in Maccabees; and as his king was indulgent to the first one, so the ruler of France will be to him."

88 I do not know if here I became too rash, but I replied to him in this meter: "Ah, now tell me: how much treasure did

91 our Lord demand from Saint Peter, before he gave the keys into his keeping? Surely he asked only, 'Follow me.'

94 Neither Peter nor the others took from Matthias gold or silver, when he was chosen for the place lost by the wicked soul.

97 Therefore stay here, for you deserve your punishment; and be sure to keep your ill-gotten coin, which made you bold against Charles.

100 And were it not that I am forbidden by my reverence for the highest keys, which you held in happy life,

103 I would use still heavier words; for your avarice afflicts the world, trampling the good and raising up the wicked.

106 Of you shepherds the Evangelist took note, when he saw her who sits upon the waters whoring with the kings;

109 quella che con le sette teste nacque,
e da le diece corna ebbe argomento
fin che virtute al suo marito piacque.

112 Fatto v'avete dio d'oro e d'argento;
e che altro è da voi a l'idolatre,
se non ch'elli uno, e voi ne orate cento?

115 Ahi, Costantin, di quanto mal fu matre,
non la tua conversion, ma quella dote
che da te prese il primo ricco patre!"

118 E mentr' io li cantava cotai note,
o ira o coscïenza che 'l mordesse,
forte spingava con ambo le piote.

121 I' credo ben ch'al mio duca piacesse,
con sì contenta labbia sempre attese
lo suon de le parole vere espresse.

124 Però con ambo le braccia mi prese;
e poi che tutto sù mi s'ebbe al petto,
rimontò per la via onde discese.

127 Né si stancò d'avermi a sé distretto,
sì men portò sovra 'l colmo de l'arco
che dal quarto al quinto argine è tragetto.

130 Quivi soavemente spuose il carco,
soave per lo scoglio sconcio ed erto
che sarebbe a le capre duro varco.

133 Indi un altro vallon mi fu scoperto.

109   she who was born with seven heads, and took strength from her ten horns as long as virtue pleased her husband.

112   You have made gold and silver your god; and what difference is there between you and the idol-worshipper, except that he prays to one, and you to a hundred?

115   Ah, Constantine, not your conversion, but that dowry which the first rich father took from you, has been the mother of so much evil!"

118   And while I was singing these notes to him, whether it was anger or conscience that was biting him, he kicked violently with both his feet.

121   I firmly believe that it pleased my leader, with such a contented smile he listened still to the sound of the true words I spoke.

124   Therefore with both arms he seized me; and when he had lifted me up to his breast, he climbed back up by the way he had come down.

127   Nor did he tire of holding me embraced, but carried me to the top of the arch that gives passage from the fourth to the fifth bank.

130   There he gently put his burden down, gently on the rough, steep ridge, which even for she-goats would be a difficult crossing.

133   From there another valley was revealed to me.

NOTES

1. O Simon Magus: With an apostrophe (the only such canto beginning in the *Inferno*; see the note to 18.1–18) Dante addresses Simon Magus, the magician from Samaria who offered the apostle Peter money for the power of the laying on of hands, conveying the Holy Spirit (Acts 8.9–24). Simon Magus gave his name to simony, the buying and selling of the sacramental powers of the priesthood, or of the priestly office itself; for Dante and his time, simony extended to nepotism in distributing church offices. The apocryphal *Acts of Peter* (Elliott) finds Simon in Rome as the chief magician of the emperor Nero; Simon is bested by Saint Peter in a series of magic competitions (based on Moses and Aaron's duel with Pharaoh's magicians); finally he flies, held up by a demon, until Saint Peter prays; then the demon must let him fall, which he does, breaking his leg in three places (there is an effective twelfth-century capital showing Simon flying and then falling head first, in the Cathedral of Autun).

2–4. the things of God . . . and for silver: Principally, but not exclusively, preaching and the sacraments, whose power is conferred with priestly office. The metaphors of marriage ("brides") and prostitution ("adulterate for gold") are not casual: the sacrament of marriage, Saint Paul says (Eph. 5.23–32), points to the mystical marriage of Christ and the Church; at his consecration a bishop puts on a ring that symbolizes his marriage to his diocese, the "bride of Christ." For fornication and prostitution as Old Testament images of priestly corruption, see the note to 1.100.

5. the trumpet must sound for you: The trumpet of epic poetry, of public denunciation, as in Hosea 8.1 (and cf. Additional Note 9), with reference also to the trumpet of the Last Judgment.

16–18. They seemed . . . baptizers: Dante's likening of the perforations in the rocky floor of this *bolgia* to the baptismal fonts of the Florentine Baptistery of San Giovanni is a famous crux, since they no longer exist (Figure 3). Early commentators differ on whether the reference is to the fonts themselves or to smaller

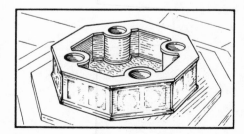

Figure 3. The baptismal font in the Pisa Baptistery.

openings, adjacent to the fonts, designed so that priests might be kept from the

crowds (mass baptisms were held during the Easter season). We follow this latter view, which accords with the pilgrim's repeated assumption of the role of priest in this canto (see the notes to lines 19–21, 46–51, and 90–117).

19–21. one of which . . . to undeceive all men: No contemporary tradition records Dante having broken any font or portion of one. In an influential note, Spitzer (1943) proposed that not a historical event, but Dante's denunciation in this canto of the corrupt Church, done with the intention of "undeceiving," or enlightening, his readers, is meant. The breaking of the font (line 20) is echoed in the violence done to the Church by Boniface (line 57; Musa). This incident, too, is an instance of lay intervention in a situation where the clergy have proved inadequate. See Additional Note 7.

21. let this be a seal: The antecedent of "this" is by no means clear (see the note to lines 19–21). In the Middle Ages, written testimony was often authenticated with a personal seal, oral testimony by an oath. Instances of personal witness by the pilgrim-poet gain prominence in the realm of fraud (e.g., 16.127–29, 18.28–33, 21.7–15, and 21.94–96); for perjury as a culminating type of fraud, see 30.112–29, with notes. See Additional Note 7.

22–24. From the mouth . . . the rest was inside: Since the holes have been explicitly compared with baptismal fonts, the immediate reference is to an inversion of the iconography of baptism, which typically showed the baptized in a font (or a river), appearing from the waist up (see 10.33, with note). Inversion is in fact a major governing principle in the canto, for simony represents a drastic inversion of values. The sinners' headlong fall has repeated Simon's as well as Satan's (see the note to line 1); once we know the sinners are popes and other clergy, it is clear that their punishment parodies the crucifixion of Saint Peter, who, according to the apocryphal *Acts of Peter,* out of humility asked to be crucified head down.

25–30. All of them had . . . from heel to toes: Fire on the feet (and "anointed" feet, at that: see the next note) involves several complex references. The most important is to the descent of the Holy Spirit into the gathered apostles at Pentecost (Acts 2), in which "there appeared to them parted tongues as it were of fire, and it sat upon every one of them" (always represented pictorially as sitting on the apostles' heads). This was traditionally accounted to be the actualizing of the Church, for from the continuing presence of the Spirit derived all the authority and power of the clergy. According to the traditional Catholic doctrine of the Church, the traditional ceremony of the ordination of priests, in which the bishop placed his hands on the postulant's head and prayed for the descent of the Spirit, was a reenactment of Pentecost and assured that each ordination was ultimately continuous with it, in an unbroken chain of contact going back to the apostles, the so-called apostolic succession (cf. French 1964).

28. oily things: In context, a clear reference to the chrism (anointing) important in four of the seven sacraments (ordination, baptism, confirmation, and extreme unction [last anointing]).

40–42. Then we came to the fourth bank . . . perforated ditch: That is, they finish crossing the bridge to the far ("the fourth") bank; then Virgil lifts the pilgrim to his hip, according to his promise in lines 34–35, and carries him to the bottom of the *bolgia*. On only one other occasion do the two descend into a *bolgia*: in Canto 23, also involving denunciation of the clergy.

45. weeping so with his shanks: The pilgrim has singled out this soul in line 32, which also prepares for the unusual expression in which the violent motions of the legs are interpreted as a sign of grief, thus as weeping.

46–51. O whatever . . . put off his death: By Florentine law, professional assassins were placed head down in a pit and buried alive. As the commentators note, according to the simile the pilgrim has adopted toward the condemned pope the role of a priest confessing a layman: the iconoclastic nature of the layman Dante's enterprise could hardly be more pithily symbolized. The imagined priest is a friar, almost certainly a Franciscan, both because the professed humility of the "lesser brothers" led them into such forms of service and also for a futher juxtaposition of humility with the corruption of the prelates; there is a sharp irony here, for while he was a cardinal, Nicholas had been the special protector of the Franciscans (the corruption of the Franciscans and Dominicans themselves is targeted in *Paradiso* 11–12).

46. you who hold your up side down: The Italian is even pithier, since *il di sù* [literally, the upper] refers both to Nicholas's position and to his values.

52–57. Are you already . . . to tear her apart: With an audacious stroke, Dante has Boniface's sins summarized and his damnation predicted by another pope in 1300, while Boniface was still alive.

Boniface VIII was born Benedetto Caetani, of a noble family, at Anagni, near Rome, in 1235. Extremely able, he rose in the Church and was made a cardinal in 1281. After the resignation of Celestine V in 1293 (see 3.59–60, with note), he was elected pope at Naples in December, 1294 and crowned on January 23, 1295. He died on October 11, 1303, in Rome.

Boniface was extremely ambitious for the Church, and his papacy was filled with conflict (for his fight with the Colonnas, a powerful Roman family, see 27.85–111, with notes). Particularly bitter was his struggle with Philip IV of France over the right to tax the French clergy. With the famous bulls *Clericis laicos* (1296) and *Unam sanctam* (1302), Boniface affirmed the supremacy of the papacy over secular rulers and excommunicated Philip; Philip had Boniface's election declared invalid and sent armed men to arrest him at Anagni in September 1303. Although he was rescued by the populace, the violence and humiliation of the experience hastened Boniface's death (see *Purg.* 20.85–90).

Dante's antagonism to Boniface would have been aroused by the pope's claims to supremacy over the emperor (refuted in *Monarchia* 3), but Dante thought Boniface utterly corrupt, guilty of having bribed his way to the papacy (see the note to lines 55–57) and of cynically engineering the Black Guelf coup in Florence in 1301 that led to Dante's exile (see 6.64–72, with note).

54. The writing lied to me: Nicholas believed Boniface was to die in 1303 (as he did). The "writing" is the book of the future, which the damned may read until the events approach (cf. 10.97–108, with note).

55–57. Are you so soon sated . . . tear her apart: A reference to the widespread accusation that Boniface VIII persuaded Celestine V to abdicate (see 3.59–60, with note) and used copious bribes to ensure his own election. The "tearing apart" of Lady Church refers to Boniface's aggressive use of simony: he treated the treasure of the Church as his own to dispose of (see Villani, *Chronicle* 8.64).

57. the lovely lady: The Church, the bride of Christ and therefore of the pope, Christ's vicar on earth (cf. lines 2–4).

62. I am not he, I am not he: The repetition answers to Nicholas's in lines 52–53. Michaela Janan, as an undergraduate, observed that in John 18.17 and 25 Peter twice says "I am not" (*non sum*, cf. *non son*), when denying Christ.

69. clothed in the great mantle: That is, he was a pope. In *Purg.* 19.103–5, Dante has another pope mention the large, sleeveless papal mantle in a passage that connects the pope's mantle with the robes worn by the hypocrites in Canto 23.

70–72. and truly I . . . myself down here: The lines identify the speaker as Nicholas III Orsini, who was pope from 1277 to 1280 (the she-bear was the emblem of the Roman Orsini family). Born shortly before 1220, he was a kinsman of the future Boniface VIII. Contemporaries thought of Nicholas as one of the first popes to practice simony and nepotism on a grand scale (Scott 1970).

73–75. Beneath my head . . . cracks of the rock: In another ironic inversion, the position of the simoniac popes, with the head of each pushing on his predecessor's feet, is a sharply focused parodic inversion of the apostolic succession (see the note to lines 25–30).

79–84. it has been a longer time . . . both him and me: Nicholas has been "planted" for twenty years (since 1280); Boniface's tenure will be shorter. Thus fewer than twenty-three years will pass from this moment (early April 1300) before Clement V, the next pope to be "planted," arrives. Clement actually died in 1314.

82–84. after him will come . . . both him and me: The "lawless shepherd" is Bertrand de Got, who as Clement V transferred the papal see from Rome to Avignon and appeased the ambition of Philip IV. Born in Gascony, Clement was bishop of Commynes by 1295 and archbishop of Bordeaux in 1299. After being elected in 1305, thanks to interference from Philip the Fair, he immediately created nine French cardinals. Crowned in Lyons, he never went to Rome, and from 1308 on kept the papal see in Avignon, beginning the "Babylonian captivity" of the papacy, which lasted until 1377. He canonized Pietro di Morrone (Celestine V) and conducted a posthumous trial of Boniface (1312). He also delayed trying Guillaume de Nogaret and Sciarra Colonna, who had attacked Boniface VIII, finally absolving them from the penalties, though not the responsibility, connected with the pope's death. Never named by Dante, Clement is identified by unflattering nicknames or periphrases. For his role in Philip's destruction of the Templars, see *Purg.* 20.91–93; for the removal of the papal see to Avignon, *Purg.* 32.157–60; for his simony, *Par.* 17.82; and for his betrayal of Henry VII, *Par.* 30.142–48.

85–86. a new Jason . . . in Maccabees: Not the Argonaut, but the brother of the high priest Onias in 2 Maccabees 4.7–8; he buys from the emperor Antiochus IV Epiphanes the high priesthood, with the promise of 440 pieces of silver. Villani (*Chronicle* 8.80) reports that Bertrand de Got, future Clement V, offered to Philip IV, in return for his support in the papal election, a tenth of all the revenues from France for five years.

88. I do not know . . . in this meter: Here Dante uses the Italian *folle*, a term used elsewhere in the *Comedy* only in reference to the possible rashness of the voyage of the pilgrim and the journey of Ulysses (see 2.35, 26.125, and *Par.*

27.82–83). "This meter" refers not only to the pilgrim's words (cf. the "shameful meter" of 7.32), but also to the appropriateness of the denunciation, its "measure."

90–117. Ah, now tell me . . . so much evil: With 16.73–76 (see notes), this passage is an important moment in the pilgrim's/Dante's gradual assumption of the role of prophet. Here, like the prophet Nathan (whose Hebrew name Dante saw as related to his own, both meaning "giving"; see Sarolli 1971), the pilgrim is confronting the mighty. It is the longest denunciation of the corrupt clergy in the poem.

90–96. how much treasure . . . the wicked soul: Dante has the pilgrim refer to two moments traditionally thought of as important in establishing the Church, in addition to Pentecost: the granting of the keys to Peter (Matt. 16.18–19) and the election of Matthias to take the place of Judas (Acts 1.26).

90. how much treasure did our Lord demand: Implicit is Dante's belief that the Church should possess no material wealth or temporal power (see *Monarchia* 3.14.3 and *Epistle* 8.2–3, "To the Italian cardinals").

93. Follow me: Matt. 4.19, Jesus' initial calling of Peter and his brother Andrew.

95. gold or silver: Dante denounces the wealth of the Church as the source of its corruption. The passages referred to are Acts 3.6, "Silver and gold I have none," spoken by Peter, and Matt. 10.9: "Do not possess gold, nor silver, nor money in your purses"; Dante cites them in his arguments against the wealth of the Church in *Monarchia* 3.9.14 (see also *Convivio* 4.11).

98–99. ill-gotten coin . . . against Charles: Dante may be referring to the (now discredited) story (Villani, *Chronicle* 7.54, 57) that Nicholas accepted a bribe to join in the plot that led to the "Sicilian Vespers" (see *Par.* 8.67 and note), the uprising that drove the Angevins from Sicily.

101. my reverence for the highest keys: Dante's piety toward the papacy as an institution is documented: see *Purg.* 20.85–90, *Epistle* 8, and *Monarchia* 3.3 and 3.14.5 (Foster 1980). But only one pope, besides Saint Peter, is found in Dante's Paradise (John XXI, Peter of Spain, the logician; that he was pope is not mentioned), and only two in Purgatory (Adrian V and Martin IV), while four popes are said to be damned (Anastasius II?, Nicholas III, Boniface VIII, and Clement V), and another probably so (Celestine V).

105. trampling the good and raising up the wicked: Again, the punishment inverts the crime (see the note to lines 73–75), which had itself inverted the proper order of things.

106–11. Of you shepherds . . . pleased her husband: Dante is drawing on the Apocalypse; see Apoc. 17.1–3, 5:

> And there came one of the seven angels . . . saying, Come, I will shew thee the condemnation of the great harlot who sitteth upon many waters, With whom the kings of the earth have committed fornication. . . . And I saw a woman sitting upon a scarlet colored beast . . . having seven heads and ten horns.

The seven heads and ten horns are usually taken to be the seven sacraments and the Ten Commandments, chief institutions of the New and Old Laws. In the New Testament, the "harlot" was associated with Babylon and pagan Rome; for Dante, as for the "Spiritual" Franciscans, she is the corrupt clergy, led by the popes, her "whoring" the Church's involvement in temporal affairs and Clement V's subservience to Philip IV. For these identifications, see *Purg.* 32.148–60, with notes.

112–14. You have made gold . . . you to a hundred: Dante has the pilgrim identify the corrupt clergy's avarice as a form of idolatry, the sin perhaps most frequently denounced by the Old Testament prophets, with whom he is closely identifying himself (line 112 is a close translation of the Vulgate text of Hosea 8.4). The identification is not original with Dante: shortly before his time, avarice and *nummulatria*, or the worship of the graven images on coins, became important targets of sermons (Camille 1989).

115–17. Ah, Constantine . . . so much evil: The Donation of Constantine was a document forged in the papal curia around 750; for centuries, it was held to be authentic even by the opponents of the popes and was proved false (on linguistic grounds) only in the fifteenth century by Lorenzo Valla and Nicholas of Cusa. According to the Donation, the emperor Constantine the Great (A.D. 288–337; emperor from 306), having been miraculously cured of leprosy by baptism at the hands of Pope Sylvester (a total fabrication) granted to the pope ("the first rich father") and his successors supreme temporal power in the West. Dante mentions the Donation on two other occasions in the *Comedy* (27.94–95 and *Par.* 20.55); in the *Monarchia* (3.10.1), he argues that Constantine's alienation of imperial power was legally invalid, its acceptance by the papacy a departure from Christ's injunction against possessions (see the note to line 95).

132. even for she-goats: Herzman and Stephany (1978) detect an ironic allusion to "sheep and goats" (Matt. 25.32) as representing the saved and the damned, respectively, at the Last Judgment. Surely "goats," the damned popes would still have a hard time of it. The popes were shepherds (see lines 83 and 106); Christ's charge to Peter to "feed my sheep" (John 21.15–17), like the gift of the keys to Peter (Matt. 16.18–19), was one of the principal texts adduced to support papal authority.

CANTO 20

1
Di nova pena mi conven far versi
e dar matera al ventesimo canto
de la prima canzon, ch'è d'i sommersi.

4
Io era già disposto tutto quanto
a riguardar ne lo scoperto fondo,
che si bagnava d'angoscioso pianto;

7
e vidi gente per lo vallon tondo
venir, tacendo e lagrimando, al passo
che fanno le letane in questo mondo.

10
Come 'l viso mi scese in lor più basso
mirabilmente apparve esser travolto
ciascun tra 'l mento e 'l principio del casso,

13
ché da le reni era tornato 'l volto,
e in dietro venir li convenia,
perchè 'l veder dinanzi era lor tolto.

16
Forse per forza già di parlasia
si travolse così alcun del tutto,
ma io nol vidi, né credo che sia.

19
Se Dio ti lasci, lettor, prender frutto
di tua lezione, or pensa per te stesso
com' io potea tener lo viso asciutto,

22
quando la nostra imagine di presso
vidi sì torta che 'l pianto de li occhi
le natiche bagnava per lo fesso.

25
Certo io piangea, poggiato a un de' rocchi
del duro scoglio, sì che la mia scorta
mi disse: "Ancor se' tu de li altri sciocchi?

28
Qui vive la pietà quand' è ben morta:
chi è più scellerato che colui
che al giudicio divin passion comporta?

CANTO 20

Fourth bolgia: *diviners—Amphiaraus—Tiresias—Arruns—Manto—*
founding of Mantua—others

1   Of a strange new punishment I must make verses
and take matter for the twentieth song in this first
canticle, which is of those submerged.

4   I was already bent over to gaze into the
uncovered depth, which was bathed with anguished
weeping;

7   and I saw people coming along the curving valley,
silent and shedding tears, at the pace taken by litanies
in this world.

10   As my gaze went lower on them, I saw that each
was marvelously twisted between the chin and the
beginning of the chest,

13   for the face was turned toward the kidneys, and
they were forced to walk backwards, since seeing
forward was taken from them.

16   Perhaps the force of paralysis at some time has
contorted someone so completely, but I have never
seen it, nor do I believe it can be.

19   So may God permit you, reader, to take profit
from your reading, now think for yourself how I
could keep dry eyes,

22   when from close by I saw our image so twisted
that the tears of their eyes were bathing their buttocks
down the cleft.

25   Surely I wept, leaning on one of the rocks of the
hard ridge, so that my guide said to me: "Are you
still one of the other fools?

28   Here pity lives when it is quite dead: who is more
wicked than one who brings passion to God's
judgment?

31   Drizza la testa, drizza, e vedi a cui
s'aperse a li occhi d'i Teban la terra,
per ch'ei gridavan tutti: 'Dove rui,

34   Anfïarao? perché lasci la guerra?'
E non restò di ruinare a valle
fino a Minòs, che ciascheduno afferra.

37   Mira c'ha fatto petto de le spalle;
perché volse veder troppo davante,
di retro guarda e fa retroso calle.

40   Vedi Tiresia, che mutò sembiante
quando di maschio femmina divenne,
cangiandosi le membra tutte quante;

43   e prima, poi, ribatter li convenne
li duo serpenti avvolti, con la verga,
che rïavesse le maschili penne.

46   Aronta è quel ch'al ventre li s'atterga,
che ne' monti di Luni, dove ronca
lo Carrarese che di sotto alberga,

49   ebbe tra ' bianchi marmi la spelonca
per sua dimora, onde a guardar le stelle
e 'l mar non li era la veduta tronca.

52   E quella che ricuopre le mammelle,
che tu non vedi, con le trecce sciolte,
e ha di là ogne pilosa pelle,

55   Manto fu, che cercò per terre molte;
poscia si puose là dove nacqu' io;
onde un poco mi piace che m'ascolte.

58   Poscia che 'l padre suo di vita uscìo
e venne serva la città di Baco,
questa gran tempo per lo mondo gio.

61   Suso in Italia bella giace un laco,
a piè de l'Alpe che serra Lamagna
sovra Tiralli, c'ha nome Benaco.

64   Per mille fonti, credo, e più si bagna
tra Garda e Val Camonica e Pennino
de l'acqua che nel detto laco stagna.

67   Loco è nel mezzo là dove 'l trentino
pastore e quel di Brescia e 'l veronese
segnar poria, s' e' fesse quel cammino.

31 Raise your head, raise it and see the one for whom the earth opened before the eyes of the Thebans, so that they all cried: 'Where are you rushing,

34 Amphiaraus? Why are you leaving the war?' And he did not stop falling downward until he reached Minos, who seizes each one.

37 Look how he has made his breast his back; because he wished to see too far ahead, now he looks backward and treads a backward path.

40 See Tiresias, who changed shape when he turned from male to female, changing all his members, every one;

43 and then he had to strike the two entangled serpents with his staff once more, before he could regain his male plumage.

46 Arruns is the one who backs up against his belly there; in the mountains of Luni, where the Carrarese hoes, who lives below,

49 he had a cave in the white marble for his dwelling, whence the view of the stars and the sea was not cut off.

52 And she who covers up her breasts, which you cannot see, with her loosened tresses, and has every hairy skin on the other side,

55 was Manto, who searched through many lands; finally she settled where I was born; therefore I wish you to listen for a little.

58 After her father departed from life, and the city of Bacchus was enslaved, for a long time she wandered through the world.

61 Up in beautiful Italy there lies a lake, at the foot of the Alps that close in Germany above the Tyrol, whose name is Benaco.

64 A thousand springs, I think, and more, bathe the land between Garda and Val Camonica and the Alps, with the water that collects in that lake.

67 In the center there is a place where the shepherds of Trento and Brescia, and the Veronese, could all give blessing, if they made the journey.

70   Siede Peschiera, bello e forte arnese
        da fronteggiar Bresciani e Bergamaschi,
        ove la riva 'ntorno più discese.

73   Ivi convien che tutto quanto caschi
        ciò che 'n grembo a Benaco star non può,
        e fassi fiume giù per verdi paschi.

76   Tosto che l'acqua a correr mette co,
        non più Benaco ma Mencio si chiama
        fino a Governol, dove cade in Po.

79   Non molto ha corso ch'el trova una lama,
        ne la qual si distende e la 'mpaluda;
        e suol di state talor esser grama.

82   Quindi passando la vergine cruda
        vide terra nel mezzo del pantano
        sanza coltura e d'abitanti nuda.

85   Lì, per fuggire ogne consorzio umano,
        ristette con suoi servi a far sue arti,
        e visse, e vi lasciò suo corpo vano.

88   Li uomini poi che 'ntorno erano sparti
        s'accolsero a quel loco, ch'era forte
        per lo pantan ch'avea da tutte parti.

91   Fer la città sovra quell'ossa morte;
        e per colei che 'l loco prima elesse,
        Mantüa l'appellar sanz' altra sorte.

94   Già fuor le genti sue dentro più spesse,
        prima che la mattia da Casalodi
        da Pinamonte inganno ricevesse.

97   Però t'assenno che, se tu mai odi
        originar la mia terra altrimenti,
        la verità nulla menzogna frodi."

100   E io: "Maestro, i tuoi ragionamenti
        mi son sì certi e prendon sì mia fede,
        che li altri mi sarien carboni spenti.

103   Ma dimmi de la gente che procede,
        se tu ne vedi alcun degno di nota;
        ché solo a ciò la mia mente rifiede."

106   Allor mi disse: "Quel che da la gota
        porge la barba in su le spalle brune,
        fu—quando Grecia fu di maschi vòta

70   Peschiera sits there, a handsome, strong fortress, to hold the front against the Brescians and the Bergamasques, where the shore around it is lowest.

73   There must fall whatever cannot stay in Benaco, becoming a river through green fields.

76   As soon as the water begins to flow, it is no longer called Benaco but Mincio, as far as Governolo, where it falls into the Po.

79   It has not flowed far before finding a depression in which it spreads out and becomes a swamp; and in the summer it is often noxious.

82   Passing there the harsh virgin saw land in the midst of the fens, uncultivated and bare of people.

85   There, to flee all human fellowship, with her servants she stayed to ply her arts, there lived, and there left her empty body.

88   The people who were scattered about later gathered to that spot, which the swamp in all directions made strong.

91   They built their city over those dead bones; and, after her who first chose the place, they named it Mantua without any other augury.

94   The people housed there used to be more numerous, before the fool of Casalodi was deceived by Pinamonte.

97   Therefore I advise you, if you ever hear any other origin given for my city, that you let no lie defraud the truth."

100   And I: "Master, your discourse is so sure and so gains my belief, that any others would be spent coals to me.

103   But among the people in this procession, tell me if you see any worthy of note; for my mind still comes back to that alone."

106   Then he told me: "That one, who from his cheek spreads his beard down over his dark shoulders, was —when Greece was emptied of males,

109 sì ch'a pena rimaser per le cune—
augure, e diede 'l punto con Calcanta
in Aulide a tagliar la prima fune.

112 Euripilo ebbe nome, e così 'l canta
l'alta mia tragedìa in alcun loco:
ben lo sai tu che la sai tutta quanta.

115 Quell'altro che ne' fianchi è così poco,
Michele Scotto fu, che veramente
de le magiche frode seppe 'l gioco.

118 Vedi Guido Bonatti; vedi Asdente,
ch'avere inteso al cuoio e a lo spago
ora vorrebbe, ma tardi si pente.

121 Vedi le triste che lasciaron l'ago,
la spuola e 'l fuso, e fecersi 'ndivine;
fecer malie con erbe e con imago.

124 Ma vienne omai, ché già tiene 'l confine
d'amendue li emisperi e tocca l'onda
sotto Sobilia Caino e le spine;

127 e già iernotte fu la luna tonda:
ben ten de' ricordar, ché non ti nocque
alcuna volta per la selva fonda."

130 Sì mi parlava, e andavamo introcque.

109   so that hardly any remained in the cradles—an
augur, and along with Calchas he determined the
point to cut the first ship's cable in Aulis.

112   Eurypylus was his name, and thus my high
tragedy sings of him at one place: you know that
well, for you know it through and through.

115   That other who is so slender in the flanks was
Michael Scot, who truly knew the game of magic
frauds.

118   See Guido Bonatti; see Asdente, who now wishes
he had attended to his leather and his thread, but
repents too late.

121   See the wretched women who left their needles, their
spindles, and their distaffs, and became soothsayers;
they cast spells with herbs and images.

124   But come along now, for Cain with his thorns now
holds the boundary of the two hemispheres and
touches the wave below Seville;

127   and already last night the moon was full: you
must remember it well, for several times it did not
harm you in the deep forest."

130   So he spoke to me, and we walked meanwhile.

NOTES

1–3. Of a strange . . . those submerged: Note the parallel with the opening of Canto 19; there is a close relation between simony (which pretends that the gifts of the Holy Spirit, of which one is prophecy, can be sold) and soothsaying. The frequency of self-conscious canto openings in the Malebolge is pointed out in the note to 18.1–18. Here Dante for the first time in the poem writes of its subdivision into canticles (*cantiche*) and cantos (*canti*).

1. strange new: The Italian *nova* has both meanings (see the notes to 6.4 and 13.73).

3. canticle: That is, the *Inferno*, translating *cantica* though Dante's term here is *canzon* (Latin *cantio*), possibly treated as an augmentative of *canto* (line 2); the cognate term *chanson* is used of long poems in Old French, as in *chanson de geste* (for the use of these terms in the early manuscripts and commentaries, see Pertile 1991). For the issue of the literary genre of the *Comedy*, see the note to 16.127–29.

3. which is of those submerged: That is, the first canticle is about the damned; Hell is often referred to as the abyss or, figurally, the Red Sea; this figural relation is made most fully explicit at the beginning of the *Purgatorio*.

9. at the pace taken by litanies: Litanies were typically religious processions begging God and the saints for help; their pace was very slow. The ironic point of the reference would seem related to the fact that the soothsayers characteristically take the future as already determined. See Additional Note 8.

11–12. marvelously twisted . . . the beginning of the chest: The violence of the distortion is partly conveyed by the order of the description, as if the head had been held still and the rest of the body twisted.

14–15. they were forced . . . taken from them: The *contrapasso* (discussed in the note to lines 37–39) is already implicit, as well as the idea that in life the soothsayers' superstition and fraudulence obstructed their capacity for accurate natural foresight.

19–25. So may God permit . . . Surely I wept: Lines 19–22 are the fourth apostrophe of the reader in *Inferno* (see the note to 8.94–96). The pilgrim's weeping here has been the subject of discussion, some commentators taking it as reflecting a specific sympathy for the diviners. We take it as expressing the pilgrim's grief at the distortion of the human body (made in the image of God), sufficient grounds for his weeping and for the reader's meditation. The mention of the pilgrim's weeping also allows time for the considerable force of our empathic discomfort to set in. See Additional Note 8.

26–30. so that my guide said . . . to God's judgment: Virgil's rebuke, too, has been variously interpreted, depending on the significance assigned to line 30. Most commentators take it as we do, as rebuking the pilgrim's grief at the punishment; other possibilities are discussed in Additional Note 8.

28. Here pity lives when it is quite dead: The commentators point to the considerable theological literature available to Dante on the nature of true compassion, appropriate only toward the living or toward the souls in Purgatory, who can change.

29–30. who is more wicked . . . God's judgment: To bring passion to God's judgment would seem to be "to refuse to accept it calmly or with satisfaction." But the meaning of line 30 is disputed; the issue is whether the lines are directed against the nature of the sin or against Dante's weeping. See Additional Note 8.

31. Raise your head, raise it: That is, stop weeping and try to understand the nature of this sin (Ramat 1976).

31–36. the one for whom . . . Minos: Amphiaraus, one of the Seven against Thebes, known to Dante in Statius's *Thebaid*. One of Statius's noblest figures, he is commanded by the king of Argos to perform augury (foretelling the future from the flight of birds) on the outcome of the war against Thebes. Later, he is the first of the Seven to die, as the earth opens and he rides in his chariot down to Hades and confronts Pluto, god of the underworld (7.688–8.126). Dante's lines conflate two passages, the words of Pluto to Amphiaraus, "quo ruis?" and the taunts of the Thebans. Amphiaraus is discussed further in Additional Note 8.

33. Where are you rushing: There is a taunting reference to the fact that Amphiaraus, having foreseen the defeat of the Greeks, including the deaths of six of the seven heroes, including himself (3.460–551), at first refuses to participate in the war against Thebes; he is compelled to do so by his greedy wife, who accepts a bribe (Dante refers to the incident in *Purg.* 12.49–51). Italian *rui* can mean both "fall" and "rush, hasten."

37–39. Look how . . . a backward path: In these lines the *contrapasso* is made explicit. The emphasis on the physical distortion of the punishment is repeated in the case of each of the five classical figures (Tiresias and Arruns, lines 40–46; Manto, lines 52–55; and Eurypylus, lines 106–13); with the moderns the insistence is dropped. For "a backward path," see *Purg.* 10.121–29.

40–45. See Tiresias . . . his male plumage: Dante knew of Tiresias's change of sex through Ovid, *Met.* 3.324–31, which he echoes in *sembiante* ("shape," line 40; cf. *Met.* 3.331), *femmina* ("female," line 41; cf. 3.326), *ribattere* and *riavesse* ("to strike again" and "to regain," lines 43 and 45; cf. 3.327, 331: *rursus* [again], *redit* [returns]). In Ovid's account, Tiresias of Thebes separates two copulating serpents with his staff and becomes a woman; seven years later he comes upon them again and again separates them, returning to male shape. When Jupiter and Juno have a dispute as to which sex has greater pleasure in intercourse, Tiresias declares that women do, whereupon Juno, angry at the revelation of the secret, blinds him. In compensation, Jupiter grants him to see the future. He was the most famous soothsayer of Greco-Roman tradition. See Additional Note 8.

45. regain his male plumage: That is, his beard; for feathers as beard, see *Purg.* 1.42, of Cato. There is also a pun on Italian *pene* [penis].

46–51. Arruns . . . the sea was not cut off: Arruns is a soothsayer in Lucan's *Pharsalia* (1.585–638) who foresees from the entrails of an ox the disastrous consequences of the civil war betweeen Caesar and Pompey, but does not tell all he sees, wrapping his prophecies in ambiguities. According to Lucan, he lived in the ruins of the city Lucca; Dante places him in the nearby mountains of Luna, where his horizons were vast (lines 50–51), in ironic contrast to his present situation, where all he can see is Tiresias's belly (Caccia 1967; Ramat 1976). His cave, too, would seem to anticipate his place in Hell.

52–56. And she who covers . . . where I was born: Tiresias's daughter Manto figures largely in Statius's *Thebaid* as his assistant. The idea that she "searched through many lands" apparently derives from *Aen.* 10.198–201, as interpreted by Servius:

> Ille etiam patriis agmen ciet Ocnus ab oris,
> fatidicae Mantus et Tusci filius amnis,
> qui muros matrisque dedit tibi, Mantua, nomen,
> Mantua dives avis. . . .

> [He, too, calls forth his troop from his father's shore,
> Ocnus, son of fate-speaking Manto and the Tuscan river,
> who gave walls to you, Mantua, and his mother's name,
> Mantua, rich in ancestors. . . .]

According to Servius, the Theban Manto came to Italy after her father's death and gave birth to Ocnus by the river god Tiber (whose source is in Tuscany).

54. every hairy skin on the other side: That is, the long hair of her head, the hair of her armpits, and her pubic hair are all turned away from the pilgrim.

58–99. After her father departed . . . no lie defraud the truth: Virgil's long digression on the foundation of his birthplace, Mantua (see 1.68–69), has excited much comment, since it has seemed to most critics to contradict the brief notice in the *Aeneid* cited in the previous note. See Additional Note 8. One of its effects is to contrast the vivid reality of the geography of Italy with the unreality of soothsaying, both ancient and modern.

58–59. After . . . the city of Bacchus was enslaved: After the war of the Seven against Thebes, the city was conquered by the Athenians under Theseus (*Thebaid* 12).

61–66. Up in beautiful Italy . . . collects in that lake: Benacus was the Latin name for the lake now known as the Lago di Garda, at the foot of the Tyrolean Alps. It is the easternmost and the largest of the lakes of northern Italy, thirty-two miles long and eleven miles wide at its widest point. Garda is a city on the eastern shore; Valcamonica is the largest of the alpine valleys north of Brescia (thus northwest of the lake); the Alps (in Dante's term, *Pennino*) stand for the territory to the north of the lake.

67–69. In the center . . . if they made the journey: In other words, the boundaries of the three dioceses of Brescia (to the west), Trento (to the northeast), and Verona (to the southeast) all meet at a point in the center of the lake (usually identified as the island of Lechi), from which each of the bishops could officially bless, since their jurisdictions overlapped there. Like the reference to litanies in line 9, the reference recalls the theme of the efficacy of prayer.

70–72. Peschiera . . . where the shore around it is lowest: Peschiera is a city at the southernmost point of the lake, controlled in Dante's time by the lords of Verona, the Scaligeri.

78. Governolo: Governolo is just over a mile north of the joining of the Mincio with the Po.

79–81. It has not flowed . . . often noxious: The swamp formed by the Mincio, eventually the site of Mantua, is about thirty-one miles south of Peschiera (some twelve miles farther, the Mincio flows into the Po). The site was unhealthy because of malaria.

82. the harsh virgin: Manto, a virgin as in Statius. This is the first departure from Vergil's account in *Aeneid* 10, which has Manto mate with the river god Tiber.

87. her empty body: After her death her body was no longer filled with her soul (cf. 9.25: "My flesh had been naked of me . . .").

88–93. The people . . . other augury: Virgil here corrects the *Aeneid* on two points: first, Tiresias's line was extinct with Manto; there is no genetic connection between it and Mantua, and Manto had no other kind of connection with the inhabitants of the region, who were "scattered"; second, Mantua was founded without recourse to the sin of divination (as might seem implied by the account in the *Aeneid*); modern theories on the founding of Mantua see the name as indigenous. See Additional Note 8.

94–96. The people housed there . . . Pinamonte: The events referred to in these lines took place in 1291, when Alberto of Casalodi, ruler of Mantua, was tricked by Pinamonte de' Buonaccolsi into withdrawing most of his (noble) supporters from the city. Pinamonte then, with the aid of the rebellious populace, took over the city and, according to the early commentators, had most of the noble families massacred.

97–99. Therefore I advise you . . . let no lie defraud the truth: Virgil's curious self-correction is discussed in Additional Note 8.

106–14. That one . . . through and through: Eurypylus is mentioned by Sinon in *Aen.* 2.114 as sent by the Greeks to the Delphic oracle to learn the future of the war; in Sinon's lying account, the oracle's discouraging reply causes the Greeks to sail for home. That Eurypylus was a soothsayer, an associate of Calchas, is Dante's reasonable enough inference from Vergil's lines, since Sinon could only be naming him to increase the verisimilitude of his account; furthermore, Servius's note can be read to mean that Eurypylus had access to the inner shrine of the Delphic temple, in which case he would have to be a priest of Apollo, like Calchas (D'Ovidio 1901).

108. when Greece was emptied of males: By the Trojan War.

110–11. along with Calchas . . . in Aulis: Dante knew from Vergil (*Aen.* 2.116–17), Servius, and Ovid (*Met.* 12.4–39) the story of how storms kept the Greek fleet in Aulis until the augur Calchas reveals that the anger of Diana must be appeased by the sacrifice of Iphigenia, young daughter of Agamemnon and Clytemnestra (Ovid's passage includes an account of prophecy from birds by which Calchas predicts the outcome of the war; it is one of the sources of Statius's account in *Thebaid* 3). It is tempting to think that Dante might have known Lucretius's description of the sacrifice of Iphigenia as one of the chief crimes caused by pagan superstition (*De rerum natura*, 1.84–101).

113. my high tragedy: Virgil is of course referring to the *Aeneid*; the contrast between the two genres represented by his poem and the *Comedy* is implied again in 21.2.

115–17. That other . . . magic frauds: Michael the Scot was in the service of the emperor Frederick II and the author of numerous treatises and translations from Greek and Arabic; he was said to have died after 1290.

118. Guido Bonatti: Guido Bonatti of Forlì was another famous astrologer and author, prominent among the Ghibellines of Romagna. Born around 1220, he served, successively, the empereror Frederick II, the Conti Guidi (see the note to 16.34–39), and Guido da Montefeltro (Canto 27); he seems to have been alive in 1296.

118–20. Asdente . . . repents too late: Dante mentions Asdente (the name probably means "toothless"), a cobbler who achieved fame as a soothsayer, as the most famous person in Parma (*Convivio* 4.16.6).

124–26. Cain with his thorns . . . touches the wave below Seville: That is, as seen from Jerusalem the moon is setting (crossing the horizon between the hemisphere of land and that of ocean) south of Seville; since according to line 127 the moon was full (i.e., directly opposite the sun) yesterday, the sun is now rising: it is the morning of Holy Saturday. Widespread popular tradition identified the image in the moon as that of Cain carrying a bundle of brambles on his back.

127–29. already last night . . . in the deep forest: The account of Dante's night in the forest in Canto 1 does not refer to the moon. In actual fact, the full moon in April 1300 took place on April 3.

130. meanwhile: Dante's word *introcque* (derived from Latin *inter hoc*) has occasioned comment because he cites it in *De vulgari eloquentia* 1.13.1 as a Florentine dialect word unworthy of the "tragic" or high style (see the note to 21.2).

CANTO 21

<table>
<tr><td>1</td><td>Così di ponte in ponte, altro parlando
che la mia comedìa cantar non cura,
venimmo, e tenavamo 'l colmo quando</td></tr>
<tr><td>4</td><td>restammo per veder l'altra fessura
di Malebolge e li altri pianti vani;
e vidila mirabilmente oscura.</td></tr>
<tr><td>7</td><td>Quale ne l'arzanà de' Viniziani
bolle l'inverno la tenace pece
a rimpalmare i legni lor non sani,</td></tr>
<tr><td>10</td><td>ché navicar non ponno; in quella vece
chi fa suo legno novo e chi ristoppa
le coste a quel che più vïaggi fece,</td></tr>
<tr><td>13</td><td>chi ribatte da proda e chi da poppa,
altri fa remi e altri volge sarte,
chi terzeruolo e artimon rintoppa:</td></tr>
<tr><td>16</td><td>tal, non per foco ma per divin' arte,
bollia là giuso una pegola spessa
che 'nviscava la ripa d'ogne parte.</td></tr>
<tr><td>19</td><td>I' vedea lei, ma non vedëa in essa
mai che le bolle che 'l bollor levava,
e gonfiar tutta, e riseder compressa.</td></tr>
<tr><td>22</td><td>Mentr' io là giù fisamente mirava,
lo duca mio, dicendo: "Guarda, guarda!"
mi trasse a sé del loco dov' io stava.</td></tr>
<tr><td>25</td><td>Allor mi volsi come l'uom cui tarda
di veder quel che li convien fuggire
e cui paura sùbita sgagliarda,</td></tr>
<tr><td>28</td><td>che, per veder, non indugia 'l partire:
e vidi dietro a noi un diavol nero
correndo su per lo scoglio venire.</td></tr>
</table>

CANTO 21

Fifth bolgia: *barrators—the Evil Claws—parley with the demons—*
strange signal

1   Thus we went from bridge to bridge, speaking of
other things my comedy does not record; and we
were at the summit when

4   we stood still to see the next cleft of Malebolge
and the next vain weeping; and I saw it to be
wondrously dark.

7   As in the Venetians' arsenal in winter the
tenacious pitch boils to recaulk their worn ships,

10   for they cannot sail; instead this man works on a
new ship, that one plugs the ribs of a craft that has
made many voyages,

13   this one repairs at the prow, this one at the stern,
another makes oars, another twists shrouds, another
patches foresail and mainsail:

16   so, heated not by fire but by God's art, a thick
pitch boiled there that clung to the banks on every
side.

19   I saw it, but in it I saw nothing but the bubbles
that the boiling brought up, and the pitch all swelling
out and subsiding deflated.

22   While I was gazing fixedly down at it, my leader,
saying: "Look out, look out!" drew me from where I
was standing.

25   Then I turned, like one eager to see what he must
escape, whom sudden fear robs of vigor,

28   and, though he looks, does not delay departure;
and I saw behind us a black devil running along the
ridge.

31   Ahi quant' elli era ne l'aspetto fero!
e quanto mi parea ne l'atto acerbo
con l'ali aperte e sovra i piè leggero!

34   L'omero suo, ch'era aguto e superbo,
carcava un peccator con ambo l'anche,
e quei tenea de' piè ghermito 'l nerbo.

37   Del nostro ponte disse: "O Malebranche,
ecco un de li anzïan di Santa Zita!
Mettetel sotto, ch'i' torno per anche

40   a quella terra, che n'è ben fornita:
ogn' uom v'è barattier, fuor che Bonturo;
del *no*, per li denar, vi si fa *ita*."

43   Là giù 'l buttò, e per lo scoglio duro
si volse; e mai non fu mastino sciolto
con tanta fretta a seguitar lo furo.

46   Quel s'attuffò, e tornò sù convolto;
ma i demon che del ponte avean coperchio,
gridar: "Qui non ha loco il Santo Volto!

49   Qui si nuota altrimenti che nel Serchio!
Però, se tu non vuo' di nostri graffi,
non far sopra la pegola soverchio."

52   Poi l'addentar con più di cento raffi,
disser: "Coverto convien che qui balli,
sì che, se puoi, nascosamente accaffi."

55   Non altrimenti i cuoci a' lor vassalli
fanno attuffare in mezzo la caldaia
la carne con li uncin, perché non galli.

58   Lo buon maestro: "Acciò che non si paia
che tu ci sia," mi disse, "giù t'acquatta
dopo uno scheggio, ch'alcun schermo t'aia;

61   e per nulla offension che mi sia fatta,
non temer tu, ch'i' ho le cose conte,
per ch'altra volta fui a tal baratta."

64   Poscia passò di là dal co del ponte;
e com' el giunse in su la ripa sesta,
mestier li fu d'aver sicura fronte.

67   Con quel furore e con quella tempesta
ch'escono i cani a dosso al poverello,
che di sùbito chiede ove s'arresta,

31   Ah, how fierce he looked! and how cruel his
bearing seemed to me with his opened wings, so
light on his feet!

34   His shoulder, which was sharp and high, was
loaded down with a sinner's two hips, and he held
hooked with his claw the sinews of both feet.

37   From our bridge he said: "O Evil Claws, here is
one of the elders of Santa Zita! Put him under, I am
going back for more

40   to that city, which is well supplied with them:
every one is a grafter there, except Bonturo; for
money there they turn 'no' into 'yes.'"

43   He threw him down and turned on the stony
ridge; and never was a mastiff loosed with more
haste to pursue a thief.

46   The sinner plunged, and came back to the surface
bottom up: but the demons hidden beneath the
bridge cried: "Here we don't show the Holy Face!

49   Here the swimming is different than in the
Serchio! So, if you don't want to feel our grapples,
don't protrude above the pitch."

52   After they made him feel the teeth of a hundred
prongs, they said: "Down here you have to dance
covered up and, if you can, grab secretly."

55   Not otherwise do cooks have their servants push
down with hooks the meat cooking in a broth, so
that it may not float.

58   My good master said to me: "So it may not appear
that you are here, squat down behind a projecting
rock to hide;

61   and no matter what harm they offer me, do not
you be afraid, for I have foreseen everything; I have
already been present at these deals."

64   Then he passed beyond the bridgehead; and as he
reached the sixth bank, he needed to have a
confident brow.

67   With the fury and tempestuous noise of dogs
coming out at a poor man, who stops and begs from
where he stands,

70 usciron quei di sotto al ponticello,
e volser contra lui tutt' i runcigli;
ma el gridò: "Nessun di voi sia fello!

73 Innanzi che l'uncin vostro mi pigli,
traggasi avante l'un di voi che m'oda,
e poi d'arruncigliarmi si consigli."

76 Tutti gridaron: "Vada Malacoda!"
per ch'un si mosse—e li altri stetter fermi—
e venne a lui, dicendo: "Che li approda?"

79 "Credi tu, Malacoda, qui vedermi
esser venuto," disse 'l mio maestro,
"sicuro già da tutti vostri schermi,

82 sanza voler divino e fato destro?
Lascian' andar, ché nel cielo è voluto
ch'i' mostri altrui questo cammin silvestro."

85 Allor li fu l'orgoglio sì caduto
ch'e' si lasciò cascar l'uncino a' piedi,
e disse a li altri, "Omai non sia feruto."

88 E 'l duca mio a me: "O tu che siedi
tra li scheggion del ponte quatto quatto,
sicuramente omai a me tu riedi."

91 Per ch'io mi mossi e a lui venni ratto;
e i diavoli si fecer tutti avanti,
sì ch'io temetti ch'ei tenesser patto:

94 così vid' io già temer li fanti
ch'uscivan patteggiati di Caprona,
veggendo sé tra nemici cotanti.

97 I' m'accostai con tutta la persona
lungo 'l mio duca, e non torceva li occhi
da la sembianza lor, ch'era non buona.

100 Ei chinavan li raffi, e: "Vuo' che 'l tocchi,"
diceva l'un con l'altro, "in sul groppone?"
E rispondien: "Sì, fa che gliel'accocchi."

103 Ma quel demonio che tenea sermone
col duca mio, si volse tutto presto
e disse: "Posa, posa, Scarmiglione!"

106 Poi disse a noi: "Più oltre andar per questo
iscoglio non si può, però che giace
tutto spezzato al fondo l'arco sesto.

70   so they came forth from under the bridge, and pointed all their grappling hooks toward him; but he cried: "Let none of you think to harm!

73   Before your hooks seize me, let one of you come forward to hear me, and then you may take counsel to grapplehook me."

76   All cried: "Let Evil Tail go!" and one stepped forth while the others stood still, and came to Virgil, saying, "What good will it do him?"

79   "Do you think, Evil Tail, that you see me here," said my master, "once already safe from all your tricks,

82   without God's will and favorable fate? Allow us to walk on, for it is willed in Heaven that I guide someone on this savage journey."

85   Then his pride fell so that he let his hook droop to his feet, and he said to the others: "Now he mustn't be gored."

88   And my leader to me: "O you, sitting among the rocks of the bridge all asquat, you can return to me safely now."

91   Therefore I moved and went to him swiftly; and the devils all started forward, so that I was afraid they would not keep the pact:

94   thus once I saw the foot-soldiers fear, coming out of Caprona under safe-conduct, seeing themselves among so many enemies.

97   I drew close to my leader with all my person, and I did not turn my eyes from their expression, which was not good.

100   They pointed their prongs, and: "Want me to nudge him," one said to the other, "on the rump?" And they replied: "Yes, give it to him in the notch."

103   But that demon who was parleying with my leader, turned swiftly about, saying, "Down, down, Tangle Head!"

106   Then he said to us: "Further along this ridge you cannot go, for the sixth arch lies all shattered at the bottom.

109   E se l'andare avante pur vi piace,
andatevene su per questa grotta:
presso è un altro scoglio che via face.

112   Ier, più oltre cinqu' ore che quest' otta,
mille dugento con sessanta sei
anni compiè che qui la via fu rotta.

115   Io mando verso là di questi miei
a riguardar s'alcun se ne sciorina:
gite con lor, che non saranno rei."

118   "Tra'ti avante, Alichino, e Calcabrina,"
cominciò elli a dire, "e tu, Cagnazzo;
e Barbariccia guidi la decina.

121   Libicocco vegn' oltre e Draghignazzo,
Cirïatto sannuto e Graffiacane
e Farfarello e Rubicante pazzo.

124   Cercate 'ntorno le boglienti pane:
costor sian salvi infin a l'altro scheggio
che tutto intero va sovra le tane."

127   "Omè, maestro, che è quel ch'i' veggio?"
diss' io, "deh, sanza scorta andianci soli,
se tu sa' ir; ch'i' per me non la cheggio.

130   Se tu se' sì accorto come suoli,
non vedi tu ch'e' digrignan li denti
e con le ciglia ne minaccian duoli?"

133   Ed elli a me: "Non vo' che tu paventi;
lasciali digrignar pur a lor senno,
ch'e' fanno ciò per li lessi dolenti."

136   Per l'argine sinistro volta dienno;
ma prima avea ciascun la lingua stretta
coi denti verso lor duca, per cenno,

139   ed elli avea del cul fatto trombetta.

109 But if you still wish to go forward, walk along this
bank: nearby is another ridge that makes a path.

112 Yesterday, five hours later than now, one
thousand two hundred and sixty-six years were
completed since the way was broken here.

115 I am sending some of these in that direction, to
see if anyone is airing himself: go with them, they
will not be troublesome."

118 "Come forward, Harlequin, Trample Frost," he
began to say, "and you, Evil Dog; and Curly Beard
command the squad.

121 Love Notch, come here, and Little Big Dragon, Big
Pig with his tusks, and Scratching Dog, and Butterfly
and crazy Ruby Face.

124 Inspect the boiling birdlime; let these be safe until
the next ridge that goes undamaged over the pits."

127 "Oh me, master, what do I see?" I said, "Ah, let us
go alone, without escort, if you know the way; I
don't ask it for myself.

130 If you are as alert as usual, don't you see how
they are grinding their teeth, and how their eyebrows
threaten treachery?"

133 And he to me: "I would not have you fear: let
them snarl as much as they please, they are doing
that for the sufferers in the stew."

136 They made left face on the bank; but first each
had bit his tongue toward their leader, as a salute,

139 and he of his ass had made a trumpet.

NOTES

1–2. Thus we went . . . does not record: For the self-conscious opening, see note to 18.1–18. "Speaking of other things" picks up the last line of Canto 20.

2. my comedy: With 16.128–29, 21.2 would give ample authority for the title of the poem, even if we lacked the unanimous testimony of the manuscripts. Following closely on Virgil's mention of his "high tragedy" (20.113), this is the second and last appearance of the word *comedìa* in the poem. The term characterizes both the style and the subject matter of the poem and, in conjunction with 20.113, contrasts them sharply with those of the *Aeneid*; its use at the beginning of the present canto is programmatic. In *De vulgari eloquentia,* Book 2, Dante had defined the highest style as the tragic, consisting of the noblest and most harmonious words, using the highest forms (the canzone and the hendecasyllable) and rhetorical constructions, and singing only the noblest subjects (the implicit model, adapted to the vernacular, is, of course, Vergil); comedy he associated with "sometimes the middle level of the vernacular, sometimes the low" (2.4.5). In the *Epistle to Can Grande* (of disputed authenticity) the genres are defined by the nature of their plots or subject matter, tragedy as "beginning happily and admirably, ending horribly," comedy as "beginning in difficulty but ending prosperously."

As Auerbach (1953) showed, the *Comedy* represents a new conception in which the many levels of subject matter, ranging from the most abject to the most sublime and apocalyptic, require all levels of vocabulary and style, from the most familiar (cf. 32.1–9), dialectal (see 20.130, with note), and obscene (cf. Canto 18 and the present one), to the most learned and technically precise, including Latinisms and neologisms.

7–18. As in the Venetians' arsenal . . . on every side: The term *arsenal* (derived from an Arabic word meaning "factory") was narrowed in Italian to mean "shipyard." In Dante's time, Venice had the most powerful navy in Europe; the site of its shipyard still exists. While formally positive (i.e., the infernal pitch is said to be like the Venetian), in fact the simile sharply contrasts the elaborate scene of organized and purposeful social activity in the Arsenal with the solitude and silence of the infernal scene (and, by implication, with the later rowdy undiscipline and futile malice of the devils). The relevance of the ship imagery to the *contrapasso* is discussed in the note to lines 53–54.

29–45. a black devil . . . to pursue a thief: This devil's function—seizing the damned at death and carrying them to Hell (frequently represented in folklore and art; see Hughes 1968)—corresponds to that of the devils mentioned in

27.113–29 and *Purg.* 5.103–14, though it might seem excluded by the scene beside the Acheron (3.70–129).

29–33. a black devil . . . light on his feet: The traditional medieval horned devils (Figure 4), perhaps to be understood in 8.83 ("rained down"), were introduced in 18.35–36, where their wings were not mentioned; their malicious sarcasms were given prominence there, however, as they will be here.

31–32. Ah, how fierce . . . how cruel: Note the parallel with 1.4, of the dark wood.

34–36. His shoulder . . . both feet: In other words, the devil has thrust his claw through the sinner's ankles, hooking his Achilles' tendons; he has then slung the sinner over one shoulder, as if he were a butcher carrying a slaughtered animal. The implicit metaphor is picked up in line 55. Kleinhenz (1982) suggests there is a parodic reference to the well-known iconographic motif of the Good Shepherd carrying the lost lamb on his shoulders.

Figure 4. A medieval devil. (Based on an illumination in a manuscript of the *Comedy*)

37. O Evil Claws: Evidently the collective name of the devils of this ditch; Dante surpasses himself in inventiveness of names in this canto (see the note to lines 118–23).

38. one of the elders of Santa Zita: Saint Zita had died around 1278 and was much venerated in her home city of Lucca; she had not yet been canonized in 1300. The elders of Santa Zita are the magistrates of the republican (and Guelf) city of Lucca. Guido da Pisa, an early commentator, identified this soul as one Martino Bottaio, a political boss, like Bonturo Dati (see the note to line 41). When Dante was writing, Lucca, like Florence, was dominated by the Black faction of Guelfs (discussed in the note to 6.64–72).

39. for more: The Italian *per anche* allows a pun on "hips" (line 35).

41. every one is a grafter there, except Bonturo: Bonturo Dati (d. after 1324) was the political boss of Lucca; the line is obviously ironic. Lucca follows Bologna (Canto 18), as the next Italian city to be denounced (see the note to 26.1–3).

42. for money there they turn 'no' into 'yes': This amounts to a definition of barratry or graft: accepting bribes to change refusal ("no") into consent (*ita* is a Latin form of "yes"; cf. *sipa,* 18.61), perhaps to what is illegal or disloyal (cf. the examples in Canto 22).

44–45. never was a mastiff . . . to pursue a thief: That is, than was the devil returning to Lucca for more thieves. The devils are also compared to dogs in lines 67–69 (see the note to 22.19–21).

46–48. The sinner plunged . . . Holy Face: The "Holy Face" was an ebony statue of the crucified Christ venerated in Lucca, supposed to have been carved by the apostle Nicodemus, except for the face, which was miraculously completed while he slept (Fallani 1976). The devils' taunt is at least two-fold, since the pitch makes the sinner black, and it is his nether cheeks that are being compared to the face of Christ (Singleton)—another parodic reference to the Crucifixion. There is probably also a reference to the fact that the "Holy Face" appeared on Lucca coins (Varanini 1989): thus no profits are to be made here.

49. the Serchio: The river near Lucca, popular for swimming in the summer, according to the early commentators.

53–54. you have to dance . . . grab secretly: There is of course nothing to grab here except the pitch itself (cf. the meiosis of avarice in Canto 7); the line is an obvious reference to the secret grabbing the sinners did in life, and it suggests one dimension of the *contrapasso*. But what is it that facilitates the grafters' thefts in life? There seems a clear reference to their positions of authority and to the public's (or their lords') presumptive trust in them. In his treatise on the unity of the Church, Augustine interprets the pitch that seals Noah's ark (a symbol of the Church) as signifying the bond of love that holds it together. Dante has transferred this idea to the traditional notion of the ship of state (already used by him in *Convivio* 4.4.5–7). Hence the relevance of the opening simile of the caulking of ships, as well as the important parallel with the simoniacs, who are being pushed down into the clefts of the rock as if they were caulking. Barratry or graft is a kind of secular equivalent of simony.

55–57. Not otherwise do cooks . . . not float: The importance of food and cooking imagery in the Malebolge is discussed in Additional Note 13.

63. at these deals: Dante's word *baratta* has been taken by most commentators as meaning "struggle" or "battle," but that *baratta* also meant "exchange" or "deal" for Dante's period is amply testified and is much more appropriate to the theme of the canto, especially since Evil Tail will try to deceive Virgil.

64–139. Then he passed . . . a trumpet: The many parallels between this episode of negotiation with devils and that in Cantos 8 and 9 have often been pointed out.

67–70. With the fury . . . from under the bridge: The simile helps set off Virgil's confidence (overconfidence? [see lines 127–35]), so different from the beggar's timidity; it is one of a series emphasizing various forms of oppression and violence—scenes of the defenseless confronted with pitiless enemies: unarmed, defeated foot soldiers (lines 94–96), a captured otter (22.36), and a mouse among cats (22.58). As Favati (1965) showed, in having the devils erupt from beneath the bridge, Dante is alluding to the trapdoor from which the devils came on stage in miracle plays, filled with humor at the devils' expense.

74. let one of you come forward: Virgil has not, it seems, recognized any of these devils or remembered their names from his earlier visit.

76. Evil Tail: The devils' names are discussed in the note to lines 118–23.

79–81. Do you think, Evil Tail . . . all your tricks: In other words, Virgil's previous descent (see 9.22–30, with notes) brought opposition and trickery from the Evil Claws (note that *vostri* [your] in line 81 is a plural), which Virgil successively warded off.

84. this savage journey: Or, way in the wilderness; the line echoes 2.142.

85–87. then his pride fell . . . mustn't be gored: Evil Tail's comic pantomime of impotence derives from the traditionally ribald treatment of devils in medieval drama, but it conceals his intention to deceive.

88–90. And my leader . . . to me safely now: The sound effects of the Italian, especially *quatto quatto* [all asquat] emphasize the pilgrim's comically undignified posture.

92. the devils all started forward: The devils are surprised to see a living person, and their blood lust is particularly stirred.

94–96. thus once I saw . . . so many enemies: As we learn only from this passage, Dante was present at the siege and surrender of Caprona, a Pisan stronghold, in August 1289, probably as one of the mounted soldiers (see note to lines 67–70). The terms of the simile involve a reversal between then and now: Dante was one of the "many enemies" then; now he is in the position of the defeated soldiers, and the devils correspond to the Florentine troops (Favati 1965); this passage and 22.1–12 constitute the only references in the *Comedy* to Dante's military careeer. See Additional Note 9.

102. give it to him in the notch: The Italian *accoccare* is formed from the noun *cocca*, the notch of an arrow or crossbow bolt, and means "to fit the notch to the bowstring." Most commentators take the allusion as generic: "let fly at him," that is, "release the arrow." But the word would seem to involve a more exact reference.

105. Tangle Head: *Scarmiglione* (Tangle Head) is formed from the verb *carminare* [to card, comb wool], plus the privative *s-*.

106–14. Further along . . . the way was broken here: Evil Tail speaks an artful mixture of truth and falsehood. It is true that the way is cut off at the *bolgia* because the bridge has fallen (lines 106–9); it is false that there is an undamaged bridge nearby. The masterful touch is in lines 112–14, whose correct—and pedantically accurate—dating of the earthquake distracts from the question of the bridges. Evil Tail remembers that since Virgil's previous visit was prior to Christ's death (9.25–27), Virgil cannot know which bridges are fallen.

112–14. Yesterday, five hours . . . the way was broken here: The way was broken by the great earthquake at Christ's death (12.31–45). "Yesterday" was Good Friday; "five hours later than now" would be noon (apparently an hour has elapsed since 20.124–29). Dante accepted Luke's statement (23.44–47) that Christ died at about noon; Christ was thought to have died in his thirty-fifth year, thus in A.D. 34. This passage dates the action of the *Comedy* as taking place in 1300 (it is the only place in the poem where the exact date is stated). Since Dante's birthday was in all probability in late May, the pilgrim has undertaken the journey in his thirty-fifth year, an additional element in the imitation of Christ that subtends the poem (discussed in the note to 1.91).

118–23. Come forward . . . Ruby Face: We translate most of the devils' names literally. Like Evil Claws (*Malebranche,* line 37), Evil Pockets (*Malebolge,* 18.1, 21.5, etc.), and Evil Tail (*Malacoda*), most of them join two words. Harlequin (*Alichino*) is the modern French form of the traditional leader of the wild infernal hunt (drawn on in 13.109–29). *Cagnazzo* (Evil Dog) is formed from *cane* and the pejorative suffix *-azzo.* *Libicocco* (Love Notch) we hypothesize to be a formation from Latin *libet* [it is pleasing] and Italian *cocca* (see line 102, with note); Spitzer (1943) argued that it was a deformation of *biricoccola,* a Tuscan word for "apricot," used in many Romance languages as a metaphor for the female organ. *Draghignazzo* (Little Big Dragon) we take as formed from *draco* [dragon], plus the diminutive suffix *-ino,* plus *-azzo.* *Ciriatto* (Big Pig) is generally taken to be derived from a Greek word for "pig." *Rubicante* (Ruby Face) is formed as a present participle. Of the twelve names, six (Evil Tail, Evil Dog, Little Big Dragon, Big Pig, Scratching Dog, and Butterfly) are explicitly bestial, like the collective name Evil Claws; several others have bestial connotations. A number of the devils' names seem to play on the names of prominent persons and families in Florence and Lucca. Scholars have amply demonstrated the basis of Dante's representation of these devils in medieval (especially French) miracle plays, in which they are ribald, sarcastic, obscene, and—of course—always defeated. Dante's names for the devils are a pastiche of names assigned to them in popular tradition and drama.

120. Curly Beard command the squad: "Squad" translates *decina* [unit of ten], the basic organizational unit of the Roman legions, to whose officer (the *decurio*) Curly Beard's new command alludes (see 22.74).

125–26. let these be safe . . . over the pits: Evil Tail's words are obviously meant as license to the devils to do as they will with the travelers, once past the next ruined bridge, but, curiously enough, if taken strictly, the words would prevent all license, since if there is no bridge, no limit is set to the travelers' safety.

127–35. Oh me, master . . . in the stew: The pilgrim reacts intuitively and directly to the devils, and he sees—correctly—that they mean harm and "threaten treachery." Virgil, however, has been taken in by Evil Tail, perhaps because of overconfidence.

132. how their eyebrows threaten treachery: The lowering and knitting of the devils' brows is referred to (cf. line 66).

135. stew: The Italian *lessi* [boiled] is usually used of boiled meat and other foods.

137–39. but first . . . made a trumpet: The leader (*duca*) of the ten is Curly Beard; it is to him the devils stick out their tongues, acknowledging his author-ity, and, as the beginning of the next canto will make clear, it is he who farts, giving the signal for their departure, all in grotesque parody of military disci-pline. Benvenuto says that the devils' grimace is called *trullizare*, explained by Camporesi (1985) as "an act miming the effort of defecation" (cf. 28.24). Roncaglia (1971) shows that the fart, like "kitchen humor," is a traditional part of low "comic" style, discussed in medieval treatises (and cf. the indignity vis-ited on the soothsayers, 20.10–24).

CANTO 22

1   Io vidi già cavalier muover campo
     e cominciare stormo e far lor mostra,
     e talvolta partir per loro scampo;

4   corridor vidi per la terra vostra,
     o Aretini, e vidi gir gualdane,
     fedir torneamenti e correr giostra,

7   quando con trombe, e quando con campane,
     con tamburi e con cenni di castella,
     e con cose nostrali e con istrane:

10   né già con sì diversa cennamella
     cavalier vidi muover né pedoni,
     né nave a segno di terra o di stella.

13   Noi andavam con i diece demoni.
     Ahi fiera compagnia! ma ne la chiesa
     coi santi, e in taverna coi ghiottoni.

16   Pur a la pegola era la mia 'ntesa,
     per veder de la bolgia ogne contegno
     e de la gente ch'entro v'era incesa.

19   Come i dalfini, quando fanno segno
     a' marinar con l'arco de la schiena
     che s'argomentin di campar lor legno:

22   talor così, ad alleggiar la pena,
     mostrav' alcun de' peccatori 'l dosso
     e nascondea in men che non balena.

25   E come a l'orlo de l'acqua d'un fosso
     stanno i ranocchi pur col muso fuori,
     sì che celano i piedi e l'altro grosso:

28   sì stavan d'ogne parte i peccatori;
     ma come s'appressava Barbariccia,
     così si ritraén sotto i bollori.

CANTO 22

Mock heroic opening—Ciampolo caught, interrogated, escapes—the pilgrim and Virgil escape

1   I have seen knights setting forth, beginning
assaults and standing muster, and sometimes
retreating to save themselves;

4   I have seen mounted men coursing your city, O
Aretines, I have seen foragers riding, tournaments
striking, and jousts running,

7   sometimes with trumpets, sometimes with bells,
with drums or signals from the tower, with things
both our own and foreign:

10   but never at so strange a pipe have I seen
horsemen or foot-soldiers setting forth, nor a ship at
a sign from land or star.

13   We were walking with the ten demons. Ah, fierce
company! but in church with the saints, in the tavern
with the gluttons.

16   My attention was all given to the pitch, to see
every condition of the moat and of the people burned
in it.

19   As dolphins do, when they signal to sailors,
arching their spines, to take measures to save their
ship:

22   so from time to time, to lessen the pain, a sinner
would show his back and hide it in less than a flash.

25   And as at the edge of a ditch the bullfrogs sit with
only their snouts showing, hiding their feet and thick
bodies:

28   so on every side did the sinners, but as Curly
Beard came near, like frogs they withdrew into the
boiling.

31   I' vidi, e anco il cor me n'accapriccia,
uno aspettar così, com' elli 'ncontra
ch'una rana rimane e l'altra spiccia;

34   e Graffiacan, che li era più di contra,
li arruncigliò le 'mpegolate chiome
e trassel sù, che mi parve una lontra.

37   I' sapea già di tutti quanti 'l nome,
sì li notai quando fuorono eletti,
e poi ch'e' si chiamaro, attesi come.

40   "O Rubicante, fa che tu li metti
li unghioni a dosso sì che tu lo scuoi!"
gridavan tutti insieme i maladetti.

43   E io: "Maestro mio, fa, se tu puoi,
che tu sappi chi è lo sciagurato
venuto a man de li avversari suoi."

46   Lo duca mio li s'accostò allato;
domandollo ond' ei fosse, e quei rispuose:
"I' fui del regno di Navarra nato.

49   Mia madre a servo d'un segnor mi puose,
che m'avea generato d'un ribaldo,
distruggitor di sé e di sue cose.

52   Poi fui famiglia del buon re Tebaldo;
quivi mi misi a far baratteria,
di ch'io rendo ragione in questo caldo."

55   E Cirïatto, a cui di bocca uscia
d'ogne parte una sanna come a porco,
li fé sentir come l'una sdruscia.

58   Tra male gatte era venuto 'l sorco;
ma Barbariccia il chiuse con le braccia
e disse: "State in là, mentr' io lo 'nforco."

61   E al maestro mio volse la faccia:
"Domanda," disse, "ancor, se più disii
saper da lui prima ch'altri 'l disfaccia."

64   Lo duca dunque: "Or dì: de li altri rii
conosci tu alcun che sia latino
sotto la pece?" E quelli: "I' mi partii,

67   poco è, da un che fu di là vicino.
Così foss' io ancor con lui coperto,
ch'i' non temerei unghia né uncino!"

31   I saw one wait, and my heart still makes me shudder at it, as sometimes one frog stays while the other jumps;

34   and Scratching Dog, who was closest, hooked his grapple in his pitchy locks and drew him up, so that he seemed to me like an otter.

37   I had learned all their names, they made such an impression on me when they were chosen and when they called to each other.

40   "O Ruby Face, see that you get your nails in him and tear his skin off!" all those cursed ones were shouting at once.

43   And I: "My master, see if you can discover who this wretch is who has come into the hands of his enemies."

46   My master stood alongside him; he asked him where he was from, and he replied: "I was born in the kingdom of Navarre.

49   My mother placed me in the service of a lord; she had generated me by a wastrel, destroyer of his wealth and of himself.

52   Then I was in the household of good king Thibaut; and there I took to barratry, for which I square accounts in this heat."

55   And Big Pig, from whose mouth on each side came a tusk like a boar's, let him feel how one of them could rip.

58   Among bad cats had the mouse arrived; but Curly Beard enclosed him with his arms, and said: "Stay over there, while I have him gripped."

61   Then he turned his face toward my master; "Ask again," he said, "if you want to know more from him before someone does him in."

64   My leader therefore: "Now say: among the other sinners under the pitch, do you know any who is Italian?" And he: "I left one,

67   a moment ago, who was from near there. Would I were still hidden with him, I'd not fear claw or crook!"

70   E Libicocco: "Troppo avem sofferto,"
disse, e preseli 'l braccio col runciglio
sì che, stracciando, ne portò un lacerto.

73   Draghignazzo anco i volle dar di piglio
giuso a le gambe; onde 'l decurio loro
si volse intorno intorno con mal piglio.

76   Quand' elli un poco rappaciati fuoro,
a lui, ch'ancor mirava sua ferita,
domandò 'l duca mio sanza dimoro:

79   "Chi fu colui da cui mala partita
di' che facesti per venire a proda?"
Ed ei rispuose: "Fu frate Gomita,

82   quel di Gallura, vasel d'ogne froda,
ch'ebbe i nemici di suo donno in mano,
e fé sì lor che ciascun se ne loda:

85   danar si tolse e lasciolli di piano,
sì com' e' dice; e ne li altri offici anche
barattier fu non picciol, ma sovrano.

88   Usa con esso donno Michel Zanche
di Logodoro; e a dir di Sardigna
le lingue lor non si sentono stanche.

91   Omè, vedete l'altro che digrigna;
i' direi anche, ma i' temo ch'ello
non s'apparecchi a grattarmi la tigna."

94   E 'l gran proposto, vòlto a Farfarello,
che stralunava li occhi per fedire,
disse: "Fatti 'n costà, malvagio uccello!"

97   "Se voi volete vedere o udire,"
ricominciò lo spaürato appresso,
"Toschi o Lombardi, io ne farò venire;

100   ma stieno i Malebranche un poco in cesso,
sì ch'ei non teman de le lor vendette;
e io, seggendo in questo loco stesso,

103   per un ch'io son, ne farò venir sette
quand' io suffolerò, com' è nostro uso
di fare allor che fori alcun si mette."

106   Cagnazzo a cotal motto levò 'l muso,
crollando 'l capo, e disse: "Odi malizia
ch'elli ha pensata per gittarsi giuso!"

70   And Love Notch said: "We've been patient too long," and he hooked one arm with his pruning knife and pulled, tearing out a muscle.

73   Little Big Dragon, too, wanted to hook him below, at the legs; at which their decurion whirled about with an evil look.

76   When they had quieted down a little, without delay my master asked the soul, who was still gazing at his wound:

79   "Who was he you say you should not have left for the shore?" and he replied, "It was Brother Gomita,

82   the one from Gallura, vessel of every fraud, who had his master's enemies in his hand and treated them so that each is thankful to him:

85   he took their money and let them go scot free, as he tells it; and in his other duties, too, he was not a small barrator, but a champion.

88   Master Michel Zanche of Logodoro keeps company with him; and their tongues never tire of speaking about Sardinia.

91   Oh me, look at this other one snarling; I would say more, but I'm afraid he's getting ready to scratch my scurf."

94   And the great officer, turning to Butterfly, whose eyes were bulging to strike, said: "Get over there, wicked bird!"

97   "If you want to see or hear," the terrified wretch began again, "Tuscans or Lombards, I can make them come;

100   but let the Evil Claws stand a little apart, so they won't be frightened of their cruelty; and I, sitting right here,

103   for one that I am, will make seven come when I whistle, as is our custom to do when one of us is a lookout."

106   At that Evil Dog lifted his snout, shaking his head, and said: "Listen to the trick he's thought of, so he can jump back in!"

109   Ond' ei, ch'avea lacciuoli a gran divizia,
rispuose: "Malizioso son io troppo,
quand' io procuro a' mia maggior trestizia."

112   Alichin non si tenne e, di rintoppo
a li altri, disse a lui: "Se tu ti cali,
io non ti verrò dietro di gualoppo,

115   ma batterò sovra la pece l'ali.
Lascisi 'l collo, e sia la ripa scudo,
a veder se tu sol più di noi vali."

118   O tu che leggi, udirai nuovo ludo:
ciascun da l'altra costa li occhi volse,
quel prima ch'a ciò fare era più crudo.

121   Lo Navarrese ben suo tempo colse;
fermò le piante a terra, e in un punto
saltò e dal proposto lor si sciolse.

124   Di che ciascun di colpa fu compunto,
ma quei più che cagion fu del difetto;
però si mosse e gridò: "Tu se' giunto!"

127   Ma poco i valse, ché l'ali al sospetto
non potero avanzar; quelli andò sotto,
e quei drizzò volando suso il petto:

130   non altrimenti l'anitra di botto,
quando 'l falcon s'appressa, giù s'attuffa,
ed ei ritorna sù crucciato e rotto.

133   Irato Calcabrina de la buffa,
volando dietro li tenne, invaghito
che quei campasse per aver la zuffa;

136   e come 'l barattier fu disparito
così volse li artigli al suo compagno,
e fu con lui sopra 'l fosso ghermito.

139   Ma l'altro fu bene sparvier grifagno
ad artigliar ben lui, e amendue
cadder nel mezzo del bogliente stagno.

142   Lo caldo sghermitor sùbito fue;
ma però di levarsi era neente,
sì avieno inviscate l'ali sue.

145   Barbariccia, con li altri suoi dolente,
quattro ne fé volar da l'altra costa
con tutt' i raffi, e assai prestamente

109   Therefore he, who had a great wealth of snares, replied: "I am really very tricky, if I procure more suffering for my own kind."

112   Harlequin could not hold back and, against the others, told him: "If you go down, I won't come after you at a gallop,

115   but beating my wings above the pitch. Let's leave the ridge and hide behind the bank, and we'll see if all by yourself you can outdo us."

118   O you who read, you will hear strange sport: each of them turned his eyes toward the other bank, and he first who had been most unwilling.

121   The Navarrese chose his moment well, planted his feet on the ground, and in one point jumped and escaped their design.

124   For that each felt the stab of guilt, but most of all he who had caused the fault; so he moved, crying: "You're caught!"

127   But it did no good, for his wings could not outspeed the other's fear; the shade dove under, and he straightened his breast to fly back up:

130   not otherwise does the duck suddenly disappear when the falcon approaches, and he goes back up, angry and ruffled.

133   Trample Frost, angered by the trick, was flying just behind him, hoping the soul would escape, eager to have a scrap;

136   and when the barrator had disappeared, he turned his talons against his fellow, and grappled with him above the ditch.

139   But the other was a full-grown hawk to grapple him, and both of them fell into the boiling pool.

142   The heat was a quick ungrappler; but not for that could they come forth, they had so enlimed their wings.

145   Curly Beard, grieving with his fellows, sent four flying to the inner bank with their hooks, and quickly enough,

148   di qua, di là discesero a la posta;
porser li uncini verso li 'mpaniati,
ch'eran già cotti dentro da la crosta.

151   E noi lasciammo lor così 'mpacciati.

148   on this side and on that, they flew to their posts;
they held out their hooks toward the viscous ones,
who were already cooked within their crusts.

151   And we left them thus entangled.

NOTES

1–12. I have seen . . . or star: Referring to the last line of Canto 21, this magnificent mock-epic simile juxtaposes the noblest (the knightly) forms of warfare and their signals with the grotesquely debased and ineffectual military discipline of the Evil Claws (the devils, it will be remembered, are at war with both God and man). At times the catalog descends from heroic assaults and reviews to retreat (line 3), mere predatory raids (line 5), and a suggestion of civil war (line 4). The simile is masterfully constructed: note the function of the repeated "vidi" [I have seen], "quando" [sometimes], and "con/a" [with/at] in articulating and gradually intensifying the accumulation of instances, and the equal division of the four terzine into two groups, one on activities, the other on their respective signals, returning at the end to horsemen, but expanding the panorama to include foot soldiers and ships as well. Essential to the effect is that the simile climaxes in ludicrous non-similarity—like the simile in 21.7–21. The topos of a list of beautiful things (including martial activities) is the basis of a well-established genre of medieval poetry, the *plazer* (see the notes to 14.30, 28.22–24).

4–5. I have seen mounted men . . . O Aretines: In a letter, now lost, quoted by Leonardo Bruni, Dante claimed to have participated as a mounted soldier in the battle of Campaldino (June 1289), in Aretine territory. There has been uncertainty as to whether *terra* (line 4) here signifies "territory" (in which case *corridori* means "scouts") or, as generally accepted today—and as regularly in Dante—"city" (in which case the reference is to civic disturbances in which horsemen—*corridori*—coursed the city to intimidate and, if possible, kill their political opponents).

6. tournaments striking, and jousts running: The distinction is between mass encounters (with swords, principally) on open fields and individual jousts (with lances) in the lists.

7. sometimes with bells: Italian cities sent forth armies accompanied by great war wagons which bore, among other equipment, great bells. The captures of such *carri* constituted major victories.

12. at a sign from land or star: The term *segno* [sign], referring to the stars, signifies "constellation": the ship would be setting forth at a certain hour (the rising or transit of a particular star or constellation), perhaps with astrological significance. The gamut of this catalog of activities and signs ends with the word *stella* [star], providing the greatest possible antithesis to the devils' signals (and one sufficiently exalted that *stelle* is the concluding word of each of the three *cantiche* of the poem).

13. the ten demons: See 21.120, with note.

14–15. in church . . . with the gluttons: This striking phrase may already have been proverbial in Dante's time; in any case it has been so ever since.

19–21. As dolphins do . . . save their ship: The traditional idea that dolphins warn sailors of approaching storms goes back at least as far as Isidore of Seville, *Etymologies* 12.6.11 (*P.L.* 82.452); it is frequently mentioned in writers contemporary with Dante. The simile contains the hidden suggestion that some kind of storm is now approaching. The frequency with which devils and sinners are compared to animals in this canto has frequently been noted: 19–21, dolphins; 25–27, 32–33, frogs; 36, otter; 56, boar; 58, cat and mouse; 96, bird; 106, dog's snout; 114, horse's gallop; 130–32, duck and falcon; 139, hawk. The devils are compared to dogs in 21.67–69 (see also the discussion of their names in the note to 21.118–23).

31. my heart still makes me shudder: Again the poet still feels the emotions of the pilgrim.

35. hooked his grapple . . . like an otter: The bases of the comparison are both the passivity of the captured otter, hanging from the hook or noose with its limbs dangling, and the sleekness of its wet fur, streaming with water (here, pitch). Line 35 is perhaps the most striking of the many sound effects in these two cantos suggesting stickiness and viscosity, partly because it combines elements of the dangers of both capture and entanglement, the grapplehooks and the pitch.

37–39. I had learned . . . to each other: One notes Dante's care to maintain the verisimilitude of the pilgrim's point of view. It is of course the pilgrim's fear (cf. 21.91–99, 127–32) that we understand to have motivated the exactness of his memory (see the note to 21.74); the commentators point out that his fear takes second place to his curiosity "when they were chosen" (21.118–23) and "when they called" (21.76, 105), and, implicitly, other occasions. Compare 25.40–45. Each of the ten demons is named once in this canto, except for Curly Beard, who is named three times (lines 29, 59, and 145).

40. O Ruby Face: Now that a sinner has been captured, the rest of the canto is filled with action and dialogue. Previously, like the pilgrim, the devils have been silent and on the alert.

45. into the hands of his enemies: Dante's term is *avversari* [adversaries], literally translating New Testament *diabolus*; we use the word "enemies" in order to preserve the politically realistic ring of the passage; it reminds us again that the infernal events are transpositions of earthly ones, probably witnessed by Dante, such as the merciless interrogations of prisoners and the fear on the faces of surrendering soldiers (21.94–96). See Additional Note 9.

48. Navarre: A small kingdom in the Pyrenees, in the south of France, integrated into that country in 1598.

50–51. she had generated me . . . and of himself: In other words, the unnamed Navarrese (to whom the early commentators attribute the name Ciampolo, or Jean-Paul) was the illegitimate son of a spendthrift who ultimately committed suicide (the punishment of both these sins is described in Canto 13). The use of the term "generated" (*generato*), usually used of a child's father, is striking when applied, as here, to the mother.

52–54. Then I was in the household . . . in this heat: Barratry is here identified as a sin characteristic of underlings; those Ciampolo mentions were servants and ministers of rulers. Civil servants of republican governments are included in the reference to Lucca (21.37–42).

52. good king Thibaut: This is probably Thibaut II, king of Navarre (1255–1270), celebrated for his valor and generosity.

57. let him feel how one of them could rip: We are not told the location of the ripping wound now inflicted by Big Pig (see line 77 and note).

58. Among bad cats had the mouse arrived: A hint of reference to beast fables, further developed in 23.4–9.

60. Stay over there . . . gripped: The line is addressed to the devils (*state* [stay] is plural); "while I have him gripped" translates the more vivid *mentr' io lo 'nforco* [literally, while I have him forked].

70. We've been patient: The Italian *abbiam sofferto* [literally, we have suffered] brings into focus the root meaning of "patient," from Latin *patior*, "to suffer," with considerable ironic force: Love Notch is impatient to *inflict* suffering.

74. decurion: See the note to 21.120.

77. gazing at his wound: This is one of the most effectively chilling moments of the canto, conveying the hallucinated atmosphere of sudden violence and the shocked amazement of its victims.

81–87. Brother Gomita . . . a champion: Galluria was one of the four administrative districts of Sardinia; according to the early commentators, Brother Gomita (a *frate godente* [see the note to 23.103]) was appointed by Nino Visconti of Pisa (see 33.13–18, with notes) as his deputy and was later hanged for his disloyalty and bribe-taking. Nothing is known of the incident related here.

83. his master's: Dante's word, *donno* (used also in line 88), from Latin *dominus*, was used in Sardinia as the equivalent of *signore*.

87. champion: Dante's word is *sovrano* [superior, sovereign].

88–89. Michel Zanche of Logodoro: Logodoro was another of the four Sardinian districts; Michele Zanche is said to have been the deputy of King Enzo

(1239–1249; d. 1272). Again, nothing specific is known of him, beyond his having been murdered by his son-in-law, Branca Doria, whom Dante places in Cocytus (33.136–47).

91–93. Oh me . . . scratch my scurf: Ciampolo's terror is real and justified, but he does not lose his presence of mind, as his slangy, contemptuous "scratch my scurf" indicates. This moment, in which he begins to manipulate the situation to his own advantage, is skillfully chosen, for he has captured everyone's attention by telling the truth (cf. 21.106–14, with notes).

97–99. If you want to see . . . Tuscans or Lombards: Virgil has inquired about Italians generally, but Ciampolo has heard him and the pilgrim converse and has recognized their respective accents. He assumes—correctly—that they will be particularly interested in sinners from their own regions (the pilgrim's interest in Tuscany needs no comment; Virgil's interest in Lombardy—compare 1.68—helps account for the digression of 20.58–91). The "question of language" permeates the Malebolge. See Additional Note 13.

106. Evil Dog lifted his snout: He smells the trick, apparently.

112–17. Harlequin . . . you can outdo us: See the note to 21.123; Harlequin's delight in pursuit befits the traditional leader of the infernal hunt. He is "against the others" in wishing to accept Ciampolo's challenge. The devils' wings and their ability to fly have not been mentioned since 21.33. They now become the focus of the action, as Harlequin's overconfidence and competitiveness lead to the discomfiture of the other devils (grotesquely lacking in "military" discipline).

118. O you who read . . . sport: The fifth of the seven addresses to the reader in the *Inferno* (see the note to 8.94–96). Dante's word *ludo* [sport, or theatrical play] is a Latinism, derived from the word used by the Romans for athletic contests and gladiatorial fights; *novo* means both "strange" and "new."

120. he first . . . most unwilling: Evil Dog (lines 106–8).

125. he who had caused the fault: Harlequin (line 112).

131. when the falcon approaches: The imagery of falcons and falconry—frequently used of angels in the *Comedy*—first appears in the poem in Canto 3 (see 3.117 and 17.127–32, with notes); it reaches explicitness in this canto just when the devils' flight ironically lands them in the pitch: as their actions show, these are fallen/falling angels.

144. they had so enlimed their wings: Dante's *inviscato* [enlimed] is derived from *visco* [birdlime], the sticky substance used to capture small birds (*inviscare* was part of the system of bird imagery in Canto 13 as well; cf. 13.55–57, with note); *impaniati* [viscous ones], line 149, equivalent to *inviscati*, is derived from *pania,* another term for the same substance.

CANTO 23

1
    Taciti, soli, sanza compagnia
n'andavam l'un dinanzi e l'altro dopo,
come frati minor vanno per via.

4
    Vòlt' era in su la favola d'Isopo
lo mio pensier per la presente rissa,
dov' el parlò de la rana e del topo,

7
    ché più non si pareggia *mo* e *issa*
che l'un con l'altro fa, se ben s'accoppia
principio e fine con la mente fissa.

10
    E come l'un pensier de l'altro scoppia,
così nacque di quello un altro poi,
che la prima paura mi fé doppia.

13
    Io pensava così: "Questi per noi
sono scherniti con danno, e con beffa
sì fatta ch'assai credo che lor nòi.

16
    Se l'ira sovra 'l mal voler s'aggueffa,
ei ne verranno dietro più crudeli
che 'l cane a quella lievre ch'elli acceffa."

19
    Già mi sentia tutti arricciar li peli
de la paura e stava in dietro intento,
quand' io dissi: "Maestro, se non celi

22
    te e me tostamente, i' ho pavento
d'i Malebranche. Noi li avem già dietro;
io li 'magino sì che già li sento."

25
    E quei: "S'i' fossi di piombato vetro,
l'imagine di fuor tua non trarrei
più tosto a me che quella dentro 'mpetro.

28
    Pur mo venieno i tuo' pensier tra ' miei,
con simile atto e con simile faccia,
sì che d'intrambi un sol consiglio fei.

CANTO 23

Imagined pursuit—slide into sixth bolgia: *the hypocrites—two Frati godenti—Caiaphas—the devil lied—Virgil's anger*

1 Silent, alone, without companions, we were walking one before, the other after, as friars minor go their way.

4 Because of the present scuffle, my thoughts had turned to that fable by Aesop where he spoke of the frog and the rat,

7 for *mo* and *issa* are not more alike than the scuffle and the fable, if one couples beginning and end with close attention.

10 And, as one thought bursts out of another, so another was born from that one, and it redoubled my former fear.

13 I considered: "These through us have suffered shame with harm, and with mockery that I believe will bitterly wound them.

16 If anger is spooled onto their ill will, they will come after us, crueler than a dog after the hare he snaps at."

19 Already I felt all my hairs curling with fear, and I kept looking back, when I said: "Master if you do not hide

22 yourself and me quickly, I am frightened of the Evil Claws. They are already behind us; I imagine them so strongly, I already hear them."

25 And he: "If I were made of leaded glass I would not catch your outer image any faster than I grasp your inner one.

28 Just now your thoughts came among mine, with similar bearing and similar face, so that I have made a single counsel of them.

31   S'elli è che sì la destra costa giaccia
che noi possiam ne l'altra bolgia scendere,
noi fuggirem l'imaginata caccia."

34   Già non compié di tal consiglio rendere,
ch'io li vidi venir con l'ali tese
non molto lungi, per volerne prendere.

37   Lo duca mio di sùbito mi prese,
come la madre ch'al romore è desta
e vede presso a sé le fiamme accese,

40   che prende il figlio e fugge e non s'arresta,
avendo più di lui che di sé cura,
tanto che solo una camiscia vesta:

43   e giù dal collo de la ripa dura
supin si diede a la pendente roccia
che l'un de' lati a l'altra bolgia tura.

46   Non corse mai sì tosto acqua per doccia
a volger ruota di molin terragno,
quand' ella più verso le pale approccia,

49   come 'l maestro mio per quel vivagno,
portandosene me sovra 'l suo petto
come suo figlio, non come compagno.

52   A pena fuoro i piè suoi giunti al letto
del fondo giù, ch' e' furon in sul colle
sovresso noi; ma non lì era sospetto,

55   ché l'alta provedenza che lor volle
porre ministri de la fossa quinta,
poder di partirs' indi a tutti tolle.

58   Là giù trovammo una gente dipinta
che giva intorno assai con lenti passi,
piangendo e nel sembiante stanca e vinta.

61   Elli avean cappe con cappucci bassi
dinanzi a li occhi, fatti de la taglia
che in Clugnì per li monaci fassi.

64   Di fuor dorate son sì ch'elli abbaglia,
ma dentro tutte piombo, e gravi tanto
che Federigo le mettea di paglia.

67   Oh in etterno faticoso manto!
Noi ci volgemmo ancor pur a man manca
con loro insieme, intenti al tristo pianto,

31   If the right bank slopes so that we can go down
into the next pocket, we will escape the imagined
pursuit."

34   He had not finished giving this advice, when I
saw them coming, with outstretched wings, not far
away, intent on seizing us.

37   My leader seized me quickly, like a mother who is
awakened by the noise and sees the flames burning
close by,

40   who takes up her son and flees, caring more for
him than for herself, not stopping even to put on her
shift:

43   and down from the neck of the hard bank, he
gave himself supine to the sloping rock that encloses
the near side of the next pocket.

46   Water has never coursed more swiftly down a
sluice to turn the wheels of a land mill, as it
approaches the paddles,

49   than did my master down that wall, carrying
me along on his breast like his son, not his
companion.

52   Hardly had his feet touched the bed of the ditch,
when the devils appeared on the bank above us; but
now there was nothing to fear,

55   for the high Providence that placed them as
ministers of the fifth ditch takes from them all power
to leave it.

58   Down there we found a painted people who were
walking with very slow steps, weeping and, by their
expressions, weary and defeated.

61   They were wearing robes with hoods pulled low
over their eyes, made in the fashion that is sewn in
Cluny for the monks.

64   On the outside they are dazzlingly gilded, but
within they are all of lead, so heavy that the ones
Frederick put on people might have been of straw.

67   Oh eternally laborious mantle! We turned once
more to the left with them, attentive to their sad
weeping,

70   ma per lo peso quella gente stanca
        venìa sì pian che noi eravam nuovi
        di compagnia ad ogne mover d'anca.

73   Per ch'io al duca mio: "Fa che tu trovi
        alcun ch'al fatto o al nome si conosca,
        e li occhi, sì andando, intorno movi."

76   E un che 'ntese la parola tosca
        di retro a noi gridò: "Tenete i piedi,
        voi che correte sì per l'aura fosca!

79   Forse ch'avrai da me quel che tu chiedi."
        Onde 'l duca si volse, e disse: "Aspetta,
        e poi secondo il suo passo procedi."

82   Ristetti, e vidi due mostrar gran fretta
        de l'animo, col viso, d'esser meco,
        ma tardavali 'l carco e la via stretta.

85   Quando fuor giunti, assai con l'occhio bieco
        mi rimiraron sanza far parola;
        poi si volsero in sé, e dicean seco:

88   "Costui par vivo a l'atto de la gola;
        e s' e' son morti, per qual privilegio
        vanno scoperti de la grave stola?"

91   Poi disser me: "O Tosco ch'al collegio
        de l'ipocriti tristi se' venuto,
        dir chi tu se' non avere in dispregio."

94   E io a loro: "I' fui nato e cresciuto
        sovra 'l bel fiume d'Arno a la gran villa,
        e son col corpo ch'i' ho sempre avuto.

97   Ma voi chi siete, a cui tanto distilla
        quant' i' veggio dolor giù per le guance?
        e che pena è in voi che sì sfavilla?"

100   E l'un rispuose a me: "Le cappe rance
        son di piombo sì grosse che li pesi
        fan così cigolar le lor bilance.

103   Frati godenti fummo e bolognesi,
        io Catalano e questi Loderingo
        nomati, e da tua terra insieme presi

106   come suole esser tolto un uom solingo,
        per conservar sua pace; e fummo tali
        ch'ancor si pare intorno dal Gardingo."

70   but because of the weight those weary people came
on so slowly that we had a new companion with
each motion of our hips.

73   Therefore I said to my leader: "Try to find
someone known by deed or name, moving your eyes
about as we walk."

76   And one who understood my Tuscan speech,
behind us, called: "Stay your feet, you who are
running so through the dark air!

79   Perhaps you will have from me what you desire."
And so my leader turned and said: "Wait, and then
walk at his pace."

82   I stood still and saw two showing in their faces
great haste of the spirit to be with me, but their
burden slowed them, and the crowded way.

85   When they had reached me, for a long time they
looked at me sidelong, without saying a word; then
they turned to each other and spoke together:

88   "That one seems alive, by the motion of his throat;
but if they are dead, by what privilege are they
exempt from the weighty stole?"

91   Then they spoke to me: "O Tuscan who have come
to the college of the sad hypocrites, do not disdain to
say who you are."

94   And I to them: "I was born and raised beside the
lovely river Arno in the great city, and I am here
with the body I have always had.

97   But who are you, whose great pain distills all I see
trickling down your cheeks? and what punishment is
in you that sparkles so?"

100   And one replied: "The orange robes are so thick
with lead that the weights make their balances creak.

103   We were Jolly Friars, and from Bologna, I
named Catalano and he Loderingo, and taken both
together by your city,

106   though the custom is to take a single man, to
preserve the peace; and we were such that it still
appears around the Gardingo."

109   Io cominciai: "O frati, i vostri mali . . ."
      ma più non dissi, ch'a l'occhio mi corse
      un crucifisso in terra con tre pali.

112   Quando mi vide, tutto si distorse,
      soffiando ne la barba con sospiri;
      e 'l frate Catalan, ch'a ciò s'accorse,

115   mi disse: "Quel confitto che tu miri
      consigliò i Farisei che convenia
      porre un uom per lo popolo a' martìri.

118   Attraversato è nudo ne la via
      come tu vedi, ed è mestier ch'el senta,
      qualunque passa, come pesa pria.

121   E a tal modo il socero si stenta
      in questa fossa, e li altri dal concilio
      che fu per li Giudei mala sementa."

124   Allor vid' io maravigliar Virgilio
      sovra colui ch'era disteso in croce
      tanto vilmente ne l'etterno essilio.

127   Poscia drizzò al frate cotal voce:
      "Non vi dispiaccia, se vi lece, dirci
      s'a la man destra giace alcuna foce

130   onde noi amendue possiamo uscirci,
      sanza costrigner de li angeli neri
      che vegnan d'esto fondo a dipartirci."

133   Rispuose adunque: "Più che tu non speri
      s'appressa un sasso che da la gran cerchia
      si move e varca tutt' i vallon feri,

136   salvo che 'n questo è rotto e nol coperchia;
      montar potrete su per la ruina,
      che giace in costa e nel fondo soperchia."

139   Lo duca stette un poco a testa china;
      poi disse: "Mal contava la bisogna
      colui che i peccator di qua uncina."

142   E 'l frate: "Io udi' già dire a Bologna
      del diavol vizi assai, tra ' quali udi'
      ch'elli è bugiardo e padre di menzogna."

145   Appresso il duca a gran passi sen gì,
      turbato un poco d'ira nel sembiante;
      ond' io da li 'ncarcati mi parti'

148   dietro a le poste de le care piante.

109   I began: "O friars, your evil . . ." but I said no more,
for into my view came one crucified to the earth with
three stakes.

112   When he saw me, he twisted himself all over,
puffing into his beard with sighs; and Brother
Catalano, who perceived it,

115   told me: "That one staked there at whom you are
looking counseled the Pharisees that it was
expedient to put one man to death for the people.

118   He is stretched naked out across the road, as you
see, so that whoever passes, he must feel his weight first.

121   And his father-in-law is laid out in the same way
in this ditch, and the others of the council that sowed
so ill for the Jews."

124   Then I saw Virgil marveling over him who was
so basely stretched cross-wise in the eternal exile.

127   Then he directed to the friar this word: "Let it not
displease you, if it is permitted, to tell us if on the
right hand some passage slopes

130   whereby we can both climb out of here, without
requiring any of the black angels to come to this
bottom to transport us."

133   So he replied: "Closer than you hope, we are
approaching a ridge that goes from the largest circle
across all the savage valleys,

136   except that in this one it is broken and does not
cover it; you will be able to climb up along the
landslide, which slopes gently up the side and is
heaped up at the bottom."

139   My leader stood a little with head bent down;
then he said: "Ill did he recount the business, who
hooks the sinners on this side."

142   And the friar: "In Bologna I once heard many
vices of the devil told, among which I heard that he
is a liar and the father of lies."

145   Then my leader walked off with great strides, his
face a little disturbed with anger; so I left the
burdened ones,

148   following the prints of his dear feet.

NOTES

1–3. Silent, alone . . . go their way: Franciscan friars went on their begging rounds in pairs, the younger following in the steps of the elder with lowered eyes. The commentators point out that the image anticipates the conventual imagery important later in the canto. The shift in tone from the ending of the last canto is striking.

4–33. Because of the present scuffle . . . the imagined pursuit: The pilgrim reacts to images in his memory, both of the scuffle and of Aesop's fables (popular in many reworkings and translations, and often used as elementary Latin textbooks); his thought is associative and combinatory, and it bears fruit in further images and even physical sensations (lines 19, 23–24). And it soon turns out that the pilgrim's imaginings are correct. On the other hand, Virgil's responses seem slow and ponderous, though he does act with dispatch in lines 37–45.

In emphasizing the pilgrim's vivid imaginings, Dante is drawing on the medieval idea of the imagination: the imaging faculty, which we share with the beasts, with its physical organ (the anterior ventricle of the brain), by which we are able to construct, associate, analyze, and combine images derived from the data of the senses, closely associated with the memory (in the rear ventricle) and with foresight. The entire passage is in fact a kind of test case for the usefulness of the body. Virgil's strangely disembodied responses here probably derive from this conception (he is close to personifying "disembodied" reason: cf. the mirror image in line 25).

4–6. that fable by Aesop: Among the dozens of versions of "Aesop" circulating in the Middle Ages (most of them going back to the Roman author Phaedrus), Dante seems to have used those deriving from the *Romulus* in Latin verse by Walter of England, of which there are a number of Old French adaptations and expansions. In the most widely circulated, a frog offers to swim a mouse across a body of water, intending to drown him; the frog ties his leg to the mouse's; when the frog tries to drown the mouse, their struggles attract a hawk, who seizes them; the frog's leg being tied to the mouse makes escape impossible for both of them. The "morality" of the fable emphasizes that the devices of the fraudulent return upon them: in the Old French *Ysopet* (Paris, I, in McKenzie and Oldfather), "barat doit conchier son mestre" [a swindle must cover its maker with shit]. Both Walter's Latin and the French versions emphasize the idea of the snare (*las*). In Marie de France's version, also based on the *Romulus,* the hawk eats the frog but lets the mouse go as too small (curiously, in her version the frog tempts the mouse out from her home in a land mill; see line 47).

7–9. for *mo* and *issa* . . . close attention: That is, the beginning and end of the scuffle are like those of the fable (*mo* and *issa* both mean "now" or "soon"; *issa/istra* is identified in 27.20–21 as Lombard; the two words are instances of identical content in different form or different dress—[see Additional Note 13]). The parallels Dante intends are not too clear, and the commentators have not reached agreement on them. In our view, the pilgrim and Virgil seem parallel to the mouse in seeking help from the devils, who would be parallel to the frog with its evil intentions; thus Ciampolo would be an inverted parallel to the hawk. Many other possibilities have been suggested.

16. If anger . . . ill will: That is, if anger is now added to the devils' permanent disposition of ill will.

25–27. If I were made of leaded glass . . . your inner one: Mirrors were made by coating one side of a sheet of glass with lead. Virgil is saying, "If I were a mirror, I would not catch the image of your body (your outer image) faster than I see your imagining or your thought (your inner image)." Virgil is close to a personification of human reason here, which operates in conjunction with the (bodily) imaging faculty.

28–30. Just now your thoughts . . . a single counsel: A striking personification of the pilgrim's and Virgil's thoughts. Virgil claims that his thoughts are just as anguished as the pilgrim's (whose "bearing and face" must be terror-stricken), but it is hard to believe him. "I have made a single counsel of them" means "I have reached a decision on their basis."

31–32. If the right bank slopes . . . the next pocket: As 19.35 has already made clear, the outer bank of a *bolgia* (i.e., the one farthest from the center) has a steeper slope than the inner one. Note that Virgil's words also serve an expository function.

40–42. not stopping even to put on her shift: That is, she is naked; her concern for her child causes her to disregard appearances entirely; the line has also been interpreted to mean the mother wears "only a shift."

44–45. he gave himself supine . . . the next pocket: That is, Virgil, holding Dante to his breast, slides down the bank into the next *bolgia*; he is "supine" because the bank is so steep that he cannot sit up as he slides, but must lie back.

46–48. Water has never coursed . . . the paddles: Dante has in mind the type of mill to which stream or river water is diverted through a system of sloping canals and sluices; as the early commentator Buti observed, this type usually has wheels smaller than those of the type set in the river itself, and therefore requires high velocity in the water. For the question of the relation of these cantos to events in Dante's life, see Additional Note 9.

55–57. the high Providence . . . power to leave it: The pilgrim at least may be presumed not to have known of this limitation in advance, partly because of the devil of 21.29–45.

58. a painted people: The expression is probably explained in line 64 (some early commentators took the expression to mean the hypocrites' faces were painted to simulate ascetic pallor). For the connection of painting and colors with fraud, see the description of Geryon, especially 17.16–18.

60. by their expressions: A reminder that the facial expressions of the hypocrites were not, in life, a reliable index of their feelings.

61–63. They were wearing robes . . . for the monks: The abbey of Cluny in Burgundy, founded in 910, was originally the chief expression of a major reform movement in Benedictine monasticism, introducing a system of centralized administration in which daughter houses, called priories, were subject to Cluny. By the time of Saint Bernard of Clairvaux (leader of another and more austere reform movement, that of the Cistercians, in the early twelfth century), Cluny was extremely powerful, with the largest church in Europe, famous for its wealth, luxury, proliferation of artistic ornament, and elaborate liturgy. Saint Bernard vehemently criticized the luxurious woolen and fur habits worn by its monks.

64–65. On the outside . . . all of lead: *Hypokrites,* the Greek etymon of *hypocrite,* derived from the verb "to judge," meant, variously, "one who gives an answer"; an "interpreter"; an "actor" (in plays and recitations); and thus a "simulator." Dante, however, is following the etymology given by the famous thirteenth-century handbook of (often fanciful) etymologies, Uguccione of Pisa's *Magnae derivationes:* "*hypocrita* derives from *hyper,* above, and *crisis,* gold, as it were *gilt over,* for on the surface and externally he appears good, but within he is evil; or *hypocrita* is derived from *hypo,* below, and *crisis,* gold, as it were *having something else beneath the gold*" (quoted by Sapegno; cf. Toynbee 1897). Dante is also drawing on the denunciations of hypocrisy in the Gospels (Matt. 6.1–6, 16–18; 7.4–5, 15; 15.1–9; and Chapter 23 in its entirety, as well as passages in the other Gospels).

65–66. so heavy . . . of straw: According to the Guelf propaganda campaign against the emperor Frederick II (see the notes to 10.119, 13.58–61), he punished traitors by encasing them in lead and then roasting them (cf. Phalaris's bull, 27.7–15).

67. Oh eternally laborious mantle: The *contrapasso* is clear: the continual alertness required for the hypocrite to conceal his true feelings (usually said to be vainglory and avarice) is symbolized by the weight of the cloak. Dante is following a tradition, which has a certain basis in the Gospels (see the note to lines 89–90), personifying hypocrisy in terms of the monastic or religious orders. In the *Romance of the Rose,* a particularly influential text, Faux-Semblant [False-Seeming] is represented as a Franciscan friar (cf. 23.1–3, with note). Note also the use of the term *manto* for the papal mantle (19.69).

70–72. because of the weight . . . motion of our hips: This is also a commentary on the difficulty hypocrites have, caught up as they are in their pretenses, in achieving repentance or actual spiritual progress.

72. with each motion of our hips: At each step.

76. my Tuscan speech: Again the emphasis on the pilgrim's regional speech (also in line 91).

82–83. two showing in their faces . . . to be with me: This is a brilliantly two-edged detail: on the assumption that these two hypocrites are "sincere" in their desire to reach the pilgrim, the irony of the *contrapasso* condemns them to great difficulty; but the lines also suggest that—in keeping with their fundamental sin—even this appearance may be misleading.

84. the crowded way: The Italian *stretta* may mean "narrow" here (cf. Matt. 7.13–14, on the "narrow way" that leads to salvation).

85. sidelong: Literally, "with oblique eye" (*con l'occhio bieco*), the traditional crooked glance of the envious (see 6.91, with note). Aquinas's *Catena aurea* on Matt.7.5 ("Thou hypocrite, cast out first the beam from thine own eye, and then shalt thou see to cast out the [straw] from thy brother's eye") quotes Augustine: "Removing from our own eye the beam of envy or malice or dissembling, then we can see to cast out the straw from our brother's eye."

89–90. by what privilege . . . from the weighty stole: The hypocrites are using legal language: "privilege" is technically a right (a law, *lex*) specific (or private) to a single person or restricted group. The "heavy stole" is of course their leaden garment. The term *stole* is used in a number of New Testament passages: in the Gospel denunciations of hypocrites (Mark and Luke), it refers to luxurious garments: "Beware of the scribes, who desire to walk in [stoles] and love salutations in the market place . . . ; who devour the houses of widows, feigning long prayer. These will receive a greater damnation" (Luke 20.46–47). In the Apocalypse (e.g., 6.11, 7.9), the white stole is the garb of the redeemed (see *Purg.* 32.81 and *Par.* 25.95, 30.129, with notes).

91. O Tuscan: The soul has recognized the pilgrim's speech as Tuscan; his apostrophe recalls Farinata's in 10.22.

91. the college of the sad hypocrites: Italian *collegio* (Latin *collegium,* a binding together) was used of many kinds of organization and usually implied a set of rules; here the hypocrite is comparing the *bolgia* of the hypocrites to a convent. The Sanhedrin (referred to in lines 122–23) could also be called a *collegio*; in *Par.* 19.110–11, Dante calls the blessed and the damned "the two colleges." "The sad hypocrites" is a quotation from the Sermon on the Mount (Matt. 6.16): "When you fast, be not like the sad hypocrites" (*hypocritae tristes*).

94–96. I was born . . . I have always had: The pilgrim's reply does not tell the hypocrites anything they have not already inferred or could infer (see line 88, and the first note to line 91).

95. the great city: In 1300 Florence was one of the two or three largest cities in Europe. Dante's term for "city" here is *villa* (cf. 1.109).

97–99. But who are you . . . sparkles so: Since lines 64–67 would seem to mean that the pilgrim has already understood the nature of the punishment in this *bolgia*; he is now being extremely disingenuous (and scornful—"sparkles" of course refers to the bright gold exterior of their robes).

100–102. The orange robes . . . make their balances creak: Catalano is comparing the structure of the human body, with the spine crossed by the shoulders and arms, to that of a traditional balance or scale; it would seem the weight causes the very bones to grind against each other. There is a rich tradition attached to this analogy, connecting the Scales of Justice (seen in the constellation Libra, associated with the virgin goddess of justice, Astraea, who returned to the sky to become the constellation Virgo, in the Middle Ages often identified with the Virgin Mary) and the figure of Christ on the Cross (satisfying God's justice; cf. lines 15–16 of Venantius Fortunatus's hymn "Vexilla regis," which is discussed in the note to 34.1–2). Thus, like the punishment of the members of the

Sanhedrin (lines 115–23), there is a clear indication that the punishment of the hypocrites is a distorted parody of the Crucifixion, punishing their corruption of justice (see the note to lines 105–8).

103. We were Jolly Friars: *Frati godenti* was the scornful popular nickname for the Cavalieri della Milizia della Beata Maria Vergine Gloriosa, a religious order founded in 1260 for the purpose of promoting civil peace; the brothers were prohibited from accepting governmental positions (but see the note to lines 105–8). The nickname reflects the fact that the order quickly achieved a reputation for corruption and self-interest.

104. I named Catalano and he Loderingo: Catalano dei Malavolti was a Guelf; Loderingo degli Andalò, one of the founders of the order, was a Ghibelline.

105–8. taken both together . . . around the Gardingo: Medieval Italian cities often appointed citizens of other cities to such posts as *podestà* (see the note to 6.96), usually singly. In 1266, in an effort to mediate the enmity between the Guelfs and the Ghibellines, Florence appointed these two jointly. Dante clearly feels that they hypocritically pretended impartiality but secretly fomented the anti-Ghibelline violence that erupted in 1267, leading to the banishment of prominent Ghibelline families and the confiscation of their property, and, in the case of the Uberti and several others, the destruction of their houses: the Uberti houses were near the Gardingo (the term means "watchtower"); the space they occupied until 1267 is now the Piazza della Signoria. Modern scholarship holds that Catalano's and Loderingo's activities were explicitly directed by the pope, Clement IV.

109. I began: "O friars, your evil: This ambiguous beginning (*mali* [evils] is plural; it could be either a noun or an adjective) is like that of the pilgrim's replies to Francesca (5.116) and to Ciacco (6.58); presumably the continuation would have been scornfully ironic. The interruption reflects the pilgrim's amazement at the sight now described (for Virgil's amazement, see line 124).

111. with three stakes: That is, one through each hand and one through both feet, as Jesus was represented as having been crucified (though with nails, not stakes).

115–23. That one staked there . . . so ill for the Jews: It is Caiaphas, the high priest and head of the Sanhedrin (the supreme council of Jerusalem), who urged the crucifixion of Jesus with the words, "It is expedient that one man die for the people" (John 11.45–52, 18.14). Dante follows the traditional interpretation, which held that Caiaphas and the others voted to condemn Jesus in order to silence his criticisms of their hypocrisy, covering their self-interest with a pretense of public concern (Caiaphas's words unwittingly alluded to the Atonement).

118–20. He is stretched . . . feel his weight first: Thus the hypocrites who voted to kill Jesus must feel the weight of the hypocrisy of all the others. This is a parodic parallel to the traditional idea that Christ on the Cross bore the weight of all men's sins (the parodic nature of the general punishment here is discussed in the note to lines 100–102). Is. 51.23 (on the humiliation of Jerusalem), "and you have placed your body as it were as a road for passers-by," is possibly being echoed here.

121. his father-in-law: Annas, Caiaphas's father-in-law, also a member of the Sanhedrin.

122. council that sowed so ill for the Jews: Like other medieval Christians, Dante considered the siege and destruction of Jerusalem by the Romans under Titus (A.D. 70), as well as the later diaspora, to be the divinely ordained punishment of the Jews for the killing of Jesus (the Gospels represent them as accepting the guilt on their heads and those of their children; e.g., Matt. 27.25). The matter is discussed at some length in *Paradiso* 7.

124–26. Then I saw Virgil . . . in the eternal exile: The miraculous aspects of the Incarnation and Atonement are apparently unknown and incomprehensible to Virgil, who is denied the Christian revelation. But the pilgrim is also amazed; see also Jer. 49.17 (on the destruction of Edom): "Every one that shall pass by it, shall be astonished and will whistle over all her wounds."

128–32. Let it not displease you . . . to transport us: Note the parallel with the ceremonious pseudocourtesy of the hypocrites in line 93. "On the right hand" is specified because their turn to the left placed the center of Hell to their right.

139–41. My leader stood . . . on this side: Virgil bends his head in thought (compare the pilgrim's bowed head in 5.109–11) as he comes to understand Evil Tail's deception (21.111). Since the beginning of the canto, he and the pilgrim have walked at a normal pace (1–33); slid to the bottom of this *bolgia* (34–51); resumed a normal pace (68–72); stood still to await the two hypocrites (81–82); and walked at the pace of the hypocrites (81). They again stand still as Virgil meditates here. Now, with an angry energy that provides welcome release from the accumulated sense of constraint, they walk rapidly toward the fallen bridge.

144. a liar and the father of lies: The hypocrite is quoting Christ's words in John 8.44: "for he [the devil] is a liar, and the father thereof [i.e., of lies]"; the phrase had become proverbial.

148. following the prints of his dear feet: A line that beautifully crystal-lizes the affection that underlies all the humor at Virgil's expense in this and the two previous cantos.

CANTO 24

1   In quella parte del giovanetto anno
che 'l sole i crin sotto l'Aquario tempra
e già le notti al mezzo dì sen vanno,

4   quando la brina in su la terra assempra
l'imagine di sua sorella bianca,
ma poco dura a la sua penna tempra,

7   lo villanello a cui la roba manca
si leva e guarda, e vede la campagna
biancheggiar tutta; ond' ei si batte l'anca,

10   ritorna in casa, e qua e là si lagna,
come 'l tapin che non sa che si faccia;
poi riede, e la speranza ringavagna,

13   veggendo 'l mondo aver cangiata faccia
in poco d'ora; e prende suo vincastro
e fuor le pecorelle a pascer caccia:

16   così mi fece sbigottir lo mastro
quand' io li vidi sì turbar la fronte,
e così tosto al mal giunse lo 'mpiastro;

19   ché, come noi venimmo al guasto ponte,
lo duca a me si volse con quel piglio
dolce ch'io vidi prima a piè del monte.

22   Le braccia aperse, dopo alcun consiglio
eletto seco riguardando prima
ben la ruina, e diedemi di piglio.

25   E come quei ch'adopera ed estima,
che sempre par che 'nnanzi si proveggia,
così, levando me sù ver' la cima

28   d'un ronchione, avvisava un'altra scheggia
dicendo: "Sovra quella poi t'aggrappa;
ma tenta pria s'è tal ch'ella ti reggia."

CANTO 24

Climb out of sixth bolgia—*seventh* bolgia: *thieves-metamorphosis*—
Vanni Fucci

1   In that part of the youthful year when the sun
tempers its locks under Aquarius and already the
nights are moving south,

4   when on the ground the frost copies the image of
her white sister, but her pen retains its temper only
briefly,

7   the peasant, his provisions running short, rises to
look, and sees the fields all white; and he strikes his
thigh,

10   goes back in his house, and complains here and
there, like a wretch who knows not what to do; then
he goes forth again and stores hope in his wicker basket
again,

13   seeing the face of the world has changed in a
short time; and he takes his crook and drives the
little sheep forth to pasture:

16   so my master made me lose confidence, when I
saw his brow so clouded, and just as quickly he
applied the plaster to the wound;

19   for, when we came to the ruined bridge, my
leader turned to me with the sweet expression I first
saw at the foot of the mountain.

22   After first having taken counsel with himself by
examining the ruin carefully, he opened his arms
and took hold of me.

25   And like one who uses judgment as he acts,
always seeming to look ahead, so, carrying me up to
the top

28   of one rock, he would look to another great
splinter, saying: "Pull yourself up to that one next,
but first test whether it will hold your weight."

31   Non era via da vestito di cappa,
     ché noi a pena, ei lieve e io sospinto,
     potavam sù montar di chiappa in chiappa.

34   E se non fosse che da quel precinto
     più che da l'altro era la costa corta,
     non so di lui, ma io sarei ben vinto;

37   ma, perché Malebolge inver' la porta
     del bassissimo pozzo tutta pende,
     lo sito di ciascuna valle porta

40   che l'una costa surge e l'altra scende.
     Noi pur venimmo al fine in su la punta
     onde l'ultima pietra si scoscende.

43   La lena m'era del polmon sì munta
     quand' io fui sù, ch'i' non potea più oltre,
     anzi m'assisi ne la prima giunta.

46   "Omai convien che tu così ti spoltre,"
     disse 'l maestro, "ché seggendo in piuma
     in fama non si vien, né sotto coltre;

49   sanza la qual chi sua vita consuma,
     cotal vestigio in terra di sé lascia
     qual fummo in aere e in acqua la schiuma.

52   E però leva sù; vinci l'ambascia
     con l'animo che vince ogne battaglia,
     se col suo grave corpo non s'accascia.

55   Più lunga scala convien che si saglia;
     non basta da costoro esser partito.
     Se tu mi 'ntendi, or fa sì che ti vaglia."

58   Leva'mi allor, mostrandomi fornito
     meglio di lena ch'i' non mi sentia,
     e dissi: "Va, ch'i' son forte e ardito."

61   Su per lo scoglio prendemmo la via,
     ch'era ronchioso, stretto e malagevole,
     ed erto più assai che quel di pria.

64   Parlando andava per non parer fievole;
     onde una voce uscì de l'altro fosso,
     a parole formar disconvenevole.

67   Non so che disse, ancor che sovra 'l dosso
     fossi de l'arco già che varca quivi,
     ma chi parlava ad ire parea mosso.

31   It was not a path for anyone wearing a cloak,
since only with difficulty, though he was light and I
was pushed from below, were we able to climb from
outcrop to outcrop.

34   And were it not that there the wall was shorter
than on the other side, I do not know about him, but
I would have been quite overcome;

37   but because all Malebolge slopes toward the
opening of the lowest pit, the nature of each valley
requires

40   that one wall be steep, the other low. Finally we
reached the point where the last rock had broken off.

43   My breath was so milked from my lungs when I
arrived there that I could go no further, but rather
sat down as soon as we arrived.

46   "From now on you will have to cast off sloth in
this way," said my master, "for one does not gain
fame sitting on down cushions, or while under coverlets;

49   and whoever consumes his life without fame
leaves a mark of himself on earth like smoke in the air or
foam in water.

52   And therefore stand up; conquer your panting
with the spirit that conquers in every battle, if it does
not let the heavy body crush it down.

55   A longer ladder must we climb; it is not enough
to have left those others behind. If you understand
me, now act so that it may help you."

58   I stood up then, pretending to be better furnished
with breath than I felt, and said: "Go, for I am strong
and bold."

61   Up along the ridge we took our way, which was
jagged, narrow, and difficult, and much steeper than
the last.

64   I was speaking as I went, so as not to seem feeble;
and then a voice came from the next ditch, unapt to
form words.

67   I do not know what it said, although I was
already mounting the arch that crosses there, but the
speaker seemed to be moved to anger.

70   Io era vòlto in giù, ma li occhi vivi
non poteano ire al fondo per lo scuro;
per ch'io: "Maestro, fa che tu arrivi

73   da l'altro cinghio, e dismontiam lo muro;
ché, com' i' odo quinci e non intendo,
così giù veggio e neente affiguro."

76   "Altra risposta," disse, "non ti rendo
se non lo far; ché la dimanda onesta
si de' seguir con l'opera tacendo."

79   Noi discendemmo il ponte da la testa
dove s'aggiugne con l'ottava ripa,
e poi mi fu la bolgia manifesta;

82   e vidivi entro terribile stipa
di serpenti, e di sì diversa mena
che la memoria il sangue ancor mi scipa.

85   Più non si vanti Libia con sua rena;
ché se chelidri, iaculi e faree
produce, e cencri con anfisibena,

88   né tante pestilenzie né sì ree
mostrò già mai con tutta l'Etïopia
né con ciò che di sopra al Mar Rosso èe.

91   Tra questa cruda e tristissima copia
corrëan genti nude e spaventate,
sanza sperar pertugio o elitropia:

94   con serpi le man dietro avean legate;
quelle ficcavan per le ren la coda
e 'l capo, ed eran dinanzi aggroppate.

97   Ed ecco a un ch'era da nostra proda
s'avventò un serpente che 'l trafisse
là dove 'l collo a le spalle s'annoda.

100   Né O sì tosto mai né I si scrisse
com' el s'accese e arse, e cener tutto
convenne che cascando divenisse;

103   e poi che fu a terra sì distrutto,
la polver si raccolse per sé stessa
e 'n quel medesmo ritornò di butto.

106   Così per li gran savi si confessa
che la fenice more e poi rinasce,
quando al cinquecentesimo anno appressa;

70 I was looking downward, but my sharp eyes
could not attain the bottom, because of the dark; and
I: "Master, when you reach

73 the next belt, let us descend from the ridge; for as
from here I hear but cannot understand, so I look
down but make nothing out."

76 "No other reply," he said, "do I give than action;
for a virtuous request should be obeyed without
discussion."

79 We came down from the bridgehead where it joins
the eighth bank, and then the pouch was made
manifest to me;

82 and I saw within it a terrible crowding of
serpents, and of such a strange kind that the memory
still curdles my blood.

85 Let Libya brag of its sands no more; for if it
produces chelydri, jaculi, and phareae, and chenchres
with amphisbaenae,

88 never did it show so many pestilences nor so
poisonous, together with all Ethiopia and what lies
beyond the Red Sea.

91 Amid this harsh and savage plenty were running
naked, terrified people, without hope of a crevice or
a heliotrope:

94 their hands were bound behind them with snakes;
these thrust through the loins their tails and
heads and were knotted in front.

97 And behold, a serpent hurled itself at one near
our bank and transfixed him where the neck is
knotted to the shoulders.

100 Neither OI nor *I* has ever been written so fast as he
caught fire and burned and was all consumed,
falling, to ashes;

103 and when he was on the ground, destroyed, the
dust gathered together by itself and instantly became
the same one again.

106 Thus the great sages profess that the Phoenix dies
and is reborn, when it approaches its five hundredth
year;

109   erba né biado in sua vita non pasce,
ma sol d'incenso lagrime e d'amomo,
e nardo e mirra son l'ultime fasce.

112   E qual è quel che cade, e non sa como,
per forza di demon ch'a terra il tira,
o d'altra oppilazion che lega l'omo,

115   quando si leva, che 'ntorno si mira
tutto smarrito de la grande angoscia
ch'elli ha sofferta, e guardando sospira:

118   tal era 'l peccator levato poscia.
Oh potenza di Dio, quant' è severa,
che cotai colpi per vendetta croscia!

121   Lo duca il domandò poi chi ello era;
per ch'ei rispuose: "Io piovvi di Toscana,
poco tempo è, in questa gola fiera.

124   Vita bestial mi piacque e non umana,
sì come a mul ch'i' fui; son Vanni Fucci
bestia, e Pistoia mi fu degna tana."

127   E ïo al duca: "Dilli che non mucci,
e domanda che colpa qua giù 'l pinse;
ch'io 'l vidi omo di sangue e di crucci."

130   E 'l peccator, che 'ntese, non s'infinse,
ma drizzò verso me l'animo e 'l volto,
e di trista vergogna si dipinse;

133   poi disse: "Più mi duol che tu m'hai colto
ne la miseria dove tu mi vedi
che quando fui de l'altra vita tolto.

136   Io non posso negar quel che tu chiedi:
in giù son messo tanto perch' io fui
ladro a la sagrestia d'i belli arredi,

139   e falsamente già fu apposto altrui.
Ma perché di tal vista tu non godi,
se mai sarai di fuor da' luoghi bui,

142   apri li orecchi al mio annunzio, e odi.
Pistoia in pria d'i Neri si dimagra;
poi Fiorenza rinova gente e modi.

145   Tragge Marte vapor di Val di Magra
ch'è di torbidi nuvoli involuto,
e con tempesta impetüosa e agra

109   in its life it eats neither grass nor grain but only
tears of incense and of balsam, and nard and myrrh
are its winding sheet.

112   And like one who falls, he knows not how, by the
force of a demon that pulls him to the earth or of
some other occlusion that can bind a man,

115   when he stands up he gazes about all dismayed
by the great anguish he has suffered, and sighs as he
looks:

118   such was the sinner when he stood up. Oh the
power of God, how severe it is, what torrents of
punishment it pours forth!

121   My leader then asked him who he was; and he
replied: "I rained down from Tuscany, not long ago,
into this fierce throat.

124   Bestial life pleased me, not human, mule that I
was; I am Vanni Fucci the beast, and Pistoia was a
worthy lair for me."

127   And I to my leader: "Tell him not to sneak off,
and ask him what sin drove him down here; for I
saw him a bloody, wrathful man."

130   And the sinner, who heard, did not feign, but
turned to me his mind and his face and was covered
with sad shame;

133   then he said: "It pains me more to be caught in the
wretchedness where you see me than when I was
taken from the other life.

136   I cannot refuse what you ask: I am placed so far
down because I stole the beautiful appointments
from the sacristy,

139   and it was falsely blamed on others. But lest you
joy in seeing me, if you ever get out of these dark
places,

142   open your ears to my message, and listen. Pistoia
first thins itself of Blacks; then Florence makes new
its laws and people.

145   Mars draws from Val di Magra a hot wind
wrapped in roiling clouds, and with impetuous, bitter
violence

148   sovra Campo Picen fia combattuto;
ond' ei repente spezzerà la nebbia
sì ch'ogne Bianco ne sarà feruto.

151   E detto l'ho perché doler ti debbia!"

148   they will fight above Campo Piceno; and he will suddenly break the cloud, so that every White will be stricken by it.

151   And I have told you this that it may grieve you!"

NOTES

1–21. In that part . . . of the mountain: With the opening of Canto 30, this is the most elaborate of the similes beginning cantos of the Malebolge (cf. Cantos 18, 21, 22, and 28). There is careful layering of levels of the cosmos: first the constellations (lines 1–3); then the earth (lines 4–6) subject to weather (lines 9–12); and finally the human figure is introduced in terms that emphasize its mutable passions (lines 10–15). Finally the foci of the simile emerge: the change of Virgil's expression (lines 17–18), compared to the melting frost, and the pilgrim's response (lines 18–21), compared to the peasant's initial dismay and later hope. Changes in the "face of the world" (line 13) parallel those in the faces of Virgil and the pilgrim.

The commentators have observed that the simile broaches metamorphosis, the dominant theme of the next *bolgia*, reached in line 70. Medieval commentators on Ovid's *Metamorphoses,* on whom Dante draws heavily in the next cantos, note that the initial events of that poem (the creation of the world, of man, of the giants, etc.) and the changes observed in the world (the seasons, the birth and death of living things) are all instances of metamorphosis, broadly understood as the changes that occur in creatures over time.

2–3. the sun tempers its locks . . . are moving south: See *Aen.* 9.638: "crinitus Apollo" [long-haired Apollo] and *Georgics* 3.303–4: "cum frigidus olim/ iam cadit extremoque inrorat Aquarius anno" [when once-cold Aquarius is already setting and bedews the last of the year]. The sun is cooling (perhaps strengthening, as steel is tempered in cold water after forging) its rays in the cold waters of Aquarius, therefore the imagined date is between January 21 and February 21, if conventional dates are used. The nights (thought of as the ideal point opposite the sun; cf. 34.5, with note) turn south at the winter solstice, when the sun turns north along the ecliptic (the Italian *al mezzo dì sen vanno* can also mean they "diminish to a half day," but with less exactitude, since only at the vernal equinox have they diminished so far).

4–6. the frost . . . only briefly: The simile is drawn from writing: the hoarfrost is like an inscription on the surface of the ground, copied from that of the snow, but it fades as the day warms up, just as real writing loses definition when the pen (for Dante a goose quill or a sharpened reed) loses its sharpness, or "temper" (the same word as in line 2). Dante's *assemprare* refers to copying into manuscripts (see *Vita nuova* 1). For parallel images see Lucan, *Pharsalia* 4.52–53, and Ex. 16.14–21. For other similes derived from writing, see line 100 and 25.64–66, and see the reference to the poet's pen at 25.143–44.

12. stores hope in his wicker basket: The import of the simile is hopeful; see also lines 20–21. By escaping from the Evil Claws the pair have overcome a serious danger (linked to the autobiographical content of the episode; see Additional Note 9). The phrase recalls Virgil's earlier description of trust as something "put in one's purse" (11.54).

13. the face of the world has changed: See Psalm 103.30: "Thou shall send forth thy spirit, and they shall be created: and thou shall renew the face of the earth." See also lines 104–5 and 144, and 25.143, with notes.

15. drives the little sheep forth: The scene has put commentators in mind of the *Bucolics* and *Georgics* of Vergil (see the note to lines 2–4); Vergil was himself thought of as a "shepherd." But the figure of "pastoral" care is also of course Christian: the shepherd of Psalm 23 [Vulgate 22] was understood to be Christ (cf. John 21.17: "feed my sheep," and the note to 19.132).

21. at the foot of the mountain: Recalling Virgil's original rescue of the pilgrim (1.63) emphasizes the hopeful tone. At lines 25–45 the wayfarers climb, rather than descend, perhaps foreshadowing the climb up the "mountain of virtue," that of Purgatory (see line 55); for the same reason, perhaps, moral commonplaces encouraging perseverance are frequent in the canto.

22–27. After first having taken counsel . . . up to the top: Virgil exhibits prudence, discretion, and fortitude, as if demonstrating the so-called cardinal virtues (prudence, justice, fortitude, and temperance).

24. took hold of me: Virgil will carry the pilgrim out of the sixth *bolgia*, that of the hypocrites, as he carried him into it when the wayfarers escaped from the Evil Claws (23.37–51) and as he did in the other case of descent into a *bolgia* (see 19.34–35).

31. a cloak: An ironic reference to the hypocrites' leaden cloaks in Canto 23.

46–57. From now on . . . that it may help you: Virgil's exhortation is based on the commonplace of the choice of Hercules at the crossroads: between the steep mountain of virtue, or the wide, inviting plain of vice; there is also an explicit reference to the climb up the mountain of Purgatory ("a longer ladder") where the notion of a mountain of virtue will be brought in more forcefully. For Hercules, see 9.98 and 25.32, with notes.

49–51. whoever consumes his life . . . foam in water: See *Aen.* 5.740, of Anchises' ghost: "tenuis fugit ceu fumus in auras" [he fled like thin smoke into the air]. But the moralizing tone of Virgil's images is biblical: see, for example, Wisdom 5.15: "For the hope of the wicked is . . . as a thin froth which is dispersed by the storm: and a smoke that is scattered abroad by the wind" (cf. Psalm 36.20). For additional images of smoke, see 25.22, 92–93, and 135, with notes.

53. the spirit . . . the heavy body: See *Aen.* 6.730–34 (quoted in the note to 10.58) and Wisdom 9.15: "For the corruptible body is a load upon the soul, and the earthly habitation presseth down the mind. . . ." Although the ideas are commonplace, Dante's mention of the relation of spirit and body, just before entering the *bolgia* of metamorphosis, is significant.

55. A longer ladder: The climb from the bottom of Hell to the surface of the earth (34.127–39); or the climb to the top of Purgatory; or both (cf. 34.82).

64–66. I was speaking . . . unapt to form words: The first information about the seventh *bolgia*, like the last (see 25.136–42, with notes), relates to speech.

69. moved to anger: The Italian can also mean "in motion"; we think the ambiguity is probably intentional, but there is an interesting textual problem here: see "Textual Variants."

82. a terrible crowding of serpents: The appropriateness of the snakes to the punishment of thieves of course derives from the account of the serpent's temptation of Adam and Eve in Gen. 3.1–7. The archetypal thief is the devil, who stealthily entered the Garden and the serpent in order to steal mankind from God (cf. Augustine, *De Genesi ad litteram* 28–29); Adam's sin included all others (murder because it caused his and Eve's deaths, theft because the fruit was forbidden, and so forth). In the *Confessions,* Augustine devotes most of Book 2 to explicating his adolescent theft of pears from a neighbor's orchard as a type of Adam's sin and of sin in general. In Jesus' parable of the sheepfold (John 10.1–18), the thief is regularly identified as the devil. See Additional Note 10.

84. the memory still curdles my blood: The early commentators understand Dante's term here (*scipa*) in various ways, taking it to mean either "divide, curdle" or "spoil."

85–90. Let Libya brag . . . the Red Sea: In the Middle Ages, Libya, Ethiopia, and Arabia (to the west, southeast, and east of Egypt, respectively) were considered inhospitable to human life because of the heat of the torrid zone (for the fabulous origin of the desert, see 17.106–11, with note). In Aristotle's works on natural science and in Pliny's *Natural History*, these areas are said to teem with often monstrous creatures; Ovid (*Met.* 4.604–20) and Lucan (*Pharsalia* 9.696–727) relate that as Perseus flew over the Sahara with the head of Medusa, the drops of its blood generated a multitude of types of serpent.

86–87. chelydri . . . amphisbaenae: This list of serpent species is taken from Lucan's list in *Pharsalia* 9.708–27 (fifteen species in twenty lines). Grandgent notes: "The *chelydri* make their path smoke, the *jaculi* are swift as darts, the *pharee* furrow the ground with their tails, the *chenchres* never follow a straight line, the *amphisbaena* has two heads."

88. pestilences: Lucan repeatedly uses the term *pestis* of the Lybian serpents that attack Cato's men (*Pharsalia* 9.614, 723, 734, and 844).

93. a crevice or a heliotrope: The Italian word for "crevice," *pertugio*, suggests an opening through which thieves might escape. Medieval lapidaries ascribe to the heliotrope-stone (the name means "sun-turner" or "sun-changer") the power of rendering its bearer invisible; in the early Italian prose *Novellino* and in Boccaccio's *Decameron* 8.3 it is imagined to permit thieves to steal with impunity. See Additional Note 10.

Although the *bolgia* is deep in Hell, Dante creates the impression of a desert landscape under a pitiless sun as the appropriate place of punishment for thieves, whose Latin name (*fur*), Isidore says, derives from the word for "dark" (*furvo, fusco*). Concealment is an essential part of Aquinas's definition of theft (*Summa theol.* 2a 2ae, q. 1, a. 66): "theft is . . . the concealed seizure of what belongs to others." Here detection is constant, inevitable (see lines 127, 130, and 132).

94–96. their hands were bound . . . knotted in front: The thieves' hands (with which they stole) are bound by the snakes. The motif of penetration and the knotting of snaky bodies suggest copulating serpents (Aristotle, *On the generation of animals* 1.7.718a18–19: "Serpents copulate by twisting round each other"). For other violent "couplings" in the *bolgia*, see 25.51–72 and 100–135.

98. transfixed him . . . to the shoulders: The serpent bites the shade at the crossing point of the spine and the shoulders (cf. 23.100–102, with note), also close to where the spinal column enters the brain. Ovid's Pythagoras, in his summary of the forms of metamorphosis, cites the belief that snakes can be formed from the spinal marrow of corpses; see *Met.* 15.389–90: "sunt, qui . . ./ mutari credant humanas angue medullas" [some believe that . . . the human marrow changes into a snake]. The reciprocal attacks of the thieves will recall another archetypal conflict: the war between serpents and humankind decreed in Gen. 3.15, as the early commentators point out.

97–111. And behold . . . its winding sheet: In the first actual metamorphosis of the *bolgia*, one of the thieves is burned to ashes and immediately reconstituted. See Gen. 3.19: "for dust thou art, and into dust thou shalt return," quoted in the burial service and in the Office for the Dead; see also Eccles. 17.31 and 41.13, Psalm 103.29–30, and the note to lines 106–11.

100. neither O nor I has ever been written so fast: Dante compares the quickness of the transformation to the time it takes to write two simple letters, which of course spell *io* (the first-person-singular pronoun, as well as the name of Io, a lover of Jove's transformed into a cow: *Met.* 1.584; see Derby Chapin 1971). The reference to writing recalls lines 4–6.

101. caught fire . . . falling, to ashes: Snake venom was often thought to include the element of fire, as in *Aen.* 7.349–56, and *Pharsalia* 9.741–42 (cf. also the note to 26.58–60).

105. became the same one again: See Vergil, *Georgics* 4.444: "in sese redit" [he returned to himself], of Proteus returning to his "original" shape after many transformations.

106–11. the great sages profess . . . its winding sheet: With the conflagration in line 100, Dante juxtaposes an antithetical comparison with the mythical Phoenix, which lives for 500 years and then immolates itself on a pyre of spices, to be reborn from its ashes. Dante's principal source is Ovid, *Met.* 15.392–407, where the Phoenix is one of Pythagoras's examples of immortality through transformation:

> Una est, quae reparet seque ipsa reseminet, ales:
> Assyrii phoenica vocant; non fruge neque herbis,
> sed turis lacrimis et suco vivit amomi.

> [One bird there is, which renews and re-sows itself,
> called Phoenix by the Assyrians; on neither grain nor grass
> it lives, but on tears of incense and balsam-oil.] (392–94)

A famous poem by Lactantius (ca. 260–ca. 325) interpreted the Phoenix as a symbol of Christ's resurrection. The implication is that, like other punishments in Hell, that of the thieves is a distorted imitation of the Crucifixion.

109. neither grass nor grain: See the quotation from Ovid in the previous note and compare *Inf.* 1.103: "Questi non ciberà terra né peltro" (of the grey-hound, the *veltro*).

112–14. like one who falls . . . can bind a man: That is, Vanni's thunder-struck attitude is like that of one who has suffered demonic possession or an epileptic fit. Christ exorcises a "dumb spirit" in possession of a boy (Mark 9.17): "Who, wheresoever he taketh him, dasheth him, and he foameth, and gnasheth with the teeth, and pineth away."

114. occlusion: Buti identifies this as a "gathering of humors, or their vapors, that enter the passageways between the heart and the brain; once these are closed, the man falls and becomes insensible." Albertus Magnus (*De animalibus* 25.7) notes that some snake poisons work "by closing the passages for the breath in the body with the thickness of its cold substance." See Additional Note 10.

124–25. Bestial life . . . Vanni Fucci the beast: Vanni Fucci was a violent member of the White Cancellieri faction of Pistoia (see the note to line 129). See Psalm 31.9: "Do not become like the horse and the mule, who have no understanding." Vanni's nickname of "beast" suggests an implied "moral" trans-formation (Vanni "acts" like a beast) (see *Convivio* 2.7.4).

126. Pistoia was a worthy lair for me: For thieves as beasts with lairs or dens, see the words of Christ, expelling the money changers from the Temple (Matt. 21.13): "you have made it a den of thieves." Dante is punning on *Pistoia* and *peste* [pestilence], used of the snakes in line 88 (cf. 25.10–12, with note).

127. Tell him not to sneak off: The action would be characteristic of the thief.

129. a bloody, wrathful man: Vanni Fucci was responsible for a number of crimes and acts of violence, the most serious being the murder, in 1293 or 1294, of Bertino de' Vergiolesi; Bertino was a relative of Foccaccia (Vanni) de' Cancellieri, a prominent White Guelf of Pistoia (see 32.63, with notes), and was killed when Foccaccia could not be found.

130. did not feign: Dante insists on the inevitable visibility of the thief here (see the note to line 93).

132. covered with sad shame: Compare Jer. 2.26: "As the thief is confounded when taken. . . ." Compare this with Virgil's cheerful expression in lines 20–21.

137. I stole: The first explicit mention of theft in the canto. For the typology of thieves in this *bolgia*, see the note to 25.50–138.

138. the beautiful appointments from the sacristy: Vanni Fucci's crime was theft of sacred objects, *furtum rei sacrae* (an established legal category). In January 1293, Vanni Fucci and others broke into the church of San Zeno in Pistoia and stole, or attempted to steal, two silver tablets with images of the Virgin and the apostles from the chapel of San Iacopo.

139. falsely blamed on others: Arrested and held for Vanni Fucci's crime was one Rampino di Francesco Foresi; he was only set at liberty in 1295, after Vanni Fucci informed on an accomplice (Vanni della Monna), with whom the treasure had been deposited; Vanni della Monna was then executed in place of Rampino. This "substitution of persons" may be related thematically to the action of the *bolgia*; see the note to 25.50–138.

142–50. open your ears . . . will be stricken by it: This deliberately obscure prophecy refers to some phase of the struggle between the Tuscan Whites and Blacks. First the Blacks are driven out of Pistoia (1301), and then Florence drives out the Whites and changes its laws (the Black coup of 1301–1302; see 6.64–72). Commentators are agreed that the "hot wind" is Moroello Malaspina, from the Val di Magra, in Lunigiana, northwest of Tuscany, and that the "roiling clouds" refer to the Tuscan Whites. Beyond that, the prophecy perhaps refers to the taking by Malaspina of the fortress of Serravalle, part of the Pistoian defenses, in 1302, perhaps to the taking of Pistoia itself by the Blacks, led by Malaspina, in 1306. The prophecy is more devastating if the definitive defeat of 1306 is meant, since the Pistoian Blacks succeeded in securing reentry into their city, whereas the Florentine Whites did not (see the note to 32.69).

In Vanni Fucci's meteorological allegory, the "hot wind," containing fire (hot and dry), and the "roiling cloud," containing water (cold and moist), collide to produce a storm. Medieval commentators on Ovid's *Metamorphoses* posit the combination and strife of elements as one of the most "basic" natural metamorphoses; concluding the canto with a meteorological one balances its opening.

144. Florence makes new its laws and people: Note the language of metamorphosis, used ironically of the change in population with the expulsion of the

Whites and the hasty revision of legislation to favor the Blacks, as if Florence were a Phoenix (see 25.143 and note).

148. above Campo Piceno: Dante and his contemporaries took the *ager Picenum*, named by Sallust as the place where Catiline was defeated in 63 B.C., to be a field near Pistoia, the scene of one of Malaspina's sorties against the Pistoian Whites.

CANTO 25

1   Al fine de le sue parole il ladro
le mani alzò con amendue le fiche,
gridando: "Togli Dio, ch'a te le squadro!"

4   Da indi in qua mi fuor le serpi amiche,
perch' una li s'avvolse allora il collo,
come dicesse "Non vo' che più diche,"

7   e un'altra a le braccia, e rilegollo,
ribadendo sé stessa sì dinanzi
che non potea con esse dare un crollo.

10   Ahi, Pistoia, Pistoia, ché non stanzi
d'incenerarti sì che più non duri,
poi che 'n mal fare il seme tuo avanzi?

13   Per tutt' i cerchi de lo 'nferno scuri
non vidi spirto in Dio tanto superbo,
non quel che cadde a Tebe giù da' muri.

16   El si fuggì che non parlò più verbo;
e io vidi un centauro pien di rabbia
venir chiamando: "Ov' è, ov' è l'acerbo?"

19   Maremma non cred' io che tante n'abbia
quante bisce elli avea su per la groppa
infin ove comincia nostra labbia.

22   Sovra le spalle, dietro da la coppa,
con l'ali aperte li giacea un draco,
e quello affuoca qualunque s'intoppa.

25   Lo mio maestro disse: "Questi è Caco,
che sotto 'l sasso di monte Aventino
di sangue fece spesse volte laco.

28   Non va co' suoi fratei per un cammino,
per lo furto che frodolente fece
del grande armento ch'elli ebbe a vicino;

CANTO 25

Seventh bolgia, *continued: Cacus—more metamorphoses—Agnello,*
Pucci Sciancato

1   At the end of his words the thief raised his hands
with both the figs, crying: "Take them, God, I'm
aiming at you!"

4   From then on snakes have been my friends,
because one of them wrapped itself around his neck,
as if to say "I won't let him say more,"

7   and another around his arms, and bound them up,
tying itself so tight in front that he could not budge.

10   Ah, Pistoia, Pistoia, why do you not decree your
incineration, so that you may not endure, since you
surpass your sowers in doing ill?

13   Through all the dark circles of Hell I saw no spirit
so proud against God, not him who fell from the wall
at Thebes.

16   He fled without saying another word; and I saw a
centaur, full of rage, come crying: "Where is he,
where is he, the unripe one?"

19   I do not think Maremma has as many water
snakes as he had on his back from the rump to
where our shape begins.

22   On his shoulders, behind his nape, lay a dragon
spreading its wings; it sets fire to any they meet.

25   My master said: "That is Cacus, who beneath the
rocks of Mount Aventine many times made a lake of
blood.

28   He does not follow the same path as his brothers,
because he fraudulently stole the great herd he found
close by;

31 onde cessar le sue opere biece
sotto la mazza d'Ercule, che forse
gliene diè cento, e non sentì le diece."

34 Mentre che sì parlava, ed el trascorse
e tre spiriti venner sotto noi,
de' quai né io né 'l duca mio s'accorse,

37 se non quando gridar: "Chi siete voi?"
Per che nostra novella si ristette,
e intendemmo pur ad essi poi.

40 Io non li conoscea; ma ei seguette,
come suol seguitar per alcun caso,
che l'un nomar un altro convenette,

43 dicendo: "Cianfa dove fia rimaso?"
Per ch'io, acciò che 'l duca stesse attento,
mi puosi 'l dito su dal mento al naso.

46 Se tu se' or, lettore, a creder lento
ciò ch'io dirò, non sarà maraviglia,
ché io, che 'l vidi, a pena il mi consento.

49 Com' io tenea levate in lor le ciglia,
e un serpente con sei piè si lancia
dinanzi a l'uno, e tutto a lui s'appiglia.

52 Co' piè di mezzo li avvinse la pancia
e con li anterïor le braccia prese;
poi li addentò e l'una e l'altra guancia;

55 li diretani a le cosce distese,
e miseli la coda tra 'mbedue
e dietro per le ren sù la ritese:

58 ellera abbarbicata mai non fue
ad alber sì, come l'orribil fiera
per l'altrui membra avviticchiò le sue.

61 Poi s'appiccar, come di calda cera
fossero stati, e mischiar lor colore,
né l'un né l'altro già parea quel ch'era:

64 come procede innanzi da l'ardore,
per lo papiro suso, un color bruno
che non è nero ancora e 'l bianco more.

67 Li altri due 'l riguardavano, e ciascuno
gridava: "Omè, Agnel, come ti muti!
Vedi che già non se' né due né uno."

31 therefore his cross-eyed deeds ended under
Hercules' club, which perhaps gave him a hundred,
but he did not feel ten of them."

34 As he was speaking, the centaur went by and
three spirits came below us, whom neither I nor my
leader perceived

37 until they cried: "Who are you?" For this reason
our talk ceased, and they alone claimed our attention.

40 I did not know them; but it happened, as it often
does by some chance, that one of them had to name
another,

43 saying: "Where has Cianfa stayed?" Therefore I, so
that my leader should pay attention, stretched my
finger from chin to nose.

46 If now, reader, you are slow to believe what I say,
that will be no marvel, for I, who saw it, hardly allow
it.

49 As I was raising my brows toward them, a serpent
with six feet threw itself on one of them and
embraced him closely.

52 Its middle feet it wrapped around his waist, with
its forefeet it seized his arms; then it pierced both his
cheeks with its fangs;

55 its hind feet it spread along his thighs, and put its
tail between them, extending it up along his loins:

58 ivy never took root on a tree so tightly as the
horrible beast grew vinelike around the other's limbs.

61 After they had adhered to each other like hot wax
and had mixed their colors, neither seemed what it
had been:

64 as, when paper burns, a dark color moves up it
preceding the flame; it is not yet black, but the white
is dying.

67 The other two were staring at him, and each cried:
"Oh me, Agnel, how you are changing! See, already
you are neither two nor one."

70   Già eran li due capi un divenuti,
         quando n'apparver due figure miste
         in una faccia, ov' eran due perduti.

73   Fersi le braccia due di quattro liste;
         le cosce con le gambe e 'l ventre e 'l casso
         divenner membra che non fuor mai viste.

76   Ogne primaio aspetto ivi era casso;
         due e nessun l'imagine perversa
         parea, e tal sen gio con lento passo.

79   Come 'l ramarro sotto la gran fersa
         dei dì canicular, cangiando sepe,
         folgore par se la via attraversa:

82   sì pareva, venendo verso l'epe
         de li altri due, un serpentello acceso,
         livido e nero come gran di pepe;

85   e quella parte onde prima è preso
         nostro alimento a l'un di lor trafisse;
         poi cadde giuso innanzi lui disteso.

88   Lo trafitto 'l mirò, ma nulla disse;
         anzi, co' piè fermati, sbadigliava
         pur come sonno o febbre l'assalisse.

91   Elli 'l serpente e quei lui riguardava;
         l'un per la piaga e l'altro per la bocca
         fummavan forte, e 'l fummo si scontrava.

94   Taccia Lucano omai, là dov' e' tocca
         del misero Sabello e di Nasidio,
         e attenda a udir quel ch'or si scocca.

97   Taccia di Cadmo e d'Aretusa Ovidio,
         ché se quello in serpente e quella in fonte
         converte poetando, io non lo 'nvidio,

100   ché due nature mai a fronte a fronte
         non trasmutò sì ch'amendue le forme
         a cambiar lor matera fosser pronte.

103   Insieme si rispuosero a tai norme
         che 'l serpente la coda in forca fesse,
         e 'l feruto ristrinse insieme l'orme.

106   Le gambe con le cosce seco stesse
         s'appiccar sì che 'n poco la giuntura
         non facea segno alcun che si paresse.

70   Already the two heads had become one, so that
      two sets of features seemed mingled in one face,
      where two heads were lost.

73   The arms became two strips from four; the thighs
      and the legs and the belly and the chest became
      members never before seen.

76   Every former appearance there was shattered; two
      and none the perverse image seemed, and off it
      moved with slow steps.

79   As the lizard, changing hedges under the great
      scourge of the dog days, seems lightning as it crosses
      the road:

82   so seemed an inflamed little serpent, livid and black
      like a grain of pepper, coming toward the bellies of
      the other two;

85   and one of them it pierced in the place where our
      first nourishment is taken; then it fell stretched out
      before him.

88   The one transfixed gazed at it but said nothing;
      rather, standing still, he yawned as if sleep or fever
      assailed him.

91   He was gazing at the serpent, and the serpent at
      him; one through his wound and the other through
      its mouth was sending forth smoke, and the smoke
      met.

94   Let Lucan now be silent, where he touches on
      miserable Sabellus and Nasidius, and let him listen to
      what the bow now looses.

97   About Cadmus and Arethusa let Ovid be silent,
      for if in his poetry he converts him into a serpent and
      her into a fountain, I do not envy him,

100   for never two natures face to face did he
      transmute so that both forms were ready to exchange
      their matter.

103   They answered each other according to this
      rule: that the serpent split its tail in two, and the
      wounded one drew his soles together.

106   His legs and thighs so adhered that soon the
      joining left no mark that could be seen.

109   Togliea la coda fessa la figura
che si perdeva là, e la sua pelle
si facea molle, e quella di là dura.

112   Io vidi intrar le braccia per l'ascelle,
e i due piè de la fiera, ch'eran corti,
tanto allungar quanto accorciavan quelle.

115   Poscia li piè di rietro, insieme attorti,
diventaron lo membro che l'uom cela,
e 'l misero del suo n'avea due porti.

118   Mentre che 'l fummo l'uno e l'altro vela
di color novo e genera 'l pel suso
per l'una parte, e da l'altra il dipela,

121   l'un si levò e l'altro cadde giuso,
non torcendo però le lucerne empie,
sotto le quai ciascun cambiava muso.

124   Quel ch'era dritto il trasse ver' le tempie,
e di troppa matera ch'in là venne
uscir li orecchi de le gote scempie;

127   ciò che non corse in dietro e si ritenne
di quel soverchio, fé naso a la faccia
e le labbra ingrossò quanto convenne.

130   Quel che giacëa il muso innanzi caccia,
e li orecchi ritira per la testa
come face le corna la lumaccia;

133   e la lingua, ch'avëa unita e presta
prima a parlar, si fende, e la forcuta
ne l'altro si richiude; e 'l fummo resta.

136   L'anima ch'era fiera divenuta,
suffolando si fugge per la valle,
e l'altro dietro a lui parlando sputa.

139   Poscia li volse le novelle spalle,
e disse a l'altro: "I' vo' che Buoso corra,
com' ho fatt' io, carpon per questo calle."

142   Così vid' io la settima zavorra
mutare e trasmutare; e qui mi scusi
la novità se fior la penna abborra.

145   E avvegna che li occhi miei confusi
fossero alquanto e l'animo smagato,
non poter quei fuggirsi tanto chiusi

109   The cleft tail took the shape the other was losing,
and its skin softened, but over there it hardened.

112   I saw both his arms withdraw into the armpits,
and the beast's two feet, which were short, lengthen
as much as the other's were shortening.

115   Then the hind feet, twisted together, became the
member which a man hides, and the other wretch out
of his had extended two feet.

· 118   While the smoke veils both of them with a new
color, generating hair on one side, and peeling it off
on the other,

121   one stood up and the other fell down, but they
did not turn aside their pitiless lanterns, under whose
gaze each was changing his snout.

124   He who was erect drew his in toward the temples,
and of the excess matter made ears that came out
over narrow cheeks;

127   what of that excess did not go to the rear became
a nose for the face and filled out the cheeks as much
as was fitting.

130   He who was lying down, extends his snout
forward and withdraws his ears into his head as the
snail does its horns;

133   and his tongue, which had previously been whole
and ready to speak, is split, and the other's forked
one is joined; and the smoke stops.

136   The soul who had become a beast fled hissing
through the valley, and the other spits as he speaks
after him.

139   Then he turned his new back on him and said to
the other: "I want Buoso to run, as I have, on all sixes
along this path."

142   Thus I saw the seventh cargo change and change
again; and here let the novelty excuse me if my pen
ever falters.

145   And although my eyes were somewhat confused
and my spirit robbed of power, the souls could not
flee so secretly

148   ch'i' non scorgessi ben Puccio Sciancato;
    ed era quel che sol, di tre compagni
    che venner prima, non era mutato;
151   l'altr' era quel che tu, Gaville, piagni.

148   that I did not see clearly Puccio Sciancato; and he
alone, of the three companions who had arrived
earlier, had not been changed;

151   the other was the one that makes you, Gaville,
weep.

NOTES

1–2. At the end of his words . . . the figs:
Vanni Fucci makes with both hands the obscene
gesture (signifying the female organ) made by
placing the thumb between the middle and index
fingers (Figure 5), pointed upward. The city of
Prato in 1297 decreed "whoever makes the figs
or shows his buttocks to heaven or to the image
of God . . . to pay ten lire each time, or be
whipped." In 1228 the citizens of Pistoia fixed
on the Carmignano tower two "figs" of marble,
aimed at Florence (Villani, *Chronicle* 6.5).

Figure 5. A fist making the "fig."

6. I won't let him say more: Vanni Fucci is silenced, but the serpents "speak"
by their action; another reference to speech and its loss (see 24.64–66, with note,
and lines 25.16, 45, 88, 94, 97, and 137).

7. bound them up, tying itself so tight: Some commentators invoke *Aen.*
2.213–24, which describes Laocoön in the coils of the sea serpents sent by the
gods; like Laocoön, Vanni Fucci has just prophesied.

10–12. Pistoia . . . surpass your sowers: The name *Pistoia* (see the note to
24.88) was sometimes said by its enemies to reflect its origin in the "pesti-
lential" revolt of Catiline (see Villani, *Chronicle* 1.32); Dante connected the
snakes/thieves with pestilence in 24.88 (see the note to 24.126). The invita-
tion to self-incineration (line 11) echoes the immolation of Vanni Fucci
(24.100–102).

15. him who fell from the wall at Thebes: Capaneus (14.46–72). Mention
of fratricidal Thebes (see line 97: founded by Cadmus with the dragon's teeth)
follows on mention of Pistoia, where the feud between the White and Black
Guelfs was said to originate.

17. a centaur, full of rage: Said in line 25 to be Cacus, although there is not
much basis for representing Cacus as a centaur; according to Virgil he was
semihomo [half-man, *Aen.* 8.194] and *semiferus* [half-beast, 8.267], gigantic (8.199),
covered with fur (8.266), and, as a son of Vulcan, able to breathe fire (8.198,
251–58). For Livy, he was merely a shepherd (1.7).

19. Maremma: This swampy coastal region was rife with snakes in Dante's day (cf. 13.7–9).

21. where our shape begins: For the meaning of this division of the body, see 12.84 and 17.82, with notes.

23–24. a dragon . . . to any they meet: The dragon on Cacus's shoulders seems to derive from the fire-breathing chimera on Turnus's helmet (*Aen.* 7.785–88). For other references to smoke, see 24.49–51 and 25.91–93, 118, and 133–35, with notes.

25–33. That is Cacus . . . ten of them: In the story as told by Livy and Vergil, Cacus stole a number of bulls and heifers from Hercules' herd; in order to conceal his theft, he dragged them by the tails into his cave under the Aventine (one of the seven hills of the future Rome). According to Vergil, Hercules tore open the mountain to find his stock, who were lowing in response to the others, and killed Cacus in spite of his smoke screen.

27. made a lake of blood: Vergil implies that Cacus both delighted in slaughter and ate human flesh (*Aen.* 8.195–97).

31. cross-eyed: More properly, "looking askance" (with envy; cf. 6.91, with note).

32. Hercules' club: The first mention of Hercules' name in Hell. Dante knew Livy's account (1.7), in which Hercules clubs Cacus to death; in the *Aeneid,* he strangles him. For Hercules' status as an analogue of Christ, see 9.54, 98, with notes.

33. gave him a hundred: The Italian means literally "gave him a hundred of them [i.e., blows]."

43. Where has Cianfa stayed: Most commentators understand Cianfa to reappear as the serpent of line 50. The early commentators identify him as Cianfa Donati, thus a member of the powerful Donati family, known from documents to have been alive in 1282 or 1283, dead by 1289. Nothing else is known about him.

45. stretched my finger from chin to nose: That is, he made the classic gesture enjoining silence, presumably because he recognizes the name Cianfa (another silencing; see the note to line 6). See Additional Note 10. For the pilgrim's curiosity, see 22.37–39.

46–48. If now, reader . . . allow it: The sixth address to the reader in the *Inferno* (see 8.94, with note), again stressing the incredibility of the events and the narrator's reliability (cf. 16.124–29 with notes, and 13.25–51).

50–138. a serpent with six feet . . . spits as he speaks after him: The precise logic of the metamorphoses as punishment of the thieves has not been fully explained; several scholars suggest that given the scholastic view of property as an extension of the person (see the note to 11.29–51), theft of the property of another would thus be appropriately punished with loss of the thief's person—that is, body. See Additional Note 10.

51–72. embraced him closely . . . were lost: For this "parodic love-kiss" (Gmelin) and its sequel, Dante draws on Ovid's narrative of the nymph Salmacis and the boy Hermaphroditus fusing into a single ambisexual being (*Met.* 4.356–88). The parallels are close; note especially Dante's simile of vine and tree (lines 58–60), and the fusion of the two forms (lines 69–72), and compare with:

> utve solent hederae longos intexere truncos
>
> . . .
>
> sic ubi complexu coierunt membra tenaci,
> nec duo sunt sed forma duplex, nec femina dici
> nec puer ut possit, neutrumque utrumque videtur
>
> [as ivies are wont to weave around tall trunks
>
> . . .
>
> thus when the limbs cohered in tight embrace
> they are not two, but a double form, so that it can be called
> neither woman nor boy, and it seems neither and both] (4.365–79)

Medieval commentators on Ovid took the episode of Salmacis and Hermaphroditus to be a representation of coitus, the fusion of the two signifying the fusing of the sperm with the mother's blood in the womb.

64. as, when paper burns . . . the white is dying: In 24.100, Vanni Fucci's reconstitution was compared to the writing of letters; here the comparison is drawn from the support for writing.

68. Agnel: The early commentators identify him as Agnello dei Brunelleschi, member of another prominent noble family. See also the note to lines 140–41.

69. you are neither two nor one: A line clearly alluding to Ovid's "neutrumque utrumque videtur" [seemed neither and both] quoted in the note to lines 51–72. For Dante, this confusion of forms parodies the union of two natures, human and divine, in Christ (see the notes to 12.12 and 83–84). There may be another reference to the Phoenix (24.107): Lactantius adapts Ovid's lines quoted above to the Phoenix as "femina seu mas . . . seu neutrum seu . . . utrumque" [female or male . . . or neither or . . . both] (the allusion is to the hermaphroditism often attributed to the risen Christ) (see 28.125).

75. members never before seen: Compare to the poet's boast of showing something never before seen (line 100) and the "novelty" (line 144) of the *bolgia*.

77–78. two and none the perverse image seemed: A variation on line 69, closer to Ovid's phrasing.

79–80. the great scourge of the dog days: The dog days, mid-July to mid-September, when the star Sirius, in Canis Major ("the greater dog," one of the hounds of Orion), rises and sets with the sun: their joining was thought responsible for the hot weather. Again, the sun's heat is associated with the thieves' punishment, as if driving the ceaseless changes (see the note to lines 91–93).

82. toward the bellies: Translating *epe* [livers]. In the Platonic tradition, the liver is the seat of appetites relating to nourishment and reproduction (see the note to 30.102).

83–84. an inflamed little serpent . . . like a grain of pepper: The pepper grain was thought to contain fire because of its sharp taste and its color (most peppercorns, originally white, green, or pink, were charred before shipping). For the association of fire and snakes, see the notes to 24.86–87 and 101–2.

85–86. the place where our first nourishment is taken: The navel. Here begins the third of the major metamorphoses in the *bolgia* (24.97–105, 25.49–78, and 25.85–138). In each, the victim is bitten at a different point: in the first, at the juncture of shoulders and neck; in the second, in the face (and the tail is thrust through the legs of the victim); and in the third, at the navel, where the fetus is nourished. Each subsequent transformation is slower and more elaborate: the first, all but instantaneous, as if a figure for the violent brevity of human life; the second is deliberate and involved, like sexual union; and the third hallucinated, laborious, and protracted, gestating unheard-of beings.

87. it fell stretched out: Ovid's Cadmus (see line 97) falls down as he is changed into a snake: "in longam tenditur alvum" [his belly became long] (*Met.* 4.576);

"in pectusque cadit pronus" [and he fell prone on his breast] (579) (see the note to line 121). For the repeated falling down in this *bolgia*, see 24.54 and 25.15, 121.

89–90. yawned . . . as if sleep or fever assailed him: Sleepiness and stupefaction are symptoms of snakebite poisoning, according to Albertus Magnus (*De animalibus* 25.7). See also Lucan, *Pharsalia* 9.815–18.

91–93. He was gazing . . . the smoke met: The reciprocal gaze and the mingling smoke seem to be mechanisms whereby the shades exchange shapes: analogies with erotic viewing, approach, embrace, consummation, and gestation are implicit. The "smoke" seems almost an active agent (perhaps related to the "spirit" that in medieval views of conception is the active principle in semen); here it pours from breaches in the body, mouth or wound. The reciprocal gazing suggests that the changing is also effected by seeing, the *form* of one thief being passed to the other via the light ("lanterns," line 122), as the light of the stars was thought to impose form on sublunary things. See also the note to lines 100–135.

94–102. Let Lucan . . . let Ovid . . . exchange their matter: The poet's boast here is an instance of a well-established literary topos in which the poet proclaims his novelty and modernity and his surpassing his models (e.g., Claudian, *In Rufinum* line 283: "taceat superata vetustas" [let antiquity, surpassed, be silent]; cited in Curtius 1953).

95. Sabellus and Nasidius: Two soldiers in Lucan's *Pharsalia* who die horrible deaths from snakebite (9.761–804): Sabellus's body is liquefied, and Nasidius's is bloated to enormous size. Sabellus's fate (compared to melting snow) may be echoed in that of Arethusa (see the note to line 97), while the loss of features in Nasidius is perhaps reflected in the current transformations.

97. Cadmus and Arethusa: Ovid's account (*Met.* 4.563–603) of the transformation into serpents of Cadmus and his wife Harmonia is Dante's principal model for the third transformation (see the notes to lines 100–135). The nymph Arethusa melted into a stream in order to escape Alpheus; but he, too, became a river and joined her (*Met.* 5.572–641).

98–99. he converts . . . I do not envy him: The line (separated in the translation, but a single line in the Italian) indicates the close identification of the portrayal of metamorphosis with the poet's linguistic power (cf. line 144 and see Additional Note 10).

100–135. two natures face to face . . . the smoke stops: Dante's order for the "exchange of matter" of the two thieves is related to the order of the transformation of Cadmus (rear legs, arms, hands, and tongue: *Met.* 4.576–89), mirroring Ovid's text as the thieves mirror each other. Dante's order is: rear legs, forelegs, hands, and penis; body hair, heads, and tongues (the stopping point; see the note to line 133). For details of Cadmus's transformation utilized in the canto, see the notes to lines 76–77, 86, 121, 123, and 133.

116. the member which a man hides: The penis (related to the figs of line 2), hidden in the rhetorical periphrasis. The hiding began with the use of fig-leaf aprons by Adam and Eve after the Fall (Gen. 3.7).

118. the smoke veils both: Compare the spewing of smoke by Cacus (see the note to line 24), allegorized as the concealment required by thieves (Fulgentius).

121. one stood up and the other fell down: The difference between erect and prone posture, or upward and downward gaze, often mentioned in these two cantos (see 24.54, 112, and 131; 25.15, 49, and 86), traditionally distinguishes human from animal; see *Met.* 1.84–86:

> pronaque cum spectent animalia cetera terram,
> os homini sublime dedit caelumque videre
> iussit et erectos ad sidera tollere vultus.

> [while other animals, prone, gaze on the earth,
> he (Prometheus) gave man a face erect, bade him see
> the heaven and lift his brow to the stars.]

122. their pitiless lanterns: See Matt. 6.22: "The light [*lucerna*] of thy body is thy eye." The reciprocal gazing here is another reference to the transformations of Cadmus and Harmonia (see line 97 and note), who must watch each other; it had been foretold that Cadmus would one day be seen as a snake ("et tu spectabere serpens," *Met.* 3.98). The pitiless gaze is related to the Medusa (see the notes to 32.130–31 and 33.55–57).

128. excess . . . a nose: Note the puns on Ovid's Latin names (Publius Ovidius Naso, the last name meaning "nose") here and at lines 45 and 97 (Sowell 1991); the name of one of Dante's chief models is repeatedly inscribed in the text.

133–35. tongue . . . is split . . . the smoke stops: Also the last act of Cadmus's transformation (*Met.* 4.586–87): "lingua repente/ in partes est fissa duas" [the tongue is suddenly split in two] (see 24.64–66 and note). The splitting of the instrument of rational speech is the end point of the third transformation. Benvenuto wisecracks that humans, not snakes, are truly "bilingual" (*bilinguis*)— that is, have lying tongues.

137. hissing . . . spits: One thief, now a serpent, hisses; the other spits clumsily with its new tongue, as if still trying to spew poison. Bestiary lore had it that human spittle was venomous to serpents, and spitting was used as an exorcistic gesture against the devil (see Boccaccio, *Decameron* 7.1.27–28).

140–41. I want Buoso to run, as I have, on all sixes: Dante's *carpone* normally means "on all fours." Buoso is variously identified by the early commentators; modern opinion inclines to see him as Buoso Donati, another member of this powerful family (see the note to line 43), a nephew of the one impersonated by Gianni Schicchi (30.40–45). L'Anonimo says that Buoso, having stolen while in office, induced the sinner speaking here, Francesco de' Cavalcanti (see the note to line 151), to steal in his place, perhaps explaining Francesco's thirst for vengeance (Momigliano in Mazzoni 1972); compare with the note to 24.99.

142. seventh cargo: The metaphor is based on the concavity of the *bolgia*, curved like a ship's hull, and the previous reference to the Libyan desert; in antiquity and the Middle Ages, sand and gravel were used as ballast for ships.

143. change and change again: In Italian, *mutare* [change] and *trasmutare* [transmute] capture the dominant note of the *bolgia* (see note to 24.1–21) and a fundamental condition of fallen humanity. After the conclusion of the previous canto (24.144) with a Florence that "makes new its laws and people," the presence here of five Florentines, three of them Black Guelfs and several from families who had converted to the Guelfs or to the Black faction, suggests that political transformation is thematized here as well.

144. if my pen ever falters: Slips of the pen are analogous, in scholastic discussions, to nature's failure to realize fully the forms imposed by the stars: "for although art acts for the sake of something, still it happens that in things made according to art mistakes are found; for sometimes the grammarian writes incorrectly" (Aquinas, *In Aristotelis Physicam* 2.14); see 24.6, the blunted "pen" of the writing of frost, and 24.100, with notes.

145. my eyes were somewhat confused: The pilgrim, gazing on so many transformations, is dazed, like the thieves themselves; for other instances in Malebolge of the pilgrim's fascination with what he sees, see 26.43–45 (implicit), 29.4–6, and 30.131–32.

148. Puccio Sciancato: This third thief (see line 35) is Puccio Galigai, called "the lame" (*sciancato*), roughly contemporaneous with the others; he had the reputation of committing "elegant" thefts and was notable for having changed parties from the Ghibellines to the Guelfs.

151. the one that makes you, Gaville, weep: The reference to Gaville iden-
tifies this thief, formerly the small serpent (line 83), as Francesco de' Cavalcanti,
known as *Guercio* [cross-eyed]. He was murdered by people from Gaville, near
Figline in the upper valley of the Arno; his death was savagely avenged by his
powerful family, making the town "weep."

CANTO 26

1   Godi, Fiorenza, poi che se' sì grande
che per mare e per terra batti l'ali,
e per lo 'nferno tuo nome si spande!

4   Tra li ladron trovai cinque cotali
tuoi cittadini onde mi ven vergogna,
e tu in grande orranza non ne sali.

7   Ma se presso al mattin del ver si sogna,
tu sentirai, di qua da picciol tempo,
di quel che Prato, non ch'altri, t'agogna;

10   e se già fosse, non saria per tempo.
Così foss' ei, da che pur esser dee!
ché più mi graverà, com' più m'attempo.

13   Noi ci partimmo, e su per le scalee
che n'avean fatto i borni a scender pria,
rimontò 'l duca mio e trasse mee;

16   e proseguendo la solinga via
tra le schegge e tra ' rocchi de lo scoglio,
lo piè sanza la man non si spedia.

19   Allor mi dolsi, e ora mi ridoglio
quando drizzo la mente a ciò ch'io vidi,
e più lo 'ngegno affreno ch'i' non soglio,

22   perché non corra che virtù nol guidi,
sì che, se stella bona o miglior cosa
m'ha dato 'l ben, ch'io stessi nol m'invidi.

25   Quante 'l villan ch'al poggio si riposa,
nel tempo che colui che 'l mondo schiara
la faccia sua a noi tien meno ascosa,

28   come la mosca cede a la zanzara
vede lucciole giù per la vallea,
forse colà dov' e' vendemmia e ara:

CANTO 26

Denunciation of Florence—eighth bolgia: *counselors of fraud—Ulysses and Diomedes—Ulysses' last voyage*

1
Rejoice, Florence, since you are so great that on sea and land you beat your wings, and your name spreads through Hell!

4
Among the thieves I found five such citizens of yours that I feel shame, and you do not rise to honor by them.

7
But if near morning one dreams the truth, you will feel, a short time from now, something of what Prato, not to speak of others, desires for you;

10
and if it had already come, it would not be early. Would it already were, since it must come! for it will weigh on me more, the older I grow.

13
We left, and up along the steps made for us earlier by the projecting bourns, my leader mounted, carrying me;

16
and as we pursued our solitary way among the splinters and rocks of the ridge, our feet could not proceed without our hands.

19
Then I grieved, and now I grieve again, when I consider what I saw, and I rein in my wit more than is my custom,

22
that it may not run without virtue guiding it, so that, if a good star or something better has given me what is good, I may not deprive myself of it.

25
As many fireflies as the peasant—resting on the hillside in the season when he who lights the world least hides from us his face,

28
when the fly gives way to the mosquito—sees down along the valley, perhaps where he harvests and plows:

31   di tante fiamme tutta risplendea
       l'ottava bolgia, sì com' io m'accorsi
       tosto che fui là 've 'l fondo parea.

34   E qual colui che si vengiò con li orsi
       vide 'l carro d'Elia al dipartire,
       quando i cavalli al cielo erti levorsi,

37   che nol potea sì con li occhi seguire
       ch'el vedesse altro che la fiamma sola,
       sì come nuvoletta, in sù salire:

40   tal si move ciascuna per la gola
       del fosso, ché nessuna mostra 'l furto,
       e ogne fiamma un peccatore invola.

43   Io stava sovra 'l ponte a veder surto,
       sì che s'io non avessi un ronchion preso,
       caduto sarei giù sanz' esser urto.

46   E 'l duca, che mi vide tanto atteso,
       disse: "Dentro dai fuochi son li spirti;
       catun si fascia di quel ch'elli è inceso."

49   "Maestro mio," rispuos' io, "per udirti
       son io più certo; ma già m'era avviso
       che così fosse, e già voleva dirti:

52   chi è 'n quel foco che vien sì diviso
       di sopra, che par surger de la pira
       dov' Eteòcle col fratel fu miso?"

55   Rispuose a me: "Là dentro si martira
       Ulisse e Dïomede, e così insieme
       a la vendetta vanno come a l'ira.

58   E dentro da la lor fiamma si geme
       l'agguato del caval che fé la porta
       onde uscì de' Romani il gentil seme;

61   piangevisi entro l'arte per che, morta,
       Deïdamìa ancor si duol d'Achille;
       e del Palladio pena vi si porta."

64   "S'ei posson dentro da quelle faville
       parlar," diss' io, "maestro, assai ten priego,
       e ripriego che 'l priego vaglia mille,

67   che non mi facci de l'attender niego
       fin che la fiamma cornuta qua vegna:
       vedi che del disio ver' lei mi piego!"

31   with so many flames the eighth pocket was all shining, as I perceived when I was where I could see its depths.

34   And as he who avenged himself with the bears saw Elijah's chariot departing, when the horses rose so steeply to Heaven

37   that he could not follow them with his eyes so as to see more than the flame alone, like a little cloud, rising up:

40   so each moves along the throat of the ditch, for none displays its theft, and every flame steals away a sinner.

43   I was standing erect on the bridge in order to see, so that if I had not grasped a projection, I would have fallen without being pushed.

46   And my leader, who saw me so intent, said: "Within the fires are the spirits; each is swathed in that which burns him inwardly."

49   "My master," I replied, "hearing you I am surer; but already it seemed to me that such was the case, and already I wanted to ask you:

52   who is in that fire that comes so divided above that it seems to be rising from the pyre where Eteocles was put with his brother?"

55   He answered me: "There within are punished Ulysses and Diomedes; thus together they go to punishment as they went to anger.

58   And within their flame they bemoan the deceit of the horse that made the gate to send forth the Romans' noble seed;

61   there within they weep for the art that makes Deidamia, though dead, still grieve for Achilles; and there they bear the punishment for the Palladium."

64   "If they can speak within those flames," I said, "master, much do I beg you, and beg again that each prayer may be worth a thousand,

67   that you not refuse to wait until the horned flame comes here: see that I bend toward it with desire!"

70   Ed elli a me: "La tua preghiera è degna
        di molta loda, e io però l'accetto;
        ma fa che la tua lingua si sostegna.

73   Lascia parlare a me, ch'i' ho concetto
        ciò che tu vuoi; ch'ei sarebbero schivi,
        perch' e' fuor greci, forse del tuo detto."

76   Poi che la fiamma fu venuta quivi
        dove parve al mio duca tempo e loco,
        in questa forma lui parlare audivi:

79   "O voi che siete due dentro ad un foco,
        s'io meritai di voi mentre ch'io vissi,
        s'io meritai di voi assai o poco,

82   quando nel mondo li alti versi scrissi,
        non vi movete; ma l'un di voi dica
        dove per lui perduto a morir gissi."

85   Lo maggior corno de la fiamma antica
        cominciò a crollarsi mormorando,
        pur come quella cui vento affatica;

88   indi la cima qua e là menando,
        come fosse la lingua che parlasse,
        gittò voce di fuori e disse: "Quando

91   mi diparti' da Circe, che sottrasse
        me più d'un anno là presso a Gaeta,
        prima che sì Enëa la nomasse,

94   né dolcezza di figlio, né la pieta
        del vecchio padre, né 'l debito amore
        lo qual dovea Penelopè far lieta,

97   vincer potero dentro a me l'ardore
        ch'i' ebbi a divenir del mondo esperto
        e de li vizi umani e del valore;

100   ma misi me per l'alto mare aperto
        sol con un legno e con quella compagna
        picciola da la qual non fui diserto.

103   L'un lito e l'altro vidi infin la Spagna,
        fin nel Morrocco, e l'isola d'i Sardi
        e l'altre che quel mare intorno bagna.

106   Io e ' compagni eravam vecchi e tardi
        quando venimmo a quella foce stretta
        dov' Ercule segnò li suoi riguardi

70 And he to me: "Your prayer is worthy of much praise, and therefore I grant it; but see that your tongue restrain itself.

73 Let me speak, for I have conceived what you wish; for perhaps they would shun, because they were Greeks, your words."

76 When the flame had come to where my leader thought it the time and place, in this form I heard him speak:

79 "O you who are two within one fire, if I deserved from you while I lived, if I deserved from you greatly or little

82 when in the world I wrote my high verses, do not move away; but let one of you tell where, lost, he went to die."

85 The greater horn of the ancient flame began to shake, murmuring, like one a wind belabors;

88 then, moving its peak here and there, as if it were a tongue that spoke, it cast out a voice and said: "When

91 I departed from Circe, who held me back more than a year there near Gaeta, before Aeneas gave it that name,

94 neither the sweetness of a son, nor compassion for my old father, nor the love owed to Penelope, which should have made her glad,

97 could conquer within me the ardor that I had to gain experience of the world and of human vices and worth;

100 but I put out on the deep, open sea alone, with one ship and with that little company by which I had not been deserted.

103 The one shore and the other I saw as far as Spain, as far as Morocco, and the island of the Sardinians and the others whose shores are bathed by that sea.

106 I and my companions were old and slow when we came to that narrow strait which Hercules marked with his warnings

109 acciò che l'uom più oltre non si metta;
da la man destra mi lasciai Sibilia,
da l'altra già m'avea lasciata Setta.

112 'O frati,' dissi, 'che per cento milia
perigli siete giunti a l'occidente,
a questa tanto picciola vigilia

115 d'i nostri sensi ch'è del rimanente
non vogliate negar l'esperïenza,
di retro al sol, del mondo sanza gente.

118 Considerate la vostra semenza:
fatti non foste a viver come bruti,
ma per seguir virtute e canoscenza.'

121 Li miei compagni fec' io sì aguti
con questa orazion picciola al cammino,
che a pena poscia li avrei ritenuti;

124 e volta nostra poppa nel mattino,
de' remi facemmo ali al folle volo,
sempre acquistando dal lato mancino.

127 Tutte le stelle già de l'altro polo
vedea la notte, e 'l nostro tanto basso
che non surgëa fuor del marin suolo.

130 Cinque volte racceso e tante casso
lo lume era di sotto da la luna,
poi che 'ntrati eravam ne l'alto passo,

133 quando n'apparve una montagna bruna
per la distanza, e parvemi alta tanto
quanto veduta non avëa alcuna.

136 Noi ci allegrammo, e tosto tornò in pianto,
ché de la nova terra un turbo nacque
e percosse del legno il primo canto.

139 Tre volte il fé girar con tutte l'acque,
a la quarta levar la poppa in suso
e la prora ire in giù, com' altrui piacque,

142 infin che 'l mar fu sovra noi richiuso."

109   so that one should not go further; on the right
       hand I had left Seville, on the other I had already left
       Ceuta.

112   'O brothers,' I said, 'who through a hundred
       thousand perils have reached the west, to this so
       brief vigil

115   of our senses that remains, do not deny the
       experience, following the sun, of the world without
       people.

118   Consider your sowing: you were not made to live
       like brutes, but to follow virtue and knowledge.'

121   My companions I made so sharp for the voyage,
       with this little oration, that after it I could hardly
       have held them back;

124   and, turning our stern toward the morning, of our
       oars we made wings for the mad flight, always
       gaining on the left side.

127   Already all the stars of the other pole I saw at
       night, and our own pole so low that it did not rise
       above the floor of the sea.

130   Five times renewed, and as many diminished, had
       been the light beneath the moon, since we had
       entered the deep pass,

133   when there appeared to us a mountain, dark in
       the distance, and it seemed to me higher than any I
       had seen.

136   We rejoiced, but it quickly turned to weeping; for
       from the new land a whirlwind was born and struck
       the forequarter of the ship.

139   Three times it made the ship to turn about with all
       the waters, at the fourth to raise its stern aloft and
       the prow to go down, as it pleased another,

142   until the sea had closed over us."

NOTES

1–3. Rejoice, Florence . . . through Hell: The text leaves it to the reader to infer the nature of the winged creature representing Florence in this bitter apostrophe. After the reptilian metamorphoses of the previous two cantos, it is natural to think of a reptile with wings: a dragon. The commentators note that an inscription in hexameters, dated 1255, still visible on the Florentine Palazzo del Bargello, describes Florence as "que mare, que terram, que totum possidet orbem" [who possesses the sea, the land, and the whole globe]; curiously, the phrase is a quotation from Lucan's *Pharsalia* 1.109, where it describes the self-destructiveness of Rome (it is quoted by Dante in *Monarchia* 2.8). The inscription continues: "per quem regnantem fit felix Tuscia tota" [through whose reign all Tuscany is made happy], to which Dante seems to allude sarcastically in line 9.

Mention of Italian cities is frequent in the Malebolge: Mantua (Canto 20), Prato (25.1–3), Venice (Canto 21), various cities of Romagna (Canto 27), and Arezzo (Canto 29); there are many denunciations: 18.58–63 (Bologna), 21.37–42 (Lucca), 25.10–15 (Pistoia), and 29.121–32 (Siena); beyond Malebolge: 33.79–90 (Pisa), 33.151–57 (Genoa), and *Purg.* 6.127–51 (Florence) (cf. Luke 10.13–15 for Jesus' denunciations of wicked cities.)

4. five such citizens of yours: Those identified in 25.43, 68, 140, 148, and 151.

7–12. But if near morning . . . the older I grow: The idea that early-morning dreams are prophetic is ancient; the commentators cite Ovid, *Heroides* 19.195–96: "namque sub auroram iam dormitante Lucina/ tempore quo cerni somnia vera solent" [for near the dawn, after the moon has set, in the time when true dreams are usually seen] (cf. *Purg.* 9.13–18 and 27.92–93). The disaster Dante predicts is not known (various possibilities have been suggested, but the text plainly states that when Dante was writing it had not yet taken place).

9. Prato: The reference is uncertain: it may be to the city of Prato, a few miles from Florence and traditionally under her control, or to Cardinal Niccolò di Prato, who excommunicated the city in 1304; we prefer the first alternative: even the traditionally most faithful subject city yearns to see Florence punished, for Tuscany is not happy.

13–15. We left . . . carrying me: In 24.79–80, the pilgrim and Virgil descended from the bridge to the bank.

19–24. Then I grieved . . . deprive myself of it: These lines, explicitly connecting grief in the moment of writing with the grief experienced in the journey (clearly penitential in nature in this instance), would seem to indicate a special relation of the poet to the sin even before it has been identified; the metaphor of spatial motion in line 22 already implicitly involves Ulysses' last voyage, which must have something to do with *unrestrained* wit.

21. rein in my wit: For the meaning of "wit" (*ingegno*), see the note to 2.7–8; note the horse metaphor.

23. if a good star or something better: The influence of the stars in Dante's nativity, to which *Par.* 22.112–14 attribute "all my wit . . . , whatever it may be" (see notes there); "or something better" refers to God's grace.

24. what is good: This phrase (Italian, *'l bene*, literally, the good) cannot refer to salvation, since salvation is never owed to the stars; it must refer to the faculty of wit itself, which may be the gift either of nature or, in certain circumstances, of grace.

25–33. As many fireflies . . . depths were revealed: The vivid simile of the fireflies, implicitly contrasting the peaceful natural scene of dusk in summer with the intense suffering of the *bolgia*, creates a sense of distance between the hillside and the valley, reducing the sinners' flames to minute proportions. Canto 24 began with an extended winter scene, also involving a peasant.

26. when he who lights the world . . . his face: When the sun is most visible, in the summertime; the first of many references to the sun in this canto.

34–39. And as he who avenged . . . rising up: A complex reference to the account of Elijah (Elias) and Elishah (Eliseus) in 2 Kings [Vulgate 4 Kings] 2.7–14:

> . . . but they two stood by the Jordan. And Elias took his mantle and folded it together, and struck the waters, and they were divided hither and thither, and they both passed over on dry ground. And when they were gone over, Elias said to Eliseus: Ask what thou wilt have me to do for thee, before I be taken away from thee. And Eliseus said: I beseech thee that in me may be thy double spirit. And he answered: Thou hast asked a hard thing: nevertheless if thou see me when I am taken from thee, thou shalt have what thou hast asked: but if thou see me not, thou shalt not have it. And as they went on, walking and talking together, behold a fiery chariot, and fiery horses parted them both asunder: and Elias went up by a whirlwind into heaven. And Eliseus saw him, and cried: My father, my father, the chariot of Israel and the driver thereof. And he saw him no more. . . . And he took up the mantle of Elias, that fell from him. . . .

The episode of the bears is related in the same chapter, verses 23–24:

> . . . as he was going up by the way, little boys came out of the city and mocked him, saying: Go up, thou bald head; go up, thou bald head. And looking back, he saw them, and he cursed them in the name of the Lord: and there came forth two bears out of the forest, and tore of them two and forty boys.

Note the motifs important in our canto: fire, whirlwind, horses/vehicle, the crossing of a body of water, and the question of seeing Elijah in the flames (cf. Eccles. 48.1: "Elias the prophet stood up as fire, and his word burned like a torch"). Implicit in Dante's comparison is the relevance to the context of the theme of prophecy, including that of the inheritance of the prophet's mantle (see Mazzotta 1979). Eliseus/Elishah (Eliseo) was the name of the brother of Dante's great-great-grandfather (*Par.* 15.136, another context involving Dante's prophetic mission).

40–42. so each . . . a sinner: The basis of the comparison is Elijah's being hidden by the flames. The metaphor of theft is discussed, in connection with line 48; it recurs in 27.127.

43–45. I was standing . . . grasped . . . without being pushed: These lines are often interpreted as being parallel to lines 21–24 (since "reining in" and "grasping" involve the hands), and thus as further emphasis on Dante's sense of being drawn to this sin.

48. each is swathed . . . burns him inwardly: In other words, the flame that hides each sinner is the externalization of the fire within him: the fire of intellect, of the malice that motivated his counsels, and of the power of his rhetoric (called by Alain of Lille, in his *Anticlaudianus,* "ignis in ore" [fire in the mouth]). The Italian *inceso* [fired within] (cf. 22.18) is, like *invola* [steals away], line 42, compounded with the preposition "in"; it is derived from Latin *incensus*, used repeatedly by Vergil to describe the burning of Troy (*Aen.* 2.327, 353, 374, 555, and 764; cf. *ardeo, ardere,* used of warriors: *Aen.* 2.316, 475, 529, and 575).

52–54. who is in that fire . . . with his brother: In Statius's *Thebaid,* Oedipus's sons, Eteocles and Polynices, kill each other at the main gate of the city; their mutual hatred divides the fire of their funeral pyre. The clear implication is that Ulysses and Diomedes now hate each other also. Dante introduced the Theban material in Canto 14, with the figure of Capaneus (lines 46–72); explicit references to it (as well as to the saga of Troy) become increasingly frequent in Malebolge and Cocytus: 20.31–45 (Amphiaraus, Tiresias) and 52–93 (Manto), 25.97–99 (Cadmus and Harmonia), 30.1–12 (Athamas), 32.10–12 (Amphion), and 130–32 (Tydeus and Menalippus). In Dante's adaptation of Augustine's paradigm of the City of God versus the Earthly City, Thebes and its modern *figura,* Florence, have replaced Rome as exemplars of the strife-ridden

Earthly City (for the foundation of Rome as the preparation of the Incarnation and the papacy, see 2.13–33).

55–56. There within are punished Ulysses and Diomedes: Ulysses is the only major Homeric figure who speaks in the *Comedy;* Dante's representation of him is an important focus of his effort to surpass the *Aeneid.*

56–57. together they go . . . to anger: In other words, being paired intensifies their punishment, just as they fired each other when they were sinning, and so incurred God's anger.

58–63. And within their flame . . . Palladium: Dante has Virgil ascribe three principal sinful acts to Ulysses and Diomedes (discussed in the note to lines 58–60); he clearly considers that Ulysses was their principal inventor, as in *Met.* 13.350–81. The first and third are based on the *Aeneid,* the second on Ovid and on Statius's *Achilleid.* Note the insistently parallel syntax of the three independent clauses, each assigned to one sin, each emphasizing the internal nature of the suffering.

58–60. And within their flame . . . noble seed: According to *Aeneid* 2, in the tenth year of the Trojan War, the Greeks pretend to sail home; they leave behind the Trojan Horse and Sinon. Sinon pretends to have been marked for sacrifice (a repetition of the events at Aulis; see the note to 20.110–11) by the hostility of Ulysses, but to have escaped; gaining the Trojans' confidence, and with many oaths to his veracity, he explains (falsely) that the theft of the Palladium (see the note to line 63) had displeased Athena, the horse being an offering to placate her. He also claims that Calchas has prophesied that if the horse is taken into Troy, Troy will bring war to Greece. The Trojans enlarge the gates vertically to admit the horse, filled with Greek soldiers, including Ulysses (medieval tradition, unlike Vergil, placed Diomedes in the horse also). Released by Sinon, Ulysses and the others open the gates to admit the rest of the Greeks. Vergil's account describes the destruction of Troy in terms of the gradual, snakelike spread of fire (see Knox 1950). In addition, the hollow horse is repeatedly described as a pregnant belly (*Aen.* 2.38, 51, 238, and 243): a fair exterior, represented as a religious offering, but pregnant with destruction. See Additional Note 13.

In Vergil's account, as in Dante's, the destruction of Troy is, of course, necessary for the founding of the new Troy, Rome, by the descendants of Aeneas (the noble seed of the Romans, line 60). The Romans eventually do take war to Greece, which they subjugate. Thus this clause, hinging on the "gate" (*porta*) that leads both into the city and out of it, shows the ultimate futility of Ulysses' and Diomedes' sin, from which God's Providence will bring forth good.

61–62. there within . . . grieve for Achilles: In Statius's version of the Achilles story (*Achilleid* 1), Achilles' mother, the sea nymph Thetis, knows of the prophecy that Achilles will die at Troy; she persuades the beardless boy to dress as a girl and hide among the daughters of King Lycomedes of the island of Scyros;

Achilles agrees because he has seen the king's daughter Deidamia, whom he soon impregnates. Calchas has seen in a trance that Achilles, necessary for the conquest of Troy, is on Scyros, and Ulysses and Diomedes go to recruit him. Posing as merchants and pretending to be spying on the Trojans, they are entertained by the king; they soon single Achilles out: their task is to persuade him to drop his own pretense (still motivated by love for Deidamia). At dinner, Ulysses' glowing account of the glories of the war visibly affects Achilles, and the next day, among many harmless gifts for the young women, Ulysses includes a spear and shield; as Achilles greedily handles them, Ulysses has a trumpet sounded; Achilles' true nature blazes forth: he burns with desire for war. Deidamia's pregnancy and the birth of Neoptolemus have so far been concealed; now the baby is brought forth, the king accepts Achilles, the wedding is celebrated, and the next morning Achilles sails off with Ulysses and Diomedes, never to see Deidamia again (*Purg.* 22.114 places her in Limbo). Ulysses' art makes Deidamia grieve, clearly, because it led to her husband's death.

Dante accurately saw that Statius, following suggestions by Ovid in *Met.* 13.162–70, established a parallel between this stratagem of Ulysses' and the Trojan Horse, involving the penetration of defenses and the bringing forth of fire from where it is hidden. Both Vergil and Ovid represent Ulysses, even more than Achilles, as the principal cause of the fall of Troy. In *Met.* 13.123–380, Ovid has Ulysses claim (rightly) that at every turning point in the war his counsel led to success; though he was only one man, he was the Greeks' steering oar (see the note to lines 85–90).

63. and there . . . Palladium: According to the *Aeneid* and the *Metamorphoses,* Ulysses and Diomedes entered Troy at night and by stealth, penetrating as far as the highest citadel, from which, after killing the guards, they carried off the statue of Pallas Athena (goddess of wisdom) on whose possession the safety of Troy was supposed to depend. According to Sinon's (lying) account in *Aeneid* 2, this act caused Athena to turn against the Greeks; he reports that when the statue was set up in the Greek camp, its eyes emitted flames and it brandished its spear and shield three times, and that from then on the Greeks' fortunes declined. Thompson (1972) suggests that Dante follows the later account according to which Ulysses and Diomedes did not steal the Palladium themselves but counseled the traitor Antenor to do so. In either case, this third sin also involves the motif of the emergence of hidden fire, as well as the use of stealth; Virgil's phrasing here is sufficiently general for the line to refer to Sinon's deceptive account of the Palladium as well as to the theft itself.

64–69. If they can speak . . . with desire: The next lines suggest that Virgil sees in the pilgrim's words only the laudable desire to hear a great Homeric figure speak. However, one should note the parallel between the pilgrim's *bending toward* the flame *with desire* and his earlier need to prevent himself from falling.

73–75. Let me speak . . . your words: The usual explanation for Virgil's idea that Ulysses and Diomedes would be repelled by Dante's speech is the traditional attribution of arrogance (including linguistic) to the Greeks. But it is always Virgil who addresses figures from classical antiquity, not the pilgrim; here there is a sharp focus on Virgil's special relation to Ulysses and Diomedes as the poet of the *Aeneid,* thus the mediator of Dante's knowledge. (Vergil's treatment of Ulysses and Diomedes in the *Aeneid* is entirely negative.)

80. if I deserved: An echo of Dido's words to Aeneas in *Aen.* 4.317–18: "si bene quid de te merui, fuit aut tibi quicquam/ dulce meum" [if I have deserved at all well of you, or anything of mine has ever been sweet to you].

84. let one of you . . . to die: Since Diomedes was supposed to have migrated to Italy and to have died there, this can only refer to Ulysses; *perduto* [lost] can refer to the fact that Ulysses' fate had been unknown, as well as to his having lost his way or being damned (cf. the fact that Elijah's body is not found: 2 Kings [Vulgate 4 Kings] 2.15–17).

85–90. The greater horn . . . cast out a voice: The emphasis on Ulysses' struggle to impart to the flame the articulatory motions of a tongue (closely related to Pier delle Vigne's struggle to speak, 13.91–92—including the references to wind) becomes even greater in the case of Guido da Montefeltro (27.7–18); note the insistent sound effects involving *m: maggior, mormorando;* see *Met.* 14.280–81 (of Circe's transformation of Ulysses' men): "nec iam posse loqui, pro verbis edere raucum/ murmur" [already I could no longer speak, but instead of words I produce a hoarse murmur]. The idea of the tongue as a flame is fundamental to the whole episode; a number of commentators have pointed to James 3.3–6:

> For we put bits into the mouths of horses, that they may obey us, and we turn about their whole body. Behold also ships, whereas they are great, and are driven by strong winds, yet are they turned about with a small helm, whithersoever the force of the governor willeth. Even so the tongue is indeed a little member, and boasteth great things. Behold how small a fire kindleth a great wood. And the tongue is a fire. . . .

All four major motifs of the canto appear in this passage: tongue, fire, horse, and ship. For the connection of flame and wind with Pentecost, see Mazzotta 1979.

90–142. When I departed . . . closed over us: Ulysses' last voyage is discussed in Additional Note 11.

90–93. When I departed . . . that name: Dante knew Ovid's account of Ulysses' stay with Circe, put in the mouth of a former follower, Macareus (*Met.* 14.233–440); line 308 states: "annua nos illic tenuit mora" [a yearlong stay held us there]. According to both Vergil and Ovid, Aeneas repeats several parts of Ulysses' voyage: he encounters the Cyclops, nears Scylla and Charybdis, and sails near Circe's dwelling, near both Cumae (where Aeneas is taken by the Sybil to the underworld) and the promontory of Gaeta, named by him for his nurse, who died there. The mention of Aeneas here calls attention to the parallel/contrast between his voyage and Ulysses'.

97. ardor: Italian *ardore* [literally, burning]. This is an important instance of the fire imagery that dominates the canto, and a major interpretive issue is whether it is to be seen as the same fire that now envelops him and has its origin within him.

98–99. to gain . . . vices and worth: Dante is adapting Horace's quotation of the beginning of the *Odyssey* (*Ars poetica* 141–42): "virum . . ./ qui mores hominum multorum vidit et urbes" [the man . . . who saw the customs of many men, and their cities]. Compare also *Epistles* 1.2.17–22.

101–2. but I put out . . . deserted: Macareus's account states that when he arrived at Circe's dwelling Ulysses had lost almost all his men and all but one ship (a principal element of the contrast between Aeneas and Ulysses established by Vergil is that Aeneas is accompanied by his entire fleet and most of his followers).

103–5. The one shore . . . by that sea: In other words, he saw all of the northern and all of the southern shore of the Mediterranean; the implication is that he circumnavigated the entire Mediterranean. No cities are mentioned (though cf. lines 110–11), nor any "human vices and worth."

107–9. that narrow strait . . . not go further: The Straits of Gibraltar. The tradition that Hercules set pillars there (the two opposing mountains) is ancient, as is the tradition that they were a prohibition, which appears, for instance, in Pindar's Fourth Nemean Ode (Kay 1980; Boitani 1992). See Additional Note 11.

110–11. on the right . . . Ceuta: Seville is on the south shore of Spain, just east of Gibraltar; Ceuta is at the tip of the African promontory opposite Gibraltar. The passage derives from Ovid's description of Daedalus's and Icarus's flight (*Met.* 8.220–25):

> . . . et iam Iunonia laeva
> parte Samos—fuerant Delosque Parosque relictae—
> dextra Lebinthos erat fecundaque melle Calymne:
> cum puer audaci coepit gaudere volatu
> deseruitque ducem caelique cupidine tractus
> altius egit iter. . . .

> [. . . and already on the left
> hand was Juno's Samos—they had left Delos and Paros behind—
> and on the right Lebynthos and Calymne rich with honey:
> when the boy began to delight in the audacious flight
> and abandoned his guide and, drawn by greed for the sky,
> flew higher. . . .]

Audaci . . . volatu [in audacious flight] lies behind Dante's *folle volo* (line 125).

112–20. O brothers . . . virtue and knowledge: Ulysses' "little oration" is clearly crucial to Dante's conception, but critics are sharply divided between those who accept Ulysses' characterization of the voyage—that it is a pursuit of the noble goals of virtue and knowledge (here critics divide further into those who applaud the pursuit and those who identify Ulysses' quite generic terms with some particular philosophical school or position Dante is rejecting: variously Neoplatonism, "humanism," and radical Aristotelianism)—and those who regard it as fraudulent, arguing that no wisdom, no knowledge of men is to be had in the "world without people," citing Seneca's *Epistle* 88, in terms of which Dante's Ulysses would have to be seen as abandoning his duties. One may reflect that Ulysses travels only on the surface of the globe, while the pilgrim goes through the center, always in contact with human souls.

113. the west: Dante's term is *l'occidente*, still close to its Latin meaning, "setting of the sun."

117. following the sun: Toward its setting.

118. Consider your sowing: That is, your descent as human beings; compare "the Romans' noble seed" (line 60).

121. sharp: There is a strong suggestion of fire imagery here; in the wake of Plato's *Timaeus* 56, fire was often identified as sharp (hence its destructiveness).

124. turning our stern toward the morning: Since the ship must be turned, its direction has not been determined until this point: they could have turned east rather than west. Iconographically, of course, the east is the direction from which illumination comes.

125. of our oars . . . flight: Many commentators have noticed the parallel of the phrase *folle volo* [mad flight] with the pilgrim's fear of a *venuta . . . folle* [mad journey] in 2.35 (also with *Par.* 27.82–83: "il varco folle d'Ulisse" [the mad path of Ulysses]). Dante is adapting a line of Vergil's describing Daedalus's flight from Crete to Italy (*Aen.* 6.18–19): "sacravit/ remigium alarum" [he consecrated the oars of his wings]. Modern scholars (Freccero 1966a; Shankland 1977) connect the reference to wings (and the reference to Daedalus) with Neoplatonic allegories of the ascent of the soul. Shankland discusses Dante's conception of the significance of his family name, Alager [wing-bearer], as one of the reasons for the importance of the Ulysses antitype.

126. always gaining on the left side: Why this should be the case is not explained, but in medieval symbolic terms it is a very bad sign, no doubt to be connected with the pilgrim's dragging left foot (1.30) and the fact that Virgil and the pilgrim usually turn to the left in Hell, to the right in Purgatory. Of course, a southwest course is necessary if Ulysses and his men are to approach the only island Dante places in the hemisphere of water, at the antipodes of Jerusalem.

127–29. All the stars . . . floor of the sea: They have passed the equator.

130–32. Five times . . . deep pass: Five months have elapsed. Commentators have pointed out that there are no references to the light of the sun after line 124, as if the voyage were taking place entirely at night.

132. the deep pass: Dante has associated the term *pass* with damnation since the beginning of the poem ("the pass that has never yet left anyone alive," 1.26–27, would seem to be the one where Ulysses perishes; cf. 5.114); the phrase *l'alto passo* [the deep pass] occurs verbatim in 2.12, referring to the pilgrim's journey to the other world.

133–35. a mountain . . . I had seen: This is, as we learn in the *Purgatorio*, the mountain at whose summit is the Garden of Eden, forbidden to man (Gen. 3.24); it also recalls the mountain of Canto 1.

136. We rejoiced . . . weeping: The line echoes James 4.9.

138. the forequarter of the ship: The Italian, "del legno il primo canto," puns on *canto;* in the first canto of the poem the pilgrim was metaphorically shipwrecked, too.

140–41. stern aloft . . . prow . . . down: Note the progression from line 124.

141. another: God.

142. until the sea had closed over us: Lines 58–60, on the Trojan Horse, draw a parallel between its penetration of the gate of Troy and the escape of Aeneas and his followers; they also establish a parallel between the Trojan Horse and Aeneas's ship: one moves inward, the other outward; one carries the seeds of destruction, the other the seeds of Rome; as Clausen (1987) points out, several of Vergil's terms for the horse are borrowed from shipbuilding. This parallel mediates a further one, fundamental to the canto, between the Trojan Horse and Ulysses' ship: both carry Greeks; both carry Ulysses and his fiery speech; one moves inward, the other outward; and both cause death.

In the sins listed in lines 58–63, Ulysses' characteristic activity has been that of imparting the fire within himself to others, for the sake of the destruction of Troy (cf. James 3.5: "Behold how small a flame sets fire to a great forest"). Ulysses' going out through the Pillars—the gate—of Hercules, to him a violent act, be-cause forbidden, is a kind of inversion of the violent entrance of the Trojan Horse into Troy, and also, in its results, a negative parallel to Aeneas's passage out the gate of Troy. Thus when the waters close around Ulysses there is a kind of im-plosion: the fire that he has loosed upon the world returns upon him, first in the form of water, then in the fire of the Malebolge. This is perhaps Dante's most elaborate version of the idea that the devices of the fraudulent are the snares that catch and punish them.

CANTO 27

1   Già era dritta in sù la fiamma e queta
        per non dir più, e già da noi sen gia
        con la licenza del dolce poeta,

4   quand' un'altra, che dietro a lei venìa,
        ne fece volger li occhi a la sua cima
        per un confuso suon che fuor n'uscia.

7   Come 'l bue cicilian, che mugghiò prima
        col pianto di colui—e ciò fu dritto—
        che l'avea temperato con sua lima,

10   mugghiava con la voce de l'afflitto,
        sì che, con tutto che fosse di rame,
        pur el pareva del dolor trafitto:

13   così, per non aver via né forame
        dal principio nel foco, in suo linguaggio
        si convertïan le parole grame.

16   Ma poscia ch'ebber colto lor vïaggio
        su per la punta, dandole quel guizzo
        che dato avea la lingua in lor passaggio,

19   udimmo dire: "O tu a cu' io drizzo
        la voce e che parlavi mo lombardo,
        dicendo: 'Istra ten va, più non t'adizzo,'

22   perch' io sia giunto forse alquanto tardo,
        non t'incresca restare a parlar meco;
        vedi che non incresce a me, e ardo!

25   Se tu pur mo in questo mondo cieco
        caduto se' di quella dolce terra
        latina ond' io mia colpa tutta reco,

28   dimmi se Romagnuoli han pace o guerra;
        ch'io fui d'i monti là intra Orbino
        e 'l giogo di che Tever si diserra."

CANTO 27

Eighth bolgia, *continued: Guido da Montefeltro, converted, but tricked*
by Pope Boniface VIII—dispute of Saint Francis and the black cherub

1   Already the flame was erect and quiet, no longer
speaking, and already it had left us with the
permission of my sweet poet,

4   when another, coming after it, made us turn our
eyes to its peak because of a confused sound coming
out from it.

7   As the Sicilian bull, which first bellowed with the
cries of him—and that was right—who had
tempered it with his file,

10   used to bellow with the voice of the afflicted one,
so that, though made of brass, still it seemed
transfixed with pain:

13   so, not having any path or outlet from its origin
within the fire, the anguished words were converted
into its language.

16   But after they had found their way up to the tip,
imparting to it that wriggling which the tongue had
given them in their passage,

19   we heard it say: "O you to whom I direct my
voice and who were just now speaking Lombard,
saying: '*Istra* you may go, I incite you no further,'

22   though I have arrived perhaps somewhat late, let
it not grieve you to stay and speak with me; you
see it does not grieve me, and I am burning!

25   If you just now fell into this blind world from that
sweet Italian earth whence I bring all my guilt,

28   tell me if the people of Romagna have peace or
war; for I was from the mountains there between
Urbino and the ridge whence Tiber is unleashed."

31   Io era in giuso ancora attento e chino,
quando il mio duca mi tentò di costa,
dicendo: "Parla tu: questi è latino."

34   E io, ch'avea già pronta la risposta,
sanza indugio a parlare incominciai:
"O anima che se' là giù nascosta,

37   Romagna tua non è, e non fu mai,
sanza guerra ne' cuor de' suoi tiranni;
ma 'n palese nessuna or vi lasciai.

40   Ravenna sta come stata è molt'anni:
l'aguglia da Polenta la si cova,
sì che Cervia ricuopre co' suoi vanni.

43   La terra che fé già la lunga prova
e di Franceschi sanguinoso mucchio,
sotto le branche verdi si ritrova.

46   E 'l mastin vecchio e 'l nuovo da Verrucchio,
che fecer di Montagna il mal governo,
là dove soglion fan d'i denti succhio.

49   Le città di Lamone e di Santerno
conduce il lïoncel dal nido bianco,
che muta parte da la state al verno.

52   E quella cu' il Savio bagna il fianco,
così com' ella sie' tra 'l piano e 'l monte,
tra tirannia si vive e stato franco.

55   Ora chi se', ti priego che ne conte:
non esser duro più ch'altri sia stato,
se 'l nome tuo nel mondo tegna fronte."

58   Poscia che 'l foco alquanto ebbe rugghiato
al modo suo, l'aguta punta mosse
di qua, di là, e poi diè cotal fiato:

61   "S'i' credesse che mia risposta fosse
a persona che mai tornasse al mondo,
questa fiamma staria sanza più scosse;

64   ma però che già mai di questo fondo
non tornò vivo alcun, s'i' odo il vero,
sanza tema d'infamia ti rispondo.

67   Io fui uom d'arme, e poi fui cordigliero,
credendomi, sì cinto, fare ammenda;
e certo il creder mio venìa intero,

31   I was still bent over intent upon him when my leader prodded my side, saying, "You speak: this one is Italian."

34   And I, having my reply already prepared, without delay began to speak: "O soul hidden down there,

37   your Romagna is not, and never was, without war in the hearts of its tyrants; but no open war did I leave there now.

40   Ravenna is as it has been for many years: the eagle of Polenta broods over it, covering Cervia with its pinions.

43   The city that underwent the long trial and made a bloody heap of the French, now finds itself beneath the green claws.

46   The old and young mastiffs of Verrucchio, who guarded Montagna ill, as they are accustomed, make drills of their teeth.

49   The cities of Lamone and Santerno are led by the lion cub in the white nest, who changes alliances between summer and winter.

52   And the city whose flank the Savio bathes, just as it lies between the plain and the mountain, so lives between tyranny and liberty.

55   Now who you are I beg you to tell us: do not be harder than others have been to you, so may your name hold up its brow in the world."

58   After the flame had roared a bit in its manner, it moved its sharp tongue here and there, and then gave forth this breath:

61   "If I believed that my reply were to a person who would ever return to the world, this flame would remain without further shaking;

64   but since never from this depth has any one returned alive, if I hear the truth, without fear of infamy I answer you.

67   I was a man of arms, and then I was a Franciscan, believing, so girt, to make amends; and surely my belief would have been fulfilled,

70   se non fosse il gran prete, a cui mal prenda!
        che mi rimise ne le prime colpe;
        e come e *qua re*, voglio che m'intenda.

73   Mentre ch'io forma fui d'ossa e di polpe
        che la madre mi diè, l'opere mie
        non furon leonine, ma di volpe.

76   Li accorgimenti e le coperte vie
        io seppi tutte, e sì menai lor arte
        ch'al fine de la terra il suono uscìe.

79   Quando mi vidi giunto in quella parte
        di mia etade ove ciascun dovrebbe
        calar le vele e raccoglier le sarte,

82   ciò che pria mi piacëa allor m'increbbe,
        e pentuto e confesso mi rendei;
        ahi miser lasso! e giovato sarebbe.

85   Lo principe d'i novi Farisei,
        avendo guerra presso a Laterano,
        e non con Saracin né con Giudei—

88   ché ciascun suo nimico era cristiano,
        e nessun era stato a vincer Acri
        né mercatante in terra di Soldano—,

91   né sommo officio né ordini sacri
        guardò in sé, né in me quel capestro
        che solea fare i suoi cinti più macri.

94   Ma, come Costantin chiese Silvestro
        d'entro Siratti a guerir de la lebbre,
        così mi chiese questi per maestro

97   a guerir de la sua superba febbre;
        domandommi consiglio, e io tacetti,
        perché le sue parole parver ebbre.

100   E' poi ridisse: 'Tuo cuor non sospetti:
        finor t'assolvo, e tu m'insegna fare
        sì come Penestrino in terra getti.

103   Lo ciel poss' io serrare e diserrare,
        come tu sai; però son due le chiavi
        che 'l mio antecessor non ebbe care.'

106   Allor mi pinser li argomenti gravi
        là 've 'l tacer mi fu avviso 'l peggio,
        e dissi: 'Padre, da che tu mi lavi

70   had it not been for the high priest, may evil take
him! who put me back into my first sins; and how
and *qua re*, I wish you to hear from me.

73   While I was the form of bone and flesh that my
mother gave me, my works were not those of a lion
but a fox.

76   The tricks and the hidden ways, I knew them all,
and I so plied their art that the fame of it went out
to the ends of the earth.

79   When I saw I had reached that part of my life
where every man should lower the sails and coil the ropes,

82   what earlier pleased me, then grieved me, and I
gave myself up repentant and shriven; ah,
miserable wretch that I am! and it would have worked.

85   The prince of the new Pharisees, making war near
the Lateran, and not against Saracens or Jews—

88   for each of his enemies was a Christian, and none
had been to take Acre nor a merchant in the Sultan's
lands—,

91   regarded neither his highest office nor holy orders in
himself, nor in me the rope that used to make its
wearers thinner.

94   But, as Constantine asked Sylvester in Soracte to
cure him of leprosy, so he asked me to teach him

97   to recover from his proud fever; he asked my
advice, and I was silent, for his words seemed
drunken.

100   Then he said again: 'Let not your heart fear:
henceforth I absolve you, if you teach me how to
raze Palestrina to the ground.

103   Heaven I can lock and unlock, as you know; for
that reason the keys are two which my predecessor
did not prize.'

106   Then his weighty arguments impelled me, for
silence seemed to me the worse course, and I said:
'Father, since you wash me

109   di quel peccato ov' io mo cader deggio,
lunga promessa con l'attender corto
ti farà trïunfar ne l'alto seggio.'

112   Francesco venne poi, com' io fu' morto,
per me; ma un d'i neri cherubini
li disse: 'Non portar, non mi far torto.

115   Venir se ne dee giù tra ' miei meschini,
perché diede 'l consiglio frodolente,
dal quale in qua stato li sono a' crini;

118   ch'assolver non si può chi non si pente,
né pentere e volere insieme puossi,
per la contradizion, che nol consente.'

121   Oh me dolente! come mi riscossi
quando mi prese, dicendomi: 'Forse
tu non pensavi ch'io löico fossi!'

124   A Minòs mi portò; e quelli attorse
otto volte la coda al dosso duro,
e poi che per gran rabbia la si morse,

127   disse: 'Questi è d'i rei del foco furo.'
Per ch'io là dove vedi son perduto,
e sì vestito, andando, mi rancuro."

130   Quand' elli ebbe 'l suo dir così compiuto,
la fiamma dolorando si partio,
torcendo e dibattendo 'l corno aguto.

133   Noi passamm' oltre, e io e 'l duca mio,
su per lo scoglio infino in su l'altr' arco,
che cuopre 'l fosso in che si paga il fio

136   a quei che scommettendo acquistan carco.

109   of that sin into which I now must fall, a long
promise with a short keeping will make you triumph
on your high throne.'

112   Francis came later, when I had died, for me; but
one of the black cherubim told him: 'Do not take him,
do not wrong me.

115   He must come down among my slaves, because
he gave the fraudulent counsel, since when, until
now, I have been at his locks;

118   for he cannot be absolved who does not repent,
nor can one repent and will together, because of the
contradiction, which does not permit it.'

121   Oh wretched me! how I trembled when he seized
me, telling me: 'Perhaps you did not think I was a
logician!'

124   He carried me to Minos; and that one twisted his
tail eight times about his hard back, and after he had
bitten it in his great rage,

127   he said: 'This is one who deserves the thieving
fire'; so that I am lost here where you see me, and
thus clothed I go tormenting myself."

130   When it had finished speaking thus, the grieving
flame departed, twisting and beating about with its
sharp horn.

133   We passed further, both I and my leader, up along
the ridge as far as the next arch, which covers the
ditch where the toll is collected

136   from those who gain cargo by putting apart.

NOTES

3. with the permission of my sweet poet: Indicating Virgil's control of Ulysses (see 26.73–75, with note); now Virgil's speech is the point of contact with the next soul to address the pilgrim.

5. made us turn our eyes to its peak: Dante again focuses attention on the point of the flame (cf. 26.68 and lines 17, 59, and 132). The idea of the tongue as goad, as in Ulysses' use of it, is implicit (see lines 61–62 and 132).

7–15. As the Sicilian bull . . . into its language: Dante found in various sources (Ovid's *Art of Love* 1.655–56; Orosius's *Seven Books against the Pagans* 1.20. 1–4) the account of how the sculptor Perillus made for Phalaris, tyrant of Syracuse, a brazen bull designed to roast criminals to death, muffling their screams so that they sounded like the bellowing of a bull; Phalaris tested the bull on Perillus himself. The explicit relevance of the simile is to correlate the soul within the flame with the victim within the bull, thus explaining the "confused sound"; but the soul within must be its fashioner: this is the same pattern pointed out in the note to 26.142, by which Ulysses' and Diomedes' devices return upon them, clear instances of "the trickster tricked." The bull is also a work of art that maliciously deceives, closely related to the "false cow" constructed by Daedalus for Pasiphaë (see 12.12–13, and *Purg.* 26.41–42) and the Trojan Horse (see Additional Note 13).

8. and that was right: See Ovid, *Art of Love* 1.655–56: "Iustus uterque fuit: neque enim lex aequior ulla est,/ quam necis artifices arte perire sua" [Both were just: nor is any law more just than for the artificers of death to perish by their own art].

9. tempered it with his file: As commentators point out, a bronze statue was sometimes filed smooth; since Horace's *Ars poetica* (line 291), the "labor of the file" (*limae labor*) has been proverbial for the labor whereby the poet polishes his verses.

10. used to bellow: Dante's verb is *mugghiare*, used also in 5.29, of the whirlwind. Reference to confusion continues the motif of Hell as Babel (see 31.78) and is relevant to the emphasis on discourse in this canto. See also lines 58 and 132 and note.

13–18. not having any path . . . in their passage: This soul finds it even more difficult to speak from within the flame than Ulysses (see 26.85–90, with note); at first all that is heard is the fire ("its language"). Eventually the "tip" of the flame acquires the motion of the tip of the tongue.

20–21. just now speaking Lombard, saying 'Istra . . .: *Istra,* here identified as Lombard, is the equivalent of *issa,* identified in 23.7 as identical in meaning with *mo,* an important word in this canto (both mean "now"); Virgil was identified by his speech as a Lombard in 22.99 also. The possibility of different "containers" having identical contents is to be correlated with that of identical containers having different contents (the condition which makes fraud possible). See Additional Note 13.

22. somewhat late: *Tardo* [late] is the same term Ulysses the character uses of himself and his companions to mean "slow" (26.106).

27. whence I bring all my guilt: Connecting the speaker with his native land prepares the correlation in lines 40–55 of his biography with the geography of Romagna.

28–30. tell me . . . unleashed: The speaker's birthplace (along with his description of his career, line 78) identifies him as Guido da Montefeltro, the most successful mercenary captain of his day; he maintained the Ghibelline hegemony in Romagna during a period when the Guelfs were in the ascendant throughout Italy. In 1293 he became duke of Urbino. Reconciled with the Church, he entered the Franciscan house at Assisi in 1296 and died there in 1298.

28. if the people of Romagna have peace or war: Like others of the damned (see 10.97–105), Guido has no knowledge of the present, which included the peace of 1299 between Guelf and Ghibelline factions in Romagna. In 1298, when Guido died, the peace was still being negotiated.

33. You speak: this one is Italian: See 26.73–75, where Virgil speaks with the Greeks Ulysses and Diomedes.

36–54. O soul . . . tyranny and liberty: Dante has the pilgrim give an account of seven cities in Romagna, including the coats of arms, each showing a beast of prey, of the ruling families.

36–39. O soul . . . did I leave there now: The lines correlate the "hidden" Guido with the violence hidden in the hearts of Romagna's rulers.

38. tyrants: "Tyrant" is used here in a broad sense for the emerging *signori* or "princes" of northern and central Italy, whose rule was based on arbitrary seizure rather than law or tradition (see 12.104). Technically, a tyrant was "one who rules a commonwealth unlawfully" (Gregory the Great); Dante, following Aristotle, writes that tyrants "do not follow laws for the common good, but attempt to twist them to their own benefit" (*Monarchia* 3.4; see also *Convivio* 4.6.27). The list of tyrants here is bracketed at the extremes of the canto by the classical Phalaris and the tyrannical Pope Boniface.

40–42. Ravenna . . . pinions: Ravenna had been under the lordship of the Guelf Guido Vecchio da Polenta, Francesca's father, since 1275; his device was a red eagle in a field of gold, hence the pinion extending as far as Cervia, "covering" it with its power. In 1283 Guido da Montefeltro lost Cervia, precious for its salt marshes, to the Polentas: the first of his defeats in the area.

43–45. The city . . . claws: Forlì, once the Ghibelline stronghold of Romagna. During the siege of the city in 1283 by a Guelf army sent by Pope Martin IV, Guido led a sortie that massacred the French knights under the count of Romagna ("a bloody heap"). Forlì passed under the control of the Ordelaffi in 1296; on their shield was the upper half of a green lion: the green claws would have been prominent.

46–48. The old . . . of their teeth: The mastiff was found on the escutcheon of a lateral branch of the Malatesta family; Dante refers to the "old mastiff" Malatesta il Vecchio (1212–1312) and his son Malatestino, who drove the Ghibellines from Rimini in 1295 and governed with notorious cruelty. Verrucchio was an ancestral castle of the Malatesta.

47. guarded Montagna ill: Montagna de' Parcitati, head of the Ghibelline resistance to the Malatesta in Rimini, was captured and murdered in prison by Malatestino in 1296, when, according to one story, Malatestino finally understood his father's repeated hint that the prisoner was "not well guarded."

48. make drills of their teeth: Dante refers to the doglike Malatestas using their fangs as drills to pierce the flesh and bone and suck blood and marrow from their subjects. Allied with the Polentas (Gianciotto Malatesta was the husband of Francesca da Polenta, Paolo Malatesta her lover; see 5.116 and note), the Malatestas were Guido's most dangerous adversaries; he had to defend Urbino against Malatestino, *podestà* of Cesena in the 1290s, several times.

49–51. Lamone . . . winter: Faenza and Imola are identified by the rivers flowing near them; these cities were frequently in and out of the hands of Maghinardo de' Pagani (see the note to lines 50–51).

50–51. lion cub . . . summer and winter: A blue lion in a white field was the device of the Pagani, whose head, Maghinardo, was notorious for fighting as a Ghibelline in Romagna, north of the Apennine chain, but as a Guelf south of it, in Tuscany (Villani, *Chronicle* 7.49): according to the early commentators, "summer" means the southern side of the mountains, "winter" the northern.

52–54. the city . . . between tyranny and liberty: Cesena, the seventh city, was under the nominal lordship of Guido's nephew Galasso da Montefeltro in 1300 but enjoyed the privileges of a free republic. The geographical position of the city between plain and slope indicates its political condition.

57. so may your name hold up its brow: Guido's name—his reputation—is here personified, as if it were the man himself; there may be implicit contrast with the animal symbolism of the tyrants (but see line 75).

61–129. If I believed . . . tormenting myself: In most of what remains of the canto, Guido responds to the pilgrim. After Guido's initial summary of his destiny (58–72), a rapid summary of his life (73–84) precedes the climactic scene with Boniface VIII (85–111): Boniface is introduced (85–93); then Guido relates the fatal interview (94–111); finally, Guido describes his damnation (112–29).

61–66. If I believed . . . I answer you: In answer to the pilgrim's promise of fame, Guido reveals his fear of infamy: he would say nothing more if he thought the pilgrim would return to earth, since he wishes to keep his reputation of having died repentant (which Dante had originally accepted; see the note to lines 79–81). Just as Guido in life gullibly believed an exaggerated promise, so here he has gullibly accepted the devil's word (cf. the inscription on the gate, 3.9). The lines are the epigraph to T. S. Eliot's epochal "Love Song of J. Alfred Prufrock."

67–72. I was . . . I wish you to hear: These lines introduce topics that recur in Guido's discourse: his fame as a soldier and strategist, which gains him Boniface's attention (67, also 78); his entry into the Franciscan order, dividing his life into "before" and "after" (67, also 83); and his reproaching the pope for derailing his amendment of life (70–71, also 84 and 91), typically couched in contrary-to-fact constructions (70, also 84 and 122–23; this construction also begins his speech, lines 61–66).

72. *qua re*: Literally, "on account of what thing." The Latin phrase, part of the scholastic formulary for logical investigation (*quod, quomodo, quare*: what, how, why?), balances the Lombardism of line 6.

73. the form of bone and flesh that my mother gave me: The "form" is the soul, the vital principle, which shapes the "bone and flesh."

74–75. my works were not those of a lion but a fox: The works of the fox are fraud, rather than open violence, the work of the lion (see 11.22–24: the two modes of *ingiuria*). Corrupt Franciscans were often depicted as vulpine in anticlerical literature and its illustrations (*Romance of the Rose*); the fox had the reputation of turning back to his old sins, as in the *Roman de Renard* (Mazzotta 1993).

78. the fame of it went out to the ends of the earth: As Mattalia notes, Guido is never named: his fame identifies him. See Psalm 18.5, "Their sound hath gone forth into all the earth," and 26.2–3. The irony of Guido's "hidden ways" becoming "famous" permeates the canto.

79–81. When I saw . . . ropes: The metaphor of the voyage of life implicitly involves Ulysses, whose last journey is the antithesis of Guido's retirement (until the pope intervenes). See *Convivio* 4.28.8:

> O miserable and vile, you that run toward this port [death] with sails aloft, and because of the driving force of the wind are shattered where you should find rest, you yourselves losing what you had traveled so far to obtain. Surely the knight Lancelot did not wish to enter port with raised sails, nor did our own most noble Latin knight Guido of Montefeltro. These noblemen did well to furl the sails of earthly activity: in their old age they surrendered to religion, setting aside all worldly pleasures and works.

For the parallels between Guido and Ulysses, see Ryan 1977.

85–93. The prince of the new Pharisees . . . the rope: Guido refers to Pope Boniface VIII, also unnamed, but reproached for being an arch-hypocrite (for the frequent denunciations of the Pharisees in the Gospels, see the note to 23.64–65 and cf. Additional Note 9), for fighting against Christians, rather than the enemies of Christendom (87–90), and for failing to respect both his own high office and priestly vocation and Guido's vows as a Franciscan.

86. war near the Lateran: That is, near Rome; Saint John in Lateran was the cathedral of Rome, the pope's see as bishop.

87–90. against Saracens or Jews . . . in the Sultan's lands: Targets for justifiable action on Boniface's part, in Dante's view, were the Muslims, who regained Saint-Jean-d'Acre, the last Christian stronghold in the Holy Land, in 1291; the Jews, traditionally regarded as enemies of Christ (see *Paradiso* 7); and merchants who continued trading with Muslims despite the ban of the Church.

94. as Constantine asked Sylvester: For this legend, see the note to 19.115–17. The simile puts Guido in the role of the pope and the pope in the role of the emperor seeking a cure; the reversal echoes the pilgrim's relation to Pope Nicholas III (see 19.46–51 and note); the relationship of Phalaris and Perillus (lines 7–12) also anticipates that of Boniface and Guido: "For just as the astute Perillus taught the astute Phalaris how to punish his enemies in a novel manner, so this clever count [Guido] taught the clever Boniface, who was a great tyrant among priests, how to use a novel piece of advice to eliminate his enemies" (Benvenuto).

97. his proud fever: Penance, including contrition, confession, absolution, and satisfaction, is preeminently the "medicinal" or "healing" sacrament (Aquinas, *Summa theol.* 3a, q. 84, a. 5), but that is not Boniface's concern.

101. henceforth I absolve you: The formula is that of absolution ("ego te absolvo"), but the language is ambiguous since "finor t'assolvo" might mean "I absolve you *as of* now" or "*until* now." For the flaws in this absolution, see lines 110–11, with note; for the emphasis on the present ("now"), see line 119 and note.

102. how to raze Palestrina: Palestrina (ancient Praeneste, twenty miles east of Rome, visible from Boniface's home town, Anagni), was a stronghold of the Colonna, the family that stood in the way of Boniface's attempts to restore the Angevins to power in Sicily and to aggrandize his patrimony in central Italy (see 19.52–57, with note). In 1297 the Colonna infuriated Boniface by stealing a large sum of money from him; he retaliated by laying siege to Palestrina. The city surrendered in 1298 on the promise of amnesty; lives were spared, but the citadel was razed (Villani, *Chronicle* 8.23). The razing of Palestrina, in a sense Guido's final military exploit, is also the symbol of his own undoing; he died in the same month and the same year. Kay (1980) points out the parallel between the fall of Palestrina and that of Troy in Canto 26.

103–4: Heaven ... the keys are two: Boniface, invoking the tradition of the keys (Matt. 16.19; see 13.58–61 and 19.91–92, with notes), implies that one key binds, the other releases. This is not Dante's view. According to Aquinas and other authorities, one key represents the discretion (*scientia*) of the confessor, the other the power of imposing penance or releasing from it (*Summa theol.* Suppl., q. 17, a. 3) (see *Purg.* 9.117–29, with notes).

104. the keys are two ... did not prize: According to contemporary accusations (repeated by Nicholas; see 19.56), Celestine V abdicated under pressure from Boniface: another boast, and a veiled threat, in the pope's words.

106. his weighty arguments impelled me: Boniface's mention of the keys (line 105) threatens damnation. Guido thinks his dilemma is between jeopardizing his salvation by giving sinful advice, and causing Boniface to use the keys to bar him from Heaven. But the "power of the keys" cannot bind the will: just as absolution works only if the sinner is penitent, the key cannot impose guilt but only temporal punishment (see Aquinas, *Summa theol.* Suppl., q. 18, a. 6). Boniface could not have kept a penitent Guido from salvation, but only (perhaps) increased his stay in Purgatory (see *Purg.* 3.133–41).

108–9. since you wash me ... I now must fall: Echoes the "penitential" Psalm 50.4: "wash me yet more from my iniquity." Guido seizes the offer of absolution (line 101): but since this is before the fact, it cannot remit sin; note the emphasis on "now" (*mo*) (see the notes to lines 20–21 and 119).

110–11. a long promise ... your high throne: The chronicle of Riccobaldo da Ferrara (as early as 1308, possibly before Dante's composition of this episode) preserves Guido's advice in language almost identical to Dante's: "Boniface said: 'only tell me how I can make them submit.' So Guido said: 'promise much, keep little of what you promise'" (Parodi 1920). Riccobaldo's account may have altered the view Dante took in *Convivio* 4.28.8 (see the note to lines 79–81). In believing Boniface, Guido himself is accepting a "long promise" that will have a "short fulfillment"; he is caught in his own trick. Note the symmetry between Boniface's short fulfillment and the long fulfillment of God's promise, on which the pilgrim is relying (cf. the note to lines 61–66).

112. Francis came later, when I had died: The jump to Guido's death mimics the suddenness of death and judgment (see the note to line 119). The motif of the dispute between devil and angel for the soul at death was common in medieval art; there is one instance in the *Inferno,* one in the *Purgatorio* (5.100–108).

113. black cherubim: In Christian angelology, the cherubim—the Hebrew means "fullness of knowledge"—were the second highest order of angels.

116. the fraudulent counsel: These words, spoken by the devil, are the only description of the sin punished in this *bolgia*; on their basis, this sin, not mentioned in Virgil's list (11.58–60), is commonly termed "false counsel," though some readers claim it is rather cunning (*astuzia*) that is targeted (Kay 1980; Ahern 1982). *Astuzia* would seem common to fraud in general, however, and it is clear also that fraudulent advice is involved in many other sins, such as pandering (cf. 18.55–57), simony (cf. 19.70–72), or sowing discord (cf. 28.106–11). What distinguishes Ulysses and Guido from the practitioners of fraud in other *bolge* would seem rather to be the use (and counseling the use) of fraud in war; the next *bolgia* punishes those who counsel resorting to violence.

119. nor can one repent and will together: The "contradiction" that snags Guido is the impossibility of making two contradictory choices in the same instant: in the "now" that separates "before" and "after." The text repeatedly hints at this contradiction by mentioning the present moment, the "now" (*istra, finor, or, mo,* and *già;* see lines 1–2, 20, 25, 39, 101, 109, and 117), and also harps on the "before" and "after" of Guido's spiritual life (lines 67, 82, 101, 108–9, and 117). Note also the frequency in the canto of words involving the sound *m,* particularly in Guido's speech, but beginning with *mugghiò,* line 7: they radiate from the *mo* of line 109 and the *morto* of line 112. See Augustine's discussion of the instant of "now" as the temporal analogue of eternity (*Confessions* 11.15–31; see Masciandaro 1970).

123. you did not think I was a logician: Devils cannot philosophize, because they cannot love wisdom, but they can use dialectic and apply the law of contradiction, a basic axiom of Aristotle's logic (see *Summa theol.* 1a, q. 58, a. 3).

129. thus clothed I go tormenting myself: The last reference to concealment (see lines 7–15, 36–39, 61–66, and 76, with notes). See Luke 12.2: "for there is nothing covered, that shall not be revealed: nor hidden, that shall not be known." Guido is still confused (cf. line 6).

131. the grieving flame departed, twisting and beating about with its sharp horn: See Wisdom 11.17: "that they might know that by what things a man sinneth, by the same also he is tormented" (Latin *torqueatur*, twisted, tortured). In Canto 28, Dante makes explicit the notion of *contrapasso* [counter-suffering] as a principle of justice in Hell. The contortions of the flame mirror those of Guido's thought; "beating about" translates *dibattendo,* which can mean "debating."

136. those who gain cargo by putting apart: That is, gain the burden of guilt by setting others at odds: those who counsel violence, the sowers of discord.

CANTO 28

1
Chi poria mai pur con parole sciolte
dicer del sangue e de le piaghe a pieno
ch'i' ora vidi, per narrar più volte?

4
Ogne lingua per certo verria meno
per lo nostro sermone e per la mente,
c'hanno a tanto comprender poco seno.

7
S'el s'aunasse ancor tutta la gente
che già, in su la fortunata terra
di Puglia, fu del suo sangue dolente

10
per li Troiani e per la lunga guerra
che de l'anella fé sì alte spoglie,
come Livïo scrive, che non erra,

13
con quella che sentio di colpi doglie
per contastare a Ruberto Guiscardo,
e l'altra il cui ossame ancor s'accoglie

16
a Ceperan, là dove fu bugiardo
ciascun Pugliese, e là da Tagliacozzo,
dove sanz' arme vinse il vecchio Alardo,

19
e qual forato suo membro e qual mozzo
mostrasse, d'aequar sarebbe nulla
il modo de la nona bolgia sozzo.

22
Già veggia, per mezzul perdere o lulla,
com' io vidi un, così non si pertugia,
rotto dal mento infin dove si trulla.

25
Tra le gambe pendevan le minugia;
la corata pareva e 'l tristo sacco
che merda fa di quel che si trangugia.

28
Mentre che tutto in lui veder m'attacco,
guardommi e con le man s'aperse il petto,
dicendo: "Or vedi com' io mi dilacco!

CANTO 28

Ninth bolgia: *sowers of discord—Mohammed—Curio—Mosca de'*
Lamberti—Bertran de Born

1　　Who could ever, even with unbound words, tell in
full of the blood and wounds that I now saw, though
he should narrate them many times?

4　　Every tongue would surely fail, because our
language and our memory have little capacity to
comprehend so much.

7　　If one gathered together all the people who ever,
on the travailed earth of Apulia, groaning poured
forth their blood

10　　on account of the Trojans, and in the long war
that took such heaped spoils of rings, as Livy writes,
who does not err,

13　　and the people who suffered wounds when
resisting Robert Guiscard, and the others whose
bones are still being collected

16　　at Ceperano, where every Apulian was a liar, and
at Tagliacozzo, where old Elard won without arms,

19　　and this one showed his perforated, this one his
truncated member, it would be nothing to equal the
wretched mode of the ninth pocket.

22　　Surely a barrel, losing centerpiece or half-moon, is
not so broken as one I saw torn open from the chin
to the farting-place.

25　　Between his legs dangled his intestines; the pluck
was visible, and the wretched bag that makes shit
of what is swallowed.

28　　While I was all absorbed in the sight of him, he,
gazing back at me, with his hands opened up his
breast, saying: "Now see how I spread myself!

433

31   Vedi come storpiato è Mäometto!
Dinanzi a me sen va piangendo Alì,
fesso nel volto dal mento al ciuffetto.

34   E tutti li altri che tu vedi qui,
seminator di scandalo e di scisma
fuor vivi, e però son fessi così.

37   Un diavolo è qua dietro che n'accisma
sì crudelmente, al taglio de la spada
rimettendo ciascun di questa risma

40   quand' avem volta la dolente strada,
però che le ferite son richiuse
prima ch'altri dinanzi li rivada.

43   Ma tu chi se' che 'n su lo scoglio muse,
forse per indugiar d'ire a la pena
ch'è giudicata in su le tue accuse?"

46   "Né morte 'l giunse ancor, né colpa 'l mena,"
rispuose 'l mio maestro, "a tormentarlo;
ma per dar lui esperïenza piena,

49   a me, che morto son, convien menarlo
per lo 'nferno qua giù di giro in giro;
e quest' è ver così com' io ti parlo."

52   Più fuor di cento che, quando l'udiro,
s'arrestaron nel fosso a riguardarmi
per maraviglia, oblïando il martiro.

55   "Or dì a fra Dolcin dunque che s'armi,
tu che forse vedra' il sole in breve,
s'ello non vuol qui tosto seguitarmi,

58   sì di vivanda che stretta di neve
non rechi la vittoria al Noarese,
ch'altrimenti acquistar non saria leve."

61   Poi che l'un piè per girsene sospese,
Mäometto mi disse esta parola;
indi a partirsi in terra lo distese.

64   Un altro, che forato avea la gola
e tronco 'l naso infin sotto le ciglia,
e non avea mai ch'una orecchia sola,

67   ristato a riguardar per maraviglia
con li altri, innanzi a l'altri aprì la canna,
ch'era di fuor d'ogne parte vermiglia,

31   See how Mohammed is torn open! Ahead of me Ali goes weeping, his face cloven from chin to forelock.

34   And all the others you see here were sowers of scandal and schism while they were alive, and therefore are they cloven in this way.

37   There is a devil back there who carves us so cruelly, putting the edge of his sword to each in this ream

40   once we have circled through the suffering road, for the wounds have closed before any confronts him again.

43   But who are you sniffing at us from up on the ridge, perhaps to delay going to the punishment decreed on your crimes?"

46   "Death has not reached him yet, nor does guilt lead him," replied my master, "into torment; but so that he may have full experience,

49   I, who am dead, must lead him through Hell down here from circle to circle; and this is as true as that I am speaking to you."

52   More than a hundred were they who, hearing him, stopped in the ditch to gaze up at me in amazement, forgetting their suffering.

55   "Now then, you who will perhaps shortly see the sun, tell Brother Dolcino, if he does not want to follow me soon down here,

58   to provide himself with enough food that the barrier of snow may give not the victory to the Novarese, which otherwise would not be easy to acquire."

61   Holding one foot lifted to walk away, Mohammed spoke this word to me; then, departing, he set it down.

64   Another, whose throat was bored through, his nose cut up to his eyebrows, and with only one ear,

67   stopping to gaze up at me in amazement with the others, first of the others opened his windpipe, which was all covered with crimson,

70   e disse: "O tu cui colpa non condanna
e cu' io vidi in su terra latina,
se troppa simiglianza non m'inganna,

73   rimembriti di Pier da Medicina,
se mai torni a veder lo dolce piano
che da Vercelli a Marcabò dichina.

76   E fa sapere a' due miglior da Fano,
a messer Guido e anco ad Angiolello,
che, se l'antiveder qui non è vano,

79   gittati saran fuor di lor vasello
e mazzerati presso a la Cattolica
per tradimento d'un tiranno fello.

82   Tra l'isola di Cipri e di Maiolica
non vide mai sì gran fallo Nettuno,
non da pirate, non da gente argolica.

85   Quel traditor che vede pur con l'uno,
e tien la terra che tale qui meco
vorrebbe di vedere essser digiuno,

88   farà venirli a parlamento seco;
poi farà sì ch'al vento di Focara
non sarà lor mestier voto né preco."

91   E io a lui: "Dimostrami e dichiara,
se vuo' ch'i' porti sù di te novella,
chi è colui de la veduta amara."

94   Allor puose la mano a la mascella
d'un suo compagno e la bocca li aperse,
gridando: "Questi è desso, e non favella.

97   Questi, scacciato, il dubitar sommerse
in Cesare, affermando che 'l fornito
sempre con danno l'attender sofferse."

100   Oh quanto mi pareva sbigottito
con la lingua tagliata ne la strozza
Curïo, ch'a dir fu così ardito!

103   E un ch'avea l'una e l'altra man mozza,
levando i moncherin per l'aura fosca,
sì che 'l sangue facea la faccia sozza,

106   gridò: "Ricordera'ti anche del Mosca,
che disse, lasso! 'Capo ha cosa fatta,'
che fu mal seme per la gente tosca."

70 and said: "O you whom guilt does not condemn, and whom I saw in Italy, if too close a resemblance does not deceive me,

73 remember Pier of Medicina, if you ever return to see the lovely plain sloping down from Vercelli to Marcabò.

76 And tell the two best men of Fano, messer Guido and Angiolello, that, if foresight is not empty here,

79 they will be thrown from their vessel in a weighted sack and drowned near Cattolica, thanks to the treachery of a wicked tyrant.

82 Between the islands of Cyprus and Maiolica Neptune has never seen so great a sin done, not by pirates, not by Argolians.

85 That traitor who sees with only one eye, who holds the city that my fellow wishes he had still to see,

88 will have them come to parley; he will bring it about that they need no vows or prayers against the Focara wind."

91 And I to him: "Show me and explain, if you wish me to carry news back up about you, who is the one of the bitter sight?"

94 Then he put his hand to the jaw of one of his companions and opened his mouth for him, crying: "This is he, and he cannot speak.

97 He, an exile, drowned Caesar's doubts, affirming that one prepared always suffers from delay."

100 Oh how dismayed Curio seemed, with the tongue cut out of his throat, he who was so bold to speak!

103 And one who had both hands cut off, lifting the stumps in the murky air so that the blood soiled his face,

106 cried: "You will remember Mosca, too, who said, alas, 'A thing done is done,' the seed of evil for the Tuscans."

109   E io li aggiunsi: "E morte di tua schiatta."
Per ch'elli, accumulando duol con duolo,
sen gio come persona trista e matta.

112   Ma io rimasi a riguardar lo stuolo,
e vidi cosa ch'io avrei paura,
sanza più prova, di contarla solo,

115   se non che coscïenza m'assicura,
la buona compagnia che l'uom francheggia
sotto l'asbergo del sentirsi pura.

118   Io vidi certo, e ancor par ch'io 'l veggia,
un busto sanza capo andar sì come
andavan li altri de la trista greggia;

121   e 'l capo tronco tenea per le chiome,
pesol con mano a guisa di lanterna;
e quel mirava noi, e dicea: "Oh me!"

124   Di sé facea a sé stesso lucerna,
ed eran due in uno e uno in due;
com' esser può, quei sa che sì governa.

127   Quando diritto al piè del ponte fue,
levò 'l braccio alto con tutta la testa
per appressarne le parole sue,

130   che fuoro: "Or vedi la pena molesta,
tu che, spirando, vai veggendo i morti:
vedi s'alcuna è grande come questa.

133   E perché tu di me novella porti,
sappi ch'i' son Bertram dal Bornio, quelli
che diedi al re giovane i ma' conforti.

136   Io feci il padre e 'l figlio in sé ribelli:
Achitofèl non fé più d'Absalone
e di Davìd coi malvagi punzelli.

139   Perch' io parti' così giunte persone,
partito porto il mio cerebro, lasso!
dal suo principio ch'è in questo troncone.

142   Così s'osserva in me lo contrapasso."

109   And I added: "And the death of your clan"; so that he, piling grief on grief, walked off like a person mad with sorrow.

112   But I remained to gaze at the host, and I saw something that I would fear, without more proof, even to retell,

115   except that my conscience makes me confident, the good companion that frees a man, if it wears the hauberk of knowing itself pure.

118   I surely saw, and it seems I still see, a torso without a head walking like the others of the sorry flock;

121   and his severed head he was holding up by the hair, dangling it from his hand like a lantern; and the head was gazing at us, saying: "Oh me!"

124   Of himself he made a lamp for himself, and they were two in one and one in two; how that can be, he knows who so disposes.

127   When he was directly at the foot of the bridge, he raised his arm far up, head and all, to bring his words close to us,

130   which were: "Now see my wretched punishment, you who go still breathing to view the dead: see if any is great as this.

133   And that you may take back news of me, know that I am Bertran de Born, he who gave the young king the bad encouragements.

136   I made father and son revolt against each other: Achitophel did no worse to Absalom and David with his evil proddings.

139   Because I divided persons so joined, I carry my brain divided, alas, from its origin which is in this trunk.

142   Thus you observe in me the counter-suffering."

NOTES

1–6. Who could ever . . . comprehend so much: Even if freed of the restrictions imposed by verse, the poet could not adequately contain in words (line 6) the scene he saw. This is the so-called inexpressibility topos (see Curtius 1953), based on such passages as *Aen.* 2. 361–62:

> Quis cladem illius noctis, quis funera fando
> explicet aut possit lacrimis aequare labores?

> [Who by speaking could unfold the slaughter of that night
> and its deaths, or equal its travails with his tears?]

and 6.625–27:

> Non, mihi si linguae centum sint oraque centum,
> ferrea vox, omnis scelerum comprendere formas,
> omnia poenarum percurrere nomina possim.

> [Not if I had a hundred tongues and mouths,
> a voice of iron, could I include all the forms of crime,
> run through the names of all the punishments.]

Compare Statius, *Theb.* 12.797–99, which lists victims of the fratricidal Theban war.

1. unbound words: Prose (Latin *oratio soluta,* unbound speech) as opposed to verse, regulated by fixed numbers and rules; in the *De vulgari eloquentia* (2.5 and 2.8) Dante compared the lines of verse in a stanza to sticks of fixed length bound together in a bundle.

7–21. If one gathered . . . the ninth pocket: The multitude of "blood and wounds" in this *bolgia* exceeds the number of all those wounded and killed in the many wars fought in the south of Italy from Roman times until the battle of Tagliacozzo (1268). The rhetorical organization of these lines may be derived from the lament for the "young king" (Henry Plantagenet, second son of Henry II of England) attributed to Bertran de Born, lines 1–5:

> Si tuit li dol el plor el marrimen
> e las dolors el dan el caitivier
> que hom anc auzis en est segle dolen
> fosson ensems, sembleran tot leugier
> contra la mort del joven rei engles.

[If all the pain and weeping and dismay
and anguish and harm and misery
that man ever had in this life of pain
were all together, they would seem light
next to the death of the young English king.]

Bertran himself appears in lines 118–42.

8. travailed earth of Apulia: Apulia refers here to the medieval kingdom of
Naples, stretching from the "heel" and "toe" of Italy as far north as the Tronto
and Garigliano rivers (near modern Ascoli and Gaeta).

10. Trojans: Of all the wars between the Trojans (the Romans, the descen-
dants of Aeneas and his followers) and the Latin tribes for control over the Ital-
ian peninsula, one of the bloodiest was the Samnite War (280 B.C.), which in-
volved the Greek mercenary Pyrrhus (see 12.135).

10–12. the long war . . . Livy writes: The second Punic, or Carthaginian,
War (218–202 B.C.). The victory of Hannibal at Cannae (216 B.C.) marked
Rome's darkest hour in its long struggle with Carthage for domination of the
Mediterranean. According to Livy (*Ab urbe condite* 22.44), Hannibal's soldiers
gleaned a bushel of rings from the corpses of the Roman dead; Orosius and
Augustine give the amount as three bushels.

14. Robert Guiscard: Born in Normandy in 1015, brother of its duke, Rob-
ert Guiscard (the surname means "sagacious" or "cunning") was in 1059 offered
Apulia and Calabria by Pope Nicholas II; he fought for twenty years to conquer
them. He died suddenly of pestilence in July 1085. (Subsequently the titles of
Apulia and Sicily were united in the person of his great-nephew, Roger I, first
of the Norman kings of the Two Sicilies.)

16. at Ceperano . . . was a liar: Frederick II's natural son, Manfred, was
defeated at Benevento in 1266 by Charles of Anjou, engaged by the pope to
establish Guelf supremacy in central and southern Italy. According to Dante's
information, the battle was lost because of the desertion of the Apulian barons,
who failed to hold positions near the pass of Ceperano, on the Liris river; Manfred
was killed on the field (see *Purg.* 3.112 and notes).

17. Tagliacozzo . . . without arms: After Manfred's defeat, the Ghibelline
cause was championed by Frederick's legitimate grandson Conradino, defeated
by Charles of Anjou at Tagliacozzo, in the rugged Abbruzzi region north-
east of Naples. The battle was very bloody, but Conradino was tricked by the
French general Elard de Valéry, who thus won "without arms"—that is, by
tactics.

22–63. Surely a barrel . . . he set it down: The interview with Mohammed is the longest in the canto. Dante accepted the medieval Christian claim that Mohammed had originally been a Christian; he treats him as a schismatic.

22–24. Surely a barrel . . . to the farting-place: Note the image of the broken container. In this canto, Dante repeatedly echoes the famous poet of the joy of battle, Bertran de Born. Compare Bertran's "Bem plai lo gais temps de pascor" [Well-pleased I am by gay Eastertime], on bodies and fortifications cleft and riven: "qan vei fortz chastels assetgatz/ els barris rotz et esfondratz" [when I see strong castles besieged and the outer walls broken and breached]. Bertran's language itself echoes the formulas for the savage wounds sustained in shock combat found in the Old French *chansons de geste* (Bertran 1986), especially the *Song of Roland*, which Dante probably read in thirteenth-century rhymed Venetian versions.

25–27. Between his legs . . . what is swallowed: The "pluck" (*corata*) is the lungs, heart, and other organs above the diaphragm; the "bag" is usually taken to mean the stomach. Mahomet's pendant intestines are suggestive of the Malebolge itself. See Additional Note 13.

29–31. with his hands . . . torn open: Italian *dilaccare* [to spread] was idiomatically used for the spreading of the thighs (cf. *lacca* [hollow, slope]; 7.16 and 12.11). This display of wounds parodies the iconography of Christ's wounds at the Last Judgment. Note the parallel between the gaping physical wounds and the gaping and staring of both the pilgrim and the punished schismatics (see lines 53–54 and 29.1–3).

31. Mohammed: In the Christian polemics that were Dante's sources of information, Mohammed was said to have been a Nestorian Christian (the Nestorians denied that Christ's divine and human natures were united) before founding Islam; thus he was thought both a heretic and a schismatic, having drawn one third of the world's believers away from the true faith.

32–33. Ali . . . his face cloven from chin to forelock: Ali was Mohammed's cousin and son-in-law. His wound suggests completion of the splitting of the body begun with the vertical slash on Mohammed; it may conceivably refer to the splitting of Islam into Sunnites and Shiites.

35. sowers of scandal and schism: Scandal (Greek *skándalon*, stumbling-block) trips others into sin (Aquinas, *Summa theol.* 2a 2ae, q. 5, a. 2; and see Augustine, *City of God* 20.5); schism, according to Aquinas, is the division (*scissura*) of the faithful by those professing to be believers. The metaphor of sowing derives from the parable of the tares in Matt. 13.24–30, 36–43 (see also lines 68, 94, 101, and 108). For the distinction between heresy and schism, see the note to 9.127–28. For the close relation between the metaphors of the body of Christ and the body politic, see Additional Note 2.

37. carves us: Dante's word *accismar* meant literally "to prepare" or "to equip"; he knew it in Bertran's "Be.m plai" (26–28): "And once the battle is joined,/ each must be prepared [*acesmatz*]/ to follow his lord willingly."

38–39. putting the edge . . . in this ream: Italian *taglio* means literally "cutting" or "slicing." Compare with Bertran, "Un sirventes," line 40: "sabra de mon bran cum talha" [they shall know how my sword can cut] and line 43: "Tot jorn resoli e retaill/ los baros" [All day I resole and reslice the barons]. In this canto where Dante makes explicit a theory of retributive punishment (see line 142), it is logical that the agent of justice (here, a devil) bear a sword: images closely contemporary with Dante (Giotto, Ambrogio Lorenzetti) show the sword as the instrument of justice. Pietro di Dante comments: "as they divided others with the word, here they themselves are now divided."

39. in this ream: A ream is a quantity of cut paper; Dante's word *risma* derives perhaps from *rame*, a brass device for cutting paper; *risma* is also a variant of *rima* [rhyme or verse], from Latin *rithimus*, associated with Gallo-Romance *rimar* [to put in a row; rive, split]. See Additional Note 12.

44. perhaps to delay . . . on your crimes: With increasing frequency in lower Hell, the pilgrim is assumed to be one of the damned. For this emphasis on the decree of punishment, see line 142, with note.

55–60. Now then, you . . . would not be easy: The charismatic Dolcino de' Tornielli, from near Novara, became the leader of the "Apostolic Brethren" after Gherardo Segarelli, their founder, was burned at the stake (1300). In 1305 Clement V ordered a crusade, recruited mainly from Novara (line 59) and Vercelli; from camps high in the mountains, the Brethren resisted until starvation forced them to a pitched battle in March 1307. Dolcino and his companion, Margaret of Trent, were captured; Dolcino's body was cruelly mutilated before he was burned at the stake at Vercelli in June 1307.

Although the Apostolic Brethren were branded as heretics by the Church, Dante places them among the schismatics; he seems to have shared most of Dolcino's doctrines in some form (Dolcino condemned the papacy and preached renewal of the Church under an emperor and a saintly pope). Apparently Dante condemns Dolcino and has him advised by Mohammed because of his leading a separate group, which makes him a schismatic, and his armed resistance to the crusaders. Eco (1980, trans. 1983) imaginatively evokes the period; Orioli (1988) offers a recent sifting of the evidence.

55–58. Now . . . with enough food: Because of Dante's use of inversion and hypallage (suspended constructions), these lines have had to be rearranged; the original order is: "Now tell Brother Dolcino that he arm himself, you who . . . if . . . , with enough. . . ." Two clauses stand between *s'armi,* "provide [literally, arm] himself" in line 55 and *vivanda* [food] in line 58.

61–63. Holding one foot . . . set it down: Again a gap in what is normally unified (see lines 55–58): walking has been suspended, like the constructions of lines 55–58; compare *Aen.* 6.546–47: "I, decus, i, nostrum; melioribus utere fatis./Tantum effatus, et in verbo vestigia torsit." [Go, our glory, go: know better fates. This much said, while speaking he turned his steps.]

64–66. Another, whose throat . . . only one ear: The mutilation of Pier da Medicina recalls that of Deiphobus; see *Aen.* 6.494–97:

> Atque hic Priamiden laniatum corpore toto
> Deiphobum vidit, lacerum crudeliter ora,
> ora manusque ambas, populataque tempora raptis
> auribus et truncas inhonesto vulnere naris.

> [But here, with his whole body torn, he saw Priam's son
> Deiphobus, and his cruelly lacerated face,
> his lips and both his hands, his ears shorn
> from his ravaged temples and his nose cut short with shameful wounds.]

(Having married Helen after the death of Paris, Deiphobus was betrayed by her and caught unarmed when Troy fell.)

68. opened his windpipe: Like Pier della Vigna, this soul speaks through his wound; the focus is on the act of speech as causing strife (see lines 35, 94, and 107, with notes).

73. remember Pier of Medicina: Piero di Aimo da Medicina is the leading candidate among several like-named members, about whom little is known, of the house of Medicina, a large village between Imola and Bologna. Benvenuto states that he sowed discord between the Malatesta and Polenta families (see 27.41, 46) by telling each inflammatory stories about the other.

74–75. the lovely plain . . . Marcabò: This plain is the entire valley of the Po, from Vercelli in the west to near Ravenna.

79–80. thrown . . . and drowned: Italian *mazzerare* is derived from *mazzera* [bundle of stones attached to fishing nets]; compare Matt. 18.6: "it were better for him [whoever scandalizes the innocent] that a millstone should be hanged about his neck, and that he should be drowned in the depth of the sea."

80. Cattolica: Site of a lighthouse overlooking the stretch of the seacoast of the March of Ancona where Guido del Cassero and Angiolello da Carignano, high-ranking nobles of Fano, were drowned.

82–84. Between the islands . . . not by Argolians: The islands of Cyprus in the eastern and Majorca in the western Mediterranean were well known to Florentines, who kept trading offices in both places. For "Argolians" meaning "Greeks," see Sinon's words in *Aen.* 2.78: "neque me Argolica de gente negabo" [nor do I deny that I am of the Argolian people], and see 30.98–129, with notes. Note the repeated geographic panoramas.

85. That traitor . . . only one eye: Malatestino's face, slashed by a sword cut and lacking one eye, seems to hint of future damnation to this *bolgia*. Christian accounts had it that Mohammed's face was also scarred by sword cuts.

86–87. the city . . . still to see: Rimini (see the note to line 99).

89–90. he will bring it about . . . against the Focara wind: The currents and winds near Cattolica were dangerous, hence prayers were often made for protection against the wind from Focara. Guido and Angiolello will need no prayers because they will be drowned.

93. the one of the bitter sight: The one mentioned in line 87.

94–95. he put his hand . . . opened his mouth: The gesture emphasizes speech as the source of discord (see lines 35 and 68, with notes). Curio was known for his venality and his glib tongue (lines 100–101); see *Pharsalia* 1.269: "Audax venali . . . Curio lingua" [Curio, bold with his venal tongue]. Piero's sarcasm echoes Lucan's moralizing over Curio's death (4.801–4): "quid prodita iura senatus/ et gener atque socer bello concurrere iussi?" [what good came to him from betraying the Senate's laws and sending Pompey and Caesar to clash in arms?]

97. an exile: Like Caesar, once having defied the Senate Curio was an exile (*Pharsalia* 1.278–79); technically this did not occur until Caesar had crossed the Rubicon.

99. one prepared always suffers from delay: The words Curio spoke to persuade Caesar to cross the Rubicon at Rimini and thus begin the civil war is one of the most famous *sententiae*, or sayings, from Lucan's poem, often quoted in the Middle Ages (*Pharsalia* 1.280–81): "tolle moras; semper nocuit diferre paratis" [do not delay: waiting always harms those who are ready] (see Dante, *Epistle* 7.5).

103. both hands cut off: Mutilation of the "executive" limbs of the body. In the *Song of Roland*, Roland is the "right arm" of Charlemagne, "le destre braz del cors" (*laisse* 45.2), a traditional relation between soldier and captain. The mutilated hands here balance the awkward walking of lines 61–63, coordinating the extremities.

106. Mosca: Mosca is the last of the five Florentines mentioned by the pilgrim to Ciacco (6.79–80) as having bent themselves to "well-doing"; he was of the Ghibelline Lamberti family, allied to the more powerful Amidei. Villani tells of how Buondelmonte de' Buondelmonti, betrothed to one of the Amidei, rejected her when offered a more appealing candidate; the Amidei, with the Lamberti and other families, urged by Mosca, decided on revenge. On Easter Sunday, 1215, Buondelmonte was dragged from his horse and stabbed to death next to the statue of Mars at the head of the Ponte Vecchio (see 13.143–51). The old chroniclers see this murder as the origin of the division of the city into Guelf and Ghibelline factions, the "beginning of its destruction."

107. A thing done is done: Literally, "a thing done has a head" (a cap, or conclusion); in short, kill him (Dino Compagni, *Cronica* 1.2.20).

108. the seed of evil for the Tuscans: Mosca's words, rather than ending the problem, unleashed violence: the *capo* was not an end of shame, but a beginning of division. For words as seeds, see lines 35, 68, 94, and 101.

109. And the death of your clan: The pilgrim caps Mosca's advice, and invokes the end, the cap, put on his kindred. In fact, the influence of the Lamberti soon waned; in 1258 they were expelled from Florence for violence.

112–42. But I remained . . . the counter-suffering: The last example of the sowing of strife is Bertran de Born, allusions to whose poetry have provided a kind of subtext for the canto; after the interview with Mohammed, this is the longest in the *bolgia*, and it provides a particularly striking conclusion.

113–17. I saw . . . knowing itself pure: Again, the poet's proof is that he "saw it"; he bears witness (see lines 1–6, 51, 71–72, and the notes to 16.124–29). Otfried Lieberknecht, in an Internet posting, cites 2 Cor. 2.12.

117. the hauberk of knowing itself pure: It is the conscience that knows itself pure—that is, blameless. Dante is adapting Saint Paul's "breastplate of justice" (Eph. 6.14) to the terminology of medieval weapons (chain mail) (cf. Saint Paul's source, Is. 59.17).

119–26. a torso . . . who so disposes: Like Mohammed's exposure of his wounds, Bertran's holding his own head parodies a type of Christian martyr: the cephalophore, who when decapitated picks up his own head and walks to his burial place (e.g., San Miniato, whose church sits above Florence; see *Purg.* 12.102).

121–22. holding . . . like a lantern: In classical epic, the severed head held aloft is a gesture of triumph (see *Aen.* 9.466; Statius, *Theb.* 9.132 and 10.452; and, of course, Perseus holding the head of Medusa).

123. Oh me: In the Italian, a rare example of *rima franta,* one rhyme combining two words; Dante may be imitating Bertran, who uses one in "Be.m plai" (quoted in the note to line 37): "to eat, drink, or sleep is not so savory as the moment I hear both sides crying 'at 'em' [*a lor*]." See Additional Note 12. For another, see 7.28: *pur lì,* rhymed with *urli* and *burli.*

125. two in one and one in two: See 25.61 and note.

128–29. he raised . . . close to us: Bertran's head is both a lantern (it sees) and a vocal conduit. A literal instance of "broken speech," since Bertran's breath is separated from its source in the lungs. For the eye as a lantern, see Matt. 6.23: "if thy eye be evil, thy whole body shall be darksome"; compare Matt. 5.29–30, on amputating members that "scandalize" one (eye and hand).

130–32. Now see . . . if any is great as this: See Lam. 1.12: "O all ye that pass by the way, attend, and see if there be any sorrow like to my sorrow." The words are spoken by the personified city of Jerusalem (see the note to 30.58–61).

131. you who go still breathing: Dante again reminds us that the pilgrim is breathing; breath is the physical image of the spirit that unifies the body. Breathing, the pilgrim distinguishes himself from the sowers of discord, who rend the unity of personal, civic, and mystical bodies.

134. Bertran de Born: Born about 1140, Bertran was lord of Hautefort, a castle in the Périgord whose ownership he disputed with his brother, whom he displaced (according to one of his biographies, through treachery). He died about 1215, a monk at the Cistercian monastery of Dalon, near Hautefort. Dante drew his information regarding Bertran's life and politics from the often fictionalized biographies, or *vidas*, of the troubadours composed in Italy in the thirteenth century. In the *De vulgari eloquentia* (2.2.9), Dante calls Bertran the preeminent poet of arms in Provençal.

135. the young king: The second son of Henry II of England (1155–1183; his older brother died at age two). He was called the young king because Henry II had him crowned in 1170 and again in 1172. Young Henry's mother, Eleanor of Aquitaine, and the French king, Louis VII, backed his demand that a substantial part of his patrimony be turned over to him. The resultant conflict among the young king, his father, and his brothers Richard and John lasted until the young king's death in 1183. His death was much lamented, perhaps less on account of his virtues than his prodigal, indeed ruinous, liberality. Some commentators have confused him with Henry II's grandson, Henry III (r. 1216–1272).

136. I made father . . . each other: One of the Provençal lives of Bertran reads:

> Always he wished them to have war with each other, the father and the son and the brother, each with the other . . . and if they made peace or called a truce, then he strove to pummel them with his satires so that they would undo the peace. (Hill and Bergin)

137–38. Achitophel . . . his evil proddings: Achitophel, counselor to King David and his son Absalom, fostered the son's sedition against his father; it resulted in Absalom's death (2 Samuel [Vulgate 2 Kings] 15.7–18.15). In the Latin chronicle by William of Newburgh (1170–1220), young Henry is called "the undutiful Absalom" (2.27). The tongue serves as goad again (see the note to 27.5).

142. the counter-suffering: "Counter-suffering" translates the Latin *contrapassum*, a rendition of the Greek *tò antipeponthón* in Aristotle's *Nicomachean Ethics* 5.5.1132b, part of a discussion of retaliation as a form of justice. Aquinas uses the term for the biblical law of retribution (*lex talionis*): *Summa theol.* 2a 2ae, q. 61, a. 4: "I answer that counter-suffering [*contrapassum*] denotes equal suffering repaid for previous action . . . this kind of justice is laid down in the Law (Ex. 21.23, 24): 'He shall render life for life, eye for eye.'" See also Deut. 19.21, Lev. 24.20, and Matt. 5.38, 7.2.

Cleft horizontally, Bertran at the end of the canto balances the vertically cleft Ali (son-in-law, head) and Mohammed (father, body) at the beginning; there is a "harmony" of cuts and slashes, of religious schism paired with secular.

The souls in this *bolgia* suffer punishments that correspond to the effects their sins have had on the body politic; thus they are figures of the body politic individually as well as collectively. This is made explicit by Bertran de Born when he says that his decapitation is the *contrapasso* for having sown discord between father and son; he speaks of his trunk as the "origin" of his head. This unexpected phrase calls attention to the special complexity of both his sin and its punishment. Henry II was both the father, the origin, of the young king and the head of the state and the family; his son was part of the body that should have been subject to Henry II, but also the future head of the state; Bertran's encouragements caused the young king to rebel, thus making illegitimate "head" against his father and ultimately aborting his rightful reign. In parting "persons so joined," Bertran doubly sinned against both the head and the trunk of the body politic.

CANTO 29

1   La molta gente e le diverse piaghe
avean le luci mie sì inebrïate
che de lo stare a piangere eran vaghe.

4   Ma Virgilio mi disse: "Che pur guate?
perché la vista tua pur si soffolge
là giù tra l'ombre triste smozzicate?

7   Tu non hai fatto sì a l'altre bolge;
pensa, se tu annoverar le credi,
che miglia ventidue la valle volge.

10   E già la luna è sotto i nostri piedi;
lo tempo è poco omai che n'è concesso,
e altro è da veder che tu non vedi."

13   "Se tu avessi," rispuos' io appresso,
"atteso a la cagion per ch'io guardava,
forse m'avresti ancor lo star dimesso."

16   Parte sen giva, e io retro li andava,
lo duca, già faccendo la risposta,
e soggiugnendo: "Dentro a quella cava

19   dov' io tenea or li occhi sì a posta,
credo ch'un spirto del mio sangue pianga
la colpa che là giù cotanto costa."

22   Allor disse 'l maestro: "Non si franga
lo tuo pensier da qui innanzi sovr'ello.
Attendi ad altro, ed ei là si rimanga;

25   ch'io vidi lui a piè del ponticello
mostrarti e minacciar forte col dito,
e udi' 'l nominar Geri del Bello.

28   Tu eri allor sì del tutto impedito
sovra colui che già tenne Altaforte,
che non guardasti in là, sì fu partito."

CANTO 29

Ninth bolgia, *continued: Virgil's rebuke—Geri del Bello—*
tenth bolgia, *falsifiers: alchemists: the Aretine—vanity of the*
Sienese—Capocchio

1   The multitude of people and their strange wounds
had so inebriated my eyes that they longed to stay
and weep.

4   But Virgil said to me: "Why do you still stare? Why
does your sight still dwell on those wretched
mutilated shades down there?

7   You did not act thus at the other pockets; think, if
you believe you could number them, that the valley
turns for twenty-two miles.

10 And already the moon is beneath our feet; little
remains of the time granted us, and there are other
things to see that you do not see."

13 "If you had attended," I then answered him, "to
the cause for which I was staring, perhaps you would
have permitted me to stay longer."

16 Meanwhile my leader walked on, with me behind
him already replying, and adding: "Within that
hollow

19 where just now I was fixing my eyes, I think a
spirit of my blood is weeping for the guilt that costs
so much down there."

22 Then said my master: "Let not your thought break
over him from now on. Attend to other things, and
let him stay there;

25 for I saw him at the foot of the bridge, pointing at
you and threatening fiercely with his finger, and I
heard him called Geri del Bello.

28 You were then so caught by him who held
Hautefort that you did not look there, and he went
off."

---

31   "O duca mio, la vïolenta morte
che non li è vendicata ancor," diss' io,
"per alcun che de l'onta sia consorte,

34   fece lui disdegnoso; ond' el sen gio
sanza parlarmi, sì com' ïo estimo,
e in ciò m'ha el fatto a sé più pio."

37   Così parlammo infino al loco primo
che de lo scoglio l'altra valle mostra,
se più lume vi fosse, tutto ad imo.

40   Quando noi fummo sor l'ultima chiostra
di Malebolge, sì che i suoi conversi
potean parere a la veduta nostra,

43   lamenti saettaron me diversi
che di pietà ferrati avean li strali;
ond' io li orecchi con le man copersi.

46   Qual dolor fora, se de li spedali
di Valdichiana tra 'l luglio e 'l settembre,
e di Maremma e di Sardigna, i mali

49   fossero in una fossa tutti 'nsembre:
tal era quivi, e tal puzzo n'usciva
qual suol venir de le marcite membre.

52   Noi discendemmo in su l'ultima riva
del lungo scoglio, pur da man sinistra;
e allor fu la mia vista più viva

55   giù ver' lo fondo, là 've la ministra
de l'alto Sire infallibil giustizia
punisce i falsador che qui registra.

58   Non credo ch'a veder maggior tristizia
fosse in Egina il popol tutto infermo,
quando fu l'aere sì pien di malizia

61   che li animali, infino al picciol vermo,
cascaron tutti—e poi le genti antiche,
secondo che i poeti hanno per fermo,

64   si ristorar di seme di formiche—
ch'era a veder per quella oscura valle
languir li spirti per diverse biche.

67   Qual sovra 'l ventre e qual sovra le spalle
l'un de l'altro giacea, e qual carpone
si trasmutava per lo tristo calle.

31   "O my leader, his violent death, as yet
unavenged," I said, "by anyone who shares the shame
of it,

34   has made him full of scorn; therefore he walked
away without speaking to me, as I judge, and that
has made me more compassionate toward him."

37   Thus we talked as far as the first place on the
ridge to show the next valley, if there were more
light there, down to its bed.

40   When we were above the last cloister of
Malebolge, so that its converts could appear to our
sight,

43   strange lamentings struck me, arrows whose iron
heads were made of pity, so that I covered my ears
with my hands.

46   What the suffering would be, if the sick from the
hospitals of Valdichiana between July and September,
and from Maremma and Sardinia,

49   were all in one ditch together: such was it there,
and a stench came from it like that from rotting
limbs.

52   We climbed down to the last bank from the long
ridge, still to the left; and then my sight was livelier

55   down toward the bottom, where the minister of
the Lord, infallible justice, punishes the falsifiers that
it registers here.

58   I do not believe it was a greater sadness to see
in Aegina the whole people sick, when the air
was so full of malice

61   that the animals, down to the little worm, all fell—
and then the ancient people, according to what the
poets firmly believe,

64   were restored from the seed of ants—than it was to
see, along that dark valley, the spirits languishing in
different heaps.

67   This one lay over another's stomach, that one over
another's shoulders, and this one crawling transmuted
himself down the evil road.

70   Passo passo andavam sanza sermone,
guardando e ascoltando li ammalati,
che non potean levar le lor persone.

73   Io vidi due sedere a sé poggiati,
com' a scaldar si poggia tegghia a tegghia,
dal capo al piè di schianze macolati;

76   e non vidi già mai menare stregghia
a ragazzo aspettato dal segnorso,
né a colui che mal volontier vegghia,

79   come ciascun menava spesso il morso
de l'unghie sopra sé per la gran rabbia
del pizzicor, che non ha più soccorso;

82   e sì traevan giù l'unghie la scabbia,
come coltel di scardova le scaglie
o d'altro pesce che più larghe l'abbia.

85   "O tu che con le dita ti dismaglie,"
cominciò 'l duca mio a l'un di loro,
"e che fai d'esse talvolta tanaglie,

88   dinne s'alcun Latino è tra costoro
che son quinc' entro, se l'unghia ti basti
etternalmente a cotesto lavoro."

91   "Latin siam noi, che tu vedi sì guasti
qui ambedue," rispuose l'un piangendo;
"ma tu chi se' che di noi dimandasti?"

94   E 'l duca disse: "I' son un che discendo
con questo vivo giù di balzo in balzo,
e di mostrar lo 'nferno a lui intendo."

97   Allor si ruppe lo comun rincalzo,
e tremando ciascuno a me si volse,
con altri che l'udiron di rimbalzo.

100   Lo buon maestro a me tutto s'accolse,
dicendo: "Dì a lor ciò che tu vuoli";
e io incominciai, poscia ch'ei volse:

103   "Se la vostra memoria non s'imboli
nel primo mondo da l'umane menti,
ma s'ella viva sotto molti soli,

106   ditemi chi voi siete e di che genti;
la vostra sconcia e fastidiosa pena
di palesarvi a me non vi spaventi."

70   Step by step we walked without speech, seeing
        and hearing the sick, who could not lift their bodies.

73   I saw two sitting propped against each other, as
        one props pan against pan to cool, both from head to
        foot all spotted with scabs;

76   and I have never seen a currycomb so plied by a
        boy awaited by his master, or by one who unwilling
        stayed awake,

79   as each one of them plied the bite of his
        fingernails on himself, for the great rage of the itch,
        which no longer has any remedy;

82   their nails tore off the scabs like knives
        scaling bream or some other fish with larger scales.

85   "O you who dismail yourself with your fingers,"
        began my leader to one of them, "and at times make
        pincers of them,

88   tell us if any Italian is among those in here, so
        may your nail suffice eternally for this work."

91   "We are Italians, whom you see so ruined here,
        both of us," one replied weeping; "but who are you
        who have asked about us?"

94   And my leader said: "I am one descending with
        this living man from ledge to ledge, and I intend to
        show him Hell."

97   Then the mutual support was broken, and
        trembling each of them turned to me, along with
        others who heard the words as if by echo.

100   My good master drew near to me, saying: "Say to
        them what you wish"; and I began, since he wished
        it:

103   "So may your memory not be stolen from human
        minds in the first world, so may it live for many
        suns,

106   tell me who you are and of what people; let not your
        filthy and disgusting punishment make you fear
        to reveal yourselves to me."

109   "Io fui d'Arezzo, e Albero da Siena,"
        rispuose l'un, "mi fé mettere al foco;
        ma quel per ch'io mori' qui non mi mena.

112   Vero è ch'i' dissi lui, parlando a gioco:
        'I' mi saprei levar per l'aere a volo';
        e quei, ch'avea vaghezza e senno poco,

115   volle ch'i' li mostrassi l'arte; e solo
        perch' io nol feci Dedalo, mi fece
        ardere a tal che l'avea per figliuolo.

118   Ma ne l'ultima bolgia de le diece
        me per l'alchimia che nel mondo usai
        dannò Minòs, a cui fallar non lece."

121   E io dissi al poeta: "Or fu già mai
        gente sì vana come la sanese?
        Certo non la francesca sì d'assai!"

124   Onde l'altro lebbroso, che m'intese,
        rispuose al detto mio: "Tra'mene Stricca,
        che seppe far le temperate spese,

127   e Niccolò, che la costuma ricca
        del garofano prima discoverse
        ne l'orto dove tal seme s'appicca,

130   e tra'ne la brigata in che disperse
        Caccia d'Ascian la vigna e la gran fonda,
        e l'Abbagliato suo senno proferse.

133   Ma perché sappi chi sì ti seconda
        contra i Sanesi, aguzza ver' me l'occhio,
        sì che la faccia mia ben ti risponda:

136   sì vedrai ch'io son l'ombra di Capocchio,
        che falsai li metalli con l'alchìmia;
        e te dee ricordar, se ben t'adocchio,

139   com' io fui di natura buona scimia."

109   "I was from Arezzo, and Albero of Siena," replied
one, "sent me to the fire; but what I died for is not
what leads me here.

112   It is true that I told him, joking: 'I could raise
myself through the air in flight'; and he, who had
eagerness but little sense,

115   wanted me to show him the art; and only because
I did not make him Daedalus, he had me burned by
one who loved him as a son.

118   But to the last pocket of the ten, for alchemy,
which I practiced in the world, Minos damned me,
who may not err."

121   And I said to my poet: "Now was there ever a
people so foolish as the Sienese? Certainly not the
French, by far!"

124   And the other leper, who heard me, replied to my
word: "Except for Stricca, he knew how to spend
moderately,

127   and Nicholas, who first discovered the rich
custom of cloves, in the garden where that seed takes
root,

130   and except for the crew for whom Caccia
d'Asciano used up his vineyard and his great
farmlands, and to whom Bedazzled displayed his
wisdom.

133   But so that you may know who seconds you
against the Sienese, sharpen your eye toward me, that
my face may answer to you:

136   then you will see that I am the shade of
Capocchio, who falsified metals with alchemy; and
you must remember, if I eye you well,

139   how good an ape I was of nature."

NOTES

1–36. The multitude . . . compassionate toward him: The first part of
the canto continues the theme of the sowers of discord (*bolgia* 9); the emphasis
on the multitude and on the pilgrim's hallucinated fixation on the wounds re-
calls the opening of the previous canto.

1–3. The multitude . . . stay and weep: For drunkenness with the spec-
tacle of blood, see Augustine's account of Alypius at the gladiatorial contests in
Confessions 6.8:

> For when he saw that blood, he drank cruelty in with it and did not turn
> away, but he fixed his sight on it and drank in fury unaware and he took
> pleasure in the wickedness of the spectacle and became drunk [inebriabatur]
> with pleasure in blood.

The pilgrim's attitude is more ambiguous, but it still involves some degree of
participation in the sin of the *bolgia*.

9. the valley turns for twenty-two miles: That is, its circumference is twenty-
two miles. Dante clearly has in mind the well-known fact that the ratio of cir-
cumference to diameter of a circle (pi) is 22:7; this means, of course, that the
diameter of this *bolgia* is seven miles. In the sixteenth century, there were several
attempts to calculate the exact dimensions of all of Hell on the basis of this indi-
cation. For the association of the number eleven with sin, see the note to 11.16–
111.

10–11. already the moon . . . granted us: Since the moon is two days past
full (20.127), the time in Jerusalem is early afternoon on Saturday. Virgil's ref-
erence to a limit on the time granted them seems a clear reference to the wide-
spread folk tradition that visits to the other world must be completed within
twenty-four hours (the journey began at nightfall on Friday; 2.1): only four or
five hours, then, remain (but see 34.96, with note). In figural terms, of course,
the arrival on the shore of the mountain of Purgatory must take place on Easter
morning.

13–21. If you had attended . . . costs so much down there: The pilgrim
claims that he was lingering in order to catch sight of one of his relatives (Virgil
identifies this relative in line 27). These lines are not inconsistent with lines
1–3; rather, they identify his desire to see his relative as itself part of the addic-
tion to bloody spectacle.

20. of my blood: It is partly the sense of the closeness, the materiality even, of the blood tie that explains the duty of exacting vengeance for the spilling of it (lines 32–33).

22. Let not your thought break over him: The metaphor has been variously explained; we interpret it as comparing Dante's relative to a rock projecting for the moment above the waves of the sea (cf. 20.3: "this first canticle, which is of those submerged"; the imagery of voyage and shipwreck has permeated the *Inferno*). Let him sink, Virgil is saying.

25–27. I saw him . . . Geri del Bello: The threatening gesture is presumably a stabbing motion. Dante's sons Jacopo and Pietro in their commentaries identify Geri del Bello, well known as an instigator of violence, as a second cousin of Dante's on his father's side; the date of his death is unknown but apparently later than 1280. Benvenuto says that the Alighieri took vengeance on Geri's killer, a member of the Sacchetti family, in 1310; Pietro Alighieri says that the families were formally reconciled in 1342. (There are detailed articles on what is known of Dante's relatives in *E.D.*)

29. Hautefort: Hautefort was Bertran de Born's castle (see the note to 28.134).

31–36. his violent death . . . compassionate toward him: The obligation of private vengeance was recognized by law in the Italian communes; vengeance was punished—in theory at least—only if it was judged excessive. Dante's position on the matter is complex: the pilgrim feels the shame of the affront (line 33) and seems to acknowledge that Geri's resentment at being unavenged is justified. At the same time, vengeance is reserved to God by the Old and New Testaments (Deut. 32.35: "Revenge is mine," quoted in Romans 12.19) and was in Dante's time a major political problem resulting from the breakdown of central authority (the empire). The temptation to avenge Geri is closely related to the sin of the *bolgia* (cf. Mosca, 28.103–11: the ruinous feud between the Amidei and the Buondelmonti, to which Dante traced all the disasters of recent Florentine history, originated in the desire for revenge).

40–45. When we were above . . . with my hands: Sounds from the new *bolgia* are said to strike the pilgrim's ears only when he reaches the point where it is fully revealed to sight, a touch characteristic of Dante's tendency to establish sharp boundaries between the parts of the other world (cf. a similar transition in 3.21–22).

40, 41. cloister, converts: Sarcastic monastic imagery, as in 23.90–91, but see the note on hospitals (lines 47–48).

43–44. strange lamentings . . . made of pity: The idea that the lamentings pierce the pilgrim with pity occasions the metaphor of their being arrows whose sharp iron points are made of pity.

46–69. What the suffering . . . down the evil road: The last *bolgia* is introduced in a manner closely parallel to the previous one (28.1–12): there the slaughter of the countless battles afflicting southern Italy, here the malaria prevalent in the marshy parts of Italy (even in the twentieth century: the Pontine marshes south of Rome and parts of the Maremma were drained only under Mussolini). Both panoramas are versions of the social consequences of fraud, the evils of the body politic. See Additional Note 13.

47–48. hospitals of Valdichiana . . . Maremma . . . Sardinia: These are all regions where malaria was particularly virulent: the Valdichiana (valley of the river Chiana, a tributary of the Arno) is in southeastern Tuscany, between Arezzo and Chiusi; the Maremma is in southwestern Tuscany. The establishment of hospitals for malaria victims was the mission of several religious orders.

57. the falsifiers that it registers here: "The falsifiers" announces the sin punished in this *bolgia*, of which, it will turn out, there are several distinct categories (hence, perhaps, the registry). Most commentators take the phrase "that it registers here" as a reference to the books in which good and bad deeds are recorded by the angels, to be read out at the Last Judgment (Apoc. 20.12), referred to also in *Par.* 19.112–13; they take "here" to mean "in this life."

58–66. I do not believe . . . different heaps: The reference is to Ovid's retelling of the myth in *Met.* 7.523–660: Aegina, a small island near Athens, was depopulated by a plague caused by Juno's anger; its king, Aeacus, begged Jupiter for help and in a dream saw the ants becoming men; his new followers appear in a manner that recalls his dream (it should be noted that Ovid's "assertion" of the myth is unusually guarded). In *Convivio* 4.27.17, Dante approvingly cites Aeacus for his appeal to God but does not mention the ants.

In Ovid's account, the plague occurs when dark clouds, hot weather, and south winds infect the springs and the lakes (533); it attacks first animals (536), and then men (552), the latter especially through the odor of the dead animals (548, 551); Dante refers only to the malignity of the air (line 60), sharpening the parallel with malaria. Ovid's description offers a number of suggestions for the heaping and indiscriminate scattering of bodies (especially lines 559–60, 570–71, 574, and 581); Dante's touch of the tiny worm dying is not in Ovid (and would seem inconsistent with the survival of the ants), though Dante may have considered it implied in the deaths of the large animals (537–81).

66. heaps: The Italian is *biche*, properly used of the heaped sheaves of harvested grain waiting to be stored (the harvest is implicitly a reference to the Last Judgment).

68–69. this one crawling transmuted himself: *Carpone* [on all fours] echoes 25.140–41, on the crawling of the new lizard. The striking "transmuted himself" (*si trasmutava*) for "transferred himself" is an anticipation of the theme of alchemy, which pretended to transmute lesser metals into gold, as well as an echo of the grotesque transmutations of the *bolgia* of the thieves.

73–84. I saw two . . . larger scales: The early commentators identified the disease from which the two are suffering as either scabies or leprosy; leprosy (in its medieval sense) seems the more likely. Bosco (*E.D.* 3, s.v. *lebbra*) cites the widely used thirteenth-century encyclopedia by Bartholomaeus Anglicus, *De proprietatibus rerum* (7.64), on one type of leprosy, called "serpentine": "it is scaly: the patient suffering from this type of leprosy easily loses the surface of his skin, which is resolved in a kind of scaliness"; Bartholomaeus also says that stench and itch are characteristic of it. Nardi (1944) suggested that the choice of this disease as the punishment for alchemists was derived from their way of considering base metals to be "diseases of gold" and lead, in particular, as the "leprosy of gold." The frenetic activity of these two sharply distinguishes them from the others so far described.

76–78. I have never seen . . . stayed awake: Two examples of extreme haste, a stable boy using the currycomb on a horse while his master waited, presumably with impatience, and one currying a horse late at night when anxious to sleep.

85. O you who dismail yourself: The metaphor implicitly compares the scabs to the circles of metal of which a coat of chain mail is fashioned. But the analogy is much closer with ancient scale armor; Dante knew Vergil's descriptions, such as *Aen.* 11.487–88 (of Turnus): "iamque adeo rutilum thoraca indutus aënis/ horrebat squamis . . ." [and already, putting on shining body-armor, he bristled with bronze scales . . .]. The comparison to the scales of snakes was natural and underlies the famous description of the armed Pyrrhus in *Aen.* 2.469–75.

109–19. I was from Arezzo . . . practiced in the world: The early commentators identify this alchemist as one Griffolino, burned at the stake in Siena before 1272 for heresy. Albero (or Alberto) of Siena was a nobleman whose existence is attested by documents, favored by the bishop—or the inquisitor— "one who loved him as a son," line 117 (the early commentators take line 117 to mean that Albero was literally the son of the bishop).

116. I did not make him Daedalus: That is, I did not teach him to fly. The allusion to Daedalus, especially in a context stressing fatherly love, suggests that Griffolino is in some sense parallel to Icarus: his overweening joke flew too high for Albero! (Cf. the references to Icarus in 17.109–11, 26.110–11.)

119. alchemy: Alchemy, then, is the first category of falsification in this *bolgia*. Medieval writers distinguish permissible alchemy (the ancestor of modern chemistry)—the effort to discover the substance common to all metals and achieve their transmutation, especially of base metals into gold—from the fraudulent variety. The notoriety of fraudulent alchemy can be gauged by the many laws against it, as well as from texts like Chaucer's "Canon Yeoman's Prologue," an exposé of a fraudulent alchemist by his servant. The cooking metaphors of the canto are related to the concoctions and reductions of alchemy.

121–23. Now was there ever . . . the French, by far: Dante also makes fun of the vanity and credulity of the Sienese in *Purg.* 13.151–54; Boccaccio (*Trattatello*) says he visited the city a number of times. The vanity of the French was proverbial.

125–32. Except for Stricca . . . Nicholas . . . the crew . . . Caccia . . . Bedazzled: These are notorious Sienese spendthrifts of the late thirteenth century (the theme relates this passage closely to the spendthrifts in 13.110–35). Stricca has been variously identified as a member of the prominent Salimbeni or Tolomei family. Nicholas may have been his brother; the spice clove, which had to be imported from the East, was extremely expensive in this period ("the garden where that seed takes root" is, of course, Siena; *appiccarsi* [literally, to adhere] is used also of two thieves in 25.61). The Italian term *brigata*, which we translate as "crew," refers to the medieval Italian custom of informal groups (apparently often of about a dozen persons, and often of both sexes, especially later in the fourteenth century) who met periodically to socialize. This one was said to have been twelve rich young men of Siena who put their entire fortunes into one fund and consumed it in twenty months, partying and banqueting; among them were Caccianemico degli Scialenghi d'Asciano and Bartolommeo dei Folcacchieri, called L'Abbagliato [Bedazzled], who is known to have repeatedly served as *podestà* of other cities and to have died in 1300.

Note the emphasis on expensive seasonings for foods in comparison with the necessities themselves. See Additional Note 13.

133–39. But so that you . . . of nature: The soul, Capocchio, now identifies himself as someone the pilgrim can recognize. Benvenuto says that Capocchio was a Florentine and possessed the academic title *magister*; Buti and others say that he and Dante studied natural science together—if so, probably *materia medica* (Dante qualified for membership in the *Arte dei Medici e Speziali* [the Guild of Physicians and Pharmacists]). Capocchio was burned at the stake in Siena in 1293; the order for payment of his executioners is recorded in the city archives.

134. sharpen your eye: The same word (*aguzzare*) used, though in a slightly different sense, of the band of homosexuals in 15.20.

139. how good an ape I was of nature: How well I could imitate nature, presumably in his imitation gold and silver, but some early commentators say that Capocchio was a famous and witty mimic. The *Romance of the Rose* seems to be one of the earliest texts to speak of art as the "ape of nature" (the metaphor is partly derogatory, since the products of art are always inferior to those of nature). Art, says Jean de Meun (lines 15999–16001),

> si garde conment Nature euvre,
> car mout voudroit fere autele euvre,
> et la contrefet conme singes.

> [watches how nature operates,
> for it would dearly wish to make such a work,
> and it imitates her like an ape.]

See Curtius 1953. All the inmates of this *bolgia* are "apes" in the sense of producing debased imitations.

CANTO 30

1   Nel tempo che Iunone era crucciata
per Semelè contra 'l sangue tebano,
come mostrò una e altra fïata,

4   Atamante divenne tanto insano
che, veggendo la moglie con due figli
andar carcata da ciascuna mano,

7   gridò: "Tendiam le reti, sì ch'io pigli
la leonessa e ' leoncini al varco!"
E poi distese i dispietati artigli,

10   prendendo l'un ch'avea nome Learco,
e rotollo e percosselo ad un sasso;
e quella s'annegò con l'altro carco.

13   E quando la Fortuna volse in basso
l'altezza de' Troian che tutto ardiva,
sì che 'nsieme col regno il re fu casso,

16   Ecuba trista, misera e cattiva,
poscia che vide Polissena morta,
e del suo Polidoro in su la riva

19   del mar si fu la dolorosa accorta,
forsennata latrò sì come cane,
tanto il dolor le fé la mente torta.

22   Ma né di Tebe furie né troiane
si vider mäi in alcun tanto crude,
non punger bestie, nonché membra umane,

25   quant' io vidi in due ombre smorte e nude,
che mordendo correvan di quel modo
che 'l porco quando del porcil si schiude.

28   L'un giunse a Capocchio, e in sul nodo
del collo l'assannò, sì che, tirando,
grattar li fece il ventre al fondo sodo.

CANTO 30

1   In the time when, because of Semele, Juno was
angry against the blood of Thebes, as she showed
once and again,

4   Athamas became so insane, that, seeing his wife
walking with his two sons on either hand,

7   he cried: "Spread the nets, so that I may catch the
lioness and her cubs at the crossing!" And then he
stretched out his pitiless claws,

10   taking the one whose name was Learchus, and
whirled him and struck his head against a rock; and
she drowned herself with her other burden.

13   And when Fortune leveled to the ground the
pride of the Trojans, all aflame, so that along with his
kingdom the king was broken,

16   Hecuba, sorrowing, wretched, and a captive, after
she saw Polyxena dead, and, grieving, had perceived
her Polydorus on the shore

19   of the sea, going mad, she barked like a dog, her
grief had so twisted her mind.

22   But neither Theban furies nor Trojan ever made
anyone so cruel, not to wound beasts, let alone
human limbs,

25   as two pallid, naked shades I saw, who ran biting
in the manner of the pig when the sty is opened.

28   One reached Capocchio and set his tusk into the
knot of his neck so that, dragging, he made him
scratch his belly on the solid floor.

31   E l'Aretin, che rimase, tremando
mi disse: "Quel folletto è Gianni Schicchi,
e va rabbioso altrui così conciando."

34   "Oh," diss' io lui, "se l'altro non ti ficchi
li denti a dosso, non ti sia fatica
a dir chi è, pria che di qui si spicchi."

37   Ed elli a me: "Quell' è l'anima antica
di Mirra scellerata, che divenne
al padre, fuor del dritto amore, amica.

40   Questa a peccar con esso così venne,
falsificando sé in altrui forma,
come l'altro che là sen va, sostenne,

43   per guadagnar la donna de la torma,
falsificare in sé Buoso Donati,
testando e dando al testamento norma."

46   E poi che i due rabbiosi fuor passati
sovra cu' io avea l'occhio tenuto,
rivolsilo a guardar li altri mal nati.

49   Io vidi un, fatto a guisa di lëuto,
pur ch'elli avesse avuta l'anguinaia
tronca da l'altro che l'uomo ha forcuto.

52   La grave idropesì, che sì dispaia
le membra con l'omor che mal converte
che 'l viso non risponde a la ventraia,

55   faceva lui tener le labbra aperte
come l'etico fa, che per la sete
l'un verso 'l mento e l'altro in sù rinverte.

58   "O voi che sanz' alcuna pena siete,
e non so io perché, nel mondo gramo,"
diss' elli a noi, "guardate e attendete

61   a la miseria del maestro Adamo;
io ebbi, vivo, assai di quel ch'i' volli,
e ora, lasso! un gocciol d'acqua bramo.

64   Li ruscelletti che d'i verdi colli
del Casentin discendon giuso in Arno,
faccendo i lor canali freddi e molli,

67   sempre mi stanno innanzi, e non indarno,
ché l'imagine lor vie più m'asciuga
che 'l male ond' io nel volto mi discarno.

31   And the Aretine who remained, trembling told
me: "That goblin is Gianni Schicchi, and in his rage
he goes treating others so."

34   "Oh," I said to him, "so may the other not set his
teeth in you, let it not be a labor to tell me who he is,
before he disappears."

37   And he to me: "That is the ancient soul of
wicked Myrrha, who became, beyond right love, her
father's lover.

40   She came to sin with him by counterfeiting herself
in another's shape, just as the other who goes off
there,

43   to gain the queen of the herd dared to counterfeit
in himself Buoso Donati, making a will and giving it
legal form."

46   And when the two rabid shades, on whom I had
kept my eyes, had passed, I turned to gaze at the
other ill-born ones.

49   I saw one made in the shape of a lute, if he had
had his groin cut from the other forked part.

52   The heavy dropsy that so unpairs the members,
with the liquid that it ill converts, that the face
does not answer to the belly,

55   made him hold his lips open, as a fevered person
does, who in his thirst turns one of them down
toward his chin and the other upward.

58   "O you who are without any punishment, and I
know not why, in this grim world," he said to us,
"gaze and attend

61   to the wretchedness of Master Adam; alive, I had
much of whatever I wished, and now, alas, I crave a
drop of water.

64   The little streams that from the green hills of the
Casentino come down into Arno, making their
channels cool and moist,

67   always stand before me, and not in vain, for their
image dries me far more than the disease that robs
my face of flesh.

70 La rigida giustizia che mi fruga
    tragge cagion del loco ov' io peccai
    a metter più li miei sospiri in fuga.

73 Ivi è Romena, là dov' io falsai
    la lega suggellata del Batista,
    per ch'io il corpo sù arso lasciai.

76 Ma s'io vedessi qui l'anima trista
    di Guido o d'Alessandro o di lor frate,
    per Fonte Branda non darei la vista.

79 Dentro c'è l'una già, se l'arrabbiate
    ombre che vanno intorno dicon vero;
    ma che mi val, c'ho le membra legate?

82 S'io fossi pur di tanto ancor leggero
    ch'i' potessi in cent' anni andar un'oncia,
    io sarei messo già per lo sentiero,

85 cercando lui tra questa gente sconcia,
    con tutto ch'ella volge undici miglia
    e men d'un mezzo di traverso non ci ha.

88 Io son per lor tra sì fatta famiglia:
    e' m'indussero a batter li fiorini
    ch'avevan tre carati di mondiglia."

91 E io a lui: "Chi son li due tapini
    che fumman come man bagnate 'l verno,
    giacendo stretti a' tuoi destri confini?"

94 "Qui li trovai—e poi volta non dierno—"
    rispuose, "quando piovvi in questo greppo,
    e non credo che dieno in sempiterno.

97 L'una è la falsa ch'accusò Gioseppo;
    l'altr' è 'l falso Sinon greco di Troia:
    per febbre aguta gittan tanto leppo."

100 E l'un di lor, che si recò a noia
    forse d'esser nomato sì oscuro,
    col pugno li percosse l'epa croia.

103 Quella sonò come fosse un tamburo;
    e mastro Adamo li percosse il volto
    col braccio suo, che non parve men duro,

106 dicendo a lui: "Ancor che mi sia tolto
    lo muover per le membra che son gravi,
    ho il braccio a tal mestiere sciolto."

70   The rigid justice that probes me takes occasion
from the place where I sinned, to put my sighs the more
to flight.

73   There is Romena, where I falsified the alloy sealed
with the Baptist, for which I left my body burned up
there.

76   But if I might see here the wicked soul of Guido
or Alessandro or their brother, for Fonte Branda I
would not trade the sight.

79   One of them has already come, if the raging
shades who run about here tell the truth; but what
does it help me, since my members are bound?

82   If I were just so light that in a hundred years I
could go one inch, I would have already set out on
the path,

85   searching through all this filthy people, although
it turns for eleven miles and is no less than one across.

88   Because of them I am among such a household:
they induced me to mint the florins that had three
carats of dross."

91   And I to him: "Who are the two wretches smoking
like wet hands in winter, lying close on your right-
hand boundary?"

94   "Here I found them—and since then they have
not even turned over—" he replied, "when I rained
down into this pit, and I do not believe they will for
eternity.

97   One is the false woman who accused Joseph; the
other is false Sinon of Troy: because of acute fever
they throw out such a stench."

100 And one of them, who perhaps resented being
named so darkly, with his fist struck him on his taut
belly.

103 That resounded as if it were a drum; and Master
Adam struck the other's face with his arm, which
seemed no less hard,

106 saying to him: "Although I am deprived of
movement by my heavy limbs, I have an arm loose
for such business."

109 Ond' ei rispuose: "Quando tu andavi
al fuoco, non l'avei tu così presto;
ma sì e più l'avei quando coniavi."

112 E l'idropico: "Tu di' ver di questo,
ma tu non fosti sì ver testimonio
là 've del ver fosti a Troia richesto."

115 "S'io dissi falso, e tu falsasti il conio,"
disse Sinon; "e son qui per un fallo,
e tu per più ch'alcun altro demonio!"

118 "Ricorditi, spergiuro, del cavallo,"
rispuose quel ch'avëa infiata l'epa;
"e sieti reo che tutto il mondo sallo!"

121 "E te sia rea la sete onde ti crepa,"
disse 'l Greco, "la lingua, e l'acqua marcia
che 'l ventre innanzi a li occhi sì t'assiepa!"

124 Allora il monetier: "Così si squarcia
la bocca tua per tuo mal come suole;
ché, s'i' ho sete e omor mi rinfarcia,

127 tu hai l'arsura e 'l capo che ti duole,
e per leccar lo specchio di Narcisso
non vorresti a 'nvitar molte parole."

130 Ad ascoltarli er' io del tutto fisso,
quando 'l maestro mi disse: "Or pur mira,
che per poco che teco non mi risso!"

133 Quand' io 'l senti' a me parlar con ira,
volsimi verso lui con tal vergogna
ch'ancor per la memoria mi si gira.

136 Qual è colui che suo dannaggio sogna,
che sognando desidera sognare,
sì che quel ch'è, come non fosse, agogna,

139 tal mi fec' io, non possendo parlare,
che disïava scusarmi, e scusava
me tuttavia, e nol mi credea fare.

142 "Maggior difetto men vergogna lava,"
disse 'l maestro, "che 'l tuo non è stato;
però d'ogne trestizia ti disgrava.

145 E fa ragion ch'io ti sia sempre allato,
se più avvien che Fortuna t'accoglia
dove sien genti in simigliante piato:

148 ché voler ciò udire è bassa voglia."

109 And he replied: "When you were going to the fire, you didn't have it so ready; but that much and more you had it when you were coining."

112 And the hydroptic: "You say true there, but you were not such a true witness where you were asked for the truth at Troy."

115 "If I spoke falsely, you falsified the coinage," said Sinon, "and I am here for one fault, but you for more than any other demon!"

118 "Remember, perjurer, the Horse," replied he of the swollen liver; "and let it be bitter to you that the whole world knows of it!"

121 "And to you bitter be the thirst that cracks," said the Greek, "your tongue, and the stagnant water that makes of your belly a hedge before your eyes!"

124 Then the coiner: "Your mouth gapes because of your disease, as usual; for, if I am thirsty and liquid swells me,

127 you have burning fever and a head that aches, and to lick the mirror of Narcissus you would not need to be invited with many words!"

130 I was all intent to listen to them, when my master said to me: "Now keep looking, for I am not far from quarreling with you!"

133 When I heard him speak to me angrily, I turned toward him with such shame that it still dizzies me in memory.

136 Like one who dreams of harm, and, dreaming, wishes he were dreaming, so that he yearns for what is as if it were not,

139 so I became, unable to speak, wishing to excuse myself, and I was excusing myself all along, though I did not think so.

142 "Less shame washes away a greater fault," said my master, "than yours has been; therefore cast off all sorrow.

145 And mind that I be always at your side, if it happen again that Fortune find you where people are in such a squabble:

148 for to wish to hear that is a base desire."

NOTES

1–27. In the time . . . when the sty is opened: This last canto of the Malebolge has perhaps the most elaborate opening, along with 24.1–21, and is a major instance of the featuring of Thebes and Troy in lower Hell (see the note to 26.52–54). Commentators have remarked on a disproportion between the atrocities in the myths and the actions of Gianni Schicchi and Myrrha. As a modern Florentine and an ancient Greek, they are correlated with Master Adam and Sinon (see the note to lines 100–129). The two are mentioned later as disseminators of news (lines 79–80).

1–12. In the time . . . her other burden: Juno, jealous of Semele (daughter of Cadmus, founder of Thebes), first destroys Semele (*Met.* 3.259–313); later, jealous of Semele's son Bacchus, she has the Fury Tisiphonē (see the note to 9.30–51) drive Athamas and his wife Ino (another daughter of Cadmus) mad (*Met.* 4.464–542). Dante sharply condenses Ovid's account; he echoes particularly lines 512–19:

> Protinus Aeolides media furibundus in aula
> clamat, Io, comites, his retia tendite silvis!
> hic modo cum gemina visa est mihi prole leaena,
> utque ferae sequitur vestigia coniugis amens:
> deque sinu matris ridentem et parva Learchum
> bracchia tendentem rapit et bis terque per auras
> more rotat fundae, rigidoque infantia saxo
> discutit ora ferox.

> [Suddenly the son of Aeolus (Athamas), mad in the midst of the palace,
> cries, "Hurrah, comrades, spread the nets here in the woods!
> here just now I saw a lioness with twin cubs."
> And he follows the footprints of his wife as if she were a beast,
> and from his mother's bosom seizes Learchus, who is laughing and
> holding out his little arms, and whirls him in the air three, four times,
> like a sling, and shatters his infant face against the hard stone
> savagely.]

The theme of violence against children is central to Canto 33.

13–21. And when Fortune . . . twisted her mind: An even more condensed epitome of events from *Met.* 13.408–575, also taking place by the sea. After the fall of Troy (the Trojan Horse figures later in the canto), the former queen, Hecuba, is enslaved by the Greeks. Sailing home, the Greeks stop in Thrace;

there Achilles' ghost demands the sacrifice of Hecuba's daughter Polyxena, over whom she utters a long lament. When she goes to the seashore for water to wash the body, she finds the body of her youngest, Polydorus, murdered by King Polymnestor (Dante drew on Vergil's version of the Polydorus story in Canto 13). She kills Polymnestor by thrusting her fingers into his eyes, and when the Thracians hurl weapons and stones at her (lines 567–69):

> . . . missum rauco cum murmure saxum
> morsibus insequitur rictuque in verba parato
> latravit conata loqui.
>
> [. . . the hurled stone she pursues with a hoarse murmur,
> biting, and, when showing her teeth as if for words,
> she barked when she tried to speak.]

Like Ovid, Dante leaves implicit Hecuba's metamorphosis into a dog (explicit in Euripides and Seneca); Athamas's claws (line 9) also suggest a beast. The medieval commentators on Ovid identify madness (alienation of mind) as one of the forms of metamorphosis.

22–27. But neither . . . sty is opened: That is, the madness of Athamas and Hecuba was not so cruel as that of these two shades. The animal references have moved from lioness and cubs (line 8) to unspecified claws (line 9) to dog (line 20) to rabid pigs (cf. 13.112–13, in a context related to this one by the catalog of Sienese spendthrifts in 29.125–32).

32. That goblin is Gianni Schicchi: This new category of falsifiers, the impersonators, suffer from rabies. Bevenuto suggests the *contrapasso*: "as madness is an alienation of the mind, so they alienated theirs by assuming the person of another." Gianni Schicchi is further identified in lines 42–45.

37–41. That is the ancient soul . . . another's shape: The story of Myrrha, who became the mother of Adonis, is told in *Met.* 10.298–502. Line 39, "al padre, fuor del dritto *amore, amica*" (cf. 5.103), makes contiguous the terms of the etymological figure (italicized), of which the second, *amica*, is placed *outside* the preceding parenthetical phrase. *Scellerata* (line 37) echoes Ovid's use of the term *scelus* [crime] to characterize Myrrha (*Met.* 10.314–15).

Jacoff (1988) points out most of the women shown in Hell have sinned sexually: Francesca (Canto 5), Thaïs (Canto 18), Myrrha (we may add Potiphar's wife); the others are Manto and the diviners (Canto 20) (see the note to 18.133–35).

41, 44. counterfeiting herself in, counterfeit in himself: Note the antithetical symmetry of the two expressions, pointed out by Torraca; the point seems to be that both have equal validity: the impersonations wrong ("falsify") both the impersonator and the one impersonated.

42–45. just as the other . . . legal form: Gianni Schicchi, who died around 1280, was a prominent member of the Cavalcanti family, famous as a mimic. No references to this story survive that antedate the *Comedy*. The early commentators relate that Simone Donati (the future father of Corso, Forese, and Piccarda) persuaded Gianni Schicchi to impersonate his dead uncle, Buoso Donati, and to dictate a will in Simone's favor; Gianni willed to himself the "queen of the herd," the most beautiful mare or mule in all Tuscany. Giacomo Puccini wrote a richly comic one-act opera on the story.

45. making a will . . . legal form: That is, before a notary and witnesses. Dante here condemns a violation of the legal norms that ensure the orderly transfer of property; compare the concern with the Sienese spendthrifts that concluded the last canto. The canto now reveals its major focus (see the note to lines 49–129).

49–129. I saw one . . . invited with many words: The major focus of the canto, and the conclusion of the Malebolge, focuses on two souls: Master Adam and Sinon. The debasing of currency (Master Adam debased the florin, the foundation of Florentine economic power) would be increasingly recognized, in the course of the fourteenth century—which saw a number of monetary crises—as a major economic problem affecting all of Europe (see Johnson 1956; Shoaf 1983). Sinon of Troy (introduced in line 98) is an instance of false testimony, like Gianni Schicchi, which in Sinon, Dante identifies as at the very root of Western history, the fall of Troy.

49–51. I saw one . . . the other forked part: That is, if one ignored the legs, the shape was that of a lute, which has an egg-shaped belly surmounted by a narrow neck (the fingerboard) that is bent back to accommodate the pegs for the strings (the metaphor thus implies that the soul is craning its neck; the lute is to be imagined with its flat face down [Figure 6]). Dante is drawing on the traditional notion of Christ on the Cross as being like a stringed instrument, his tendons stretched on the wood (Heilbronn 1983); this is a particularly rich instance of an infernal punishment parodying the Crucifixion (cf. the notes to 23.100–102, 118–20 and

Figure 6. A lute, face down.

Additional Note 16). The drum of lines 102–3 would consist of skin stretched on a wood frame.

52–57. The heavy dropsy . . . the other upward: According to medieval medical writers, the type of dropsy from which Master Adam is suffering, *timpanite* [drum dropsy], bringing intense thirst, is caused by a malfunction of the liver, which normally converts the food, already "cooked" by the heat of the stomach and broken down into an intermediate liquid (*omor*, line 53), into blood, which the heart then distributes to the rest of the body; the malfunction creates impure humors that distend the belly while the other members, especially the face, lose flesh (the face "does not reply to"—is out of proportion with—the belly: the harmony, or tempering, of the fluids of the body is disrupted, so that the body is like a discordant musical instrument; see Spitzer 1963). As the commentators point out, these lines are characterized by unusual terms and harsh sounds, especially in rhyme: *lëuto* [lute], *ventraia* [belly], *dispaia* [unpairs]—the last two apparently coinages of Dante's (cf. *discarno* [lose flesh], line 69); all refer to the belly or lower body (cf. *anguinaia* [groin], *forcuto* [forked], lines 50–51).

57. turns one of them . . . the other upward: Thus the lips, too, are "unpaired" by the disease.

58–129. O you . . . with many words: The scene with Master Adam moves gradually from his learned, self-pitying effort to elicit sympathy to the futile exchange of malicious taunts and blows with Sinon. Uniquely among the souls of the other world, in this scene Master Adam entirely forgets his dialogue with the pilgrim. Master Adam's fixation on revenge, and its role in his damnation, is similar to Ugolino's. For Master Adam's importance in the Malebolge as a whole, see Additional Note 13.

58–90. O you . . . three carats of dross: Master Adam's first speech is eleven terzinas, thirty-three lines long. At its center, with *ma* [but], line 76 (to what does the "but" refer?), the focus becomes his hatred and desire for vengeance.

58–61. O you . . . to the wretchedness of Master Adam: These lines echo the famous passage in Lam. 1.12 (echoed by Dante also in *Vita nuova* 7 and in 28.130–32—Bertran de Born's opening words; Lam. 1.1 is echoed in *Vita nuova* 29, 1.2 in *Inf.* 8.77), spoken by the personified Jerusalem after the destruction of the city in 586 B.C.:

> O vos omnes qui transitis per viam,
> adtendite et videte si est dolor sicut dolor meius;
> quoniam vindemiavit me, ut locutus est Dominus in die irae furoris sui.

[O you all who pass by in the road,
attend and see if there is any sorrow like my sorrow,
for the Lord has harvested me according to his word in the day of his anger
    (trans. R. M. D.).]

Figurally the fall of Jerusalem, like the destruction of Sodom, looks forward to the Last Judgment; tropologically these lines were interpreted as expressing the fear of damnation. That Bertran de Born and Master Adam quote the same biblical passage, one spoken by a personification of the body politic, itself points to the central theme of these cantos.

61. Master Adam: One Adam of England is identified in a legal document of 1277 as a "familiar" (that is, a member of the household) of the Conti Guidi of Romena; a chronicler relates that a representative of the Conti Guidi was burned in Florence in 1281 for circulating counterfeit coins.

62–63. alive, I had . . . drop of water: Dante is drawing on the parable of the rich man and Lazarus (Luke 16.19–31): the rich man dies and, burning in Hell, sees in the bosom of Abraham (in Heaven) the beggar Lazarus, "full of sores" in life, whom he had spurned. He begs to have Lazarus dip the tip of a finger in water and bring it to him, and when Abraham replies that the gulf between Heaven and Hell is absolute, the rich man begs him to have Lazarus warn his five brothers; Abraham refuses, for "if they hear not Moses and the Prophets, neither will they believe, if one rise again from the dead."

64–75. The little streams . . . burned up there: The Casentino is a mountainous region east of Florence, including the upper basin of the Arno, in Dante's time under the control of the Conti Guidi (see the note to 16.34–39), of whose castle at Romena the ruins still exist. The image of the streams intensifies Master Adam's thirst at several metaphorical levels beyond the literal: they are an image of the health and innocence of the earth, contrasting sharply with Master Adam's disease, and they imply the idea of baptism and its renewal of childlike innocence, present also in the other image referred to, that of the Baptist stamped on the florin. The supreme irony of the passage is that the very place where he sinned and the products of his sin, if Master Adam had attended to them, could have led him to repentance and salvation. Master Adam's name, of course, is itself a reminder of the theological context; he should have remembered the biblical Adam when he was in the Edenic Casentino (on his offspring, see the notes to lines 79–90 and 118–20).

67. always stand before me: Dante has in mind the classical precedent for such torments, Tantalus (*Met.* 4.458–59): "tibi, Tantale, nullae/ deprenduntur aquae, quaeque inminet, effugit arbor" [no waters, Tantalus, can be caught by you, and the tree above you flees].

70–72. The rigid justice . . . the more to flight: In other words, God's justice probes Adam internally by causing the image of the streams to be ever present to him; to dismiss it is beyond his power. Thus the true image of the streams torments the producer of false images (i.e., counterfeit coins).

72. to put my sighs the more to flight: To make him sigh (pant) more frequently.

73–74. where I falsified the alloy sealed with the Baptist: In order to counterfeit florins, Master Adam had to imitate a distempered digestive system: first he cooked and refined gold, producing a liquid (parallel to the first digestion in the stomach); then he contaminated the gold by adding dross (parallel to the malfunction of the liver); finally, placing cast disks of the contaminated gold in a die or matrix, with blows of a hammer he imprinted on them the outer form of the florin—on one side, the Florentine lily, and on the other, the city's patron saint (see 13.143–50, with notes), John the Baptist; this imprinting is parallel to the liver's final production of blood (see Durling 1981a). The alloy of the florin is "sealed with the Baptist" to testify (cf. line 45) to the correct weight and composition of the coin. Master Adam's term *lega* [alloy] also means "league" or "covenant"; both refer to the social bond that his crime violates (11.56) and are additional reminders of the Baptist's call to repentance.

Medieval writers thought of money as the blood of the body politic; in their conception the heart was a reservoir, and blood flowed outward from the heart like a river (the idea of the circulation of blood is much later). Master Adam is an image of a distempered body politic (see 28.142, with note, and Additional Note 13).

76–90. But if I might see . . . three carats of dross: Like the first half of his speech, this half ends with the specification of his sin, this time even more precise. Italian *battere* [to strike, to mint] refers to the hammer blow on the matrix. The three carats of dross made Master Adam's florins weigh twenty-one carats instead of twenty-four.

78. for Fonte Branda . . . trade the sight: Several candidates have been suggested for what must have been a famous spring. Master Adam's hatred is so strong that he would prefer to witness his enemies' suffering than to have his thirst relieved. This amounts to preferring vengeance to salvation.

80. if the raging shades . . . tell the truth: In other words, Gianni Schicchi and Myrrha—and presumably the other impersonators—are able to speak and disseminate information.

81. but what does it help . . . members are bound: Another "but," whose referent is worth considering. The Italian *che mi val* means literally "what is it worth to me" (cf. coins) or "what power does it give me" (cf. 22.127). There is an important pun in *legate* [bound], from the same root as *lega* (see note to lines 73–74): his limbs are incapable of motion, made of a contaminated alloy, and bound by God's judgment (in fact, he is a bondslave to the Old Law; he is the Pauline Old Man of Romans 5.14–19, 6.6, and 7.17–24).

86–87. although it turns . . . one across: In 29.9 Virgil told the pilgrim that the circumference of the ninth *bolgia* was twenty-two miles; the diameter of this tenth is half of the previous, thus three and a half miles.

88. household: The Italian term is *famiglia* (see the note to 15.22); Master Adam's contemptuous use of it expresses his pride in his learning and high social status; we are also reminded that all the damned are members of Satan (see Additional Note 2) and ultimately his servants. In the clear allusions to the biblical Adam in Master Adam's name and the scene of his sin, we also have allusions to the idea of the human family, all descended from him.

90. dross: Italian *mondiglia* derives from *mondare* [to cleanse]; it is the remnant after cleansing.

91–93. Who are the two . . . right-hand boundary: The pilgrim's tone is sarcastic, both in his vivid simile and in his metaphoric use of "boundary"—as if Master Adam's belly were so huge as to constitute a geographic region (another reminder of the symbolism of the body politic). The two souls' metaphorical "smoking like wet hands" also reduces them in size next to Master Adam. The vapor identifies them as suffering from a fourth disease, thus as a fourth category of falsifier: the symptoms of their disease are those of what medieval writers identify as "putrid fever" (Contini 1953).

97–99. One is the false woman . . . such a stench: Both Potiphar's wife and Sinon are formally guilty of perjury. The story of Potiphar's wife, who tried to seduce Joseph and, when he refused, accused him of attempting to rape her, is told in Gen. 39.7–21. Sinon's role in inducing the Trojans to take the horse into the city is discussed in the note to 26.58–60. The "stench" (Italian *leppo*: related to words for "fat," it seems meant to evoke the smell of burning fat) is the "smoke" of lines 92–93 (cf. 17.3: Geryon "makes the whole world stink," with note). The issue of perjury is closely related to the counterfeit florin: the Baptist on it is bearing false witness to its quality.

These last two souls mentioned in the Malebolge are protagonists of two major events in the (for Dante) parallel histories of the two chosen peoples: Joseph's success in Egypt (which led to the enslavement of the Jews and the Exodus) and the fall of Troy (which led to the founding of Rome) (see the note to lines 1–27).

100–129. And one of them . . . with many words: The famous flyting (exchange of taunts) between Master Adam and Sinon moves from blows (one each) to verbal taunts (four for Master Adam, three for Sinon); the taunts progress from naming sins to naming punishments in purely physical terms, thus gradually downward, each echoing and mirroring the previous one, until reaching Narcissus and his mirror. Vergil's Sinon, like Master Adam, is of noble birth, a comrade and close relative (*Aen.* 2.86) of King Palamedes of Nauplia. The progressive degradation of their high status is part of the savage irony. The representation of the damned in this canto begins and ends with the crazy violence of paired souls (cf. 32.43–51 and 124–32).

102–3. with his fist . . . a drum: Sinon's blow establishes a relation between Master Adam's belly and the Trojan Horse, for it alludes to Laocoön's spear (*Aen.* 2.50–53):

> . . . validis ingentem viribus hastam
> in latus inque feri curvam compagibus alvum
> contorsit. Stetit illa tremens, uteroque recusso
> insonuere cavae gemitumque dedere cavernae.

> [. . . with his great strength he hurled a huge spear
> against the beast's side, its belly curved with ribs.
> It stood there trembling, and when the womb was struck
> the hollow caverns resounded and gave a moan.]

The terms referring to Master Adam's belly (*l'epa croia* [his taut liver], *ventraia* [belly], line 54) resound onomatopoetically, like *tamburro* [drum], related to the name of his disease.

102. on his taut belly: Here, as in 25.82 and 30.119, Dante uses *epa*, from the Greek word for "liver" (*epar*), to refer to the belly; for the importance of the liver to Master Adam's disease, see the notes on lines 52–57 and 73–74.

104–11. and Master Adam . . . when you were coining: As Sinon's taunt shows, Master Adam's blow to his face is an analogue of the hammer blow that stamps the coin.

112–14. You say true there . . . at Troy: The two falsifiers—one of words, the other of coins—are now condemned to speak only truths, but they are bitter truths that only intensify their pain.

117. for more than any other demon: Sinon is referring to the multitude of false florins coined by Master Adam. As the terminology of minting and the digestion metaphor suggest, there was an analogy between coining and reproduction in the Aristotelian theory: the formal principle in the father's seed stamps the father's form on the mother's blood. Master Adam's contaminated florins are thus also, at another level, his evil offspring (cf. line 48: "li altri mal nati," and 3.115: "il mal seme d'Adamo").

118–20. Remember, perjurer, the Horse . . . knows of it: The complexity of Sinon's sin allows Master Adam to derive two taunts from it (as Sinon did from his). The fact that the whole world (all the descendants of Adam; cf. Sinon's last taunt) knows of Sinon refers to what is perhaps the most painful side of his punishment; the lower in Hell, the more unwilling souls are to be remembered on earth.

123. a hedge before your eyes: An obstacle to sight (like the hill for which the Pisans cannot see Lucca; 33.29–30), emblematic of Master Adam's inability to see beyond himself.

124–29. Your mouth gapes . . . with many words: Answering Sinon's references to his (Adam's) tongue and belly, Master Adam names Sinon's mouth and head, continuing the correlation between belly and face established by the two blows that began the quarrel.

128–29. to lick . . . with many words: That is, Sinon is just as thirsty as Master Adam; the "mirror of Narcissus" is a surface of water, like the pond where Narcissus (named in the *Comedy* only here) fell in love with his own image and died of desire for it (*Met.* 3.370–503). The allusion to the standing water of Narcissus's pool brings the episode to a close with a parallel to the streams of the Casentino of lines 64–66. The entire relation of Master Adam and Sinon has been specular—they are reflections of each other: this is their infernal Narcissism, fixated on the image of their own despair and damnation (see the note on the Medusa, Tydeus, and Menalippus in 32.130–31).

130–48. I was all intent . . . a base desire: The two cantos of the falsifiers are thus framed by two rebukes of the pilgrim by Virgil (see 29.1–12), the second considerably more severe. The commentators point out that the entire flyting had taken place under the aegis of a "comic-realistic" stylistic mode related to the abusive *tenzone* (also a flyting) with Forese Donati of Dante's youth (cf. *Purg.* 23.115–20), which the present passage far surpasses in energy and abusiveness, and to which Dante would be in a sense bidding farewell (its authenticity has, however, recently been questioned).

131–32. Now keep looking . . . quarreling with you: Dante's term for "look" (*mirare*) was, as he knew, the etymon of a common word for "mirror," *miraglio*. The pilgrim's gazing is a form of mirroring (cf. 32.54), and if he and Virgil quarreled, they would be a reflection of Sinon and Master Adam.

134–35. such shame that it still dizzies me: The shame still agitates him. The pilgrim's capacity for intense shame, resting on his ability to see himself critically, distinguishes him from the falsifiers.

136–41. Like one who . . . did not think so: The description of a dream-like, hallucinatory state, within the function of lines 130–48, replaces the blood-drunkenness of the opening of Canto 29 with a confusion whose function is to bring the pilgrim back to himself.

145–47. And mind . . . such a squabble: Virgil is very close here to being a personification of the pilgrim's faculty of reason—that is, of his ability to *reflect* on his actions, essential to freeing himself from the debased specularity of the *bolgia*.

CANTO 31

1   Una medesma lingua pria mi morse
       sì che mi tinse l'una e l'altra guancia,
       e poi la medicina mi riporse:

4   così od' io che solea far la lancia
       d'Achille e del suo padre esser cagione
       prima di trista e poi di buona mancia.

7   Noi demmo il dosso al misero vallone
       su per la ripa che 'l cinge dintorno,
       attraversando sanza alcun sermone.

10   Quiv' era men che notte e men che giorno,
       sì che 'l viso m'andava innanzi poco;
       ma io senti' sonare un alto corno

13   tanto ch'avrebbe ogne tuon fatto fioco,
       che, contra sé la sua via seguitando,
       dirizzò li occhi miei tutti ad un loco.

16   Dopo la dolorosa rotta, quando
       Carlo Magno perdé la santa gesta,
       non sonò sì terribilmente Orlando.

19   Poco portäi in là volta la testa,
       che me parve veder molte alte torri;
       ond' io: "Maestro, dì, che terra è questa?"

22   Ed elli a me: "Però che tu trascorri
       per le tenebre troppo da la lungi,
       avvien che poi nel maginare abborri.

25   Tu vedrai ben, se tu là ti congiungi,
       quanto 'l senso s'inganna di lontano;
       però alquanto più te stesso pungi."

28   Poi caramente mi prese per mano,
       e disse: "Pria che noi siam più avanti,
       acciò che 'l fatto men ti paia strano,

CANTO 31

The giants—Nimrod—Ephialtes—Antaeus lowers them to Cocytus

1   One and the same tongue first stung me so that
both my cheeks were stained, and then held out the
medicine to me:

4   so I hear that the spear of Achilles and his father
was the cause first of ill and then of good reward.

7   We turned our backs on the wretched valley, up
along the bank that girds it round, crossing over
without further speech.

10   Here it was less than night and less than day, so
that my sight did not pierce far ahead; but I heard
the sound of a horn so loud

13   that it would make any thunder feeble, which
drew my eyes straight to one place, following its
path backward.

16   After the dolorous rout, when Charlemagne lost
the holy company, Roland did not sound his horn so
terribly.

19   I had not long held my head turned there, when I
seemed to see many high towers; therefore I: "Master,
say, what city is this?"

22   And he to me: "Because your sight traverses the
shadows from too far away, your imagining is
blurred.

25   You will see clearly, when you reach it, how sense
is deceived by distance; therefore drive yourself a
little further."

28   Then he took me affectionately by the hand and
said: "Before we are any closer, so that the fact may
seem less frightening to you,

31 sappi che non son torri, ma giganti,
  e son nel pozzo intorno da la ripa
  da l'umbilico in giuso tutti quanti."

34 Come, quando la nebbia si dissipa,
  lo sguardo a poco a poco raffigura
  ciò che cela 'l vapor che l'aere stipa:

37 così, forando l'aura grossa e scura,
  più e più appressando ver' la sponda,
  fuggiemi errore e cresciemi paura,

40 però che, come su la cerchia tonda
  Montereggion di torri si corona,
  così la proda che 'l pozzo circonda

43 torreggiavan di mezza la persona
  li orribili giganti, cui minaccia
  Giove del cielo ancora quando tuona.

46 E io scorgeva già d'alcun la faccia,
  le spalle e 'l petto e del ventre gran parte,
  e per le coste giù ambo le braccia.

49 Natura certo, quando lasciò l'arte
  di sì fatti animali, assai fé bene
  per tòrre tali essecutori a Marte.

52 E s'ella d'elefanti e di balene
  non si pente, chi guarda sottilmente
  più giusta e più discreta la ne tene;

55 ché dove l'argomento de la mente
  s'aggiugne al mal volere e a la possa,
  nessun riparo vi può far la gente.

58 La faccia sua mi parea lunga e grossa
  come la pina di San Pietro a Roma,
  e a sua proporzione eran l'altre ossa;

61 sì che la ripa, ch'era perizoma
  dal mezzo in giù, ne mostrava ben tanto
  di sovra, che di giugnere a la chioma

64 tre Frison s'averien dato mal vanto,
  però ch'i' ne vedea trenta gran palmi
  dal loco in giù dov' omo affibbia 'l manto.

67 "*Raphèl maì amècche zabì almì,*"
  cominciò a gridar la fiera bocca,
  cui non si convenia più dolci salmi.

31   know that they are not towers, but giants, and
they are in the pit, around its rim, from the navel
downward, all of them."

34   As, when mist dissolves, the gaze little by little
makes out the shape of what the vapor-thickened air
had hidden,

37   so, boring through the thick dark atmosphere,
drawing closer and closer to the edge, my error fled
and my fear grew;

40   for, as above its circling walls Montereggione is
crowned by towers, so there above the bank that
circles the pit

43   towered with half their persons the horrible
giants, whom Jove still threatens from the sky when
he thunders.

46   And I already discerned the face of one, his
shoulders and breast, and a large part of his belly,
and down his sides both his arms.

49   Nature surely, when she left off the crafting of
animals like those, did well to deprive Mars of such
instruments.

52   And if she has not repented of elephants and
whales, whoever considers subtly will hold her more
just and more discreet;

55   for where sharpness of mind is joined to evil will
and power, there is no defence people can make
against them.

58   His face seemed as long and broad as the pine
cone of Saint Peter in Rome, and to that proportion
were his other bones;

61   so that the bank, which was his apron from the
waist down, left so much of him exposed above it
that to reach his mane

64   three Frisians would have boasted idly, for I saw
thirty great spans down from the place where the
mantle is clasped.

67   "*Raphèl maì amècche zabì almì,*" the fierce mouth
began to shout, for no gentler psalms befitted it.

70   E 'l duca mio ver' lui: "Anima sciocca,
tienti col corno, e con quel ti disfoga
quand' ira o altra passïon ti tocca!

73   Cércati al collo, e troverai la soga
che 'l tien legato, o anima confusa,
e vedi lui che 'l gran petto ti doga."

76   Poi disse a me: "Elli stessi s'accusa:
questi è Nembrotto per lo cui mal coto
pur un linguaggio nel mondo non s'usa.

79   Lasciànlo stare e non parliamo a vòto;
ché così è a lui ciascun linguaggio
come 'l suo ad altrui, ch'a nullo è noto."

82   Facemmo adunque più lungo vïaggio,
vòlti a sinistra; e al trar d'un balestro
trovammo l'altro assai più fero e maggio.

85   A cigner lui qual che fosse 'l maestro
non so io dir, ma el tenea soccinto
dinanzi l'altro e dietro il braccio destro,

88   d'una catena che 'l tenea avvinto
dal collo in giù, sì che 'n su lo scoperto
si ravvolgëa infino al giro quinto.

91   "Questo superbo volle esser esperto
di sua potenza contra 'l sommo Giove,"
disse 'l mio duca, "ond' elli ha cotal merto.

94   Fïalte ha nome, e fece le gran prove
quando i giganti fer paura a' dèi;
le braccia ch'el menò, già mai non move."

97   E io a lui: "S'esser puote, io vorrei
che de lo smisurato Brïareo
esperïenza avesser li occhi mei."

100   Ond' ei rispuose: "Tu vedrai Anteo
presso di qui, che parla ed è disciolto,
che ne porrà nel fondo d'ogne reo.

103   Quel che tu vuo' veder più in là è molto,
ed è legato e fatto come questo,
salvo che più feroce par nel volto."

106   Non fu tremoto già tanto rubesto
che scotesse una torre così forte
come Fïalte a scuotersi fu presto.

70   And my leader toward him: "Foolish soul, be content with your horn, give vent with that, when anger or some other passion touches you!

73   Feel at your neck, and you will find the thong that holds it, o befuddled soul, and there it is, curving across your breast like a bow."

76   Then he said to me: "Himself accuses himself; that is Nimrod, because of whose evil thought the world no longer speaks one language.

79   Let us leave him alone and not waste speech, for to him every language is like his to others, unknown."

82   Therefore we took a longer path, turning to the left; at the distance of a cross-bow shot we found the next, much fiercer and larger.

85   Who was the master to bind him I cannot say, but one arm was held in front and the right arm behind him,

88   by a chain wrapped about him from the neck down, so that on what we saw of him it made five full turns.

91   "This proud one wished to prove his power against highest Jove," said my leader, "and thus is he rewarded.

94   His name is Ephialtes, and he performed great deeds when the giants made the gods afraid; the arm he struck with then, he never moves."

97   And I to him: "If it can be, I would wish my eyes to have experience of the immense Briareus."

100   And he replied: "You will see Antaeus near here, who speaks and is unbound; he will place us at the bottom of all wickedness.

103   He whom you wish to see is much further over there, and he is bound and shaped like this one, except that his face seems fiercer."

106   Never could rough earthquake so violently shake a tower as Ephialtes suddenly shook himself.

109   Allor temett' io più che mai la morte,
     e non v'era mestier più che la dotta,
     s'io non avessi viste le ritorte.

112   Noi procedemmo più avante allotta,
     e venimmo ad Anteo, che ben cinque alle,
     sanza la testa, uscia fuor de la grotta.

115   "O tu che-ne la fortunata valle
     che fece Scipïon di gloria reda
     quand' Anibàl co' suoi diede le spalle—

118   recasti già mille leon per preda,
     e che, se fossi stato a l'alta guerra
     de' tuoi fratelli, ancor par che si creda

121   ch'avrebber vinto i figli de la terra:
     mettine giù, e non ten vegna schifo,
     dove Cocito la freddura serra.

124   Non ci far ire a Tizio né a Tifo;
     questi può dar di quel che qui si brama;
     però ti china e non torcer lo grifo.

127   Ancor ti può nel mondo render fama,
     ch'el vive, e lunga vita ancor aspetta,
     se 'nnanzi tempo grazia a sé nol chiama."

130   Così disse 'l maestro; e quelli in fretta
     le man distese, e prese 'l duca mio,
     ond' Ercule sentì già grande stretta.

133   Virgilio, quando prender si sentio,
     disse a me: "Fatti qua, sì ch'io ti prenda."
     Poi fece sì ch'un fascio era elli e io.

136   Qual pare a riguardar la Carisenda
     sotto 'l chinato, quando un nuvol vada
     sovr'essa sì ched ella incontro penda:

139   tal parve Antëo a me che stava a bada
     di vederlo chinare, e fu tal ora
     ch'i' avrei voluto ir per altra strada.

142   Ma lievemente al fondo che divora
     Lucifero con Giuda ci sposò;
     né, sì chinato, lì fece dimora,

145   e come albero in nave si levò.

109 Then more than ever I feared death, and the fright alone would have sufficed, had I not seen his bonds.

112 We walked further then, and we came to Antaeus, who rose a good five ells, not counting his head, out of the pit.

115 "O you who once—in the fortunate valley that made Scipio the heir of glory when Hannibal and his men turned tail—

118 brought in a thousand lions as your catch, and, if you had been present at your brothers' great war, it seems some still believe

121 the sons of earth would have been victorious: set us down, and do not disdain to do so, where the cold locks in Cocytus.

124 Do not make us go to Tityos or to Typhon: this man can give what here is desired; therefore bend down and do not twist your snout.

127 He can still repay you with fame in the world, for he is alive and expects long life still, if grace does not call him before his time."

130 So spoke my master; and he in haste stretched out his hands, whose powerful grip Hercules once felt, and grasped my leader.

133 Virgil, when he felt himself gripped, said to me: "Come here, that I may hold you." Then he made one bundle of himself and me.

136 As Garisenda appears from below the leaning side when a cloud passes above it so that it seems to fall:

139 so Antaeus appeared as I stood waiting to see him bend over, and that was a time when I would have wished to go by another road.

142 But lightly he set us down on the bottom that devours Lucifer with Judas; nor did he remain bent over,

145 but like the mast of a ship he raised himself.

1–6. One and the same . . . good reward: Compare the opening of Canto 24, on a change in Virgil's attitude toward the pilgrim.

1–3. One and the same tongue . . .the medicine to me: Virgil functions like conscience, reproaching ("stung") but also limiting the self-criticism (offering "medicine"): see Deut. 32.39: "I will strike, and I will heal"; and Tobit 13.2: "For thou scourgest and thou savest: thou leadest down to hell, and bringest up again."

4–6. the spear of Achilles and his father . . . good reward: Dante is alluding to Ovid's *Art of Love* (4.43–48):

> Discite sanari, per quem didicistis amare,
> una manus vobis vulnus opemque feret:
> vulnus in Herculeo quae quondam fecerat hoste
> vulneris auxilium Pelias hasta tulit.

> [Learn to be cured from the same who taught you to love,
> one hand will bring you both wound and remedy:
> having once wounded the enemy, the son of Hercules (Telephus),
> the Pelian spear brought help for the wound.]

According to the myth, only Achilles' spear could heal a wound it had inflicted. The troubadors and later medieval poets understood *Pelias* as a reference to Peleus, Achilles' father, rather than to Mount Pelion. The first of a series of epic references in the canto.

7–11. turned our backs . . . my sight did not pierce far ahead: The wayfarers enter what seems a large plain, which, according to 30.86–87, must be something less than three miles in diameter.

10. less than night and less than day: Twilight; for possible meanings of this time of day, see the note to 34.5.

14–15. drew my eyes . . . following its path backward: The pilgrim's curious backward following of the sound of the horn perhaps echoes the *Song of Roland* (lines 1765–67), when the sound of Roland's tardy horn blasts finally reaches the main army, recalling them: "The horn could be heard far away: Charles heard it, going through the passes . . . so did the Franks hear it."

16–18. After the dolorous rout . . . his horn so terribly: According to the *Song of Roland*, when Charlemagne's rear guard, led by Roland (Orlando) and Oliver, is ambushed in the pass of Roncesvalles, Roland delays signaling for help until too late to save his companions, who are slaughtered to a man (see 32.122 and note). The deaths of Roland, Oliver, Turpin, and others signal the end of "the holy company," the peers or paladins of France, as in line 1735: "Oi nus defalt la leial cumpaignie" [Today we lose the loyal company] (see line 71 and note).

20–21. many high towers . . . what city is this: The appearance of a city recalls the approach to the city of Dis; compare 9.67–72. Dante's word for "city" here (*terra*) also means "earth" (see also the notes to lines 31–43, 120–21).

22–26. Because your sight traverses . . . deceived by distance: Dronke (1986) found an interesting parallel in the famous treatise on optics by Witelo (thirteenth century), who gives the example of a tower seen through "murky air" in twilight, as a classic instance of visual misjudgment (see *Purg.* 29.47–53).

31–44. not towers . . . the horrible giants: The pilgrim's error transforms the giants into the towers of a city, and this error informs the simile in line 40. Note that "towered" in line 43 may also be taken transitively, meaning that the giants crown the bank with towers and thus are towers. Allegorically, both giants and towers traditionally stand for pride: see Wisdom 14.6: "from the beginning . . . when the proud giants perished," and Augustine, *City of God* 16.3: "Therefore he [Nimrod] with his people began to erect a tower against the Lord, by which his impious pride was signified." See also lines 107, 121, and Additional Note 14.

32. in the pit . . . from the navel downward: Note the parallelism of the giants with Farinata, exposed "from the waist upward" (cf. *King Lear* 4.6.125–26: "But to the girdle do the gods inherit,/ Beneath is all the fiend's"). For this division of the body, see 17.19–24, 32.34, with notes, and Additional Note 2.

40–41. above its circling walls . . . towers: The small fortress of Montereggione stands on a low hill eight miles northwest of Siena; fourteen towers, reduced in height since Dante's day, still surmount the

Figure 7. The walls of Montereggione.

walls (Figure 7). The walls and towers were built after 1260, when the Sienese defeated the Florentine Guelfs at Montaperti; when the emperor Henry VII marched toward Florence in 1312, Montereggione harassed his movements.

Nearly circular, with towers evenly spaced, Montereggione is compared to the last redoubt of Hell, imagined as a city, Dis (8.68), with outer walls (Cantos 8 and 9), defensive ditches (Malebolge) around the central fortress (the pit of Cocytus with its giant-towers), and Satan at the lowest point of the central pit (the "tower"), all upside-down (see 18.10–18 and 34.6–7, with notes).

44. Jove still threatens . . . when he thunders: A reference to the classical war of the giants against the gods, when the giants attacked Olympus (see the note to lines 94–95). Jupiter's name of the "thunderer" (*tonans*) had been a standard epithet for the Christian God in Christian Latin poetry from the time of Prudentius (fourth century) (see 14.52–60 and note, also line 92).

49–51. Nature . . . such instruments: Dante takes the size of the giants to be historical, on the basis of Gen. 6.4:

> Now giants were upon the earth in those days. For after the sons of God went in to the daughters of men, and they brought forth children, these are the mighty men of old, men of renown.

This verse was the basis of the traditional euhemeristic interpretation (see Baruch 3.26–28). The giants no longer exist because Nature, God's minister, stopped fashioning them, depriving Mars of such *essecutori* [literally, executors].

55. where sharpness of mind . . . evil will and power: See Aristotle, *Politics* 1.1.1253a: "just as man is the best of the animals if perfected in virtue, so, if he is separated from law and justice, he is the worst of all, for he owns the weapons of reason." The combination of malice, destructive violence, and misused intelligence is an argument for the last portion of Hell being the zone of "mad brutishness" (see 11.82–83, with notes).

59. the pine cone of Saint Peter: The bronze pine cone, now about thirteen feet high, may once have stood near the Campus Martius in Rome (in Saint Peter's in Dante's time, it is now in the Belvedere Gardens).

60. to that proportion were his other bones: Reckoning the size of giants from their "remains" was a traditional puzzle; Augustine reports finding a human tooth 100 times normal size (*City of God* 15.9). Dante's recourse to subjective factors in measurement (cf. "seemed as long and broad") make calibrations pointless; the numerous stated measurements in lower Hell (the size of Hell itself, of the individual *bolge*, of the giants, of Satan) are not consistent (Gilbert 1945; Kleiner 1989; Kirkham 1990). The giants' disproportion here may itself be a judgment: they are out of scale, like the pine cone Dante uses to measure them: see Aristotle (*Ethics* 5.3.1131b16): "the just is the proportional, the unjust is what violates the proportion." See also lines 64, 83, 84, and 113.

61. his apron from the waist down: Dante's metaphor uses the biblical word, *perizoma* [apron], for the fig leaves that Adam and Eve used after the Fall to conceal their sexual parts (Gen. 3.7). Along with pride, the giants embody a rebel-lious sexuality: Gen. 6.4 was sometimes taken to mean that the rebel angels mated with women to produce giants; in Vergil (*Aen.* 6.580) the giants are the spawn of earth (*Titania pubes*: the "young," but also the "genitals," of Earth); the crime of the giant Tityos was his attempt to rape Latona, the mother of Apollo and Diana (Servius on *Aen.* 6.595), while for Fulgentius and the mythographic tra-dition, Antaeus signifies the rebellious sexual libido, because of his contact with the earth (Rabuse 1961).

64. three Frisians . . . thirty great spans: Dante relied on encyclopedia accounts of Frisians as "a people of strength, tall of body, of fierce and harsh spirit" (cf. Terlingen 1965).

66. where the mantle is clasped: Perhaps a reference to giants as "great and mighty men"; only the rich wore cloaks.

67–81. Raphèl . . . unknown: The first giant named is Nimrod (Nembrotto), king of Babylon (Gen. 10.9–10). Dante based the idea that Nimrod was a giant, God's adversary, and the builder of the Tower of Babel (Gen. 11.1–9), on Augustine's *City of God* (16.3–5), which followed the Old Latin translation of the Greek Septuagint version: "Nebroth . . . began to be a giant on the earth." In the same passage, Augustine understood the Greek to mean "against the Lord."

Dante's version of the confusion of tongues (Gen. 11.7–9) in the *De vulgari eloquentia* (1.7.7) is unusual:

> For community of language remained only of those engaged in the same activity; for instance, all architects had the same language, all those rolling stones had the same language, all those preparing stones had the same lan-guage. . . . However many were the varieties of activity directed to the work, by the same number of languages the human race is divided; and the more highly placed their activity, the more rudely and barbarously they now speak.

This is the logic by which Nimrod, king and director of the entire undertaking, is left entirely alone, with a language no one but he understands.

67. Raphèl maì amècche zabì almì: Attempts to decipher Nimrod's babble (Guerri 1909; Lemay 1963) have not persuaded. As Plutus's language (cf. 7.1) seems a hash of Greek, Nimrod's language sounds Semitic. Dronke (1986) points to the tradition of invented languages, used largely for comic effect in Church plays at Twelfth Night and Easter.

69. no gentler psalms befitted it: As the book of Psalms was taken as a model for "the unity of a well-ordered city bound by concordant variety" (Augustine, *City of God* 17.14), there is an implicit contrast with Babel (see the note to lines 70, 74).

70, 74. Foolish soul, befuddled soul: On the Earthly City (Hell), see *City of God* 16.4: "This city, which is called confusion, is that very Babylon . . . for Babylon, interpreted, means confusion."

71. be content with your horn . . . touches you: Nimrod's expression is of passion, not intellect. This is perhaps a final glance at Roland, whose pride kept him from sounding the horn; see *Song of Roland*, line 1171: "you did not deign to sound your horn." Throughout the canto, Dante interweaves the giants with heroes of epic (Achilles, Roland, Scipio, and Hercules), "great and strong men." Achilles and Hercules are classical (often allegorized); Scipio and Roland, historical (Scipio a Roman hero, Roland a Christian one).

76. evil thought: See Gen. 11.4, words attributed by Augustine to Nimrod: "Come, let us make a city and a tower, the top whereof may reach to heaven: and let us make our name famous before we be scattered abroad into all lands."

79–81. not waste speech . . . unknown: Nimrod can neither understand nor be understood by anyone (see the note to lines 67–81). The juxtaposition of the confusion of Babel and the "speaking in tongues" of Pentecost was a commonplace of medieval biblical exegetes (cf. Barański 1989; see the note to line 69).

85. Who was the master to bind him: Dante's reflection evokes passages like Job 39.10: "canst thou bind the rhinoceros . . . ," and 40.20–21; the "master" is presumably God (see 15.12), perhaps the archangel Michael.

86. one arm was held . . . behind him: The focus on the arm follows Vergil (see *Aen.* 6.583–84, quoted in the note to lines 94–95); compare Job 38.15: "the high arm shall be broken."

91. This proud one . . . against highest Jove: This links the giants with Lucifer's attempt to rise above his creator (see 7.12 and 34.35, with notes) (see the note to lines 94–95).

94–95. Ephialtes . . . the gods afraid: The second giant the pilgrim sees is Ephialtes: he and his brother were sent by their father Neptune to pile Mount Ossa and Mount Pelion (in Macedonia) on top of each other in order to reach Mount Olympus and displace the gods (*Aen.* 6.583–84): "qui manibus magnum rescindere caelum/ adgressi superisque Iovem detrudere regnis" [who with their hands tried to destroy great Heaven, and to thrust Jove down from his high realm].

On the gods' fear of the giants, see the notes to 14.52–60 and 31.120–21.

98. immense Briareus: See Statius, *Theb.* 2.596: "immensus . . . Briareus." Virgil's words (lines 103–5) indicate that Briareus is not hundred-handed (see *Aen.* 10.565–66), but merely huge.

100–101. Antaeus ... who speaks and is unbound: This third giant was not among those who attacked the gods (see the note to lines 94–95), which perhaps explains his not being bound. Dante read in Lucan (*Pharsalia* 4.593–660) how Antaeus devastated crops, men, and beasts in the valley of Zama, in North Africa, until Hercules arrived to challenge him: in order to conquer, Hercules had to keep Antaeus from contact with his mother, Earth, who strengthened him: so Hercules held him aloft in his arms and crushed him (see line 132).

107. shake a tower: A giant compared to a tower again (see the notes to lines 31–44, 136–38).

108. Ephialtes suddenly shook himself: Confirming Virgil's judgment on his ferocity, Ephialtes produces a metaphorical earthquake: ancient mythology attributed earthquakes and volcanic eruptions to giants, bound in Tartarus or under Mount Aetna after their defeat (cf. lines 91–95). The giants have so far in this canto received historical (they truly existed), euhemerist (they signify powerful, violent men), and physical explanations (they signify earthquakes).

109. I feared death: See 1.7 and 34.25, with notes.

115–29. O you ... before his time: Virgil's speech to Antaeus, who does not speak (though in line 101 he is said to be able to do so), is an aretalogy or enumeration of his great deeds, followed by a petition: a formula associated with praying to the gods (Dronke 1986). Virgil uses hyperbole or exaggeration (the thousand lions, mentioned in *Pharsalia* 4.601–2; the notion that the giants would have won if Antaeus had been present) to flatter Antaeus, then offers praise and fame in return for setting them down in the bottom of Hell.

115–17. the fortunate valley ... turned tail: Zama, in North Africa, where Publius Cornelius Scipio defeated Hannibal and broke the power of Carthage, establishing Roman control of the Mediterranean. Zama is "fortunate," and Scipio inherited glory, because of this victory, which conferred on him the title Africanus.

120–21. it seems some still believe ... victorious: Vergil, with a careful double qualifier (cf. 12.42), alludes to *Pharsalia* 4.595–97: "caeloque pepercit,/ quod non Phlegraeis Antaeum sustulit arvis" [She (Earth) spared the gods when she did not raise up Antaeus on the field of Phlegra]. For the giants associated with Earth (Italian *terra*, meaning both "earth" and "city"), see the notes to 20–21, 31–44, 41, and 100–101.

123. where the cold locks in Cocytus: See 32.2–3, 23–24 and 34.52 and 117, with notes. In his *Commentarii* 1.10, Macrobius notes that Cocytus means "sorrow." See Additional Note 2.

124. to Tityos or to Typhon: In classical myth, Tityos (see the note to line 61) was stretched out on a plain and bound (his body covered nine acres) while a vulture fed on his liver (cf. *Aen.* 6.595–97). Typhon was punished for attacking the gods by being buried under Mount Aetna, where his shakings appear as volcanic activity (also called Typhoeus; see *Par.* 8.70).

129. if grace does not call him before his time: The remark links the pilgrim to Scipio Africanus the Younger, who Cicero's *Somnium Scipionis* said would have become the most important man in Rome but that his fate was cut short, for Scipio died under mysterious circumstances in his fifty-sixth year, 129 B.C.;) the identification would be exploited by Boccaccio in his biography of Dante. See the association of the pilgrim with the hero Hercules, in the note to line 132.

132. whose powerful grip Hercules once felt: The pilgrim now feels Antaeus's grip, as Hercules did when wrestling with him: Hercules' grip was fatal to Antaeus (see the note to lines 100–101). Although unbound, Antaeus must obey the higher law that protects Virgil and the pilgrim.

This is the final reference to Hercules (most are implicit) in the *Inferno* (see 9.98–99, 12.67–69, 17.97, and 25.31–32, with notes) and the one in which the pilgrim and the hero are most closely identified.

135. he made one bundle of himself and me: Literally, a sheaf or *fascis*, also the symbol of Roman authority. There are a number of parallels here with the passage on Geryon (17.79–96) and the descent along Satan (34.70–81).

136. As Garisenda appears . . . it seems to fall: Having begun with the pilgrim's confusion of the giants with towers, the canto concludes by comparing Antaeus to a leaning tower that appears to fall when a cloud passes behind it (the "tower" does in fact "fall," in that the giant bends over). The Garisenda tower, built in Bologna in 1110 and still standing, though reduced in height, is 10.6 feet out of the perpendicular at its crest and 160 feet high; the Asinelli tower next to it, 320 feet high, was built in 1109.

Dante supposed that the Garisenda had been built for private warfare; modern opinion is that it was built by the city. But most such towers in the Italian cities were built by the warring clans; in Dante's day, Bologna bristled with more than 100 of them. By repeatedly associating his giants with towers, Dante makes them symbols both of the pride that scaled Heaven (Satan; the tower of Babel; Pelion on Ossa) and of the resistance to Roman law and authority implicit in the prevalence of private war in northern and central Italy. Cantos 32 and 33, which closely concern civil strife, also involve the tower motif. For the linguistic issue, see Ascoli 1990.

142. the bottom that devours Lucifer with Judas: For the implications of "devour" here, see 34.55–56.

145. like the mast of a ship he raised himself: Compare *s'ergea* [he was rising up], of Farinata (10.35). This is the next to last (see 34.48) of the references to ships in lower Hell (cf. 16.134, 17.100, 21.7–15, 22.12, 25.142, 26.100–142, 27.81, and 28.79; cf. 7.13–14). The full-rigged ship (masts, spars, and sails) was often mentioned as a figure of pride (cf. Platas [7.13–15] and the note to 27.79–81).

CANTO 32

1   S'ïo avessi le rime aspre e chiocce
come si converrebbe al tristo buco
sovra 'l qual pontan tutte l'altre rocce,

4   io premerei di mio concetto il suco
più pienamente; ma perch' io non l'abbo,
non sanza tema a dicer mi conduco:

7   ché non è impresa da pigliare a gabbo
discriver fondo a tutto l'universo,
né da lingua che chiami mamma o babbo.

10   Ma quelle donne aiutino il mio verso
ch'aiutaro Anfïone a chiuder Tebe,
sì che dal fatto il dir non sia diverso.

13   Oh sovra tutte mal creata plebe
che stai nel loco onde parlare è duro,
mei foste state qui pecore o zebe!

16   Come noi fummo giù nel pozzo scuro
sotto i piè del gigante assai più bassi,
e io mirava ancora a l'alto muro,

19   dicere udi'mi: "Guarda come passi!
Va sì che tu non calchi con le piante
le teste de' fratei miseri lassi."

22   Per ch'io mi volsi, e vidimi davante
e sotto i piedi un lago che per gelo
avea di vetro e non d'acqua sembiante.

25   Non fece al corso suo sì grosso velo
di verno la Danoia in Osterlicchi,
né Tanaï là sotto 'l freddo cielo,

28   com' era quivi; che se Tambernicchi
vi fosse sù caduto, o Pietrapana,
non avria pur da l'orlo fatto cricchi.

CANTO 32

1   If I had harsh and clucking rhymes such as befit the dreadful hole toward which all other rocks point their weight,

4   I would press out the juice from my concept more fully; but because I lack them, not without fear do I bring myself to speak;

7   for it is no task to take in jest, that of describing the bottom of the universe, nor one for a tongue that calls mommy or daddy.

10   But let those ladies aid my verse who helped Amphion enclose Thebes, so that the word may not be different from the fact.

13   Oh beyond all others ill-created throng who dwell in the place of which it is hard to speak, better had you here been sheep or goats!

16   When we were down in the dark well, far below the giant's feet, and I was still gazing at the high wall,

19   I heard one say to me: "Watch how you step! Walk so that you do not trample with your feet the heads of your wretched weary brothers."

22   I turned then and saw before me and beneath my feet a lake to which icy cold gave the appearance of glass and not of water.

25   So thick a veil was never made over its course by the Austrian Danube in winter, nor by the Don under its freezing sky,

28   as was there; and if Tamberlic should fall on it, or Pietrapana, at its edge it would not even creak.

31   E come a gracidar si sta la rana
        col muso fuor de l'acqua, quando sogna
        di spigolar sovente la villana,

34   livide insin là dove appar vergogna
        eran l'ombre dolenti ne la ghiaccia,
        mettendo i denti in nota di cicogna.

37   Ognuna in giù tenea volta la faccia;
        da bocca il freddo, e da li occhi il cor tristo
        tra lor testimonianza si procaccia.

40   Quand' io m'ebbi dintorno alquanto visto,
        volsimi a' piedi, e vidi due sì stretti
        che 'l pel del capo avieno insieme misto.

43   "Ditemi, voi che sì strignete i petti,"
        diss'io, "chi siete?" E quei piegaro i colli;
        e poi ch'ebber li visi a me eretti,

46   li occhi lor, ch'eran pria pur dentro molli,
        gocciar su per le labbra, e 'l gelo strinse
        le lagrime tra essi, e riserrolli.

49   Con legno legno spranga mai non cinse
        forte così, ond' ei come due becchi
        cozzaro insieme, tanta ira li vinse.

52   E un ch'avea perduti ambo li orecchi
        per la freddura, pur col viso in giùe,
        disse: "Perché cotanto in noi ti specchi?

55   Se vuoi saper chi son cotesti due,
        la valle onde Bisenzo si dichina
        del padre loro Alberto e di lor fue.

58   D'un corpo usciro; e tutta la Caina
        potrai cercare, e non troverai ombra
        degna più d'esser fitta in gelatina:

61   non quelli a cui fu rotto il petto e l'ombra
        con esso un colpo per la man d'Artù,
        non Focaccia, non questi che m'ingombra

64   col capo sì ch'i' non veggio oltre più,
        e fu nomato Sassol Mascheroni:
        se tosco se', ben sai omai chi fu.

67   E perché non mi metti in più sermoni,
        sappi ch'i' fu' il Camiscion de' Pazzi,
        e aspetto Carlin che mi scagioni."

31   And as the frog sits croaking, with its muzzle out
of the water, at the season when the peasant woman
often dreams of gleaning,

34   the grieving shades, livid, were in the ice up
to where shame appears, playing the tune of the
stork with their teeth.

37   Each held his face turned down; from their
mouths the cold, from their eyes their wicked hearts
exact testimony among them.

40   When I had looked around myself a little, I looked
down at my feet and saw two so pressed together
that the hair of their heads was mingled.

43   "Tell me, you who so press your breasts together,"
I said, "who are you?" And they bent back their necks;
and when they had turned their sight up to me,

46   their eyes, which had previously been wet within,
dripped tears over their features, and the cold
pressed the tears into the eyes and locked them up.

49   Board with board clamp never bound so tight; and
they like two goats butted together, such anger
overcame them.

52   And one who had lost both ears to the freezing,
still with his face turned down, said: "Why do you
mirror yourself in us?

55   If you want to know who those two are, the valley
where the Bisenzio descends belonged to their father
Albert and to them.

58   From one body they were born; and you can
search through all Caina and not find a soul worthier
to be fixed in gelatine,

61   not him whose breast and shadow were pierced
by one blow from the hand of Arthur, not Focaccia,
not this one who so encumbers me

64   with his head that I cannot see any further, and
his name was Sassol Mascheroni: if you are Tuscan,
you know who he was.

67   And so you won't have me make any more
speeches, know that I was Camiscion de' Pazzi; and I
await Carlino to excuse me."

70   Poscia vid' io mille visi cagnazzi
        fatti per freddo, onde mi vien riprezzo,
        e verrà sempre, de' gelati guazzi.

73   E mentre ch'andavamo inver' lo mezzo
        al quale ogne gravezza si rauna,
        e io tremava ne l'etterno rezzo,

76   se voler fu o destino o fortuna,
        non so, ma, passeggiando tra le teste,
        forte percossi 'l piè nel viso ad una.

79   Piangendo mi sgridò: "Perché mi peste?
        se tu non vieni a crescer la vendetta
        di Montaperti, perché mi moleste?"

82   E io: "Maestro mio, or qui m'aspetta,
        sì ch'io esca d'un dubbio per costui;
        poi mi farai, quantunque vorrai, fretta."

85   Lo duca stette, e io dissi a colui,
        che bestemmiava duramente ancora:
        "Qual se' tu che così rampogni altrui?"

88   "Or tu chi se' che vai per l'Antenora
        percotendo," rispuose, "altrui le gote,
        sì che, se fossi vivo, troppo fora?"

91   "Vivo son io, e caro esser ti puote,"
        fu mia risposta, "se dimandi fama,
        ch'io metta il nome tuo tra l'altre note."

94   Ed elli a me: "Del contrario ho io brama.
        Lèvati quinci e non mi dar più lagna,
        ché mal sai lusingar per questa lama!"

97   Allor lo presi per la cuticagna
        e dissi: "El converrà che tu ti nomi
        o che capel qui sù non ti rimagna."

100   Ond' elli a me: "Perché tu mi dischiomi,
        né ti dirò ch'io sia né mosterrolti,
        se mille fiate in sul capo mi tomi."

103   Io avea già i capelli in mano avvolti,
        e tratti glien' avea più d'una ciocca,
        latrando lui con li occhi in giù raccolti,

106   quando un altro gridò: "Che hai tu, Bocca?
        non ti basta sonar con le mascelle,
        se tu non latri? qual diavol ti tocca?"

70   Then I saw a thousand faces made doglike by the
cold, whence I shudder, and always shall, at frozen
fords.

73   And while we were walking to the center toward
which all weight collects, and I was trembling in the
eternal chill,

76   if it was wish or destiny or fortune, I do not
know, but, pacing among the heads, I struck my foot
hard in the face of one.

79   Weeping it scolded me: "Why do you pound me?
if you are not here to increase the vengeance for
Montaperti, why do you bother me?"

82   And I: "My master, now wait for me here, so that
I can be freed from a doubt by him; then you can
hurry me as much as you will."

85   My leader stopped; and I said to that one, who
was still cursing violently: "Who are you, to
reproach others so?"

88   "Now who are you, to walk through Antenora
striking," he said, "others' cheeks, so that, if you were
alive, it would be too much to bear?"

91   "I am alive, and it can be precious to you," was my
reply, "if you wish fame, that I place your name
among my other notes."

94   And he to me: "The opposite is what I'm greedy
for. Get up from here, and stop pestering me, for you
flatter badly here in this swamp!"

97   Then I seized him by the scalp and said: "You will
have to name yourself or not a hair will be left up
here."

100   Then he to me: "Though you scalp me, I will not
tell you who I am nor show you, though you
fall on my head a thousand times."

103   I had already wrapped his hair around my hand
and had torn out more than one tuft of it, he barking
with his eyes kept down,

106   when another shouted: "What's wrong with you,
Bocca? isn't it enough to play tunes with your jaws,
that you have to bark, too? What devil is tickling
you?"

109   "Omai," diss' io, "non vo' che più favelle,
malvagio traditor, ch'a la tua onta
io porterò di te vere novelle."

112   "Va via," rispuose, "e ciò che tu vuoi conta;
ma non tacer, se tu di qua entro eschi,
di quel ch'ebbe or così la lingua pronta.

115   El piange qui l'argento de' Franceschi:
'Io vidi,' potrai dir, 'quel da Duera
là dove i peccatori stanno freschi.'

118   Se fossi domandato: 'Altri chi v'era?'
tu hai dallato quel di Beccheria
di cui segò Fiorenza la gorgiera.

121   Gianni de' Soldanier credo che sia
più là con Ganellone e Tebaldello,
ch'aprì Faenza quando si dormia."

124   Noi eravam partiti già da ello,
ch'io vidi due ghiacciati in una buca,
sì che l'un capo a l'altro era cappello;

127   e come 'l pan per fame si manduca,
così 'l sovran li denti a l'altro pose
là 've 'l cervel s'aggiugne con la nuca:

130   non altrimenti Tidëo si rose
le tempie a Menalippo per disdegno,
che quei faceva il teschio e l'altre cose.

133   "O tu che mostri per sì bestial segno
odio sovra colui che tu ti mangi,
dimmi 'l perché," diss' io, "per tal convegno,

136   che se tu a ragion di lui ti piangi,
sappiendo chi voi siete e la sua pecca,
nel mondo suso ancora io te ne cangi,

139   se quella con ch'io parlo non si secca."

109 "Now," I said, "I don't want you to say any more, wicked traitor, for to your shame I will carry back true news of you."

112 "Get lost," he replied, "and tell what you will; but do not be silent, if you escape from here, about him whose tongue was so loose just now.

115 He bewails the silver of the French here; 'I saw,' you can say, 'him from Duera, down there where the sinners keep cool.'

118 If you were asked, 'Who else was there?' beside you is that Beccheria whose throat-piece Florence sawed through.

121 Gianni de' Soldanier I believe is over there with Ganelon and Tebaldello, who opened Faenza when it slept."

124 We had already left him, when I saw two frozen in one hole so that one head was a hat to the other;

127 and as bread is eaten by the starving, so the one above put his teeth to the other, there where the brain joins the nape:

130 not otherwise did Tydeus gnaw Menalippus' temples in his rage, than this one did the skull and the other things.

133 "O you who show by such a bestial sign your hatred over him you are eating, tell me why," I said, "with this pact,

136 that if you justly complain of him, when I know who you are and what his sin, in the world above I shall repay you for it,

139 if that with which I speak does not dry up."

NOTES

1–12. If I had . . . from the fact: As in 28.1–6, the poet disclaims the ability to describe what he sees, in this case the bottom of Hell, the center of the cosmos. The poet does indeed find "harsh and clucking rhymes," but the question of how language can "suit" a place of such horror remains through these final cantos.

1. harsh and clucking rhymes: As in English, the Italian for "clucking" (*chioccio,* also used at 7.2) is onomatopoetic, like numerous other words in the canto (see lines 9, 30, 35, and 105). That the significance of onomatopoetic words is their sound, their acoustic "matter," suits them to the dense material center of the cosmos. Dante's word *rime* means both "rhymes" and "verses" (see *Convivio* 4.2.12: *rima* is "all the speaking that falls in numbers and regulated time and rhymed consonance").

2–3. the dreadful hole . . . point their weight: The pilgrim approaches the center of the earth, the focus of the weight of the geocentric universe. See Cicero, *Somnium Scipionis* 4.9: "And that one that is ninth, in the middle—the earth—is the lowest and does not move, and on it the weight of all the others is borne" (see 11.64–65, 31.123, 34.111, and lines 73–74).

4. press out the juice from my concept: An image from wine or oil making, in which screw-driven presses squeeze the juice from the fruit; this is a well-established image of the Last Judgment (based on the imagery of Matthew 13, 20, and 24 and on Apoc. 14.18–20). Implicit here is the idea that the poet's concept creates pressure within him; note the relation of this pressure to the pressure driving tears from the souls (lines 38–39), and the weight bearing down on the center of the earth.

7. to take in jest: Dante's word for "jest" is *gabbo,* the name of a Provençal literary genre (the *gab* [mockery]) consisting, as the name suggests, of mockery, challenges, and boasting (Ahern in *Lectura Dantis Californiana*). The canto has much sardonic "gallows humor."

8. describing the bottom of the universe: "Describing" means both "narrating in words" and "circumscribing," as if with compasses, "as if the poet were building the bottom of Hell in describing it" (Singleton); see "enclosing" in line 11.

9. a tongue that calls mommy or daddy: Describing Hell is no child's play. As this and the next canto will prove, it is also not a task for a tongue that speaks the tender words between child and parent, expressing natural love; in these cantos, natural human relations are banished. Such words as *mamma* and *babbo* are in *De vulgari eloquentia* 2.7.4 explicitly excluded from the "tragic" style (see the note to 21.2). See line 139 and note.

10. those ladies . . . who helped Amphion enclose Thebes: In his second invocation to the Muses ("those ladies"; the first is 2.7), Dante alludes to the poet Amphion, who, like Orpheus, charmed inanimate objects with the help of the Muses. In the traditional story (found in Horace, Statius, Macrobius, and Brunetto Latini), Amphion's poetry causes the rocks to move to form the walls of Thebes. Dante is also echoing Statius, who compares himself, as author of the *Thebaid,* with Amphion (*Achilleid* 1.13); Dante, too, "must join rhyme to rhyme in order to wall up the city of Hell" (Benvenuto). The motif of the ponderous rocks enclosing Thebes repeats the theme of weight and pressure in lines 3–5.

12. so that the word . . . from the fact: Platonic tradition (*Timaeus* 29b; see Boethius, *Consolation* 3.12.38) recommends there be resemblance (Boethius says "consanguinity") between words and the things they describe.

15. better had you here been sheep or goats: That is, animals without rational souls. See Matt. 26.24: "it were better for him, if that man had not been born" (said of Judas, who was to betray Christ). For sheep and goats in the context of judgment, see Matt. 25.32–33 (and line 50). See also 19.132 and note.

17–18. far below . . . the high wall: This suggests that the giants must be standing on a ledge of rock well above the pit of Cocytus itself. Allegorically speaking, to be "under the feet" of the giants means to be under the mass of earth that the giants—"sons of the earth"—represent; the giants were compared to a circle of walls (31.40–44).

21. your wretched weary brothers: Since Italian often omits possessives, Dante's *de' fratei* [of the brothers] is ambiguous. The speaker may be claiming brotherhood with the pilgrim, referring to the other damned as his "brothers," or, if he is one of the sons of Alberto of Mangona (lines 40–42), simply referring to himself and his brother. In any case, the mention of brotherhood is ironic: it is those who betrayed kinsmen who are punished here.

23–24. a lake . . . not of water: Medieval science held that ice frozen long enough became rock crystal; the cold was thought of as pressure, "squeezing out the moisture" (Albertus Magnus; see Durling and Martinez 1990).

25–27. So thick a veil . . . freezing sky: Both the Danube and the Don (Tanaï) run into the Black Sea; the Danube through modern Austria and Hungary, the Don through Ukraine. For Italians, these were typical far northern rivers, known to freeze over in winter, mentioned as such by Macrobius (*Commentarii* 2.7.20).

28–29. if Tamberlic should fall on it, or Pietrapana: Tamberlicchi or Tambernicchi is thought to be Mount Tambura in the Apuan Alps near Lucca, in northwestern Tuscany; Pietrapana (or Petra Apuana) is in the same range. The geography has shifted from the faraway Thebes, Danube, and Don, to the familiar (and see 33.30). The circle of the traitors is heavily populated with Tuscans who were nearly contemporaries of Dante (see line 66).

The imagined falling of mountains recalls the attempt of the giants to pile Pelion on Ossa (see the note to 31.94–95).

31–33. as the frog . . . dreams of gleaning: The simile strikes the only lyrical, bucolic note in these harsh cantos; for other bucolic similes, see 25.1–21 and 26.25–30.

34. up to where shame appears: The image of the souls buried in ice to their necks (shame appears in the neck and head) recalls other "immersion" images (see 8.53, 12.116–17, 17.9, 31.32–33).

36. playing the tune of the stork: The stork's name in Latin (*ciconia,* pronounced *kikónia*) was originally onomatopoetic, reflecting the idea that storks made sound by clacking their beaks (cf. *Met.* 6.96: "crepitante ciconia rostro" [the stork with rattling beak]) (see lines 106–8 and 139, with notes).

37. held his face turned down: For this posture, expressing shame, see 25.121 and note; see 32.45, 53, and 105. Almost wholly immersed in the dense matter of the center of the universe, these souls can barely lift their faces upward in the typically human attitude.

38–39. from their mouths . . . exact testimony among them: The chattering of teeth is the testimony exacted by the cold, the weeping is that exacted by their guilt; the souls are testifying before each other (*tra lor*). The emphasis on eyes and mouth will dominate the canto. The passage establishes a relation between the cold and the force of the traitors' grief: the external cold and pressure lock in expression, while the internal pressure of grief squeezes it out: the souls are pressed between the two. The cold is of course also the coldness of heart (the "stony heart" of Ezek. 11.19 and 36.26) that made them traitors.

41. I looked down at my feet: The attitude of the pilgrim's head now matches that of the traitors.

41–42. two . . . the hair of their heads was mingled: See Statius, *Theb.* 12.385–86: "amplexu miscent avide lacrimasque comasque" [embracing, they greedily mingle both tears and hair]. In *Par.* 32.68–72, Esau and Jacob (for Augustine, archetypes of the two cities) are said to be distinguished by the color of their hair (as in Gen. 25.25).

43. you who so press your breasts together: Gmelin calls lines 43–48 a "parodic love-kiss" (also describing 25.54). In many medieval illustrations of the zodiac, the Twins of Gemini (often identified as Castor and Pollux) were represented embracing; Castor and Pollux were emblems of fraternal love, as the

Theban brothers were of fraternal hatred (see the note to 26.52–54). See Paolo and Francesca, the first paired souls in Hell, whose destiny was sealed by a kiss in 5.136–38 (cf. lines 58, 61–62 and notes).

47–50. and the cold . . . so tight: A prime example of the idea of cold exerting pressure.

48. locked them up: The antecedent of "them" (*li*) is "eyes" in line 46.

49–50. Board with board . . . so tight: A brilliant example both of the violent harshness invoked in lines 1–12 and of spatial construction: in normal word order, the logic is *spranga non cinse mai legno con legno così forte* [clamp never bound board with board so tightly], but the inversion makes the two words for "board" contiguous (*legno legno*), surrounded by *con . . . spranga* (as if "with . . . a clamp").

51. they like two goats butted together: For the goat signifying the reprobate, see line 15 and note. In *Theb.* 4.397–400, the duel of Eteocles and Polynices is foreseen in terms of a fight between bulls:

> . . . similes video concurrere tauros;
> idem ambobus honos unusque ab origine sanguis
> ardua conlatis obnixi cornua miscent
> frontibus alternaque truces moriuntur in ira.

>   [I see matching bulls run at each other;
> alike in honor, and of one blood,
>   their brows colliding, they mingle proud horns as they strive,
>   and, savage in mutual rage, they die.]

54. Why do you mirror yourself in us: Often taken in a weak sense ("why do you stare?"); but reference to the glassy ice (line 24) and to the pilgrim's imminent imitation of the traitors' violence (lines 98–105) make the reference much richer (see the note to 30.131–32).

56–57. where the Bisenzio descends . . . and to them: The Bisenzio flows into the Arno near Signa, ten miles downriver from Florence; in its valley were located Vernia and Cerbaia, castles belonging to Count Alberto of Mangona. The old commentators say that Count Alberto's two sons, Napoleone and Alessandro, fought over their inheritance and ultimately killed each other (date uncertain, between 1282 and 1286). In 1280, the brothers had been formally reconciled, exchanging the kiss of peace (see line 43 and note).

58. From one body they were born: The expression compresses the brothers back to their single origin; compare the note to line 51, and *Theb.* 11.407–8 on the duel of Eteocles and Polynices: "stat . . . unius ingens/ bellum uteri" [behold . . . the great strife of a single womb].

58. Caina: Named by Francesca in 5.107 as the destination of her killer (her husband Gianciotto), Caina is named for Cain, who killed his brother Abel out of envy and was exiled, branded with a mark to prevent anyone from killing him (Gen. 4.8–15) (see the note to 10.67–69). For Augustine, Cain was the founder of the Earthly City of ambition, rivalry, and fratricide: in this sense, Caina is part of the foundation of Hell itself.

60. a soul worthier to be fixed in gelatine: Gallows humor: the ice is like jellied aspic (these words [*gelo, gelatina, jellied*] are all derived from Latin *gelu* [frost, cold], and the speaker adopts an inverted criterion of worth among the "worst souls in Hell" (see line 69 and note; 33.124 and note).

61–62. him whose breast . . . the hand of Arthur: Dante refers to the prose *Mort le roi Artu* [Death of King Arthur] (conclusion of the Vulgate Cycle, to which belongs the *Lancelot*, the book read by Paolo and Francesca; see 5.127–28 and note). In the *Mort*, Arthur kills Mordred with a savage lance thrust: "and the story says that, after the lance was removed, a ray of sunlight passed through the wound. . . ." Officially Arthur's nephew, Mordred was in fact Arthur's son by his sister Morgan le Fay; he betrayed Arthur by attempting a coup d'état while Arthur was in France, warring upon Lancelot.

63. Focaccia: Vanni de' Cancellieri of Pistoia, said by the early chroniclers to have murdered his father or uncle. He was blamed by the Florentines as the originator of the division between Whites and Blacks.

63–64. who so encumbers me with his head: The souls are obstacles and encumbrances to one another (as they are literally stumbling blocks, "scandals," for the pilgrim; see line 78). Compare Master Adam, his sight blocked by his belly (30.123), and the Pisans (33.29–30).

65. Sassol Mascheroni: A member of the Florentine family of the Toschi, he murdered his uncle's only son for the sake of an inheritance, which fell to Sassolo when the uncle died shortly thereafter. He was punished by being rolled through the city in a barrel full of nails, and then beheaded (l'Anonimo).

68. Camiscion de' Pazzi: Alberto or Umberto Camiscione, one of the Pazzi of the Valdarno; he is said to have killed his kinsman Ubertino for his castles.

69. I await Carlino to excuse me: This soul will be "excused" because Carlino de' Pazzi, also a relation, will be so much worse. Dino Compagni (*Chronicle* 2.28) reports that Carlino, holding a fortress for the White Guelfs, betrayed it for money, in a move that undermined the White exiles' 1302 campaign (see Petrocchi 1984) (cf. the note to 24.142–50).

70. faces made doglike: Dante's word here (*cagnazzo*) is obscure. It seems to mean "purple," the color of a dog's lips and nose (for other dog imagery, see line 105 and 33.78); for the devil named Cagnazzo, see the note to 21.118–23.

72. frozen fords: The pilgrim now passes from Caina to the next zone, Antenora (see line 88). Commentators note that Dante's putting two lists of five persons each in this canto (lines 55–69, 116–23) recalls a technique of the *sirventese*, described in *Vita nuova* 6, which lists names of contemporary persons (cf. "Io son venuto al punto de la rota," lines 53–58).

76. wish or destiny or fortune: Recalls 15.46; note the addition of "wish" to the usual formula.

78–123. I struck my foot . . . Faenza when it slept: This remarkable episode, with the pilgrim tearing out the hair of a traitor who will not identify himself, is a main focus of the canto. With the pilgrim's betrayal of brother Alberigo (33.109–50), it is the most striking instance in the *Inferno* of the pilgrim's becoming involved in the sins he is visiting. It does not follow, however, that the vengeance meted out is unjust; the pilgrim's role is suited to the place where pity is dead, among those who have violated all bonds.

The episode also explores the pilgrim's (and the poet's) deep identification with the factional politics of his day. He acts on his own (82–85) and is taken for one of the dead traitors (90) or as the avenger (80–81) of the treachery that decided a particularly bloody battle (Montaperti; see 10.32–33 and 85–87, with notes); he is even taken for a devil (108; cf. 33.110–11).

78. I struck my foot: This kick (cf. lines 19–21) makes the traitor's head a "stumbling block," a "scandal" (see 28.35, with note, and Matt. 13.41). The kick also recalls the blow on the cheek the Gospel urges us to forgive (Matt. 5.39). The principles of love and retaliation are sharply juxtaposed in the next canto.

80–81. vengeance for Montaperti: Not named until line 106, the speaker is Bocca degli Abati, notorious for striking off the hand of the Guelf standard-bearer at the decisive moment of the battle of Montaperti, causing the Guelf defeat. Bocca, a Ghibelline, had remained in Florence after the expulsion of his party in 1258, pretending to sympathize with the Guelf cause.

87. Who are you, to reproach others: See Matt. 7.4: "How sayest thou to thy brother: Let me cast the mote out of thy eye; and behold a beam is in thine own eye?" See Additional Note 15.

88. Antenora: The second subdivison of the ice, for those who betray nation, city, or party, is named after Antenor, the Trojan lord and companion of Aeneas. In the tradition of Troy stories represented by the *Roman de Troie*, Antenor is a traitor who helps the Greeks take the city; tradition makes him the founder of Padua.

91–94. I am alive . . . what I'm greedy for: Dante offers this traitor a bargain or pact, to exchange fame for his revelation of his identity; the soul violently rejects it (see the note to line 135).

97–105. Then I seized . . . eyes kept down: Dante's canzone "Così nel mio parlar voglio esser aspro," one of the *rime petrose* or "stony rhymes," lines 66–78, imagines seizing the lady by the hair and making violent love to her (see Durling and Martinez 1990). Other echoes of these poems, which use harsh rhymes to invoke the hardness of crystal and risk the peril of petrifaction by a Medusa-like lady, occur in lines 1–12 and 22–23.

106–8. What's wrong . . . tickling you: Bocca, whose name means "mouth" (note the emphasis on all the sounds he makes), is betrayed by another of the traitors.

113–23. do not be silent . . . when it slept: Bocca, his name revealed, takes his own revenge (and dictates some of the poem), revealing the identities of five more traitors, like Camiscione in lines 55–69.

116. him from Duera: Buoso da Duera of Cremona. During the campaign of Charles of Anjou against Manfred (1265; see 28.16 and note), Buoso used French gold to bribe the Marchese Pallavicino and the Lombard Ghibellines to allow the passage of the French troops toward Parma, "because of which the people of Cremona, in a fury, destroyed the lineage of those of Duera" (Villani, *Chronicle* 7.4).

117. where the sinners keep cool: The expression *star fresco* [to be in for it] may have already been proverbial in Dante's day; it has been so ever since.

119. that Beccheria: Tesauro di Beccheria of Pavia, abbot of Vallombrosa and papal legate in Florence for Pope Alexander IV. After the Ghibellines were expelled in July 1258, he was seized by the Florentines on charges of conspiring with the exiles. Although many doubted his guilt, he was tortured and beheaded; the Florentines were excommunicated by the pope.

121. Gianni de' Soldanier: After the defeat of Manfred in 1266, the Florentine Gianni de' Soldanieri became a Guelf in order to secure power (Villani, *Chronicle* 7.14). The Soldanieri were an old Ghibelline family that suffered heavily in the proscriptions of 1302, which included Dante.

122. Ganelon: With Judas, the archetypal medieval traitor. According to the Old French *Song of Roland,* Ganelon, Roland's stepfather, was bribed by the Saracen king Marsilio (at Saragossa) to betray his stepson and the whole rear guard of Charlemagne's army, causing the massacre of Roncesvalles (see 31.16–18 and notes). After the battle, Ganelon was tried, found guilty, and torn apart by four horses.

122. Tebaldello: A member of the Ghibelline Zambrasi family of Faenza; he avenged a private grudge against the Lambertazzi, a Bolognese family that had taken refuge there after their expulsion from Bologna in 1274. On the morning of November 13, 1280, Tebaldello opened the gates of Faenza to the Bolognese Guelfs, who entered the city and massacred their enemies.

125. two frozen in one hole: At close quarters, like Napoleone and Alessandro (line 41). A series of puns, focused on the mouth, speech, and eating, links Dante's word for "hole," *buca* (in Latin, "mouth"), Bocca's name (106), and the first word of the next canto (33.1), "mouth" (*bocca*).

127. as bread is eaten by the starving: The verb here, *manduca*, is identical with the vulgar Latin *manducare*, used in the New Testament of the Eucharistic meal (see Luke 22.11, 15; John 6.54) (see 33.59–63 and notes). For cannibalism and "mad bestiality," see the note to 11.81–83.

129. there where the brain joins the nape: Dante's word (*nuca*) is an Arabic medical term for the point where the brain joins the spinal marrow in the vertebral column (Nardi 1944).

130–31. not otherwise did Tydeus . . . in his rage: See *Theb.* 8.745–64: dying of a wound from Menalippus's spear, the hero Tydeus asks for the head of his killer, whom Tydeus has also cut down with a spear-cast. For him, Menalippus's severed head is a version of the Medusa: the mirror showing him his own death (see the note to 33.55–57). When it is brought to him, Tydeus, goaded by the Fury, falls on it and gnaws at it, just as Minerva is bringing the laurel wreath to honor his valor (8.760–61): "atque illum effracti perfusum tabe cerebri/ aspicit et vivo scelerantem sanguine fauces" [she gazes at him, soaked with gore from the shattered brain, defiling his mouth with living blood]. She turns away. Tydeus's hatred drives off his "immortal glory" (note *cappello*, line 126, which can mean "wreath").

130, 134. did . . . gnaw . . . you are eating: In both cases, Dante uses the reflexive pronoun (*si rose, ti mangi*), emphasizing the ferocity of the eater.

133. such a bestial sign: The expression "bestial sign" is an oxymoron, since beasts, lacking reason, are not able to signify.

135. with this pact: Instead of the fame he offered Bocca, here the pilgrim promises infamy for the eater's enemy. Dante's word for "pact" is *convegno* [convention] (cf. Shoaf 1988).

139. if that with which I speak does not dry up: If his tongue does not dry—that is, if he stays alive. References to the mouth or to speech have been frequent in this canto (see lines 6, 9, 14, 36, 38, 107–8, 115, and 116).

CANTO 33

1   La bocca sollevò dal fiero pasto
quel peccator, forbendola a' capelli
del capo ch'elli avea di retro guasto.

4   Poi cominciò: "Tu vuo' ch'io rinovelli
disperato dolor che 'l cor mi preme
già pur pensando, pria ch'io ne favelli.

7   Ma se le mie parole esser dien seme
che frutti infamia al traditor ch'i' rodo,
parlare e lagrimar vedrai insieme.

10   Io non so chi tu se' né per che modo
venuto se' qua giù; ma fiorentino
mi sembri veramente quand'io t'odo.

13   Tu dei saper ch'i' fui conte Ugolino,
e questi è l'arcivescovo Ruggieri:
or ti dirò perché i son tal vicino.

16   Che per l'effetto de' suo' mai pensieri,
fidandomi di lui, io fossi preso
e poscia morto, dir non è mestieri;

19   però quel che non puoi aver inteso,
cioè come la morte mia fu cruda,
udirai, e saprai s'e' m'ha offeso.

22   Breve pertugio dentro da la muda
la qual per me ha 'l titol de la fame,
e che conviene ancor ch'altrui si chiuda,

25   m'avea mostrato per lo suo forame
più lune già, quand' io feci 'l mal sonno
che del futuro mi squarciò 'l velame.

28   Questi pareva a me maestro e donno,
cacciando il lupo e ' lupicini al monte
per che i Pisan veder Lucca non ponno.

CANTO 33

Antenora, continued: Ugolino's account of his death—denunciation
of Pisa—Ptolomea: traitors to guests: Brother Alberigo—denunciation
of Genoa

1   That sinner lifted up his mouth from his savage
     meal, wiping it on the hairs of the head he had
     wasted from behind.

4   Then he began: "You wish me to renew desperate
     grief that already presses my heart merely thinking,
     before I speak of it.

7   But if my words will be seed to bear the fruit of
     infamy for the traitor I gnaw, you will see me speak
     and weep together.

10   I know not who you are nor in what manner you
     have come down here; but truly, you seem to me a
     Florentine when I hear you.

13   You are to know that I was Count Ugolino and
     this is the Archbishop Ruggieri: now I will tell you
     why I am such a neighbor to him.

16   That by effect of his evil thoughts, trusting him, I
     was taken and then killed, there is no need to say;

19   but what you cannot have heard, that is, how
     cruel my death was, you shall hear, and you shall
     know if he has injured me.

22   A small aperture within that mew which because of
     me has the name of Hunger, and where others must
     still be shut,

25   had shown me through its opening several moons
     already, when I dreamed the evil dream that rent the
     veil of the future for me.

28   This man appeared to me master and lord,
     hunting the wolf and his little cubs on the mountain
     for which the Pisans cannot see Lucca.

31 Con cagne magre, studïose e conte
Gualandi con Sismondi e con Lanfranchi
s'avea messi dinanzi de la fronte.

34 In picciol corso mi parieno stanchi
lo padre e ' figli, e con l'agute scane
mi parea lor veder fender li fianchi.

37 Quando fui desto innanzi la dimane,
pianger senti' fra 'l sonno i miei figliuoli,
ch'eran con meco, e dimandar del pane.

40 Ben se' crudel, se tu già non ti duoli
pensando ciò che 'l mio cor s'annunziava;
e se non piangi, di che pianger suoli?

43 Già eran desti, e l'ora s'appressava
che 'l cibo ne solëa essere addotto,
e per suo sogno ciascun dubitava;

46 e io senti' chiavar l'uscio di sotto
a l'orribile torre, ond' io guardai
nel viso a' mie' figliuoi sanza far motto.

49 Io non piangëa, sì dentro impetrai:
piangevan elli; e Anselmuccio mio
disse: "Tu guardi sì, padre! che hai?"

52 Perciò non lagrimai, né rispuos' io
tutto quel giorno né la notte appresso,
infin che l'altro sol nel mondo uscìo.

55 Come un poco di raggio si fu messo
nel doloroso carcere, e io scorsi
per quattro visi il mio aspetto stesso,

58 ambo le man per lo dolor mi morsi;
ed ei, pensando ch'io 'l fessi per voglia
di manicar, di sùbito levorsi,

61 e disser: "Padre, assai ci fia men doglia
se tu mangi di noi: tu ne vestisti
queste misere carni, e tu le spoglia."

64 Queta'mi allor per non farli più tristi;
lo dì e l'altro stemmo tutti muti:
ahi dura terra, perché non t'apristi?

67 Poscia che fummo al quarto dì venuti,
Gaddo mi si gittò disteso a' piedi,
dicendo: "Padre mio, ché non m'aiuti?"

31 With lean, eager, alert bitches, he had put
Gualandi with Sismondi and Lanfranchi before his
face.

34 In brief course the father and his sons seemed to
tire, and I seemed to see the sharp fangs tearing their
flanks.

37 When I awoke before the dawn, I heard my sons,
who were with me, crying in their sleep and asking
for bread.

40 You are surely cruel if you do not already grieve,
thinking what my heart was announcing to me; and
if you are not weeping, about what do you usually
weep?

43 They were already awake, and the hour was
drawing near when our food used to be brought to
us, and each was afraid because of his dream;

46 and I heard them nailing up the door at the base
of the horrible tower, hence I looked into the faces
of my sons without a word.

49 I was not weeping, I so turned to stone within:
they were weeping; and my Anselmuccio said: 'You
have such a look, father! what is it?'

52 Therefore I did not shed tears, nor did I reply all
that day or the night after, until the next sun came
forth into the world.

55 When a little ray had entered our dolorous prison,
and I perceived on four faces my own appearance,

58 both my hands I bit for rage; and they, thinking
that I must be doing it out of a desire to eat,
suddenly stood up

61 and said: 'Father, it will be much less pain for us
if you eat of us: you clothed us with this wretched
flesh, so do you divest us of it.'

64 I quieted myself then, so as not to make them
sadder; that day and the next we were all mute: ah,
hard earth, why did you not open?

67 After we had reached the fourth day, Gaddo
threw himself stretched out at my feet, saying: 'My
father, why do you not help me?'

70   Quivi morì; e come tu mi vedi,
vid' io cascar li tre ad uno ad uno
tra 'l quinto dì e 'l sesto; ond' io mi diedi,

73   già cieco, a brancolar sovra ciascuno,
e due dì li chiamai, poi che fur morti.
Poscia, più che 'l dolor, poté 'l digiuno."

76   Quand' ebbe detto ciò, con li occhi torti
riprese 'l teschio misero co' denti,
che furo a l'osso, come d'un can, forti.

79   Ahi Pisa, vituperio de le genti
del bel paese là dove 'l *sì* suona,
poi che i vicini a te punir son lenti,

82   muovasi la Capraia e la Gorgona
e faccian siepe ad Arno in su la foce,
sì ch'elli annieghi in te ogne persona!

85   Che se 'l conte Ugolino aveva voce
d'aver tradita te de le castella,
non dovei tu i figliuoi porre a tal croce.

88   Innocenti facea l'età novella,
novella Tebe, Uguiccione e 'l Brigata
e li altri due che 'l canto suso appella.

91   Noi passammo oltre, là 've la gelata
ruvidamente un'altra gente fascia,
non volta in giù, ma tutta riversata.

94   Lo pianto stesso lì pianger non lascia,
e 'l duol che truova in su li occhi rintoppo
si volge in entro a far crescer l'ambascia;

97   ché le lagrime prime fanno groppo
e, sì come visiere di cristallo,
rïempion sotto 'l ciglio tutto il coppo.

100   E avvegna che, sì come d'un callo,
per la freddura ciascun sentimento
cessato avesse del mio viso stallo,

103   già mi parea sentire alquanto vento;
per ch'io: "Maestro mio, questo chi move?
non è qua giù ogne vapore spento?"

106   Ond' elli a me: "Avaccio sarai dove
di ciò ti farà l'occhio la risposta,
veggendo la cagion che 'l fiato piove."

70   There he died; and as you see me, I saw the three
fall one by one between the fifth day and the sixth;
and I,

73   already blind, took to groping over each of them,
and for two days I called them, after they were dead.
Then fasting had more power than grief."

76   When he had said that, with eyes askance he took
the wretched skull in his teeth again, which were
strong against the bone, like a dog's.

79   Ah, Pisa, shame of the peoples of the lovely land
where *sì* is spoken, since your neighbors are slow to
punish you,

82   let Capraia and Gorgona move and make a barrier
at the mouth of Arno, so that it may drown every
person in you!

85   For if Count Ugolino was reported to have
betrayed your fortresses, you should not have put his
sons on such a cross.

88   Their young age, O new Thebes, made Uguiccione
and Brigata innocent, and the other two my song
names above.

91   We passed further, where the freezing rudely
swathes another people, not bent over but with
heads thrown back.

94   Weeping itself prevents weeping there, and the
sorrow that finds a block over the eyes turns back
within to increase the pain;

97   for the first tears make a knot and, like crystal
visors, fill all the cup below the brow.

100   And although, as if by a callus, because of the
cold every feeling had ended its stay on my face,

103   already I seemed to feel some wind; for which I:
"My master, who moves this wind? is not every
vapor extinguished down here?"

106   And he to me: "Soon you will be where your eye
will give you the answer, when you see the cause
raining down this breath."

109   E un de' tristi de la fredda crosta
gridò a noi: "O anime crudeli
tanto che data v'è l'ultima posta,

112   levatemi dal viso i duri veli,
sì ch'ïo sfoghi 'l duol che 'l cor m'impregna
un poco, pria che 'l pianto si raggeli."

115   Per ch'io a lui: "Se vuo' ch'i' ti sovvegna,
dimmi chi se', e s'io non ti disbrigo,
al fondo de la ghiaccia ir mi convegna."

118   Rispuose adunque: "I' son frate Alberigo,
i' son quel da le frutta del mal orto,
che qui riprendo dattero per figo."

121   "Oh," diss' io lui, "or se' tu ancor morto?"
Ed elli a me: "Come 'l mio corpo stea
nel mondo sù, nulla scïenza porto.

124   Cotal vantaggio ha questa Tolomea,
che spesse volte l'anima ci cade
innanzi ch'Atropòs mossa le dea.

127   E perché tu più volontier mi rade
le 'nvetrïate lagrime dal volto,
sappie che, tosto che l'anima trade

130   come fec' ïo, il corpo suo l'è tolto
da un demonio, che poscia il governa
mentre che 'l tempo suo tutto sia vòlto;

133   ella ruina in sì fatta cisterna.
E forse pare ancor lo corpo suso
de l'ombra che di qua dietro mi verna;

136   tu 'l dei saper, se tu vien pur mo giuso:
elli è ser Branca Doria, e son più anni
poscia passati ch'el fu sì racchiuso."

139   "Io credo," diss' io lui, "che tu m'inganni,
ché Branca Doria non morì unquanche,
e mangia e bee e dorme e veste panni."

142   "Nel fosso sù," diss' el, "de' Malebranche,
là dove bolle la tenace pece,
non era ancora giunto Michel Zanche,

145   che questi lasciò il diavolo in sua vece
nel corpo suo, ed un suo prossimano
che 'l tradimento insieme con lui fece.

109   And one of the grievers of the icy crust cried to me: "O souls so cruel that you are given the last place,

112   lift from my eyes the hard veils, so that I may give vent a little to the anguish that gathers in my heart, before my tears freeze up again."

115   Therefore I to him: "If you wish me to help you, tell me who you are, and if I do not extricate you, may I have to go down to the bottom of the ice."

118   He replied therefore: "I am Brother Alberigo, I am he of the fruits of the evil orchard, and here I receive a date for every fig."

121   "Oh," said I to him, "now are you already dead?" And he to me: "How my body may fare up in the world, I have no knowledge.

124   Ptolomea has this advantage, that often the soul falls here before Atropos has sent it off.

127   And that you may more willingly shave the glassy tears from my eyes, know that, as soon as the soul betrays

130   as I did, its body is taken over by a demon, who then governs it until his time has all revolved;

133   the soul falls down into this cistern. And perhaps the body still appears up there of the shade who is wintering here behind me;

136   you must know of him, if you have just now come down here: he is ser Branca Doria, and years have passed since he was closed in like that."

139   "I believe," I told him, "that you are deceiving me, for Branca Doria is not yet dead, and he eats and drinks and sleeps and wears clothes."

142   "Up in the ditch," he said "of the Evil Claws, there where the sticky pitch is boiling, Michel Zanche had not yet arrived,

145   when this one left a devil in his stead, in his body and that of a relative of his who committed the betrayal along with him.

148   Ma distendi oggimai in qua la mano,
aprimi li occhi." E io non gliel' apersi;
e cortesia fu lui esser villano.

151   Ahi Genovesi, uomini diversi
d'ogne costume e pien d'ogne magagna,
perché non siete voi del mondo spersi?

154   Ché col peggiore spirto di Romagna
trovai di voi un tal, che per sua opra
in anima in Cocito già si bagna,

157   e in corpo par vivo ancor di sopra.

148   But stretch out your hand to me now, open my eyes." And I did not open them for him; and it was courtesy to treat him boorishly.

151   Ah, men of Genoa, foreign to every decent usage, full of every vice, why have you not been exterminated from the world?

154   For with the worst spirit of Romagna I found such a one of yours, that for his deeds in soul he already bathes in Cocytus,

157   and in the body he seems still alive up above.

NOTES

1–3. his mouth . . . from behind: The emphatic opening of the canto, focusing especially on the sinner's "mouth" (*bocca*; cf. the note on 32.106–8), follows immediately, without proem, on the pilgrim's words at the end of Canto 32. The episode begins and ends with his "savage meal." Note the featuring of an etymological figure (*capelli . . . capo*) parallel to that in 32.126 (*capo . . . cappello*).

4–75. You wish . . . than grief: This "oration" of Count Ugolino (identified in line 13) is, with Francesca da Rimini's and Ulysses', probably the most famous in the *Comedy*. With them, Ugolino is the classic model for the Romantic view of Dante's damned as great-souled and rising above the background of Hell and the theological categories of sin. In Ugolino's case, the consuming desire for revenge was seen as the expression of the father's outrage at his children's suffering. Recent opinion has moved to another extreme: Russo (1967) has argued that Ugolino's term *dolore* [grief, pain] is to be interpreted exclusively in terms of the desire for revenge; Bárberi–Squarotti (1971) has analyzed Ugolino's speech as cynically contrived so as to obscure his guilt and attract to himself the pathos of the children. A major issue has been the interpretation of line 75.

4–21. You wish . . . if he has injured me: The proem of Ugolino's oration: the painfulness of speaking (4–6); the greater intensity of his desire to bring infamy on his enemy (7–9); his identification of the pilgrim as familiar with the publicly known events (10–18); and the announcement of his subject, his own death (19–21).

4–6. You wish me . . . before I speak of it: Ugolino is echoing the words with which Aeneas begins his account of the fall of Troy (*Aen.* 2.3, 6–8, 12–13):

> Infandum, regina, iubes renovare dolorem. . . .
> quis talia fando
> Myrmidonum Dolopumve aut duri miles Ulixi
> temperet a lacrimis? . . .
> quamquam animus meminisse horret luctuque refugit,
> incipiam.

> [You bid me renew, O queen, unspeakable grief. . . .
> speaking such things, who
> of the Myrmidons or the Dolopes, or what soldier of cruel Ulysses
> could refrain from tears? . . .
> although my spirit shudders to remember and shrinks from this grief,
> I will begin.]

The allusion suggests the larger political context of Ugolino's tragedy. That Ugolino's grief "presses" (*preme*) on his heart continues the motif of pressure set up by 32.1–12 (cf. especially 32.4: *premerei* [I would press]).

7–9. But if my words . . . speak and weep together: The metaphor is complex: it amounts to saying that Ugolino accepts the pact with the pilgrim, who is to repeat his story among the living; at that point Ruggieri will gain infamy. Thus Ugolino's words are to be the seed; the pilgrim's memory, the earth where it is planted; the text of lines 4–75, the plant; and infamy, the fruit. This is the first of the series of references in the canto to the Sermon on the Mount (Matthew 5–7) (see the note to line 120).

9. speak and weep together: Mouth and eyes. The phrase conspicuously echoes 5.126, where Francesca says, "I will do as one who weeps and speaks."

11–12. a Florentine when I hear you: Like Farinata (10.25–27), Ugolino has recognized the pilgrim's city, not merely his region, by his speech.

13–18. I was Count Ugolino . . . no need to say: As a Florentine, the pilgrim must know of these events; they took place when Dante was in his early twenties. Ugolino uses the past tense of himself ("I was") and the present tense of Ruggieri ("this is"), placing his own guilt in the past, Ruggieri's in the present.

Ugolino della Gherardesca, count of Donoratico, was born in the first decades of the thirteenth century. Gmelin's outline of events is succinct:

> Ugolino was descended from an old Longobard Ghibelline family with rich possessions in the region of Pisa. He had been the representative of the Hohenstaufen in Sardinia, but after their downfall he returned to Pisa and joined the Guelf party, in the hope of gaining control of Pisa with their help. Later, when the Pisan Ghibellines under the leadership of the archbishop, Ruggieri degli Ubaldini, became dominant again, he negotiated with them in order to drive out his own grandson Nino Visconti, but he was treacherously lured into the city by the Archbishop, arrested, and imprisoned. Dante, who was a friend of Nino Visconti (he placed him among the negligent rulers in *Purgatorio* 8), could have heard the entire story from him.

Ugolino, two of his sons, and two (according to some sources, three) grandsons were imprisoned in July 1288 and probably died in March 1289. It is possible but unlikely that Dante was badly informed about the identity of those in the tower with Ugolino. The changes, making all four of them children (rather than two grown men and two adolescents), are probably deliberate.

Dante places both Ugolino and Ruggieri (a typical pairing of lay and cleric,

Guelf and Ghibelline) in Antenora (see the note to 32.88) as betrayers of party; that they are not in Ptolomea (the third section of Cocytus, for traitors to guests) is assured by the clarity of the transition in line 92.

15. such a neighbor: "Thou shalt love thy neighbor as thyself" (Matt. 22.37–40, 5.43–48): another in the series of allusions to the Sermon on the Mount (Matthew 5–7). The intimate enmity parodies the social bonds on which the city rests.

22–25. A small aperture . . . several moons already: That is, through a small opening or window Ugolino had been able to see the waxing and waning of the moon a number of times (it is not clear that he can see the sun). A mew (Italian, *muda*) is a room for molting hawks, dark so as to keep them quiet; Buti suggests that the city's eagles had been kept there. After the deaths of Ugolino and his children, the tower became known as the Torre della fame [Hunger Tower]; it was used as a prison until 1318. This stone tower with a small window (like an eye) is a version of the image of the body as a prison (see the note to 10.58–59).

26–27. I dreamed the evil dream . . . for me: The most famous "rent veil" is that of the Temple in Jerusalem, rent at Christ's death (see the note to 12.31–45); Ugolino's language is biblical and apocalyptic. His assertion that the dream was "evil" is discussed in Additional Note 15.

28–36. This man . . . tearing their flanks: Ugolino's dream occurs just before dawn (line 37), at the time for prophetic dreams (26.7–12). It shows Ruggieri as master of the hunt for the wolf and his cubs (Ugolino and his sons), on Monte Pisano or Monte San Giuliano, both between Pisa and (Guelf) Lucca (the recurrent motif of blocked sight; see the note to 32.63–64). The bitches recall those of the infernal hunt in 13.124–29; Gualandi, Sismondi, and Lanfranchi were powerful Pisan Ghibelline families. The dream sums up events so far and predicts Ugolino's and his sons' deaths; the dogs' fangs repeat the motif of teeth. Ugolino sees himself as a wolf, the traditional enemy of man.

38–39. I heard my sons . . . asking for bread: The Italian diminutive *figliuoli* already suggests that the children are small; they are never represented as asking for food while awake. This is another allusion to the Sermon on the Mount (Matt. 7.9–10).

40–42. You are surely cruel . . . usually weep: This highly rhetorical appeal to the pilgrim's pity, belied by Ugolino's own failure to weep (lines 49–50), is a chief basis for the claim that Ugolino's speech is cynically self-aggrandizing (see the note to lines 4–75).

41. what my heart was announcing to me: Because of the importance of the Annunciation (to Mary), Ugolino's use of the term *annunziava* is laden with irony.

45. each was afraid because of his dream: Each of the children, then, has also had a dream, perhaps a prophetic one.

46–47. I heard them . . . horrible tower: According to the chroniclers, not only was the tower nailed up, its keys were thrown into the river.

47–50. hence . . . they were weeping: The causal relation implied by the Italian *onde* [hence] is extremely loose; Ugolino means, it would seem, that he was so overwhelmed by the event that he is incapable of speaking: he can only stare at the children. The contrast between his silent rigidity and their expressiveness is the focus of the account.

50–51. my Anselmuccio . . . what is it: Anselmuccio was the legal name of Ugolino's fifteen-year-old grandson (Ugolino is also a diminutive, of Ugo, but still the count's name). The use of the name here suggests that the affectionate diminutive (-*uccio*) is used for a very small child, incapable of grasping the implications of events.

52. Therefore: Ugolino represents his silence here and later as the expression of forbearance, since the only things he could say—expressions of his despair and his hatred for Ruggieri—would only upset the children more (cf. line 64).

55–57. When a little ray . . . my own appearance: The sun's light makes it possible for him to see the children's faces. His "own appearance" (cf. *Theb.* 8.753, of Tydeus looking at Menalippus's head: "seseque agnovit in illo" [and he recognized himself in him]; see the note to 32.130–31) has several implications. It signifies the children's family resemblance to himself; it suggests that he can see the progress of their starvation, can read both his and their deaths inscribed in their faces. For this moment and the Medusa, see Additional Note 15.

58. both my hands I bit for rage: Italian *dolore,* which we here translate as "rage," includes suggestions of sorrow, grief, anger, desire for revenge, and, here, guilt. Ugolino's first turning to stone and then biting his hands are stages of his becoming what we find in Cocytus; see Filippo Argenti (8.62–63), who "turned on himself with his teeth." Of course, Ugolino's biting his hands does express, along with its other complexities, his hunger for justice against Ruggieri; compare with Matt. 5.6.

59–63. they, thinking . . . divest us of it: The children are represented as not understanding their father's agony because of their youth and innocence. Lines 62–63 echo Job 1.21: "Naked came I out of my mother's womb, and naked shall I return thither: the Lord gave, and the Lord hath taken away. . . . blessed be the name of the Lord." The commentators point out that their offer of their flesh as food involves allusion to the Eucharist. See Additional Note 15.

The Italian *spogliare* means both "to take away" and "to undress" (cf. 3.114). *Manicar* [to eat], like *manducare* (32.127), is a familiar dialect word; in *De vulgari eloquentia* 1.13.2, Dante identifies it as Florentine and excludes it from the "tragic" style (cf. the notes to 32.1–12).

67. After we had reached the fourth day: The sun has risen, then, and the inmates of the tower can see each other again.

69. My father, why do you not help me: As the commentators point out, these words echo Jesus' last words as reported by Matthew and Mark: "Eli, Eli, lamma sabachthani, that is, My God, my God, why hast thou forsaken me?" (Matt. 27.46).

70–72. There he died . . . and the sixth: Gaddo dies on the fourth day, the others on the fifth and sixth days. Medieval readers would have been alert to the fact that Christ's death took place on the sixth day of the week.

72–74. I, already blind . . . after they were dead: Ugolino calls them for two days: he lives, then, into the eighth day, when presumably he dies— Macrobius had written that a man cannot live more than a week without food. The commentators have seen the ironic parallel with the week of the Creation; there is also a negative parallel with Christ's resurrection, which took place on the day after the Sabbath (in the Middle Ages the number eight was universally associated with baptism and resurrection).

75. Then fasting had more power than grief: "Grief" translates *dolor*, which includes the complexities noted at line 58. The line is ambiguous: his rage could not kill him, but on the eighth day his hunger did; or: hunger overcame his grief, and he fed on the children's bodies. There has been much debate about this line. See Additional Note 15.

76. with eyes askance: Ugolino's eyes are *torti* [twisted], past participle of the verb Dante uses of Ciacco in 6.91 to describe the characteristic oblique gaze of envy and in 30.21 of doglike madness.

78. like a dog's: The vivid image picks up the several comparisons of the souls in Cocytus to dogs (32.70, 105, and 108), as well as the dogs of Ugolino's dream. Here part of the point is the adaptation of dogs' teeth to grinding bones. The wolf is implied also: Ugolino and Ruggieri are instances of *homo homini lupus*: men who have become wolves to others.

79–90. Ah, Pisa . . . my song names above: The poet's calling down of punishment on Pisa recalls God's destruction of Sodom, not to speak of the Flood. The method, flooding Pisa by blocking the mouth of the Arno with the two small offshore islands of Capraia and Gorgona, imagines a closing in of rock and the formation of a lake parallel to that of Cocytus or Thebes (see 32.10, with note). The names *Capraia* [Goat Island] and *Gorgona* seem to have appealed to Dante for their association with the damned (who are goats to be separated from the sheep; Matt. 25.33) and with the Medusa. He is remembering Christ's words in Matt. 18.6: "But he that shall scandalize one of these little ones that believe in me, it were better for him that a millstone should be hanged about his neck, and that he should be drowned in the depth of the sea" (see the note to 28.79). The next-to-last denunciation of an Italian city in the *Inferno* (see lines 151–57).

80. the lovely land where *sì* is spoken: In *De vulgari eloquentia*, Dante classifies the Romance languages on the basis of the word used for "yes" (cf. 18.61, 21.42); this was already traditional. The traitor, of course, says an everlasting "no."

85–88. For if Count Ugolino . . . on such a cross: While *podestà* of Pisa in 1285, Ugolino ceded several Pisan castles to Lucca and Florence (Guelf cities), apparently with the intention—successful, in fact—of weakening their alliance with Genoa against Pisa. Later the Pisan Ghibellines charged that this was done treacherously. Even if true, the charge could not justify the killing of his sons (*porre a croce* can mean simply "to torture," but after line 69 the reference to Christ's cross is unmistakable).

88–90. Their young age . . . my song names above: Uguiccione was a son of Ugolino's; Nino, called "il Brigata," was a grandson. One should note that Dante's denunciation of the starving of the children validates Ugolino's denunciation of Ruggieri (lines 7–9 and 19–21), as does God's making him the instrument of Ruggieri's punishment.

The Italian juxtaposes two different senses of the word *novello* [new, young]. Pisa is a "new Thebes" because its wickedness rivals that of Thebes, the most wicked city of antiquity; and it is a "young Thebes" in terms of the mythographic tradition that identified it as a Theban colony (Zampese 1989). For Dante's references to the saga of Thebes, see the notes to 26.52–54, 30.1–27; for denunciations of Italian cities, including Genoa, 33.151–57, see the note to 26.1–3.

91–93. We passed further . . . heads thrown back: In both Caina (32.31–72) and Antenora (32.73–33.90), the souls can protect their eyes by lowering their heads; they also face away from the wind. Now we enter Ptolomea, reserved for those who have murdered guests.

94–99. Weeping itself . . . below the brow: The exquisite painfulness of the "crystal visors" is due in part to the fact that, as Dante knew, water expands when it forms ice. This is a particularly uncomfortable version of the insistence in these cantos on the idea of pressure. The tropological significance of the "crystal visors" is probably that the malice and hatred of these sinners have blocked their ability to see anything else; it is a continuation of the theme of blocked sight, a version of the "beam" of the Gospel (Matt. 7.3): "And why seest thou the mote that is in thy brother's eye; and seest not the beam that is in thy own eye?" See also Matt. 6.22–23: "The light of thy body is thy eye. . . . But if thy eye be evil thy whole body shall be darkness. If then the light that is in thee be darkness: the darkness itself, how great shall it be!" The note to line 148 discusses the probable source for the visors in the Gospel of John. As part of a helmet, the visors refer ironically to the "armor of God" (Eph. 6.13–17), which includes "the helmet of salvation."

104–5. who moves . . . extinguished down here: The pilgrim asks *who*—rather than *what*—moves the wind (it is explained in 34.49–52). The accepted theory of winds was that they resulted from the heat of the sun evaporating moisture (hence "vapor") and from the consequent differences in temperature (as in 9.67–68); earthquakes were caused by winds trapped underground (3.131–33). But "down here" all heated air ("vapor") is chilled ("extinguished," since the element of fire has been removed).

110–14. O souls so cruel . . . freeze up again: In contrast with the ferocious energy of Ugolino, this last and most wicked soul is apparently suffering so intensely that he entreats souls he supposes even more merciless than himself.

The swelling of the heart with sorrow and the gathering of tears are coalesced here, as if the pressure on the eyes reaches the heart itself. The generative imagery (*impregna* [impregnates]) is continued in lines 118–20.

115–17. If you wish . . . bottom of the ice: The pilgrim has already encountered Bocca degli Abbati's resistance to revealing his identity (32.94–105). His promise here is of course fraudulent, since he has realized that he and Virgil will descend through the ice; his betrayal of the betrayer (lines 149–50) is already prepared; he will violate this pact (see the note to 33.149–50).

118–20. I am Brother Alberigo . . . every fig: Alberigo, a leading member of the Manfredi of Faenza, a prominent Guelf family, was a *frate godente* (see the notes to 23.103–8). In 1285 he invited to dinner several relatives from whom he had formerly been estranged in a dispute over land; at the end of the meal, his words "Vengan le frutta" [Let the fruits come] were the signal for the assassins who then murdered his relatives, including one who tried to hide under Alberigo's cloak. Various phrases like "the fruits of friar Alberigo" became proverbial soon after, as did Dante's "fruits of the evil orchard," if it was not already so when he wrote.

120. a date for every fig: Dates being more expensive than figs, the phrase means "better than I gave" (cf. the proverbial phrase to give or receive "pan per focaccia" [bread for shortbread]). Maintaining the fruit metaphor, Dante is making scornful play on the name *Alberigo* as related to the word for "tree" (*albero*) and draws on the Sermon on the Mount (Matt. 7.16–20), especially:

> Do men gather grapes of thorns or figs of thistles? Even so every good tree bringeth forth good fruit, and the evil tree bringeth forth evil fruit. . . . Wherefore by their fruits ye shall know them.

121. are you already dead: Brother Alberigo was still alive in the spring of 1302, in Ravenna, where he made a will; he seems to have died around 1307.

122–23. How my body . . . no knowledge: This sinner seems even more ignorant of the present than is usual (see 10.100–108).

124–33. Ptolomea . . . into this cistern: The name of this third division of Cocytus is derived from the Ptolemy, king of Egypt, who permitted the murder of his guest, the defeated Pompey the Great, possibly also from the Ptolemy of 1 Macc. 16.11–16, who murdered his father-in-law and two brothers-in-law when they were his guests. Dante's bold imagining of a demon's taking over the body of these traitors is probably heterodox, but it draws on the account of Judas in Luke 22.3: "And Satan entered into Judas," as well as popular tradition (see below).

126. Atropos: One of the three Fates; Clotho was said to spin the thread of one's life, Lachesis to measure it, and Atropos to sever it.

133. cistern: A cistern is a well or a reservoir for drinking water.

134–38. perhaps the body . . . closed in like that: Branca Doria, member of a famous noble family of Genoa, invited his father-in-law, Michele Zanche, to dinner and had him killed along with those who accompanied him. According to some, this took place in 1275; according to others, in 1290. Michele Zanche was mentioned by Ciampolo as always talking about Sardinia (22.89–90).

135. wintering here behind me: Italian *vernare* can mean "to spend the winter," but the phrase may be even more sardonic, since *vernare* can also mean "to sing in the spring" (used of birds); there could be a reference to the "stork's tune" (32.36) of chattering teeth.

140–41. Branca Doria . . . and wears clothes: Branca Doria outlived Dante; he was still alive in 1325. Dante's words seem to echo a phrase from Caesarius of Heisterbach's dialogue in which one interlocutor expresses surprise at the idea that a certain Landgraf Hermann was possessed: "I did not think a human body, without a soul, could eat, drink, and sleep" (cited in Biagioni 1957).

148. But stretch out your hand to me: What Brother Alberigo asks is an analogue (like the pilgrim's gesture toward Brunetto Latini in 15.29) of a gesture of Jesus—for instance, in Matt. 8.3 (of the healing of a leper): "and Jesus, extending [*extendens*] his hand, touched him." The allusion suggests that Dante may have developed his idea of the crystal visors on the basis of the mud visor in the healing of the man blind from birth: "[Jesus] spat on the ground, and made clay of the spittle, and spread the clay on his eyes, And said to him, Go, wash in the pool of Siloe. . . . He went, therefore, and washed, and he came seeing" (John 9.6–7).

149–50. And I did not . . . to treat him boorishly: That is, to have lightened in any way the suffering of this wicked soul would have been a lapse; true *cortesia* (behavior appropriate to the court of a ruler, in this case, God) here requires what in other circumstances would be its reverse (the behavior of a peasant, a *villano*).

151–57. Ah, men of Genoa . . . up above: The denunciations of Italian cities in the *Inferno* are listed in the note to 26.1–3; this is the last of them.

CANTO 34

1　　　"*Vexilla regis prodeunt inferni*
verso di noi; però dinanzi mira,"
disse 'l maestro mio, "se tu 'l discerni."

4　　　Come, quando una grossa nebbia spira
o quando l'emisperio nostro annotta,
par di lungi un molin che 'l vento gira:

7　　　veder mi parve un tal dificio allotta;
poi per lo vento mi ristrinsi retro
al duca mio, ché non lì era grotta.

10　　Già era, e con paura il metto in metro,
là dove l'ombre tutte eran coperte,
e trasparien come festuca in vetro.

13　　Altre sono a giacere; altre stanno erte,
quella col capo e quella con le piante;
altra, com' arco, il volto a' pié rinverte

16　　Quando noi fummo fatti tanto avante
ch'al mio maestro piacque di mostrarmi
la creatura ch'ebbe il bel sembiante,

19　　d'innanzi mi si tolse e fé restarmi,
"Ecco Dite," dicendo, "ed ecco il loco
ove convien che di fortezza t'armi."

22　　Com' io divenni allor gelato e fioco,
nol dimandar, lettor, ch'i' non lo scrivo,
però ch'ogne parlar sarebbe poco.

25　　Io non mori' e non rimasi vivo:
pensa oggimai per te, s'hai fior d'ingegno,
qual io divenni, d'uno e d'altro privo.

28　　Lo 'mperador del doloroso regno
da mezzo 'l petto uscia fuor de la ghiaccia;
e più con un gigante io mi convegno

CANTO 34

*Judecca: traitors to lords and benefactors—Satan—Brutus, Cassius,
and Judas—descent past the center—climb to Purgatory*

1 　　　*"Vexilla regis prodeunt inferni* toward us;
therefore look ahead," said my master, "to see if you
discern him."

4 　　　As, when a thick mist breathes, or, when our
hemisphere is all night, a mill appears from afar that
the wind is turning:

7 　　　so I seemed to see such an edifice there; then,
because of the wind, I shrank behind my leader, for
there was no other shelter.

10 　　　I was already—and fearfully I set it in meter—
where the shades were all covered, and they
appeared like straws in glass.

13 　　　Some are lying; others are vertical, this with head
above, that with feet; some, like bows, turn their
faces toward their feet.

16 　　　When we had moved so far ahead that it pleased
my master to show me the creature who had once
been beautiful,

19 　　　he removed himself from in front of me and made
me stop, saying: "Behold Dis, and behold the place
where you must arm yourself with courage."

22 　　　How then I became frozen and feeble, do not ask,
reader, for I do not write it, and all speech would be
insufficient.

25 　　　I did not die and I did not remain alive: think
now for yourself, if you have wit at all, what I
became, deprived of both.

28 　　　The emperor of the dolorous kingdom issued from
the ice at the mid-point of his breast; and I am more
to be compared with a giant

31 che i giganti non fan con le sue braccia:
vedi oggimai quant' esser dee quel tutto
ch'a così fatta parte si confaccia.

34 S'el fu sì bel com' elli è ora brutto,
e contra 'l suo fattore alzò le ciglia,
ben dee da lui procedere ogne lutto.

37 Oh quanto parve a me gran maraviglia
quand' io vidi tre facce a la sua testa!
L'una dinanzi, e quella era vermiglia;

40 l'altr' eran due, che s'aggiugnieno a questa
sovresso 'l mezzo di ciascuna spalla
e sé giugnieno al loco de la cresta:

43 e la destra parea tra bianca e gialla;
la sinistra a vedere era tal, quali
vegnon di là onde 'l Nilo s'avvalla.

46 Sotto ciascuna uscivan due grand' ali,
quanto si convenia a tanto uccello:
vele di mar non vid' io mai cotali.

49 Non avean penne, ma di vispistrello
era lor modo; e quelle svolazzava,
sì che tre venti si movean da ello;

52 quindi Cocito tutto s'aggelava.
Con sei occhi piangëa, e per tre menti
gocciava 'l pianto e sanguinosa bava.

55 Da ogne bocca dirompea co' denti
un peccatore, a guisa di maciulla,
sì che tre ne facea così dolenti.

58 A quel dinanzi il mordere era nulla
verso 'l graffiar, che talvolta la schiena
rimanea de la pelle tutta brulla.

61 "Quell' anima là sù c'ha maggior pena,"
disse 'l maestro, "è Giuda Scarïotto,
che 'l capo ha dentro e fuor le gambe mena.

64 De li altri due c'hanno il capo di sotto,
quel che pende dal nero ceffo è Bruto—
vedi come si storce, e non fa motto—

67 e l'altro è Cassio, che par sì membruto.
Ma la notte risurge, e oramai
è da partir, ché tutto avem veduto."

31 than the giants with his arms: see now how great
must be the whole that fits with such a part.

34 If he was as beautiful then as now he is ugly,
when he lifted his brow against his Maker, well must
all grieving proceed from him.

37 Oh how great a marvel did it seem to me, when I
saw three faces on his head! One was in front, and
that was crimson;

40 the others were two, and they were joined to the
first above the midpoint of each shoulder, and came
together at the crest:

43 and the right one seemed between white and
yellow; the left was such to see as those who come
from beyond the cataracts of the Nile.

46 Beneath each one came out two great wings, such
as befitted so great a bird: sea-going sails I never saw
so large.

49 They did not have feathers; their mode was like a
bat's; and he was fanning them, so that three winds
went out from him:

52 by them Cocytus was frozen. With six eyes he
was weeping, and down three chins dripped the
tears and the bloody slobber.

55 In each of his mouths he was breaking a sinner
with his teeth in the manner of a scutch, so that he
made three suffer at once.

58 To the one in front the biting was nothing next to
the clawing, for at times the spine remained all
naked of skin.

61 "That soul up there who has the greatest
punishment," said my master, "is Judas Iscariot, with
his head inside, waving his legs outside.

64 Of the other two whose heads are below, he who
hangs from the black muzzle is Brutus—see how he is
convulsed, but does not say a word—

67 and the other is Cassius, who seems so powerfully
built. But the night is rising again, and now we must
depart, for we have seen everything."

70   Com' a lui piacque, il collo li avvinghiai;
ed el prese di tempo e loco poste,
e quando l'ali fuoro aperte assai,

73   appigliò sé a le vellute coste;
di vello in vello giù discese poscia
tra 'l folto pelo e le gelate croste.

76   Quando noi fummo là dove la coscia
si volge, a punto in sul grosso de l'anche,
lo duca, con fatica e con angoscia,

79   volse la testa ov' elli avea le zanche,
e aggrappossi al pel com' om che sale,
sì che 'n inferno i' credea tornar anche.

82   "Attienti ben, ché per cotali scale,"
disse 'l maestro, ansando com' uom lasso,
"conviensi dipartir da tanto male."

85   Poi uscì fuor per lo fóro d'un sasso,
e puose me in su l'orlo a sedere;
appresso porse a me l'accorto passo.

88   Io levai li occhi e credetti vedere
Lucifero com' io l'avea lasciato,
e vidili le gambe in sù tenere;

91   e s'io divenni allora travagliato,
la gente grossa il pensi che non vede
qual è quel punto ch'io avea passato.

94   "Lèvati sù," disse 'l maestro, "in piede:
la via è lunga e 'l cammino è malvagio,
e già il sole a mezza terza riede."

97   Non era camminata di palagio
là 'v' eravam, ma natural burella
ch'avea mal suolo e di lume disagio.

100   "Prima che de l'abisso mi divella,
maestro mio," diss' io quando fui dritto,
"a trarmi d'erro un poco mi favella:

103   ov' è la ghiaccia? e questi com' è fitto
sì sottosopra? e come, in sì poc' ora,
da sera a mane ha fatto il sol tragitto?"

106   Ed elli a me: "Tu imagini ancora
d'esser di là dal centro, ov' io mi presi
al pel del vermo reo che 'l mondo fóra.

70 As it pleased him, I clung to his neck; and he watched for time and place, and when the wings were fully open

73 he took hold of the furry sides; from tuft to tuft then he descended between the thick hair and the frozen crust.

76 When we came to where the thigh is hinged, exactly at the widest of the hips, my leader, with labor and difficulty,

79 turned his head to where he had his shanks, and clung to the pelt like one who climbs, so that I supposed we were returning into Hell again.

82 "Hold fast, for by such stairs," said my master, panting like one weary, "must we depart from so much evil."

85 Next he went forth through the hole in the rock, and placed me sitting on the rim; then he extended his careful step to me.

88 I raised my eyes, thinking to see Lucifer as I had left him, and I saw that he extended his legs upward;

91 and if I labored in thought then, let the gross people ponder it who do not see what point it was that I had passed.

94 "Rise up," said my master, "on your feet; the way is long and the path is difficult, and already the sun has reached mid-tierce."

97 That was no walk through a palace where we were, but a natural cavern that had uneven ground and lacked light.

100 "Before I am uprooted from the abyss, my master," said I, when I was erect, "speak to me a little to help me out of error.

103 Where is the ice? and he, how is he fixed so upside down? and how, in so little time, has the sun made the passage from evening to morning?"

106 And he to me: "You imagine that you are still on the other side of the center, where I laid hold on the fur of this evil worm that gnaws the world.

109   Di là fosti cotanto quant' io scesi;
quand' io mi volsi, tu passasti 'l punto
al qual si traggon d'ogne parte i pesi.

112   E se' or sotto l'emisperio giunto
ch'è contraposto a quel che la gran secca
coverchia, e sotto 'l cui colmo consunto

115   fu l'uom che nacque e visse sanza pecca;
tu haï i piedi in su picciola spera
che l'altra faccia fa de la Giudecca.

118   Qui è da man, quando di là è sera;
e questi, che ne fé scala col pelo,
fitto è ancora sì come prim' era.

121   Da questa parte cadde giù dal cielo;
e la terra, che pria di qua si sporse,
per paura di lui fé del mar velo,

124   e venne a l'emisperio nostro; e forse
per fuggir lui lasciò qui loco vòto
quella ch'appar di qua, e sù ricorse."

127   Luogo è là giù da Belzebù remoto
tanto quanto la tomba si distende,
che non per vista, ma per suono è noto

130   d'un ruscelletto che quivi discende
per la buca d'un sasso ch'elli ha roso
col corso ch'elli avvolge, e poco pende.

133   Lo duca e io per quel cammino ascoso
intrammo a ritornar nel chiaro mondo;
e sanza cura aver d'alcun riposo

136   salimmo sù, el primo e io secondo,
tanto ch'i' vidi de le cose belle
che porta 'l ciel, per un pertugio tondo.

139   E quindi uscimmo a riveder le stelle.

109   You were on that side while I descended; when I
turned, you passed the point toward which the
weights all move from every direction.

112   And now you are beneath the hemisphere
opposite the one covered by the dry land, and under
whose high point died

115   the man who was born and lived without sin; you
have your feet on a little sphere that makes the other
face of the Judecca.

118   Here it is morning, when there it is evening; and
this one, who gave us a ladder with his fur, is still
fixed as he was earlier.

121   On this side he fell down from Heaven; and the
dry land, which previously extended over here, for
fear of him took the sea as a veil,

124   and came to our hemisphere; and perhaps what
does appear on this side left this empty space in
order to escape from him, and fled upward."

127   There is a place down there, removed from
Beelzebub as far as the width of his tomb, known not
by sight, but by the sound

130   of a little stream that descends through a hole in a
rock eroded by its winding course, and it is not
steep.

133   My leader and I entered on that hidden path to
return to the bright world; and, without taking
care for rest at all,

136   up we climbed, he first and I second, until I saw
the beautiful things the heavens carry, through a
round opening.

139   And thence we came forth to look again at the
stars.

NOTES

1–7. *Vexilla regis* . . . such an edifice there: The first, preliminary view of Satan, too distant to be made out clearly in the darkness. He is compared to a mill (another image of the harvest, traditionally associated with the Last Judgment; cf. the note to 32.4). Compare the pilgrim's first view of the giants (31.19–27).

1–2. *Vexilla regis prodeunt inferni* toward us: "The standards of the king of Hell go forth toward us." The first three Latin words of line 1 are the opening of a hymn by Venantius Fortunatus (535–600) in praise of the Cross:

> Vexilla regis prodeunt,
> fulget crucis mysterium
> quo carne carnis conditor
> suspensus est patibulo.

> [The standards of the king go forth:
> the mystery of the Cross shines,
> by which, in the flesh, the creator of flesh
> was hung upon the gibbet.]

The *vexillum* (from *veho* [to transport]) was the standard of a Roman legion, carried into battle. In the hymn, the word refers to the crosses carried in processions; Virgil's satirical application of it to Satan (the reference is to his wings, lines 46–52) emphasizes the fact that Satan is immobilized and alludes to the traditional idea that his punishment is a debased parody of the Crucifixion (see the notes to lines 39–45, 54, and 70–93, and Additional Note 16). The hymn was sung at feasts of the Cross (November 14, May 3) and at vespers (it is now evening) during the last weeks of Lent.

5. when our hemisphere is all night: When it is midnight in Jerusalem, in Dante's thinking, it is night over all the hemisphere of land, which extends from the Ganges to Gibraltar (180 degrees of longitude, in his geography; Jerusalem is its midpoint [Figure 8]). As Virgil will observe in line 68, "night," the ideal point of midnight, circling opposite the sun, "is rising" (that is, the sun is setting), always in Jerusalem.

6–7. a mill . . . such an edifice: The dimly perceived waving of Satan's wings seems like the turning sails of a windmill. Windmills were common in the Tuscan landscape (cf. 23.46–48 and note). Dante's word for "building" (*dificio*, edifice) could be used of almost any large structure: a stone building, a siege tower, a machine like a windmill, a ship or part of a ship (the flax brake in line 56 is called a *dificio* in L'Ottimo). The term strengthens the connection with the giants, first perceived as towers.

10. fearfully I set it in meter: Compare *Aen.* 2.204: "horresco referens" [I shudder to relate it]; said of the approach of the serpents that killed Laocoön (see 25.7 and note).

11. the shades were all covered: The traitors in this last zone of Cocytus, Judecca (named for Judas; see line 117), are wholly embedded in the ice; they can make no sound, nor can Satan, his mouth being otherwise engaged (line 55).

12. like straws in glass: Cassell (1984) links this detail to Satan described as a windmill in line 6: the traitors are the "chaff," "straw," "cockles," or "tares" that are rejected at the harvest (cf. Matt. 13.30–40; Augustine, *City of God* 20.9).

18. the creature who had once been beautiful: Satan had been called Lucifer [Light-bearer], because he was the most beautiful of the angels.

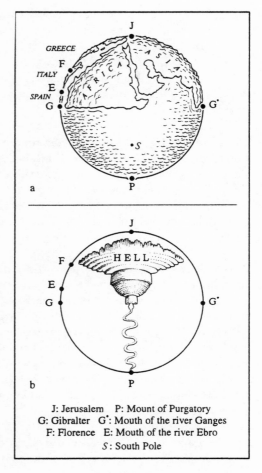

J: Jerusalem   P: Mount of Purgatory
G: Gibralter   G˙: Mouth of the river Ganges
F: Florence   E: Mouth of the river Ebro
S : South Pole

Figure 8. The relative positions of Gibraltar, Jerusalem, the Ganges, and Purgatory.

20. Behold Dis: "Dis" names both Satan (11.65 and 12.39) and the city of lower Hell (8.68; see *Aen.* 6.127): conflating the names contributes to the identification of the body of Satan with the infernal Earthly City (see Additional Note 2). The expression *Ecco Dite* also parodies the presentation of Christ to Pilate (John 19.5): "Ecce homo" [Behold the man].

21. you must arm yourself with courage: Echoing the entry into Hell (see 3.13–15, with note).

22–27. How then I became . . . deprived of both: The last of the seven addresses to the reader in the *Inferno* (see the note to 8.94–96). In the essentialist metaphysics to which Dante subscribed, evil is not a positive quality but a defect, a lack of good, thus of being. That Satan is the most evil of creatures means for Dante that he possesses the least reality; insofar as he does have positive existence, however, Satan, like everything else, is good (for Dante, this means that Satan carries out God's justice and, in his elaborate, parodic parallels with God and the crucified Christ, is a chief "sign" of the divine). The pilgrim's loss of strength when confronted with Satan expresses in part the paradoxical power of Satan's "lack" ("deprived" in line 27 alludes to the idea of evil as privation).

25. I did not die and I did not remain alive: This moment is the culmination of the penitential imitation of Christ in the descent into Hell, symbolically the pilgrim's death to sin, that is, the death of the "old man," leading to the reversal of direction from descent to ascent (from the descent in humility to the ascent in justification, from the experience of sin to the recovery of original justice, which is the subject of the *Purgatorio*; see Freccero 1965b) (see the note to 1.91).

28–67. The emperor . . . so powerfully built: After the careful, suspenseful preparation of the first twenty-eight lines, we now have the full, formal description of Satan (on the fall of the angels, see 3.7, with note). He is now the ugliest of creatures (line 34). His very ugliness is parodic of God: his three faces parody the Trinity (various correlations have been offered between God's power, wisdom, and love [see 3.5–6, with note] and the colors of Satan's three faces); he is suspended, without physical contact with his "realm," in a parody of God's transcendence of creation; his power over Hell is maintained through the wind from his wings, a parody of the Spirit of God, which in Gen. 1.2 "moved over the face of the waters."

28. The emperor of the dolorous kingdom: God is "that emperor who reigns on high" (1.124), "the king of the universe" (5.91). For the "dolorous [*doloroso*] kingdom," compare 3.1 "the grieving [*dolente*] city," and 3.2 "the eternal sorrow [*dolore*]."

29. at the mid-point of his breast: Compare this to the giants (31.33, 43) and Farinata (10.33); as Cassell (1984) observes, this connects Satan, like Farinata, with the iconography of baptism (see the note to 10.33).

30–31. I am more to be compared with a giant than the giants with his arms: This proportion yields a Satan towering about 600 to 1,300 feet (50 to 100 stories) over the ice. Even using the smaller dimensions, the pilgrim obviously would not be able to see detail on human figures (lines 55–69) at such distances; this is not realism.

35. when he lifted his brow against his Maker: When he rebelled (see 10.35–36, with note).

36. well must all grieving proceed from him: The use of the term *procedere* alludes to the Neoplatonic terminology whereby the universe is the result of "procession" from the One.

39–45. crimson . . . cataracts of the Nile: All three are related to the cru- cified Christ: the crimson, to his blood; the off-white, to his flesh; the black, to his bruises. Freccero (1965b) showed that Dante is drawing here on a well-es- tablished tradition of "the devil on the Cross" (*diabolus in patibulo*).

45. from beyond the cataracts of the Nile: From Ethiopia; the falls divide the upper from the lower Nile (cf. 16.105, with note). For the exceptional quali- ties of the Nile, see the note to *Purg.* 28.121–33.

46–52. Beneath each one . . . Cocytus was frozen: Satan is the source of impotence, ignorance, and hate, as the Trinity is of Power, Wisdom, and Love.

46–48. wings . . . sea-going sails: For the devils as birds, see 21.29–33 and 22.112–44, with notes. Satan was the highest of the seraphs, the highest order of angels, which have six wings (Is. 6.2): "the one had six wings . . . with two they covered his face, and with two they covered his feet, and with two they flew" (cf. Apoc. 4.8). Wings as sails link Satan to Icarus (cf. note to 17.106–11) and Ulysses (cf. 26.125, with note), typical overreachers. See also 31.145, with note.

49. like a bat's: In Aesop's fable, the bat, punished for having betrayed the birds to the land animals, becomes an outcast, neither fully bird nor fully land animal, neither of the day nor of the night: a creature of twilight.

54. the tears and the bloody slobber: Parodying the blood and water that flowed from the pierced side of Christ (John 19.34); compare "Vexilla regis," line 12: "manavit unda et sanguine" [blood and water flowed], and the tears of the Old Man of Crete, which become the rivers of Hell (14.112–17).

56. in the manner of a scutch: The scutch or flax-brake has a hinged wooden paddle fitting into a slotted piece beneath it. Raw flax, placed between the two pieces, is crushed when the paddle descends, separating woody parts from the strands that can be combed and spun into linen. The scutch was a recent inven- tion (the first recorded examples are from Holland in the early fourteenth cen- tury). The Italian word (*maciulla*) is usually considered a diminutive of *machina*; see also the mill (lines 6–7); the scutch, too, is a harvest implement.

61–67. That soul . . . powerfully built: The three souls in Satan's mouths are obviously thought to be receiving the worst punishments in Hell, after Satan's: those who betrayed Christ (Judas) and Julius Caesar (Brutus and Cassius). The correlation derives from the familiar one between Church and Empire, the goals of God's providential ordering of history since the beginning (see 2.13–31, with notes). Dante thought of the empire as entrusted with governing all men, just as Christ redeemed all men, and he thought of Julius Caesar as chosen to be the first emperor.

The spectacle of the devil eating damned souls (and often excreting them, too) is frequent in journeys to the other world (Morgan 1990) and visual representations of Hell (Hughes 1968); in the Florentine Baptistery, Satan's three heads (two of them snake's heads) are eating sinners in the manner imagined here. The parodic relation to the Eucharist is obvious. Dante is also associating Satan and Cocytus with the Saturn of mythology, who devoured his children, and the planet Saturn, which is responsible for floods, freezing, and death, and which inclines men toward treachery (see the note to 13.143–50, Rabuse 1958, and Durling and Martinez 1990).

That only in Cocytus, the very bottom of Hell, we find its emperor (34.1) is probably the most important single instance of the inversion and Babel-like confusion of Hell. Like Satan himself, Hell is many-headed: the pilgrim and Virgil entered by a speaking (inscribed) Hellmouth in Canto 3, Limbo and the circle of the lustful are versions of the human head, and Satan is the titular head of the realm (see the note to lines 70–93).

63. his head inside . . . his legs outside: Judas Iscariot is distinguished from Brutus and Cassius by having his head and upper body in Satan's maw: perhaps reflecting John 13.27 (Gmelin): "and after the morsel [the Last Supper], Satan entered into him" (see the note to 33.124–33), and that he hanged himself (cf. the note to 13.107, and cf. the position of the damned popes, 19.22–24).

65. Brutus: Marcus Junius Brutus, a Stoic and disciple of Cato (see 14.13–15, with note), obtained pardon and preferment from Caesar after the civil war. With Cassius he led the conspiracy to assassinate Caesar in 44 B.C.

66. does not say a word: Brutus restrains evidence of his suffering, as a Stoic should; or perhaps his is a "brutish" silence; note the topic of silence.

67. Cassius: Gaius Cassius Longinus, like Brutus, was pardoned by Caesar after the civil war. After Caesar's death, he and Brutus fought Octavian and Mark Antony at Philippi; Octavian and Antony won when Cassius, mistakenly thinking the battle lost, had himself killed. There is no good explanation of why Cassius is "powerfully built," unless as a physical counterpart to Brutus's stoicism.

68. the night is rising again: See the note to line 5. If night is rising for the hemisphere of land, we have reached the end of the first full day of the journey, the evening of Holy Saturday; the pilgrim and Virgil entered Hell on the evening of Good Friday (cf. 2.1 and 21.112–14, with notes).

70–93. As it pleased him . . . that I had passed: In making Satan himself the way out of Hell, Dante audaciously combines several notions that underlie his treatment of the pilgrim's journey. First, Satan's punishment is an analogue of the Crucifixion (see the note to lines 39–45): thus Satan can be made to stand for Christ and the Cross. As in 12.31–45 (see note), Christ is "the Way." Second, the pilgrim's journey is an imitation of Christ; in the climb down and then up Satan, the travelers enact an imitation of Zachaeus's climbing of the sycamore to see Christ enter Jerusalem (Luke 19.3–4). This was regularly interpreted as an analogue of the Crucifixion (since Christ climbed the Cross, in the medieval conception; see also the note to lines 39–45). The midpoint of the cosmos (often compared with the point of intersection of the Cross in commentaries on Romans 8.38–39; see the note to 8.82–117) is the place of conversion. It is of course the power of the Cross that enables the travelers to use Satan's fur as a ladder (Freccero 1965b). See Additional Note 16.

At line 70, the exact midpoint of the canto, the wayfarers begin the climb down Satan's flank to the broadest part of the hips; there Virgil reverses direction, so that his head is now toward Satan's legs; since he has by now passed the central point, he is climbing away from the center; but the pilgrim thinks he is climbing up into Hell. Brown (1959) pointed out that this point corresponds to Satan's anus.

75. between the thick hair and the frozen crust: Satan does not touch the ice: he is suspended, with the weight of the cosmos holding him in place (see the note to lines 28–67, and line 123).

79. shanks: The same word used of the inverted popes, 19.45. Whether *elli* [he] (line 79) refers to Satan or to Virgil has been disputed (see Hatcher and Musa 1970).

82. by such stairs: The tufts of Lucifer's fur (*vello,* line 74); shaggy fur was a regular feature of medieval devils. The image of stairs (with the same rhymes, at the same line numbers) is used for the ride on Geryon, 17.82; compare 34.119. In 24.55, it was made clear that the stairway or ladder is a major symbol of the *Comedy,* expressing the hierarchical structure of the universe and the stages of the pilgrim's way through it.

90. I saw that he extended his legs upward: Having passed the central point, the travelers now see Satan from the other side. Still in line with Jerusalem, they are now directly under the antipodes of Jerusalem, the mountain of Purgatory (at the center of the hemisphere of water, which does not coincide with the Southern Hemisphere, as the hemisphere of land does not coincide with the Northern; at the antipodes of Jerusalem, the mountain of Purgatory would in modern terms be at 144°45' W, 31°45' S, some thousand miles south of the Marquesas) (Figure 8).

96. already the sun has reached mid-tierce: At line 68, it was evening, about 6:00 P.M., Jerusalem time. Now, since the wayfarers are in the opposite hemisphere, it is morning, and the sun, not mentioned as the indicator of time since Canto 1, has reached the point in the sky corresponding to about 8:30 A.M. (for the so-called canonical hours, see *Purg.* 1.1–9, with notes).

100–126. Before I am uprooted . . . and fled upward: The pilgrim asks three questions: where is the ice? why is Satan upside down? and how can it be morning? All three derive from the pilgrim's confusion of hemispheres, as Virgil points out in his reply.

106–26. You imagine . . . fled upward: Virgil explains that the pilgrim is now under the zenith opposite to that of Jerusalem, under which ("under whose high point," i.e., zenith) Christ was crucified (lines 114–15). Jerusalem was thought the center of the hemisphere of land (after Ezek. 5.5: "I have set her in the midst of the nations"). The shift in hemispheres explains the change in time (cf. line 68).

Virgil goes on to explain (lines 121–26) that there was once land in what is now the hemisphere of water, but that at Satan's approach (line 123) it fled to the other hemisphere, entirely covering the other hemisphere with dry land (lines 123–24), whereas the more southerly hemisphere remained almost entirely water (see 26.117 and the note to 26.126). "What does appear on this side" refers to the mountain of Purgatory, whose matter, Virgil speculates, may have come from the cavity where they stand ("this empty space," line 125; cf. lines 97–99).

108. this evil worm that gnaws the world: Virgil's image makes the earth seem an apple, with Satan the worm within it; see 6.22 for Cerberus, "the great worm."

110–11. the point . . . from every direction: The fourth mention of this point in the *Inferno* (the others are 11.64, 32.2–3, and 73–74), and the third mention of the weights.

115. the man who was born and lived without sin: This is the last of the periphrastic references to Christ in Hell, where he is never named directly, except by the pilgrim in 19.91; Virgil's description of Christ once again omits his divinity (see the notes to 4.53 and 12.31–45 and Additional Note 16).

117. Judecca: Judecca (see line 11, with note) is not named within Hell.

121. on this side he fell down from Heaven: Dante imagines Satan falling from the zenith of the mountain of Purgatory to the center of the earth. Dante believed in absolute directions (up, down, left, right); Satan must have fallen in the absolute downward direction. (This is a version of Plato's and Aristotle's doctrine of absolute directions; see Freccero 1959.)

130–33. a little stream . . . hidden path: Since the rivers of Hell derive from the Old Man of Crete (14.112–20), this stream probably derives from the rivers of the Earthly Paradise (see *Purg.* 28.25). Many rivers (e.g., the Nile, the Alpheus of Sicily) were thought to travel large distances underground.

136. up we climbed: Dante's freedom with chronology is evident, since this climb takes as long as the descent (twenty-four hours).

137–38. the beautiful things . . . through a round opening: Compare Ugolino's sightings of the moon through the narrow opening in his tower (33.22, 55), and see 1.37–40. Note the contrast between the "beautiful things" (line 137) and Lucifer, named after the "morning star" (cf. Is. 14.12).

139. to look again at the stars: In the open air at last, after the constriction and confinement of Hell, they are able to see the chief beauty of the cosmos; compare Psalm 8.4–5 (as translated from the Vulgate):

> For I will behold thy heavens, the works of thy fingers: the moon and the stars which thou hast founded. What is man that thou art mindful of him? or the son of man that thou visitest him?

Each of the three *cantiche* of the poem ends with the word *stelle*.

ADDITIONAL NOTES

1. Autobiography in the *Divine Comedy*

(After Canto 2)

As early as the second line of the poem, Dante invites us to consider the *Comedy* as autobiographical. The pilgrim who will travel through the other world is at one level an Everyman, an instance of *quisquis salvandus* [whoever is to be saved]; one of the most original aspects of the poem, however, is Dante's clear insistence that the universal aspects of his (or anyone's) experience reveal themselves, paradoxically, in what is most rootedly individual and historically concrete. Thus Beatrice does operate in the pilgrim's experience as the embodiment of various principles (most fundamentally, divine revelation), but Dante insists that his experience of them reached him through the medium of his love for the historical Beatrice and his memory of her after her death.

Charles Singleton's (1954) distinction betweeen the "journey there" (the pilgrim's path through the other world) and the "journey here" (Dante's—or Everyman's—actual historical journey in the real world) provides help. As Singleton observes, Dante's statements about allegory (in the *Convivio* and, if it is his, the *Epistle to Can Grande*) insist on allegory as a relation, a parallel between two or more sets of events, whether fictional events with true referents ("allegory of the poets") or real, historical events figurally related to other historical events ("allegory of the theologians"). In either case it is the parallels of events between the "journey there" and the "journey here" to which we must be alert.

Without becoming involved in the endless debates about the authenticity of the *Epistle to Can Grande* or whether Dante's is an "allegory of the poets" or an "allegory of the theologians," or some mixture of the two (in our view, a poet of Dante's greatness and originality escapes all rigid categories; see the excellent discussions in Van Dyke 1985), it is clear that the narrative of the *Comedy* is a fictional transposition into the terms of the poem not only of Dante's spiritual crisis (represented by his being lost in the dark wood) and its resolution, but also in some sense of his entire experience of life.

The poem privileges a particular aspect of experience: his encounters with persons who impressed or influenced him in some way, in Hell primarily those from whom he learns the nature of various sins and the potentiality for the same sins within himself. In addition to writers, these are (1) actual persons known personally by Dante; (2) historical persons known to him indirectly; and (3) mythical figures known to him through his reading (which of course he treats with extraordinary, revisionist freedom). The encounters with these figures were *events* in Dante's experience, and when they appear in the poem they take the form of events there, most characteristically, in the *Inferno*, events in which the souls reveal themselves by speaking (and in a sense "confessing") to the pilgrim or to his guide. Since these confessions take place in the other world, they reveal some ultimate truth about the speakers: the pilgrim relives his experience, reinterprets it in the light of his spiritual crisis.

Dante places the time of his spiritual crisis in the spring of 1300, just before his term as one of the priors of Florence brought him to the forefront of events, into direct conflict with the long-term aims of Pope Boniface VIII, and ultimately to permanent exile from his beloved city. The various prophecies made in the poem may well reflect a foreboding, already growing in 1300, about the turn his life was to take in 1302. In any case, exile, the central disaster of Dante's life, impinges on the journey to the other world, and on the crisis of 1300, at every point. (One of the most interesting parts of the *Inferno*, from this point of view, is Cantos 21–23, discussed in Additional Note 9.) Whatever may have been the "actual" inner events of 1300 that are reflected in the poem, it seems that in Dante's view they brought him a new sense of being chosen, sent into politics to bear witness to the truth and to combat "the spirits of wickedness in the high places" (Eph. 6.12), without fear of the cost.

R.M.D.

2. The Body Analogy, 1

(After Canto 11)

From the perspective of Canto 11 it becomes possible to identify an important emerging pattern: Hell has a structure analogous to that of the human body. The pilgrim and Virgil begin their descent through Hell at what corresponds to the head (the traditional entrance is, after all, Hellmouth, which "speaks" in its inscription). Limbo, associated with memory (see the note to 4.69), is thereby associated with the traditional seat of memory, the rear ventricle of the brain. This understanding is clearly present in Boccaccio's remarks on Limbo, explaining that Virgil, as Reason, "was sent from the limbo of the microcosm, which is the brain, above which there is nothing of our body except the skull and the scalp" (*Esposizioni*, pp. 134–35). The sin of Paolo and Francesca is associated with the eyes and the front ventricle of the brain, traditional seat of imagination and foresight (see notes to 5.113, 130–31, 133, and 141–42). Gluttony is, as Ciacco says, the sin of the gullet (see the note to 6.53); the sullen seem located in a way that refers to the spleen.

The walls of Dis mark the entrance to what corresponds to the human breast, seat of the sins of violence. Note the emphasis on Farinata's posture, mentioning breast first (10.35), visible from the waist up. Dante's placing the punishment of heresy here has caused some puzzlement, because of Virgil's failure to mention it in Canto 11: in our view, this placing reflects the fact that both in biblical language and in Aristotelian physiology, the seat of reason, wisdom, and, for Christians, faith, is the heart or breast. Also, it is with the breast/heart that the *obstinate* heretic stands against (Latin *obsto*) God's law (see the note to 9.61–63). For the other sins of violence, see the notes to 12.47, 13.37–39, 14.8–39, and 94–120. For the sins of fraud, see Additional Note 13.

The basis of Dante's analogy is triple. First is the traditional notion (it originates in Plato and permeates political thinking in Christian times as well) of the body politic: the idea that the state is analogous to the human body, and thus to the principle that orders it, the human soul (see MacKinnon 1989). One of the most famous statements of the analogy known to Dante is the Roman historian Livy's account of the fable told by the patrician Menenius Agrippa to the Roman plebs in rebellion against the Senate (*Ab urbe condita* 2.32.8–33.1):

> "At the time when human beings were not fully unified, as they are now, but the various parts of the body had each their own mind and were able to speak, the rest of the parts of the body complained of the belly, angry that their pains, their labor and ministry had to provide everything, while the belly, resting lazily in the midst of them, did nothing but enjoy the pleasures they provided; therefore they agreed that the hands would bring no food to the mouth, the mouth would not accept it if brought, the teeth would not chew it. Because of their anger, while they intended to subdue the belly with hunger, the members themselves, indeed the whole body, became extremely sick. From this it became clear that the belly's service was hardly unimportant and that it nourished them as well as being nourished, giving back to each part of the body what it needed to live and prosper, dividing fairly among the veins of the body the blood that it fashioned by digesting the food." They say that by comparing the two situations he showed how the anger of the plebs against the senate was sedition within the body [politic] and thus mollified their spirits. Negotiations then began to establish harmony, and among the conditions agreed on were that the plebs would have their own magistrates. . . .

Dante knew the elaborate version of the fable by John of Salisbury (*Policraticus* 5 and 6), for whom the head of the body politic is the king, the heart is the senate and nobility, the stomach and intestines are the taxgatherers and treasurers; the idea of money as the blood of the body politic is already implicit in John (for further discussion, see Durling 1981a).

The classical idea of the body politic was adapted to the Church by the Christian theologians, beginning with Saint Paul, for whom the Church—that is, the community of believers (therefore of those saved)—is the mystical body of Christ, of which Christ is the head and the believers the members, joined together by love (1 Cor. 12.12–27; Eph. 5.29–30). By a natural extension, then, the damned became seen as the members of the body of Satan, of which Satan is the head. In the thirteenth century, the body politic also began to be spoken of as a "mystical body"—for example, by Vincent of Beauvais (1250) (Kantorowicz 1957).

The third basis is the traditional Platonic allegory of the underworld that goes back to Servius's commentary on the *Aeneid*, Macrobius's *Commentarii* on the *Dream of Scipio* (1.10.9–12), and beyond. Macrobius writes:

> Those who among the various peoples have founded religious ceremonies have denied that the underworld is anything but our bodies themselves, enclosed in which our souls suffer a prison ugly in its darkness, horrible with its filth and blood. This they have called the tomb of the soul, the pit of Dis, the underworld, and everything which superstition believed to be there, they have endeavored to place in ourselves and our human bodies: the river of oblivion they assert to be nothing other than the error of the soul which forgets the majesty of the previous life enjoyed before being thrust into the body, and which believes that there is life only in the body. In a similar interpretation they considered Phlegethon to be the burning of angers and greeds, Acheron to be whatever deed or word causes remorse, according to human changeability, Cocytus whatever drives men to grief and tears, Styx whatever immerses human souls in the gulf of hatreds. Even the description of punishments they believed to be taken from human experience, considering the vulture *tearing forever at his liver* [*Aen.* 6.598] to be nothing other than the torments of conscience. . . .

(Macrobius goes on to give explanations of the punishments of Tantalus and Ixion that treat them as metaphors for their respective sins.)

It is easy to see how the angry and sullen in Canto 7 are versions of the Neoplatonic allegory. But Dante has made the parallel between Hell and the human body structural and specific, rather than generic and merely moralistic, as in Servius and Macrobius. And in Christian tradition, Hell is Babel/Babylon or confusion: Hell and the devils are portrayed as a grotesque disorder of body parts. Dante continually associates sins with the misuse and/or malfunctioning of parts of the body, often in the sense of inversion (as when lust, associated with the lower body, dominates reason, located in the head; Satan may be the head of Hell, but he is located at its anus).

The descent into Hell is also a descent into increasing materiality: while in the upper circles souls are driven by the wind or are mere "emptiness," by the time we reach the last cantos of Malebolge and Cocytus the sense of their materiality has increased immeasurably. This pattern is closely related to the Neoplatonic notion of the underworld as signifying the descent into bodily existence, combined with Saint Paul's conception of "the body of this death" (Romans 7.24), the heavy, material, mortal body which the damned never transcend. In the *Purgatorio* and *Paradiso*, a central theme will be the ascent toward higher and higher levels of immateriality, and the "glorified body" (1 Cor. 15.35–55) will be a central concern.

It should be evident from the above that throughout the *Comedy* there is a persistent problematizing of the human body and the soul's relation to it. A full discussion of Dante's conception of the relation of body and soul must be postponed until the *Purgatorio*, where it is a major explicit focus. Even in the *Inferno*, however, where the "body of death" is at the center of attention, there is no simple identification of the body itself with evil. Attention is constantly directed to the ways in which sin distorts the body as well as the soul, and also to the tantalizing question—to which Dante's approach is highly original—of the relation of the individual body to the collectivities in which it is involved, also conceived as bodies: the body politic, the body of Satan, the body of Christ. See also Additional Note 13:

R.M.D.

3. The Old Man of Crete

(Canto 14)

The statue itself has a double origin. The most important source is the dream of Nebuchadnezzar (Dan. 2.31–35):

> Thou, O king, sawest, and behold there was as it were a great statue: this statue, which was great and high, tall of stature, stood before thee, and the look thereof was terrible. The head of this statue was of fine gold, but the breast and the arms of silver, and the belly and the thighs of brass: And the legs of iron, the feet part of iron and part of clay. Thus thou sawest, till a stone was cut out of a mountain without hands: and it struck the statue upon the feet thereof . . . and broke them to pieces. Then was the iron, the clay, the brass, the silver, and the gold broken to pieces together, and became like the chaff of a summer's threshingfloor, and they were carried away by the wind: and there was no place found for them: but the stone that struck the statue, became a great mountain, and filled the whole earth.

Daniel interprets the statue as representing the succession of empires, beginning with Nebuchadnezzar's (the gold), to ultimate destruction. The Christian interpreters saw the dream both as a prophecy of the coming of Christ and as an allegory of the present state of humanity (Richard of Saint Victor saw the gold head as symbolic of freedom of the will; Bosco). Dante has combined the biblical statue with Ovid's account of the successive ages of gold, silver, brass, and iron (*Met.* 1.89–150). That the statue is of an old man is Dante's addition, as is the crack.

The other source of Dante's myth is the rich cluster of associations surrounding the island of Crete, traditionally thought to be in the center of the Mediterranean (for Minos, Pasiphaë, the Minotaur, and Daedalus, see the note to 12.12). In the *Aeneid*, when the Trojans are told to "seek out your ancient mother," they at first understand the reference to be to Crete; when they settle there, however, a plague attacks them and the vegetation (3.137–42):

subito cum tabida membris
corrupto caeli tractu miserandaque venit
arboribusque satisque lues et letifer annus.
Linquebant dulcis animas aut aegra trahebant
corpora; tum sterilis exurere Sirius agros,
arebant herbae et victum seges aegra negabat.

[when suddenly on our members,
because of the corrupted region, there came a lingering, wretched
sickness, and on the trees and the sown crops, a death-bringing season.
Men left sweet life or dragged about sick
bodies; then Sirius burned the sterile fields,
the grass dried up, and the sick grain denied us food.]

(Aeneas's household gods inform him that the "ancient mother" was Italy, not Crete; the Trojan race had a double origin.) From these lines and an earlier reference to Crete as deserted (*Aen.* 3.122–23), Dante drew the idea of it as a waste land. Note the parallels with the fiery plain, Sodom, and Libya: sterility and fire from the heavens.

Dante also draws on the incident related by Augustine (taken from Pliny the Elder's *Natural History*) of the exhuming on Crete of a gigantic, erect body, thought to be that of Orion or another mythological figure. Crete (thought by Latin writers to be related to Latin *creta*, "clay" or "chalk") was traditionally the birthplace of Zeus (lines 100–102), chosen by Rhea to hide him from his father Saturn, who devoured his children; to hide his cries she had the Curetes dance, pound their weapons, and shout. Ancient traditions, known to Dante through Augustine and others, had the Cretans claim Zeus was buried there as well.

Commentators are agreed that Dante's statue represents the successive ages of human history, beginning with the golden, or prelapsarian. The crack in all the parts below the head refers to the *vulneratio naturae*, the wound in man's nature resulting from Adam's sin. Thus the Old Man of Crete would be a symbol of the "old man" of Pauline tradition ("our old man is crucified with [Christ], that the body of sin may be destroyed" [Romans 6.6]; cf. Eph. 4.22–24: "put off the old man"), human nature afflicted with sin and powerless to save itself (hence the tears that form the four rivers of Hell). The statue's having its back toward Damietta (in Egypt, a chief port of entry into the Muslim lands) and its face toward Rome "as toward its mirror," has been variously explained, both positively and negatively.

It seems clear that the statue is also a representation of the present state of humanity (in a Thomist view, more optimistic than an Augustinian one): its intellect whole, still golden in spite of the Fall, but its lower nature suffering the *vulneratio naturae*. The iron and clay feet have sometimes been interpreted as referring to the empire and the papacy respectively.

The Old Man of Crete has an important relation to the overall body analogy in the *Inferno*. Like the body of Satan, it is a representation of both the history of mankind and its present state, expressed in terms of the human body (cf. the hemisphere of light in Limbo, representing enlightenment, and the statue's head of gold, for instance). Like the body of Satan, again, it is subterranean.

R.M.D.

4. Dante and Brunetto Latini

(Canto 15)

The prominent persons identified as guilty of the sin of Sodom in this canto—Brunetto, Priscian, Accursio, and Mozzi—are not identified as homosexuals in any known sources that are independent of Dante. Therefore, the question whether they are placed here for homosexuality or for some other transgression has occasioned debate over the last half-century; recently the debate has become particularly intense (Kay 1978; Armour 1991). We hold with the traditional, majority view (that the sin is indeed homosexuality) for the following reasons.

Dante uses the term *Soddoma* [Sodom] to refer to homosexuality in *Purg.* 26.40, conformably with his use in the *Inferno* of the same term for "sins against nature" (11.48, 50). In Dante's milieu, the "sin against nature" was the most frequent and widespread way of referring to homosexuality (cf. 15.81, "banished from human nature"). It was proverbial, too, that homosexuality was particularly common among clerics (cf. 15.106). And the reference in 15.114 to "protended muscles," though susceptible of several interpretations, is most naturally taken as a reference to sexual exertions. In any case, the tradition of taking the sin of the inhabitants of Sodom in Genesis 19 to be sexual is well founded in the biblical text and established in Christian exegesis in such authors as Clement of Alexandria and Tertullian (second–third centuries), Augustine (fourth–fifth centuries), Gregory the Great (sixth–seventh centuries), and the law code of the emperor Justinian (sixth century); scholastics like Albertus Magnus and Aquinas took it for granted.

Beyond this, interpretation is bound to be less obvious. Pequigney (1991), relying on a traditional iconography of urban homosexuality, argues that the references to furtive glances, nude sports, and nocturnal bands add up to conscious representation of a homosexual milieu. In this vein, several of Brunetto's remarks might be seen as equivocal (see lines 65–66, 71–72), a view that Avalle (1977) and Ahern (1991) possibly corroborate. Compounding the issue is the fact that in Dante's day, as often since, homosexuality "dare not speak its name" (Piero di Dante calls it "mute"); this may help explain the lack of explicitness in the canto: reticence and indirection are themselves traditionally intrinsic to homosexuality (line 104 would fit this view).

The question may be approached also by way of the metaphorical language of the canto. As several commentators observe (e.g., Freccero 1991), the pilgrim's relation to Brunetto (as to Virgil) is spoken of as that of a son to a father (e.g., lines 31, 37, and 83). Not of course a natural father: what in another context might be a "mere" metaphor for the relationship of a mentor and a disciple is here charged with irony, for Brunetto's repeated claims to a figurative fathering of the pilgrim take place against the background of the sterility of Sodom. Ancient and medieval philosophers often spoke of the relation of teacher and pupil as the imposition of form on (passive) matter, applying this central Aristotelian category to social relations as well as to metaphysics, art, perception, memory, knowledge, and sexual generation (in which, according to Aristotle, the male seed imposed form on the female matter; see *Purgatorio* 25, with notes). The generative imagery even involves the idea of writing, in which letters, like seeds, are sown in a furrow on the page. Thus a whole nexus of imagery—form and matter, sexual generation, sealing and its variant coining, writing (see Canto 30 and Additional Note 13)—is involved in such moments as the pilgrim's testimony that Brunetto left his "kind paternal image" (line 84) in his memory and taught him (*insegnavate* [taught], etymologically "signed," line 83) "how man becomes eternal." There may be a reference here to Brunetto's having specifically trained or shaped his memory (Brunetto translated the part of Cicero's *De inventione* concerning the art of memory; the title of his encyclopedia, *Treasure*, was a standard metaphor for memory).

Thus we discern three families of metaphor applied by the text to the pilgrim: the pilgrim as "seed," "plant," or "fruit"—that is, the pilgrim as metaphorically generated by Brunetto's moral, intellectual, and political example; the pilgrim as bearer of Brunetto's seal or imprint; and the pilgrim as keeper of the "treasure" of Brunetto's knowledge and of his writings. In each case, Brunetto's predicament is that although he may wish to assert the strong sense of the metaphor, in each case his sin thwarts him, forcing the discourse back to the merely figurative or, at worst, to ironic commentary on his homosexuality. His claimed paternity can only be figurative, for sodomy is a fruitless sowing (14.8–9). His "sealing" of the pilgrim persists in the pilgrim's memory of him (lines 82–83), but his own burned appearance defaces his good memory (lines 25–28); his writings, though frequently echoed by the poet (line 87; see the note to line 50), are destined to be digested into the *Comedy*, a much greater "treasure" (cf. *Par.* 1.11) that will overshadow Brunetto's (see lines 88–90) and in which Brunetto's reputation will be destroyed.

In the metaphorical links between sodomy and agriculture, sealing/coining, and writing, Dante's account of Brunetto reveals its derivation from the antihomosexual tradition represented most prominently by the late-twelfth-century poet, preacher, and theologian Alain of Lille, whose *De planctu naturae* [Complaint of nature] (Alain of Lille 1978, 1980) was echoed by Jean de Meun in the *Romance of the Rose*. In speeches attributed to Venus or Genius (representatives of natural generation), both writers condemn sodomy as a male refusal to impose form on the receptive material in the womb of the female, to coin new images of the father (see *Romance of the Rose*, lines 19629–87). The homosexual, says Venus in the *De planctu* (1.27–30),

> . . . strikes on an anvil where no seed is coined.
> The hammer shrinks from its own anvil;

the idea signs no matter in the matrix,
rather the ploughshare plows a sterile shore.

In these terms, Brunetto's insistence on his figurative paternity would betray a desire to "seal" or "coin" his disciple not merely metaphorically but by way of vice. Abuse of metaphor is one of Alain's accusations against the sodomites, for sodomy can be expressed by disorders in other forms of activity, and especially rhetorical language (1.23–26):

> . . . this trope cannot be called a metaphor.
> This figure falls better under the vices.
> He is overmuch the logician through whom
> a simple twist of art makes nature's laws perish.

R.L.M.

5. Dante and Homosexuality

(Canto 16)

In *Inferno* 15 and 16, Dante sets forth, though in very compressed form, a complex and nuanced view of homosexuals and homosexuality. Crucial to his view is the distinction between experiencing homosexual desires (or, for that matter, heterosexual ones) and acting on them. Dante of course knew Vergil's second Eclogue, in which the shepherd Corydon yearns for the lovely boy Alexis; if on that account he attributed to Vergil homosexual leanings, he nonetheless classes him with the virtuous pagans who "did not sin" (4.33–39).

It is difficult not to read Cantos 15 and 16 as an acknowledgment that Dante had felt such desires; in 16.46–51 the language is particularly strong: he is "greedy to embrace them," and "If I had been protected from the fire [that is, if there were no punishment for homosexual acts], I would have *thrown myself* down there among them" (italics added); the translation is literal. He feels such desires (and they seem to impinge strongly also in his relation to his teacher Brunetto; see especially 15.22–30), but he does not act on them.

Dante acknowledges the biblical prohibition of homosexuality (Genesis 19; see the notes to 14.8–39). But he remembers that adultery is also forbidden (adultery was traditionally understood to include unmarried sexual relations and even excessively passionate relations between married persons). In the *Purgatorio*, the last purification is that of lust (Cantos 25–27). Dante's treatment there of homosexual lust is identical with his treatment of heterosexual lust; even the numbers of souls undergoing the purgation seem equal. And while Dante subjects the homosexuals in Hell to a particularly savage punishment (based, of course, on the biblical one), he grants those he meets there high status as benefactors of the city and, in the case of Brunetto, of himself personally. He represents the Florentine aristocrats as examples of high, generous courtesy and civic spirit and has Virgil endorse his reverence for them (16.15–18).

There is, however, sharp social commentary in both cantos. The homosexuals are classed in different groups. According to Brunetto Latini's account of his crowd as consisting of literary and clerical homosexuals, and since the three Florentines of Canto 16 are from the high nobility, it is evident that the groups are distinct according to class and that Dante is presenting what amounts to an incipient sociology of homosexual styles. We are invited to compare their ways; the strutting of the aristocrats, compared with that of wrestlers who eye each other looking for possible holds, is based on sharp observation, as is the attribution to the literary group of much more subdued behavior, such as nocturnal walks, and the scrutiny to which they subject the pilgrim.

One striking element of Dante's treatment is his having Iacopo Rusticucci attribute his own homosexual activity to the frustration generated by his relationship with his "fierce wife"; this acknowledgment of the possibility of extenuating circumstances, like other aspects of Dante's nuanced treatment of the theme, is a far cry from the bitterness of other medieval treatments of homosexuality.

R.M.D.

6. Geryon's Spiral Flight

(Canto 17)

In addition to his triple nature, Dante's Geryon is a swimmer surfacing, a skiff backing out of its mooring, a beaver dangling its tail, a swimming eel, a descending falcon, an arrow shot from a bowstring, and—most significantly—a ladder or stairway. Like the many similes in the canto, this variety suggests the complications of fraud. But the variety also has a clear focus: Geryon's varying motion (Cambon 1963). There are three accounts of Geryon's motion (16.130–36, 17.100–17, and 17.127–36). In the first and last, when Geryon approaches and departs, he moves in a straight line; but in the central instance, when he bears the pilgrim, he both turns and descends: that is, his motion combines straight-line and circular patterns. Geryon's flight, which is compared to that of Icarus and to Phaëthon's ill-fated attempt at driving the chariot of the sun, is the emotional climax of the episode and marks the midpoint of the *Inferno*.

In a notable essay, John Freccero (1961a) observed that the motion of the pilgrim on Geryon's back, and generally throughout the poem, is a spiral one (the pilgrim is always circling, but also descending or ascending); he associated this motion with the typically spiral motion of an incarnate soul (according to the traditional Platonic–Aristotelian idea), which combines the circular motion of the self-moved with the straight-line motion of becoming. He also pointed out that spiral motion is preeminently exemplified by the sun, whose path over the course of the year is a spiral, circling every day around the earth but gradually moving north or south between the solstices (cf. *Convivio* 2.5). These two motions of the sun illustrate the two fundamental motions of the cosmos according to Plato's *Timaeus*: the movement of the Same (that of the whole celestial sphere, the daily motion) and that of the Other or Different (the motions of the planets, thought of as going backward along the ecliptic, thus "against" the motion of the Same). Later in the poem, Dante describes the sun's track and the two cosmic motions more elaborately (*Purg.* 4.61–66; *Par.* 10.1–12), and Virgil will explicitly invoke the sun as the guide (cf. *Purg.* 13.13–21).

Like the celestial motions, Virgil's instructions are twofold: to make wide circles and to avoid a steep descent. Virgil's instructions to Geryon (17.97–98) in fact draw on the advice that Phoebus and Daedalus give their sons (see the notes to lines 106–11), in nearly identical words (*Met.* 2.136–40: "inter utrumque tene" [hold between the two]; 8.203–6: "inter utrumque vola" [fly between the two]). With the words he has his Daedalus utter (17.111: "mala via tieni" [You're on a bad course]), Dante reminds us that both Phaëthon and Icarus disregard paternal advice to take the "middle" way, neither too high nor too low, neither too far to one side or the other (thus vertical and horizontal components), reflecting the classical idea of virtue—the basis of Aristotle's ethical system—as the temperate course between extremes. That the sun's regular orbit is the course Phaëthon should have followed is explicit in Ovid's text (cf. *Met.* 2.130–33), which describes an oblique (thus spiral) path, the result of the "proper" course of the sun struggling against the swift daily motion. And indeed "la strada che mal non seppe careggiar Feton" [the road that Phaëthon could not drive along, to his hurt] is what Dante calls the ecliptic, the sun's annual track, in *Purg.* 4.72 (cf. the figure on p. xv).

The sun is not visible in *Inferno* 17, nor anywhere within Hell itself, where time is told by the moon (cf. 10.81). But the sun was glimpsed, and mentioned as a guide, before entering Hell (1.17–18) and will be referred to just after leaving it (34.96). Yet the sun is *present* in the sense that the motion Virgil imposes on Geryon is congruent with solar motion: in other words, though Phaëthon strayed from the sun's path, Geryon follows it. By mentioning the Milky Way (the scorch mark, Ovid says, left by Phaëthon's flight), Dante suggests that the pilgrim's solar path leads in fact to the abode of the blessed: it was a commonplace that the Milky Way was the road to Heaven (cf. *Met.* 1.168; cf. Dante's use of the Milky Way in *Par.* 14.99, 25.18).

The similes describing the pilgrim's fear refer to the danger of loss of control of the pilgrim's "vessel"; the concern governs the entire canto. In Ovid's fables, Icarus and Phaëthon fall into water (the Icarian sea and the Po); this is anticipated by the opening nautical simile for Geryon, comparing him to a swimmer surfacing after detaching a sea anchor, and hints that the pilgrim might be drowned in the figural watery abyss of Hell (cf. 20.3). Ending the episode, the imagined falconer bewails the "fall" of his bird ("Oh me, you are coming down," 18.129) as if watching Icarus or Phaëthon tumble down (*not* an Ovidian detail). And, crucially, the pilgrim's removal of his girdle anticipates the references to Phaëthon's loss of the reins restraining the solar chariot and Icarus's loss of his wings (the line numbers correspond, 106–11 in each case). These disconnections culminate with the pilgrim's loss of any visual reference "except that of the beast," echoing Phaëthon's terror when he can see only fierce zodiacal animals (chiefly the Scorpion, cousin to scorpion-tailed Geryon). However, from this complete disorentiation the pilgrim, despite being mounted on the image of fraud, regains his bearings, thanks precisely to the spiral descent Virgil has imposed: the wind in the pilgrim's face, the sound of the torrent beneath, and the visual sighting of the torments below all indicate by sensible means that the pilgrim is both turning and descending (Ovid's Phaëthon, by contrast, panics when he looks down). In other words, even when completely at the mercy of fraud, reliance on the guidance of reason (and its guarantor, divine grace) affords the route by which the realm of fraud can be entered and traversed (see notes on the cord, 16.106).

As commentators observe, the "winged man" returns later in the poem as an image *in bono* for the pilgrim's upward flight (Shankland [1975] observed that the Alighieri coat of arms probably bore a pair of wings: *Alagherius* meant literally "wing-bearer"). The Neoplatonic view of Daedalus's flight as an escape from the prison of the body was adapted by early Christians to represent the soul's flight to heaven (Courcelle 1944; see also Boethius, *Consolation* 4.4); and the soul's guidance of a chariot back to its origin was adopted by Ambrose, Augustine, and Boethius (*Consolation* 3.9.19) from Neoplatonic versions of Plato's myth (*Phaedrus* 246–48), influenced by the chariot-ascensions of Enoch and Elijah in the Bible.

In addition to the threat of fraud and the risks of pride, the pilgrim's anxiety may reflect the fact that here the pilgrim's journey transcends that of Vergil's Aeneas (Benvenuto de' Rambaldi was the first to note it: "he was extending his flight . . . beyond that treated by Vergil, who was his father. . . ."); Aeneas and the Sybil do not venture into Tartarus, but instead turn right toward Elysium (see the note to 9.132; also Prov. 22.28). The passage on Geryon stands midmost between the pilgrim's difficult entrance to Dis and the harrowing descent below the giants (Canto 31), both dramatic transitions where the poet exceeds the Vergilian model. But if Virgil fails before Dis, it is precisely Virgil who here bends Geryon to the correct path. If, as recent views assert (Ferrucci 1971; Barolini 1992), the fantastic Geryon stands for the poet's imagination—or for the multiform poem itself—then it is the voice of Virgil that makes Geryon negotiable for the pilgrim, that (in allegory) directs Dante's Gothic imagination with classical discipline.

As Geryon fuses multiple images in himself, he also summarizes a number of images of the pilgrim's journey. We have stressed his role as vehicle, but Geryon is suggestive also in his function as stairway or ladder (cf. 17.82, echoed at 34.82), a link in the pilgrim's climb down and up the "golden staircase" or "golden chain" of the hierarchical medieval cosmos (see Introduction). The golden chain was also understood by Plato and the Stoics (and possibly by Boethius: cf. *Consolation* 2.8 and 3.2) as the ecliptic: that is, the path of the sun along the ecliptic during the year—Phaëthon's path—fundamental to the order of temporal existence on earth (cf. *Par.* 10.1–12). Thus in having Geryon "tamed" by Virgil so that he furnishes passage for the pilgrim, Dante joins two comprehensive images for cosmic order—the great chain and the two celestial motions—to furnish the pilgrim with a golden clew through the labyrinth of Hell.

R.L.M.

7. Boniface's Church

(Canto 19)

The name of Simon Magus, similar to that of the first pope, Simon Peter, introduces a parodic, inverted Church that often has been described (French 1964; Scott 1970; Herzman and Stephany 1978). As our notes suggest, this inverted Church, Boniface's Church as Dante saw it, parodies the idea of the apostolic succession and the scriptural passages that authorized the papacy and episcopacy. As Scott observed, the "slot" reserved for damned popes also parodies the throne of Peter, representing the pope's headship over the whole Church and thought of as resting on the "rock" of Peter, the foundation of the Church itself (Matt. 16.18).

The allusion to Pentecost in the flames that lick the feet of the damned Pope Nicholas serves to remind us that the "power" of the Church, its ability to help the faithful to salvation by the remission of sins, lay in its administration of the seven sacraments, sometimes thought of in Dante's day as linked to the seven gifts of the Spirit; only priests had full sacramental powers. In this canto, Dante alludes unmistakably to six of the seven sacraments: to Holy Orders (the vehicle of the apostolic succession, which Simon Magus wished to buy); to Marriage (which signifies the mystery of Christ's marriage to the Church, which bishops imitate); to Penance (the pilgrim is like the assassin's confessor); in the reference to flames on "oily things," to Confirmation and Extreme Unction, sacraments whose principal "matter" is oil (fortifying the soul, respectively, for the militant life and for death); and to Baptism; reference to the Eucharist is more difficult to discern. The allusions to Baptism are equally important with those to Holy Orders: Baptism is the "door" or "gateway" of the Church, since through it believers are received into the faith; it is prominent in the comparison of the holes where the popes are punished with the circular niches provided in the Florentine Baptistery for the officiants (though the meaning of the passage is disputed, the reference to Baptism is explicit). A principal irony is that while the baptismal font is the entrance to the Church, thus to freedom, these holes are the reverse: each leads to a kind of eternal oubliette.

Dante's panorama is broader still, however: in addition to the emphasis on Christ's institution of the Church, it is also represented as foreordained from the Creation, an idea suggested in the reference to Wisdom, traditionally the second Person of the Trinity, invoked as the artificer of the *bolgia* itself: the seven-pillared palace of Wisdom is the archetype of all church buildings (Durandus 1.1.26), and Solomon's Temple is the archetype of the Church in the dedication liturgy for new churches (cf. Wisdom 9.8). The Old Testament figure of the Church, the priesthood and temple of Israel, is remembered (in corrupt form) with the allusion to the corruption of the high priest from Maccabees. The Donation of Constantine, which introduced the wealth and temporal power that Dante held to be the principal disease of the Church, provides the emotional climax of the canto, which is closely linked to apocalyptic prophecy in the comparison of the Church to the Whore of the Apocalypse (see *Purgatorio* 32–33), a frequent practice of the radical Franciscan preachers. The Church—and its corruption by its adulterous spouses—is described from Creation to Last Judgment in a comprehensive account to which Dante the poet might well set his name and his seal.

This is what Dante appears to do through the enigmatic anecdote in which he admits to breaking a baptismal font for a good purpose and "sets his seal," his personal signature, to his confession of the act. The metaphor of sealing is closely related to baptism itself, in which, as in Holy Orders and Confirmation, the Holy Spirit was thought to impose on the soul an indelible "character" or seal (for this reason, these sacraments could not be repeated). The poet's assertion of having rescued someone drowning in a baptismal font also alludes to the understanding of baptism as including the risk of spiritual death (for instance, the Red Sea, which drowned the pursuing Egyptians), from which the newly baptized Christian is saved by being reborn in the Holy Spirit. If we follow Spitzer (1943) in taking Dante's anecdote figuratively, as referring to the text of the canto, the anecdote would signify the poet's attempt to save sinners by attacking the corrupt Church—by breaking down the door, so to speak, which (as here in Hell) has become the entrance to a tomb (19.7). Such a reading of his action follows Dante's statement that "just as a wax impression gives clear evidence of what seal made it, though the seal itself is never seen, so we should not wonder that we must look for the divine will by visible signs, for even our human wills can be detected by others only through signs" (*Monarchia* 2.2.8, trans. Schneider).

R.L.M.

8. Dante and the Classical Soothsayers

(After Canto 20)

A number of puzzling questions are raised by this canto, which has been the subject of a good deal of recent discussion. First, there is some uncertainty as to the nature of the sin being punished. In Canto 11, Virgil alluded to "caster[s] of spells" (*chi affattura*, line 58), who here are mentioned only in passing (line 123). Is Dante treating both divination and magic as kinds of fraud? If so, this would be consistent with their position in the Malebolge. Or is he treating them as branches of black magic? It is striking that except for 9.22–27 and possibly 11.58, black magic is not mentioned in the *Comedy*, unless in *Inferno* 19 (see the note to 19.1) or here.

Dante may have thought that pagan soothsaying involved the agency of demons, in addition to superstition and fraudulence. This was the traditional view in Augustine and other writers (Augustine's view was that the demons' prophecies were/are always inherently fraudulent). In *Par.* 17.31–33, Dante refers to the foretelling of the future:

> . . . per ambage, in che la gente folle
> già s'inviscava pria che fosse anciso
> l'Agnel di Dio che le peccata tolle
>
> [. . . in ambiguities, in which the deluded people used to entangle themselves, before the Lamb of God was killed, who takes away our sins]

This passage is reconcilable with the traditional belief that the pagan oracles were silenced at the death (or birth) of Christ, and that the agency of demons had been involved in them; it by no means imposes the view, however, and can mean simply that Christianity did away with superstition and brought a more rational understanding of experience.

On balance, then, it would seem that we are to regard soothsaying and magic as merely fraudulent exploitations of superstition, as the "game of magic frauds," lacking any supernatural aspect. Amphiaraus, Manto, Arruns, and Eurypylus are easily accounted for in this view: we are to regard them euhemeristically—that is, as historical personages who practiced fraud, perhaps even deceiving themselves, and around whom popular imagination and the poets' feignings wove false myths. But what, then, are we to make of Tiresias's two changes of sex? Did they "actually" take place? Is Virgil mistaken in asserting that they did? If so, this would be the only place in the poem where the character Virgil is mistaken about a "historical" fact. (Interestingly, Vergil's poetry nowhere mentions Tiresias.) At least one early commentator (Guido da Pisa) solved the problem by identifying Tiresias as a hermaphrodite.

The five classical figures represent the four great Roman poets whom Dante most admires. To what extent are they to be regarded as tainted by these sinful practices? The cases of Virgil, Ovid, and Lucan, all of whom are in Limbo, whose occupants are emphatically said not to have sinned (4.34), suggests that Dante thought it possible to represent pagan superstitions in poetry without guilt. Statius's long condemnation of augury (*Theb.* 3.351–65) may have influenced his notion that Statius embraced Christianity.

One of the most debated issues is the meaning of Virgil's rebuke of the pilgrim's weeping, especially in lines 29–30. Scholars who hold that the lines rebuke the pilgrim for the sin of divination interpret line 30 to mean "he who believes God's judgments can be changed, can be made passive" (Parodi 1908; Hollander 1980, 1983). The problem with this interpretation (aside from the contortion it imposes on the admittedly none too clear Italian) is that it does not seem to fit the sin. The five pagan diviners are not characterized in Dante's sources as wishing to change the will of the gods; rather, they consider the future fated, irrevocable, and therefore knowable. Dante considered this view characteristic of paganism: while the pagans did not believe that prayer could affect future events (cf. *Aen.* 6.376), Christians do; he even has Virgil assert that in pre-Christian times God did not heed pagan prayers (*Purg.* 6.28–42; see *Purgatorio* 16 and 23 on the relation between God's foreknowledge and human freedom).

A less forced interpretation of Virgil's rebuke is the one we adopt: "he who brings passion to God's judgments [does not accept them calmly]." This connects the pilgrim's weeping here with a major theme of the *Inferno*, his grief at the spectacle of damnation: of the virtuous pagans, Francesca, Ciacco, Pier delle Vigne, the counselors of violence, and so forth. (It is not true, as is sometimes asserted, that the pilgrim is nowhere else rebuked for this; cf. 29.4–6.)

Another puzzle in the canto is the long digression on Manto, in which Dante has Virgil correct the *Aeneid*; Manto is now a "harsh virgin," not the mother of Ocnus; also, Virgil's account of the founding of Mantua (lines 58–99) does not mention the passage in *Aeneid* 10 that he is correcting, though he implicitly characterizes it as a lie. The problem is compounded by the fact that *Purg.* 22.113 places the "daughter of Tiresias" in Limbo (at least one critic [Kay 1978a] sees the contradictions as merely apparent and intended by Dante to sharpen our critical reading). There is a tendency in Italy to see the canto as shielding Virgil against the imputation of necromancy; the tendency on this side of the Atlantic is to see it as an attack on him (Hollander and Barolini 1990).

Virgil's limitations are emphasized in the Malebolge (see also Cantos 21–23); but by definition he knows more than the historical Vergil and is always correcting him, at least implicitly: the Hell he shows the pilgrim differs in countless ways from those in the *Aeneid*. Canto 20 is certainly one of the places in the poem where it is clearest that the Virgil who is guiding Dante through Hell (and later through Purgatory) does not coincide with the historical Vergil. No doubt part of the explanation of its anomalies is that they are to remind the reader of the distinction and of the oversimplifications in the view taken in Canto 4 of the other classical poets, though at the same time they avoid any major dislocation of the dramatic fiction whereby Virgil "is" the soul of the historical Vergil.

A particularly interesting aspect of Canto 20 is that it repeatedly emphasizes the textuality, the fictive nature, of both the *Aeneid* and the *Comedy* as distinct from their authors. It opens with an unusual reference to the subdivisions (cantos and *cantiche*) of Dante's poem; it has Virgil characterize the *Aeneid* as a "high tragedy"; and it is followed by the contrasting, programmatic reference to Dante's poem as a "comedy" (see 21.1–3, with notes). Virgil's conspicuous reference to his "high tragedy"—and to Dante's close knowledge of it—occurs, oddly, in connection with Eurypylus (lines 106–14), a character mentioned in the *Aeneid* only in passing (by Sinon, in the lying account he gives the Trojans of the horse). Although critics have probably exaggerated the problem posed by Eurypylus (Dante would indeed seem to be showing off his knowledge of a minor point; see the notes to lines 106–14), it is no doubt significant that the attribution of antithetical literary genres to the *Aeneid* and the *Comedy* occurs in connection with an antithesis between soothsaying (classical) and prayer/prophecy (biblical and Christian): a central issue in Dante's view both of the historical Vergil and of his character Virgil is the status of the fourth Eclogue, which the *Purgatorio* interprets as foretelling the coming of Christ. How is it that Virgil is not saved? The question is discussed in the notes to *Purgatorio* 21 and 30.

R.M.D.

9. Autobiography in Cantos 21–23

There is a particular density of autobiographical reference in these cantos, both explicit and implicit. Commentators have observed, for instance, that they are the only cantos in the entire *Comedy* in which Dante refers to his military service in the summer of 1289 (21.94–96, 22.4–5), and his experience of war and of its cruel humor does seem to have contributed largely to the hellish atmosphere of the eighth *bolgia*. These cantos are noteworthy for relating the longest stay in any of the Malebolge (two entire cantos and fifty-seven lines of a third), for containing the second of Dante's two programmatic uses of the term *comedìa* in the *Comedy* (21.2; the first is 16.128), and for having the only clear statement of the fictional date of the action (21.112–14).

There is another respect in which this fifth—central—*bolgia* of ten has a special place in the Malebolge. After the armed coup d'état of the Black party in Florence in November 1301, Dante, one of the most prominent and active among the Whites, was charged with having used his position as prior (mid-June to mid-August 1300) for personal profit, with having maliciously denied aid to "Charles of Anjou" (Valois?) and Boniface VIII, and with having conspired against the Blacks of Pistoia. On hearsay evidence, he was convicted and declared a "falsifier and barrator" in January 1302: he was barred from public office permanently, assessed a large fine, and banished for two years; when he did not pay the fine within the allotted three days, his property was declared forfeit; in March 1302, he was condemned to be burned alive if found in Florentine territory. Dante repeatedly and scornfully denied the charges, stating that his innocence was known to all; around 1315 he rejected amnesty, refusing to confess to crimes he had not committed.

The visit to the *bolgia* of the barrators, the encounter with the Evil Claws, and the narrow escape into the *bolgia* of the hypocrites is some kind of commentary on the false charge of barratry and the circumstances of Dante's going into exile. One level is very easy to decipher: when the cynical Charles of Valois gave the followers of Corso Donati (the leader of the Blacks) license to rampage in Florence, we know from Dino Compagni's *Chronicle* that a number of them arrested and tortured wealthy citizens (not necessarily members of the White party) in order to extort money. The sadistic devils are in part a transposition into the poem of the corrupt, sadistic thugs who followed Corso and manufactured the charges against Dante. Luigi Pirandello suggested that the fart that ends Canto 21 is a satirical reference to the trumpet fanfares that accompanied the public proclamation of charges and sentences (cf. 19.5).

Perhaps, as many commentators believe, the relation of the episode to the events of Dante's life is merely generic; to have been falsely tried and condemned for barratry in absentia is in itself a narrow escape. And it is certainly clear that Dante's personal experience of the multiple forms of fraud underlies all of the Malebolge (in Additional Note 13, we discuss their culmination in the issues of false currency and false testimony). But the emphasis in Cantos 21–23 on a dramatic, narrow escape from capture, *if* autobiographical, strongly suggests that Dante had at some point been within the grasp of his enemies. Perhaps on the way home from Rome he encountered a Florentine patrol who at first did not understand who he was; or perhaps such an episode occurred during one of the Whites' incursions into Florentine territory in 1302 or 1303. These are of course speculations, but not entirely without basis.

One of the most ironic touches in the whole sequence is the fact that Virgil and the pilgrim find safety from the devils in the *bolgia* of the hypocrites, described in strongly monastic and clerical terms: their robes are like those of the monks of Cluny, they are a *collegio* (23.91) and thus parallel to both the Sanhedrin of New Testament times, who are prominently featured, and the College of Cardinals of Dante's time. As Dante makes clear in countless passages in the poem, in his eyes the papal Curia was the most pernicious center of hypocrisy in Christendom (the principal denunciations of the papacy and the Curia are 19.88–123 and *Par.* 27.19–66). He also makes it plain (beginning with 6.68–69), that the chief hypocrite in Rome and the chief author of Florence's misfortunes, as well as of his own, was Pope Boniface VIII, whom he calls "the prince of the new Pharisees" in 27.85: Boniface, who "sells Christ all day long," is a kind of follower of the high priest Caiaphas. Perhaps, as Leonardo Bruni asserts, Dante was indeed in Rome in October 1301 as a member of the embassy to Boniface and heard of the coup only in Siena on his way home; if so, he may have come to regard leaving Rome safely as his decisive escape. On the other hand, perhaps the elaborate, sanctimonious hypocrisy of the Curia was Dante's protection against the open violation of his status as ambassador.

R.M.D.

10. Time and the Thief

(Cantos 24–25)

Dante pays great attention to theft in the Malebolge: in addition to the thieves of the seventh *bolgia*, embezzlers (Cantos 21–22), usurers (Canto 17), and counterfeiters (Canto 30) were also recognized in the Middle Ages as akin to thieves; the last two sins "frame" the Malebolge (and see also "thievish fire," 27.127, perhaps recalling how the counselors concealed their motives). Dante's emphasis reflects that theft directly violates a basic principle of justice, the distribution to all of what each deserves (see Aquinas, *Summa theol.* 2a 2ae, q. 66, a. 6: "theft is contrary to justice, which grants to each his own"). Dante's vision of a society dominated by theft as a nest of vipers (cf. ibid) might also summarize his reaction to the banking and commercial activity of Florence, a place of monetary "change" and "exchange" (see 25.142: "mutare e trasmutare") where the almighty gold florin was dominant (Ferrante 1986).

But all this does not explain why Dante chose to punish some of the thieves by turning them into snakes: more to the point, the mutations ensue, in two cases, from embraces that resemble acts of copulation. If, as Hollander (1984a) suggests, the three main transformations parody the Resurrection of the flesh, the Incarnation of Christ, and the fashioning of humankind from the slime of the earth (all three mysteries might ultimately be signified, for medieval readers, by the Phoenix named in lines 106–11), they are no less clearly representations of the generation and corruption found in nature: Vanni Fucci acts out the return to dust of the human life cycle (Gen. 2.7 and Eccles. 17.32); Agnello and Cianfa portray the blending of male and female attributes in offspring; technically, theirs is a hermaphroditic union, in which male and female are evenly balanced, hence Dante's choice of this myth, and see Aristotle, *On the generation of animals* 1.23 (731a10–14: "For when they [sexed animals] need to generate, they leave off being separate and are united . . . this is plainly seen when they are uniting and copulating, one animal being produced out of the two of them"); finally, Guercio and Buoso demonstrate the articulation of the fetus in gestation by the formal principle, or "hot spirit" (*pneuma, spiritus*) in the seminal fluid—the process is double, transforming a human into a serpentine body and vice versa, each acting reciprocally on the other according to established Aristotelian principles of generation and corruption; see *On generation and corruption* 1.10.328a-b.

That the cantos stage a mimesis of generation and corruption explains many details: mention of the Libyan desert, fertile in snakes because of its exposure to the sun (Lucan, *Pharsalia* 9.689–733, 854–56); mention—unique in Dante's works—of both male and female sexual organs (25.2 "the figs," a common metaphor; 25.116, "what man hides") and of the umbilical cord (25.85–86). The serpent not only was the form of the traditional enemy, who brought death and all our woe to Adam and Eve (Gen. 3.15), but might be generated from the spinal marrow of a corpse (*Met.* 15.389–90). The female viper, moreover, was reported by the bestiaries to conceive when the male spat its seed into her mouth (see 25.138); she then decapitated him, and the offspring gnawed their way out of the mother, killing her. Such nightmarish procreation confirms the views of Mattalia and of Klein (1981) that the thieves' embraces are pseudo-erotic; at a deeper level, it also illustrates Economou's (1976) claim that Dante alludes, through the references in this canto to pens, letters, paper, and writing, to the figure of Genius, traditionally the "scribe" of Nature, who writes out the course of individual human lives (the ancient Roman *genius* was the tutelary spirit of the fecundity of a family or clan). That the generation of humans is like the combination of syllables in a word was remarked by Aristotle (*On the generation of animals* 722a31).

The frequency of allusion to Ovid's *Metamorphoses* in both cantos may alert us to the fact that Dante's interspecies transmutations exemplify not only incessant flux, but also metempsychosis, the passage of the soul from body to body (often of different species). This is represented as a form of immortality by Pythagoras the philosopher in his great speech in the last book of the *Metamorphoses*, whose account of how "everything is changed . . . all things are in flux" underlies Cantos 24 and 25 (Pythagoras mentions both the Phoenix and the pool of Salmacis, among other connections). Since sexual generation, for Augustine (*City of God* 15.16) as for Aristotle (*On the generation of animals* 731b25–732a12), is nature's best attempt to render its works immortal—if not as individuals, then as species—it might be concluded that the sexual imagery of the *bolgia* parodies both metempsychosis and sexual generation (Pythagoras also describes human gestation, and the "ages of man") insofar as they are failed attempts at escaping the destructive effects of time, "the devourer of things" (*Met.* 15.235), on the human composite of soul and body. For if thieves break in, steal, and take away—their Latin name *fur* was interpreted by Justinian's law code as derived from *auferre*, *ablatio* [bearing away]—time also conventionally "bears away" all things (*Met.* 15.197; Boethius, *Consolation* 4.6.32; and see 25.109). The thieves are punished by being "taken away" by the action of the very processes that express the human subjection to, and attempt to overcome, time. We can defend this general approach by noting that Dante brackets the episode with the cosmic machinery of temporal effects (24.1–21) and with a triple rhyme on "time" (*tempo*; 26.8–12), where the word means chronological time ("di qua da picciol *tempo*" [a short time from now]), then an expected event ("non saria per *tempo*" [it would not be early]), and finally the aging of the poet himself ("com' più m'at*tempo*" [the older I grow]). Both the opening simile, which pans from the constellations to a fleeting glimpse of Virgil's face (cf. *Met.* 15.199–213), and Vanni Fucci's transformation, which although it occurs instantaneously is compared to the long-lived Phoenix (whose cycle of self-reproduction was the longest in nature), outline a panorama of time measured by intervals long and short. This, as Aristotle says in his *Physics* (8.3.4), is nature as the principle of movement and change, which necessarily transpires over time [see also *Summa theol.* 1a, 2ae, q 32, a. 2c]. Thus, too, Virgil's sententious reference (24.51) to human life as transitory like smoke or foam (see Wisdom 2.2, 5.14, etc.).

By bearing things away, the thief emulates the work of time; thus the thieves are subject to time's thievery in violently accelerated form. But this does not exhaust Dante's conception. The enigmatic line 24.93, noting that the thieves find no crevice or "heliotrope" that would help them disappear, is a clue to the eschatological allegory of the canto: according to the bestiaries, snakes seek out narrow crevices in the rock (*foramina petri*) in order to rub off their old skins; this mutation is compared to the regeneration of baptism or moral conversion (see Augustine, *City of God* 16.26). In the seventh *bolgia* regeneration is negative, a descent into beasts (Derby Chapin 1971), and the thieves' wish to disappear expresses, instead, the fantasy of escaping detection by the all-seeing sun of Justice, Christ, signified in the *bolgia* by the solar bird, the Phoenix (see Malachi 4.3, highly relevant here). The counter-suffering is thus governed by the contrast, noted above, between sexuality and metempsychosis as natural and mythical attempts to attain immortality and what Dante held to be its true form, achieved through the Resurrection of Christ. This contrast is brought home to the thieves in their constant discovery and seizure by each other, through which they experience the reiterated, unexpected arrival of the moment of judgment, which comes, according to scripture, like a "thief in the night" (see 1 Thess. 5.2, 2 Peter 3.3–13, and Apoc. 3.3).

In view of this elaborate program, we disagree with views (e.g., Hawkins 1980) that see Dante's art in these cantos as dialectically excessive, thematizing the risk to the poet of pride in his own mastery. Rather, Dante requires all his art to represent, as an elaborate trope for theft, the futile war of generation against time. The rivalry with Lucan and Ovid, in addition to recognizing the masterful precedence of these poets in accounting for time and process, is itself an instance of how poets are necessarily caught up in generation, how the poet's art must, Phoenix-like, renew the tradition as it is gnawed away by the "envy of time" (*Met.* 15.234–35). The poet, too, must be a kind of thief in order to renew the lineage of poetry, and no less than the Genius of generation must the poetic *ingegno* [genius] inscribe new words on the flowing pages of time. But as a Christian poet Dante can also be a thief in the Christological sense and come not only to strive, imitate, and surpass, but also to judge.

R.L.M.

11. Ulysses' Last Voyage

(Canto 26)

Although the story of Ulysses' last voyage seems to be essentially Dante's invention, it draws upon a number of traditions—for instance, that Ulysses sailed into the Atlantic and founded Lisbon—and passages in ancient authors known to Dante, perhaps most notably Ovid and Seneca. Ovid has Ulysses' former follower Macareus relate to Aeneas his desertion of Ulysses after the stay with Circe (*Met.* 14.436–40):

> Resides et desuetudine tardi
> rursus inire fretum, rursus dare vela iubemur.
> Ancipitesque vias et iter Titania vastum
> dixerat et saevi restare pericula ponti.
> Pertimui, fateor, nactusque hoc litus adhaesi.
>
> [Lazy and slow from inactivity,
> we are ordered to set out over the sea, to hoist our sails again.
> Circe had predicted that our way would be uncertain
> and our journey vast, and that there remained the dangers of the cruel deep.
> I grew utterly afraid, I confess, and escaping I clung to this shore.]

This passage provided the starting point Dante gives to Ulysses' narrative (he does not envisage Ulysses' returning home but rather beginning his long journey at the end of his stay with Circe), and it may have suggested "vecchi e tardi" [old and slow] (line 106), the idea of Ulysses' being deserted by some of his men (lines 101–2), as well as the idea of shipwreck awaiting them (cf. *restare, Met.* 14.439) on a vast surface.

Seneca's skeptical discussion of the usefulness of the study of literature in-cludes an attack on learned speculations on the story of Ulysses, which probably draws on a traditional Stoic topos (*Epistula ad Lucilium* 88.6–7):

> You inquire where Ulysses wandered, rather than preventing us from for-ever wandering? There is no time to hear whether he was tossed about be-tween Italy and Sicily or beyond the world known to us (for he could not have wandered about for so long in so small a space): for storms of the spirit toss us about every day, and wickedness drives us into all of Ulysses' misfor-tunes. There is no lack of beauty to solicit our eyes, or of enemies; over here there are cruel monsters who delight in human blood, over here in-sidious flatteries for our ears, over here shipwrecks and just as many varieties of misfortune. Teach me this: how to love my fatherland, how to love my wife, my father, how to reach, though shipwrecked, these virtuous goals.

There is no reason to suppose that Dante was ignorant of the tradition of Ulysses' return home and his death at the hands of his son by Circe, Telegonus: he could have known it from Dictys Cretensis, Benoît de St. Maure, or Guido delle Colonne; Benvenuto, writing late in the century, says that even children and the illiterate know the story. Rather, it would seem, Dante wished to provide an ending more in keeping with his conception of the hero.

Commentators have been sharply divided about the significance for Dante of Ulysses' voyage and its relation to the sins for which he is explicitly condemned. Not surprisingly, a significant body of opinion has always seen it as embodying a heroic devotion to the investigation of truth (Tennyson's dramatic monologue "Ulysses" derives from this tradition; its leading postwar exponent has been Mario Fubini; see his 1976 *E.D.* article). Various more recent opinions see Ulysses' voy-age as an instance of vain curiosity (condemned by Augustine, for instance, in *Confessions* 10.35); as magnanimous though impossible; as intellectually presump-tuous; as aspiring to forbidden knowledge; as an instance of some form of "hu-manism" or non-Christian philosophy. Kay (1980) argues that Ulysses is seeking immortality in the forbidden Isles of the Blest but conceals the fact from his men.

Scott (1971) has the most thorough discussion of the many parallels, both explicit and implicit (and all negative), that Dante sets up between Ulysses and other figures: the pilgrim, Aeneas, Elijah, Cato of Utica, and Solomon (these are discussed in the notes to 26.91–93; *Purg.* 1.73–75 and 130–32; and *Par.* 14.103–8 and 27.82–83; the parallels with Guido da Montefeltro are discussed in the notes to Canto 27); there is no doubt that Ulysses' voyage provides the most important and frequently recalled antitype to the pilgrim's own voyage through the other world. Most commentators since Croce (1921) agree that Ulysses is a kind of negative alter ego for Dante, an apotropaic punishing of something to which he felt particularly drawn, though there is no agreement as to what it was. Barolini (1992) argues that the parallel lies in Dante's claim to speak for God (see the notes to Canto 17, and Additional Note 6), but she does not explore the claims to prophecy implicit in the canto in this connection or the passages where the duty of writing the poem is laid on the pilgrim, such as *Par.* 17.106–42 and 27.40–66.

To us it does not seem possible to dissociate the Ulysses of the last voyage from the Ulysses of Troy; the metaphoric structure of the sins listed by Virgil is continued in the pattern of his voyage (see, in particular, our note to line 142). European ventures westward into the Atlantic were already beginning in Dante's day; most notable perhaps was the lost Vivaldi brothers' expedition of 1291 (Nardi 1949). From a contemporary point of view, we find it striking that Dante's powerful imagining (even prophetically using the term *new land—nova terra,* line 137— for a discovery) attributes the characteristic European/Western thirst for exploration to a figure already established, in the Latin tradition, as representing ruthless and faithless military destructiveness.

The remarkable polyvalence of Dante's myth is far from having been exhausted. Lotman (1980), though he believes Dante saw Ulysses' voyage as ethically neutral, remarks:

> Dante saw in [Ulysses] the traits specific to the scientific consciousness and the general cultural climate of the coming age: the separation between science and morality, between discoveries and their results, between science and the personality of the scientist. . . . Finding himself on the threshold of a new epoch, Dante saw one of [its] fundamental dangers.

A recent survey of the avatars of Ulysses is Boitani 1992.

R.M.D.

12. The Poetry of Schism

(Canto 28)

From the beginning of the canto (lines 5–6), Dante identifies both language and thought as containers, literally a "bosom" (line 6, *seno*). The poet's verses might be thought of as "walls" keeping in their "content": Brunetto Latini compares verse, bound to its rules, to the bound stakes of a palisade (*Trésor* 3.10); Mohammed's slashed abdomen, compared to a barrel with its staves missing, alludes to the containing function of language: the formal container is breached, and its "contents" spill out. More fundamentally, Latin rhetoricians divided the rhetorical period (Cicero called it "circuitum orationis" [the circuit of the sentence]) into *membra* [member] and *caesa* [literally, cuts]. Canto 28 illustrates this fundamental opposition in that its "content" is a heap of slashed body parts (see the note on *risma,* line 39, and the irony of Mosca's use of *capo,* line 107). The dialectic of binding and cutting also characterizes Dante's first mention of the punishment in the *bolgia* (27.132), juxtaposing retribution as the imposition of a load (*acquistan carco*) with the sowers' act of putting asunder (*scommettendo*). Such a mapping of the disarticulations of linguistic entities over disarticulations of the human body is fundamental to Dante's mimesis of violence in Canto 28, where (as later in Canto 32) the "word [does] not differ from the fact."

The canto's opening section (lines 7–21) displays unusual rhetorical complexity and marked metrical and phraseological roughness. Consecutive enjambents (run-on lines), polysyndeton (repeated use of conjunctions), and multiple subordinate clauses within syntactic periods (Beltrami 1985) give the effect of coils of phrasing that run over the limits of verse and exceed the capacity of a normal breath; indeed, the comparison opened in line 7 is not closed until line 20 ("if were gathered . . . would not equal"). The "circuit of speech" is here stretched beyond its limit; the protest of inadequacy—the inexpressibility topos—is not merely rhetorical. Line 21 itself separates noun and modifier (*modo . . . sozzo*), and such gaps in syntax recur: lines 22–24 suggest, with a clause inserted between the elements of the comparison, the staved-in barrel described, while lines 55–58 separate verb and object and 61–63 interrupt the performance of Mohammed's step (illustrating the gap in lines 55–58).

The same principle of coordinating word and fact determines that the trope that relates parts to wholes, synechdoche, should heap up fragments of bodies in the same twenty-one lines. Blood, wounds, bones, and scattered members stand for whole bodies; the bushel of rings figures the heaps of Roman dead at Cannae. Sheer accumulation replaces the functional articulation of parts of the living, organic body. This implicit, scattered body signifies a history of human groups at war: Trojans and Latians (a proto–civil war); Troy and Carthage (Mediterranean war between rival empires of antiquity); Robert Guiscard and Byzantium (near-contemporary Mediterranean war among Christians from the extremes of Europe); and finally the "civil" war of Christendom between emperor and papacy. The list covers the span of time Dante would have recognized as historical (753 B.C.–A.D. 1268).

In the body of the canto the breaking of the symbolic bodies of human community are signified: Mohammed rends the "seamless garment" of the Church, Curio destroys the civil body of Rome (cf. Lucan, *Pharsalia* 10.416–17: "Latium sic scindere corpus/ dis placitum" [thus it pleased the gods to rend the body of Italy]), and Mosca sows discord in Florence. Bertran's inflammatory poems break the bond between king and heir that itself signifies the bond of ruler and ruled. These bodies are dismembered in a scheme dictated by the symmetry of the larger discourse unit (the canto) itself: the chief body parts, head and trunk, are twice separated, at each extreme of the canto; midmost we find smaller wounds, external and internal, to the head (Pier da Medicina, Curio; and see line 107), bracketed by notation of the limbs, or extremities: in Mosca's case, recision of the hands, executive members of the rational mind; in Mohammed's, his disjointed step. The spectacle of dismemberment also evokes again the sinner's key utterance: holding up his stumps, Mosca repeats his infamous words, and Pier da Medicina handles Curio like a ventriloquist's dummy, repeating his fateful words; Curio's severed tongue, at the central point of the canto, focuses speech and wound at a single locus. This poetic and rhetorical balancing of dismemberment is framed by the double enunciation of the counter-suffering itself, by Mohammed (lines 34–36) and later by Bertran (lines 139–42). The counter-suffering has in fact an intrinsically poetic structure: according to Aristotle (*Ethics* 5.5.1132b), reciprocation or counter-suffering is unsuited to civic life; it is an excess of balance (Mazzotta 1993), thus typified by Rhadamanthus, the harsh judge of the underworld. Aristotle quotes a distich of Hesiod (fragment 286 in Diels) that medieval commentators recognized as poetry: "If a man suffer what he has done, then justice is rendered, sum for sum." Poetic justice is a harsh justice (Freccero 1984).

Although Dante echoes the violent poetry of the Old French war epics, the martial epics of Lucan and Statius, and several gruesome passages in the *Aeneid*, his poetry of discord springs most directly from his imitation of Bertran de Born, the poet he identifies elsewhere as master of the genre of the martial lyric. Of Bertran's forty-seven attributed poems (Bertran 1986), nearly half describe or refer to the wounds produced by mounted shock combat; if we include reference to sieges and war in general, the count of poems describing or calling for battle rises to twenty-six. A number of allusions (often pointed out; see the notes and the martial diction of verses 28, 55, and 117 observed in Bertran) and verbal devices in Canto 28 suggest that Dante understood Bertran's poetry not only as divisive but as itself wilfully displaying kinds of dismemberment: note, for example, the *rima franta* [broken rhyme] of verse 124, inspired by Bertran (see our note, and Picone 1979) and Dante's use of echoes from Bertran's "half-sirventes" (a poem cut in half, *Miez sirventes*). Indeed, Bertran claims that he is in harmony with strife, not peace ("Ab gerra m'acort,/ q'ieu non teing ni crei/ negun'autra lei" [I'm attuned to war, for I do not hold nor believe any other law]), and thus opposes the principles of concord that harmonize the universe. In Bertran's oeuvre, Dante found an already elaborated poetics of schism.

Couching several of his calls to war in the form of the *plazer* (a genre in which the poet describes what pleases him), Bertran goes so far as to boast that his poems help precipitate conflict: this frequent marking of the causal link between word and wielded weapon, which is also remarked in the biographies (*vidas*) of the poet, might have earned Bertran his harsh treatment at Dante's hands (Barolini 1984):

> Lo coms m'a mandat e mogut . . .
> q'ieu fassa per lui tal chansso
> on sion trencat mil escut
>
> [The count has commanded and urged me . . .
> to make him a song such that
> a thousand shields will be slashed] (Bertran 1986)

The final line of Canto 27 (27.136), giving a preview of the counter-suffering, modifies a line from Bertran's sirventese "Non puosc mudar mon chantar non esparga" [I can't keep myself from scattering my song], which deploys a similar antithesis: "Anta l'adutz e de pretz lo descarga/ gerra. . . ." [it [war] brings him shame and discharges him of honor]. Given the reference to scattering, this verse might be taken as the fitting epitaph for Dante's Bertran and his poetry of schism.

R.L.M.

13. The Body Analogy, 2: The Metaphorics of Fraud
(After Canto 30)

In the body analogy governing the structure of Hell, the circles of fraud correspond to the belly. The analogy is particularly pronounced in the Malebolge, where we find countless references to the processes and products of the human digestive system and to their analogues, as well as to a number of diseases thought in Dante's time to result from disorders of digestion. Several of the Malebolge are filled with fluids, and many of the punishments involve sharply focused parodies of cooking and digestion, such as those of the flatterers, who are immersed in shit (Canto 18); the simoniacs, who are burned by oily flames (Canto 19); the barrators, who are cooked in pitch (Cantos 21–22); the thieves, who undergo changes and exchanges of form, incineration, and agglutination (Cantos 24–25); the falsifiers, discussed in the notes to Canto 30.

The belly of Hell is the appropriate place for the punishment of fraud because, traditionally, knowledge or truth is like food: it nourishes the soul. Food and knowledge are associated in Genesis 3, when Adam and Eve eat the forbidden fruit; Saint Paul develops the analogy at some length in 1 Corinthians 3: the new Christian is a babe in the Spirit and must be nourished with milk—easier doctrine—until he is ready for meat. Fraud, on the other hand, is a form of poison, though the devices of the fraudulent may taste sweet at first. The food metaphor recurs frequently in the *Comedy*, drawing upon the countless ancient and medieval texts that elaborate various forms of the analogy (for further discussion, see Durling 1981a).

The food metaphor is inherent in much of the traditional metaphorics of fraud. The trickster "cooks up" his scheme, and once the victim has "swallowed" the story, the victim is "caught" in it: the deceiver seeks to make the victim swallow what will then swallow the victim. This tropic reversal of container and thing contained pervades Dante's entire treatment of fraud and provides the retributive pattern: the devices of the fraudulent return upon them and the spinner is caught in his own web, which turns out to be part of the larger web spun by the greater spider, Satan. Seen from above, the Malebolge resembles a huge spider web, as well as being a kind of blocked distortion of the winding path of the intestines.

The categories of container and thing contained are thus basic to Dante's analysis of fraud. His two chief instances of fraud are the Trojan Horse and the counterfeit coin (see the discussions in the notes to Cantos 26 and 30); they would seem to be correlated in part as *external* fraud, used in war against an enemy, and *internal* fraud as a distemper of society. Both are understood in terms of a disparity between container—external appearance or wrapping (integument, *involu-*

crum: the face)—and inner contents (the belly), which do not "respond" to it (cf. 30.54), as in a true votive offering or a genuine coin they do. If the horse carries the Greek soldiers who will burn Troy, the counterfeit florin carries three carats of dross, which inflate and infect the economy. In both horse and coin, the issue of false witness is central: Sinon swears to the religious purpose of the horse; the florin is imprinted with the emblems of the state (the lily) and of the patron saint in order to testify that it is made of twenty-four–carat gold (its value depends directly on that of the metal).

In the medieval terms of Dante's analysis, the dual structure of integument versus content is inherent in language itself, whose necessity derives from the existence of the body (for men must have an external, physical means of signifying their inner thoughts and feelings). The relation of integument and content is thus analogous to that between body and soul. To be expressed, thoughts must be clothed (or enclosed) in words, which have outer, physical form, and inner meaning (*mo* and *issa* are different in outer form, but identical in inner meaning, 23.7). Lying is possible because the body can conceal or misrepresent the soul, and because understanding of meaning (intention) is always inferential: just as his face may not reveal what is in his heart, our interlocutor may not "mean what he says"—that is, the true meaning, the content or intent, of his words may be different from their outer guise. Thus in the Malebolge, the question of the nature of language is ever-present: this is all the more the case because of the social nature of language, insisted on repeatedly, for instance in references to regional and municipal dialects, and the importance of the various forms of fraud in the sickness, as Dante sees it, of the body politic. Since language itself is always problematic, it is clear that such is the case for Dante's poetry as well: the relation between allegory and fraud is one of tension, and the issue is never far from the surface in the *Comedy*.

R.M.D.

14. Dante's Political Giants

(Canto 31)

Dante names six giants: Nimrod, Ephialtes, Antaeus, Briareus, Typhon, and Tityos. The last three are only mentioned: the first three, whom the pilgrim sees, refer to distinct episodes of gigantomachy: Nimrod's attempt to scale Heaven with the tower of Babel (a biblical episode); the attack of the giants against Mount Olympus in Thessaly (in Macedonia) in a bid to overthrow Jupiter (the episode from pagan myth); and the struggle between Hercules and Antaeus in North Africa (a mythic episode within Lucan's "historical" poem, the *Pharsalia*: for this as an allegory of the civil war in northern Africa, see the note to lines 120–21). Rabuse (1961) showed that the three episodes have clear political reference, each being linked to one of the empires of pride and arrogance: Babylon, the Macedonian Greece of Alexander the Great, and Carthage, thought of either as antagonists or as temporary substitutes of Dante's legitimate, providentially inspired "Roman" empire in its march toward world sovereignty. See Orosius, *Seven Books against the Pagans*, 2.1.3–6:

> and by the same ineffable plan at the four cardinal points of the world, four chief kingdoms preeminent in distinct stages, namely: the Babylonian kingdom in the East, the Carthaginian in the South, the Macedonian in the North, and the Roman in the West. Between the first and last of these, that is, between the Babylonian and the Roman, as it were, between an aged father and a little son, the intervening and brief kingdoms of Africa and Macedonia came as protectors and guardians, accepted by the power of time, not the law of inheritance.

In declaring Rome providential, transcending the other empires, Dante is, of course, subverting Orosius's scheme.

R.L.M.

15. Ugolino

(Cantos 32–33)

A principal key to the interpretation of Ugolino's narrative is the contrast between his stony silence and the words and actions of the children. It has been understood, correctly, that Ugolino's inability to free himself from his vengeful hatred of Ruggieri already expresses his damnation. But critics have been so caught up in their reaction against the excesses of the Romantic interpretation stemming from De Sanctis that they have discarded its chief contribution—that both motifs are there: Ugolino's savage hatred, which seals his damnation, and his love for his children, which, because he is justifiably outraged by their murder, paradoxically further feeds his hatred and thus his damnation. One should keep clearly in mind, however, that Dante's text insists again and again that God validates Ugolino's moral outrage; it shows God's justice using Ugolino's hatred as the instrument of the punishment of Ruggieri. One of the object lessons Ugolino represents is the consequence of forgetting "Judge not, that you be not judged. For with what judgment you judge, you shall be judged, and with what measure you mete, it shall be measured unto you" (Matt. 7.1–2; all quotations in this note are from the King James Version).

The episode is in fact permeated with references to the Sermon on the Mount (Matthew 5–7). In a whole series of respects Ugolino is shown as going against its precepts. Though he does hunger after justice (Matt. 5.38), he does not forgive his enemies, let alone bless them or pray for them (Matt. 5.44–47, 9.11), and therefore he himself is unforgiven (Matt. 6.15); and he has forgotten the "supersubstantial bread" of the Lord's Prayer (Matt. 6.10). He is obsessed with the morrow, watching from day to day the slow progress of his own and the children's deaths, forgetting "Take no thought for the morrow, for the morrow will take thought for itself. Sufficient unto the day is the evil thereof" (Matt. 6.33–34). He has forgotten the heavenly father's loving solicitude: "Ask, and you shall receive; seek, and you shall find; knock, and it shall be opened to you. . . . Or what man is there among you, of whom if his son ask bread, will he give him a stone? . . . If you then, being evil, know how to give good gifts to your children, how much more will your father who is in heaven give good gifts to them that ask him" (Matt. 7.7–11).

Most of all, Ugolino has forgotten the analogy between earthly fathers and the heavenly father, whose single most elaborate statement in the New Testament is the Sermon on the Mount. The analogy is in fact a principal key to the episode; the significance of the children's words and actions can only be fully understood in terms of it. Everything they say and do shows that in Dante's terms they are saved: they express loving concern and inquire into his trouble (lines 50–51); they express grief at his agony and offer their flesh for him to eat (in a clear reference to the Eucharist), in which they echo Job's words, often cited as the model for the believer's correct attitude of trust and submission to the will of God; Gaddo echoes the last words of Christ on the Cross. The children both speak to their earthly father as if he were the representative of the heavenly father (as, of course, the analogy in the Sermon on the Mount implies), and, in expressing concern and offering food, act toward him as if they, not he, were the fathers.

It is not merely that the status of the children as Christ-figures deepens Ugolino's guilt. The point is rather that in Dante's terms they do in fact represent Christ, and their love embodies Christ's compassion and his offer of salvation. What the analogy invites Ugolino to do is to accept the reversal of roles already implicit in their words and to treat them as the representatives of Christ. Salvation is as close to him as asking for his children's forgiveness, which they have implicitly already offered. Thus when Ugolino looks into his children's faces and sees only death and his guilt, he makes them a version of the Medusa: he does not weep, he turns to stone. But if he could respond to the children's love, if he could see in their dying but loving faces the reflection of Christ's, he would be saved. But he himself must become as a little child (Mark 10.13–15), become truly *Ugolino*.

The conception of the Medusa Dante is drawing on here derives from Statius's *Thebaid,* in which Tydeus (one of the Seven against Thebes), who has mortally wounded Menalippus but has been mortally wounded by him also, commands his followers to bring him the severed head of his enemy: he watches the life drain from Menalippus's staring eyes, seeing the image of his own death. In his rage he gnaws on the head; Statius's text is evasive, but Tydeus's target appears to be Menalippus's eyes. As this occurs, Minerva, who was bringing Tydeus a hero's eternal crown, averts her eyes and departs (8.716–66).

Much ink has been spilled on the question of whether line 75 implies cannibalism on Ugolino's part, an idea that surfaces in the nineteenth century (De Sanctis [1869] was apparently the first to point out that the line is ambiguous). In support of the cannibalism hypothesis can be adduced the *Thebaid* reference, the repeated emphasis on eating and teeth, the cannibalism of the punishment itself, the punishment of Judas, Cassius, and Brutus in Satan's mouths (also a kind of parody of the Eucharist), and the many references to the myth of Saturn (as in the figure of Satan), who ate his children until his wife substituted stones. Contini (1965) adduced a number of medieval texts showing that such events were often considered characteristic of tragedy (and the *Epistle to Can Grande*—of disputed authenticity—cites Seneca's tragedies, of which the most famous was the *Thyestes*, as typically tragic). As Contini said, accepting the idea "may add horror, but not the poetry of horror," and does not perhaps much affect the basic significance of the episode.

R.M.D.

16. Christ in Hell

(After Canto 34)

Christ is ever-present in Dante's Hell. There are not a great many explicit references, but implicit ones occur in virtually every canto and in fact provide the entire rationale of the pilgrim's journey. The first explicit reference is part of the inscription on the gate in Canto 3: Hell was made by "Divine Power, Highest Wisdom, and First Love." All three of these terms—*Potestate, Sapïenza,* and *Amore*—were traditionally recognized as among the names of God and refer to the persons of the Trinity. "Wisdom" refers to the second person, the Son, the Logos, "through whom were all things made," identified with Christ in the first chapter of the Gospel of John. (One may observe, in this connection, that the repeated references by the narrating poet to the exactitude and ingenuity of the punishments in Hell [e.g., 14.6, 19.10–12] imply Christ as both Wisdom and Judge.)

It is only partly true, then, as is frequently asserted, that Christ and God are not named in Hell. In addition to the gate, Beatrice's mention of God in 2.91, Nessus's in 12.119, and Francesca's use of one of Christ's titles ("*King* of the universe," 5.91), perhaps the clearest instance comes in the pilgrim's denunciation of the corrupt papacy, addressed to Nicholas III in 19.90–92: "Now tell me, how much treasure did our Lord demand from Saint Peter, before he gave the keys into his keeping?"

A majority of the direct references to Christ are made by Virgil, and they are noteworthy in that they all omit any reference to Christ's divinity. It is evident that Virgil does not really know who Christ is. They refer to Christ's Harrowing of Hell (4.52–63, 12.37–38), to his Second Coming and Last Judgment (6.94–99), and, in the last instance within the *Inferno,* to his life and death in general (34.114–15). In other passages which do not mention Christ, Virgil refers to God (1.124–29), to the gate left permanently open after the Harrowing of Hell (8.125–26), and to the valley of Jehoshaphat, scene of the Last Judgment (10.10–12); these are of course indirect references to Christ also. Although the most detailed of Virgil's references to Christ is the first (4.52–63), the most important is probably that in 12.37–38, for it enables the pilgrim and the reader to connect the landslide between the circles of heresy and violence with the earthquake at Christ's death, although Virgil himself is unable to do so.

In addition to that in Canto 12, Foster (1970) noted four references to Christ's passion and death: 21.106–14, where the devil Evil Tail states that the next bridge over the Malebolge fell in what turns out to be the same earthquake and falsely suggests that there is another still standing nearby; 23.133–38, where the hypocrite explains to Virgil and the pilgrim that the ruins of the bridge afford a ladder; 23.111 and following, where Caiaphas, the high priest who hypocritically advised that Christ be put to death, is crucified in the way and must feel the weight of everyone's hypocrisy as they tread upon him; and 34.1, the quotation of Venantius Fortunatus's hymn in praise of the Cross, "Vexilla regis prodeunt."

All five of these references to the Passion have to do with the path the pilgrim and Virgil follow through Hell. Without the earthquake at Christ's death, the cliff in Canto 12 would be impassable; likewise, the absence of a bridge over one of the pits of fraud is the occasion of Evil Tail's effort to entrap the travelers, and Satan himself provides the ladder by which the travelers leave Hell. In all these instances, as our notes have observed, Dante has in mind Christ's words in John 14.6: "I am the way, the truth, and the life. No man cometh unto the Father save by me." Two of the most basic and largest questions about the *Inferno* are involved: Why does the pilgrim have to go through Hell? How is he to do so? The two answers are virtually identical: the pilgrim must descend through Hell in imitation of Christ's death: he must humble himself, penitentially experience his kinship with the damned, and die to sin, according to the pattern set forth by Saint Paul in Romans 6.3–4: "Know ye not, that all we who are baptized in Jesus Christ were buried with him by baptism into death: that as Christ is risen from the dead by the glory of the Father, so we also may walk in newness of life."

We are reminded of Christ's being the Way at key moments: at the descent to the circle of violence (since the Crucifixion was in Dante's eyes the worst act of violence ever committed, and all others in some sense repeat it), in the circle of the hypocrites (and Caiaphas and the other members of the Sanhedrin undergo the irony of being literally *the way*, almost its pavement), and at the last crossing, in connection with the figure of the devil on the cross, for the descent down Satan's side is the culmination of the pilgrim's penitential imitation of Christ in Hell, and it leads to the central crossing from the hemisphere of Jerusalem to that of Purgatory. The pilgrim, then, as one who must imitate Christ, who is following Christ, is a *figure*, an analogue of Christ; and only the example of Christ, and the power of the crucified Christ, can get him through. In a sense the idea of Christ as the Good Shepherd (parodied by a devil in Canto 21; see the note to lines 34–36) is implicit throughout.

In showing us the punishments of the damned, the pilgrim's journey prefigures the Day of Judgment (in fact the writing of the poem itself, with its apocalyptic focus on the "Last Things," does so, and the poet is an even more dramatic analogue to Christ the Judge than is the pilgrim). The direct references to the Last Judgment all pursue the question asked by the pilgrim in the first of them (Canto 6): Will the sufferings of the damned be greater, the same, or less after the Last Judgment? In Canto 6, Virgil explains that their sufferings will increase when body and soul are reunited, since their natures as human beings will be more complete. This is the emphasis also in the three later references: the heretics' tombs will be closed (10.10–12) and their intellects will be empty (10.106–8); alone among all the damned the suicides will not be reunited with their bodies (13.103–8).

As one might expect, then, the pilgrim's confrontations with the damned prefigure their future confrontation with Christ the Judge at the Last Judgment, "face to face," as 1 Corinthians has it, and, in *Inferno* 10, "I had fixed my eyes on his" (line 34). This idea is not insisted upon equally in the various episodes, of course, but two aspects of virtually all the encounters draw on the connection. As Ramat (1976) observed:

> One of the fundamental unifying principles of the *Inferno* is that each sinner . . . is alone, closed in his own remembrance, which is limited to a crucial image which Justice has chosen or to the eternal memory of his sin, and in any case to a perpetual renewal of grief. . . . The damned sinner then speaks openly the discourse that ceaselessly goes on within him, that discourse and not another. . . .

The sinner makes a kind of confession to the pilgrim; he must speak true by his lights (cf. 18.51–57): and, as the resurrected dead will do at the Last Judgment (see Apoc. 20.12–15), we the living overhear. And it is noteworthy that in a number of cases—Ugolino and Master Adam are the most obvious—what the sinners relate is the moment of their blind rejection of Christ's call to repentance and salvation, just as they will have to do at the Last Judgment. Once mercy is rejected, justice is merciless, but it is important to remember that, for Dante, even the worst of the damned have chosen damnation *in spite of* Christ's efforts to save them.

Second, the encounters are prefigurations of the Last Judgment because without exception they increase the suffering of the damned. "No greater pain is there than to remember the happy time in wretchedness," says Francesca; the simoniac Pope Nicholas wildly kicks his burning feet as the pilgrim denounces his corruption; and the thief Vanni Fucci says, "It pains me more to be caught in the wretchedness where you see me than when I lost the other life." One of the clearest examples is that of Caiaphas (23.112–13):"When he saw me, he twisted himself, puffing into his beard with sighs." His suffering is increased, as the commentators point out, because he realizes that this living man will testify among the living, and his hypocrisy has been useless: this is exactly what will occur at the Last Judgment, when all will know his sin.

Another aspect of Caiaphas's punishment is emphasized. Just as, ironically, he must bear the weight of all hypocrites' sin, so also he is crucified. His punishment is a clear—and, of course, overdetermined—parodic analogue of the Crucifixion of Christ, like that of Satan himself (see the note to 34.39–45). It might appear that Satan and Caiaphas are special cases, and of course in a sense they are. But a moment's reflection will show that every punishment in Hell, as Dante conceives it, must be a distorted reflection of the Crucifixion, even though it is only in certain cases that he chooses to emphasize the fact. Dante accepted Saint Paul's theory of the Atonement as set forth in the Epistle to the Romans—that is, that Christ's death on the Cross paid the punishment demanded by Justice for all men's sins. The Crucifixion fully satisfies the Old Law, which Jesus sums up in the Sermon on the Mount, quoting Exodus, as "an eye for an eye, a tooth for a tooth." The penalty imposed on each soul in Hell must then be, in due proportion, analogous to the Crucifixion, and "an eye for an eye, a tooth for a tooth" equals, clearly enough, the famous principle of *contrapasso,* the exact fitting of punishment to crime. The analogy with the Crucifixion is not always insisted on, but there are clear references to it in 13.107–8, 19.22–24, 21.46–48, 23.100–102 and 118–20, 24.106–11, 27.103–4, 28.29–31, 30.49–51, and 33.87.

Some of the most emphatic references to the analogy between punishments in Hell and Christ's death come in Canto 10; there are very clear references to his burial and resurrection, for instance when the pilgrim observes that "all the covers [of the tombs] are lifted and no one is standing guard" (10.7–9). When Farinata and Cavalcante stand up in their tomb, they are enacting an abortive analogue both of Christ's resurrection and of the general resurrection of the dead, which they have denied. Furthermore, the immobile figure of Farinata, visible from the waist up, alludes to the famous iconographic motif called the *Imago pietatis*: in this respect Farinata is a kind of dark reflection, an *umbra,* of the dead Christ and the sanctified Host. Other focused references to the Eucharist occur in Cantos 33 and 34.

The pilgrim, then, is imitating Christ's death in his descent through Hell; the pilgrim is an analogue of Christ the Judge at the Last Judgment; the punishments of the damned are negative analogues to Christ's Crucifixion and sometimes, in closely analogous ways, of his Resurrection. All the examples cited are two-sided: they point in two directions, damnation and salvation; they can be understood in two ways, *in malo* and *in bono.* For the damned, Christ, whose mercy they rejected, is the Judge who condemns them to fruitless imitation of his Incarnation, death, and Resurrection; but for the pilgrim, Christ is the principle that makes passage through Hell, and escape from Hell, possible. The lessons are directed at the reader. On the negative side, *in malo,* the reader is to learn to fear God's justice: "O vengeance of God, how much must you be feared by everyone who reads what was made manifest to my eyes" (14.16–18). But on the positive side, *in bono,* the reader is to learn to see and trust Christ everywhere, even in the depths of Hell, "though I walk in the midst of the shadow of death," as the psalmist put it. This is the great difference between the pilgrim and Virgil; this is the reason the pilgrim can confront Satan himself, while the author of the *Aeneid,* in Dante's view, was blocked at the gate of Dis.

R.M.D.

TEXTUAL VARIANTS

We list here, with brief comments, passages where we have adopted readings rejected by Petrocchi.

3.31. We depart from the Petrocchi reading, *error*, in favor of *orror*, even though *orror* may be a *lectio facilior; error* sacrifices the powerful sensory vividness of the bristling hair.

8.111 Petrocchi's "modal conjunction" *(che,* deriving, like *ché,* from Latin *quid,* and not orthographically distinguished in Dante's day) seems a needless sophistication here, though we adopt it in 8.64 and 30.132.

11.28. The context seems clearly to imply the definite article. The traditional reading here is "de' violenti" [of the violent]; as Petrocchi himself established, Dante's practice is best interpreted in such cases as *d'i;* Petrocchi's *di* seems arbitary here.

14.48. We adopt the traditional reading here *(maturi* [ripen]); Petrocchi's *marturi* [inflict pain] seems clearly a *lectio facilior* and sacrifices both a striking metaphor and a very characteristic sarcasm.

16.102. We accept the traditional *dovria . . . esser* [there should be], as opposed to Petrocchii's *dovea . . . esser* [there was to have been], which some of the early commentators explained by supposing that the Conti Guidi had once planned to build a castle at San Benedetto delle Alpi; but *mille* [a thousand], which they took to mean "a thousand people," is clearly the correlative of *una scesa* [one descent], meaning that there is a single cataract when the river is in spate, but a thousand stages of descent when it is not.

19.45. The context clearly requires *che sì piangeva* [who was weeping so]—line 32 has identified Nicholas as "wriggling more" than the others—rather than Petrocchi's *che si piangeva* [who was weeping].

24.69. Like other modern editors, we adopt Pietro di Dante's emendation *ad ire* for the widely attested *ad ira,* which seems the *lectio facilior;* however, the meaning he asserts, "to go," seems redundant with *mosso* [moved], which if complemented would seem to require an expression of ethos. We incline to the view that *ire* is the plural of *ira* [anger], though such usage would admittedly be un-precedented.

26.14. This is a vexed passage, for the manuscripts, giving *fatto* [made], do not provide the agreement of past participle (normal in Dante), which would re-solve the difficulty (i.e., *fatte* would indicate that the stairs—[*scalee*, feminine] had been "made" by the projections; *fatti* would indicate that "we" [*ne*, mascu-line] had been "made"—pale, if *iborni* is accepted as a neologism based on the Latin *eburneus* [ivory-colored]). We follow the traditional reading, rather than Petrocchi's *che n'avea fatto iborni,* which seems forced.

BIBLIOGRAPHY

Reference Works

Enciclopedia dantesca. 1970–1983. Umberto Bosco, director. Edited by Giorgio Petrocchi. 6 vols. Rome: Treccani.

Brieger, Peter, Millard Meiss, and Charles S. Singleton. 1969. *Illuminated Manuscripts of the Divine Comedy*. 2 vols. Bollingen Series 81. Princeton, N.J.: Princeton University Press.

Devoto, Giacomo, and Gian Carlo Oli. 1971. *Dizionario della lingua italiana*. Florence: Le Monnier.

Toynbee, Paget. 1968. *A Dictionary of Proper Names and Other Notable Matters in the Works of Dante*. Revised by Charles S. Singleton. Oxford: Clarendon Press.

Works by Dante

La Commedia secondo l'antica vulgata. 1966–1967. Edited by Giorgio Petrocchi. 4 vols. Milan: Mondadori.

The Convivio. 1908. Translated by Philip H. Wicksteed. 2nd ed. Temple Classics. London: Dent.

Convivio. 1988. Edited by Cesare Vasoli and Domenico De Robertis. In *Opere minori*. *Tomo I/2*. Milan: Ricciardi.

The Banquet. 1989. Translated by Christopher Ryan. Saratoga, Calif.: ANMA Libri.

De vulgari eloquentia. 1979. Edited by Pier Vincenzo Mengaldo. In *Opere minori*. *Tomo II*. Milan: Ricciardi.

Epistole. 1979. Edited by Arsenio Frugoni and Giorgio Brugnoli. In *Opere minori*. *Tomo II*. Milan: Ricciardi.

Latin Works. 1929. Translated by A. G. Ferrers Howell and Philip H. Wicksteed. Temple Classics. London: Dent.

Monarchia. 1979. Edited by Bruno Nardi. In *Opere minori*. *Tomo II*. Milan: Ricciardi.

On World-Government (*De Monarchia*). 1957. Translated by Herbert W. Schneider. 2nd ed. Indianapolis: Bobbs Merrill.

Opere minori. Tomo II. 1979. Milan: Ricciardi.

Opere minori. Tomo I/2. 1988. Milan: Ricciardi.

Rime. 1946. Edited by Gianfranco Contini. 2nd ed. Turin: Einaudi.

Dante's Lyric Poetry. 1967. Edited by Kenelm Foster and Patrick Boyde. 2 vols. Oxford: Clarendon Press.

Vita nuova. 1980. Edited by Domenico De Robertis. Milan: Ricciardi.

The New Life. 1867. Translated by Charles Eliot Norton. Boston: Houghton Mifflin.

The Vita Nuova. 1969. Translated by Barbara Reynolds. Harmondsworth: Penguin.

Commentaries on the *Divine Comedy*

Alighieri, Pietro. 1845. *Petri Allegherii super ipsius genitoris Comoediam Commentarium.* Edited by Vincentio Nannucci. 3 vols. Florence: Piatti.

Bambaglioli, Graziolo de'. 1915. *Il commento dantesco di Graziolo de' Bambaglioli dal Colombino di Siviglia con altri codici confrontato.* Savona: Bertolotto.

Benvenuto da Imola. 1885. *Benvenuti de Rambaldis de Imola Comentum super Dantis Aldigherij Comoediam.* Edited by I. P. Lacaita. 5 vols. Florence: Barbèra.

Boccaccio, Giovanni. 1965. *Esposizioni sopra la Comedia di Dante.* Edited by Giorgio Padoan. In vol. 6 of *Tutte le Opere di Giovanni Boccaccio,* edited by Vittore Branca. Milan: Mondadori.

Bosco, Umberto, and Giovanni Reggio, eds. 1988. *La Divina Commedia.* 3 vols. Florence: Le Monnier.

Buti, Francesco da. [1858–1862] 1989. *Commento di Francesco da Buti sopra la Divina Commedia di Dante Allighieri.* Edited by Crescentino Giannini. 5 vols. Pisa: Nistri.

Chiavacci Leonardi, A. M. 1991. *Commedia. Volume primo: Inferno.* Commentary by Anna Maria Chiavacci Leonardi. Milan: Mondadori.

Commento alla Divina Commedia d'anonimo fiorentino del secolo XIV. 1866–1874. Edited by Pietro Fanfani. Bologna: Romagnoli.

Chiose anonime alla prima cantica della Divina Commedia di un contemporaneo del poeta. 1865. Edited by Francesco Selmi. Turin: Stamperia realeo.

Fallani, Giovanni. 1993. *Dante Alighieri: Tutte le opere.* Commentaries by Giovanni Fallani, N. Maggi, and S. Zennaro. Rome: Newton.

Giovanni di Serravalle. 1891. *Translatio et comentum cum texto italico totius libri Dantis Aldigherii Fratris Iohannis de Serravalle.* Edited by Marcellino da Civezza and Teofilo Domenichelli. Prato: Giachetti.

Gmelin, Hermann. 1954. *Die göttliche Komödie: Kommentar.* 3 vols. Stuttgart: Klett.

Grandgent, C. H., ed. 1933. *La Divina Commedia di Dante Alighieri.* Rev. ed. Boston: Heath.

Guido da Pisa. 1974. *Expositiones et glose super Comediam Dantis facte per Fratrem: Guidonem Pisanum.* Edited by Vincenzo Cioffari. Albany: State University of New York Press.

Lana, Jacopo della. 1866. *Comedia di Dante degli Allagherii col commento di Jacopo della Lana bolognese.* Edited by Luciano Scarabelli. Bologna: Tipografía rede.

L'Ottimo. 1827–1829. *L'Ottimo Commento della Divina Commedia.* Edited by Alessandro Torri. Pisa: Capurro.

Mattalia, Daniele, ed. 1960. *La Divina Commedia.* 3 vols. Milan: Rizzoli.

Mazzoni, Francesco. 1967. *Saggio di un nuovo commento alla Divina Commedia, canti I–III.* Florence: Sansoni.

————, ed. 1972. *La Divina Commedia. Inferno. Con i commenti di Tommaso Casini-Silvio Adrasto Barbi e di Attilio Momigliano. Introduzione e aggiornamento bibliografico-critico di Francesco Mazzoni.* Florence: Sansoni.

Pézard, André, ed. 1979. *Oeuvres complètes.* 4th ed. Paris: La Pléiade.

Sapegno, Natalino, ed. 1957. *La Divina Commedia.* Milan: Ricciardi.

Scartazzini, L., and G. Vandelli, eds. 1968. *La Divina Commedia.* 20th ed. Milan: Hoepli.

Singleton, Charles S., trans. 1970. *The Divine Comedy.* 3 vols. Bollingen Series 80. Princeton, N.J.: Princeton University Press.

Lecturae Dantis

Lectura Dantis Americana: Inferno. 1989– . Philadelphia: University of Pennsylvania Press.

Lectura Dantis Californiana: Inferno. In preparation.

Lectura Dantis neapolitana: Inferno. 1986. Edited by Pompeo Giannantonio. Naples: Loffredo.

Lectura Dantis scaligera: Inferno. 1967. Florence: Le Monnier.

Lectura Dantis Virginiana: Dante's Divine Comedy. Introductory Readings: Inferno. 1990. Charlottesville: University of Virginia Printing Office.

Letture classensi. 1966– . Ravenna: Longo.

Letture dantesche: Inferno. 1955. Edited by Giovanni Getto. Florence: Sansoni.

Nuove letture dantesche: Inferno. 1966–1968. Florence: Le Monnier. [Sponsored by the Casa di Dante, Rome.]

Primary Texts

Alain of Lille. 1955. *Anticlaudianus: Texte critique avec une introduction et des tables.* Edited by R. Bossuat. Textes philosophiques du moyen-âge. Paris: Vrin.

––––––. 1978. *"De Planctu Naturae."* Studi medievali 19:797–879.

––––––. 1980. *The Plaint of Nature.* Translated, with commentary, by James J. Sheridan. Toronto: Pontifical Institute of Medieval Studies.

Albertus Magnus. 1890–1899. *Opera omnia.* Edited by Auguste Borgnet. 38 vols. Paris: Vivès.

Augustine of Hippo. 1948. *S. Aurelii Augustini Confessionum libri XIII.* Edited by Iosephus Capello. Turin: Marietti.

––––––. 1960. *Confessions.* Translated by John K. Ryan. Garden City, N.Y.: Doubleday, Image Books.

––––––. 1963. *The City of God.* Abridged and translated by J. W. C. Wand. Oxford: Oxford University Press.

––––––. 1981. *De civitate Dei libri XXII.* Edited by Bernard Dombart and Alfons Kalb. 5th ed. 2 vols. Stuttgart: Teubner.

Bastin, Julia. 1929–1982. *Recueil général des Isopets.* 3 vols. Paris: Champion.

Bertran de Born. 1986. *The Poems of the Troubadour Bertran de Born.* Edited by William D. Paden, Jr., Patricia H. Stäblein, and Tilde Sankovich. Berkeley: University of California Press.

Biblia Sacra iuxta Vulgatam clementinam. 1965. Edited by Alberto Colunga and Lorenza Turrado. 4th ed. Madrid: Biblioteca de los autores cristianos.

Boccaccio, Giovanni. 1974. *Trattatello in laude di Dante.* Edited by Pier Giorgio Ricci. In vol. 3 of *Tutte le opere di Giovanni Boccaccio,* edited by Vittore Branca, 423–538, 848–911. Milan: Mondadori.

––––––. 1976. *Decameron.* Edited by Vittore Branca. In vol. 4 of *Tutte le opere di Giovanni Boccaccio,* edited by Vittore Branca. Milan: Mondadori.

Boethius. 1957. *Anicii Manlii Severini Boethii Philosophiae Consolatio.* Edited by Ludwig Bieler. Turnholt: Brepols.

Bonaventura of Bagnoregio. 1953. *The Mind's Road to God.* Translated by George S. Boas. New York: Liberal Arts Press.

Bruni, Leonardo. 1904. "La vita di Dante." In *Le vite di Dante, Petrarca, e Boccaccio scritte fino al secolo decimosesto,* edited by Angelo Solerti. Milan: Vallardi.

Compagni, Dino. 1993. *Cronica delle cose occorrenti ne' tempi suoi.* Edited by Gabriella Mezzanotte. Milan: Mondadori.

Contini, Gianfranco, ed. 1960. *Poeti del duecento.* 2 vols. Milan: Ricciardi.

Durand, Guillaume. 1859. *Rationale divinorum officiorum.* Naples: Dura.

Elliott, J. K. 1993. *The Apocryphal New Testament: A Collection of Apocryphal Christian Literature in an English Translation.* Oxford: Clarendon Press.

Guillaume de Lorris and Jean de Meun. 1970. *Le Roman de la rose.* Edited by Félix Lecoy. 3 vols. Paris: Champion.

Hill, R. T., and Thomas G. Bergin. 1973. *Anthology of the Provençal Troubadours.* Revised by Thomas G. Bergin. 2nd ed. 2 vols. New Haven, Conn.: Yale University Press.

The Holy Bible, translated from the Latin Vulgate [Douay version]. 1989. Rockford, Ill.: Tan.

John of Salisbury. 1909. *Policraticus.* Edited by C. C. J. Webb. 2 vols. Oxford: Clarendon Press.

Johnson, Charles. 1956. *The De moneta of Nicholas Oresme and the English Mint Documents.* London: Nelson.

Justinian. 1877. *Corpus iuris civilis.* Vol. 1, *Institutiones et Digestum.* Edited by Paul Krueger and Theodor Mommsen. Berlin: Weidmann.

———. 1987. *Institutes.* Translated, with an introduction, by Peter Birks and Grant McLeod. Ithaca, N.Y.: Cornell University Press.

Kim, H. C. 1973. *The Gospel of Nicodemus: Gesta Salvatoris. Edited from the Codex Einsiedlensis, Einsiedlen Stiftsbibliothek, MS 326.* Toronto: Pontifical Institute of Medieval Studies.

Latini, Brunetto. 1948. *Li livres dou Tresor.* Edited by Francis J. Carmody. University of California Studies in Modern Philology, vol. 22. Berkeley: University of California Press.

———. 1960. *Il tesoretto.* In vol. 2 of *Poeti del duecento,* edited by Gianfranco Contini. Milan: Ricciardi.

Livy. [1914] 1964. *Titi Livi Ab urbe condita.* Edited by Robert Seymour Conway and Charles Flamstead Walters. Vol. 1, bks. 1–5. Oxford: Clarendon Press.

Lucan. 1926. *M. Annaei Lucani Belli civilis libri X.* Edited by A. E. Housman. Cambridge, Mass.: Harvard University Press.

Macrobius. 1970. *Commentarii in Somnium Scipionis.* Edited by I. Willis. Vol. 2 of *Opera.* Leipzig: Teubner.

Marie de France. [1884] 1974. *Die Fabeln.* Edited by Karl Warnke. Geneva: Slatkine.

Martianus Capella. 1983. *Martianus Capella.* Edited by James Willis. Leipzig: Teubner.

McKenzie, Kenneth, and William A. Oldfather. 1921. *Ysopet, Avionnet: The Latin and French Texts.* Urbana: University of Illinois Press.

Micha, Alexandre, ed. 1978–1983. *Lancelot: Roman en prose du XIIIᵉ siècle.* 9 vols. Textes littéraires français. Geneva: Droz.

Ovid. [1961] 1992. *P. Ovidi Nasonis Amores, Medicamina faciei femineae, Ars amatoria, Remedia amoris.* Edited by E. J. Kenney. Oxford: Clarendon Press.

———. 1991. *Metamorphoses.* Edited by William S. Anderson. Stuttgart: Teubner.

Paton, Lucy Allen, trans. 1929. *Sir Lancelot of the Lake: A French Prose Romance of the Thirteenth Century. Translated from MS. in the Bibliothèque Nationale (Fonds français, 344).* New York: Harcourt, Brace.

Paulus Orosius. 1964. *The Seven Books Against the Pagans.* Translated by Roy J. Deferrari. Washington, D.C.: Catholic University of America Press.

Plato. 1937. *Plato's Cosmology: The "Timaeus" of Plato.* Translated, with a running commentary, by F. M. Cornford. London: Routledge & Kegan Paul.

———. 1961. *The Collected Dialogues, Including the Letters.* Edited by Edith Hamilton and Huntington Cairns. Bollingen Series 71. Princeton, N.J.: Princeton University Press.

Pseudo-Dionysius. 1987. *Pseudo-Dionysius: The Complete Works.* Translated by Colm Luibheid. Foreword, notes, and translation collaboration by Paul Rorem. New York: Paulist Press.

La Queste del saint Graal. Roman du XIIIᵉ siècle. 1949. Edited by Albert Pauphilet. Les Classiques français du moyen-âge. Paris: Champion.

Sacrobosco, Giovanni. 1949. *The Sphere of Sacrobosco and Its Commentators.* Edited by Lynn Thorndike. Chicago: University of Chicago Press.

Seneca. 1965. *L. Annaei Senecae Ad Lucilium epistulae morales.* Edited by L. D. Reynolds. 2 vols. Oxford: Clarendon Press.

————. [1986] 1991. *L. Annaei Senecae Tragoediae. Incertorum auctorum Hercules [Oetaeus], Octavia.* Edited by Otto Zwierlein. Oxford: Clarendon Press.

Servius. 1887–1923. *Servii grammatici qui feruntur in Vergilii carmina commentarii.* Edited by G. Thilo and H. Hagen. 3 vols. Leipzig: Teubner.

The Song of Roland. 1978. Translated by Frederick Goldin. New York: Norton.

Statius. [1906] 1965. *P. Papini Stati Thebais et Achilleis.* Edited by H. W. Garrod. Oxford: Clarendon Press.

Thomas Aquinas. 1872–1884. *Opera omnia.* Edited by S. E. Fretté. 34 vols. Paris: Vivès.

————. 1980. *Opera omnia.* Edited by Roberto Busa, S.J. 7 vols. Stuttgart: Frommann, Holzboog.

Vergil. [1900] 1955. *P. Vergili Maronis Opera.* Edited by F. A. Hirtzel. Oxford: Clarendon Press.

Villani, Giovanni. 1906. *Chronicle.* Translated by Rose E. Selfe. London: Constable.

————. 1990. *Nuova Cronica.* Vol. 1. Edited by Giuseppe Porta. Parma: Guanda.

William of Newburgh. [1856] 1964. *Historia rerum anglicarum.* Edited by Hans Claude Hamilton.Vaduz: Kraus Reprint.

Modern Works

Abrams, Richard. 1986. "Against the *Contrapasso*: Dante's Heretics, Schismatics, and Others." *Italian Quarterly* 27:5–19.

Ahern, John. 1982. "Dante's Slyness: The Unnamed Sin of the Eighth Bolgia." *Romanic Review* 73:275–91.

————. 1990. "'Nudi grammantes': The Grammar and Rhetoric of Deviation in *Inferno* XV." *Romanic Review* 82:466–82.

Alessio, Gian Carlo, and Claudia Villa. 1984. "Per *Inferno* I, 67–87." In *Vestigia: Studi in onore di Giuseppe Billanovich*, edited by Rino Avesani, Mirella Ferrari, Tino Foffano, Giuseppe Frasso, and Agostino Sottili, 1:1–21. Rome: Edizioni di storia e letteratura.

Al-Sabah, Rasha. 1977. "*Inferno* XXVIII: The Figure of Muhammad." *Yale Italian Studies* 1:147–61.

Armour, Peter. 1983. "Brunetto: The Paternal Paterine?" *Italian Studies* 38:1–38.

———. 1991. "The Love of Two Florentines: Brunetto Latini and Bondie Dietaiuti." *Lectura Dantis* 9:60–71.

Ascoli, Albert R. 1989. "The Vowels of Authority (Dante's *Convivio* IV.vi.3–4)." In *Discourses of Authority in Medieval and Renaissance Literature*, edited by Kevin Brownlee and Walter Stephens, 23–46, 255–62. Hanover, N.H.: University Press of New England.

———. 1990. "'Neminem ante nos': Historicity and Authority in the *De vulgari eloquentia*." *Annali d'italianistica* 8:186–231.

Auerbach, Erich. 1953. *Mimesis: The Representation of Reality in Western Literature*. Translated by Willard Trask. Princeton, N.J.: Princeton University Press.

Avalle, D'Arco Silvio. 1975a. *Analyse du récit de Paolo et Francesca (Dante Alighieri, "Enfer," V)*. Schriften und Vorträge des Petrarca-Instituts Köln, vol. 27. Krefeld: Scherpe Verlag.

———. 1975b. *Modelli semiologici nella Commedia di Dante*. Milan: Bompiani.

———. 1977. "'Nel terzo girone del settimo cerchio.'" In *Ai luoghi di delizia pieni*, 82–106. Milan: Ricciardi.

Bacchelli, Riccardo. 1954. "Da Dite a Malebolge: La tragedia delle porte chiuse e la farsa dei ponti rotti." *Giornale storico della letteratura italiana* 131:1–32.

Baker, David J. 1974. "The Winter Simile in *Inferno* 24." *Dante Studies* 92:77–90.

Barański, Zygmunt G. 1989. "Dante's Biblical Linguistics." *Lectura Dantis* 5:105–431.

Bárberi-Squarotti, Giorgio. 1971. "L'orazione del conte Ugolino." *Lettere italiane* 23:3–28.

Barchiesi, Marino. 1973. "Catarsi classica e 'medicina' dantesca." In *Letture classensi*, 4:11–124.

Barkan, Leonard. 1975. *Nature's Work of Art: The Human Body as Image of the World*. New Haven, Conn.: Yale University Press.

———. 1988. *The Gods Made Flesh: The Renaissance*. New Haven, Conn.: Yale University Press.

Barolini, Teodolinda. 1984. *Dante's Poets: Textuality and Truth in the "Comedy."* Princeton, N.J.: Princeton University Press.

———. 1990. "*Inferno* XX." In *Lectura Dantis Virginiana*, 262–74.

————. 1992. *The Undivine Comedy: Detheologizing Dante*. Princeton, N.J.: Princeton University Press.

Bates, Richard, and Thomas Rendall. 1989. "Dante's Ulysses and the Epistle of James." *Dante Studies* 107:33–44.

Beltrami, Pietro G. 1985. "Metrica e sintassi nel canto XXVIII dell'*Inferno*." *Giornale storico della letteratura italiana* 162:1–26.

Bernocchi, M. 1974–1976. *Le monete della repubblica fiorentina*. 4 vols. Florence: Olschki.

Biagioni, Luigi. 1957. "Frate Alberigo dei Manfredi aus Faenza in der Romagna." *Deutsches Dante Jahrbuch* 34–35:102–35.

Boitani, Piero. 1992. *L'ombra di Ulisse: Figure di un mito*. Bologna: Il Mulino.

Bosco, Umberto. 1967. *Dante vicino: Contributi e letture*. Rome: Sciascia.

Boyde, Patrick. 1971. *Dante's Style in His Lyric Poetry*. Cambridge: Cambridge University Press.

————. 1981. *Dante Philomythes and Philosopher: Man in the Cosmos*. Cambridge: Cambridge University Press.

Boyers, Hayden. 1926. "Cleavage in Bertran de Born and Dante." *Modern Philology* 24:1–3.

Brown, Norman O. 1959. *Life Against Death*. Middletown, Conn.: Wesleyan University Press.

Brownlee, Kevin. 1984. "Phaëthon's Fall and Dante's Ascent." *Dante Studies* 102:135–44.

Caccia, Ettore. 1967. "Canto XX." In *Lectura Dantis Scaligera: Inferno*, 673–720.

Cambon, Glauco. 1963. "Examples of Movement in the *Divine Comedy*: An Experiment in Reading." *Italica* 40:108–31.

Camille, Michael. 1989. *The Gothic Idol: Ideology and Image-Making in Medieval Art*. Cambridge: Cambridge University Press.

Camporesi, Piero. 1985. *La casa dell'eternità*. 2nd ed. Milan: Garzanti.

Capitani, Ovidio. 1980. "Riferimento storico e pubblicistica nel commento di Bruno Nardi alla *Monarchia* dantesca." In *Letture classensi*, 9–10:217–45.

Carroll, John S. [1904] 1971. *Exiles of Eternity: An Exposition of Dante's Inferno*. Port Washington, N.Y.: Kennikat.

Carruthers, Mary. 1990. *The Book of Memory: A Study of Memory in Medieval Culture*. Cambridge: Cambridge University Press.

Cassell, Anthony K. 1984. *Dante's Fearful Art of Justice*. Toronto: University of Toronto Press.

———. 1989. *Lectura Dantis Americana: Inferno I*. Philadelphia: University of Pennsylvania Press.

Clausen, Wendell. 1987. *Vergil's "Aeneid" and the Traditions of Hellenistic Poetry*. Berkeley: University of California Press.

Contini, Gianfranco. 1953. "Sull XXX dell'*Inferno*." *Paragone* 54:3–13. [Reprinted in Contini 1976, 159–70.]

———. 1965. "Filologia ed esegesi dantesca." *Rendiconti dell'Accademia nazionale dei Lincei* 362. 7.1:18–37. [Reprinted in Contini 1976, 113–42.]

———. 1970. *Varianti e altra linguistica: Una raccolta di saggi*. Turin: Einaudi.

———. 1976. *Un'idea di Dante: Saggi danteschi*. Turin: Einaudi.

Corti, Maria. 1989. "On the Metaphors of Sailing, Flight, and Tongues of Fire in the Episode of Ulysses (*Inferno* 26)." *Stanford Italian Review* 9:33–48.

Courcelle, Pierre. 1944. "Quelques symboles funéraires du néoplatonisme latin: Le vol de Dédale—Ulysse et les Sirènes." *Revue des études anciennes* 46:65–93.

———. 1955a. "Interprétations néo-platonisantes du livre *VI* de l'*Enéide*." In *Entretiens sur l'Antiquité classique: Recherches sur la tradition platonicienne*, 3:95–136.

———. 1955b. "Les pères de l'église devant les enfers virgiliens." *Annales d'histoire doctrinale et littéraire du moyen-âge* 30:5–74.

———. 1965. "Tradition platonicienne et traditions chrétiennes du corps-prison (*Phédon* 62 b; *Cratyle* 400 c)." *Revue des études latines* 43:407–43.

———. 1967. *La Consolation de Philosophie dans la tradition littéraire: Antécédents et postérité de Boèce*. Paris: Etudes Augustiniennes.

Croce, Benedetto. 1921. *La poesia di Dante*. Bari: Laterza.

Curtius, Ernst Robert. 1953. *European Literature and the Latin Middle Ages*. Translated by Willard Trask. Bollingen Series 36. New York: Pantheon Books.

Damon, Phillip W. 1967a. "Dante's Ulysses and the Mythic Tradition." In *Medieval Secular Literature: Four Essays*, edited by W. Matthews, 25–45. Berkeley: University of California Press.

———. 1967b. "Geryon, Cacciaguida, and the Y of Pythagoras." *Dante Studies* 85:15–33.

Daniélou, Jean. 1964. *Primitive Christian Symbols*. Translated by Donald Attwater. Baltimore: Helicon.

Davis, Charles T. 1957. *Dante and the Idea of Rome*. Oxford: Clarendon Press.

———. 1967. "Brunetto Latini and Dante." *Studi medievali* 8:421–50.

———. 1976. "Veltro." In *Enciclopedia dantesca*, 5:908–12.

———. 1984. *Dante's Italy and Other Essays*. The Middle Ages. Philadelphia: University of Pennsylvania Press.

De Robertis, Domenico. 1981. "In viaggio coi demòni." *Studi danteschi* 53:1–29.

De Sanctis, Francesco. 1869. "Ugolino." In *Nuovi saggi critici*, 665–83. Naples: Morano.

———. 1957. *De Sanctis on Dante: Essays*. Translated and edited by Joseph Rossi and Alfred Galpin. Madison: University of Wisconsin Press.

Derby Chapin, D. L. 1971. "Io and the Negative Apotheosis of Vanni Fucci." *Dante Studies* 89:19–31.

Doob, Penelope Reed. 1990. *The Idea of the Labyrinth from Classical Antiquity Through the Middle Ages*. Ithaca, N.Y.: Cornell University Press.

D'Ovidio, Francesco. 1901. *Studi sulla Divina Commedia*. Milan: Sandron.

Dronke, Peter. 1986. *Dante and Medieval Latin Traditions*. Cambridge: Cambridge University Press.

Durling, Robert M. 1975. "'Io son venuto': Seneca, Plato, and the Microcosm." *Dante Studies* 93:95–129.

———. 1981a. "Deceit and Digestion in the Belly of Hell." In *Allegory and Representation: Selected Papers from the English Institute, 1979–80*, edited by Stephen J. Greenblatt, 61–93. Baltimore: Johns Hopkins University Press.

———. 1981b. "Farinata and the Body of Christ." *Stanford Italian Review* 2:1–34.

Durling, Robert M., and Ronald L. Martinez. 1990. *Time and the Crystal: Studies in Dante's "Rime petrose."* Berkeley: University of California Press.

Eco, Umberto. 1980. *Il nome della rosa*. Milan: Bompiani.

———. 1983. *The Name of the Rose*. Translated by William Weaver. San Diego: Harcourt Brace Jovanovich.

Economou, George D. 1976. "The Pastoral Simile of *Inferno* XXIV and the Unquiet Heart of the Christian Pilgrim." *Speculum* 51:637–46.

Erickson, Carolly. 1976. *The Medieval Vision: Essays in History and Perception.* New York: Oxford University Press.

Fallani, Giovanni. 1976. *Dante e la cultura figurativa medievale.* 2nd ed. Bergamo: Minerva Italica.

Favati, Guido. 1965. "Il 'jeu de Dante' (Interpretazione del canto xxi dell'*Inferno*." *Cultura neolatina* 25:34–52.

Fengler, Christie K., and William A. Stephany. 1981. "The Capuan Gate and Pier della Vigna." *Dante Studies* 99:221–42.

Ferrante, Joan. 1986. "Good Thieves and Bad Thieves: A Reading of *Inferno* XXIV." *Dante Studies* 104:83–98.

Ferrucci, Franco. 1971. "*Comedía*." *Yearbook of Italian Studies* 1:29–52.

Fido, Franco. 1986. "Writing Like God—or Better?: Symmetries in Dante's 26th and 27th Cantos." *Italica* 63:250–64.

Foster, Kenelm. 1957. *God's Tree: Essays on Dante and Other Matters.* Oxford: Blackfriars.

———. 1970. "Cristo." In *Enciclopedia Dantesca*, 2:262–69.

———. 1980. *The Two Dantes and Other Studies.* Berkeley: University of California Press.

Freccero, John. 1959. "Dante's Firm Foot and the Journey Without a Guide." *Harvard Theological Review* 52:245–81.

———. 1960. "Dante and the Neutral Angels." *Romanic Review* 51:3–14.

———. 1961a. "Dante's Pilgrim in a Gyre." *PMLA* 76:169–71.

———. 1961b. "Satan's Fall and the *Quaestio de Aqua et Terra*." *Italica* 38:99–115.

———. 1962. "Dante's 'per sé' Angels." *Studi danteschi* 39:3–38.

———. 1965a. "Infernal Inversion and Christian Conversion (*Inferno* XXXIV)." *Italica* 42:35–41.

———. 1965b. "The Sign of Satan." *Modern Language Notes* 80:11–26.

———. 1966a. "Dante's Prologue Scene." *Dante Studies* 86:1–25.

———. 1966b. "The River of Death: *Inferno* II, 108." In *The World of Dante: Six Studies in Language and Thought*, edited by S. Bernard Chandler and J. A. Molinaro, 25–42. Toronto: University of Toronto Press.

———. 1972. "Medusa: The Letter and the Spirit." *Yearbook of Italian Studies* 2:7–10.

———. 1977. "Bestial Sign and Bread of Angels (*Inferno* 32–33)." *Yale Italian Studies* 1:53–66.

———. 1983. "The Significance of *Terza Rima*." In *Dante, Petrarch, Boccaccio: Studies in the Italian Trecento in Honor of Charles S. Singleton*, edited by Aldo S. Bernardo and Anthony L. Pellegrini, 3–17. Binghamton, N.Y.: Medieval and Renaissance Texts and Studies.

———. 1984. "Infernal Irony: The Gates of Hell." *Modern Language Notes* 99:769–86.

———. 1986. *Dante: The Poetics of Conversion*. Edited by Rachel Jacoff. Cambridge, Mass.: Harvard University Press.

———. 1988. "Ironia e mimesi: Il disdegno di Guido." In *Dante e la Bibbia: Atti del Convegno Internazionale promosso da 'Bibbia.' Firenze, 26–27–28 settembre 1986*, edited by Giovanni Barblan, 41–54. Florence: Olschki.

———. 1991. "The Eternal Image of the Father." In *The Poetry of Allusion: Virgil and Ovid in Dante's "Comedy,"* edited by Rachel Jacoff and Jeffrey Schnapp, 62–76. Stanford: Stanford University Press.

French, Reginald. 1964. "Simony and Pentecost." *Annual Report of the Dante Society of America* 82:67–94.

Friedman, John B. 1972. "Antichrist and the Iconography of Dante's Geryon." *Journal of the Warburg and Courtault Institutes* 35:108–22.

Fubini, Mario. 1966. *Il peccato di Ulisse e altri scritti danteschi*. Milan: Ricciardi.

———. 1976. "Ulisse." In *Enciclopedia Dantesca*, 5:803–9.

Gardiner, Eileen. 1989. *Visions of Heaven and Hell Before Dante*. New York: Italica.

Gilbert, Allan H. 1945. "Can Dante's *Inferno* Be Exactly Charted?" *PMLA* 60:287–306.

Gregory, Tullio. 1992. *Mundana sapientia: Forme di conoscenza nella cultura medievale*. Rome: Edizioni di storia e letteratura.

Guerri, Domenico. 1904. "'Papé Satàn, Papé Satàn aleppe' (*Inferno* VII, 1)." *Giornale dantesco* 12:138–42.

———. 1909. "Il nome di Dio nella lingua di Adamo secondo il XXVI del *Paradiso* e il verso di Nembrotto nel XXXI dell'*Inferno*." *Giornale storico della letteratura italiana* 54:65–76.

Guzzardo, John. 1987. *Dante: Numerological Studies*. New York: Peter Lang.

Hardt, Manfred. 1973. *Die Zahl in der Divina Commedia*. Frankfurt am Main: Athenäum Verlag.

Hatcher, Anna Granville, and Mark Musa. 1964. "Lucifer's Legs." *PMLA* 79:191–99.

———. 1970. "Aristotle's 'matta bestialità' in Dante's *Inferno*." *Italica* 47:366–72.

Hawkins, Peter S. 1980. "Virtue and Virtuosity: Poetic Self-Reference in the *Commedia*." *Dante Studies* 98:1–18.

Heilbronn, Denise. 1983. "Master Adam and the Fat-Bellied Lute (*Inf.* XXX)." *Dante Studies* 101:51–65.

Herzman, Ronald B., and William B. Stephany. 1978. "'O miseri seguaci': Sacramental Inversion in *Inferno* XIX." *Dante Studies* 96:39–65.

Higgins, David. 1973. "Cicero, Aquinas and St. Matthew in *Inferno* XIII." *Dante Studies* 93:61–94.

Hollander, Robert. 1969. *Allegory in Dante's "Commedia."* Princeton, N.J.: Princeton University Press.

———. 1973–1975. "The Invocations of the 'Commedia.'" *Yearbook of Italian Studies* 2:235–40.

———. 1980. *Studies in Dante.* Ravenna: Longo.

———. 1982. "Dante's 'Book of the Dead': A Note on *Inferno* XXIX 57." *Studi danteschi* 54:31–51.

———. 1983. *Il Virgilio dantesco: Tragedia nella Commedia.* Florence: Olschki.

———. 1984a. "Dante's Georgic (*Inf.* XXIV, 1–21)." *Dante Studies* 102:111–21.

———. 1984b. "*Inferno* XXXIII, 37–74: Ugolino's Importunity." *Speculum* 59:549–55.

———. 1984c. "Virgil and Dante as Mind-Readers (*Inferno* XXI and XXIII)." *Medioevo romanzo* 8:85–100.

———. 1985. "Ugolino's Supposed Cannibalism." *Quaderni d'italianistica* 6:64–81.

Holmes, George. 1986. *Florence, Rome, and the Origins of the Renaissance.* Oxford: Clarendon Press.

Hughes, Robert. 1968. *Heaven and Hell in Western Art.* New York: Stein and Day.

Jackson, Margret. 1971. "'Forse tu non pensavi ch'io loïco fossi': Traces of Formal Logic in the *Divina Commedia*." *Romance Philology* 24:563–71.

Jacoff, Rachel. 1988. "Transgression and Transcendence: Figures of Female Desire in Dante's *Commedia*." *Romanic Review* 79:129–42.

————, ed. 1993. *The Cambridge Companion to Dante*. Cambridge: Cambridge University Press.

Jacoff, Rachel, and Jeffrey Schnapp, eds. 1991. *The Poetry of Allusion: Virgil and Ovid in Dante's "Comedy."* Stanford: Stanford University Press.

Jacoff, Rachel, and William A. Stephany. 1989. *Lectura Dantis Americana: Inferno II*. Philadelphia: University of Pennsylvania Press.

Jacomuzzi, Angelo. 1972. *Il palinsesto della rettorica e altri studi danteschi*. Florence: Olschki.

Kantorowicz, Ernst H. 1957. *The King's Two Bodies: A Study in Mediaeval Political Theology*. Princeton, N.J.: Princeton University Press.

Kaulbach, Ernest N., S.S. 1968. "*Inferno* XIX, 45: The 'Zanca' of Temporal Power." *Dante Studies* 86:126–35.

Kay, Richard. 1978a. "Dante's Double Damnation of Manto." *Res Publica Litterarum* 1:113–28.

————. 1978b. *Dante's Swift and Strong: Essays in "Inferno" XV*. Lawrence: Regents Press of Kansas.

————. 1980. "Two Pairs of Tricks: Ulysses and Guido in Dante's *Inferno* XXVI–XXVII." *Quaderni d'italianistica* 1:107–24.

————. 1985. "The Spare Ribs of Dante's Michael Scot." *Dante Studies* 103:1–14.

————. 1988. "Astrology and Astronomy." In *The "Divine Comedy" and the Encyclopedia of Arts and Sciences*, edited by Giuseppe Di Scipio and Aldo Scaglione, 147–62. Philadelphia: Benjamin Johns.

Kirkham, Victoria. 1992. "Eleven Is for Evil: Measured Trespass in Dante's *Commedia*." *Allegorica*: 27–50.

Kirkpatrick, Robin. 1987. *Dante's "Inferno": Difficulty and Dead Poetry*. Cambridge: Cambridge University Press.

Klein, Robert. 1981. *Form and Meaning: Essays on the Renaissance and Modern Art*. Translated by Madeline Jay and Leon Wieseltier. Princeton, N.J.: Princeton University Press.

Kleiner, John. 1989. "Mismapping the Underworld." *Dante Studies* 107:1–31.

Kleinhenz, Christopher. 1973–1974. "Dante's Towering Giants." *Romance Philology* 27:269–85.

————. 1982. "Iconographic Parody in *Inferno* 21." *Res Publica Litterarum* 5:125–37.

————. 1988. "*Inferno* 8: The Passage Across the Styx." In *Lectura Dantis*, 3:23–40.

Knox, Bernard M. W. 1950. "The Serpent and the Flame: The Imagery of the Second Book of the *Aeneid*." *American Journal of Philology* 71:379–400.

Lansing, Richard H. 1974. "Submerged Meaning in Dante's Similes (*Inferno* XXVII)." *Dante Studies* 94:61–69.

————. 1981. "Dante's Concept of Violence and the Chain of Being." *Dante Studies* 99:67–87.

Larner, John. 1980. *Italy in the Age of Dante and Petrarch, 1216–1380*. Vol. 2 of *Longman History of Italy*. London: Longman.

Le Goff, Jacques. 1986. *Your Money or Your Life*. Translated by Patricia Ranum. New York: Zone Books.

Lemay, Richard. 1963. "Le Nemrod de l'*Enfer* de Dante et le *Liber Nemroth*." *Studi danteschi* 40:57–128.

Leo, Ulrich. 1951. "The Unfinished *Convivio* and Dante's Rereading of the *Aeneid*." *Mediaeval Studies* 13:41–64.

————. 1962. "Zum 'rifacimento' der 'Vita nuova.'" *Romanische Forschungen* 74:281–317.

Livi, Giovanni. 1918. *Dante, suoi primi cultori, sua gente e Bologna*. Bologna: Licinio Cappelli.

Looney, Dennis. 1990. "*Inferno* VII." In *Lectura Dantis Virginiana*, 82–92.

Lotman, Jurij. 1980. "Il viaggio di Ulisse nella *Divina Commedia* di Dante." In *Testo e contesto: Semiotica dell'arte e della cultura*, edited by Simonetta Salvestroni, 81–102. Bari: Laterza.

Lovejoy, Arthur O. 1936. *The Great Chain of Being: A Study of the History of an Idea*. The William James Lectures on Philosophy and Psychology, 2nd ser. Cambridge, Mass.: Harvard University Press.

Lucchesi, Valerio. 1987. "Epicurus and Democritus: The Ciceronian Foundations of Dante's Judgement." *Italian Studies* 42:1–19.

MacKinnon, Patricia L. [1988] 1989. *The Analogy of the Body Politic in Saint Augustine, Dante, Petrarch, and Ariosto*. [Ph.D. diss., University of California at Santa Cruz]. Ann Arbor: University Microfilms.

Martinez, Ronald L. 1995. "Troubadours and Italy." In *Handbook of Troubadours*, edited by F. R. P. Akehurst and Judith H. Davis, 279–94. Berkeley: University of California Press.

Masciandaro, Franco. 1970. *La problematica del tempo nella "Commedia."* Ravenna: Longo.

———. 1979. "Appunti sulla corda di Gerione e la cintura-serpente della dialettica." *Revue des études italiennes* 25:259–72.

Mazzoni, Francesco. 1953. Review of *Il canto XI dell'Inferno*, by Bruno Nardi. *Studi danteschi* 31:209–14.

———. 1986. "Il canto XI dell'Inferno." In *Lectura Dantis neapolitana: Inferno*, 171–200.

Mazzotta, Giuseppe. 1979. *Dante, Poet of the Desert: History and Allegory in the "Divine Comedy."* Princeton, N.J.: Princeton University Press.

———. 1993. *Dante's Vision and the Circle of Knowledge*. Princeton, N.J.: Princeton University Press.

McGinn, Bernard. 1972. *The Golden Chain: A Study in the Theological Anthropology of Isaac of Stella*. Washington, D.C.: Cistercian Publications.

Mercuri, Roberto. 1984. *Semantica di Gerione: Il motivo del viaggio nella "Commedia" di Dante*. Rome: Bulzoni.

Miller, Clarence H. 1984. "Hercules and His Labors as Allegories of Christ and His Victory over Sin in Dante's *Inferno*." *Quaderni d'italianistica* 5:1–17.

Mitchell, Charles. 1951. "The Lateran Frescoes of Boniface VIII." *Journal of the Warburg and Courtauld Institutes* 14:1–6.

Moore, Edward. [1887] 1963. *Studies in Dante*. 4 vols. Oxford: Clarendon Press.

Morgan, Alison. 1990. *Dante and the Medieval Other World*. Vol. 8 of *Cambridge Studies in Medieval Literature*. Cambridge: Cambridge University Press.

Morpurgo, Giacomo. 1926. *Dalle sue lettere e dai suoi libretti di guerra: Dai primi studi*. Florence: Le Monnier.

Musa, Mark. 1964. "Aesthetic Structure in the *Inferno*, Canto XIX." In *Essays on Dante*, edited by Mark Musa, 145–71. Bloomington: Indiana University Press.

———. 1974. *Advent at the Gates: Dante's "Comedy."* Bloomington: Indiana University Press.

Musseter, Sally. 1978. "*Inferno* xxx: Dante's Counterfeit Adam." *Traditio* 34:427–35.

Najemy, John. 1982. *Corporatism and Consensus in Florentine Electoral Politics*. Chapel Hill: University of North Carolina Press.

Nardi, Bruno. 1944. *Nel mondo di Dante*. Rome: Istituto Grafico Tiberino.

———. 1949. *Dante e la cultura medievale: Nuovi saggi di filosofia dantesca*. 2nd ed. Bari: Laterza.

————. 1955. "Il canto XI dell'*Inferno*." In *Letture dantesche: Inferno*, 191–207.

————. 1966. *Saggi e note di critica dantesca*. Milan: Ricciardi.

————. 1967. *Saggi di filosofia dantesca*. 2nd ed. Florence: La Nuova Italia.

Nassar, Eugene P. 1993. "The Iconography of Hell: From the Baptistery Mosaic to the Michelangelo Fresco." *Dante Studies* 111:53–105.

Noakes, Susan. 1968. "Dino Compagni and the Vow in San Giovanni: *Inferno* XIX, 16–21." *Dante Studies* 86:41–63.

————. 1988. *Timely Reading: Between Exegesis and Interpretation*. Ithaca, N.Y.: Cornell University Press.

Noonan, John T. 1957. *The Scholastic Analysis of Usury*. Cambridge, Mass.: Harvard University Press.

Olschki, Leonardo. 1940. "Dante and Petrus de Vinea." *Romanic Review* 31:105–11.

Orioli, Ranieri. 1988. *Venit perfidus heresiarcha: Il movimento apostolico-dolciniano del 1260 al 1307*. Rome: Istituto storico per il Medioevo.

Owen, D. D. R. 1970. *The Vision of Hell: Infernal Journeys in Medieval French Literature*. Edinburgh: Scottish Academic Press.

Padoan, Giorgio. 1959a. "I canto degli Epicurei." *Convivium* 27:12–39.

————. 1959b. "Il mito di Teseo e il cristianesimo di Stazio." *Lettere italiane* 11:432–57.

————. 1960. "Ulisse 'fandi fictor' e le vie della Sapienza." *Studi danteschi* 37:21–61.

————. 1961. "'Colui che fece per viltà il gran rifiuto.'" *Studi danteschi* 38:75–128.

————. 1970. "Il Limbo dantesco." In *Letture classensi*, 3:187–217.

————. 1977. *Il pio Enea, l'empio Ulisse*. Ravenna: Longo.

————. 1993. *Il lungo cammino del "Poema sacro."* *Studi danteschi*. Florence: Olschki.

Pagliaro, Antonino. [1953] 1967. *Ulisse: Ricerche semantiche sulla Divina Commedia*. Messina: D'Anna.

Palgen, Rudolf. 1969. *Dantes Luzifer*. Munich: Max Huebner Verlag.

Panofsky, Erwin. 1957. *Gothic Architecture and Scholasticism*. New York: Meridian Books.

Paratore, E. 1968. *Tradizione e struttura in Dante*. Florence: Sansoni.

Parodi, E. G. 1908. "La critica della poesia classica del xx. canto dell'"Inferno."' *Atene e Roma* 11:193–95, 237–50.

———. 1911. Review of *Una pagina dantesca: Notizie inedite sil conte frate Guido da Montefeltro (c. 1222–1281)*. Estratto dall'*Archivum francescanum historicum*, fasc. II, anno II, 1910, 19 pp, by P. Girolamo Golubovich, O.F.M. *Bullettino della Società Dantesca Italiana* 18:262–74.

———. 1920. *Poesia e storia nella Divina Commedia: Studi critici*. Naples: Perrella.

———. 1955. "Il canto xx dell'Inferno." In *Letture dantesche: Inferno*, 377–91.

Patch, Howard R. 1950. *The Other World, According to Descriptions in Medieval Literature*. Cambridge, Mass.: Harvard University Press.

Pequigney, Joseph. 1991. "Sodomy in Dante's *Inferno* and *Purgatorio*." *Representations* 36:22–42.

Perrus, Claudine. 1989. "Le Jeu des diables (*Inferno*, xxi–xxii)." *Chroniques italiennes* 17:11–34.

Pertile, Lino. 1991. "*Canto—Cantica—Comedia* e l'Epistola a Cangrande." In *Lectura Dantis Virginiana*, 9:105–23.

Petrocchi, Giorgio. 1969. *Itinerari danteschi*. Bari: Adriatica.

———. 1984. *Vita di Dante*. Bari: Laterza.

Pézard, André. 1948. "Du *Policraticus* à la *Divine Comédie*." *Romania* 70:163–91.

———. 1950. *Dante sous la pluie de feu*. Paris: Vrin.

———. 1958. "Le Chant des géants." *Centre Universitaire Mediterranée: Annales* 13:185–210.

Picone, Michelangelo. 1979. "I trovatori di Dante: Bertran de Born." *Studi e problemi di critica testuale* 19:71–94.

Pirandello, Luigi. 1968. "La commedia dei diavoli e la tragedia di Dante." In *Opere*. Vol. 6, *Saggi, poesie, scritti vari*, edited by M. Lo Vecchio, 343–61. Milan: Mondadori.

Psaki, Regina. 1990. "*Inferno XXIII*." In *Lectura Dantis Virginiana*, 297–306.

Rabuse, Georg. 1958. *Der kosmologische Aufbau der Jenseitsreiche Dantes: Ein Schlüssel zur Göttlichen Komödie*. Graz: Hermann Böhlaus Nachf.

———. 1961. "Dantes Antäus-Episode, der Höllengrund und das Somnium Scipionis." *Archiv für Kulturgeschichte* 43:18–51. [Reprinted in Rabuse 1976a, 76–112.]

———. 1966. "I corpi celesti, centri di ordinamento dell'immaginazione poetica di Dante." *Annali dell'Instituto Universitario Orientale di Napoli*, Sezione romanza, 8:215–44. [Reprinted in Rabuse 1976a, 272–87.]

———. 1972. *Die goldene Leiter in Dantes Saturnhimmel.* Schriften und Vorträge des Petrarka-Instituts Köln, no. 25. Krefeld: Scherpe.

———. 1973. "Les Paysages astrologiques de la Divine Comédie." In *Gesammelte Aufsätze zu Dante*, edited by Erika Kanduth, Fritz Peter Kirsch, and Siegfried Löwe, 331–47. Stuttgart: Wilhelm Braumüller.

———. 1976a. *Gesammelte Aufsätze zu Dante.* Edited by Erika Kanduth, Fritz Peter Kirsch, and Siegfried Löwe. Stuttgart: Wilhelm Braumüller.

———. 1976b. "Saturne et l'échelle de Jacob." *Annales d'histoire doctrinale et littéraire du moyen-âge* 45:7–31.

Ramat, Raffaello. 1976. *Il mito di Firenze e altri saggi danteschi.* Florence: D'Anna.

Reade, W. H. V. 1909. *The Moral System of Dante's "Inferno."* Oxford: Clarendon Press.

Roncaglia, Aurelio. 1971. "Lectura Dantis: Inferno XXI." *Yearbook of Italian Studies* 1:3–28.

———. 1981. "L'invenzione della sestina." *La metrica* 2:1–41.

Rorem, Paul. 1993. *Pseudo-Dionysius: A Commentary on the Texts and an Introduction to Their Influence.* New York: Oxford University Press.

Russo, Vittorio. 1967. *Sussidi di esegesi dantesca.* Naples: Liguori.

Ryan, Lawrence V. 1976. "*Stornei, Gru, Colombe*: The Bird Images in *Inferno* V." *Dante Studies* 94:25–45.

———. 1977. "Ulysses, Guido, and the Betrayal of Community." *Italica* 54:227–49.

Salvemini, Gaetano. 1901–1902. Review of *Le istituzioni giuridiche medievali nella "Divina Commedia,"* by Gino Arias. *Bullettino della Società Dantesca Italiana* 9:112–22.

Sansone, Mario. 1967. "Cavalcanti, Cavalcante de'." In *Enciclopedia dantesca*, 1:891.

———. 1970. "Farinata." In *Enciclopedia dantesca*, 2:804–9.

Sarolli, Gian Roberto. 1971. *Prolegomena alla "Divina Commedia."* Florence: Olschki.

Scott, John A. 1970. "The Rock of Peter and *Inferno* XIX." *Romance Philology* 27:462–79.

———. 1971. "*Inferno* XXVI: Dante's Ulysses." *Lettere italiane* 23:145–86.

————. 1977. *Dante magnanimo: Studi sulla "Commedia."* Florence: Olschki.

Segre, Cesare. 1986. "Il canto XV dell'*Inferno*." In *Lectura Dantis neapolitana: Inferno,* 259–68.

Shankland, Hugh. 1975. "Dante's 'Aliger.'" *Modern Language Review* 70:764–85.

————. 1977. "Dante's 'Aliger' and Ulysses." *Italian Studies* 32:21–40.

Shanzer, Danuta. 1989. "The Punishment of Bertran de Born." *Yearbook of Italian Studies* 8:95–97.

Shoaf, Richard A. 1975. "Dante's *colombi* and the Figuralism of Hope in the *Divine Comedy*." *Dante Studies* 93:27–59.

————. 1983. *Dante, Chaucer, and the Currency of the Word.* Norman: Oklahoma University Press.

————. 1988. "The Crisis of Convention in Cocytus: Allegory and History." In *Allegoresis: The Craft of Allegory in Medieval Civilization,* edited by J. Stephen Russell, 157–69. New York: Garland.

Silverstein, Theodore. 1937. "Did Dante Know the Vision of St. Paul?" *Harvard Studies and Notes in Philology and Literature* 19:231–47.

Simonelli, Maria P. 1993. *Lectura Dantis Americana: Inferno III.* Philadelphia: University of Pennsylvania Press.

Singleton, Charles S. 1954. *Dante's Commedia: Elements of Structure.* Cambridge, Mass.: Harvard University Press.

————. 1965. "The Vistas in Retrospect." In *Atti del Congresso internazionale di studi danteschi (20–27 aprile 1965),* 279–304. Florence: Sansoni.

————. 1966a. "Campi semantici dei canti xii dell'*Inferno* e xiii del *Purgatorio*." In *Miscellanea di studi danteschi,* edited by the Instituto di letteratura italiana, 11–22. Genoa: Bozzi.

————. 1966b. "'O Simon Mago.'" *Modern Language Notes* 80:92–99.

Sowell, Madison U., ed. 1991. *Dante and Ovid: Essays in Intertextuality.* Binghamton, N.Y.: Medieval and Renaissance Texts and Studies.

Spitzer, Leo. 1937. "Bemerkungen zu Dantes *Vita nuova*." *Publications de la Faculté de lettres de l'Université d'Istanbul,* II 1:162–208.

————. 1942. "Speech and Language in *Inferno* XIII." *Italica* 19:77–104.

————. 1943. "Two Dante Notes: I. An Autobiographical Incident in *Inferno* XIX. II. Libicocco." *Romanic Review* 34:248–62.

————. 1963. *Classical and Christian Ideas of World Harmony: Prolegomena to an Interpretation of the Word 'Stimmung.'* Edited by Anna G. Hatcher. Baltimore: Johns Hopkins University Press.

————. 1976. *Studi italiani.* Edited by Claudio Scarpati. Vol. 4 of *Letteratura e cultura dell'Italia unita.* Milan: Vita e Pensiero.

Stefanini, Ruggero. 1990. "Canto XXVI." In *Lectura Dantis Virginiana,* 332–50.

————. 1992. "Spunti di esegesi dantesca: Due contrappassi (*Inf.* VI e XIX) e due cruces (*Purg.* XXVII 81 e *Par.* XXXII 139)." In *Forma e parola: Studi in memoria di Fredi Chiappelli,* edited by Dennis J. Dutschke, Pier Massimo Forni, Filippo Grazzini, Benjamin R. Lawton, and Laura Sanguineti White, 45–65. Rome: Bulzoni.

Stephany, William A. 1982–1983. "Pier della Vigna's Self-Fulfilling Prophecy: The Eulogy of Frederick II and *Inferno* XIII." *Traditio* 38:193–212.

Sturm, Sara. 1972. "Structure and Meaning in *Inferno 26.*" *Dante Studies* 92:93–106.

Terlingen, Jan. 1965. "Dante e il mito dei Frisoni." *Revue des études italiennes* 11:422–38.

Thompson, David. 1972. "A Note on Fraudulent Counsel." *Dante Studies* 92:149–52.

————. 1974. *Dante's Epic Journeys.* Baltimore: Johns Hopkins University Press.

Toynbee, Paget. 1897. "Dante's Obligations to the *Magnae Derivationes* of Uguccione da Pisa." *Romania* 26:537–54.

————. 1965. *Dante Alighieri's Life and Works.* 4th ed. Edited by Charles S. Singleton. New York: Harper & Row.

Trovato, Mario. 1976. "Il contrapasso nell'ottava bolgia." *Dante Studies* 94:49–60.

Tucker, Dunstan J., O.S.B. 1960. "In exitu Israel de Aegypto: *The Divine Comedy* in the Light of the Easter Liturgy." *American Benedictine Review* 11:43–61.

Vance, Eugene. 1986. *Mervelous Signals: Poetics and Sign Theory in the Middle Ages.* Lincoln: University of Nebraska Press.

Van Dyke, Carolynn. 1985. *The Fiction of Truth: Structures of Meaning in Narrative and Dramatic Allegory.* Ithaca, N.Y.: Cornell University Press.

Varanini, Giorgio. 1989. "Dante e Lucca." In *Dante e le città dell'esilio: Atti del Congresso Internazionale di Studi, Ravenna (11–15 settembre 1987),* edited by Guido di Pino, 91–114. Ravenna: Longo.

Waley, Daniel. 1988. *The Italian City Republics.* 3rd ed. London: Longman.

Wilkins, Ernest Hatch. 1955–1956. "Dante's Celestial 'Scaleo': Stairway or Ladder?" *Romance Philology* 9:216–22.

————. 1959. "Cantos, Regions, and Transitions in the *Divine Comedy*." In *The Invention of the Sonnet and Other Studies in Italian Literature*, 103–10. Rome: Edizioni di Storia e Letteratura.

Yowell, Donna L. 1986. "Ugolino's 'bestial segno': The *De vulgari eloquentia* in *Inferno* XXXII-XXXIII." *Dante Studies* 104:121–43.

Zaleski, C. 1987. *Otherworld Journeys: Accounts of Near-Death Experience in Medieval and Modern Times*. New York: Oxford University Press.

Zampese, Christina. 1989. "'Pisa novella Tebe': Un indizio della conoscenza di Seneca tragico da parte di Dante." *Giornale storico della letteratura italiana* 166:1–21.

Ziolkowski, Jan. 1985. *Alain of Lille's Grammar of Sex: The Meaning of Grammar to a Twelfth-Century Intellectual*. Speculum Anniversary Monographs, vol. 10. Cambridge, Mass.: Medieval Academy of America.

INDEX OF ITALIAN, LATIN, AND OTHER
WORDS DISCUSSED IN THE NOTES

References are to notes, by canto and lines, or to Additional Notes (*A.N.*) by number.

INDEX OF PASSAGES
CITED IN THE NOTES

References are to notes, by canto and lines, or to Additional Notes *(A.N.)* by number.

INDEX OF PROPER NAMES
IN THE NOTES

References are to notes, by canto and lines, or to Additional Notes (A.N.) by number.

Aaron: 19.1 and passim
Abati, Bocca degli: 32.80–81 and
    passim; 33.115–17
Abbruzzi: 28.17
Abraham: 14.8–39; 30.62–63
Absalom: 28.137–38
Accorso, Francesco d': 15.110
Acheron (river): 2.108; 3.70–78, 77–78,
    91–93; 21.29–45
    moralized: A.N. 2
Achilles: 5.65–66; 12.71; 26.61–62;
    30.13–21; 31.4–6, 71
Achitophel: 28.137–38
Acquacheta (river): 16.94–102
Acre, Saint Jean d': 4.129; 27.87
Actaeon: 13.130
Acts of Peter: 19.1, 22–24
Adam: 1.30; 3.115; 4.52–63; 6.109–11;
    13.26; 14.8–39; 24.82; 25.116;
    30.64–75 and passim; 31.61;
    A.N. 3; A.N. 13
Adam of England: 30.61
Adam, Master: 30.1–27 and passim;
    32.63–64
Adimari (Florentine family): 8.61
Adonis: 30.37–41
Adrian V, pope: 19.101
Adriatic Sea: 5.93
Aeacus: 29.58–66
Aegina (island): 29.58–66
Aeneas: 1.73–74; 2.13, 14–15, 26–27,
    126; 3.13–15, 59–60, 91–93;
    4.115–17, 121, 124; 5.61–62,
    82–84; 7.22–25; 8.27, 65, 68–69;
    9.38–42, 132; 13.32; 14.61–66;

    15.46–48, 82; 26.58–60, 80;
    28.10; 33.4–6; A.N. 6
    parallel with Ulysses: 26.90–93,
    101–2, 142; A.N. 11
Aeolus: 30.1–12
Aeschylus: 4.88
Aeson: 18.83–96
Aesop, fables: 22.58; 23.4–33
    of bat: 34.49
    of frog and mouse: 23.4–6, 7–9
Aetna, Mount: 14.52–60; 31.108, 124
Africa, North: 31.100–1; A.N. 14
Africanus (title): 31.115–17, 129
Agamemnon: 4.121; 20.110–11
Ahern, John: 27.116; 32.7
Alain of Lille. *See also* Index of passages
    cited
    Anticlaudianus: 26.48
    De planctu Naturae: 15.106–8
Alberigo, brother: 32.78–123; 33.110–
    14 and passim
Albero da Siena: 29.109–20
Albert the Great. *See also* Index of
    passages cited
    On Minerals: 32.22–23
    Super Matthaeum: 12.41–43
Alberto da Mangona: 32.20–21 and
    passim
Aldobrandi, Tegghiaio: 6.79–80; 16.40–
    42 and passim
Alessandro da Mangona: 32.20–21 and
    passim
Alexander IV, pope: 32.119
Alexander the Great: 12.107; 14.31–36;
    A.N. 14

INDEX OF PROPER NAMES
IN THE TEXT AND TRANSLATION

Only the actual occurrences of proper names are listed here. Both Dante's forms and those used in modern English are indexed; the main entry is in English, with Dante's Italian in parentheses. References are by canto and line number.